HUMAN RESOURCE MANAGEMENT
IN LOCAL GOVERNMENT:
CONCEPTS AND APPLICATIONS
FOR HRM STUDENTS AND PRACTITIONERS

JAMES A. BUFORD JR., PH.D.
Auburn University
Troy State University

JAMES R. LINDNER, PH.D.
Texas A&M University

SOUTH-WESTERN
TM
THOMSON LEARNING

Australia · Canada · Mexico · Singapore · Spain · United Kingdom · United States

Human Resource Management in Local Government:
Concepts and Applications for HRM Students and Practitioners
by James A. Buford Jr., and James R. Lindner

Publisher: Dave Shaut
Senior Acquisitions Editor: Charles McCormick Jr.
Developmental Editor: Mardell Toomey
Senior Marketing Manager: Joseph A. Sabatino
Media Technology Editor: Diane M. Van Bakel
Media Production Editor: Robin K. Browning
Production Editor: Amy S. Gabriel
Manufacturing Coordinator: Sandee Milewski
Photography Manager: Cary Benbow & Rik Moore
Photo Credits: Kevin McCrea; Digital Stock; PhotoDisc, Inc.
Internal Design: Craig Ramsdell, Ramsdell Design
Cover Design: Rik Moore
Production House: Trejo Production
Printer: R.R. Donnelley & Sons Company, Willard Manufacturing Division

Printed in the United States of America
1 2 3 4 5 03 02 01 00

For more information contact South-Western, 5101 Madison Road, Cincinnati, Ohio, 45227 or find us on the Internet at *http://www.swcollege.com*

For permission to use material from this text or product, contact us by
• **telephone: 1-800-730-2214**
• **fax: 1-800-730-2215**
• **web: http://www.thomsonrights.com**

Library of Congress Cataloging-in-Publication Data

Buford, James Ansel, Jr.

Human resource management in local government : concepts and applications for HRM students and practitioners / James A. Buford Jr., James R. Lindner.

p. cm.

Includes bibliographical references and index.

ISBN: 0-324-06156-0

   1. Local government—United States—Personnel management. 2. Civil service—United States—Personnel management. I. Lindner, James R., II. Title.

JS358.B78 2001

352.6'213'0973—dc21

00-068778

For Hugh, Allen, Alec, and Nick

BRIEF CONTENTS

CONTENTS

PREFACE

Human Resource Management in Local Government: Concepts and Applications for HRM Students and Practitioners evolved from a 1991 book published by the Auburn University Center for Governmental Services: *Personnel Management and Human Resources in Local Government.* That book was the text in an accreditation program for HR managers in local government using the content outline for the body of knowledge of what was then called the Personnel Accreditation Institute (PAI) of the American Society for Personnel Administration (ASPA). Despite limited printing and marketing, the first book was very successful and gained widespread acceptance in local governments throughout the United States. Since then, emerging issues, a rapidly expanding knowledge base, and new approaches to the way human resource activities are managed have made it necessary to revise and update virtually every topic. Our current work, *Human Resource Management in Local Government: Concepts and Applications for the HRM Students and Practitioners,* has really become a different book rather than a new edition because of these substantive changes. We believe this is the most current and useful text available for those who want to learn more about HR management in a local government setting. This text is specific, detailed, and comprehensive in its approach. HR topics and activities that are most important to local governments are covered in considerable depth. For example, the complexities of the legal environment in local government and the potential for liability are greater than in the private sector. Further, all employees of local government have workplace rights provided in the U.S. Constitution. Moreover, certain units such as police and fire are especially vulnerable to challenges in such areas as selection, promotion, and administration of wage and hour requirements.

Accordingly, there is much more analysis and discussion of employment law and its application to HR activities in this text than might be found in a more general HR text. For HR-related areas that are highly specialized (such as health, safety, and security) or not applicable to all local governments—collective bargaining, for example—coverage is more streamlined and traditional. Every effort has been made to make this text as readable and valuable as possible to a broad group of HR students and professionals while maintaining the integrity of each topic presented.

This text successfully combines sound theory and concepts with relevant and interesting practical applications. While each topic is supported with detailed examples of HR practice, procedures and methods are viewed only as a *means to an end* rather than ends in themselves. The reader is challenged to consider alternative approaches in this changing field, and strong emphasis is given to effective HR management that is driven by strategic objectives.

This text is written for students who are enrolled in management, human resource management, and public administration courses, at both the undergraduate and graduate levels. It is also an indispensable reference for professional already working in local and state government. It is used as an authoritative guide to preparing for professional certification examinations by the Human Resource Certification Institute (HRCI) or the Public Human Resource Certification Council (PHRCC). The text provides content coverage of both the HRCI content outline and the PHRCC competency model, which are reproduced in the appendix.

ORGANIZATION OF THE BOOK

The part and chapter sequence of the book is consistent with the flow of HR management activities. Each part is designed as a self-contained unit to facilitate self-study, classroom instruction, and presentation in workshops and seminars. Because no component of HR is practiced in isolation, substantial cross-referencing provides coherence and a central unifying theme.

Part 1, "Understanding Human Resource Management," introduces the reader to the nature of HR management in a local government setting and identifies the various HR activities. This part also presents a review of historical developments that have shaped contemporary HR and examines in considerable detail the statutes, regulations, and constitutional provisions of employment law.

Part 2, "Organizational Considerations," deals with the behaviors and attitudes that predict what people are likely to do and examines the HR implications of motivation, satisfaction, and leadership in building a high-performance organization. Also covered is the strategic nature of HR planning and how policy guidance shapes the development of HR systems and processes.

Part 3, "Staffing," begins with a discussion of how work is organized into jobs or other work assignments, the techniques of job analysis, and how information from job analysis is used in designing and validating selection tests and other procedures. This part continues with a discussion of recruiting and concludes with a detailed examination of the components of a legal and effective selection process.

Part 4, "Developing Employees and Measuring Work Contributions," covers orientation, skills training, and development, including evaluation of these activities. This is followed by a discussion of the nature and uses of performance appraisal and how appraisal systems are designed and implemented to accurately assess work contributions and provide a basis for both developmental activities and administrative decisions.

Part 5, "Compensating Employees," focuses first on the design of a pay structure that supports the organization's strategic objectives and is internally consistent and externally competitive. This part continues with a discussion of individual pay systems, the factors used to reward employees for their service, skills, and work contributions, and considerations in the development of a benefits package. Finally, this part covers how the compensation program should be administered to ensure compliance with legal requirements and policy guidelines.

Part 6, "Enhancing Employee Relations and Providing Security," discusses how organizations can build effective relationships between management and employees by anticipating typical problems and having programs in place to deal with issues when they arise. This part also addresses labor relations in local government and covers the collective bargaining process as it is carried out in states that have legislation based on the federal model. Also included in this part is a general overview of the nature of safety, health, and security programs.

Part 7, "Moving Toward the Future," contains the final chapter, which examines the state of HR management in local government and provides ways of thinking about how HR professionals can best respond to current and emerging challenges.

LEARNING-ORIENTED FEATURES

An effort has been made throughout the book to provide a balance between theory and practice. Toward this end a number of features are designed to enhance understanding of concepts and principles and to illustrate applications in a local government setting.

- **Opening Vignettes.** These real-world events are designed to capture the reader's interest, establish the chapter theme, and raise issues that are important to local governments. An emphasis is placed on HR's contribution to organizational effectiveness.
- **Internet Resources.** The Internet has become a vital tool for HR professionals in virtually all practices. Accordingly, each chapter contains a number of websites to direct readers to the latest on-line information, examples, and research.
- **Exhibits.** Each chapter contains numerous exhibits such as graphic materials, charts, data, and summaries of current research. Each exhibit is keyed to specific text material and designed to explain and reinforce HR concepts and principles.
- **HR Highlights.** These boxed features appear in every chapter and are carefully developed to involve the reader in the material that is being discussed by raising issues, applying concepts, and comparing alternative approaches in a real-world situation.
- **Summaries.** Each chapter concludes with a concise summary of the material presented. These summaries are designed to reinforce learning by reiterating the main points of each topic in a logical and thorough manner.
- **Questions for Review and Discussion.** Each chapter includes relevant questions to help the reader assess his or her own understanding of the topics covered. These questions call for an analysis and application of the concepts and principles discussed in the chapter.
- **Questions for Critical Thinking.** Provided as an appendix (Appendix A), these questions will bring about lively, provocative classroom discussions for those using this text in an academic or training setting.
- **Endnotes.** Citations of academic and practitioner journals, government doc-

uments, and books credit the source of key text material and are also used to
indicate where additional information is available.

- **Appendices.** Because many readers keep their HR text as a reference source,
  we have included at the end of the book a full set of appendices that will pro-
  vide a useful reference for the future:
  A. Questions for Critical Thinking (see description above)
  B. Content Outline of the HR Body of Knowledge as set forth by the Human
      Resource Certification Institute
  C. Selected Competencies in the IPMA HR Competency Model
  D. Organizations and Government Agencies in HR Management
  E. Publications in HR Management
  F. Annual Report Form EEO-4
  G. Job Description for HR Director in Small Municipality

ACKNOWLEDGMENTS

No book is exclusively the work of the individuals who are listed as authors. The
authors are grateful to have had the assistance of many people. A special acknowledgment goes to the following individuals who served as chapter coauthors in their area
of expertise: Barbara M. Montoya, J.D., Montgomery (Alabama) City–County Personnel Board (employment law, Chapter 3); Arthur G. Bedeian, Ph.D., Louisiana State
University (organizational behavior, Chapter 4); Ronald L. Robinson, Ph.D., Troy
State University–Fort Benning (recruiting, selection, and test validation, Chapter 9);
Kim Dooley, Ph.D., and Tim Murphy, Ph.D., Texas A&M University (training and
development, Chapter 10); and Gene Armistead, Ph.D., Montgomery (Alabama)
Water Works and Sanitary Sewer Board (occupational health and safety, Chapter 16).

The authors are especially grateful to those who provided reviews and helpful
suggestions and comments. We are also grateful to other academicians and professionals who furnished ideas, contributed material, or provided assistance.

Suzanne Burnette
Lee-Russell Council of Governments

Jaime Castillo, Ph.D.
New Mexico State University

Karen Cason
Montgomery, Alabama City–County Personnel Board

Richard Chackerian, Ph.D
Florida State University

Tina Chiappetta
International Personnel Management Association

Mohammad Chizari, Ph.D.
Tarbiat Modarres University

Diana J. Clark, Ph.D.
Decisions, Inc. Consultants

Nikki Conklin, Ph.D.
The Ohio State University

Kathy Cox, Ph.D.
The Ohio State University

Cheryl Cunningham
Office of U.S. Representative Bob Riley

Floyd Decker
Yarger, Decker & McDonald

Larry Dooley, Ph.D.
Texas A&M University

Bernie Erven, Ph.D.
The Ohio State University

Margaret Fitch-Hauser, Ph.D.
Auburn University

Johnna Flowers, LPC, LMFT
Auburn, Alabama

Bill Giles, Ph.D.
Auburn University

Sherry Gorden
Riverbed Chapter of SHRM

Teresa Harless
Town of Blacksburg, Virginia

William H. Holley, Ph.D.
Auburn University

Mark T. Imperial, Ph.D.
University of Indiana

Suzette Jelinek, Ed.D.
Auburn University

Paul Johnson, Ed.D.
City of Tifton, Georgia

Ron Karren, Ph.D.
University of Massachusetts

Richard C. Kearney, Ph.D.
East Carolina University

Phyllis Mason, PHR
University of Rio Grande

Warren McCord, Ph.D.
Auburn University

Dana McPherson
City of Phenix City, Alabama

Randall Miller
City of Selma, Alabama

Donald L. Mims, CPA
Montgomery County, Alabama

Theresa Murphrey, Ph.D.
Texas A&M University

Randy Nickolaus
City of Eureka, California

Dwight R. Norris, Ph.D.
Auburn University

Steve Reeves, SPHR, IPMA-CP
City of Auburn, Alabama

Sarah Shiffert
*International Personnel
Management Association*

Kyle Steadham
City of Irving, Texas

Anne Stewart
Auburn University

Debbie Tankersely
*International Personnel
Management Association*

Ron Tejeda
Burgin Lumber Company

Christine D. Townsend, Ph.D.
Texas A&M University

Dorman Walker, Esq.
Balch & Bingham LLP

Ted Wheeler
Pike County, Ohio

Roger S. Wolters, Ph.D.
Auburn University

Carol K. Woolbright, Ed.D.
Troy State University–Phenix City

Diana Young
City of Cincinnati, Ohio

Special recognition goes to research assistants Ginger Hallmark, Scott Landrum, and Margaret Nanson and graduate students Tonia Dousay, Rebecca Garren, Edmund Jones, Ann Oliver, and Sabrina Tuttle. Becky Wells provided technical assistance, particularly during the planning and development stages of the book. Thanks to Debbie King, who provided a "special touch" to each and every chapter, and to Kenny Stroud, who kept the information flowing.

Back at the firm, Yolanda Jackson deserves thanks and praise for both support and service to clients while her alleged leader was working on this project. Dee Dee Harper, president of Ellis-Harper, was gracious about the time that went into this project, even though the hours were nonbillable.

The encouragement and support of academic administrators at institutions where the authors are faculty members or hold affiliations meant a great deal. These include Sharon Oswald, head, Department of Management, Auburn University; Aaron Lucas and Charles White, directors, Southeast Region, University College, Troy State University; and Edward Hiler, vice chancellor and dean, College of Agriculture and Life Sciences, Dick Creger, executive associate dean, Academic Programs, and Glen Shinn, department chair, Agricultural Education, Texas A&M University.

The authors very much appreciate the work of the team at South-Western who helped to develop and produce this work. They include Mardell Toomey, developmental editor, Charles McCormick, acquisitions editor, Amy S. Gabriel, production editor, and Sandee Milewski, manufacturing coordinator. Appreciation also goes to Rik Moore and Craig Ramsdell for their book designs, and to Margaret Trejo for managing the typesetting and editorial work.

Finally, on the home front Betty Buford and Cheri Lindner deserve accolades just for putting up with us during this project. But they did much more than that and their support and encouragement in our life and work is deeply appreciated.

ABOUT THE AUTHORS

DR. JAMES A. BUFORD JR.

Dr. Buford is director of Ellis-Harper Management, a human resource consulting firm, and adjunct professor of Management at Auburn University. He also serves on the faculty of Troy State University–University College and is affiliated with the Center for Local Government Studies. He earned the B.S.F. and M.S. degrees from Auburn University and the Ph.D. from the University of Georgia. Dr. Buford is certified by both HRCI and PHRCC.

Dr. Buford has authored or coauthored three other texts and more than 75 articles and papers. His work has appeared in many of the leading HR management journals. In addition to his research, teaching, and continuing education activities he has consulted widely with organizations in the areas of selection, performance appraisal, and compensation. His clients include numerous cities and counties. Dr. Buford also serves as an expert witness in HR cases brought in federal courts.

At Auburn University Dr. Buford held both administrative and faculty assignments and received several awards, including the Auburn Alumni Association Award for Excellence in Extension Education. He was involved in the development of one of the first accreditation programs in the United States for local government HR professionals. He also writes creative nonfiction, including two critically acclaimed collections of essays.

DR. JAMES R. LINDNER

Dr. Lindner is assistant professor in the department of Agricultural Education and member of the Graduate Faculty at Texas A&M University. His research interests include HR management, distance education, and planning and needs assessment. Dr. Lindner teaches both graduate and undergraduate courses (on-campus and distance), including a course in HR management. He earned the B.S. and M.B.A. degrees at Auburn University and the Ph.D. at The Ohio State University and is certified by HRCI.

Dr. Lindner has authored or coauthored more than 50 articles and papers and two textbooks. He has received a number of awards for his research and teaching, including the Epsilon Sigma Phi Early Career Service Award and the Agricultural Communicators in Education Silver Award for Technical Publication. In addition to his research and teaching activities, Dr. Lindner collaborates with Ellis-Harper Management and the Center for Local Government Studies in a variety of consulting and educational programs.

Within his department's distance education work group at Texas A&M, Dr. Lindner is developing and teaching courses delivered entirely at a distance via distance education technologies in the joint doctoral program (*http://doc-at-a-distance.tamu.edu*) of Texas A&M and Texas Tech Universities.

ANCILLARY PRODUCTS

Instructor's Manual with Test Bank (ISBN 0-324-11966-6)—The instructor's manual includes chapter overviews for each chapter in the main text, teaching suggestions, answers to end-of-chapter "Review and Discussion" questions, and discussion of "Critical Thinking" questions found in Appendix A. The test bank includes true/false, multiple-choice, and essay questions.

Website—*http://buford.swcollege.com*

We offer support products and features for students, practitioners, and instructors.

PART 1
UNDERSTANDING HUMAN RESOURCE MANAGEMENT

Human resource management is an action-oriented and exciting field that seeks to ensure the effective use of human talent to achieve the goals of organizations. Before examining a series of distinct HR activities, it is useful to gain an overall perspective. Chapter 1 introduces the reader to the nature of HR management in a local government setting and identifies the various HR activities. Chapter 2 provides a review of historical developments that have shaped contemporary HR. Chapter 3 examines in considerable detail the statutes, regulations, and constitutional provisions of employment law.

CHAPTER 1
AN INTRODUCTION TO
HUMAN RESOURCE MANAGEMENT

A DAY IN THE LIFE

Doug Watson arrived at work early and reviewed the items that were on his agenda for that day. For 18 years Doug has served as the city manager of Auburn, Alabama, a progressive and growing city with a population of approximately 40,000. The city operates under the council-manager form of government and has 650 regular and temporary employees. In 1998 the City Council adopted "Auburn 2020," a visionary strategic plan that addressed how the city would deal with anticipated issues and challenges of the next 20 years.

Everything on Doug's agenda was related to plan objectives for this year and for the five-year period. For example, he needed to check on the implementation of improved procedures in Revenue Office, especially the conversion to a new business tax software program. In reviewing the progress on construction of the new library, he thought about the greatly expanded services that would soon be available. Another important item involved developing additional capabilities in information technology. Later that day he would be meeting with the chair of an employee task force charged with identifying needs and opportunities involving the geographic information system (GIS), including the sharing of databases among city departments and outside entities. This project would not be fully implemented for two more years, but he needed to make sure everything was on track. He would spend some time dealing with public safety issues including review of plans to provide increased police patrolling and build a fifth fire station to serve a rapidly growing area. Finally he would be receiving a report from the Parks and Recreation Department regarding the status of a therapeutic recreation program for citizens with disabilities. Doug saw potential major benefits to the city in all these initiatives, which is why he picked up the phone and called Steve Reeves, the human resource director.

INTRODUCTION

The issues faced by Doug Watson illustrate an important fact. Local governments employ many kinds of resources, but without people (human resources) they would not be able to accomplish their purposes or even exist. Human resource management is fundamentally about people in the organization—how they are selected, what they are assigned to do, the way they are treated, and how their contributions are measured and rewarded.

Working effectively with people requires an understanding of concepts of organizational management and human behavior and knowledge relating to how systems can be designed to accomplish objectives in the various human resource activity areas. It is also useful to understand how modern human resource management has evolved as a natural consequence of grouping people together, whether in governmental settings or shops and factories. Chapter 2 is a brief history of human resource management. This introductory chapter addresses the following topics: organizational resources and productivity, contemporary HR management challenges, HR management activities, modern HR management in local government, and HR management accountabilities.

ORGANIZATIONAL RESOURCES AND PRODUCTIVITY

An organization can be defined as a group of people (whether two or two thousand or more) working together in a coordinated effort to achieve a set of objectives. There are many different types of organizations in society, all having different sets of objectives. For example, a for-profit corporation employs people in producing marketable goods or services, a university aims at the creation and transmission of knowledge, and a church strives for spiritual ends. The objective of the organization known as local government is to deliver services such as the administration of justice, fire protection, education, roads, utilities, and recreation.

Regardless of the type of organization, its success in achieving objectives is a function of how well its resources are managed. These include financial, physical, information, and human resources. Financial resources include funds from various sources used to pay for the cost of operation. Physical resources include materials, supplies, buildings, and equipment. Information resources are data used by the organization. Human resources are managerial, professional, and operating employees.

Organizations such as local governments improve by using their resources more efficiently and effectively. *Effective* means delivering the right services in a way that citizens feel is appropriate. *Efficient* means that the organization delivers the services at the lowest cost. Productivity is the ratio of outputs (services) to inputs (people, revenue, equipment, etc.). Through gains in productivity, local government managers can reduce costs and conserve resources, thus giving citizens a fairer return for their tax dollars.

Many local governments do an excellent job of realizing opportunities from financial and physical resources. For example, a city government would likely devote considerable time and effort in estimating revenues and allocating funds among various budget categories. Appropriate financial controls would be used to monitor expenditures. Likewise, new technology such as a computer-aided design system would be adopted if an analysis showed that street planning could be accomplished at less cost. Local governments are also becoming much better in using information resources in planning activities such as traffic engineering, zoning, and expansion of services.

In the final analysis, however, the wise use of financial, physical, and information resources, and the productivity of the organization as a whole, depend on effective and efficient functioning of **human resources**. It is, after all, people who do the work. **Human resource management** deals with the design and implementation of systems in an organization to ensure the efficient and effective use of human talent to accomplish organizational goals.[1]

Human resources and human resource management are relatively modern terms. The traditional term *personnel* does not really capture the vitality and potential of individuals in the organization; moreover, personnel management (or administration) suggests activities with a clerical and reactive orientation. The term *human resources* better describes employees as unique assets, capable of growth in abilities, while human resource management suggests a dynamic, proactive approach. Accordingly the authors will use the human resource(s) terminology, occasionally shortened to **HR** or **HRM** throughout this book. The top individual will be referred to as the human resource or HR manager and the organizational unit will be called the HR department.

CONTEMPORARY HR MANAGEMENT CHALLENGES

The environment for HR management is constantly changing. In recent years a number of developments have had major implications. Some of the most important include workforce demographics and diversity, competition in the market for services, and the pervasive impact of information technology.

WORKFORCE DEMOGRAPHICS AND DIVERSITY

http://www.hrconsultant.com/hrm/glossary.html
Stern and Associates provides a glossary of human resource management terms, jargon, acronyms, and concepts.

Until recently, the U.S. workforce was quite homogeneous. Even after Title VII of the Civil Rights Act was passed in 1964, different demographic groups tended to remain segregated by organizational level and occupational category. In the past 15 years, however, the workforce has changed dramatically.[2] Although African Americans are still the largest minority group, the percentage of Asian and Hispanic workers is growing more rapidly. It is estimated that by 2008 approximately 30 percent of workers will be nonwhite. More women are working, with the increase coming from families in which both spouses have jobs and families headed by single parents. Both women and minorities have been advancing to higher-level jobs. Another important demographic is age. In the United States and other developed countries people are living longer, and families are having fewer children. The median age will increase to 41 by 2008. This is reflected in the age distribution of the workforce, with people in the 40–64 age bracket showing the greatest increase. The educational level of workers has continued to rise, even though at the lower end of the spectrum, HR professionals and writers point out that many workers are still not able to read, write, and solve simple math problems.[3] Exhibit 1-1 illustrates significant demographic trends affecting the workforce. While barriers to job mobility still exist, there is no question that the workforce has become much more diverse.

Along with demographic changes, employee values have also evolved.[4] The baby boom generation began to enter the American workforce in the mid-1960s and is still the largest identifiable group in most organizations. Its members came of age during the period including the sexual revolution, the civil rights movement, and the assassination of national leaders such as President John F. Kennedy and Dr. Martin Luther King. Finally, they shared, in one form or another, the Vietnam experience. As the baby boomers came into their own, the traditional assumptions that

EXHIBIT 1-1

TRENDS IN
WORKFORCE
DEMOGRAPHICS
BY RACE/
ETHNICITY, SEX,
AND AGE,
1998–2008

Workforce Characteristic	1998	2008	Change
White, Non-Hispanic	73.6	69.7	–3.9
African American	11.6	12.2	+0.6
Asian and Other	4.5	5.6	+1.1
Hispanic Origin	10.3	12.5	+2.2
Male	53.7	52.5	–1.2
Female	46.3	47.5	+1.2
Age 16–24	15.4	15.8	+0.4
Age 25–39	36.4	30.8	–5.6
Age 40–64	45.0	50.0	+5.0
Age 65–74	2.7	2.9	+0.2
Age 75 and Older	0.5	0.5	NC

Source: U.S. Department of Labor, Bureau of Labor Statistics, Employment Projections 1998–2008.

had shaped employer-employee relations for decades no longer applied. The traditional "work ethic" that emphasized hard work, respect for authority, and material success began to be replaced by a concern for quality of life and autonomy. For many workers, especially dual-career couples and single parents, achieving a balance between work demands and family responsibilities is very important. The newest cohort, born between 1963 and 1981, known as Generation X, now composes about 20 percent of the U.S. workforce. Recent studies have suggested that contrary to certain stereotypical portrayals (such as having a greater concern with money), GenXers and boomers are more alike than different.

Although workplace diversity is a positive outcome of fair employment legislation, better education and health care, and changing attitudes, it creates its own challenges. Many of the approaches currently used in organizing and managing the workforce were developed when groups of employees tended to be much more homogeneous.[5] When issues arise or incidents occur, the management response often fails to solve the problem or even makes things worse. The HR task is to maintain awareness of prevailing values and attitudes that characterize the workforce in general, while being sensitive to the needs and concerns related to race, gender, religion, culture, and other dimensions of diversity. It is also important for HR to be proactive by identifying issues likely to arise and design programs to enhance employee relations and resolve problems.

COMPETITION IN THE MARKET FOR SERVICES

Local government was once viewed as the only source of a number of essential services to its citizens. It was, quite literally, "the only game in town." Today there is increasing sentiment that many of these services could be provided more efficiently by other organizations or at least that competition is a good thing. Privatization, also known as outsourcing, contracting-out, partnering, and to some degree, employee leasing, means that an outside organization or individual has been hired to perform what was once considered a government responsibility. The list ranges from education to waste collection to prisons.[6] If a government cannot satisfy its customers in any activity, there is always someone who will propose to do it better and for less. Recent management approaches such as **total quality management** (**TQM**) and **reengineering** have a strong customer service orientation.

Total quality management or TQM is an approach to management that is based on the work of W. Edwards Deming in postwar Japan.[7] TQM employs statistical methods and benchmarking of products and services against industry standards to ensure continuous quality improvement of organizational activities. Other components of TQM, sometimes referred to as **Theory Z**, include participative management, employee empowerment, and a focus on customer satisfaction.[8] In local government there is often a direct link between the unit providing the service (education, waste collection, street maintenance, etc.) and the individual or household receiving it. Reengineering and its public sector counterpart**, reinventing government**, goes beyond TQM and uses process as a major organizing principle. In the typical task-centered organization, like jobs are grouped into functional departments and departments into divisions. Reengineering requires management to visualize the collection of activities needed to create an output (the process) and then assign the work to teams without regard to functional lines.[9]

An important HR issue related to competition arises when certain employees are faced with the prospect of losing their jobs. In addition to assisting affected individuals with the transition, HR must promote the idea among both employees and managers that like it or not, competition is now a fact of life. Competition also has ethical dimensions involving HR management, which will be addressed in a later section. HR programs facilitate TQM by designing jobs that give lower-level employees the authority to make operating decisions, especially those employees who deal directly with citizen-customers. HR contributes to reengineering by creating an environment for change and developing nontraditional approaches to HR areas (especially compensation) that support reengineering initiatives.

INFORMATION TECHNOLOGY

As recently as the 1980s, information technology or IT was seen as a way to make business and government more efficient. Now IT has become the driving force in the economy. In fact, no organization of any size can even operate without computers. The obvious application for HR is the human resource information system (HRIS) used to collect, organize, store, and retrieve data on employees. Formerly a records management tool, an HRIS routinely provides information on forecasting, planning, career management, and evaluating the HR function.[10]

Other applications of IT include job analysis, recruiting, training, internal communications, collective bargaining, research, and the use of specialized programs to facilitate HR activities such as building a pay structure or developing an affirmative action plan. Computers can allow employees in certain areas to perform all or part of their jobs at home and to electronically transmit work products. In general, work in the "service industries" (such as local government) has involved a high degree of social interaction. It was through social skills and technical knowledge that employees contributed and gained personal fulfillment. Increasingly, however, IT is being used to mediate transactions between service providers and customers using electronic menus and websites.[11] Finally IT raises important privacy issues related to e-mail, the Internet, and databases containing sensitive information. IT will continue to transform the nature of work in ways we cannot yet comprehend. Noted authority Arthur B. Shostack puts it quite well. How all of this will affect HR, he says, "staggers the mind."[12]

In late 1999 the Long Range Strategic Planning Committee of the International Personnel Management Association discussed what they felt would be the key issues faced by public sector professionals during the period 2000–2005. The following list is the result of that discussion:*

TOP HR TRENDS

1. **Information Technology**—Developing new IT applications such as electronic commerce and communications, automation/ paperless processes, reduction in administrative processing time and cost.
2. **Business Partner/Internal Consultant Role of HR Management**—Aligning HR objectives with strategic plans and working with line management on creative approaches to HR issues.
3. **Labor-Management Relations**—Forming cooperative partnerships with unions.
4. **Work Life Issues**—Humanizing the workplace by balancing work and family through telecommunicating, flextime, etc.
5. **Shifting Demographics**—Managing diversity and coping with labor pool shortages and shorter tenure of workers.
6. **Leadership Development**—Focusing on employee development, retraining, and continuous learning.
7. **Compensation Packages**—Designing alternative pay structures such as skill-based pay and gainsharing and new benefits programs such as defined contribution retirement plans.
8. **Selection Processes**—Shifting from knowledge, skills, and abilities to behaviors.
9. **Decentralization**—Shifting decision making to point-of-contact with customers.
10. **Managing Change**—Responding to downsizing, accountability, politicization, and privatization, building flexibility in systems and processes, and delegating HR authority to line managers.

*Globalization of HR was omitted because of limited application to local governments.

Source: "Top HR Trends," *IMPA News* 69 (September 1999), 1.

HR MANAGEMENT ACTIVITIES

Organizational performance in local government is enhanced by accomplishing goals related to productivity, quality, and processes.[13] Productivity (closely related to efficiency, discussed earlier) is measured by output per employee; for example, the amount of solid waste collected by a sanitation helper over a time period. Productivity is important in controlling the costs of government services. The quality (or effectiveness) of the service provided is also important. If the government gains a reputation for poor service quality (employees skip houses along their routes or spill garbage on customers' lawns), it will be seen as less effective. Finally, the design of various operational processes of government (such as solid waste collection and disposal) influences both productivity and quality. For instance, the process might be improved by modifying the collection routes and changing from a job-based arrangement of tasks to work teams.

Because it is people who perform the work and design the processes, HR management contributes to the accomplishment of these goals in all aspects of organizational performance. To facilitate this contribution, HR management is composed of several groups of related activities. The following is a brief overview of these activities as they will be addressed in following chapters.

COMPLYING WITH LAWS AND REGULATIONS

The legal environment influences all HR activities. Equal employment opportunity encompasses the federal laws and guidelines that address employment discrimination based on race, sex, disability, and other prohibited classifications. Another important area concerns laws that apply to other employment issues such wages and hours, income sufficiency, workplace health and safety, and collective bargaining. The final area involves constitutional rights and protections that extend to the workplace for employees of local government. These areas are covered in Chapter 3. Additional details on applications of laws and regulations to HR activities are provided in Chapters 8, 9, 11, 14, 15, and 16.

DEALING WITH ORGANIZATIONAL CONSIDERATIONS

In local government, local people must work effectively as individuals and in group settings. Clearly, the organization benefits when employees want (are motivated) to perform their tasks. Employee motivation is a consequence of forces operating in the person and in the environment. Job satisfaction, which is related to motivation, involves employee attitudes. While high levels of satisfaction do not necessarily lead to high performance, job dissatisfaction has a negative effect on motivation. Motivation and satisfaction are greatly influenced by managerial philosophy and leadership. The HR implications of motivation, satisfaction, and leadership in building a high-performance organization are covered in Chapter 4 with additional applications in Chapter 13.

Successful organizations are those that plan. HR planning has several dimensions. First, planning should have a strategic perspective rather than focus on techniques. Policies should be developed to ensure that HR decisions support the organization's mission and strategic objectives. Having adequate human resource information systems (HRIS) to provide accurate and timely information is essential. A vital element of planning is to anticipate requirements and make provisions to deploy people where they are needed. The nature of HR planning and types of plans are examined in Chapter 5. How policy guidance shapes the development of HR systems and processes is illustrated particularly in Chapters 8 through 14 and 16.

STAFFING

The purpose of staffing is to provide an adequate supply of human resources to accomplish the work of the organization. First, the work must be logically organized into jobs or other work assignments. Job (or work) design involves determining the specific tasks and responsibilities to be carried out by each member of the organization. Organizing and designing jobs is covered in Chapter 6.

Job analysis is the systematic investigation of work content and worker qualifications. Information from job analysis is used in planning, selection, training, performance appraisal, and compensation and is a requirement for validation of instruments such as tests, structured interviews, and performance appraisal forms. Job analysis is the basis for job descriptions and job specifications. Chapter 7 discusses the techniques of job analysis.

Recruiting is necessary to generate a sufficiently large number of applicants to fill available jobs. If this process is not carried out, the organization may not have a pool of qualified candidates that match job requirements. The selection process is a series of steps that are designed to ensure that the best-qualified applicants are ultimately hired. The process must ensure that all selection procedures meet legal requirements. Recruiting and selection activities are covered in Chapters 8 and 9.

DEVELOPING EMPLOYEES AND MEASURING WORK CONTRIBUTIONS

Each new employee of local government represents a considerable investment even before he or she reports to work. But human resources should be viewed as assets that should increase in value. This begins with orientation and skill training as necessary. As jobs evolve and change, ongoing retraining accommodates the new requirements. Development is concerned with preparing employees for assignments beyond the immediate responsibilities of their jobs. Effective training is based on a systematic process beginning with needs assessment and includes an evaluation component. The training process is covered in Chapter 10.

Assessing work contribution using formal performance appraisal systems can benefit both the organization and the employee whose performance is rated. Performance ratings can be used for both developmental and administrative purposes. However, when used to justify actions such as promotion and discharge, performance appraisal instruments are considered "tests" and must meet legal requirements. Effective performance appraisal also requires that managers and supervisors understand and carry out their responsibilities. The design and administration of performance appraisal systems are examined in Chapter 11.

COMPENSATING EMPLOYEES

Compensation is probably the most important factor affecting why people decide to work at one organization over another. The responsibility of management is to design a compensation program that attracts and retains a qualified workforce, motivates employees to put forth their best efforts, and achieves optimum returns for the dollars spent. The first task is to design a pay system that supports the organization's strategic objectives and is internally consistent and externally competitive. The pay system is the centerpiece of the compensation program, but there are additional tasks. Procedures must be developed to reward employee contributions fairly and equitably. It is also necessary to design and offer employees a package of services and programs known as employee benefits. The program must be competently administered to comply with laws and regulations and carry out the organization's compensation policies. Compensation activities are covered in Chapters 12 and 13.

ENHANCING EMPLOYEE RELATIONS AND PROVIDING SECURITY

To ensure the continuing contribution of the workforce to organizational objectives, HR management has additional responsibilities. The relationship between management and employees must be handled effectively. Employee problems must be anticipated and programs should be in place to resolve these problems, proactively where possible but also through the use of disciplinary procedures. These topics are covered in Chapter 14.

Although there is no federal law governing labor relations in the public sector, the federal Labor Management Relations Act (as amended) serves as a model for states that have comprehensive labor laws applying to public sector organizations such as local governments. Such laws include the right of public employees to form unions for collective bargaining and impose a duty on the part of the employer to bargain with the union on wages, hours, and other conditions of employment. These laws typically establish a state agency to determine the bargaining unit, hold elections, certify the union, determine codes of unfair practices, and administer procedures. The role of unions in compensation is discussed in Chapter 13, and Chapter 15 covers the full labor relations process in local government.

Finally, the physical and mental health and safety of employees are major concerns. Traditional safety programs focus on elimination of unsafe acts and working conditions. Because of the increasing number of incidents of workplace violence, workplace security is also a major concern. Activities associated with these responsibilities are discussed in Chapters 16.

MOVING TOWARD THE FUTURE

The early part of the book covers individual HR functions and activities. The final part is concerned with how they fit together and are linked with the organization's strategic objectives. Chapter 17 examines the state of HR management in local government and provides ways of thinking about how HR professionals can best respond to current issues and prepare for emergency challenges.

MODERN HUMAN RESOURCE MANAGEMENT IN LOCAL GOVERNMENT

Local governments generally operate based on a model that follows classical concepts of organization and management. While the HR function has basic features of this model, other factors are also important in understanding how the function is carried out in this setting. These include the partnership between HR management and line management, the pressure of HR to respond to changing conditions and increased demands, and institutional arrangements that are unique to government entities.

LINE, STAFF, AND AUTHORITY

http://www.aspanet.org
The American Society for Public Administration (ASPA) is the largest public administration organization and provides a variety of member and nonmember services.

The concepts of line and staff are important in understanding the operation of human resource management in any organizational structure. The line refers to those units that are directly involved with the production of the organization's goods or services. Manufacturing, service, and governmental organizations all have line units. Examples are the finishing department in a manufacturing operation, the loan department of a bank, and the fire department of a city. Line managers customarily exercise **authority**, which is the right to command action from others.

In contrast, the staff functions in an advisory capacity to serve the line units of the organization. The primary goal of these individuals and departments is to assist and provide support to line departments in attaining objectives efficiently and effectively. Research and development, finance, public relations, and HR management are examples of departments that normally function in a staff capacity. The staff investigates, researches, and advises, but exercises authority only in certain situations, which will be explained.

It should be stressed, however, that HR management should not be viewed as an area in which staff specialists work with technical matters and line managers fill out forms. As illustrated in Exhibit 1-2, managers, supervisors, and in many cases, operating employees throughout the organization are partners in all HR activities.

EXHIBIT 1-2

EXAMPLES OF PARTNERSHIP ROLES
AND RESPONSIBILITIES IN HUMAN
RESOURCE MANAGEMENT

HR Area or Activity	HR Professionals	Line Managers	Employees
Managing Strategically	• Work closely with line managers to develop HR policies based on mission and strategic objectives. • Control HR policies.	• Work closely with HR professionals to contribute to development of HR policies based on mission and strategic objectives. • Comply with HR policies.	• Understand mission and strategic objectives. • Comply with procedures and instructions.
Complying with Laws and Regulations	• Maintain technical knowledge of employment law. • Build legal requirements into HR systems and procedures. • Monitor legal compliance indicators and statistics.	• Maintain working knowledge of employment law. • Follow guidelines when engaged in supervisory activities that have high legal risk. • When necessary seek HR advice from HR professionals. • Treat employees fairly.	• Understand employment rights. • Notify management when problems are encountered. • Treat coworkers with respect.
Building High-Performance Workplace	• Assess organizational climate. • Train line managers on motivation and leadership.	• Implement motivational techniques. • Match leadership "style" to situation.	• Focus on contributions. • Accept supervisory leadership.
Hiring, Developing, and Compensating Employees	• Coordinate recruiting activities. • Develop and validate selection tests. • Assess training needs. • Design training and development programs. • Develop and validate performance appraisal system. • Develop and maintain pay structures. • Design benefits plan. • Carefully analyze problems and issues, giving full consideration to objectives of line managers. • Advise and assist line managers.	• Evaluate applicants on job-related factors. • Orient new employees. • Arrange for employee training. • Establish performance expectations and counsel employees. • Observe and measure work contributions. • Recommend pay adjustments based on contributions. • When necessary, seek advice from HR professionals. • Offer suggestions to improve systems and procedures.	• Learn requirements of job and performance expectations. • Take advantage of opportunities to build personal capabilities. • Work diligently to achieve objectives.

EXHIBIT 1-2 (CONTINUED)

EXAMPLES OF PARTNERSHIP ROLES
AND RESPONSIBILITIES IN HUMAN
RESOURCE MANAGEMENT

HR Area or Activity	HR Professionals	Line Managers	Employees
Maintaining Effective Employee Relations	• Assess organizational climate. • Develop programs to deal with common employee problems and enhance employee relations. • Advise and assist line managers. • Counsel seriously troubled or potentially violent employees or coordinate referrals. • Establish progressive disciplinary procedures.	• When dealing with employee performance issues consider impact of personal situation. • Intervene and conduct limited counseling activities. • Request assistance from HR professionals with seriously troubled or potentially violent employees. • Discipline employees fairly.	• Comply with rules of workplace conduct. • Voice concerns. • Seek and accept assistance with problems. • Treat coworkers with respect. • Practice self-discipline.
Providing Health, Safety, and Security	• Develop workplace safety and health programs. • Design workplace security systems. • Design emergency procedures for accidents and incidents.	• Identify and correct unsafe acts and working conditions. • Involve employees in implementing workplace safety programs. • Maintain workplace security. • Initiate emergency procedures in case of accident or incident.	• Comply with safety rules. • Report safety and security violations, accidents, and incidents. • Participate on safety committees.

Source: Based in part on partnership model in Susan E. Jackson and Randall S. Schuler, *Managing Human Resources,* 7th ed. (Cincinnati: South-Western, 2000).

RELATIONSHIPS WITH LINE MANAGEMENT

The HR manager often reports to a top manager such as a city manager or county administrator. Within this reporting relationship HR management has four specific roles in its partnership with line management. These are service, advisory, policy control, and employee advocacy.[14]

PROVIDING SERVICES

Certain activities are performed as direct services to line management. For example, the Fair Labor Standards Act imposes certain requirements on local governments. The HR department is typically responsible for implementation of the provisions of the act, keeping appropriate records, and making reports. In fact, a number of HR activities are so complex that to do them properly, line managers would have to neglect their other essential functions. In this role HR management must become the authority on laws, regulations, policies, and procedures and ensure that technical and administrative issues are addressed in a timely manner and do not become a burden to operating departments.

That slogan was used recently by the U.S. Army to make the point to potential recruits that the peacetime Army is more than KP, Saturday inspections, and boring training exercises; rather it offers an interesting and challenging career. The same could be said for HR man-

BE ALL THAT YOU CAN BE

agement in local government. Like the Army, the public sector as a whole is breaking away from its old bureaucratic habits and creating innovative, performance-based organizations. In many cases HR management has more involvement and visibility than its counterpart in the supposedly more attractive business environment.

In Logan, Utah, Bruce Adams, the city's assistant personnel director, points out that much of his time is spent working with city departments to implement the city's strategic objective of being responsive to the public. For Adams, HR work in local government provides a variety of experiences not found in other organizations. "We have a zoo, public utility, police department, public library, court, and many other services to the city," he says. "I get the opportunity to learn about a wide variety of occupations. I wouldn't want to go into a widget factory and learn 12 positions inside out." Adams also suggests that the higher profile of HR work in local government provides challenges not faced by other HR professionals. Because the exposure is so much greater, there is constant pressure to maintain professional competence. When a wrong decision is made, the taxpayers will be among the first to know. "It's easy for word to get back to a local paper and make front-page news, whereas in the private sector, mistakes can go more unnoticed," he adds.

As local governments have changed to become mission driven and customer focused, HR management is much more appealing (and demanding). For the HR professional the work can provide a rewarding career. The slogan "be all that you can be" is certainly appropriate.

Source: Carla Joinson, "Public Sector HR: Leaving Bureaucracy Behind," *HR Magazine* 45 (June 2000), 78–85.

COUNSELING AND ADVISING

In this capacity the human resource staff advises line managers in the conduct of HR activities. For example, a construction supervisor in the public works department would likely rely on the expertise of the HR department when preparing for a counseling session with an equipment operator whose job performance needs to improve. In another case the advice could center on the feasibility of establishing an assessment center to identify candidates for promotions in the fire department. In performing this role, HR management should understand the situation, consider the viewpoint and goals of line managers, and offer practical approaches. Reciting the HR "conventional wisdom" is not especially helpful.

IMPLEMENTING AND CONTROLLING POLICIES

As mentioned earlier, HR management is a staff function and does not exercise line authority. In some situations, however, achieving policy objectives and complying with legal guidelines are so important that the department must have a direct influence on line management decisions. Therefore, in these situations the HR department is given functional authority. This is a right that an individual or department has over specific activities undertaken by other departments. When it exercises functional authority the HR department does more than advise; it gives instructions to line management. Examples are requiring the use of structured interviews when selecting applicants, approving pay rates for new hires, and ensuring that proper procedures are followed when employees are terminated. In performing this role, HR management must be both diplomatic and credible or it will be perceived as imposing unnecessary, bureaucratic obstacles to the goals of line management.

ADVOCATING EMPLOYEE CONCERNS

One of the enduring roles of HR is in representing employee concerns to line management. For example, a firefighter may believe that his service in the National Guard has caused him to be passed over for promotion because his attendance at monthly drills creates problems with the duty schedule. A clerk in the finance department receives what she considers to be an unfair performance rating because a computer problem caused a report to be late. HR can provide a support structure and "safety valve" to deal with these kinds of workplace issues. Effective performance in this role requires taking an even-handed approach. The objective is not to "take the employee's side" but to resolve the problem.

ORGANIZING THE HUMAN RESOURCE UNIT

Except in very small units of government or other organizations, there is usually an identifiable individual with direct responsibility for human resource management. Larger units have a human resource department, or civil service board or commission. In either case the term *human resource manager* is used in this book to refer to the individual who, in a staff capacity, is responsible for personnel/human resources activities. This may be an individual with another title (for example, county clerk) who has only a part-time HR assignment. At the other extreme, the human resource manager may be the head of a large department with several subordinate managers and large numbers of operating employees.

The HR function evolves over time in a somewhat predictable manner. At some stage of growth in an organization, HR activities become a burden to line departments and are assigned full- or part-time to at least one employee. This typically takes place as the total number of employees approaches 100. At approximately 200 employees an HR department usually emerges. The **human resource/staff ratio** is the number of full-time equivalent employees assigned to HR for each 100 employees on the payroll.

A recent study by the Bureau of National Affairs indicates that median human resource/staff ratios have remained stable over the last five years, ranging from 0.9 to 1.0.[15] A ratio of 1.0 is often used as a rule of thumb but can be somewhat misleading. As might be expected, there are economies of scale in HR management because the same activities are spread over larger numbers of employees. The study also found that the ratio declined from 1.3 (for up to 250 employees) to 0.5 (2,500 or more employees). The ratio depends on the number of responsibilities included under the HR function, which often includes payroll and benefits administration, safety, and in-house communications. The list has come to include such diverse activities as credit union, food service, facilities management, child care center, and motor pool.[16] Every organization is different, and rather than apply ratios, the approach should be to match skills and staff with organizational needs.

Human resource departments in local government are organized in many different ways. Exhibit 1-3 shows a large city civil service department that is broken down into a number of divisions. The divisions are segmented into subunits based on specific activities. Virtually all of the people assigned to these subunits specialize in one particular activity. Exhibit 1-4 on page 18 shows the organization of a city-county personnel board in a medium-sized jurisdiction. The unit is much smaller, but a considerable amount of specialization still exists. Finally, members of the human resource department in the small jurisdiction shown in Exhibit 1-5 on page 19 are, by necessity, HR generalists who must cover a broad range of activities.

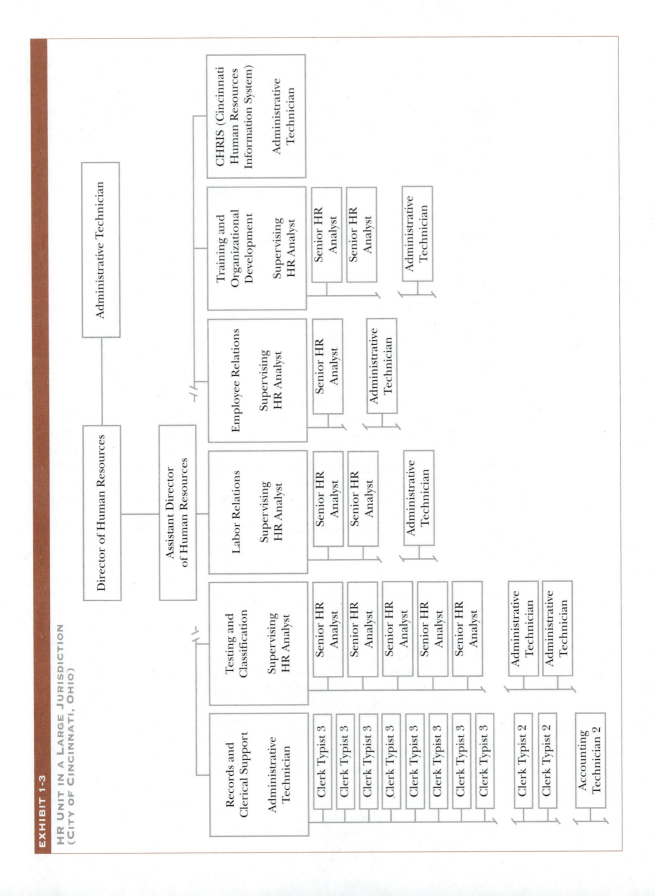

EXHIBIT 1-3

HR UNIT IN A LARGE JURISDICTION
(CITY OF CINCINNATI, OHIO)

Human resource departments in local government tend to be structured around a core of typical responsibilities such as employment, training and development, compensation and benefits, employee relations, and payroll/HRIS. It should be noted that TQM, reengineering, privatization, and continually expanding IT applications discussed earlier tend to create a more decentralized, egalitarian organization where the emphasis is on team performance. As the role of HR shifts to facilitate this type of culture it may also be necessary for the HR structure to change from the traditional model to one that focuses on teamwork, consulting, and customer service.[17]

INSTITUTIONAL ARRANGEMENTS

The two basic models for the HR function in local government can be best explained in the context of the **reform movement** (discussed in some detail in Chapter 2).[18] In the early 1900s, reform meant protection of public servants from undue political influence. More specifically, reform was a response to the cynical use of spoils patronage by political machines of large cities. In this context reform meant **neutral competence**, exemplified by an independent civil service board or commission. Currently, the reform movement emphasizes that elected officials should have the authority necessary to carry out the mandates of the electorate. Accordingly, the term **executive responsibility** suggests an HR function in which the chief executive maintains a high degree of control. It is important to note that neutral competence and executive responsibility are not either-or classifications. Local governments display wide variation along this personnel continuum.

In the civil service system, the HR function is administered by a board or commission with comprehensive policy-making, administrative, and appellate powers. The commission members are elected or appointed independently of the chief executive of the jurisdiction. The authority for local civil service systems may be contained in the state constitution or enacted as a state law. In states where cities and counties have "home rule," the authority may be a local charter adopted by popular vote, a resolution by the governing body, or local ordinance. In this type of system the commission typically has authority over a majority of employees, the HR administrator, and department heads. In other words, the organization and management of the workforce is based on merit standards and is protected from arbitrary political decisions.

The advantage of a civil service system is that the arrangement promotes fairness and removes excessive political interference from HR activities. On the other hand, the organizational separation and apolitical nature of boards and commissions are often viewed as obstacles to efficiency. In fact, the large, specialized HR organizations that generate complaints of bureaucratic inflexibility tend to be civil service systems.

In the integrated model, the HR function reports to the chief executive of the jurisdiction. This model came with the city manager movement and is one of the tenets of nonpartisan reform of local government. In this arrangement the HR administrator and department heads are appointed by and work at the pleasure of the chief executive; however, lower-level managers and operating or "classified" employees are often covered by a **merit system**. The integrated model often provides for citizen involvement through appeals boards and oversight committees; however, these bodies are typically advisory in nature and without "rule-making" authority. This model facilitates managerial innovation and accountability by allowing the chief executive to exert control over individuals in policy-making positions.

An integrated HR function is considered more responsive in that officials have

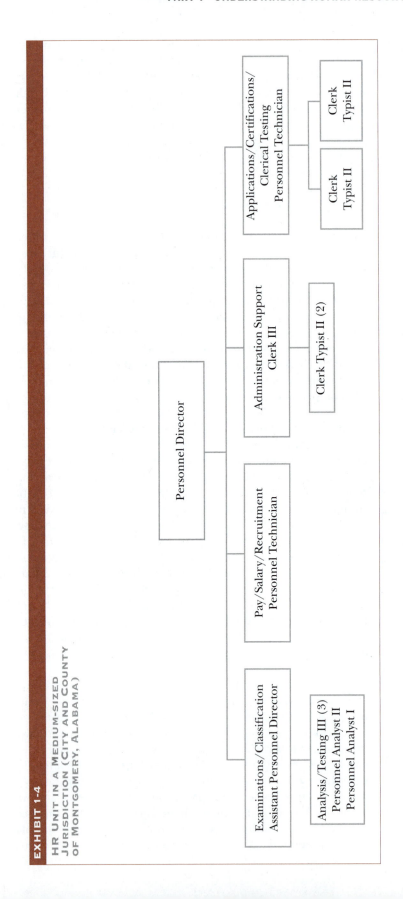

EXHIBIT 1-4

HR UNIT IN A MEDIUM-SIZED
JURISDICTION (CITY AND COUNTY
OF MONTGOMERY, ALABAMA)

EXHIBIT 1-5

HR UNIT IN A SMALL JURISDICTION
(CITY OF EUREKA, CALIFORNIA)

Human Resources Director

Human Resources Manager
- Supervision of daily operations
- Development of HR policies and procedures
- Advice to departments on technical or complex problems
- Safety management
- HR projects
- Management of sensitive or difficult HR and labor issues

HR Analyst I & II
- Staffing
- Test development
- Orientation and training
- Compensation and classification studies
- Benefits administration
- Explanation of HR policies and procedures
- Labor negotiations assistance and support

HR Assistant
- Position announcement and recruiting
- Workers compensation claims processing
- Compilation of data
- Reports and records management
- Scheduling, arrangements, and contact with applicants
- Office and clerical services

greater latitude in making HR decisions affecting the programs they were elected to carry out. On the other hand, it can result in excessive politicization of the HR function. (The latter-day reformers, of course, would disagree. Apparently, the original reasons for establishing independent agencies—the prevention of corruption, bossism, and spoilsmanship—do not apply to them.)

The development of a satisfactory institutional arrangement for HR management in local government presents formidable difficulties and trade-offs. There is no simple solution. As stated by the writers of a major public personnel text:

> *Deep-seated and intractable social and political problems cannot be resolved with organizational cosmetics. The tension between the society's desire for depoliticized, merit-oriented public services and its interest in enabling its elected representatives to effectuate their policies is likely to make the nature of institutional arrangements for public personnel administration subject to constant reevaluation and modification for many decades to come.*[19]

HR MANAGEMENT ACCOUNTABILITIES

As the traditional personnel orientation has shifted to a human resources focus, the visibility and influence of HR management has also increased. But this enhanced status comes with a set of expectations. Some of these expectations are new, while others have always existed but deserve reinforcement. Recent accountabilities are associated with the strategic partnership aspect of HR management. Professional qualifications and ethics have always been central tenets of HR management, but the number and complexity of HR issues and their ethical implications continue to increase.

PROFESSIONAL ACCOUNTABILITIES

It is now generally accepted that HR management is based on a substantial body of specialized and technical knowledge. As the authors of a popular HR text put it quite well, the idea that "liking to work with people" is the major qualification necessary for success is a myth.[20] Individuals who make HR management their career field are expected to have a foundation in a number of competency areas including organizational management, employment, training and development, compensation, employee and labor relations, health and safety, and employment law. Both the HR Competency Model of the International Personnel Management Association (IPMA) and the Content Outline of the HR Body of Knowledge of the Human Resource Certification Institute (HRCI) are shown in the Appendix.

http://www.shrm.org
The Society for Human Resource Management (SHRM) is the largest HR generalist organization and provides a variety of member and non-member services.

The broad range of issues faced by HR professionals suggest that knowledge equivalent to a college degree is probably essential and that certification is highly desirable. The IPMA introduced its public sector certification HR program in 1999. Certification is earned by completing a written examination based on the HR Competency Model and having an acceptable training and experience rating.[21] Although the Society for Human Resource Management (SHRM) has offered certification for a number of years (refer to Chapter 2), the IPMA certification is also appropriate for HR professionals in local government.

http://www.ipma-hr.org/
The International Personnel Management Association (IPMA) is an organization that provides human resource leadership, professional development, information, and services for the public sector.

HR professionals also need to continually update their knowledge in a field that is constantly changing. For example, a text that was published even three years ago would not include recent developments in a number of activity areas such as compensation ("gainsharing" as a way to reward team performance in local government) and in the legal environment (three Supreme Court decisions on sexual harassment). During the next few years new issues will arise and the knowledge base will expand; accordingly this text also has a limited "shelf life." Involvement in professional associations is one of the best ways to maintain technical proficiency. The IPMA best addresses HR issues and concerns unique to the public sector while SHRM deals with areas of general interest (and is more likely to have a local chapter). HR professionals should review the professional literature including on-line information (both IPMA and SHRM maintain websites). They should also seek personal professional development by attending seminars and workshops.

STRATEGIC PARTNERSHIP ACCOUNTABILITIES

During the 1980s strategic management became prominent. Strategic management begins with a mission statement and the identification of the areas in which the organization has unique capabilities in providing products and services (its "distinctive competence"). Strategic management requires organizations to conduct an analysis of internal strengths and weaknesses and external opportunities and threats (known as a SWOT analysis) and develop strategic objectives to guide activities in all departments or strategic business units (SBUs). While the concept and methodologies of strategic management were originally associated with business organizations, they are increasingly used by public sector organizations including local governments.[22]

Although local governments are not businesses, they must manage their human resources in a "business-oriented" manner. That involves designing HR systems and processes that are driven by the government's mission and strategic objectives.[23]

During the next few years the term *metric* will become an increasingly familiar part of the lexicon of HR management. In this context the term refers to quantifiable standards of measurement for various HR activities—in other words, numbers with dollar signs attached. Met-

rics are essential to demonstrating the value of HR practices to both internal and external stakeholders. Efficiency metrics include turnover, absenteeism, productivity, and intellectual capital. It is also important to devise metrics that address value creation and effectiveness. This type of metric can be applied to any HR activity by determining the cost, the time to do it, the quantity and quality involved, and the human reaction. Finally, cutting edge HR departments are beginning to use a variation of return on investment (ROI), an established financial metric. The HR version of ROI is calculated by assigning monetary values to a program and dividing the value by the cost. Standard HR formulas and ratios have been developed by such organizations as the Saratoga Institute in Santa Clara, California, and Performance Resources Organization in Birmingham. Local governments can also develop their own metrics programs. In any case, as the pressure for fiscal accountability and quantitative assessment continues, accountability will continue to build. Jac Fitz-enze, chairman of the Saratoga Institute, offers these words of wisdom to HR professionals: "You can't define yourself if you don't have the data."

Source: Robert J. Grossman, "Measuring Up," *HR Magazine* 45 (January 2000), 29–35.

Quite often, however, HR activities are carried out using procedures and techniques that have gained a certain legitimacy based on familiarity and acceptability and because they lead to some end result. But that result may not contribute to objectives and may even conflict with objectives. For example, a local government may have an objective of having employees expand job boundaries and a pay structure with narrow grades (this illustration is not uncommon). The need for HR managers to be guided by strategic objectives in such areas as selection, training, performance appraisal, and compensation in order to align activities with strategic objectives is emphasized throughout this book, but there is another important accountability.

Assume that HR management implements a skill-based pay system and replaces the narrow pay grades with pay "bands." It now becomes necessary to evaluate the new system. There were likely significant costs incurred in development and implementation, probably requiring an increase in wages. It is anticipated that these costs will be offset by productivity gains and a reduction in the number of employees required to accomplish the work. After a suitable time has elapsed, HR management should be able to document whether or not the new system resulted in net financial benefits. HR management is expected to evaluate all activities in terms of costs and benefits, and ultimately to justify its own existence as a strategic contributor rather than as a line item in the budget.

ETHICAL ACCOUNTABILITIES

In deciding what is "ethical," most people rely to some extent on rules of right conduct in everyday life: don't lie, cheat, or steal, do practice the "golden rule," and so forth. Following these precepts also avoids legal difficulties. A manager, however, has an obligation to pursue the goals of the organization, and the ethical issues are more complex. Additional guidelines are needed.[24]

In an organizational setting, legitimate decisions are made based on three criteria. From a "business" perspective a correct decision is one that benefits the organization. Since organizational activities take place in a legal framework, a correct decision is one that complies with the law. But not everything that benefits the organization and complies with the law is "right." There are fundamental values of society and organizational and professional standards that must be taken into account, especially in a government setting. Therefore a correct decision is one that follows moral principles. An ethical decision is one that integrates all three criteria.

A recent survey of HR professionals found a number of problem areas including employment decisions based on favoritism, sex discrimination and harassment, failure to maintain confidentiality, nonperformance factors used in appraisals, and arrangements with vendors and consultants resulting in personal gain.[25] While many of these problems have legal implications, they all have negative effects on morale and organizational performance. Decisions that led to these problems generally failed on all criteria. It is not realistic to suggest that HR management can impose a system that eliminates these kinds of problems, all of which illustrate behavior that is clearly unethical. Moreover, in many situations the ethical issues are more complex, or the criteria conflict with each other.

For example, should an employee be dismissed (as the rules require) for repeated incidents of being late for work? Possibly so, because the organization has a legitimate interest in employees being present for duty and a legal right to enforce reasonable rules. But what if he is a single parent with a sick child? Moral principles suggest that the organization should have compassion and consider his situation. Maybe he should be given another chance. Assume that another employee was recently terminated for the same reasons, but there were no extenuating circumstances. What if the recently terminated employee is a member of a protected group? The decision to temper justice with mercy could result in a charge of discrimination and even a lawsuit. Even though the organization would probably prevail, there will be significant costs and negative publicity.

Competition in the market for government services, discussed earlier, also has ethical dimensions.[26] Contracting and/or outsourcing such services can save taxpayers' money and the practice is legal. However, when government performs these services the employees have rights founded in "merit principles," which came out of the civil service reform movement and date back to the Pendleton Act of 1883 (see Chapter 2). The essence of merit is selection of individuals based on competence and protection from partisan political abuse. What happens to the employees who are laid off? Perhaps they will be hired by a contractor with connections to elected officials and do the same work for lower pay, minimum benefits, and little job security. But to impose requirements that contractors comply with all of the traditional requirements of merit systems defeats the purpose of contracting the service. Moreover, the fact that political considerations were factored into the selection of the contractor does not necessarily equate to political corruption.

HR professionals face these kinds of ethical dilemmas on a continuing basis. They should, of course, assess the immediate and long-term consequences of their actions and decisions. They should also consider the effects on the personal lives of employees and their families. Both SHRM and IPMA have adopted codes of ethics that contain useful guidelines. The IPMA principles and values statement (code of ethics) is shown in Exhibit 1-6. In many cases the government will have adopted a resolution that includes statements of values and ethics. Besides adhering to personal and professional ethical standards, HR professionals should contribute to the development of policies that stress fair treatment, workplace rights, and respect for human dignity. They can also make a strong impact by pointing out the negative consequences of unethical acts and decisions.

EXHIBIT 1-6

IPMA CODE OF
PROFESSIONAL
PRINCIPLES AND
STATEMENT OF
VALUES

- To support the Association's goal and objectives for developing the human re-source management professional and the public's understanding of the role of human resource management.
- To maintain the highest standards of professional competence and of professional and personal conduct.
- To respect the dignity of all individuals, and to protect people's right to fair and equitable treatment in all aspects of employment without regard to race, sex, reli-gion, age, national origin, disability, or any other non-merit, non-job-related fac-tor, and to promote affirmative action.
- To support my employer's legitimate efforts for a qualified and productive work-force to accomplish my employer's mission.
- To emphasize the importance of addressing the impact of management plans and decisions on people.
- To support, mentor, and counsel individuals pursuing a career in human resource management.
- To treat as privileged and confidential information accepted in trust.
- To uphold all federal, state, and local laws, ordinances, and regulations, and en-deavor to instill in the public a sense of confidence and trust about the conduct and actions of my employer and myself.
- To avoid a conflict of interest.
- To not compromise, for personal gain or benefit or special privilege, my integrity or that of my employer.

Source: International Personnel Management Association (October 5, 1991). Used by permission.

SUMMARY

Human resource management is fundamentally about people in organizations— how they are selected, what they are assigned to do, the way they are treated, and how their contributions are measured and rewarded. The objective of the organiza-tion known as local government is to deliver services such as the administration of justice, fire protection, education, roads, utilities, and recreation.

The environment for HR management is constantly changing. In recent years there have been a number of developments that have major implications. Some of the most important include workforce demographics and diversity, competition in the market for services, and the pervasive impact of information technology.

Organizational performance in local government is enhanced by accomplish-ing goals related to productivity, quality, and processes. HR management con-tributes to the accomplishment of these goals in all aspects of organizational per-formance. To facilitate this contribution, HR management is composed of several groups of related activities. These include planning, complying with laws and regu-lations, designing jobs and staffing the organization, developing employees and measuring work contributions, and enhancing employee relations and providing security.

Modern HR management in local government is a staff function and operates based on classical concepts of organization and management; however, managers, supervisors, and, in many cases, operating employees throughout the organization are partners in all HR activities. HR departments in local government tend to be structured around a core of typical responsibilities such as employment, training and development, compensation and benefits, employee relations, and payroll/ HRIS. As the role of HR shifts to facilitate this type of culture it may also be necessary for the HR structure to change from the traditional model to one that focuses on teamwork, consulting, and customer service.

Institutional arrangements for local government are best explained in the context of the reform movement. Originally reform was a response to the cynical use of spoils patronage by political machines of large cities. The term *neutral competence* is associated with an independent civil service board or commission. Currently, the reform movement emphasizes that elected officials should have the authority necessary to carry out the mandates of the electorate. Accordingly, the term *executive responsibility* suggests an HR function in which the chief executive maintains a high degree of control. It is important to note that neutral competence and executive responsibility are not either-or classifications. Local governments display wide variation along this continuum.

As the traditional personnel orientation has shifted to a human resources focus, the visibility and influence of HR management has also increased. But this enhanced status comes with a set of expectations. Some of these expectations are new, while others have always existed but deserve reinforcement. Recent accountabilities are associated with the strategic partnership aspect of HR management. Professionalism and ethics have always been central tenets of HR management, but the number and complexity of HR issues and their ethical implications continues to increase.

QUESTIONS FOR REVIEW AND DISCUSSION

1. How is the productivity of financial, physical, and information resources in units of local government related to the productivity of human resources?
2. What are the implications of the HR challenges discussed in this chapter?
3. What are the major sets of HR activities? Identify the activities in each set.
4. Briefly explain how HR responsibilities are shared between the HR staff and line managers.
5. Design an organizational structure for the HR unit in a city with 500 employees.
6. Compare and contrast the terms *neutral competence* and *executive responsibility*. Which type of institutional arrangement exemplifies each term?
7. In what ways do associations such as IPMA contribute to professional development in the HR field?
8. Discuss the following statement: "Although local governments are not businesses, they must manage their human resources in a "business-oriented" manner.
9. What three criteria must be considered in making an ethical decision? How should these criteria be balanced in resolving the ethical dilemmas that were discussed?

ENDNOTES

[1] Robert L. Mathis and John H. Jackson, *Human Resource Management*, 9th ed. (Cincinnati: South-Western, 1999), 4.

[2] Demographic statistics and trends are based on U.S. Department of Labor, Bureau of Labor Statistics, *Employment Projections 1998–2008.*

[3] Arthur Sherman, George Bohlander, and Scott Snell, *Managing Human Resources* (Cincinnati: South-Western, 1998), 24–25.

[4] This discussion draws on Stephen P. Robbins, *Organizational Behavior,* 8th ed. (Upper Saddle River, N.J.: Prentice-Hall, 1998), 136–137. See also Carole L. Jurkiewicz, "Generation X and the Public Employee," *Public Personnel Management* 29 (Spring 2000), 55–74.

[5] Susan E. Jackson and Randall S. Schuler, *Managing Human Resources* (Cincinnati: South-Western, 2000), 32.

[6] Jay M. Shafritz, Norma M. Riccucci, David H. Rosenbloom, and Albert C. Hyde, *Personnel Management in Government,* 4th ed. (New York: Dekker, 1992), 413–415.

[7] For a technical discussion of TQM see W. Edwards Deming, *Quality, Production and Competitive Position* (Cambridge, Mass.: MIT Center for Advanced Engineering Study, 1992).

[8] For applications of TQM to local government see Douglas J. Watson and Bettye B. Burkhalter, "Developing a Theory Z Culture in Local Government," *Public Personnel Management* 21 (Fall 1992), 401–409, and entire issue 25 (Winter 1996).

[9] See Michael J. Hammer and James Champy, *Reengineering the Corporation* (New York: HarperCollins, 1993); and David E. Osborne and Ted Gabler, *Reinventing Government: How the Entrepreneurial Spirit Is Transforming the Public Sector* (Reading, Mass.: Addison Wesley, 1992). See also Patricia A. Compton, "Process Engineering Formula for Success for the Future," *Public Personnel Management* 25 (Summer 1996), 257–264; and Lizanne Lyons and Anthony D. Vivenzio, "Employee Involvement in Seattle: Reengineering Government in a City Lacking a Financial Crisis," *Public Personnel Management* 27 (Spring 1998), 93–102.

[10] Bill Roberts, ""Making Employee Data Pay," *HR Magazine* 44 (November 1999), 86–96; and Kenneth A. Kovach and Charles E. Cathcart Jr., "Human Resource Information Systems (HRIS): Providing Business with Rapid Access, Information Exchange and Strategic Advantage," *Public Personnel Management* 28 (Summer 1999), 275–283.

[11] Jackson and Schuler, 57.

[12] Arthur B. Shostak, "Professing HR Trends," *HR Magazine* 44 (November 1999), 49–59.

[13] Mathis and Jackson, 10–11.

[14] Sherman, Bohlander, and Snell, 29.

[15] Bureau of National Affairs, *Bulletin to Management,* "Human Resource Activities, Budgets and Staffs," SHRM-BNA Survey No. 65, June 29, 2000, S-13.

[16] Carla Joinson, ". . . and Other Duties as Assigned," *HR Magazine* 45 (February 2000), 66–72.

[17] Carla Joinson, "Changing Shapes," *HR Magazine* 44 (March 1999), 40–48.

[18] Victoria E. Johnson and David Sink, "Personnel Reform in Consolidated Metropolitan Government: Executive Responsibility and Neutral Competence," *Public Personnel Management* 15 (Spring 1986), 11–21; Shafritz et al., 47–54. See also Katherine C. Naff and John Crum, "Merit, Management and Neutral Competence: Lessons from the U.S. Merit Systems Protection Board, FY 1988–FY 1997," *Public Administration Review* 60 (March/April 2000), 111–122.

[19] Shafritz et al., 62.

[20] Mathis and Jackson, 32.

[21] International Personnel Management Association, "IPMA Public Sector Human Resources (HR) Certification," *http://www.ipma-hr.org/training/certification.html* (August 2000).

[22] See, for example, Mark H. Moore, *Creating Public Value: Strategic Management in Government* (Cambridge, Mass.: Harvard University Press, 1997); and Steven Cohen and William Eimicke, *Tools for Innovators: Creative Strategies for Managing Public Organizations* (San Francisco: Jossey-Bass, 1998).

[23] David Ulrich, "A New Mandate for Human Resources," *Harvard Business Review* 76 (January/February 1998), 124–134.

[24] This section draws on John C. Boatright, *Ethics and the Conduct of Business,* 2d ed. (Englewood Cliffs, N.J.: Prentice-Hall, 1997), 1–27. A comprehensive discussion of ethical issues in an employment setting is found in Part III, 109–257.

[25] Commerce Clearing House, "1991 SHRM/CCH Survey," *Human Resource Management Service* (June 26, 1991).

[26] James P. Piffner, "The Public Service Ethic in the New Public Service Personnel Systems," *Public Personnel Management* 28 (Winter 1999), 541–553. Other articles in this special ethics edition cover a number of issues relevant to HR management in local government.

CHAPTER 2
HISTORICAL DEVELOPMENT OF THE HUMAN RESOURCE FUNCTION

THE PAST IS PROLOGUE

In 1854 Ulysses S. Grant, who had served with distinction in the Mexican War, decided to resign his commission and return to his home in Missouri. In 1859, after several unsuccessful business ventures, he sought an appointment as county engineer. Grant believed that his degree in military (civil) engineering from the U.S. Military Academy and his army experience with roads and bridges qualified him for the position. Because he did not have the right political connections, his application was rejected.

Source: Brooks Simpson, *Ulysses S. Grant: Triumph Over Adversity* (New York: Houghton Mifflin, 2000), 61–72.

As the 19th century was drawing to a close, the quality of working-class life was quite dismal. Pay was low and 12-hour days and six-day weeks were common. The work was hard and conditions in the plants were poor and often dangerous. Workers had no employment rights or benefits. The Knights of Labor, which had recently achieved limited success in bargaining on their behalf with employers for better wages and working conditions, was in decline. Workers were expected to show up and do their jobs, day after day, year after year until they were too old to work, became injured, or contracted an occupational disease, whichever came first.

Source: William H. Holley and Roger S. Wolters, *The Labor Relations Process*, 6th ed. (Homewood Ill.: Dryden, 2001, forthcoming).

Despite having received a liberal education in the best American and European schools, Frederick W. Taylor decided to learn the trade of machinist. In 1878 he took a position in the plant of Midvale Steel Company in Philadelphia and rose to the position of chief engineer. Taylor devoted much of his time to analyzing the nature of shop work and came to the conclusion that a very large percentage of both labor and material was wasted through inefficient organization and supervision of work.

Source: Harold Koontz and Cyril O'Donnell, *Principles of Management* (New York: McGraw-Hill, 1955), 20.

Although the principle of employment based on "merit" dates from the passage of the Pendleton Act in 1883, the issue of how much workers should be paid was not addressed at that time. Political and personal favoritism continued to be the basis for determining the duties and pay of public employees until well into the 20th century.

Source: Jay M. Shafritz, Norma M. Riccucci, David K. Rosenbloom, and Albert C. Hyde, *Personnel Management in Government*, 3d ed. (New York: Dekker, 1992), 134.

During World War II, large numbers of women worked in factories because most able-bodied men were serving in the armed forces and there was a labor shortage. The contribution of "Rosie the Riveter" to the war effort was legendary. During that time the War Department had reluctantly agreed to train a group of black fighter pilots at Mouton Field in Tuskegee, Alabama. These pilots, known as the "Tuskegee Airmen," distinguished themselves in combat with the 99th Fighter Squadron. After the war, however, Rosie had to give up her job to a man who would earn higher pay for the same work, and few of the Tuskegee Airmen were able to find employment in the rapidly growing air transportation industry.

Source: Paula Watson, "All Guts for Old Glory, One Woman's Choice for Woman of the Century Is *Rosie the Riveter*," *Dallas Morning News* (December 29, 1999) and Herbert E. Carter, "The Legacy of the Tuskegee Airmen," *National Forum* 75 (Fall 1995), 10–16.

INTRODUCTION

As Chapter 1 pointed out, much of the work of society is accomplished by organizations. Organizations began to replace individual work patterns during the mid-18th century because of the advantages of specialization and division of labor, a management principle that is identified with the Industrial Revolution in England. In addition to shops and factories, the principle was applied in other settings such as the Prussian Army and the British Civil Service. As the examples illustrate, a natural consequence of grouping workers together was the need for better ways and means of selecting workers, designing jobs, providing pay, and attending to the welfare of the workforce. As these needs were addressed, the activities of what is now called human resource management began to appear. Such activities tended to emerge in the sector (public or private) where a particular need or concern was first identified and were adopted in the other sector when the benefits became apparent. Some activities that came later followed this pattern while others emerged in both sectors at about the same time. A comprehensive history of human resource management would trace the effects of hundreds of social, economic, and political factors beginning in the 1700s. This chapter is a brief overview of key developments.[1]

THE BEGINNINGS

Although HR management as a specialized function did not begin to emerge until the early 1900s, its antecedents can be traced to developments that took place throughout the 19th century. As public and private organizations became larger and more complex, issues related to employment and working conditions became a major concern of reformers. In the public sector the focus was on employment practices based on "merit," while the industrial reformers sought to improve the workers' lives, both on and off the job.

FROM ELITISM TO SPOILS

http://www.nlc.org/
The National League of Cities (NCL) is an organization that strives to strengthen and promote cities as centers of opportunity, leadership, and governance.

Discussion of the history of human resource management in government customarily, and rightly, focuses on the **spoils system** vs. the **merit system**, and the superiority of the latter.[2] The first six presidents of the United States maintained an unofficial but effective merit system. With some exceptions, their appointments to public office were based on considerations of character and fitness, and removals were made for cause. The public service was elitist in that the values of these presidents tended to restrict it to members of the better-educated class. By the late 1820s, however, a strong public reaction to the elitism of the early presidents had developed. Many Americans felt that the time had come to "democratize" the public service and bring in people from all social classes. Thus, the elitist period, which began with George Washington, came to an end with John Quincy Adams.

The notorious "spoils era" in the federal service began in 1829 with President Andrew Jackson and lasted for more than 50 years. President Jackson has been somewhat overvilified as originator of "spoils patronage," since it was already solidly established in many state and local governments where political "bosses" controlled appointments. Abuses such as using workers in partisan activities and requiring salary kickbacks to fund the operation of political machines were commonplace. But ultimately it was disenchantment with the corrupted federal service that provided the impetus for reform.

THE REFORM MOVEMENT

In 1865 Congressman Thomas A. Jenkes introduced a number of bills designed to curb the patronage power of the president, and the **reform movement** became a major political issue. By the late 1870s a number of federal, state, and city associations were formed to press the reform agenda. Congress remained recalcitrant, however, and it was not until President Garfield was assassinated by a disgruntled officeseeker in 1881 that reform was accomplished. The "great day" came on Janu-

---

While President Andrew Jackson is associated with political patronage, it is doubtful that he ever used the word *spoils*. The most celebrated statement and apparently the one that led to the term *spoils system* was made by Senator William L. Marcy of New York in 1832 during a debate with Henry Clay:

JACKSON NEVER SAID IT

It may be, sir, that the politicians of the United States are not so fastidious as some gentlemen are, as to disclosing the principles on which they act. They boldly preach what they practice. When they are contending for victory, they avow their intention of enjoying the fruits of it. If they are defeated, they expect to retire from office. If they are successful, they claim, as a matter of right, the advantages of success. They see nothing wrong with the rule, that *to the victor belongs the spoils* . . . [emphasis added].

Source: Quoted in Jay M. Shafritz et al., *Personnel Management in Government*, 3d ed. (New York: Dekker, 1992), 9.

EXHIBIT 2-1	
MAJOR FEATURES OF THE PENDLETON ACT	• Established the U.S. Civil Service Commission, an executive agency composed of three bipartisan commissioners appointed by the president. • Required open competitive examinations, probationary periods, and protection from political pressures (merit system procedures) in various departments composing approximately 10 percent of the federal service. • Authorized the commission to supervise the conduct of examinations and make investigations to determine the degree of departmental enforcement of its rules. • Authorized the president to extend merit system coverage by executive order.

Source: Jay M. Shafritz et al., *Personnel Management in Government*, 4th ed. (New York: Dekker, 1992), 29–30.

ary 16, 1883, when the Pendleton Act establishing the U.S. Civil Service Commission was signed by President Chester A. Arthur.[3] The major features of the act are shown in Exhibit 2-1. While the Pendleton Act was not a total victory for reformers, it signaled a change in direction from spoils to merit in the federal service and was the beginning of what has been called the era of "government by the good."[4]

A secondary result of the movement for reform in the federal service was a model of progressive personnel practices for state and local government. In 1895, Chicago became the first major city to establish a civil service commission.[5] In addition to appointments, another major issue to be addressed was the payment of wages and salaries. Wages had been determined individually, with personal favoritism playing a major part. A system of evaluating various jobs was needed. Following the lead of the U.S. Civil Service Commission, Chicago also became in 1912 the first city to establish a position classification and pay system.[6] Subsequently, many units of local government adopted classification plans, still the predominant form of job evaluation in cities and counties. Although by the 1920s most states and many large cities had moved away from spoils patronage, reform in local governments progressed at a slower pace. For example, it was 1935 before Jefferson County (Birmingham), Alabama, established a merit system.[7]

THE INDUSTRIAL WELFARE MOVEMENT

The counterpart in the private sector to the spoils system in government service was the economic system of **laissez-faire** capitalism, which developed with the Industrial Revolution.[8] The idea that a "winner" (official, owner, manager, etc.) should have practically unlimited freedom of action and control over subordinates was reinforced in the late 19th century by the philosophy of Social Darwinism, which incorrectly applied the genetic theories of Charles Darwin to social and economic situations. Employees were thought to have lost the struggle for dominance and were expected to submit to the wishes of owners and managers, who had prevailed in the struggle for "survival of the fittest." In the factories hours were long, wages were low, and working conditions were very poor. Management was very much opposed to labor unions and during the late 1880s played a major role in discrediting the Knights of Labor, which had achieved modest success in bargaining with employers on behalf of unskilled workers.

Still, however, some in management believed that their position carried with it an obligation to make things better for the working class. The concerns of these reformers led to the **industrial welfare movement**, which focused on improving conditions for employees both in the workplace and in their lives away from the job. Firms began to establish positions to assist workers with education, housing, medical care, and related matters. These **welfare secretaries** or social secretaries were the first of several types of personnel specialists in such areas as employment, training, and safety.

Thus in both business and government it can be seen that the various personnel activities were beginning to appear. As their benefits became obvious to employers, grouping them together was the next logical step. Although this was some years away, the foundation for the personnel function was now in place.

THE EMERGENCE OF PERSONNEL MANAGEMENT

While the reform movements in both the public and private sectors led to a number of personnel activities, for most of these activities there was no underlying body of knowledge or set of principles. Accordingly practice was an art, largely based on trial and error. Research on task design and worker efficiency, along with the application of psychology in work settings, were the precursors of the "science" of personnel management. These developments and the achievements of the reform movements led to the development of personnel management as a professional field and to the establishment of personnel departments in industry and government.

SCIENTIFIC MANAGEMENT AND THE EFFICIENCY MOVEMENT

The late 1800s saw the rise of the efficiency movement. Both the public and private sectors were heavily influenced by the thinking of Frederick W. Taylor. His book, *The Principles of Scientific Management*, published in 1911, emphasized planning, job design, and efficiency.[9] He believed that all tasks should be analyzed and that management has a responsibility to determine how each task can be performed in the "one best way" by each worker. Taylor's four principles of **scientific management** are shown in Exhibit 2-2. The concerns of scientific management were translated into standardization of positions and the development of task instructions, job standards, and pay related to performance.

The contemporaries of Taylor in the efficiency movement included Frank and Lillian Gilbreath, who pioneered time and motion study, and Henry Gantt, who developed the Gantt Chart, still used in work scheduling. Although Taylor himself recognized the humanitarian and motivational aspects of the worker's role, scientific management heavily emphasized planning and simplification of tasks. Employees who actually performed the tasks were often regarded as cogs in a machine.

The application of scientific management to the government sector was carried on by **bureaus of municipal research**, which were unique to the public domain.[10] Most notable was the New York Bureau of Municipal Research, established in 1906. These bureaus were privately sponsored and financed and derived their strength and influence from the fact that they were outside the government. The bureau movement thus evoked a sense of citizen responsibility, right, and participation quite unlike the application of scientific management in business. The bureaus also were the antecedent of university-based centers and institutes of government.

EXHIBIT 2-2	
TAYLOR'S PRINCIPLES OF SCIENTIFIC MANAGEMENT	1. Development of a true science of managing, complete with clearly stated laws, rules, and principles to replace old rule-of-thumb methods. 2. Scientific selection, training, and development of workers; whereas in the past, workers were randomly chosen and often untrained. 3. Enthusiastic cooperation with workers to ensure that all work is performed in accordance with scientific principles. 4. Equal division of tasks and responsibilities between workers and management.

Source: Frederick W. Taylor, *The Principles of Scientific Management* (New York: Harper, 1911).

EARLY INDUSTRIAL PSYCHOLOGY

While Taylor and others were concerned with finding the best ways for workers to perform tasks, researchers in **industrial psychology** were studying how to design selection procedures that would match workers' qualifications with jobs. By 1890 the Civil Service Commission was beginning to develop intelligence and trade tests. In 1913 Hugo Munsterberg published *Psychology and Industrial Efficiency*, which described studies in selecting streetcar motormen and telephone switchboard operators.[11] He later developed the concept of statistical validity, a technique for measuring how well an employment test predicts future job performance. During World War I, the U.S. Army developed the Army Alpha and Beta tests to place recruits in appropriate military specialties. Research into assessment devices that accurately measure applicants' abilities and motivation continues to this day.

ESTABLISHMENT OF PERSONNEL DEPARTMENTS

By the early 1900s, along with continued developments in worker efficiency and employment testing, specialized personnel activities such as employment, safety, wage administration, pensions, and employee welfare were being grouped into administrative units. In 1917 Standard Oil of New Jersey created a personnel and training department to coordinate several related programs. This was considered the model for the personnel departments that were beginning to be established in industry.[12] During that time civil service departments in state and local governments were also adding activities, often beginning with classification and pay systems, discussed earlier.

As these departments were established, a framework for the development and dissemination of knowledge to support their work began to appear.[13] By 1920 Ordway Tead was teaching a personnel course at Columbia University, and in 1922 Tead and Henry Metcalf published *Personnel Administration*, the first comprehensive textbook in the field.[14] The authors' example of a personnel department is shown in Exhibit 2-3. The foundations of classification and pay were set forth by a congressional commission in 1920 and codified in the federal Classification Act of 1923.[15] Included in these principles was the standard of equal pay for equal work, a precept that would take 40 more years to become established in personnel practice and employment law. Professional journals also began to appear in the field. For example, the *Journal of Personnel Research* (now called *Personnel Journal*) was first published in 1922.

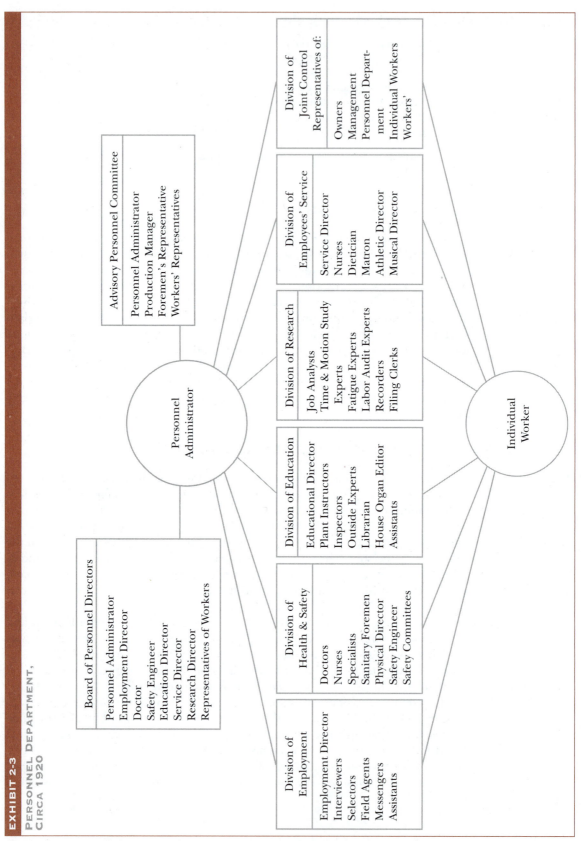

EXHIBIT 2-3
PERSONNEL DEPARTMENT, CIRCA 1920

Board of Personnel Directors

Personnel Administrator
Employment Director
Doctor
Safety Engineer
Education Director
Service Director
Research Director
Representatives of Workers

Advisory Personnel Committee

Personnel Administrator
Production Manager
Foremen's Representative
Workers' Representatives

Personnel Administrator

Individual Worker

Division of Employment

Employment Director
Interviewers
Selectors
Field Agents
Messengers
Assistants

Division of Health & Safety

Doctors
Nurses
Specialists
Sanitary Foremen
Physical Director
Safety Engineer
Safety Committees

Division of Education

Educational Director
Plant Instructors
Inspectors
Outside Experts
Librarian
House Organ Editor
Assistants

Division of Research

Job Analysis
Time & Motion Study
Experts
Fatigue Experts
Labor Audit Experts
Recorders
Filing Clerks

Division of Employees' Service

Service Director
Nurses
Dietician
Matron
Athletic Director
Musical Director

Division of Joint Control
Representatives of:

Owners
Management
Personnel Department
Individual Workers
Workers'

Source: Ordway Tead and Henry C. Metcalf, *Personnel Administration* (New York: McGraw-Hill, 1920), 38.

COMING OF AGE

During the next 30 years the personnel function evolved into a collection of core activities that continue to this day. Major influences on theory and practice included the **human relations movement**, labor legislation, World War II, and the peacetime economic boom.

THE HUMAN RELATIONS MOVEMENT

Scientific management and the efficiency movement produced significant advances in personnel management through focusing closely on positions and on efficient task performance. The human relations movement broadened the focus, showing the importance of interpersonal and social factors in organizational productivity. One of the most important breakthroughs resulted from a series of studies conducted at the Hawthorne Works of the Western Electric Company between 1924 and 1932.[16] Known as the Hawthorne experiments, the studies were designed to assess the effects of lighting and ventilation on worker productivity. In one experiment, production increased when lighting was improved, but it continued to increase when lighting was reduced. Other unexplained outcomes began to appear. It became clear that factors other than working conditions were operating, and social scientists were brought in. The most notable was Elton Mayo, who with his colleagues continued the research with a new emphasis on group behavior and workers' feelings.

The major contribution of the Hawthorne experiments was evidence that the "one best way" was too simplistic. The work showed very clearly that social interactions among employees and with management had a great influence on worker productivity. Further experimentation confirmed the importance of teamwork, cooperation, and participative management.

LABOR LEGISLATION

Although labor unions such as the Knights of Labor (KOL) had always existed in the United States, they were not seen as legitimate by management, which had no legal obligation to bargain with them over such issues as wages and working conditions. The laws and court system, along with public opinion, were hostile to union tactics, especially strikes. During the Great Depression public opinion began to shift, and in 1935 the Wagner Act established the rights of industrial employees to form unions and to bargain collectively with management. National unions such as the American Federation of Labor (AFL) and the Congress of Industrial Organizations (CIO) were able to organize large numbers of workers in mass production industries and greatly improve wages and working conditions.[17] The Wagner Act also provided the basic model for the labor relations process that would later develop in the public sector. The Fair Labor Standards Act, passed in 1938, was not to apply to local government until almost 50 years later. Nevertheless, most cities and counties took the cue from private industry and paid the minimum wage. Many also voluntarily paid overtime for all hours worked over 40 in a week.

SPECIALIZATION OF PERSONNEL ACTIVITIES

By the 1940s the personnel function was responsible for a diverse collection of activities. These activities developed into specialized areas such as employment, compensation, and employee relations, each with its own specialized body of knowledge. In 1940, for example, Sears, Roebuck and Company began conducting surveys to determine employees' attitudes about their jobs and the company. Through the use of research methods developed by social scientists, the company was able to identify key areas of employee dissatisfaction and focus on potential problem areas.[18] During this period quantitative methods of job evaluation called point factor plans were being developed to establish wage structures. Slightly modified versions of these early plans are still being used.[19]

WORLD WAR II AND THE POSTWAR BOOM

With the onset of World War II the U.S. economy was rapidly converted to the production of war materiel. Personnel departments aided the war effort by administering wage regulations, managing a workforce that now included large numbers of women, and facilitating worker productivity. At the same time the armed forces had to classify millions of enlistees into various military occupations, and testing was used on a scale never before seen.

When the war ended, many feared a depression, but instead there was an economic boom. There were good jobs available for returning veterans, and the end of wage controls and rationing meant that most people would finally share in the American Dream. With the merger of the AFL and CIO the labor movement reached its high-water mark. There were concerns, however, that all groups were not sharing equally, especially women, minorities, and older persons. Women generally earned less than men for performing the same work. Although the civil rights movement during the 1950s dramatically changed public attitudes regarding race discrimination, African Americans continued to have a low economic status.

INCREASING INFLUENCE OF THE LEGAL ENVIRONMENT

As it became apparent that these issues were connected to the workplace, national social policy began to focus on the employment relationship. Major federal legislation was passed in the area of fair employment and many states adopted laws providing for collective bargaining by government employees.

FEDERAL EQUAL EMPLOYMENT LAWS

During the 1950s and early 1960s employment testing had become popular and was generally considered to be a fair method of selection. In 1963 the highly publicized case of *Myart v. Motorola* caused personnel practitioners, industrial psychologists, and test publishers to deal with a whole set of new concerns. For example, many tests were improperly administered, culturally and racially biased, and not related to job performance.[20] Recognition grew that the most pervasive discriminatory effects might result from seemingly neutral practices such as tests, education and experience requirements, and height and weight standards, practices that also would perpetuate effects of past discrimination. In 1964, after much debate, Congress passed the Civil Rights Act, a landmark piece of social legislation. Title VII of the act, along with several major Supreme Court decisions, required employers to revise selection practices and eliminate barriers to job mobility. The provisions of Executive Order 11246 required private firms that contracted with the federal government to have affirmative action plans (AAPs). Other private and governmental organizations also developed AAPs, some on a voluntary basis and others because of federal court orders and consent decrees. Other equal employment legislation during the 1960s included the Equal Pay Act (1963) and the Age Discrimination in Employment Act (1967). These laws applied to private industry at the time of their passage, but within a few years coverage was extended to local governments.

REGULATION OF LABOR RELATIONS IN THE PUBLIC SECTOR

http://www.natat.org
The National Association of Towns and Townships (NATaT) is an organization that educates law-makers and public policy officials about issues and opportunities facing small town governments.

The 1960s also saw a number of labor disputes at the federal level, including strikes and the implementation of Executive Order 10988, which provided the framework for labor relations in the federal government. By then a number of states had passed labor legislation affecting local government, modeled after the basic process established by the Wagner Act of 1935 as amended by later federal laws including the Taft-Hartley Act (1947) and the Landrum-Griffin Act (1959). The right to strike against a public employer remains a major issue and is usually prohibited or limited.

CHANGING EMPHASIS OF CIVIL SERVICE REFORM

By the 1970s the Civil Service Commission had come under severe criticism for inefficiency, concentration of power in the federal bureaucracy, and lack of opportunities for minorities and women. The emphasis of the reform movement changed from protecting government employees from spoils patronage to providing the president with more authority to carry out electoral mandates. The Civil Service Reform Act of 1978 brought about major changes and also had a major influence on the personnel function in state and local government. The Civil Service Commission was replaced by the Office of Personnel Management (OPM), an independent agency intended to work closely with the president to manage the personnel aspects of the federal bureaucracy. The director is appointed by the president and confirmed by the Senate. The act also created the Merit Systems Protection Board (MSPB), with general oversight functions.

REFORM IN STATE AND LOCAL GOVERNMENT

The reform movement also tended to change how the personnel function was organized and managed in state and local government. The term *executive responsibility* was used to describe a model in which the personnel function reports to the

---

The goal of making the federal service more responsive to executive leadership was accomplished by the Civil Service Reform Act of 1978, but the pressure for reform had been building for 40 years. With the election of Franklin D. Roosevelt in 1932 and the New Deal, the role of government shifted from providing well-established services to initiating programs and change. In 1937 President Roosevelt's Committee on Administrative Management, known as the Brownlow Committee, reported that the Civil Service System was an impediment to the president's ability to carry out his electoral mandate, and that the executive branch should have more authority over personnel management. The later Commissions on Organization of the Executive Branch of Government, chaired by former president Herbert Hoover (the Hoover Commissions), came to essentially the same conclusions in reports issued in 1949 and 1955.

LATTER-DAY REFORM

Source: Frederick C. Mosher, *Democracy in the Public Service* (New York: Oxford, 1982), 83–85.

chief executive officer of the jurisdiction. The model (discussed in detail in Chapter 1) came with the city manager/county administrator movement and is one of the tenets of nonpartisan reform of local government. In this arrangement the chief executive appoints and may dismiss the personnel administrator and department heads. Lower-level managers and operating or "classified" employees, however, are often covered by a merit system. Allowing the chief executive to exert control over individuals in policy-making positions is designed to promote innovation and accountability.

MERIT SYSTEM PRINCIPLES

Another feature of the Civil Service Reform Act was to write into law the set of **merit system principles** shown in Exhibit 2-4. These principles apply directly only to the federal government; however, they provide an excellent expression of national policy to state and local governments. Notice several areas that apply particularly in the public sector, such as those relating to political coercion and "whistle-blowing." Another interesting aspect is the endorsement of the concept of equal pay for work of equal value (comparable worth). This issue also has major implications for local governments.

EXHIBIT 2-4

MERIT SYSTEM PRINCIPLES

1. Recruitment should be from qualified individuals from appropriate sources in an endeavor to achieve a workforce from all segments of society, and selection and advancement should be determined solely on the basis of relative ability, knowledge, and skills, after fair and open competition which assures that all receive equal opportunity.
2. All employees and applicants for employment should receive fair and equitable treatment in all aspects of personnel management without regard to political affiliation, race, color, religion, sex, marital status, age, or handicapped condition, and with proper regard for their privacy and constitutional rights.
3. Equal pay should be provided for work of equal value, with appropriate consideration of both national and local rates paid by employers in the private sector, and appropriate incentives and recognition should be provided for excellence in performance.
4. All employees should maintain high standards of integrity, conduct, and concern for the public interest.
5. The federal workforce should be used efficiently and effectively.
6. Employees should be retained on the basis of adequacy of their performance, inadequate performance should be corrected, and employees should be separated if they cannot or will not improve their performance to meet required standards.
7. Employees should be provided effective education and training in cases in which such education and training would result in better organizational and individual performance.
8. Employees should be protected against arbitrary action, personal favoritism, or coercion for partisan political purposes, and prohibited from using their official authority or influence for the purpose of interfering with or affecting the results of an election or nomination for election.
9. Employees should be protected against reprisal for the lawful disclosure of information which the employee reasonably believes evidences a violation of any law, rule or regulation, or mismanagement, a gross waste of funds, and abuse of authority, or a substantial and specific danger to the public health or safety.

Source: Civil Service Reform Act at 5 U.S.C. § 2301.

Ironically, leadership to state and local governments was effectively dropped from the executive mandate in the 1980s. The Intergovernmental Personnel Act of 1970 provided for federal assistance designed to strengthen state and local personnel systems in line with merit principles. Up until 1980 the Bureau of Intergovernmental Personnel Programs did a commendable job in this area and also published a much-needed series of resource materials for local governments. During the 1980s, however, research and demonstration projects, training grants, and similar activities were severely curtailed due to lack of funds.

PROFESSIONALIZATION OF PERSONNEL MANAGEMENT

By the 1970s, the field of personnel management had become well established, but practitioners were faced with a field that was complex, interdisciplinary, and constantly changing. Their professional competence was a matter of growing concern. The issue was addressed by professional societies, particularly the American Society of Personnel Administration (ASPA), which changed its name in 1990 to the Society for Human Resource Management (SHRM), and the International Personnel Management Association (IPMA), by local government organizations such as the National League of Cities and the National Association of Counties, and by colleges and universities.

http://www.theroundtable.org/
The Public Employees Roundtable promotes interest in public service careers and provides links to local government websites.

CERTIFICATION PROGRAMS

In 1974 ASPA (SHRM) established the Personnel Accreditation Institute (now Human Resource Certification Institute). This initiative promoted professional development in two major ways. It identified a body of knowledge pertaining to the field and provided a means for personnel professionals to certify their knowledge and competence. Practitioners, academicians, and consultants with the requisite combination of education and experience can now earn certification as a Generalist–Operational Level, Generalist–Policy Level, or as a Specialist–Policy Level. Credentials are earned by passing a comprehensive examination. Additional certification programs were also established in HR specialty areas including compensation, training and development, benefits, and safety.

EDUCATIONAL REQUIREMENTS FOR PRACTITIONERS

Colleges and universities had for many years offered academic courses and curricula that provided a foundation of knowledge in personnel management. By the 1970s many larger organizations required a bachelor's degree for a beginning job in personnel and encouraged those without the necessary educational background to enroll in appropriate academic courses. Some colleges and universities also began to offer continuing education courses in management for local governments through institutes of government and similar organizations. These programs were often sponsored by state affiliates of the national local government organizations mentioned above. For example, in 1976 the Center for Governmental Services at Auburn University, in cooperation with the Alabama Association of County Commissioners, began to offer workshops in classification and pay and employment law to county officials. These activities ultimately led to the establishment of a formal certification program for city and county personnel managers. The program was keyed to HRIC requirements and was taught by certified professionals.[21]

THE MODERN ERA

The term *modern era* has a generational significance; therefore this section summarizes developments that have taken place during the past 20 years, including the shift to a human resources focus, the strategic approach to HR management, and how HR management increasingly displays the characteristics of a profession. The section concludes by examining the many similarities as well as some important differences in HR management between the public and private sectors.

THE HUMAN RESOURCES FOCUS

By the 1980s the term *human resources* had begun to appear, often as a suffix to the more familiar "personnel," as an indication of the increased role and scope of the function. The term also represented a change in emphasis from activities that were essentially reactive (such as examination, position classification, and administration of work rules) to activities that were more proactive (such as employee development, quality of worklife initiatives, and job enrichment). By the early 1990s human resources had become established in the literature and was the official name of most departments in both the public and private sectors. As previously noted, ASPA became SHRM and the name of its publication was changed from *Personnel Administrator* to *HR Magazine*. The IPMA retains the older designation along with its publication, *Public Personnel Management*. It should be noted, however, that articles in that journal use the term *human resources* with increasing frequency, and that both the term and what it represents seem to have taken hold.

http://www.cce.cornell.
edu/programs/
restructuring
**Restructuring Local
Government is an article
on some of the techniques
local governments can use
to improve service delivery,
such as decentralization
and introducing
competition.**

THE STRATEGIC APPROACH TO HR MANAGEMENT

Also during the 1980s, strategic management (discussed in Chapters 1 and 5) became prominent. Strategic management begins with the development of a mission and vision and the determination of organizational resources and capabilities. The organization then prepares a strategic plan to guide activities in all departments. While the concept and methodologies of strategic management were originally associated with business organizations, they are increasingly used by public sector organizations including local governments.[22] Even though local governments are not businesses, they must manage their human resources in a "business-oriented" manner. That involves designing HR systems and processes that are driven by the government's mission and strategic objectives. A strategic approach is essential in meeting challenges brought by workplace demographics and diversity issues, competition in the "market" for government services, and the pervasive influence of information technology (discussed in Chapter 1).

HR MANAGEMENT AS A PROFESSION

The various contributors to HR management such as researchers, writers, consultants, and practitioners have, for many years, been regarded as "professionals." Moreover, the area of HR management increasingly has the characteristics of a "profession." These include a recognized body of knowledge, ongoing research and publication of results, certification requirements, and codes of ethics. In 1999 the IPMA developed a competency model for HR professionals in the public sector and established a certification program (for details, see Chapter 1). However, HR management differs from certain other professions such as law and medicine in one important way. Human resource practitioners, not being self-employed and lacking either the protection or control of legal or licensing sanctions tied directly to professional bodies, must owe ultimate loyalty to their employing organizations rather than to professional or ethical obligations. The key word is *obligations*. A city HR director could subvert the IPMA Code of Ethics by basing a promotion decision on political considerations rather than on merit principles and have no fear of sanctions. A city attorney who knowingly violated the Code of Professional Responsibility by withholding a relevant document during pretrial discovery procedures would be subject to disciplinary action by the state bar association.

COMPARISON OF PUBLIC AND PRIVATE SECTOR HR FUNCTIONS

As it has evolved, the human resource function in the public sector, including local government, is not, in many important aspects, greatly different from its counterpart in the private sector.[23] In other words, although the two have arisen from different beginnings and developed along different evolutionary tracks, many of the distinctions have become blurred and the similarities have become more apparent. For example, the idea that a job in the public sector was a guarantee of lifetime employment (certainly not characteristic in the private sector) has been substantially discredited by the reform movement and developments such as privatization of government services. State and local government merit systems are being revamped to provide more administrative discretion regarding performance appraisal and demotion and dismissals for unsatisfactory work.

The factor of leadership turnover, often cited as a major difference between sectors, is less significant than in the past. Corporate mergers and acquisitions have had a major impact in the private sector. Hostile takeovers in particular often lead to changes in HR management that are sudden and traumatic. On the other hand, the executive responsibility model (discussed above) gives newly elected officials a major influence in HR management. But the factor that has had the greatest influence is undoubtedly the legal environment. In the 1970s and 1980s the coverage of all major EEO laws and regulations was extended to the public sector. In 1985 the U.S. Supreme Court brought all functions of local government under the provisions of the Fair Labor Standards Act. In 1990 the Americans with Disabilities Act established employment rights for citizens with physical and mental disabilities.

There are, of course, important differences between sectors, particularly in the case of local government. While this is changing, a local government is still less subject to the discipline of a "market" for its services. It is constrained mainly by taxpayers who elect public officials. Private sector goals tend to be more measurable because they can be stated in terms of profit and loss, units produced, sales volume, and similar objective measures. Officials of local governments must aggregate and facilitate the viewpoints of diverse and often conflicting interests. Goals tend to be ambiguous and performance requirements are often not clear. Another difference is that permanent employees of a governmental unit generally have more rights in their jobs, including the right to due process.

There are also differences between sectors in the application of certain EEO laws and regulations. Major differences exist in both federal and state laws that regulate labor relations and health and safety. Finally, there are unique institutional arrangements in the public sector. A human resource function administered by an independent board or commission (discussed in Chapter 1) is common in many medium-sized to large units of local government. The idea of human resource decisions being made outside the executive chain of command would be anathema in private enterprise.

Public vs. private comparisons are an interesting intellectual exercise, but they often miss the point, which is that the two sectors face, in similar environments, the common organizational issue of identification and resolution of practical problems. Variables such as size, financial resources, quality of leadership, and employee motivation cut across both sectors. The goal of HR management in any setting is to attract and develop the human talent necessary to accomplish the mission of the organization.

SUMMARY

Although HR management as a specialized function did not begin to emerge until the early 1900s, its antecedents can be traced to developments that took place throughout the 19th century, most notably the achievements of reform movements in both the public and private sectors. By the 1890s, following the lead of the federal government, state and local governments had begun to replace spoils patronage with merit systems. In industry positions such as welfare secretaries were being established to improve the life of workers, both on and off the job.

While the reform movements had led to a number of personnel activities, for most of these activities there was no underlying body of knowledge or set of principles. Research on task design and worker efficiency, along with the application of psychology in work settings, were the precursors of the "science" of personnel management. By the 1920s these developments and the achievements of the reform movements had led to the development of personnel management as a professional field and to the establishment of personnel departments in industry and government.

During the next 30 years the personnel function evolved into a collection of core activities that continue to this day. Major influences on theory and practice included the human relations movement, labor legislation, and World War II. When the war ended, many feared a depression, but instead there was an economic boom. There were concerns, however, that all groups were not sharing equally in the prosperity, especially women, minorities, and older persons.

As it became apparent that these issues were connected to the workplace, national social policy began to focus on the employment relationship. During the 1960s major federal legislation was passed in the area of fair employment, including the Equal Pay Act, Civil Rights Act (Title VII), and the Age Discrimination in Employment Act. Many states also adopted laws providing for collective bargaining by government employees.

By the 1970s the focus of the civil service reform movement changed from protecting government employees from spoils patronage to providing the president with more authority to carry out electoral mandates. The Civil Service Reform Act of 1978 brought about major changes and also had a major influence on the personnel function in state and local government. Also during the 1970s, professional issues received major emphasis. Certification programs were established and many larger government organizations began to require a college degree for a beginning job in personnel. Colleges and universities established continuing education programs for local government practitioners, often keyed to certification requirements.

By the 1980s the term *human resources,* had begun to appear, often as a suffix to the more familiar *personnel,* as an indication of the increased role and scope of the function. A strategic approach to HR management became essential to align HR activities with the organization mission and objectives and to meet various challenges. The area of HR management has increasingly become characterized as a "profession."

As it exists today the HR function in local government in many respects is similar to its counterpart in other public and private settings. Although there are some important differences in how certain HR activities are performed in local government, the goal of HR management in any setting is to attract and develop the human talent necessary to accomplish the mission of the organization.

QUESTIONS FOR REVIEW AND DISCUSSION

1. What were the achievements of the reform movements in government and industry during the 19th century?
2. Briefly describe the contributions of scientific management and early industrial psychology to the HR field.
3. Identify the activities that were brought together to form the first personnel departments in industry and government.
4. When did employment discrimination become a major social issue? Identify the major equal employment opportunity laws that were passed during that period.
5. Describe the recent emphasis of civil service reform. What are the implications for local government?
6. Discuss, in general terms, the evolution of personnel/human resource management as a professional field.
7. What is implied by the term *strategic approach* to HR management?
8. As it has evolved, how is HR management in local government similar to its counterpart in other settings? How is it different?

ENDNOTES

[1] The organization and content of this chapter draws on the work of a number of writers. Historical implications are a major theme in Jay M. Shafritz et al., *Personnel Management in Government*, 4th ed. (New York: Dekker, 1992). Additional historical context is provided by Frederick C. Mosher, *Democracy in the Public Service*, 2d ed. (New York: Oxford, 1982) and Charles Cooke, *Biography of an Ideal* (Washington, D.C.: U.S. Civil Service Commission, 1958). Wendell L. French includes a major section on the history of HR management in *Human Resources Management*, 4th ed. (Boston: Houghton Mifflin, 1998).

[2] This discussion is based on Cooke, 7–53.

[3] Cooke, 53.

[4] Mosher, 57.

[5] Shafritz et al., 21.

[6] Shafritz et al., 134.

[7] Brenda V. Digges and Robert R. Freelund, "From Spoils System to Merit System—60 Years of Progress in Jefferson County, Alabama," *Public Personnel Management* 26 (Winter 1997), 559–564.

[8] French, 27–29.

[9] Frederick W. Taylor, *The Principles of Scientific Management* (New York: Harper & Brothers, 1919).

[10] Mosher, 74–75. See also Lawrence J. O'Toole, Jr., "Harry F. Byrd, Sr., and the New York Bureau of Municipal Research: Lessons from an Ironic Alliance," *Public Administration Review* 46 (March/April 1986), 113–123.

[11] Hugo Munsterberg, *Psychology and Industrial Efficiency* (Boston: Houghton Mifflin, 1913).

[12] French, 35–36.

[13] French, 36–37.

[14] Ordway Tead and Henry C. Metcalf, *Personnel Administration* (New York: McGraw-Hill, 1920).

[15] Shafritz et al., 136–137.

[16] William J. Dickson, "Hawthorne Experiments," *Encyclopedia of Management*, 2d ed. (New York: Van Nostrand Reinhold, 1973), 298–302.

[17] William H. Holley and Roger S. Wolters, *The Labor Relations Process*, 6th ed. (Homewood, Ill.: Dryden, 2001, forthcoming).

[18] French, 30.

[19] George T. Milkovich and Jerry M. Newman, *Compensation*, 6th ed. (Boston: Irwin/McGraw-Hill, 1999), 122.

[20] Evelyn M. Idelson, *Eliminating Discrimination: A Compelling National Priority* (Washington, D.C.: Equal Employment Opportunity Commission, 1979), II-1; and H. C. Lockwood, "Testing Minority Applicants for Employment," *Personnel Journal* 42 (April 1963), 356–360.

[21] James A. Buford Jr., *Personnel Management and Human Resources in Local Government* (Auburn University: Center for Governmental Services, 1s991), 11.

[22] Mark H. Moore, *Creating Public Value: Strategic Management in Government* (Cambridge, Mass.: Harvard University Press, 1997), and Steven Cohen and William Eimicke, *Tools for Innovators: Creative Strategies for Managing Public Organizations* (San Francisco: Jossey-Bass, 1998).

[23] See, for example, J. Norman Baldwin, "Public vs. Private: Not the Different, Not the Consequential," *Public Personnel Management* 16 (Summer 1987), 181–183.

CHAPTER 3
THE LEGAL ENVIRONMENT OF
HUMAN RESOURCE MANAGEMENT

SEE YOU IN COURT

Employees and applicants who believe their legal rights have been violated can be expected to seek redress from enforcement agencies and the courts. The following are selected cases involving local governments that were settled during 1999 and 2000. In most instances the employer did not acknowledge any wrongdoing.

- Lee County (Tampa), Florida, agreed to pay about $500,000 to two toll bridge collectors and their wives to settle an age discrimination and retaliation lawsuit brought by the Equal Employment Opportunity Commission on their behalf. The lawsuit, which was brought in 1999, alleged that a 60-year-old male was constructively discharged after filing an internal complaint because the promotion was given to a man in his 20s. His supervisor was fired at age 65 after giving evidence in an internal investigation of the complaint. The men's wives were included in the settlement because the EEOC had alleged that the county had refused to consider them for their husbands' jobs in retaliation for their husbands' actions. (*EEOC v. Lee County*, M.D. Fla., No. 99-248-CIV-FTM-24D, 2000)
- The U.S. Court of Appeals for the 4th Circuit upheld a trial court's award of $260,000 in compensatory and punitive damages in a sexual harassment lawsuit brought under Title VII of the Civil Rights Act. The case was brought against a North Carolina Sheriff Department alleging that the chief deputy had harassed a female employee from 1992 to 1995. (*Carter v. Barker*, 4th Cir. No. 99-1433)
- A U.S. district court ordered the city of Houston to pay fire department dispatchers and arson investigators $6.2 million and firefighters $4.4 million for unpaid overtime wages and later awarded $2.8 million in legal fees. The lawsuit consolidated 2,600 claims alleging that the city had violated the Fair Labor Standards Act. (*Vela v. Houston*, S.D. Tex., No. H-97-3471, 1999 and 2000)

- In Holyoke, Massachusetts, a police officer who had been suspended for violation of 11 department rules relating to release of information alleged in federal court that the suspension violated his First Amendment rights to free speech. The court determined that one of the rules was a facially unconstitutional "gag order" and that another excessively prohibited otherwise permissible speech. The court issued an injunction prohibiting the police department from enforcing the rules. (*Wagner v. City of Holyoke,* D. Mass., No. 98-30170-MAP, 2000)

Source: Bureau of National Affairs, *Government Employee Relations* 38 (1871, 1872, 1873, July and August 2000).

INTRODUCTION

These examples illustrate only a few of the ways in which organizations can encounter legal issues in the workplace. Laws and regulations cover almost every aspect of the employment relationship and many are quite complex. Understanding and complying with these mandates is a shared responsibility of HR and line management, and the consequences of not meeting this responsibility are very serious. Answering and possibly litigating a charge is time consuming and expensive even if the organization prevails. When the organization loses (or agrees to a settlement), the remedy imposed by an enforcement agency or a court usually adds to the cost in terms of back pay, damages, court costs, attorney fees, etc. Other consequences include unfavorable publicity and damage to employee relations through loss of trust.

There are five major components of the legal environment: The first component consists mainly of laws passed by Congress as an expression of national social policy, such as Title VII of the Civil Rights Act of 1964, which addresses employment discrimination. Also, however, certain presidential executive orders apply to employment practices in local government. Federal laws and executive orders are called **statutory law**. The federal court system provides the second component by interpreting the law, such as by determining intent and coverage, and occasionally deciding constitutional questions. Rulings by federal appeals courts and the U.S. Supreme Court set important precedents, such as the decision in *Griggs v. Duke Power Company*, which established the framework for litigation brought under Title VII. The collective set of court decisions in an employment area are the **case law**. The next component involves regulations issued by federal agencies established to enforce the law. These regulations are revised and updated as necessary to comply with major court decisions and are considered authoritative sources of information on compliance practices. An example would be the "Uniform Guidelines on Employee Selection Procedures," which applies to Title VII. The term often applied to agency regulations is **administrative law**. Certain basic rights set forth in the U.S. Constitution apply also to the employment relationship in local government. Thus an important component of the legal environment is **constitutional law**. Finally, state laws and local ordinances establish a body of law that may contain additional provisions or extend coverage in employment matters but may not conflict with federal laws, constitutional requirements, or federal court rulings. This component of the legal environment is known as **common law**. This chapter will focus mainly on federal statutory and constitutional law, case law, and administrative law.

In discussing the legal environment it is useful to consider first the area of equal employment opportunity and the federal laws and guidelines that address employment discrimination based on race, sex, disability, and other prohibited classifications. Another important area concerns laws that apply to other employment issues such wages and hours, income sufficiency, workplace health and safety, and collective bargaining. The next area covers in some detail the constitutional rights and protections that extend to the workplace for employees of local government. The final area discusses the nature and scope of state employment laws.[1] Major topics addressed in this chapter are: federal regulation of discrimination in employment, federal regulation of the workplace and employment relationship, constitutional provisions that apply to employees of local government, and state employment laws.

FEDERAL REGULATION OF EMPLOYMENT DISCRIMINATION

The first federal laws affecting fair employment were passed in the era following the Civil War. However, the most important comprehensive federal legislation aimed at securing **equal employment opportunity (EEO)** has been a series of acts beginning in the early 1960s. Of these, the most encompassing is Title VII of the Civil Rights Act of 1964, as amended by the Equal Employment Opportunity Act of 1972. Other major laws include the Equal Pay Act of 1963, the Age Discrimination in Employment Act of 1967, and the Americans with Disabilities Act of 1990.

TITLE VII OF THE CIVIL RIGHTS ACT OF 1964

Title VII is the basic federal law expressing national policy to prohibit discrimination on the basis of race, color, national origin, religion, or sex in all aspects of employment and by all organizations with 15 or more employees. Title VII was extended to cover federal, state, and local public employers and educational institutions by the Equal Employment Opportunity Act of 1972. Title VII states:

> It shall be an unlawful employment practice for an employer (1) to fail or refuse to hire or to discharge any individual or otherwise to discriminate against any individual with respect to compensation, terms, conditions, or privileges of employment because of such individual's race, color, religion, sex, or national origin; or (2) to limit, segregate or classify his employees in any way that would deprive or tend to deprive any individual of employment opportunities or otherwise adversely affect his status as an employee because of such individual's race, color, religion, sex or national origin.[2]

http://www.eeoc.gov/
The U.S. Equal Employment Opportunity Commission (EEOC) provides comprehensive information and guidance regarding equal opportunity in employment through administrative and judicial enforcement of the federal civil rights laws and through education and technical assistance.

The effect of Title VII is to establish of groups of people identified by race, color, religion, sex or national origin who are "protected" from unfair employment practices. Thus, a black who applies for a job in a predominantly white organization is a member of a protected group, as is a woman who applies for a job that is male dominated. The concept of protected groups was extended by the Age Discrimination in Employment Act of 1967 to people over 40 years of age and by the Vocational Rehabilitation Act of 1973 and Americans with Disabilities Act of 1990 to disabled citizens.

Decisions made by federal appeals courts and the U.S. Supreme Court have interpreted the intent of Congress as to how the law is to be carried out. Title VII and other fair employment laws are administered by the U.S. Equal Employment Opportunity Commission (EEOC), an independent federal agency. The commission has issued guidelines on selection procedures; sex, national origin, and religious discrimination; affirmative action; and sexual harassment. These guidelines carry considerable weight with the courts in employment discrimination cases.

Thus, there is a body of statutory, administrative, and case law that provides a basic standard for fair employment.

All local governments covered by Title VII are required to keep specified records relating to employment actions. Organizations with more than 100 employees and smaller jurisdictions on a rotating sample basis must submit an annual report form to the EEOC, indicating by race, sex, and national origin employment by major functions, job classifications, and salary levels. These reports are used by the EEOC and by all other federal agencies as a primary indicator of EEO compliance. Employers also are required to place EEO posters in conspicuous places to provide information on the law to all employees and applicants.

INTERPRETATION OF THE LAW

When Title VII was enacted in 1964, many employers believed that discrimination consisted of conscious, overt acts of ill will or bias, or of identifiable unequal treatment of specific individuals or groups, mainly on the basis of their race. This type of discrimination is known as *disparate treatment* and is, of course, prohibited by Title VII, as is discrimination based on color, sex, religion, or national origin. Overt acts of bias and unequal treatment diminished after 1964; however, discrimination remained a problem. The key HR practice on which attention focused as a source of nonovert discrimination was employment testing. During the 1950s and early 1960s testing had become popular and was generally considered to be a fair method of selection. In 1963 the highly publicized case of *Myart v. Motorola* caused HR practitioners, industrial psychologists, and test publishers to deal with a whole set of new concerns. For example, many tests were improperly administered, culturally and racially biased, and unrelated to job performance.[3] Recognition grew that the most pervasive discriminatory effects might result from seemingly neutral practices such as tests, education and experience requirements, and height and weight standards, practices that also would perpetuate effects of past discrimination. Debate in Congress led to the passage of the Tower Amendment, which states:

> . . . nor shall it be an unlawful employment practice for an employer to give and to act upon the results of any professionally developed ability test provided that such test, its administration or action upon the results is not designed, intended or used to discriminate because of race, color, religion, sex and national origin.[4]

In a decision specifically interpreting the language and intent of the Tower Amendment, the landmark 1971 Supreme Court ruling in *Griggs v. Duke Power Co.* established the present legal standard of discrimination under Title VII: practices must be measured by their *consequences* and *effects*, not merely by motive or intent.[5] In deciding the case, the Court legitimized the EEOC "Guidelines" (now the 1978 "Uniform Guidelines") as having practically the force of law in selection discrimination cases.[6] The case involved an employer whose requirements of a high school diploma and minimum score on two aptitude tests led to a disproportionately low number of promotions for minority workers. The Court held that employment practices that have an adverse effect on minority applicants must be job related. The Court specifically stated:

> Under the Act, practices, procedures, or tests, neutral on their face, and even neutral in terms of intent, cannot be maintained if they operate to "freeze" the status quo of prior discriminatory practices . . . If an employment practice which operates to exclude [African Americans] cannot be shown to be related to job performance the practice is prohibited . . . Congress directed the thrust of the Act to consequences of employment discrimination, not simply the motivation.[7]

In *Griggs*, the Court established, and a subsequent series of decisions affirmed, that employment practices or standards, which operate to exclude groups protected by Title VII, are illegal and must be eliminated, unless the employer can demonstrate that they are required by "business necessity." Another interpretation made in *Griggs* concerns the term *professionally developed* tests. This means that a test must meet validity standards, not merely be "developed by a professional." "Business necessity" has been defined in *Griggs* and subsequent decisions to require demonstration by the employer that a practice is essential for effective job performance.

Griggs and related court decisions have thus established a second definition of discrimination. **Disparate treatment** occurs when persons protected by the law are treated differently from other employees or job applicants. That is, disparate treatment involves decision rules with a racial or sexual premise, and is on its face intentional discrimination. **Disparate impact** is typically unintentional and involves decision rules that have unequal racial or gender *consequences,* so that barriers are erected that appear to be neutral but have the effect of screening out a disproportionate number of minority applicants.

RECENT DEVELOPMENTS

During the period 1988–1990 a number of U.S. Supreme Court decisions favored employers by making it more difficult for plaintiffs to use statistics in making cases and easing evidentiary standards for showing business necessity. After much debate Congress passed and the president signed the Civil Rights Act of 1991 as an amendment to Title VII. The act strengthened existing protections and provided additional remedies. Key features of the legislation include the following:

*   Making discrimination illegal whenever it is a motivating factor in an employment decision even though the same decision would have been made in the absence of the discriminatory motive.

In Aesop's fable "The Fox and the Stork," both were offered a vessel of milk. The vessel had a long neck, which presented no problem for the stork because of his bill. The fox, however, try as he might, could not get the milk and went away hungry. Former U.S. Supreme Court

FAIRNESS—FOR THE FOX *AND* THE STORK

Chief Justice Warren E. Burger, in delivering the *Griggs* decision, used this fable to illustrate why the court will not permit so-called color blind employment practices that have the appearance of fairness, but disproportionately screen out minorities and are not related to job performance:

> What is required by Congress is the removal of artificial, arbitrary and unnecessary barriers to employment when the barriers operate invidiously to discriminate on the basis of racial or other impermissible classification. Congress has now provided that tests or criteria for employment or promotion may not provide equality of opportunity only in the sense of the fabled offer of milk to the stork and the fox. On the contrary, Congress has now required that the posture and condition of the job sector be taken into account. It has—to resort again to the fable—provided that the vessel in which the milk is offered be one all sectors can use. [Title VII] proscribes not only overt discrimination but practices that are fair in form, but discriminatory in operation . . .

Source: *Griggs v. Duke Power Company,* 401 U.S. 430 (1971).

- Allowing plaintiffs to make a prima facie case of discrimination by establishing either that a single employment practice or that a *group* of employment practices results in a disparate impact.
- Specifying that defendants in a disparate impact case have a burden of proof (rather than an easier burden of *production)* in showing business necessity.
- Defining business necessity as bearing a substantial and demonstrable relation to effective job *performance.*
- Facilitating prompt and orderly resolution of challenges to employment practices implementing litigated or consent decrees, with a general goal of ensuring that once an order is entered, it is final.
- Providing that a jury may award compensatory and/or punitive damages where the defendant engaged in an unlawful employment practice with "reckless or callous indifference to the federally protected rights of others."
- Encouraging the use of alternative dispute resolution procedures.[8]

ENFORCEMENT AND REMEDIES

The EEO liability process is set in motion when a potential charging party contacts the EEOC by phone, letter, or office visit and provides detailed information on the nature of the charge.[9] Exhibit 3-1 indicates the number and types of charges made during recent years. The EEOC will make an initial assessment of the allegations. If a charge is filed, the EEOC will send a copy of the charge to the employer. If there is a state or local agency that handles the type of discrimination claimed, a copy will be sent to that agency for possible resolution. If the charge is not resolved, the EEOC will reassume jurisdiction. Based on the results of the intake investigation the charge may be dismissed or assigned to an investigator to obtain additional evidence. A charge may also be referred for mediation in the alternative dispute resolution program (see below). A charge may be settled at any point in the process, or the EEOC may complete the investigation and make a determination of "reasonable cause" or "no cause."

Where "reasonable cause" is found after an investigation, the EEOC must seek to reach an agreement through conciliation that will eliminate all aspects of discrimination. Legal remedies required in a conciliation agreement are similar to those required by the courts and are adapted to specific findings of discrimination. They include ending discriminatory practices and systems; instituting nondiscriminatory practices and systems; and providing specific financial and other remedies to make victims of discrimination "whole," that is, placing them where they would have been had discrimination not occurred. Specific remedies include hiring, reassignment, promotion, training, retroactive seniority rights, back pay, and other compensation and benefits. Title VII authorizes back pay up to two years prior to filing a charge. Numerical remedies, setting goals for race, national origin, and sex and timetables for hiring, training, and promotions, are frequently used. Where conciliation is unsuccessful, the EEOC can litigate against both public and private employers or issue the charging party a private "right to sue." A charging party may also obtain this authorization at any time during the process, even if the EEOC finds for the employer.

In court cases, determination of which party carries the burden of producing evidence or of proving a case is very important. In Title VII cases, shifting evidentiary burdens have been designed to aid courts and litigants in arranging the presentation of evidence. In all cases, the *final* burden of proof lies with the plaintiff; that is, the person (employee or applicant) who claims an employer has violated the law. At various stages of the court process in Title VII cases, however, the burden of producing evidence shifts from one party to the other. The

EXHIBIT 3-1

U.S. EQUAL EMPLOYMENT
OPPORTUNITY COMMISSION CASES,
FISCAL YEARS 1992–1999

	FY 1992	FY 1993	FY 1994	FY 1995	FY 1996	FY 1997	FY 1998	FY 1999
Total charges[a]	72,302	87,942	91,189	87,529	77,990	80,680	79,591	77,444
Race	29,548	31,695	31,656	29,986	26,287	29,199	28,820	28,819
Sex	21,796	23,919	25,860	26,181	23,813	24,728	24,454	23,907
Disability[b]	1,048	15,274	18,859	19,798	18,046	18,108	17,806	17,007
Age	19,573	19,809	19,618	17,416	15,719	15,785	15,191	14,141
Retaliation	11,096	13,814	15,853	17,070	16,080	18,198	19,114	19,694
National origin	7,434	7,454	7,414	7,035	6,687	6,712	6,778	7,108
Religion	1,388	1,449	1,546	1,581	1,564	1,709	1,786	1,811
Equal Pay Act	1,294	1,328	1,381	1,275	969	1,134	1,071	1,044

[a] The number for total charges reflects the number of individual charge filings. Because individuals often file charges claiming multiple types of discrimination, the number of total charges for any given fiscal year will be less than the total of the eight types of discrimination listed.
[b] EEOC began enforcing the Americans with Disabilities Act on July 26, 1992.

Source: U.S. Equal Employment Opportunity Commission, "Charge Statistics FY1992 Through FY1999," *http://www.eeoc.gov/stats/charges.html* (September 5, 2000).

table presented in Exhibit 3-2 gives an overview of the required sequence, indicating the kinds of evidence that must be presented, as taken from various EEO court cases.

For disparate treatment cases, as shown in the table, the plaintiff has the first burden, set forth by the U.S. Supreme Court in *McDonnell-Douglas v. Green*,[10] and must establish a **prima facie** case of discrimination by showing that he or she belongs to a protected group; applied and was qualified but rejected; and the position remained open. If the plaintiff succeeds in establishing this prima facie case, the burden shifts to the defendant (stage 2). In order to shift the burden back, the defendant must present a legitimate, nondiscriminatory reason for its decision (otherwise, the defendant loses the case). The defendant's second burden was established in *Texas Department of Community Affairs v. Burdine*.[11]

Finally, if the defendant is successful in stage 2, the plaintiff again carries the burden in stage 3 and must show that the defendant's reason is actually a pretext for discrimination. This requires evidence of other discriminatory treatment by the employer, either against the plaintiff personally or against the plaintiffs' group in general. The third burden in disparate treatment cases was also established in *Burdine* and clarified in *St. Mary's Honor Center v. Hicks*.[12]

As the table indicates, the sequence for disparate impact cases is similar. The first and second burdens were established in the *Griggs* case, discussed above. The plaintiff can establish a prima facie case and shift the burden to the defendant by offering statistical evidence of a kind and degree sufficient to show that a practice or group of practices has caused the exclusion of applicants

EXHIBIT 3-2

SEQUENCE OF EVIDENCE AND
PROOF IN TITLE VII CASES

Evidentiary Burden	Disparate Treatment Cases	Disparate Impact Cases
First Burden (plaintiff)	Show that: • The person is a member of a protected group, *and* • The person applied for a job for which he or she was qualified, *and* • Despite being qualified, the person was rejected, *and* • After rejection the employer continued to seek other applicants with similar qualifications.	Show that: • One or more employment practices has an adverse effect on members of a protected group, *and* • The protected group represents a pool of qualified applicants.
Second Burden (defendant)	Provide: Legitimate, nondiscriminatory reason(s) for the rejection.	Show that: • The practice is justified by business necessity, *or* • The procedure or test has been validated in accordance with the "Uniform Guidelines."
Third Burden (plaintiff)	Show that: The defendant's reason(s) were a pretext for discrimination.	Show that: An alternative selection practice that meets the employer's needs but has less adverse impact is available.

for jobs or promotion because of their membership in a protected group. The defendant must now show that the practice in question is job related or required by business necessity. The Civil Rights Act of 1991 specified that this is a burden of proof. Finally, in stage 3, the plaintiff must now show that there is an alternative requirement that will serve the employer's interest in efficient and trustworthy workmanship without an undesirable effect on the protected group. The plaintiff's third burden in a disparate impact case was set forth in *Albemarle Paper Co. v. Moody.*[13]

ALTERNATIVE DISPUTE RESOLUTION

Title VII encourages parties to avoid litigation and resolve charges of discrimination through **alternative dispute resolution (ADR)**.[14] Actually, most cases are settled before trial, either by agreements worked out by employers and persons making complaints or through EEOC conciliation, discussed above. There are various forms of ADR including negotiation, mediation, fact finding, and arbitration. The form most favored by the EEOC is mediation.

Mediation is an informal process during which an impartial third party, the mediator, assists the disputing parties in reaching a mutually acceptable settlement. The mediator is not a judge and does not make a decision or impose a solution; rather the mediator identifies issues, encourages dialogue, clarifies misunderstandings, and explores solutions. The EEOC has entered into agreements with nonprofit organizations to provide qualified mediators who typically serve without pay or for a nominal fee. If the dispute cannot be resolved, the charge may be processed as above, or other ADR techniques may be used, such as arbitration.

A major advantage of ADR is its flexibility. The disputing parties control how the dispute will be resolved, the procedures to be used, and whether decisions reached will be binding. In ADR programs sponsored by the EEOC, agreements reached through mediation are considered enforceable. Arbitration decisions, known as "awards," are usually binding whether the EEOC is involved or not. Other advantages of ADR include reducing caseloads of enforcement agencies and the courts and reaching more timely settlements. ADR is also appropriate for resolving charges brought under other laws enforced by the EEOC including the Age Discrimination in Employment Act, Equal Pay Act, and Americans with Disabilities Act, discussed below. ADR is also used in labor issues, discussed in a later section and in Chapter 15.

REVERSE DISCRIMINATION

In that underemployment of women and minorities can lead to a prima facie case of discrimination under the disparate impact model, local governments face a dilemma. So-called reverse discrimination can occur when, in an effort to meet employment utilization goals, members of protected groups are hired or promoted while better-qualified majority applicants are rejected. Title VII does not *require* preferential treatment of women and minorities to correct imbalances in the workforce. However, there are three situations in which this issue may arise: court orders, consent decrees, and voluntary affirmative action programs.

When an employer loses a Title VII case, the trial court may impose hiring and promotion goals when this is deemed necessary to overcome the effects of past discrimination. In this situation, of course, the employer has a defense against a charge of reverse discrimination. Often, however, the employer and the plaintiff(s) avoid trial by mutually agreeing to a settlement that contains such goals. These settlements, known as "consent decrees," are approved by the courts.

Voluntary affirmative action programs (discussed in detail in Chapter 8) might also be considered to constitute reverse discrimination. The Supreme Court has, however, established that voluntary programs designed to improve the utilization of women and minorities may not substantially disadvantage nonminority applicants and employees. The Court has ruled that affirmative action goals are appropriate where:

- They are based on a "manifest imbalance" between the proportion of a minority (females) in an employer's workforce and the qualified minorities (females) in the local labor force.
- They are not inflexible "quotas."
- They do not unnecessarily infringe on the interests of whites (males).
- They do not require the discharge of whites (males).
- They do not create an absolute bar to the advancement of whites (males).
- They do not deny any innocent employee the benefits of his or her seniority.
- They are temporary and are designed to end as soon as the proportion of minorities (females) in the employer's workforce approximates the proportion of qualified minorities (females) in the local labor force.
- They ensure that objective qualifications of minorities (females) selected under affirmative action are substantially equal to whites (males) who are passed over.[15]

SEX DISCRIMINATION

Title VII was passed to deal with race discrimination; the addition of sex as a prohibited classification was actually the unintended outcome of a parliamentary maneuver used by opponents of the legislation. Moreover, sex stereotypes, particularly those concerning women, continue to be socially acceptable. Nonetheless, even though the law may still be ahead of prevailing attitudes, depriving people of employment opportunities based on sex is illegal.[16] Prohibited activities include sex-related job requirements, sex-plus discrimination, benefits discrimination, and sexual harassment.

SEX-RELATED JOB REQUIREMENTS. The exclusion of one sex from a particular job is illegal unless sex is a "bona fide occupational qualification" (discussed below). It is also illegal to restrict job mobility by engaging in job placement practices that perpetuate occupational segregation. For example, some organizations have an unwritten policy of "channeling" all female applicants into traditionally female classifications. Another area of discrimination is imposing arbitrary physical requirements that tend to screen out or exclude women. These include minimum height, weight, and strength (for example, heavy lifting) standards. This does not mean that organizations cannot establish physical requirements. It means that all physical requirements must be based on job-related factors and applied uniformly.

SEX-PLUS DISCRIMINATION. This type of discrimination occurs when a subgroup of one sex (usually female) is deprived of employment opportunities. Examples include refusing to hire women with small children, wives of students, unwed mothers, and so forth. Note that the actions do not adversely affect all women, only a subgroup of women. But they are illegal unless they also apply to men. Such classifications are based on generalizations about the behavior of women as compared to men. Perhaps the most important contemporary area of sex-plus discrimination involves employee benefit plans.

BENEFITS DISCRIMINATION. In 1978 Congress amended Title VII with the Pregnancy Discrimination Act. This act prevents employers from requiring women to take unpaid leaves of absence or resign because of pregnancy. The act also provides that employers must grant sick leave for pregnancy-related illnesses (for example, morning sickness) and for childbirth if sick leave is granted for other medical conditions.[17] It is important to note, however, that this act does not provide full employment benefits. For example, a woman who uses up her sick leave could be terminated if the employer could justify the decision through business necessity. Another legal protection for women relates to retirement benefits. Previously some organizations required women to contribute more to their pension funds than men, based on a longer life expectancy. In 1978 the U.S. Supreme Court ruled that this practice violated Title VII.[18]

SEXUAL HARRASSMENT. The EEOC issued sex discrimination guidelines for the first time in 1980, defining **sexual harassment** as an illegal form of sex discrimination. Under these guidelines sexual harassment is defined as unwelcome advances, requests for sexual favors, and other verbal or physical conduct occurring in an employment context. The EEOC and the courts recognize two distinct types of sexual harassment, namely *quid pro quo* and hostile work environment.[19]

Quid pro quo is a Latin term meaning "for value received" and occurs when a supervisor or other person able to affect the terms and conditions of employment coerces or attempts to coerce an employee to grant a sexual favor in exchange for a reward (promotion, pay increase, desirable assignment, etc.) or to avoid an adverse action (firing, layoff, increased workload, undesirable assignment, etc.).

http://fairmeasures.com/sh.html
Fair Measures provides information on sexual harassment for employers and employees.

A hostile work environment occurs when workplace conduct of a sexual nature reaches a level that is offensive to a reasonable person. This includes verbal conduct (telling offensive jokes, making offensive remarks, or making unwelcome advances), physical conduct (unwelcome touching), and visual conduct (offensive pictures, posters, and written material).[20] In 1986 the U.S. Supreme Court ruled in *Meritor v. Vinson* that a hostile work environment was actionable even if there are no negative employment consequences, and that an economic effect is not required for sexual harassment to exist.[21]

According to the EEOC the employer is liable for a hostile work environment if it knew or should have known that the harassment was taking place unless it can show that it took immediate corrective action. In *quid pro quo* sexual harassment the employer is automatically or strictly liable for the acts of its agents and supervisors regardless of whether it knew or should have known of their occurrence. However, the *Meritor* decision provided that an employer may avoid liability if it can show that a supervisor who is charged with a hostile work environment was not acting as an "agent" of the employer. The decision also rejected a complaint procedure that required the victim to complain first to her supervisor (whom she had accused of sexual misconduct).

In *Harris v. Forklift Systems* the Court defined a "reasonable person" as one with the "perspective of the victim."[22] Since over 80 percent of complaints are made by women, this has the practical effect of establishing a "reasonable woman" standard in determining the type of conduct that will be viewed as contributing to a hostile work environment. In order to settle the conflict in the federal Circuit Courts of Appeal, the Supreme Court recently issued decisions in two cases that provide standards for determining an employer's liability when supervisors are involved in a hostile work environment. In *Faragher v. City of Boca Raton* the Court ruled that an employer is subject to "vicarious liability" for a hostile environment created by a supervisor unless it established and clearly communicated procedures for handling complaints and the employee failed to follow the procedures.[23] If, however, the harassment resulted in a tangible employment action there is no defense and the employer is strictly liable for the actions of the supervisor. In *Burlington Industries, Inc. v. Ellerth* a tangible employment action is defined as a "significant change in the employment status, such as hiring, firing, failing to promote, reassignment with significantly different responsibilities, or a decision causing a significant change in benefits."[24] Finally, in *Oncale v. Sundowner Offshore Services*, the Court allowed for same-sex lawsuits in sexual harassment cases.[25]

It is important for organizations to understand that they are responsible for the conduct of their employees and supervisors and may also be held responsible for the conduct of nonemployees with access to the workplace. Some organizations believe that the proper approach is the less said the better, and calling attention to the issue only creates problems where none existed before. This attitude is counterproductive and greatly increases potential liability.[26] The EEOC and the courts require employers to take the opposite approach by sensitizing employees, uncovering misconduct, and taking remedial action.

BONA FIDE OCCUPATIONAL QUALIFICATIONS

Title VII provides for excluding applicants on the basis of religion, sex or national origin in certain situations. For example, it would be permissible to specify that a woman be hired for the position of jail matron. These exceptions are known as bona fide occupational qualifications, or BFOQs. The BFOQ defense is most often used when it is necessary to select applicants on the basis of sex. Both the courts and the EEOC have defined this concept in rather narrow terms, and its use is limited to obvious situations, such as jail matron. BFOQ cannot be used to justify certain generally held beliefs that result in sex segregated job classifications, such as "women do not have the strength to be equipment operators," or "males are not suited for secretarial jobs." The BFOQ defense can never be used to justify excluding applicants on the basis of race.

APPLICATION OF TITLE VII IN HR ACTIVITIES

Title VII covers employment decisions in a number of HR activities. Specific applications to hiring practices including affirmative action programs and the requirements of the "Uniform Guidelines" are discussed in Chapters 8 and 9. Performance ratings, when used as the basis for employment decisions, are considered "tests" within the meaning of Title VII. Chapter 11 covers the requirements of legally defensible performance appraisal systems along with several important court cases. Title VII also addresses disparate treatment in pay. A detailed analysis of this topic, including another series of court cases, is contained in Chapter 13. Finally, an effective employer response to diversity issues including sexual harassment is discussed in Chapter 14.

THE AGE DISCRIMINATION IN EMPLOYMENT ACT OF 1967

The Age Discrimination in Employment Act (ADEA) prohibits age-based discrimination against persons over 40 years old in all aspects of employment.[27] Like Title VII, the ADEA prohibits discrimination against a legally protected group in hiring, compensation, discharge, or other terms, conditions, or privileges of employment, and generally prohibits mandatory retirement at any age. The legal process follows generally the disparate treatment theory discussed above. Employers are required to maintain specified records and to make such records available for inspection by compliance officers. Employers also must post in conspicuous places specified notices outlining rights under the act.

The act does not prohibit otherwise unlawful actions when age is a bona fide occupational qualification (BFOQ). Use of the BFOQ defense in local governments usually involves public safety personnel, where age qualifications are used in both hiring and mandatory retirement. The U.S. Supreme Court has held that this exception was intended to be very narrow, and age qualifications must be justified by business necessity. In order to justify a maximum hiring age (typically 30–45), employers cannot rely on cost alone; but some courts have allowed age-related cost considerations such as training requirements. In the case of mandatory retirement age (typically 50–60), the employer must show a significant relationship between increased age and a decrease in public safety.

The other defense available to an employer is to justify employment decisions with legitimate, nondiscriminatory reasons not based on age. Reasonable factors other than age (RFOA) provided for in the ADEA include poor job performance, misconduct, lack of qualifications, diminished ability, elimination of the job, reductions in force, and similar job-related reasons.

The act is enforced by the EEOC, which follows the same process as for charges made under Title VII, discussed above. When a violation is found, an attempt must be made to achieve voluntary compliance through conciliation. If such an attempt is unsuccessful, either the individual(s) affected or the EEOC may file a lawsuit. Suits must be brought within two years of the discriminatory act or, in the case of a willful violation, within three years. Individuals may sue for employment, reinstatement, promotions, pay as a result of discrimination (including back wages and fringe benefits), attorney's fees, court costs and, in the case of willful violations, liquidated (double) damages. Litigation is usually aimed at ending an employer's violations of the act in addition to the remedies above; however, courts may grant other necessary relief, depending on the situation. In addition to enforcement activities, the EEOC conducts programs to encourage employment on the basis of ability rather than age and to resolve specific problems. The ADEA applies mainly to disparate treatment in selection and pay, discussed in Chapters 8, 9, and 13.

THE EQUAL PAY ACT OF 1963

Enacted as an amendment to the Fair Labor Standards Act, the Equal Pay Act (EPA) requires that men and women employed in the same establishment receive equal pay (including fringe benefits) for jobs that involve substantially equal skill, effort, and responsibility and are performed under similar working conditions.[28] The work need not be identical, merely substantially equal. The EPA is concerned solely with wage discrimination based on gender. The act exempts from its provisions wage differentials arising from seniority or merit systems, systems that measure earnings by quantity or quality of production, and any other systems based on factors other than gender. The act is enforced by the EEOC and the process and remedies are essentially the same as for the Age Discrimination in Employment Act discussed previously. For further discussion of the EPA, see Chapter 13. As stated above, pay discrimination also is prohibited under Title VII. In *Gunther v. County of Washington* the Supreme Court ruled that work does not have to be equal to bring a charge of pay discrimination based on race, color, sex, religion, national origin, or age.[29] This issue is also discussed in Chapter 13.

THE AMERICANS WITH DISABILITIES ACT OF 1990

A major civil rights initiative of the 101st Congress was the passage of the Americans with Disabilities Act (ADA) of 1990.[30] The ADA provides broad-based discrimination protection for the disabled (preferable to the term *handicapped)*. While local governments are not explicitly defined as "employers" in Title I (employment), they are covered by the provisions of Title II (public services), which contains a general provision prohibiting discrimination on the basis of **disability**. The act is patterned on other federal civil rights laws and supplements existing protections afforded by the Vocational Rehabilitation Act of 1973 (discussed below). The act defines a disabled person as "one who has a physical or mental impairment which substantially limits one or more life activities; or has a record of such an impairment; or is regarded as having such an impairment."

http://www.usdoj.gov/
crt/ada/adahom1.htm
The U.S. Department of
Justice ADA home page
provides comprehensive
information on the
Americans with Disabilities
Act and guidelines
for compliance.

The ADA prohibits employment discrimination against qualified individuals with disabilities, defined as persons who can with "reasonable accommodation" perform the essential functions of a particular job. The standard for determining whether reasonable accommodation must be made in the employment of a person with a disability is whether it would cause "undue hardship" to the employer. Discrimination is prohibited in all areas, including selection, promotion, compensation, transfer and recruitment, advertising, hiring and termination, and other terms and conditions of employment.

One issue, which is certain to become increasingly important, is the status of applicants and employees with respect to Acquired Immune Deficiency Syndrome (AIDS). In 1987 the U.S. Supreme Court held that a contagious disease should be considered a disability (or handicap), and persons impaired by such diseases are protected from discrimination if otherwise qualified.[31] The case concerned a schoolteacher who was dismissed after the third relapse of tuberculosis. The Court held that decisions motivated by "fear of infection" are discriminatory.

OTHER COMPREHENSIVE FAIR EMPLOYMENT LAWS

The Immigration Reform and Control Act of 1986 (IRCA) contains a number of antidiscrimination provisions.[32] The IRCA covers employers with four or more employees. It protects all aliens from employment discrimination based on national origin and establishes a new protected class based on citizenship status. The IRCA is enforced by the U.S. Department of Justice, Office of Special Counsel for Immigration Related Unfair Employment Practices.

Although used less frequently following the application of Title VII to local governments, the Civil Rights Acts of 1866 and 1871 are still important. The Civil Rights Act of 1866 provides that all persons have equal protection of the laws (that is, the same as white citizens). This law has been used to sue public employers for race discrimination.[33] The Civil Rights Act of 1871 prohibits local government officials from acting under color of local law or custom to deprive citizens of constitutional rights.[34] Discrimination suits may be brought under either of these laws separately or concurrently with actions under Title VII. These statutes have different time and procedural requirements and may carry additional remedies. An overview of the features of major fair employment laws is provided in Exhibit 3-3.

LAWS AND EXECUTIVE ORDERS PROHIBITING DISCRIMINATION AS A CONDITION FOR RECEIVING FEDERAL FUNDS

A number of federal laws prohibit discrimination in federally funded programs. Many acts creating such programs contain specific requirements, while some refer to other laws. In most cases, the requirements affecting employment practices are based on compliance with Title VII and related comprehensive laws. Cities and counties that contract with the federal government are covered by the Vietnam Veterans Readjustment Assistance Act of 1974 and are required to engage in affirmative action. Also, Executive Order 11246 (1965) may have significant bearing on local government.

Discrimination on the basis of handicap is prohibited by the Vocational Rehabilitation Act of 1973, as amended.[35] Two sections of the act apply to local government employment. Section 504 prohibits discrimination against handicapped persons in employment, services, participation in, and access to all programs receiving federal financial assistance. The Department of Health and Human Services (HHS) has responsibility for developing and coordinating uniform regulatory standards for all federal agencies under this section. It also administers regulations covering its own funded programs through its Office of Civil Rights (OCR). Section 503 of the act prohibits discrimination in employment by federal contractors and subcontractors. This section is enforced by the Office of Federal Contract Compliance Programs (OFCCP), U.S. Department of Labor, which has issued regulations requiring such employers to take affirmative action in employment of the handicapped. As a practical matter, the important provisions of this act are contained in the Americans with Disabilities Act discussed above.

EXHIBIT 3-3

COMPREHENSIVE FAIR
EMPLOYMENT LAWS

Law	Effect on HR Management
Civil Rights Act of 1964, Title VII as amended in 1972, 1978, 1991, and 1994	Prohibits employment discrimination based on race, color, religion, or national origin. Prohibits retaliation against employee or applicant for making complaint or filing charge. Prohibits sexual harassment. Cases can be made alleging intentional discrimination (disparate treatment) or systemic discrimination (disparate impact).
Equal Pay Act of 1963	Requires employers to offer equal pay to males and females performing equal work unless differentials are based on seniority, merit, quality or quantity of production, or other factors not related to sex.
Age Discrimination in Employment Act of 1967 as amended in 1986 and 1990	Prohibits employment discrimination based on age over 40. Generally prohibits mandatory retirement. Generally prohibits maximum hiring age.
Americans with Disabilities Act of 1990	Prohibits employment discrimination based on disability. Requires employers to offer reasonable accommodation to otherwise qualified applicants and employees with disabilities.
Immigration Reform and Control Act of 1986 as amended in 1990 and 1996	Prohibits employment discrimination against legal aliens based on citizenship status.
Civil Rights Act of 1866	Prohibits employers from denying persons (employees and applicants) equal protection of the laws.
Civil Rights Act of 1871	Prohibits local government officials from acting under color of local law or custom to deprive citizens of constitutional rights.

Issued in 1965, presidential Executive Order 11246 (with its amendments) prohibits discrimination in all employment practices by federal contractors, subcontractors and federally assisted construction contractors on the basis of race, color, religion, sex, national origin, physical handicap, or veteran's status.[36] In addition, certain employers are required to take affirmative action to ensure that applicants and employees are treated without discrimination. Affirmative action required under the order specifically includes persons who are handicapped and veterans. Local government employment is covered under the order when such agencies or their instrumentalities participate in or work on or under a government contract or subcontract or hold such a contract.

The executive order is administered and enforced by the Office of Federal Contract Compliance Programs (OFCCP), U.S. Department of Labor, which has issued detailed regulations for "result-oriented" programs to eliminate discrimination and to encourage equal employment opportunities. It covers any contract or subcontract over $10,000 within any 12-month period. Contractors are required to take affirmative action to employ and advance all qualified persons and to eliminate specified discriminatory practices. They must notify labor organizations and must include a standard EEO clause in all covered contracts, subcontracts, and purchase orders. Their employment plans and practices are subject to periodic compliance reviews by the OFCCP.

While few small- to medium-sized cities and counties actually contract with the federal government, virtually all counties have Cooperative Extension Service employees. State Cooperative Extension Services receive funds allocated by the Extension Service, U.S. Department of Agriculture, to designated land-grant colleges and universities to provide services to farmers, youth, homemakers, and other special segments of the community. Their staff employment practices are covered by nondiscrimination requirements under Executive Order 11246, Title VI of the Civil Rights Act, and additional department regulations.[37]

Each state Cooperative Extension Service (CES) organization is required to develop a detailed equal opportunity program and affirmative action plan for progress to be submitted to the Extension Service as a condition of funding. These plans include specific goals and timetables for minorities and women in all job categories. They require state CES organizations to develop procedures for identifying and eliminating practices that discriminate or perpetuate discriminatory impact, to establish effective internal EEO complaint systems, and to submit updated annual reports to the Extension Service, which reviews them for needed changes and improvements. The Extension Service also conducts audits and compliance reviews of extension practices and affirmative action plans, using Title VII legal standards to determine compliance.

GOVERNMENT REGULATION OF THE WORKPLACE AND THE EMPLOYMENT RELATIONSHIP

Another important aspect of the legal environment involves laws and regulations that address employment and workplace issues other than discrimination, including compensation, safety and health, and collective bargaining. Because they are more specific in their application these laws are only briefly covered in this section. More complete details are provided in later chapters as indicated.

LAWS APPLYING TO COMPENSATION

A major law on compensation is the Fair Labor Standards Act (FLSA), which establishes minimum wages, maximum hours, overtime pay, restrictions on child labor, and record-keeping requirements.[38] The FLSA originally applied only to the private sector, but in 1985 the U.S. Supreme Court decision in *Garcia v. San Antonio Metropolitan Transit Authority* extended coverage to virtually all functions of state and local government.[39] The Family and Medical Leave Act (FMLA) is designed to provide employees with job protection in cases of family or medical emergencies.[40] An eligible employee is entitled to 12 weeks of unpaid leave for birth or adoption; serious health condition of a spouse, parent, or child; or the employee's own serious health condition. While on leave, employees retain all previously earned seniority and employment benefits. Both the FLSA and the FMLA are enforced by the Wage and Hour Division of the U.S. Department of Labor. The regulations pertaining to these laws are quite complex. More complete details on these laws are contained in Chapter 13.

Other federal regulation of compensation involves mandatory employee benefits. Local governments are required to provide coverage under Social Security and Medicare or offer a plan that pays a similar retirement income. The Social Security Act also established a national federal-state unemployment insurance program for individuals who become unemployed through no fault of their own. Most states require payment of benefits for 26 weeks, with extended federally funded benefits of 13 weeks. Workers' compensation (not a federal mandate but compulsory in 47 states) is designed to provide income and medical benefits to employees who are injured on the job. Employers must fund this benefit according to state guidelines. Mandatory benefits are also discussed more fully in Chapter 13.

LAWS APPLYING TO EMPLOYEE HEALTH AND SAFETY

The legal framework for employee health and safety involves workers' compensation laws (mentioned above and discussed in Chapter 13) and the federal Occupational Safety and Health Act (OSHA).[41] OSHA provisions do not apply to local governments in their role as employers. However, the act provides that any state desiring federal approval for programs dealing with the private sector must provide a similar program for state and local government employees. OSHA is administered and enforced by the Occupational Safety and Health Administration. Chapter 16 covers the responsibilities of local governments in dealing with this area.

LAWS APPLYING TO COLLECTIVE BARGAINING

Although there is no federal law governing labor relations in the public sector, the federal Labor Management Relations Act (as amended) serves as a model for states that have comprehensive labor laws applying to public sector organizations such as local governments. Such laws include the right of public employees to form unions for collective bargaining and impose a duty on the employer to bargain with the union on wages, hours, and other conditions of employment. These laws typically establish a state agency to determine the bargaining unit, hold elections, certify the union, determine codes of unfair practices, and administer procedures including a wide range of alternative dispute resolution (ADR) procedures. The role of unions

Laws that regulate HR management are complex enough when considered individually. The degree of complexity increases greatly when situations raise questions under several different laws. One such occurrence is when a worker requests a leave of absence for an illness or an injury. If the request is not handled properly, an employer could be exposed to liability under the Americans with Disabilities Act, the Family and Medical Leave Act, and state workers' compensation laws, which have overlapping provisions and are enforced by different agencies. This area is often called the "Bermuda Triangle" of employment law.

THE BERMUDA TRIANGLE

Because there are several different factors that must be analyzed, HR managers should use a multitrack approach and decision model. A simplified overview is shown below:

1. Determine the law(s) that cover the employer.
2. For each law, determine if the employee is covered.
3. Define the injury or illness (i.e., "disability," "serious health condition," or "compensable injury").
4. Determine the benefit(s) that the employer is required to provide.

The approach still requires the HR manager to be familiar with the details of each applicable law and possibly the terms of a collective bargaining agreement. However, considering each element of the problem in a logical sequence both reduces the complexity of the process and increases the likelihood that the ultimate decision will be correct.

Source: Stephen S. Zashin, "The Leave of Absence Puzzle: Fitting the Pieces Together," *Public Personnel Management* 26 (Winter 1997), 471–481.

in compensation is discussed in Chapter 13, and Chapter 15 covers the full labor relations process in local government. Refer to Exhibit 3-4 for a summary of legislation regulating the workplace and the employment relationship.

CONSTITUTIONAL ISSUES OF LOCAL GOVERNMENT EMPLOYMENT

Local government must also be concerned with constitutional constraints upon the treatment of public employees. This section examines the constitutional status of employees from several important perspectives. The discussion is largely based on and in part condensed and adapted from the work of noted authority David H. Rosenbloom.[42]

CONSTITUTIONAL DOCTRINES IN PUBLIC EMPLOYMENT

At one time the constitutional status of government employees was covered by the doctrine of privilege. Under this doctrine it was accepted that since there was no constitutional right to government employment, it was a "privilege" to hold a gov-

---

EXHIBIT 3-4

MAJOR LAWS REGULATING THE WORKPLACE
AND THE EMPLOYMENT RELATIONSHIP

Law	Effect on HR Management
State Workers' Compensation Laws Note: Laws provide generally uniform coverage.	Requires employers to establish an insurance program to cover expenses incurred by an employee for a work-related injury or disease.
Social Security Act of 1935 (numerous amendments)	Participating employers are required to offer retirement, unemployment, benefits for dependents, and Medicare. Nonparticipating employers are required to offer comparable plan.
Fair Labor Standards Act of 1938 (numerous amendments)	Establishes minimum wage. Generally requires payment of one-and-one-half times the regular rate for non-exempt employees who work more than 40 hours in a workweek (certain special provisions apply to local governments). Establishes executive, administrative and professional exemptions. Restricts child labor.
Family and Medical Leave Act of 1993	Requires employers to provide eligible employees up to 12 weeks of unpaid leave for childbirth, adoption, caring for a sick family member or close relative, serious health condition, or similar family exigency.
Occupational Safety and Health Act of 1970	Through the Occupational Safety and Health Administration, establishes and enforces mandatory job safety and health standards. These standards do not apply to local governments in their role as employers, but states that gain approval for private sector programs must set standards for local governments that are as effective as the federal standards.
National Labor Relations Code, including Acts of 1935, 1947, and 1959.	The code, while not applying directly to the public sector, serves as a general model for state legislation establishing procedures for local government workers to organize and bargain collectively with employers over wages, hours, and other terms and conditions of employment.

ernment job.[43] Under this approach, governments were free to abridge almost all employment and retention rights of their employees. The doctrine of privilege has been eroded both by the extension of federal laws to the public sector and by various court decisions. As the previous discussion has shown, a person who feels that he or she has been treated unjustly can file a charge of discrimination based on race, color, religion, national origin, sex, age, or disability. However, current judicial doctrine grants employees constitutional protections whether or not they are members of a "protected" class. The proverbial "white male under 40," for example, may still claim constitutional rights.

DUE PROCESS REQUIREMENTS

In 1972 the U.S. Supreme Court in *Board of Regents v. Roth* set forth the grounds upon which a dismissed public employee could assert a right to due process under the 14th Amendment. These include:

- The employee has a property interest in the job.
- The dismissal violates an employee's liberty interest.
- The dismissal was in retaliation for the exercise of protected substantive constitutional rights.[44]

These conditions have significant impact on the employment relationship in local government. Typically, a property interest in a public employee's job is established when an employer and employee enter into a binding and legally enforceable employment agreement or contract. Such agreements may be written, oral, or even implied. Examples include teachers with "tenure" and civil service employees who have permanent status. A liberty interest involves a person's reputation as it affects his or her employability. Thus an employee who suffers embarrassment and injury to his or her reputation resulting from a dismissal or forced resignation can assert a deprivation of liberty. Finally, the employee may exercise rights such as freedom of speech or assembly. An employee could claim, for example, that an adverse public or private statement about an employer was protected under the First Amendment.

Due process is a systematic, orderly procedure in which the individual has a right to be fully informed of and be heard concerning action that is pending against him or her. **Procedural due process** has been interpreted as requiring that the employee have an opportunity to object to a proposed action before a fair, neutral decision maker (which need not be a judge). **Substantive due process** focuses on the content of the action. If the action involves a fundamental right (such as free speech), the employer must provide substantive due process and show a compelling or overriding interest in the action.[45]

A constitutionally protected property interest in employment must be based on state law. For example, in *Bishop v. Wood*, a case decided in 1976, the Supreme Court upheld the dismissal of a North Carolina police officer for unsatisfactory performance without a due process hearing. Although he was classified as a "permanent" employee by a local ordinance, the Court ruled that he could not claim a property interest in his job.[46] In 1985, however, the Court ruled in *Cleveland Board of Education v. Laudermill* that a security guard who was discharged for lying on his application form was entitled to a hearing because he had a property interest under an Ohio civil service statute.[47]

In *Bishop*, the Court also ruled that because there was no public disclosure of the reasons for dismissal, the employee's liberty interests were not violated. An employer can avoid liability for violation of an employee's liberty interest by not disclosing reasons for discharging an employee. This applies also to constructive discharge, where an employee is either pressured or allowed to resign as an alternative to being terminated.

Finally, the Supreme Court requires due process where a dismissal involves substantive constitutional rights. In *Mt. Healthy School District Board of Education v. Doyle*, the Court ruled that an untenured teacher dismissed for repeated incidents of what the board viewed as unprofessional conduct could establish a claim for reinstatement if the decision to dismiss him was based on his exercise of rights protected by the First Amendment.[48]

Even though the public employee's constitutional rights to due process are limited, HR management should probably afford such protections. While procedural due process may not always be a constitutional right, allowing an employee facing termination to present his or her side of the story is always good HR policy.

EQUAL PROTECTION

Equal protection of the laws is also derived from the Fourteenth Amendment.[49] In an employment setting, equal protection requires similarly situated groups to be treated similarly unless a legitimate government interest is involved. Courts have held that employment decisions having an adverse effect will be considered valid if there is a rational basis relating to the government interest. In 1976 the Court in *Washington v. Davis* required plaintiffs to show a discriminatory purpose in order to successfully challenge a written examination, which had a harsh racial impact.[50] This decision suggests that human resource practices having a disparate impact on protected groups, when challenged on constitutional grounds, will generally be upheld unless they have a discriminatory intent. Recall, however, that issues involving disparate impact alone can be litigated under Title VII. Recent activity in this area has focused on the constitutionality of affirmative action ordered by lower courts as a remedy for violations of the Civil Rights Act of 1871. In 1987 the Court in *U.S. v. Paradise* upheld a 50 percent promotional quota for qualified African Americans imposed on the Alabama Department of Public Safety. This was based on a 1972 decision that determined that Alabama had unconstitutionally excluded African Americans from its force of state troopers for almost 40 years.[51]

While equal protection is mainly concerned with race, local governments should avoid discrimination based on other arbitrary classifications of employees, whether or not they have "protected group" status under existing laws.[52] For example, unfavorable treatment of homosexuals would be considered illegal unless an employee acted in such a way as to cause a disruption of operations. A practical way to deal with the issue might be to follow the "don't ask—don't tell" approach used by the military.

FREE SPEECH

The public employee's right to free speech is broadly protected. In *Pickering v. Board of Education* the U.S Supreme Court held that the public employee's freedom of expression can be abridged only in specific situations. These include speech that would impair discipline and harmony in the workplace, breach confidentiality, impede job performance, or jeopardize close personal loyalty. Somewhat related to confidentiality is the issue of an employee's use of special or privileged information. A file clerk, for example, may have access to information that though not in itself confidential is not generally available to others. It is generally considered that an employee may not make use of such information for personal gain or in ways that would damage the organization. This Supreme Court decision, *Pickering v. Board of Education,* also provides protection for activities described as "whistle-blowing."[53] Later the Court addressed the general issue of nonpartisan free speech in *Rankin v. McPherson.*[54] In that case a probationary employee was dismissed for a statement in regard to the unsuccessful attempt to assassinate President Reagan (". . . if they go for him again, I hope they get him."). The Court ruled that consideration must be given to the employee's authority and public accountability in determining whether such speech is grounds for dismissal. Constitutional protection, however, does not extend to purely partisan expression.

FREEDOM OF ASSOCIATION

Freedom of association includes the right to join organizations, especially unions and political parties. Public employees may also join protest movements, advocacy groups, and even organizations that are regarded by some as extremist, such as militias, as long as they do not participate in illegal activities. Public employees also have the right not to join an organization. In *Elrod v. Burns*, the U.S. Supreme Court overturned the dismissal of non–civil service Republican employees in the Sheriff's Office of Cook County, Illinois, when the Republican sheriff was replaced by a Democrat.[55] To justify such dismissals, employers must show that partisan affiliation is strongly related to job performance.

Freedom of association also applies where government employees are represented by a labor union and nonunion members in the bargaining unit are required to pay a "fair share" of union expenses. This is called the "agency shop" and has been held to be constitutional. In 1986, however, the Court established guidelines on the assessment of agency shop fees. The Court ruled in *Chicago Teachers Union v. Hudson* that nonunion members had the right to an explanation of the basis for the fee and could prevent the union from spending any part of the fee for political action.[56] For a more complete discussion of union security see Chapter 15.

THE RIGHT TO PRIVACY

The employee right to privacy derives from the Fourth Amendment, which protects citizens from unreasonable searches and seizures, and the Fifth Amendment protection against self-incrimination. A major question involving the right to privacy focuses on drug testing. Local governments are becoming more concerned about substance abuse and organizational losses resulting from absenteeism, accidents, and poor performance. Many substances can be detected through tests such as urinalysis. Such testing of employees, particularly random or blanket testing, raises constitutional questions.

Previously, a key issue, which had divided the federal appeals courts, was whether public employee drug testing is ever permissible absent evidence of employee drug abuse or impairment. The 1989 decision in *National Treasury Employees Union v. Von Raab* makes it clear that even reasonable suspicion is not always required, at least where public safety or other "compelling" government interest outweighs any "diminished expectation of privacy" of the employees being tested.[57] Since *Von Raab,* the Court has denied review in cases challenging random drug testing of police officers and transit employees. It is likely, however, that the constitutionality of workforce testing in general will continue to be measured on a case-by-case basis.

Beyond public safety, transit, and other safety-sensitive employee groups, there is no clear indication by the Court that broad-based testing programs will be sanctioned. Thus testing of other employee groups should be limited to situations where there is "reasonable suspicion" that the employee is using illegal drugs (this is a lesser standard than "probable cause," which must indicate a greater probability of accuracy). A similar line of reasoning applies to other types of workplace searches. Since public employees are entrusted with significant responsibilities, and the consequences of their misconduct or incompetence can be severe, it is sufficient to establish reasonable suspicion as the basis for a search. The U.S. Supreme Court decision in *O'Connor v. Ortega* suggests that searches to retrieve work-related materials or to investigate violations of workplace rules do not abridge the public employee's right to privacy.[58]

http://www.law. cornell.edu/ The Legal Information Institute contains "Law about . . .", a section on employment law, including U.S. Supreme Court decisions.

Another zone of privacy derived from the Fourth Amendment involves the confidentiality of employee records and communications. This includes information stored in electronic databases accessible through human resource information systems (HRIS), e-mail, Internet usage, and information stored in personal computer hard drives. Privacy legislation addressing the constitutional question applies to federal agencies, but employers in the private sector are not prohibited from accessing and using this information. It seems intuitive, however, that local governments should be sensitive to these concerns. They should limit access to human resource files and not disclose information without consent. A related issue is the right of employees and applicants to inspect their files and in some cases challenge derogatory information, which is covered by federal and state laws. This topic is discussed more fully in Chapter 9.

LIBERTY

The broad issue of public employees' "liberty" (as distinguished from a liberty interest involving a person's reputation) has been the subject of considerable litigation. Issues involving employees' liberty include mandatory maternity leaves, dress codes and grooming standards, and residency requirements. Mandatory maternity leave is now prohibited by Title VII, discussed earlier. In regard to dress and grooming codes, the Court has tended to allow restrictions unless they are arbitrary, capricious, or unfairly enforced. The most recent decision was *Goldman v. Weinberger*, which upheld the right of the U.S. Air Force to enforce its dress code.[59] Finally, the Court upheld the constitutionality of residency requirements for firefighters in *McCartny v. Philadelphia Civil Service Commission*.[60]

PERSONAL LIABILITY OF PUBLIC OFFICIALS

A public official who violates either the constitutional or statutory rights of employees is also exposed to personal tort liability. *Tort* is a French word referring to a "private wrong" for which an individual may sue to recover damages when a duty owed to that individual is breached.[61] The basis for tort liability of state and local officials is the Civil Rights Act of 1871, which provides that persons acting under color of state law are liable to the injured party "in an action at law, suit in equity, or other proper proceeding for redress."[62] At one time the courts provided immunity to public officials acting in good faith, without malicious intent to harm. In 1975 and 1982, however, the U.S. Supreme Court in *Wood v. Strickland* and *Harlow v. Fitzgerald* extended the limits of liability. In *Harlow* the Court held that a state or local public official is not immune from liability if his or her conduct violates "clearly established

EXHIBIT 3-5

CONSTITUTIONAL AMENDMENTS
THAT REGULATE EMPLOYMENT
IN LOCAL GOVERNMENT

Constitutional Amendment	Effect on HR Management
First Amendment (1791)	Protects freedom of expression and association. Generally prohibits adverse action against employees based on exercise of free speech (certain exceptions apply). Prohibits adverse action against employees based on membership (or nonmembership) in organizations such as unions and political parties.
Fourth Amendment (1791)	Protects property interest in job of employees who have been granted permanent status under state law. Prohibits dismissal of such employees without procedural due process (substantive due process is required if dismissal is based on the exercise of substantive constitutional rights). Prohibits employers from disclosing reasons for dismissal without due process. Prohibits adverse treatment of employees based on race or other arbitrary classification such as sexual orientation.
Fourteenth Amendment (1868)	Protects employee privacy. Requires employers to establish reasonable suspicion prior to conducting workplace searches. Generally prohibits random or blanket drug testing of employees (certain exceptions apply).

statutory or constitutional rights of which a reasonable person would have known."[63] This increased exposure to personal liability lawsuits suggests that public officials, including HR managers, should both become knowledgeable about legal rights of employees and develop procedures (for example, review processes) to respond to situations where these rights are in question.[64] An overview of constitutional provisions that regulate local government employment are contained in Exhibit 3-5.

STATE EMPLOYMENT LAWS

A number of states have employment laws. In many cases these laws provide for an agency to process and resolve discrimination complaints, which may be made directly or referred by the EEOC, as discussed previously. In general, state laws have the same objectives as federal laws, but often have additional requirements or extend coverage. Many states, for example, have laws that go beyond the Equal Pay Act in providing pay equity for women. State laws may also extend the coverage of federal laws, for example by establishment of additional "protected classes." It is also common for states to provide additional overtime provisions by modifying the 40-hour week threshold contained in the Fair Labor Standards Act to an eight-hour day or to require double-time pay in certain situations.

State laws are also important in dismissals because they can serve as a basis for lawsuits alleging wrongful discharge. The common-law doctrine of employment at will means that the employment relationship can be terminated at-will by either party, and some state statutes apply the at-will doctrine to public employees. In many states, however, statutory or constitutional provisions give permanent job rights to certain types of employees (employees who have completed a probationary period, teachers with tenure, etc.). Where these provisions cover local governments, employees can acquire property interests in their jobs. As discussed above, once a property interest is determined to exist, an employee who is discharged is entitled to procedural due process.

State contract laws and court interpretations are also important.[65] Many state courts have ruled that employers have entered into implied contracts with their employees by procedures contained in employee handbooks, policy manuals, and other documents. Courts have also ruled that oral statements of supervisors and managers may also have the effect of legal contracts. Most written and oral statements promise that employees can be terminated only for "just cause" and after a hearing. In addition, state courts may rule that an implied covenant of good faith and fair dealing applies to employment. Various state laws also prohibit discharges based on filing workers' compensation claims, serving on juries, refusing to commit perjury, refusing to commit acts that violate state law, and exposing law violations (whistle-blowing). Even in the absence of a particular law, state courts are increasingly siding with employees in wrongful discharge claims.

Another issue covered by state laws is preemployment and workforce drug and alcohol testing. While workforce testing is also a constitutional issue, as has been discussed, some state laws restrict employer testing of both applicants and employees. States with restrictive laws tend to prohibit drug testing except in specific situations. States with permissive laws tend to permit testing provided acceptable procedures are used.[66] Employers generally have the right to test employees based on a probable cause or reasonable suspicion standard.[67]

SUMMARY

Laws and regulations cover almost every aspect of the employment relationship and many are somewhat complex. Understanding and complying with these mandates is a shared responsibility of HR and line management, and the consequences of not performing this responsibility are very serious. The legal environment of HR management in local government is defined by federal statutes (statutory law), federal court decisions (case law), and administrative regulations (administrative law), by constitutional provisions (constitutional law), and by state and local laws and ordinances (common law).

The area of equal employment opportunity includes the federal laws and guidelines that address employment discrimination based on race, sex, disability, and other prohibited classifications. Major laws include Title VII of the Civil Rights Act, the Equal Pay Act, the Age Discrimination in Employment Act, and the Americans with Disabilities Act. Other laws and executive orders apply in specific situations. Courts have established two types of discrimination claims. Disparate treatment occurs when persons protected by the law are treated differently from other employees or job applicants. That is, disparate treatment involves decision rules with, for example, a racial or sexual premise, and is on its face intentional discrimination. Disparate impact is typically unintentional and involves decision rules that have unequal racial or sexual *consequences*. Barriers that are erected appear to be neutral but have the effect of screening out a disproportionate number of minority applicants.

Another important area concerns laws that apply to other employment issues such as wages and hours, income sufficiency, workplace health and safety, and collective bargaining. Major laws include the Fair Labor Standards Act, the Family and Medical Leave Act, and the Occupational Safety and Health Act. Although there is no federal law governing labor relations in the public sector, the federal Labor

Management Relations Act (as amended) serves as a model for states that have comprehensive labor laws applying to public sector organizations such as local governments.

Certain basic rights set forth in the U.S. Constitution apply also to the employment relationship in local government. The Fourteenth Amendment provides that employees subject to termination generally have a right to due process. The First Amendment protects workplace speech and provides freedom of association, including the right to join unions and other organizations. The Fourth Amendment regulates workplace searches and seizures such as drug testing and addresses other privacy concerns.

A number of states have fair employment laws that have the same intent as federal laws but may impose added requirements or extend coverage. Many state courts have ruled that employee handbooks, policy manuals, and related documents are enforceable contracts. Also, many state laws regulate drug testing by employers.

QUESTIONS FOR REVIEW AND DISCUSSION

1. Define the terms *statutory law*, *case law*, and *administrative law* and give an example of each.
2. Which equal employment opportunity laws apply to all units of local government?
3. What is "disparate impact"? Explain how the *Griggs* decision has made this concept so important.
4. How can cities and counties improve the utilization of women and minorities without engaging in reverse discrimination?
5. What three named acts constitute sexual harassment?
6. What is the definition of a person with a disability?
7. Which law establishes the minimum wage and the 40-hour workweek?
8. Explain what is meant by a "property interest" in a job. How is it acquired? What employment rights does it confer?
9. An employee of Acme Manufacturing Company stated publicly that the general manager was incompetent and needed to be replaced. The employee was terminated. Could a city employee be terminated for making the same statement about the mayor? Why or why not?
10. A county is about to implement a program of requiring all employees to submit to random drug testing. On what grounds could this program be challenged?
11. Explain the relationship between federal and state employment laws.
12. Give two examples of how state laws and court decisions have eroded the doctrine of employment at will.

ENDNOTES

[1] For a comprehensive analysis of the background of federal fair employment laws, see Evelyn M. Idelson, *Eliminating Discrimination in Employment: A Compelling National Priority* (Washington, D.C.: U.S. Equal Employment Opportunity Commission, July 1979). An excellent review of legal practice is given by Ivan E. Bodensteiner and Rosalie Berger Levinson in *State and Local Government Civil Rights Liability*, (Eagan, Minn.: West, 2000). vols. 1, 2, and 3 as updated.

[2] Civil Rights Act of 1964, Title VII, Section 703(a), at 42 U.S.C. §§ 2000 et seq. See also Idelson, IV-1 and 2.

[3] Idelson, II-1, and H. C. Lockwood, "Testing Minority Applicants for Employment," *Personnel Journal* 42 (April 1963), 356–360.

[4] Civil Rights Act, Title VII, Section 703(b), at 42 U.S.C. § e-2.

[5] *Griggs v. Duke Power Co.*, 401 U.S. 430 (1971).

[6] Equal Employment Opportunity Commission, Civil Service Commission, Department of Labor, and Department of Justice, Adoption by Four Agencies of "Uniform Guidelines on Employee Selection Procedures," 43 Federal Register 38,290–38,309 (August 25, 1978).

[7] *Griggs*, at notes 11, 14, and 17.

[8] Civil Rights Act of 1991, amendment to Title VII at scattered sections of 42 U.S.C.

[9] For more coverage of Title VII charge processing and litigation, see U.S. Equal Opportunity Commission, *Employer EEO Responsibilities*, April 2000 (revised), Q1-3, and Bodensteiner and Levinson, 5:25–31 and 5:32–37.

[10] *McDonnell Douglas Corp. v. Green*, 411 U.S. 792 (1973).

[11] *Texas Dept. of Community Affairs v. Burdine*, 450 U.S. 248 (1981).

[12] *St. Mary's Honor Center v. Hicks*, 509 U.S. 502 (1993).

[13] *Albemarle Paper Co. v. Moody*, 422 U.S. 405 (1976).

[14] Administrative Dispute Resolution Act of 1990 at 5 U.S.C. 571–584.

[15] *United States v. Weber*, 443 U.S. 193 (1979); *Wgant v. Jackson Board of Education*, 476 U.S. 267 (1986); and *Johnson v. Transportation Agency, Santa Clara County, California*, 480 U.S. 616 (1987); see also Robert K. Robinson, Joseph G. P. Paolillo, and Brian J. Reithel, "Race-Based Preferential Treatment Programs: Raising the Bar for Establishing Compelling Government Interests," *Public Personnel Management* 27 (Fall 1998), 349–352, and S. N. Colamery, *Affirmative Action: Catalyst or Albatross* (Commack, N.Y: Nova Science, 1998), 1–41.

[16] For an analysis of recent court cases involving sex discrimination, see Paul S. Greenlaw, John P. Kohl, and Robert D. Lee, Jr., "Title VII Sex Discrimination in the Public Sector in the 1990s: The Court's View," *Public Personnel Management* 27 (Fall 1998).

[17] Pregnancy Discrimination Act of 1974, amendment to Title VII at 42 U.S.C. § 2000e(k).

[18] *Los Angeles Department of Water & Power v. Manhart*, 435 U.S. 702, 98 S. Ct. 1370, 55 L. Ed. 2d 657 (1978).

[19] 29 C.F.R. § 1604.11(a).

[20] For every federal circuit court's definition of hostile environment see *Red Mendoza v. Borden, Inc.*, 195 F.3d 1238 (1999).

[21] *Meritor Savings Bank v. Vinson*, 106 U.S. 2399 (1986).

[22] *Harris v. Forklift Systems, Inc.*, 114 S. Ct. 367 (1993).

[23] *Faragher v. City of Boca Raton*, 524 U.S. 775, 118 S. Ct. 2275 (1998).

[24] *Burlington Industries v. Ellerth*, 118 S. Ct. 2257 (1998).

[25] *Oncale v. Sundowner Offshore Services, Inc.*, 523 U.S. 75 (1998).

[26] John D. Canoni, "Sexual Harassment: The New Liability," *Risk Management* 46 (January 1999), 12–17, and Marjorie A. Johnson, "Use Anti-Harassment Training to Shelter Yourself from Suits," *HR Magazine* (October 1999) 7–81, and Bodensteiner and Levinson, 5:16.

[27] Age Discrimination in Employment Act of 1967 at 29 U.S.C. §§ 621 et seq.; see also Bodensteiner and Levinson, 7:01–36.

[28] Equal Pay Act of 1963 at 29 U.S.C. §§ 201 et seq. See also Timothy S. Bland, "Equal Pay Enforcement Heats Up," *HR Magazine* 44 (July 1999), 138–145, and Bodensteiner and Levinson, 6:01–23.

[29] *Gunther v. County of Washington*, 452 U.S. 161 (1981).

[30] Americans with Disabilities Act of 1990 at 42 U.S.C. §§ 12101–17, 12201–13. See also Bodensteiner and Levinson, 8:05–50.

[31] *School Board of Nassau County v. Arline*, U.S. Supreme Court Docket No. 85-1277 (1987). See also Jeffrey A. Mello, *AIDS and the Law of Workplace Discrimination* (Boulder, Colo.: Westview, 1995).

[32] Immigration Reform and Control Act of 1986 at 8 U.S.C. § 1324(a).

[33] Civil Rights Act of 1866 at 42 U.S.C. § 1981. See also Idelson, IV-6.

[34] Civil Rights Act of 1871 at 42 U.S.C. § 1983. See also Idelson, IV-6.

[35] Vocational Rehabilitation Act of 1973 at 29 U.S.C. §§ 706, 793, 794. See also Bodensteiner and Levinson, 8:05.

[36] Executive Order 11246, Revised Order No. 4, 41 C.F.R. Part 60.

[37] 7 C.F.R. Part 18.

[38] Fair Labor Standards Act of 1938 at 29 U.S.C. §§ 201–216. Interpretations issued by the U.S. Department of Labor include 29 C.F.R. Parts 511–800.

[39] *Garcia v. San Antonio Metropolitan Transit Authority*, U.S. 1055. Ct 1005.

[40] Family and Medical Leave Act of 1993 at 29 U.S.C. §§ 2601 et seq.

[41] Occupational Safety and Health Act of 1970 at 29 U.S.C. §§ 654 et seq.

[42] Unless otherwise cited, this presentation and all court cases discussed in regard to constitutional issues follows Jay M. Shafritz et al., *Personnel Management in Government*, 4th ed. (New York: Dekker, 1992), 277–318 and David H. Rosenbloom, "What Every Public Personnel Manager Should Know About the Constitution," in Steven W. Hays and Richard C. Kearney, eds., *Public Personnel Administration*, 3d ed. (New York: Prentice Hall, 1995), 20–36 (citations of 47 court cases are found on 35–36).

[43] Shafritz et al., 283–287, and Rosenbloom, 21–23.

[44] *Board of Regents v. Roth*, 48 U.S. 564 (1972), and Rosenbloom, 32.

[45] Roger L. Miller and Gaylord A. Jentz, *Business Law Today*, 5th ed. (Cincinnati: West, 2000), 26–27.

[46] *Bishop v. Wood*, 426 U.S. 341 (1976).

[47] *Cleveland Board of Education v. Laudermill*, 470 U.S. 532 (1985), and Rosenbloom, 32.

[48] *Mt. Healthy School District Board of Education v. Doyle*, 429 U.S. 274 (1977), and Rosenbloom, 33.

[49] Rosenbloom, 49–52.

[50] *Washington v. Davis*, 426 U.S. 229 (1976).

[51] *United States v. Paradise*, 94 L. Ed. 2d 203 (1987).

[52] Bodensteiner and Levinson, 1:15.

[53] *Pickering v. Board of Education*, 39 U.S. 75 (1947), and Rosenbloom, 42.

[54] *Rankin v. McPherson*, 97 L. Ed. 2d. 315 (1987), and Rosenbloom, 22–25.

[55] *Elrod v. Burns*, 427 U.S. 347 (1976), and Rosenbloom, 26.

[56] *Chicago Teachers Union v. Hudson*, 89 L. Ed. 2d 232, and Rosenbloom, 26.

[57] *National Treasury Employee's Union v. Von Raab*, 109 U.S. 1384 (1989); see also Charles V. Dale, *Governmentally Mandated Drug Testing: Legal and Constitutional Developments* (Washington, D.C.: Congressional Research Service, May 6, 1997).

[58] *O'Connor v. Ortega*, 94 L. Ed. 2d 714 (1987), and Rosenbloom, 27.

[59] *Goldman v. Weinberger*, 475 U.S. 503 (1986).

[60] *McCartny v. Philadelphia Civil Service Commission*, 424 U.S. 645 (1976), and Rosenbloom, 29.

[61] John D. Ashcroft and Janet Ashcroft, *Law for Business* (Cincinnati: West, 1999), 20–21.

[62] Civil Rights Act of 1871 at 42 U.S.C. § 1983.

[63] *Wood v. Strickland,* 420 U.S. 308 (1975), and *Harlow v. Fitzgerald,* 457 U.S. 800 (1982), and Rosenbloom, 33–34.

[64] Rosenbloom, 33–34, and Bodensteiner and Levinson, 1:36-41.

[65] For a comprehensive discussion of employment contract law, see Steven C. Kahn, Barbara Berish Brown, and Michael Lanzarone, *Legal Guide to Human Resources* (Boston: Warren, Gorham & Lamont, 1999), 8:1–52.

[66] For a review of state drug testing laws see John M. Moorwood, "Drug Testing in the Private Sector and Its Impact on Employees' Right to Privacy," *Labor Law Journal* 45 (December 1994), 731–748.

[67] In reference to state courts see Jonathan A. Segal, "Will Drug Testing Pass or Fail in Court?" *Personnel Journal* 75 (April 1996), 141–44.

PART 2
ORGANIZATIONAL CONSIDERATIONS

Human resource management is carried out in organizations—social units composed of people. For the organization to be successful, it must analyze HR needs in light of its mission and strategic objectives. Chapter 4 deals with the behaviors and attitudes that predict what people are likely to do and examines the HR implications of motivation, satisfaction, and leadership in building a high-performance organization. Chapter 5 presents the broad scope of HR planning, discusses the nature and use of various planning tools, and explains how policy guidance shapes the development of HR systems and processes.

CHAPTER 4
BEHAVIORAL FOUNDATIONS OF HUMAN RESOURCE MANAGEMENT

NATIONAL CHAMPIONSHIP

Citizens of the town of Blacksburg, Virginia, home of Virginia Tech, are rightly proud of the Hokies, whose 11-0 record during the 1999 football season earned them an invitation to the Sugar Bowl and the opportunity to play for the national championship. Although the football team came up a little short, there was another national championship being decided that year. Over the past few years, Blacksburg, which has a population of approximately 42,000, has emerged as a leader among cities its size in efficiency and cost-effectiveness of operations and excellence in the quality of its services. In 1999 the town won the IPMA Excellence Award for small organizations.

This achievement can be attributed to a number of factors, but probably the most important is that Blacksburg built an organizational culture that emphasizes employee commitment, effective leadership, and a high value on service to customers. For example, line managers, with facilitation by the Human Resources Division, acquired leadership skills and committed themselves to a participative approach that empowers employees and involves them in decision making. The new employee orientation program was revamped to promote socialization into the work environment and included a "buddy system." Training programs were keyed to address capacity building and career development needs. Regularly scheduled offerings include a variety of topics from job skills to communications and diversity. An awards process was initiated to recognize employees for noteworthy accomplishments in such areas as safety, training, operations, and customer service. Employees earn points that can be used to purchase leave days or gifts from downtown merchants. Cross-functional process improvement teams were established to work with citizens on service delivery and customer satisfaction. The pay system was redesigned to reward individual and team performance and to encourage employees to acquire new skills. Effective benefits cost control measures were implemented, enabling the town to continue to offer a benefits package that is attractive to employees and financially sound.

Most local governments have employees and managers who are individually competent in their jobs. What distinguishes the town of Blacksburg is *organizational competence.* This was brought about by approaches as shown above that tap into the latent forces that influence human behaviors and attitudes to build maximum performance and contributions.

Source: "1999 Agency Awards for Excellence," *IPMA News* 65 (August 1999), 5–6.

INTRODUCTION

The Blacksburg example illustrates how HR professionals work with line managers to create a high-performance organization. This chapter is about what people do in organizations and how their behaviors and attitudes affect organizational performance, a field of study known as **organizational behavior** or **OB**. The field includes a large number of topics, and an in-depth examination of each is beyond the scope of a text in HR management. However, there is general agreement that effective HR management must deal with certain key areas of OB. It is important to understand the forces that induce (or motivate) an employee to exert energy and effort in achieving organizational objectives. It is also useful to review the link, if any, between an employee's emotional response (or degree of satisfaction) with elements present in the work climate and his or her job performance. Ultimately, however, it is line managers in their interactions with employees who have the greatest influence on the work environment. Therefore it is necessary to address management philosophy and leadership. This chapter surveys motivation (content and process approaches), job satisfaction for appropriate work outcomes, and management philosophy and leadership.[1]

MOTIVATION: BASIC CONSIDERATIONS

What induces people to want to work at a particular place on a particular job and want to do that job well? A new city planner, for example, may have a graduate degree and substantial expertise in the field and have a general interest in good city planning. However, if the person has no interest in spending a great deal of time with the city planning commission, real estate developers, and private citizens attempting to mediate controversial zoning issues, he or she will likely not be motivated to actually do the work and will not be effective. The crucial issue is how people can be induced to see the goals of the organization as their own and to put forth the effort required to achieve them.

Most people are familiar with stereotypical military scenes (often humorous) in which a drill instructor "motivates" (loudly) a sleepy recruit to fall out for reveille, or an airborne sergeant "motivates" (with his foot) a reluctant paratrooper trainee to jump from a plane. The authors have, in their pasts, been similarly "motivated." These are, of course, not really examples of motivation at all, but of force and threat to compel behavior. At the same time, the military also offers familiar images of genuine motivation. Especially in elite units such as the airborne, soldiers often develop intense pride in and loyalty to the unit and are willing to risk their lives and endure extreme hardship to help carry out the assigned mission. Such individuals, in other words, have accepted the goals of their organizations as their own. They are motivated.

Human motives are based on a variety of drives, desires, wishes, and similar

http://www.mapnp.org/
library/guiding/
motivate/motivate.htm
The Management Assistance Program for Nonprofits provides links to numerous articles and research findings on employee motivation theory and application in both the for-profit and non-profit sectors, including local governments.

forces often called needs. **Motivation** is a predisposition to behave in a purposeful manner to satisfy specific, unmet needs. For example, an employee in the Parks and Recreation Department with a desire to control other people (need for power) might apply for the position of park superintendent. If a solid waste supervisor wanted to become known as an authority on his or her subject matter (need for recognition), one expected behavior would be to present a talk to a conference on sanitary landfills. Motivation, as can be seen, is an "inner state." Thus, managers cannot, from the outside, directly "motivate" someone. Managers can, however, use employees' motivations to instill *esprit de corps*, to influence employees to actually want to achieve the purposes of the group. The more managers understand motivation, the better they are able to influence that behavior so that it will be consistent with and support organizational objectives.

CONTENT APPROACHES TO MOTIVATION

The content approach to motivation focuses on what causes individuals to act in a certain way. Theories using this approach attempt to answer such questions as "What forces prompt people to behave as they do?" Following this approach, if one wants to understand what motivates people, one must identify their needs. The two content theories that have generated the most interest are Maslow's need hierarchy theory and Herzberg's two-factor theory.

NEED HIERARCHY THEORY

Abraham Maslow's need hierarchy theory is one of the most popular and widely known theories of motivation.[2] According to Maslow, people are motivated to satisfy five categories of needs: *physiological* needs (food, shelter, clothing, etc.), *safety needs* (security, freedom from threat, avoidance of pain, etc.), *social needs* (friendship, affection, acceptance, etc.), *esteem needs* (recognition, respect, responsibility, etc.), and *self-actualization* needs (creativity, realization of one's potential, self-expression, etc.). These needs are arranged in a hierarchy of ascending importance, from low (physiological) to high (self-actualization).

Maslow contended that a "lower" need must be satisfied before the next "higher" need could motivate behavior. For example, a person's safety needs would have to be satisfied before the next level of need (social) could motivate behavior. Thus, the strength of any need is determined by its position in the hierarchy and by the degree to which it and all lower needs have been satisfied. Satisfaction of a need, however, triggers dissatisfaction at the next higher level. This sequence repeats itself until the highest level of the hierarchy (self-actualization) is reached. Maslow also suggested that a person could progress down as well as up the various need levels. Thus, sudden unemployment could shift one's concern from a pursuit of personal recognition to a preoccupation with providing for home and family.

Although Maslow's concept is intuitively appealing, the theory has not been supported by research.[3] First, researchers have been unable to reproduce the five needs levels, suggesting instead that there are no more than two or three levels. Second, although people do generally place a great deal of emphasis on satisfying their lower-level needs (for example, hunger, thirst, sex), research suggests that once these needs are satisfied most people do not necessarily climb Maslow's need hierarchy in the proposed manner.

Despite its questionable validity as a complete account of motivation, Maslow's theory is useful to managers. It is clear that motivation is determined by multiple needs, and needs can be identified and addressed. Thus, esteem needs can be satisfied by an awards program in which outstanding performers receive a certificate. It should be stressed that different people have different needs, and also that an individual's needs are likely to change over time. It is a manager's responsibility to create a climate in which people have opportunities to satisfy whatever needs are important to them. Failure to do this is likely to lead to frustration, reduced output, and increased turnover.

THE TWO-FACTOR THEORY

A second significant content theory of motivation was developed by Frederick Herzberg.[4] Traditionally, managers had viewed job satisfaction and job dissatisfaction as opposite ends of the same continuum. In research based on interviews with accountants and engineers, Herzberg found that the factors producing job satisfaction were entirely separate from those producing job dissatisfaction. That is, although an unpleasant work environment might be a reason given for job dissatisfaction, a pleasant work environment was not likely to be cited as a reason for job satisfaction. Herzberg concluded, therefore, that a two-factor theory was needed to explain employee motivation.

Herzberg labeled the factors that produced job satisfaction *motivators*. His analysis indicated these factors are directly related to job *content*, reflecting a need for personal fulfillment. He labeled the factors that led to job dissatisfaction *hygienes*, and found they are related more to the work setting, or job context, than to job *content*.

Herzberg concluded that only motivators produce job satisfaction, whereas hygienes merely prevent job dissatisfaction. The two-factor theory basically reduces Maslow's five need levels to two. Herzberg's hygienes are roughly equivalent to Maslow's three lowest need categories. Similarly, his motivators are roughly equivalent to Maslow's two highest needs, esteem and self-actualization. Exhibit 4-1 compares Herzberg's motivator and hygiene factors with Maslow's hierarchy of needs.

Like the hierarchy of needs theory, the two-factor theory has been criticized on several grounds.[5] The research methodology was considered inadequate to support the conclusions. Certain factors, such as supervision, achievement, and pay, have been shown to be important for both satisfaction and dissatisfaction. Also, because Herzberg's subjects were accountants and engineers, it is not known if the theory applies to workers in different economic and educational categories.

Nevertheless, Herzberg's theory carries valuable managerial implications. First, a person can be satisfied and dissatisfied at the same time. A recent study of municipal employees found that both employees and supervisors tended to be satisfied with certain aspects of their jobs, such as the chance to learn new things, but generally dissatisfied with the pay.[6] Second, practical experience suggests that Herzberg's theory explains why certain actions, such as improved working conditions, often do not improve motivation. Improved hygiene factors may not strike at the root of the motivation problem at all. Finally, Herzberg's ideas are evident in many successful programs like those in Blacksburg where jobs were redesigned to provide opportunities for achievement, recognition, responsibility, advancement, and personal growth.

EXHIBIT 4-1

A COMPARISON OF MASLOW'S
NEED HIERARCHY THEORY AND
HERZBERG'S TWO-FACTOR THEORY

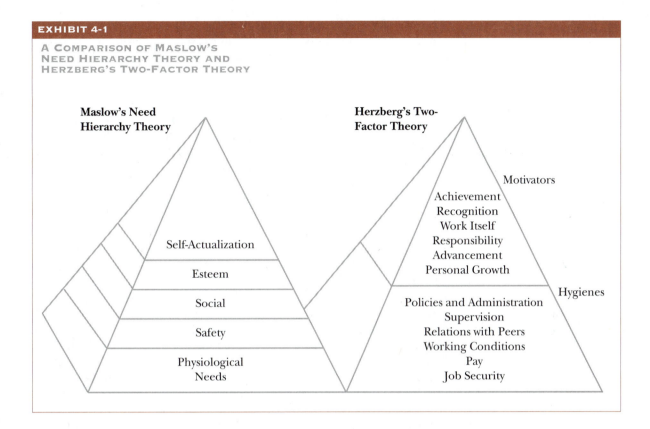

Maslow's Need Hierarchy Theory

- Self-Actualization
- Esteem
- Social
- Safety
- Physiological Needs

Herzberg's Two-Factor Theory

Motivators
- Achievement
- Recognition
- Work Itself
- Responsibility
- Advancement
- Personal Growth

Hygienes
- Policies and Administration
- Supervision
- Relations with Peers
- Working Conditions
- Pay
- Job Security

PROCESS APPROACHES TO MOTIVATION

While the content approach concerns what within people motivates them to behave in a certain way, the process approach concerns how people are motivated. Process theories focus on the direction or choice of behavioral patterns. The process theories that have generated the most interest are Vroom's expectancy theory, Adams's equity theory, Skinner's reinforcement theory, and Locke's goal-setting theory.

EXPECTANCY THEORY

Expectancy theory is perhaps the most respected motivation theory. As set forth by Victor H. Vroom, expectancy theory is based on the belief that people will act to maximize their rewards.[7] The theory holds that motivation is determined by two elements, the *belief* that effort will be rewarded and the *value* attached to specific rewards.

Beliefs, or expectancies, can be separated into two types. They are *Expectancy* (or Expectancy 1), the belief that effort will lead to performance, and *Instrumentality* (also known as Expectancy 2), the belief that performance will result in a desirable outcome. Expectancy is actually a belief in personal effectiveness; that is, that an individual can perform well if he or she makes the effort. Instrumentality is the belief that work contributions will be identified, accurately measured, and appropriately rewarded. The opposite, of course, may be true in either case. A person may feel that working harder does not produce better results or that higher performance is not directly related to rewards. In such a situation, a person would be low in both Expectancy 1 and Expectancy 2.

The second determinant of motivation is *valence*, which is the value placed on an outcome (reward). It can be either positive or negative. Thus, a person may attach a negative value to an outcome (for example, being fired); or a positive value (for example, being promoted). The more positive the value, the more likely a person will be highly motivated. The more negative the value, the less likely a person will be highly motivated. The operation of expectancy theory is shown below:

$$\text{Motivation} = (\text{Expectancy 1}) \ (\text{Expectancy 2}) \ (\text{Valence})$$

The following example illustrates how Vroom's expectancy theory works on the job. A police detective questions suspects, interviews witnesses, inspects crime scenes, and so forth. The more of these tasks he carries out (as opposed to taking long coffee breaks), the more cases he is likely to solve. Thus, there is a direct relationship between effort and performance (Expectancy 1). Since the city has a merit pay plan, this performance will be reflected in a good pay raise; that is, there is a direct relationship between performance and rewards (Expectancy 2). Finally, the detective has a child entering college in the fall and his household budget is already strained. Hence, the detective is eager to get a pay raise. In expectancy terms, he values the increased income (valence). Overall, expectancy theory is generally considered one of the better frameworks for both understanding motivation and determining the value attached to rewards. Interestingly, the study mentioned above suggested that local government employees are more concerned with job security, pay, and personal advancement than with benefiting society, teamwork, or autonomy.[8]

This is not to say that expectancy theory is without criticism.[9] Researchers have found that the complexity of expectancy theory makes it very difficult to test, and practitioners have found that this complexity makes its practical application difficult. Critics note that human decision makers are incapable of processing the information required to know all alternative outcomes, their likelihood of occurrence, or their desirability, even if such information were available.

Expectancy theory carries several valuable managerial implications, however. Employees must believe that they have the necessary competencies to achieve objectives. This issue was addressed in Blacksburg with the training program. Desired performance must be clearly linked to rewards as illustrated by the pay system designed to reward contributions. Finally, rewards must be meaningful to employees. By understanding individual employee needs, managers can match them to rewards for maximum motivation.

EQUITY THEORY

A second process theory of motivation is based on the work of J. Stacy Adams. Generally known as equity theory, it attempts to explain people's satisfaction with outcomes and to predict resulting changes in their behavior.[10] Equity theory defines motivation in terms of the perceived equity between the effort a person puts into a job and what he or she receives in return, especially as compared to other persons in similar positions. Equity theory holds that (1) perceived inequity creates tension within a person; (2) this tension motivates a person to restore equity; and (3) the strength of the resulting behavior will vary directly with the magnitude of the perceived inequity.

The theory is concerned with equity, which is not the same as equality. An individual may perceive his or her outcomes to be exactly equal to outcomes gained by another and still perceive inequity. Equity is attained when the ratio of an individual's perceived outcomes to inputs equals the ratio of the other person's outcomes to inputs. That is:

$$\frac{\text{Outcomes/Self}}{\text{Inputs/Self}} = \frac{\text{Outcomes/Other}}{\text{Inputs/Other}}$$

For example, a person who considers himself or herself to be exerting moderate efforts and receives a moderate pay increase may perceive equity with a coworker who exerted great effort and receives a large pay raise. Their outcomes are different, but their ratios of outcomes/inputs are equal. Perceived inequity may exist when a person judges his or her outcomes (for given inputs) as being either *too low* relative to another, or as being excessive relative to another. Pay is of course only one of many factors that may enter the equity equation. Other possible input/outcome factors include experience/promotion opportunities, productivity/recognition, or seniority/coworker esteem.

Examples of perceived inequity are quite common. For instance, consider the situation in which new employees receive starting salaries as high or higher than persons with many years of service. Although this may be necessary to attract top-quality candidates, the practice is almost inevitably seen as inequitable. There appears to be little doubt that people become distressed, and thus motivated to act, when they feel they are being treated inequitably. In efforts to restore equity, people may do one or more of the following.[11]

ALTER INPUTS. People may increase or decrease their inputs, depending upon whether the perceived inequity is advantageous or disadvantageous. For instance, underpaid employees may work less, while those who are overpaid may work harder.

ALTER OUTCOMES. The lawsuits brought by women, persons over 40, and minorities against organizations are examples of attempts to alter outcomes. Federal and state legislation prohibiting pay discrimination is designed to address this type of inequity.

LEAVE THE FIELD. People who feel inequitably rewarded may seek to find a more favorable balance of outcomes to inputs elsewhere. An accountant, for example, may decide to leave a government job for the private sector when he or she realizes what counterparts in accounting firms are earning.

RATIONALIZE THE SITUATION. People may attempt, consciously or unconsciously, to adjust their perceptions of equity or inequity. An equipment operator who feels that merit raises in the public works department are based on favoritism may adopt the attitude that things work the same way with construction firms.

Equity theory is intuitively appealing and has received a great deal of attention. Its popularity can be partially explained by its ease of understanding and commonsense appeal. It is also generally supported by research, but with some qualifications.[12] First, inequities created by overpayment have not been shown to have a significant impact on worker behavior (one of the authors, in developing pay systems for local governments, has accumulated considerable anecdotal evidence that supports this conclusion). Other investigations have revealed that a small part of the working population actually prefer that their outcome/input ratio be less than the referent comparison (anecdotal evidence also suggests that the term "small" is quite accurate).

Managers should be aware that people make equity comparisons, and when they feel they are treated inequitably, attitude and performance problems may be expected. Since rewards are judged in a relative rather than an absolute fashion, it is important to influence employee perceptions of equity by making inputs required for outcomes as explicit as possible.

REINFORCEMENT THEORY

Reinforcement theory is based largely on the work of B. F. Skinner. Its guiding principle is that human behavior is a function of its consequences.[13] Stated more formally, behaviors that result in desirable consequences will likely recur; those that result in undesirable consequences will be less likely to recur. This last statement is popularly referred to as "Thorndike's Law of Effect."[14] The application of Thorndike's Law of Effect to work settings is referred to as **behavior modification** or **operant conditioning**. This theory focuses on influencing behavior through positive or negative reinforcement (rewards or punishments).

Various schedules of reinforcement are possible.[15] The *fixed interval* schedule provides reinforcement at predetermined times regardless of behavior. A good example is the monthly paycheck. Performance under a fixed interval schedule tends to be poor. A *variable interval* schedule provides reinforcement at random times. An example of this would be a solid waste supervisor who makes unannounced visits at the county landfill, giving praise or blame as appropriate. When employees do not know when their boss is coming, they will tend to maintain a reasonably high level of effort. In a *fixed ratio* schedule, reinforcement is applied after a predetermined number of behaviors, such as in the Blacksburg example, where employees earned points that could be used to purchase paid leave or other items. Finally, there is a *variable ratio* schedule, which is the most powerful schedule in terms of reinforcement. This type of reinforcement is programmed like a slot machine, and an employee has no idea when a behavior will be rewarded. While this kind of reinforcement schedule is too complex to use in a pay plan, it works very well for such rewards as praise and recognition.

Reinforcement theory is unquestionably the most controversial of the motivation theories. Critics charge that it ignores the social processes that exist in any human system (recall the Hawthorne studies), as well as individual employee differences. It is too rigid and programmed in its methods, failing to consider the importance of individual needs, expectancies, and valences. Reinforcement overemphasizes the importance of external outcomes (for example, pay and promotions) and ignores the role of internal outcomes (for example, feelings of accomplishment and recognition) that result from simply doing a task. Finally, the theory raises ethical concerns. Many critics feel the use of punishment and the term *behavior modification* itself smacks of employee manipulation. They fear behavior modification may be used to exploit employees.

Even in view of these criticisms, reinforcement is a legitimate motivation theory and carries several important implications for managers. First, behavior that is rewarded will be repeated, and conversely. Thus, it is important for managers to state which behaviors will be rewarded and which will not. Rewards must be based on levels of performance. Identical rewards, such as across-the-board pay increases, reinforce mediocre and low performance and weaken high performance. Finally, if desired performance is not rewarded at all, it will diminish and eventually cease.

EXHIBIT 4-2

FEATURES OF SELECTED PROCESS
THEORIES OF MOTIVATION

Motivational Theory	Description	Key Issues
Vroom's Expectancy Theory	Motivation is the product of *expectancy*, *instrumentality*, and *valence*.	• Employee assessments of their own ability are important. • Performance must be linked to rewards (line of sight). • Rewards must be meaningful.
Adams's Equity Theory	Employees are motivated when they believe that their *reward/contribution ratio* is equal to the ratio of a *referent other*.	• Rewards must be allocated consistently and fairly among employees. • Employee perceptions are very important.
Skinner's Reinforcement Theory	Behaviors that are *rewarded* will recur and those that are not rewarded or punished will be discontinued.	• Performance must be tightly coupled to desired behaviors. • Rewards must closely follow demonstration of desired behavior.
Locke's Goal-Setting Theory	*Performance goals* influence greater intensity and duration of performance.	• Performance goals should be specific and challenging. • Performance must be linked to rewards (line of sight).

Source: Based in part on George T. Milkovich and Jerry M. Newman, *Compensation*, 6th ed. (Boston: Irwin/McGraw-Hill, 1999), 276–278.

GOAL-SETTING THEORY

The goal-setting theory of motivation is based on the work of Edwin A. Locke and his colleagues.[16] The theory suggests that specific, challenging goals are more likely to lead to desirable behaviors than vague goals such as "do your best." To illustrate the operation of this theory in a work setting, consider a situation in which the public works director of a city announces to the unit heads that there have been too many lost-time accidents and "you need to pay more attention to safety." The unit heads may appear to agree, but this is not really a goal. It would be better to establish specific expectations, such as holding weekly safety meetings, monitoring the worksite and enforcing safety rules, and properly completing accident reports.

To be effective, goals should be stated in terms of observable behaviors or outcomes, including a time limit where possible. Feedback on goal-directed performance is essential because it provides a standard against which employees can measure their performance. Also, positive feedback on the attainment of goals gives an employee a sense of achievement and recognition. It is important to note, however, that the effectiveness of goal setting is reduced if goal achievement is not connected to rewards that the employee sees as valuable, or if the rewards system is perceived to be unfair (note the relationship of goal setting theory with expectancy and equity theories discussed above).[17] Exhibit 4-2 compares the features of expectancy, equity, reinforcement, and goal-setting theories of motivation.

JOB SATISFACTION

It is necessary to distinguish between motivation and **job satisfaction,** since the terms are often confused. Certainly, satisfaction of needs is an important element of motivation. It is most useful, however, to consider job satisfaction as being concerned with people's attitudes about their work rather than with their efforts to fill a need or seek rewards. Locke, for example, defines job satisfaction as "the pleasurable emotional state resulting from the appraisal of one's job as achieving or facilitating one's job values."[18] Thus, a recreation center employee may like (be satisfied with) the assignment to work with young people, or a heavy equipment operator may feel the pay is too low (be dissatisfied). Stated another way, satisfaction is in the past tense, involving outcomes already experienced; motivation suggests the present, where a person is striving toward an outcome. As pointed out in the discussion of Herzberg's motivation theory, a person may be highly satisfied and not motivated, or the reverse may be true. Job satisfaction and motivation are often related, however. A highly motivated person with low job satisfaction may look for another job.

While a strong case can be made that high levels of motivation are associated with high performance, the case regarding job satisfaction is not so clear. It has often been assumed that satisfied workers perform better, but research has not provided strong support for this idea. In fact there are probably many satisfied employees whose performance is only mediocre. Job satisfaction is now believed to be more the result of job performance than its cause. The reasoning for this concerns the rewards system. If better performance leads to higher rewards, such as recognition, pay, and promotion, and these rewards are seen as fair, the result is greater satisfaction.[19] An employee strives to satisfy other, more specific needs, and job satisfaction is thus a consequence of an appropriate motivating environment and not directly a motivating cause.

http://www.calib.com/
nccanch/pubs/
usermanuals/supercps/
satisfy.htm
Caliber and Associates
provides detailed
information on increasing
job satisfaction and
preventing burnout of
child protective services
caseworkers.

JOB SATISFACTION AND WORK OUTCOMES

Job satisfaction (or dissatisfaction) thus has a limited, but significant, relation to job performance and the efficient functioning of the organization. Job satisfaction is a desirable outcome in itself because of its positive impact on attendance, retention, and prosocial "citizenship" behaviors such as helping coworkers, helping customers, and being cooperative.[20] Managers must especially be aware of the very strong relationship shown by research between job dissatisfaction and certain specific problems. One important relationship that has been established is that job dissatisfaction is related to excessive turnover. Other negative consequences of job dissatisfaction include absenteeism, defensive behaviors, and poor performance.[21] All of these problems are costly; for example, the cost of replacing an employee, in terms of recruitment, selection, and training, is several times the average monthly salary. Thus, efforts to increase job satisfaction are usually excellent investments.

BUILDING JOB SATISFACTION

Job design (discussed in Chapter 5) has a major impact on job satisfaction. Generally, when employees have greater self-direction and the opportunity to perform interesting and challenging work, satisfaction is increased. These aspects of jobs have to do with job content and are related to Herzberg's motivator factors. As might be expected, Herzberg is an advocate of job enrichment as a job design strategy to increase satisfaction. To some workers, however, the environmental aspects of their

Motivation and satisfaction are different things that affect performance in different ways. An understanding of both is important in taking management action that attracts and keeps workers and induces those workers to put forth their best efforts. The chart below illustrates some significant ways in which motivation and satisfaction affect employees.

MOTIVATION VS. SATISFACTION

Motivation	Satisfaction
Is an employee's drive to perform on the job.	Is an employee's feeling about the job.
Comes from an employee's "inner state."	Comes from an employee's expectation and job values.
Is measured by the degree to which the job fulfills the employee's wants, needs, and desires.	Is measured by the employee's attitudes (favorable or unfavorable) about various aspects of the job.
When present, the employee is "turned on," and strives to achieve work expectations.	When present, the employee experiences a feeling of contentment and well-being
When absent, the employee experiences a lack of fulfillment and is likely to put forth only enough effort to meet minimum job standards.	When absent, the employee experiences a feeling of alienation and is likely to be absent, be late, complain, or quit.
Individual preferences vary widely among individuals and change over time.	Preferences can usually be identified for groups of employees and remain rather stable over time.
Can be influenced by management action directed at job **content** (achievement, recognition, etc.) or behavioral **process** (pay for performance).	Can be influenced by management action directed at job **context** (improved working conditions, competitive level of pay, etc.).

jobs may be more important. These aspects include Herzberg's hygiene factors, such as pay and benefits, relationships with others, and working conditions. Note how Blacksburg addressed these factors by involving employees in decision making, fostering relationships, providing competitive pay, and offering attractive benefits.

The collective perception of employees regarding these and similar factors is the **organizational climate**. Both research and experience indicate that organizational climate is related to organizational performance; thus programs designed to build job satisfaction should have a positive benefit. Such programs should be based on a climate survey that measures job satisfaction levels in various dimensions such as pay, promotional opportunities, task clarity and significance, skills utilization, organizational commitment, and relationships with supervisors and coworkers.[22] The HR department may design a questionnaire or use a commercially available instrument. The IPMA Center for Personnel Research has sample surveys collected from various organizations available to members.[23] Survey information can be very useful, especially in identifying sources of employee dissatisfaction. For example, counselors at a county youth detention facility were exhibiting a number of indicators of low morale including grievances, absenteeism, and high turnover. Management believed that the major problem was low pay. During this time a new HR director from the private sector with a background in employee relations was added to

Satisfaction surveys are designed to capture the intensity of employee attitudes and feeling in key areas. In conducting this kind of research both the focus of the survey and the method of collecting data are important. It is recommended that surveys have a specific theme (one year it may be pay, the next, supervision, etc.). Rather than use open-ended questions or ask for yes-no answers, employees should be asked to indicate whether they agree with carefully selected statements as shown below:

MEASURING EMPLOYEE SATISFACTION

1. My supervisor keeps me informed about matters affecting me.
    Strongly disagree   1   2   3   4   5   Strongly agree
2. I trust my supervisor to be fair in enforcing work rules and taking disciplinary action.
    Strongly disagree   1   2   3   4   5   Strongly agree
3. I feel free to go to a "higher boss" than my immediate supervisor to discuss any problems that are bothering me.
    Strongly disagree   1   2   3   4   5   Strongly agree
4. My supervisor is friendly and helpful.
    Strongly disagree   1   2   3   4   5   Strongly agree

The overall mean value of responses to these and other statements is a measure of the degree of satisfaction with the area of supervision. Moderate to high agreement (means 3 and above) would indicate that employees are generally satisfied. Low agreement (mean less than 3) would be a cause for concern because it would indicate that supervision is causing dissatisfaction.

Source: Maureen Smith, "Measuring Employee Satisfaction Through Surveys," *IPMA News* 65 (March 1999), 15–16. Survey items listed were developed by HR Solutions, Inc., a Chicago-based consulting firm.

the staff. A survey revealed a number of areas of dissatisfaction including pay, promotion opportunities, organizational communications, and the administration of work rules. Based on these findings the center improved its pay program and modified a number of its other policies. As a result, turnover was significantly reduced.[24]

This example illustrated the appropriate management response to the job satisfaction issue. While pay is often a source of dissatisfaction and was undoubtedly linked to the high turnover at the facility, the HR director understood that other factors were probably involved. The major benefit of an accurate assessment of organizational climate is that it allows management to identify and improve areas of dissatisfaction. The key word is *improve*. Recall that satisfaction is mainly concerned with hygiene factors, which have limited motivational value. For example, improving the general level of pay to market levels would be sufficient to remove dissatisfaction. For pay to be a motivator, further increases should be based on job performance (pay-for-performance systems are discussed in Chapter 13).

MANAGEMENT PHILOSOPHY AND LEADERSHIP

Both management philosophy and leadership are key aspects of organizational performance. Management philosophy involves the fundamental values held by the executive leadership and elected officials. Leadership styles and behaviors are the way managers at all levels implement the management philosophy through their interaction with employees.

MANAGEMENT PHILOSOPHY

Management philosophy in local government consists of a set of guiding principles that influence decisions and activities in a number of areas such as type and quality of services provided, priorities, resource allocations, and importantly, how human resources will be managed. Management philosophy is important because managers at all levels tend to take their cues from higher management. If a city manager has a hierarchical, "top down" orientation and believes employees must be closely supervised, department heads and lower line managers will tend to be autocratic and controlling. On the other hand, if the city manager's views are egalitarian and he or she believes that employees should have a voice in matters concerning their work (such as job/work assignments, training, performance appraisal, pay, benefits, and discipline), lower-level managers will tend to model their behavior on this philosophy. Another important aspect of management philosophy is ethics, discussed in Chapter 1. When the executive management of a government is committed to high ethical standards, the outcomes of whatever leadership behaviors are employed will generally be more positive.

LEADERSHIP

The organizational manager by definition occupies a leadership position. He or she is responsible for establishing a direction or focus for the organization and for influencing individual or group activities toward achievement of chosen objectives. However, leadership is an elusive quality, and the factors that underlie the success or failure of a leader are not perfectly understood. The problematic nature of leadership is well shown in the sign on a supervisor's desk: "There they go. I must hurry and catch up with them, for I am their leader."[25]

The supervisor's sign especially points up the difficulty of leadership in modern public sector organizations, in which the leader's range of control is limited by legal and policy considerations. Nevertheless, leadership is basic to organizational management. Research and experience in the field have provided useful knowledge regarding effective leadership practice and helpful insights regarding leadership training and the selection of managers for leadership positions.

THE LEADER'S ASSUMPTIONS ABOUT PEOPLE

A key ingredient in the understanding of effective leadership is the realization that managers who hold different assumptions about the people who report to them will behave differently toward those people as well. Writing in the late 1950s, Douglas M. McGregor was one of the first to explore this factor.[26] McGregor explained that if managers assume that people generally dislike work and wish to avoid responsibility (a common assumption), they will treat subordinates accordingly. McGregor called these Theory X managers. Another kind of manager tends to assume that people generally want to use their capacities and energies to the fullest extent, at work as well as at play, and under the right conditions will not only accept but seek responsibility. These managers, whom McGregor called Theory Y managers, will treat subordinates quite differently.

Theory X managers are likely to be *autocratic* leaders. They will rely on coercion, discipline, and penalties to accomplish objectives. Theory Y managers are likely to be *democratic* leaders. They will emphasize self-management and encourage subordinates to seek responsibility and share in decision making. The irony is that, consistent with reinforcement theory, the managers' assumptions tend to create what is assumed. Treat a person as a loser (or winner), and he or she is likely to be conditioned to act like one. McGregor called this result a self-fulfilling prophecy.

Theory X and Theory Y, of course, represent two extremes, and most local government managers would fall somewhere in between. The major contribution of McGregor's work is the insight that managers do tend to hold different assumptions, and that a manager (leader) influences a leadership situation by his or her assumptions about people.

THE NATURE OF EFFECTIVE LEADERSHIP

Leadership is the art of influencing the behavior of others toward the attainment of goals and is closely connected with management philosophy. Attempts by researchers to determine the nature of leadership have resulted in a vast amount of literature and a number of important theories. This section very briefly outlines approaches to leadership based on traits, behaviors, and situational forces and summarizes representative theories.[27]

LEADERSHIP TRAITS. Early attempts to understand leadership centered on determining the specific traits (distinctive physical or psychological characteristics) that make a person an effective leader. It was believed that if these traits could be identified, other individuals should be able to acquire them through training and experience. In other words, leadership could be learned. Later studies suggest that this is not usually the case; however, it is generally believed that such attributes as intelligence, ambition, integrity, self-confidence, and job-related knowledge are required for effective leaders.[28]

Other studies have focused, with better results, on behavioral and situational approaches to leadership.

LEADERSHIP BEHAVIORS. Underlying behavioral approaches is the assumption that effective leaders utilize a particular behavioral style that causes others to follow them. Research has indicated certain consistent relationships between patterns of leadership behavior and group performance. These studies generally concluded that managers who had most success as leaders followed what Rensis Likert called the "participative-group" approach.[29] In this approach, managers have complete trust and confidence in subordinates, use rewards on the basis of group participation, encourage group participation in broad goal setting and decision making, and encourage upward, downward, and lateral communication. Note, for example, the features of both Theory Y and participative leadership in the Blacksburg example. Although Likert's work is almost 40 years old, his ideas are prominent in the move away from traditional "top-down" management in local government toward more egalitarian and process-oriented approaches.[30]

SITUATIONAL FORCES. Later studies, while building on the behavioral approach, focused much more intensively on situational perspectives. The central theme of these studies is that the appropriate blend of leadership behaviors depends on conditions and forces present in the work situation. In other words, while a participative style may be ideal, it is not always appropriate. In local government many situations can arise that call for a directive or even autocratic style. Examples include responses to emergencies in the police and fire services, but others are less obvious. A water superintendent is expected to insist that laboratory tests be performed correctly. The most important contribution of these studies is in pointing out the significance of situational factors and showing that it is inaccurate to speak without qualification of "effective" leaders.

http://www.andromeda.
rutgers.edu/~ncpp
The National Center for Public Productivity is a research and public service organization that helps federal, state, local, and not-for-profit agencies in further improving their capacity to provide quality services.

There is a wide disparity between research-based knowledge and prescriptions for leadership success. Most studies indicate rather clearly that effective leadership requires an understanding of human behavior, knowledge of the capabilities of subordinates, and the ability to

WHY IS LEADERSHIP TRAINING INEFFECTIVE?

select and carry out the type of leadership behavior that is appropriate to the situation. Yet many leadership training courses are built around the popular literature, which offers simplistic, one-dimensional approaches.

The U.S. Army invests heavily in leadership training, very little of which is the type depicted in war movies. Quoting from the manual:

> Bear in mind that competent leaders mix elements of all these styles [directing, participative, transformational, etc.] to match the place, task and the people involved. Using different leadership styles in different situations or elements of the same style in the same situation isn't inconsistent. The opposite is true: if you use only one leadership style, you're inflexible and will have difficulty operating where the style doesn't fit.*

The point is this: No single set of rules or techniques will suffice for the successful leader. There are no quick fixes, either in a military setting or in a civilian organization.

*U.S. Army, *Army Leadership: Be, Know, Do* (Washington D.C.: Department of the Army, FM-22-100, 1999), 3: 15–16.

Source: Contributed by Carol K. Woolbright, Associate Professor of Educational Leadership, Troy State University—Phenix City.

The HR department can improve the effectiveness of organizational leadership in a number of ways. The department should be actively involved in the selection process so that the prospective manager is placed in an assignment that matches his or her competencies. Coaching and counseling can help new managers adjust to the workplace culture. Finally, training and development programs should emphasize selecting the leadership behavior appropriate to the situation rather than promote the idea that there is one "best" style of leadership.[31]

SUMMARY

Content approaches to motivation hold that employees strive to satisfy multiple needs, from the physiological to higher needs such as esteem and personal growth. Process approaches focus on the "how" rather than the "what" of motivation. Expectancy theory stresses the relationship between the belief that effort will be rewarded and the value attached to rewards. Equity theory holds that people are motivated by comparisons (perceived inequities) between their own ratio of job outcomes to inputs and those of others. Reinforcement theory stresses the importance of appropriately scheduling rewards in motivating performance.

Job satisfaction, the attitudes people have about their work, affects work outcomes. Lack of job satisfaction indicates an inadequate motivational environment and is associated with problems such as absenteeism and turnover. Job design offering interesting tasks and self-direction builds job satisfaction.

Leadership is influenced by assumptions about people. Theory X managers, assuming people are lazy and dislike work, use control and/or coercion. Theory Y managers, who assume people are willing and self-directed, use democratic methods. Behavioral approaches distinguish employee-centered vs. job-centered leadership styles. Situational approaches stress a match between leadership style and job situation. The most successful leaders are flexible, adapting to the job and employee context. This finding must be considered in selection, placement, training, and performance appraisal of managers.

QUESTIONS FOR REVIEW AND DISCUSSION

1. Consider Maslow's hierarchy of needs. Which need is important to you at this point in your life?
2. A popular interpretation of Herzberg's motivator/hygiene theory suggests that pay is not a motivator. Do you agree?
3. Consider the expectations placed on you by your superior for this fiscal year. Can you accomplish these things if you make the effort? Will accomplishing them lead to a merit raise, promotion, or other specific reward?
4. Carefully distinguish between motivation and satisfaction. Can a person be satisfied and not motivated?
5. How might an organization measure and deal with job dissatisfaction?
6. Examine the various aspects of your job and pick out the one that you like the least and probably perform the most poorly. What type of behavior modification could your organization use so that you will be motivated to do better?
7. Why is an understanding of leadership so important to a local government manager?
8. Review Theories X and Y and determine your own assumptions about people. Give examples of how your attitudes are reflected in your behavior.

ENDNOTES

[1] This chapter draws on Stephen P. Robbins, *Organizational Behavior*, 8th ed. (Upper Saddle River, N.J.: Prentice-Hall, 1998), especially 130–202 and 344–385.

[2] Abraham Maslow, "A Theory of Human Motivation," *Psychological Review* 50 (July 1943), 370–396, and *Motivation and Personality*, 2d ed. (New York: Harper and Row, 1970).

[3] Robbins, 171.

[4] Frederick Herzberg, Bernard Mauser, and Barbara B. Snyderman, *The Motivation to Work* (New York: Wiley, 1959), and Herzberg, *Work and the Nature of Man* (Cleveland: World, 1996).

[5] Robbins, 173.

[6] Carole L. Jurkiewicz and Tom K. Massey Jr., "What Motivates Municipal Employees: A Comparison Study of Supervisory vs. Non-Supervisory Personnel," *Public Personnel Management* 26 (Fall 1997), 367–378.

[7] Victor H. Vroom, *Work and Motivation* (New York: Wiley, 1964).

[8] Jurkiewicz and Massey, 367.

[9] Robbins, 189.

[10] J. Stacy Adams, "Toward an Understanding of Inequity," *Journal of Abnormal and Social Psychology* 67 (1963), and Richard T. Mowday, "Equity Theory Predictions of Behavior in Organizations," in Richard M. Steers and Lyman W. Porter, eds., *Motivation and Work Behavior*, 3d ed. (New York: McGraw-Hill, 1983), 91–112.

[11] Based on Robbins, 185.

[12] Robbins, 187.

[13] B. F. Skinner, *Science and Human Behavior* (New York: Free Press, 1953).

[14] Edward L. Thorndike, *Animal Intelligence* (New York: Macmillan, 1911), 244.

[15] Robbins, 72–75.

[16] Edwin A. Locke and Gary P. Latham, *A Theory of Goal Setting and Task Performance* (Englewood Cliffs, N.J.: Prentice-Hall, 1990).

[17] Robbins, 181.

[18] Edwin A. Locke, "What Is Job Satisfaction?" *Organizational Behavior and Human Performance* 5 (1970), 484–500.

[19] Edward L. Lawler III and Lyman W. Porter, "The Effects of Performance on Job Satisfaction," *Industrial Relations* (October 1967), 20–28, and Wendell L. French, *Human Resources Management* (Boston: Houghton Mifflin, 1998), 109–110. See also Jurkiewicz and Massey, 371–372.

[20] Katherine A. Karl and Cynthia L. Sutton, "Job Values in Today's Workforce: A Comparison Between Public and Private Sector Employees," *Public Personnel Management* 27 (Winter 1988), 515–528.

[21] Robbins, 155–156, and French, 111.

[22] Yaun Ting, "Determinants of Job Satisfaction of Federal Government Employees," *Public Personnel Management* 26 (Fall 1997), 311–335.

[23] Maureen Smith, "Measuring Employee Satisfaction," *IPMA News* 65 (March 1999), 15–16.

[24] The illustration used is based on a project conducted by the authors during 1994–1995 with a county youth development center.

[25] This slogan is on a deskplate distributed by the Pfizer Corporation.

[26] Douglas M. McGregor, *The Human Side of Enterprise* (New York: McGraw-Hill, 1960).

[27] For a comprehensive discussion of organizational leadership see Robbins, 344–385.

[28] See, for example, Shelly A. Kirkpatrick and Edwin A. Locke, "Leadership: Do Traits Matter?" *Academy of Management Executive* 5 (May 1991), 48–59.

[29] Rensis Likert, *New Patterns of Management* (New York: McGraw-Hill, 1961), and *The Human Organization: Its Management and Value* (New York: McGraw-Hill, 1962).

[30] Richard White, "The High Performance Organization that Lexington Built," *Public Management* 80 (June 1988), 16–20.

[31] Robert J. Grossman, "Ensuring a Fast Start," *HR Magazine* (July 1999), 32–38.

CHAPTER 5
PLANNING AND
POLICY DEVELOPMENT

THINKING FORWARD

Hennepin County is the largest of the seven counties that compose the metropolitan area of Minneapolis and St. Paul, Minnesota. Because of its size it is also a major employer in the state with 28 departments and over 11,000 employees. Through its strategic planning process, the county Human Resources Department became aware that the county was likely to lose 30 percent of its current workforce over the next 10 years due primarily to the retirement of its baby boom employees. Replacing such a large number of employees was anticipated to result in significant cost. Besides the direct cost of replacement and training, there would be a decline in productivity and a major loss of institutional knowledge.

On the other hand, effective strategic planning had bought the county some time. The Human Resources Department not only knew how many employees would become eligible to retire, it also knew where the retirements would have the greatest impact. To best position the county to deal with potential losses, the department has incorporated strategies to address employee retention and development as a top priority. A number of strategic initiatives were developed, all focusing on becoming an "employer of choice."

For example, the county developed a set of leadership competencies emphasizing the manager's role as a coach, mentor, and employee developer. Another initiative was the development of a corporate university to guide the development and communication of the county's core values (operational, service, and staff excellence). Dual career tracks are being designed to allow the county to reward and retain the best technical talent without requiring a move into management.

The idea behind these and other initiatives is to have qualified replacements on board and ready to move into roles that will be vacated by the baby boomers. Granted, being the employer of choice is a strategy that may not be appropriate for every local government. For example, increasing the pay for senior-level administrative and professional employees would mean that many of them would continue to work beyond the time they are eligible for retirement. The county could also begin to contract out various critical functions. The key is to have a strategy in place.

It is obvious from a review of workforce demographics that the baby boom generation will soon begin to leave the workforce in large numbers. Effective HR planning, as in Hennepin County, surfaces this as well as other key issues and allows organizations to create their future rather than react to situations as they arise. All local governments will have to face the impending exit of the boomers—now, or at their retirement parties.

Source: Rudy Viscasillas, "Retaining Your Top Talent by Becoming the Employer of Choice," *IPMA News* 65 (March 1999), 14.

INTRODUCTION

Planning in general and strategic planning in particular is one of the most widely used productivity-improvement tools used by local governments. Effective planning has positive benefits for both organizations and employees. Organizations benefit from increased capabilities to deliver more and better services at lower cost. Employees benefit from increasing their competencies and value to current and future employers.[1] For a local government as a whole and for each unit within the organization, planning is the most basic of all management functions and is the responsibility of all managers. Planning should be the basis from which all managerial decisions are made. Therefore, HR managers must have a good understanding of planning concepts in order to perform their duties. The failure to plan results in random activities not directed toward defined strategic objectives. Unplanned activities cannot be controlled, since control involves correcting deviations from plans. Planning should never be thought of as a process used only occasionally or when one is not engaged in the "real work" of management.

Topics covered in this chapter include: planning and strategic planning approaches, need for planning by local government, standing HR plans (policies, procedures, and rules), human resource planning (managing staffing demand and supply), and human resource information systems.

PLANNING APPROACHES

Two approaches to organizational and long-term planning are traditional planning and strategic planning. Although both approaches focus on setting and achieving goals, strategic planning represents a shift in the context in which objectives are set. The primary focus of planning is on achieving specified goals. With strategic planning the focus is on achieving strategic objectives that detail how a local government can achieve its mission. As Chapter 1 noted, HR management has an increasing responsibility for designing and implementing HR systems and processes that are aligned with the organization's strategic plans and objectives.

When a strategic planning approach is used, all HR strategic objectives should be based on how the outcomes will impact the entire organization, not just the HR department. Therefore, HR strategic objectives related to job design, recruiting, selecting, staffing, training, appraising, compensating, and so on should be established and achieved with a local government's mission in mind. Throughout this book the authors attempt to describe how HR activities can be tied to a local government's strategic objectives. With regard to establishing policies, procedures, rules, human resource plans, and human resource information systems, the authors recommend local government HR managers think strategically and focus on how the attainment of HR-related strategic objectives will help the local government achieve its mission.

TRADITIONAL PLANNING

Planning has been traditionally defined as the process of determining organizational objectives and selecting a future course of action for their accomplishment. A typical planning process includes the following six steps: determining a management philosophy, establishing objectives, developing premises, making decisions, implementing a course of action, and evaluating results.[2]

STRATEGIC PLANNING

Strategic planning is critical to the strategic management approach discussed in Chapter 1. Strategic planning can be defined as the process of determining strategic objectives and actions needed to achieve a local government's mission through those objectives. There are five general steps in the strategic planning process: defining a local government's mission; conducting an environmental scan of a local government's internal strengths and weaknesses and external opportunities and threats (SWOT analysis); establishing strategic objectives, strategies, and tactics; implementing a course of action; and evaluating results and processes.[3] Exhibit 5-1 depicts the five steps.

WHAT IS DIFFERENT ABOUT PLANNING IN LOCAL GOVERNMENTS?

Local governments are increasingly developing and implementing strategic plans in response to external relations, management responsibilities, budgeting, and human relations and in light of the need for improved performance and increased public accountability.

External relations. Planning in a local government is usually an open process. The public, constituents, and interest groups often play a vital and sometimes vocal role in helping local governments develop, implement, and evaluate plans. Additionally, the media take much more interest in covering governmental planning efforts than in covering business.

Management responsibilities. Managers who have administrative responsibility for program planning and evaluation, service delivery systems, program and project management, and performance measurement must also deal with political and constituent demands and concerns. Additionally, providing services often takes precedence over cost efficiency.

Budgeting. Budgeting cycles in government require much greater lead time than in the private sector. This means that operational planning has to be done far in advance, and greater emphasis must be placed on contingency plans if planning assumptions turn out to be wrong. Further, budgeting plans are often tied to political and not strategic issues.

Human relations. The special nature of government services makes planning for human resources, organization culture, internal communications, and labor relations different. Government employees may have constitutional rights that private sector employees do not. Employees may be in a position to manipulate planning efforts because governments often have a monopoly on the work being performed.

Source: Adapted from Theodore H. Poister and Gregory D. Streib, "Strategic Management in the Public Sector," *Public Productivity & Management Review* 22 (March 1999), 308–325.

EXHIBIT 5-1

STRATEGIC
PLANNING
PROCESS

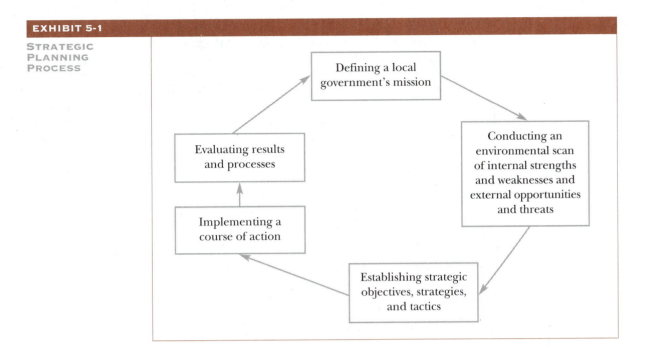

DEFINING THE MISSION

Strategic plans are derived from an organizational purpose or mission. A mission is a local government's reason for being. It should also reflect the importance people attach to the local government's work. The foundation for local governments is often found in enabling legislation, local, state, and federal laws, codes, and regulations, and to a great extent the publics it serves. Within these constraints, local governments must answer this question: "What is our purpose?" This may be more difficult than is readily apparent, because differing and sometimes conflicting interpretations may arise. Regardless, the question must be answered. Unfortunately, some local governments never clarify their purpose to their staff, their clientele, or other organizations. This failure results in lack of direction, waste and duplication of effort, and loss of confidence by society. On the other hand, if the mission is clearly communicated and understood by all concerned, it is possible to develop clear and meaningful plans. A local government's purpose (mission statement) should be articulated in writing and publicly displayed.

CONDUCTING AN ENVIRONMENTAL SCAN

The essence of strategic planning is a strategic analysis or environmental scan of internal **s**trengths and **w**eaknesses and external **o**pportunities and **t**hreats, or SWOT. A SWOT of a local government's internal capabilities is needed to effectively implement its mission, strategies, and objectives. A scan of a local government's external environment is needed to identify certain trends and forces that could have real or perceived impacts on operations.

Drawing conclusions from SWOT analysis serves two purposes in the light of a local government's mission, strategies, and objectives. First, it facilitates the statement of problems that come from identified weaknesses within the organization and from threats noted in the external environment. Second, the analysis provides necessary information to formulate strategic objectives.

ESTABLISHING STRATEGIC OBJECTIVES

Before any course of action is undertaken, strategic objectives should be clearly determined, understood, and stated. Strategic objectives provide guidelines for action by directing and channeling staff efforts. They establish constraints by prescribing both what should and what should not be done. An organization that commits to one strategic objective may reduce its discretion to pursue other strategic objectives. For example, a commitment to serve a need for leisure time activities with additional employees in the parks and recreation department reduces the financial resources available to hire police officers.

Strategic objectives also provide a legitimizing basis for justifying an organization's existence. Citizens, legislators, special interests, and society at large must believe that the unit of government has a legitimate right to continue its activities. If its strategic objectives are deemed appropriate, an organization will enjoy a greatly enhanced ability to obtain resources and support from its environment. To the extent that strategic objectives are clearly understood, they offer direct standards for measuring performance. Finally, strategic objectives are an important source of motivation. The incentive of being identified with a "winning team" is a strong inducement to perform.

IMPLEMENTING A COURSE OF ACTION

Once strategic objectives have been established, they must be implemented. Implementation is an ongoing challenge that involves the understanding and commitment of management in order to accomplish the established strategic objectives. While this sounds intuitively obvious, the implementation phase is inherently unpredictable and presents significant problems in government.[4] These include diversion of resources, deflection of policy goals, coping activities of politically accountable administrators, dissipation of energy caused by "game playing," nonpurposive program assembly delays, the necessity for collective decisions, and dysfunctional negotiations. The key to successful implementation is to establish strategic objectives that support the organization's mission and are strong enough conceptually to withstand this constantly shifting set of political and social pressures.

A good illustration of the implementation problem in local government is affirmative action. A business firm seeking to qualify as a government contractor would develop an affirmative action plan (AAP) as a management decision. That such plans are normally implemented successfully is evidenced by compliance reviews by the Office of Federal Contract Compliance Programs. A city government would develop a voluntary affirmative action plan to expand opportunities for minorities and women as a political decision. But the details of implementing the plan are considerably more difficult for the city government.

For the business firm a hiring goal in a particular job group is the result of a straightforward (albeit tedious) set of calculations. The CEO expects the HR department and subordinate line management to use "all reasonable efforts" to attain the goal, preferably before the next visit by the OFCCP compliance officer. For the city government the appropriateness of having a goal at all will likely be a major issue among administrators, employees, job applicants, and citizens whose real or perceived interests are adversely affected. The objections of these actors can be translated into bureaucratic resistance, charges of "reverse discrimination," and political counterpressures. As a result, actual implementation may not progress very much past the platitudes of public officials and the phrase "Affirmative Action Employer" added to job announcements.

EVALUATING RESULTS AND PROCESSES

Finally, strategic plans should be evaluated. Evaluation is necessary to provide feedback concerning the progress of a plan. Alterations in plans are almost certain. If projected results do not occur, the strategic objectives of a plan may be unrealistic, planning premises may be inaccurate, or the chosen plan of action may be inappropriate. Managers should view the need for these alterations as a learning experience and should not feel guilty when unforeseen conditions or events require corrective action. This aspect of evaluation is considered a normal and predictable activity encountered by managers at all levels. It is also very important to maintain the integrity of the evaluation process. Very few activities show only positive results on objective evaluation. As noted above, negative results are to be expected and offer opportunities for corrective action. Thus, policy makers must resist self-serving evaluations that accumulate "evidence" in favor of programs that may be failing.[5]

NEED FOR PLANNING IN LOCAL GOVERNMENT

Strategic planning is a very important area of management in all types of organizations. The private (corporate) sector has a long history of strategic planning, although it is relatively new at the local government level.[6] Governments have been increasingly interested in strategic planning as a result of various crises in the public sector. As a process, strategic planning in local government has been shown to be highly effective. Brooks noted that "the Miami-Dade Department of Solid Waste Management's successful strategic plan . . . enabled it to overcome a crisis driven by environmental compliance costs and private-sector competition. The department has since regained market share, reduced prices, restored financial viability and improved its bond rating."[7] For several reasons, local governments are engaging in planning activities and many have developed strategic plans and strategic objectives to achieve those plans.[8]

First is the shift away from bureaucratic decision making to a focus on results. The public increasingly demands better services along with increased accountability. Governments that are responding effectively to this changing environment empower citizens by transferring control from the bureaucracy to the community and measuring their performance by outcomes rather than inputs. They are driven by their missions—not by their rules and regulations. They anticipate situations before they emerge rather than react to problems. They also redefine the people who use their services as customers and offer them choices.

Second, governments are expected to be more socially responsible now than in the past. Although their performance has improved, stakeholder expectations have increased at an even greater rate. Local governments are expected to do much more than meet their traditional legal and economic obligations. Both managers and employees are held to higher ethical standards than their counterparts in the public sector.[9] Ensuring equal access to programs and services and increasing participation in government affairs has a high priority. Staffing has become much more complex, involving such issues as diversity, quality of worklife, workplace demographics, work processes, and technology.

Finally, technological advances have tended to destabilize existing systems. Information technology, in particular, is being invented, dispersed, adopted, and abandoned at an increasing rate. As governments deal with downsizing, rightsizing, reengineering, and reinventing their organization, integration of information systems is key.[10] When more technological variables are introduced, management must redress the balance through planning. For instance, the geographic information system (GIS) is a tool used in urban planning to improve the input, storage, retrieval, analysis, and presentation of data on maps, reports, and plans. The operation and ultimate success or failure of such a system, however, depends on competencies of the person operating the system. The head of the planning department will encounter employees with the following attitudes: (1) The GIS is essential to my job; (2) The GIS is nice and fun to have; (3) The GIS is OK; and (4) I liked the old paper-and-pencil method better. Where employees fall on this spectrum will largely determine the effectiveness of the new technology. While it is true that the new system is faster and more accurate than the old system, it is also true that operating the new system requires better-trained employees. The training must be planned, which is one of the reasons that human resource management has come to occupy such an important role.

Today there is hardly a situation in modern life that does not involve action by some level of government. County and municipal governments have been affected by growth of state and federal activities and have themselves taken on a multiplicity of initiatives. Thus local government encounters difficulties in coordination and implementation undreamed of in the past and quite unlike those encountered in the private sector. The accomplishment of politically determined objectives requires increasingly sophisticated planning.

http://www.pti.nw.dc.us/
Public Technologies, Inc.
provides information on
how local governments can
benefit through use of
information technologies.

STANDING PLANS FOR HUMAN RESOURCES

Human resource management plays a leading role in two aspects of organizational planning: development of standing plans to provide guides for HR activities, and human resource planning, which seeks to ensure that the organization has the right people in jobs. **Standing plans** are used repeatedly in managerial situations that occur again and again. That is, standing plans take the form of policies, procedures, and rules.[11]

POLICIES

A **policy** is a general statement that serves to guide decision making. Policies establish parameters within which certain decisions are to be made. These parameters purposely provide broad guidelines that are subject to interpretation, thus requiring managers to exercise discretion in policy application. Two principal advantages are incorporated within the concept of a policy:

- time is saved by making advance decisions about situations that are likely to occur; and
- consistency is assured in how similar situations are decided.

Policies define the boundaries within which decisions are made and ensure that decisions will be consistent with established objectives. They are a means of encouraging initiative, but only within certain limits. Policies give a unified structure to other types of plans and permit the delegation of authority without loss of control. Major policies involve organization structure, services provided, finance and taxation, and other basic issues. Functional policies are derived from major policies to shape and guide such functions as HR management and finance. Since policies are designed as guides to decision making, they must allow for some discretion; otherwise, they are merely rules.

EXHIBIT 5-2

TYPICAL HUMAN
RESOURCE POLICY
AREAS

Attendance and Time Off
- Hours of work
- Holidays
- Vacation and leave

Employment
- Equal Employment Opportunity/
  Affirmative Action
- Requisition and recruitment
- Background investigations
- Interviewing
- Preemployment physicals
- Nepotism
- Employment of aliens
- Appointments
- Probationary period
- Layoffs and recalls
- Access to personnel files

Compensation
- Job evaluation
- Wage and salary surveys
- Pay administration
- Benefits and services

Termination
- Discharge
- Voluntary separation
- Retirement

Training and Development
- Orientation
- On-the-job training
- Formal training
- Employee educational assistance

Performance Appraisal
- Purposes of appraisal
- Appraisal administration
- Review of ratings
- Right of appeal

Work Rules and Discipline
- Work rules
- Disciplinary actions
- Appeals and grievances

Safety and Health
- Safety program
- Workers' compensation
- Contagious diseases
- Employee wellness program
- Employee assistance program

While policies should be written statements, they may be implied from the actions of management. Such "unwritten" policies can be beneficial and even essential; however, there is a danger that managerial decisions not intended to set precedents may be interpreted as policy. Thus an organization may be plagued with numerous "unwritten" policies that are religiously followed but have no legitimacy. It is a good practice to periodically review policies at all levels and remove those that are outdated or unnecessary, including "unwritten" policies.

A well-written, up-to-date HR policy manual should be developed by all organizations. A list of typical HR policy areas is shown in Exhibit 5-2.

PROCEDURES

A **procedure** (sometimes called a minor policy) is a guide to action followed to achieve a given purpose. Similarity exists between a procedure and a policy because both are intended to influence certain decisions. Exhibit 5-2 lists broad HR policy areas such as compensation and training and development. The topics listed under each broad policy area are matters that require procedures. In contrast to a policy, a procedure addresses itself to a single decision that prescribes exactly what actions are to be taken in a specific situation; little room is left for discretion. Consequently, a degree of assurance that all similar situations will be handled in a predictable manner exists when a procedure has been established. Once a procedure becomes routine, a manager is free to concentrate on solving problems that require more thought; however, procedures must be reviewed and revised periodically to ensure their continued appropriateness within an organization.

The need for procedures arises when an organization wishes to establish a standard method of handling routine activities. Procedures are guides to action rather than thinking. They often spell out a series of steps arranged in a predetermined best order. A good procedure ensures that required actions can be performed in the most efficient way with savings in both time and cost. Procedures also ensure that all necessary steps are accomplished, providing a structure for carrying out policies with a minimum of inconvenience and delay.

RULES

A **rule** specifies what is required of an individual; little room is left for interpretation. This type of standing plan either prescribes or prohibits action by specifying what may or may not occur in a given situation; a time period is not usually specified. A rule is narrow in scope and application compared to other types of standing plans. The only element of choice affecting a rule is whether it applies in a given situation.

A rule is distinct from a policy and a procedure; however, it is based on policy and often part of a procedure. Rules should be carefully distinguished from policies. Policies allow and encourage managerial discretion; rules do not. Many organizations think they have policies but merely spell out rules. By their very nature, rules repress thinking and should be used only when people cannot be allowed to use discretion.

THE HIERARCHY OF POLICIES, PROCEDURES, AND RULES

The standing plans discussed above may be viewed as a hierarchy where the apex is a major policy. Each subordinate plan is derived from and supports the one at the higher level. Each succeeding level places additional limits on management's freedom to act.

This relationship can be shown by an illustration. The payment of wages and salaries is shaped and guided by the compensation policy. The policy spells out the organization's compensation objectives and outlines the responsibilities of various levels of management in achieving these objectives. An example is shown in Exhibit 5-3. Note that the area of discretion is quite broad. For example, a structure of pay grades is to be based on job evaluation. These structures will be adjusted based on market conditions. However, the type of job evaluation plan to be used is not indicated, nor does the policy state how often wage and salary surveys are to be conducted. These decisions are delegated to the HR manager.

Obviously, the policy alone does not establish the methods for handling the various activities in the organization's compensation program. Let us assume that the HR department has evaluated all jobs, conducted a wage and salary survey, and established a pay grade structure that reflects the labor market (as provided for in the policy). But additional guidance is still needed. For example, Joe Smith has been selected to fill the job of water treatment plant operator. What is his starting salary?

In order to determine the answer to this question, a procedure is needed to cover various situations such as initial hire, reemployment, promotion, and so forth. An example of such a procedure is shown in Exhibit 5-4. The area of discretion is

EXHIBIT 5-3

SAMPLE
COMPENSATION
POLICY

It is the policy of the city that compensation will be externally competitive, internally equitable, and performance based. Jobs will be formally evaluated and placed in pay grades in terms of relative value to the city. Each pay grade will be assigned an appropriate pay range including minimum, midpoint, and maximum. Pay ranges will be adjusted based on changing economic and competitive factors as determined by periodic wage and salary surveys. Individual wage and salary adjustments will be based on job performance appraisal. Compensation programs will be carried out in accordance with federal and state laws and regulations as these apply to wages and hours, employment relationships, overtime, equal pay for equal work and nondiscrimination based on race, color, national origin, religion, sex, age, disability, or other impermissible classification. Responsibilities for compensation management are outlined below:

Executive Management (City Manager):
1. Review and approve classification and pay plan.
2. Review and approve compensation procedures.
3. Review matters for which authority has not been otherwise delegated or is an exception to a policy.

Operating Management (Department Heads):
1. Administer wages and salaries of personnel under his or her supervision within approved budgets and in accordance with procedures established by this policy.
2. Review and appraise the performance of each member of his or her staff periodically and base recommended increases on guidelines contained in merit pay procedures.

HR Manager:
1. Develop and maintain an internally equitable and competitive pay structure.
2. Develop evaluation systems that will group positions of substantially comparable content into salary grades; develop procedures for establishing pay rates of classified employees.
3. Develop classification and pay plans for job groups. Maintain files of class specifications.
4. Maintain such records as may be required to facilitate salary administration, provide adequate control of salary costs, and comply with provisions of the Fair Labor Standards Act.
5. Develop procedures for compliance with Equal Pay Act, Title VII of the Civil Rights Act and appropriate state laws.
6. Review all deviations from established salary administration procedures.

For an in-depth discussion on compensation policy and other types of HR policies see Richard J. Simmons, *Employee Handbook and Personnel Policies Manual,* 7th ed. (Van Nuys, Calif.: Castle, 2000).

more specifically defined; however, there is still some measure of flexibility. For example, Item 2 provides that an experienced person can be started anywhere between the minimum and the midpoint of the range for the pay grade.

Finally, the procedure contains certain rules; for example, no person can receive a starting salary that is less than the minimum for the pay grade. The only persons who can receive a starting salary above the midpoint are those who are reemployed or have been promoted.

EXHIBIT 5-4

SAMPLE
PROCEDURE FOR
ESTABLISHING
PAY RANGES FOR
CLASSIFIED
EMPLOYEES

1. An employee possessing the minimum qualifications for the job to which he or she is appointed will normally begin at the minimum salary for the pay grade; no person, however, may receive less than the minimum.

2. The rate of pay for new employees with related experience and/or additional qualifications may be above the minimum salary but not greater than the midpoint of the pay grade, as determined by the HR director.

3. The rate of pay for a person who has a previous employment record with the county will be established by the HR director, taking into consideration changes in the pay range since the employee was terminated, number and years of intervening experience, and prior length of service in the classification. The rate of pay shall not exceed the maximum for the grade.

4. When an employee is promoted, a fully qualified person will receive at least the minimum salary for the grade. However, the new salary must be as much above the minimum salary as necessary to provide a 10 percent increase, or the maximum for the grade, whichever is less.

5. Exceptions to these procedures require authorization of the county administrator.

HUMAN RESOURCE PLANNING

Human resource planning (HRP), an activity that has received increasing attention within the past several years, is the process that attempts to maintain at all times an appropriate staff of qualified employees for achieving objectives. HRP has been linked with increases in **organizational capacity,** that is, the ability of a local government to pursue and maintain a competitive advantage for the products and services it offers.[12] One way that human resource departments add value to the organization, thus creating a competitive advantage, is to position human resources as a **core competency**.[13] For a local government's human resources to become a core competency, it must attract, maintain, and motivate highly competent employees; this is the focus of HRP. Such planning must consider both future **demand** for various types of employees and internal and external **supply** of these employees. The process, that is, includes forecasting staffing needs, comparing them to current staff composition, and determining the number and types of staff to be recruited, promoted, or phased out. Effective human resource planning requires the gathering and evaluation of a great deal of information. Ideally it should be a continuous activity coordinated by an HR department with input from line managers.

FORECASTING DEMAND FOR HUMAN RESOURCES

The first step in human resource planning is to forecast the need for employees in various job categories. This should be based on the organization's strategic plan. For example, a city may be planning to annex several rapidly growing residential areas in the next five years. This probably means that more employees will be needed in the police and fire departments. On the other hand, the city may also be considering "privatization" of solid waste collection and disposal. If this is the case, fewer employees will be needed in the sanitation department and more employees may be needed to manage the contract.

Techniques for forecasting staffing needs range from simple and informal to highly sophisticated. Assume we need to know the number of employees that will be needed in the public safety division five years from now. Techniques that might be used include managerial forecasting, the Delphi technique, and trend analysis.

MANAGERIAL FORECASTING

The judgment of line managers is employed in **managerial forecasting**, either from top down or from bottom up. In a top-down approach, the director of public safety could request estimates from the police and fire chiefs. In a bottom-up approach, lower-level managers (chief of detectives, fire operations officer) could provide estimates that would be refined and consolidated through a series of reviews. Another way to obtain the information is for the human resources department to survey operating managers at the appropriate level with a questionnaire. The idea behind this technique is that since most employment decisions are made by line managers, they are the ultimate experts about staffing needs in their units.

THE DELPHI TECHNIQUE

Considered one of the most effective planning methodologies, the **Delphi technique** is a method for developing a consensus of expert opinion.[14] The first step is to obtain the cooperation of a panel of experts. In addition to managers, the panel would probably include outside experts; for example, the chairman of the planning commission and the executive director of the Chamber of Commerce might be appropriate choices. Panel members are asked to respond to a carefully designed questionnaire. The response of each individual is weighted by some measure of relative importance such as previous accuracy or influence on the situation. The summarized information is then reported to the experts in the form of a second questionnaire. This process is repeated until general agreement is obtained.

TREND ANALYSIS

The assumption of **trend analysis** is that past patterns can be used to predict the future. In simplest terms, the number of employees in the division is determined for each year of a base period (for example, five years) and the rate of change is projected into the future. For example, if the number of employees increased during 1996–2001 by an average of seven per year to a present strength of 200, by the year 2006 the division will need 235 employees. A variation of this method would be to relate the number of employees to an appropriate variable such as population or area. For example, planners might find that each increase of 1,000 in population generates 2.3 employees in public safety. Statistical methods including **regression** and **correlation** analyses are used in trend analysis.

Using these forecasts as a basis, the human resources department can now develop specific plans. A **staffing table** lists the estimated future number of vacancies in each type of job, as shown in Exhibit 5-5. While these tables are only approximations, they allow the human resources department to become more proactive—that is, anticipating a need and taking advance action to avoid having to react to a crisis. For example, a review of Exhibit 5-5 shows that 15 entry-level firefighters must be hired during the year.

ASSESSING THE SUPPLY OF HUMAN RESOURCES

In addition to forecasting the future needs for employees, human resource planning is concerned with assessing and monitoring potential sources of supply for employees to fill these needs. These include both internal sources (employees) and external sources (persons to be recruited from the labor market). Because effective

EXHIBIT 5-5

A PARTIAL STAFFING TABLE
FOR A CITY GOVERNMENT

Code	Job Title	Department	Estimated Vacancies by Month												Total
			1	2	3	4	5	6	7	8	9	10	11	12	
111	Customer Service Representative	Utilities		2							3			2	7
215	GIS Technician	Planning				1									1
305	Firefighter	Fire		3		3		3		3		3			15
365	Fire Engineer	Fire	1											1	2
385	Company Officer	Fire												1	1
405	Heavy Equipment Operator	Public Works				2		2							4
640	Athletic Supervisor	Parks & Rec									1				1

assessment of staffing supply sources requires collecting and processing large amounts of information, specialized Human Resource Information Systems (HRISs) have been developed to facilitate the activity.

INTERNAL STAFFING SOURCES

In estimating the potential internal human resource supply, the objective is to project what the workforce might look like at some future time. This requires analyses of two types of movements. Movements out of the organization (attrition) occur through retirements, resignations, dismissals, deaths, and disabling injuries and illnesses. One methodology used to estimate human resource movement out of and within an organization is called **Markov analysis**.[15] Markov analysis shows the number of employees who stay in a particular job from year to year, as well as the number of employees who move out of and within the organization. The output of a Markov analysis is visually depicted as a Markov or transition matrix as shown in Exhibit 5-6. For a sanitation worker, during a given year there is a 67 percent chance of being a sanitation worker in a year, a 7 percent chance of being promoted to crew leader, a 7 percent chance of being transferred to equipment operator, and a 20 percent chance of leaving the organization. Although the example used one year, a Markov analysis can be used with any time frame.

Two other important tools, succession charts and skills inventories, are used to identify present employees who can be transferred or promoted to fill expected openings.

Succession charts list various key positions and display information on their incumbents and the readiness of different candidates for promotion to the positions. The city manager might want plans for filling future vacancies in the parks and recreation department, for example. The necessary information would be obtained from both HR records and immediate superiors. A portion of a succession chart is shown in Exhibit 5-7. Note that the chart enables management to assess the number of potential replacements, their skills, and also the potential effect of losses due to retirements, promotions, and other causes. For example, Exhibit 5-7 indicates that the position of parks and recreation director could be filled by an inter-

EXHIBIT 5-6

MARKOV MATRIX FOR A COUNTY TRANSPORTATION DEPARTMENT

2001 \ 2002	Transportation Superintendent	Assistant Superintendent	Crew Leader	Mechanic	Maintenance Worker	Sanitation Worker	Equipment Operator	Exit
Transportation Superintendent (n = 1)	100% / 1	0 / 0	0 / 0	0 / 0	0 / 0	0 / 0	0 / 0	0 / 0
Assistant Superintendent (n = 2)	0 / 0	100% / 2	0 / 0	0 / 0	0 / 0	0 / 0	0 / 0	0 / 0
Crew Leader (n = 3)	0 / 0	33% / 1	33% / 1	0 / 0	0 / 0	0 / 0	0 / 0	33% / 1
Mechanic (n = 2)	0 / 0	0 / 0	50% / 1	0 / 0	50% / 1	0 / 0	0 / 0	0 / 0
Maintenance Worker (n = 5)	0 / 0	0 / 0	0 / 0	20% / 1	40% / 2	0 / 0	0 / 0	40% / 2
Sanitation Worker (n = 15)	0 / 0	0 / 0	7% / 1	0 / 0	0 / 0	67% / 10	7% / 1	20% / 3
Equipment Operator (n = 3)	0 / 0	0 / 0	0 / 0	0 / 0	0 / 0	33% / 1	33% / 1	33% / 1
Forecasted Supply	1	3	3	11	3	11	2	

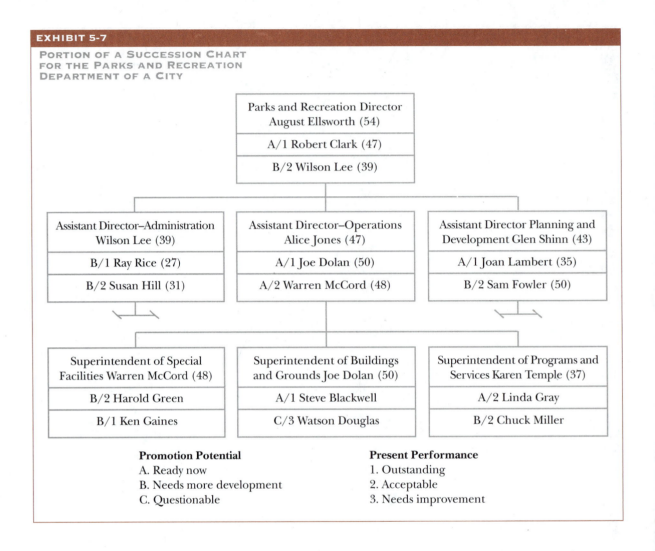

EXHIBIT 5-7

PORTION OF A SUCCESSION CHART
FOR THE PARKS AND RECREATION
DEPARTMENT OF A CITY

Parks and Recreation Director
August Ellsworth (54)

A/1 Robert Clark (47)

B/2 Wilson Lee (39)

Assistant Director–Administration
Wilson Lee (39)

B/1 Ray Rice (27)

B/2 Susan Hill (31)

Assistant Director–Operations
Alice Jones (47)

A/1 Joe Dolan (50)

A/2 Warren McCord (48)

Assistant Director Planning and
Development Glen Shinn (43)

A/1 Joan Lambert (35)

B/2 Sam Fowler (50)

Superintendent of Special
Facilities Warren McCord (48)

B/2 Harold Green

B/1 Ken Gaines

Superintendent of Buildings
and Grounds Joe Dolan (50)

A/1 Steve Blackwell

C/3 Watson Douglas

Superintendent of Programs and
Services Karen Temple (37)

A/2 Linda Gray

B/2 Chuck Miller

Promotion Potential
A. Ready now
B. Needs more development
C. Questionable

Present Performance
1. Outstanding
2. Acceptable
3. Needs improvement

nal candidate instead of an outside candidate. If, however, no one from within an
organization is qualified, the chart would alert the city manager to the fact that a key
vacancy could occur.

Skills inventories collect and consolidate basic information about all the organization's employees. In its simplest form, a skills inventory includes a list of the
names and qualifications of employees. The main advantage of a skills inventory is
that it provides a means to evaluate quickly and accurately the skills that are available from within the organization. For example, to be promoted to lieutenant in the
fire department, a firefighter must have completed fire officer and instructor certifications. Data from a skills inventory could be used to develop a list of persons eligible for promotion. Information from a skills inventory is useful for making other
decisions, such as whether an organization's current employees have the necessary
competencies to begin a new service. A skills inventory also aids in planning future
employee training and management development programs.

Because the type of information required about prospective managers differs
from that about operating employees, some organizations maintain a separate

management inventory. In addition to biographical data, a management inventory may contain performance history and potential for advancement. Skills and management inventories can be generated from manually compiled forms and index cards but are especially suited for inclusion in computerized Human Resource Information Systems.

EXTERNAL STAFFING SOURCES

http://www.census.gov/
The U.S. Census Bureau is the preeminent collector and provider of timely, relevant, and quality data about the people and economy of the United States.

It is usually impossible to fill every future opening with present employees. This is particularly true of entry-level jobs. Non-entry-level jobs may also be difficult to fill from internal sources, especially when a jurisdiction is growing, or if the organization fails to train and develop its employees.

Labor market analysis is used to monitor external staffing sources. The analysis should first consider the general availability of persons in the recruitment area who have requisite skills. If the unemployment rate is high, it will be relatively easy to acquire new employees. Under conditions of full employment, the organization will need to attract applicants who work for others. Basic information on the characteristics of the labor force for each county in the United States can be obtained from national, state, and local sources (see Exhibit 5-8). The data are provided by categories such as managerial, clerical, and machine operators. Information on population, education, employment, and occupational status is also included. Information developed in labor market analysis is usually also available by race, sex, and national origin. This information is extremely useful in designing affirmative action programs (discussed in detail in Chapter 8).

http://www.bls.gov/
The Bureau of Labor Statistics is the principal fact-finding agency for the federal government in the broad field of labor economics and statistics.

Another important factor in labor market analysis is consideration of local area training institutions or programs capable of training persons in the requisite skills. These include high schools, community colleges, vocational schools, and programs such as those conducted by the Workforce Investment Partnership Act. These institutions and programs provide a continuous flow of qualified persons into the job market. Moreover, it is often possible to work with appropriate officials to tailor curricula and programs to meet specific needs.

EXHIBIT 5-8

DATA SOURCES FOR LABOR MARKET ANALYSIS

The U.S. Census Bureau, Bureau of Labor Statistics, Regional BLS information offices, state and local departments of development, state and local employment services, and state and local departments of education collect and provide a variety of data regarding labor market information.

America's Career InfoNet (ACINet), whose development was sponsored by the U.S. Department of Labor, provides users with a variety of occupational, demographic, and labor market information at the local, state, and national levels. It provides data on occupational competencies, tasks, education and training requirements, wages, and trends and includes an occupation-specific collection of links to other Internet resources. Following is an example of labor market data available from ACINet.

The number of HR managers in local governments is projected to grow by 12 percent over the next 10 years. In Texas, the number of HR managers across all industries is projected to grow by 24 percent over the next 10 years. In the U.S., the number of HR managers across all industries is projected to grow by 19 percent over the next 10 years.

The average wage for an HR manager: U.S. $49,000; Texas $49,200; College Station, TX $45,300; Houston, TX $51,100; and Lubbock, TX $32,900.

Source: *http://www.acinet.org/acinet/* (August 16, 2000).

USE OF HUMAN RESOURCE INFORMATION SYSTEMS

Human resource planning requires a vast amount of information and data. **Human resource information systems (HRISs)** provide local governments with a systematic procedure for collecting, storing, maintaining, and retrieving information and data related to their human resources.[16] Most HRISs include the use and integration of computers and other information technologies (IT). An HRIS may be as simple as handwritten time cards or as complex as computerized expert systems. The ultimate success or failure of a local government's HRIS is based on the ability of the organization and its employees to use the system to make better decisions. Advances in HRIS technology is enabling HR to focus more on planning and strategic issues and less on processing data.[17]

PURPOSE OF HRIS

The two major purposes of an HRIS are improving human resource decision making and reducing processing costs and time. Most attention to date has focused on improving operational efficiency or doing tasks faster with fewer people. Word processors, spreadsheets, databases, and other vendor software programs are examples of IT tools that are helping local government do more with less. Scanning technology, Internet and intranet applications, as well as automated record keeping systems are also being incorporated into HRIS in an effort to increase operational efficiency. To more fully realize the potential of HRIS, local governments need to take advantage of its strategic and planning applications.[18] HRIS can help organizations extend the planning horizon—the period in which planning can be done with a high degree of reliability. For example, construction of a five-year Markov matrix for a planning department can be automated by an HRIS. Use of HRIS to conduct trend analysis can forecast the need for additional employees in the department.

COMPONENTS OF HRIS

The three basic components of an HRIS are data and information input, maintenance, and output. A Human Resource Information System (HRIS) captures data about people and converts these facts into useable information. The data that can be entered into an HRIS is virtually unlimited. There is a tendency to include as much data as possible, in case it may be needed at some future time; however, this is time consuming and not cost-effective. It is important to identify which data are likely to be needed for planning and reporting purposes, and include only information that can contribute to a legitimate purpose. A list of possible categories and data elements is shown in Exhibit 5-9.

Many cities and counties are using information technologies to help employees and the public assess their local governments' resources and services. The city of Westminster, Colorado, has an intranet from which employees can access over 300 forms and current information,

LOGGING ON TO YOUR LOCAL GOVERNMENT

search for information, and complete and send internal forms from over 600 of the city's personal computers. Further, job seekers can use the city's Internet site to access, complete, and submit an on-line job application or download the form and submit it in person. Information about employee benefits is also available on-line.

Source: David Puntenney, "City Intranet," in Christine Ulrich, ed., *Ideas in Action: A Guide to Local Government Innovation* (Washington, D.C.: International City/County Management Association, Spring 2000), mgt-4; and *http://www.ci.westminster.co.us/*.

EXHIBIT 5-9

CATEGORIES AND
DATA EXAMPLES
FOR A HUMAN
RESOURCE
INFORMATION
SYSTEM (HRIS)

- Employee data: name, address, telephone number, Social Security number, date of birth, race, citizenship, gender, military experience, marital status, date of hire.
- Job data: title, salary grade, FLSA status, department, location, job description, supervisor.
- Compensation and reviews: FLSA status, EEO classification, pay period, work schedule, hours per week, compensation history, current wage, date of next review, name of reviewer, results of review, wage increases and bonuses.
- Applicant tracking: applicant information, applicant status, recruiting statistics, source statistics.
- Benefits and retirement: vacation and sick leave, medical, dental, vision, life, pension plan, tax-deferred accounts, dependents, beneficiaries, disability, ADA, workers' compensation, FMLA.
- Training and orientation: orientation manual, employee handbook, organization policy and procedure manual, employee education, employee competencies, courses taken, certifications, continuing education courses, other forms of training, cross-training, in-house training.
- Attendance and performance: hours and days worked, overtime, tardiness, critical incidents, disciplinary actions, grievances filed.

The input data sources for an HRIS include HR records, transactions, and employees themselves. Keeping data in proper form and up to date can be accomplished by networking the system to appropriate data sources. For example, a transaction such as a wage increase is entered into the payroll system and updates the HRIS automatically. However, it is not possible to automate all data sources. Employees must be responsible for updating certain parts of their records. An employee who completes a course at a community college would need to notify the human resources department so that the skills inventory part of the HRIS could be updated. This would also be true for changes of address, medical and health items, and similar data. Most HRIS software is capable of producing a wide range of standardized reports and can be programmed to produce special reports as needed.

DESIGNING AND IMPLEMENTING AN HRIS

The first step in designing an HRIS is to specify what the system is supposed to do.[19] The following questions should be addressed in designing an HRIS:

- What type of data will be collected?
- How much data will be collected?
- How will the data be collected?
- When will the data be collected?
- Who will use the systems?
- How will people access the systems?
- How will the system be updated and maintained?

The answers to these questions will help guide the project team to hardware, software, training, and security needs.

The second step in designing an HRIS is to implement the system. The following guidelines can be used to help local government implement a system.[20]

1. Break the entire project into several smaller projects.
2. Assemble the necessary resources before beginning the project.

3. Evaluate several systems before committing to one.

4. Communicate problems about the new system to everyone involved and those who will be using the system.

5. Plan for any additional staff needed to operate and maintain the system once it is implemented.

6. Break implementation tasks into projects that can be completed within a two-week period.

7. Keep abreast of legal and security issues throughout the life of the project.

8. Openly communicate all progress to everyone involved and those who will be using the system.

9. Decentralize decision making to appropriate management levels.

10. Implement the most important and basic elements of the system first before dealing with the "bells and whistles."

http://www.ihrim.org/
The International Association for Human Resource Information Management (IHIRM) provides articles and information on the application of human resource information systems.

The final step in designing an HRIS is to evaluate the system. Is the system functioning as designed? Do the benefits of the system outweigh the costs?

TRAINING

As noted earlier, it is essential to train those who will use the HRIS and managers as well. Training can be done by external or internal trainers. Research suggests that training programs conducted by internal staff result in greater employee satisfaction with the system.[21]

SECURITY AND OTHER CONSIDERATIONS

Questions remain as to whether the cost of buying, using, and maintaining a computerized HRIS is offset by increases in productivity.[22] What is clear, however, is that information technologies are changing how managers input, maintain, and use human resource information and data.

A final point on HRIS is that it obviously accumulates a great deal of information about an individual. The federal government and many state governments have passed laws intended to protect the privacy rights of employees. The security of computerized HR records is a major problem, and access should be limited to persons with a need to know. Employees should also have the right to review their HR records and challenge information they believe is incorrect.

SUMMARY

Planning provides organizational direction and helps managers cope with change. Planning in general and strategic planning specifically is one of the most widely used productivity improvement strategies. HR systems and processes should be aligned with the organization's strategic plans and objectives.

Steps in the strategic planning process are defining a mission, conducting a SWOT analysis, establishing strategic objectives, implementing a course of action, and evaluating results. Planning activities in HR should support the overall strategic objectives and strategic plan of the organization. Strategic planning is needed in local government because of the increased social responsibility of governments, the destabilizing effects of technological advances, and the complex growth in government initiatives.

The human resources department develops standing plans and human resource plans. Standing plans—policies, procedures, and rules—cover recurring situations and are used over and over. A policy is a general statement that guides decision making. Procedures are a guide to action in implementing a policy. A rule either prescribes or prohibits specific action.

Human resource planning strives to provide an adequate workforce for achieving objectives. Techniques used to forecast need or demand for employees include managerial forecasting, the Delphi technique, and trend analysis. Human resource planning also must project the supply of employees from both internal and external sources. Markov analysis enables management to project the internal supply of employees. Succession charts enable management to assess the qualifications of current staff as possible replacements for key positions. Skills inventories collect and consolidate information about the organization's human resources. Labor market analysis yields information on availability of workers from external sources. Human Resource Information Systems (HRISs) facilitate strategic decision making (effectiveness) and increase operational efficiency.

QUESTIONS FOR REVIEW AND DISCUSSION

1. Briefly describe the five general steps in the strategic planning process.
2. Describe the relationship between HR systems, processes, and activities and strategic planning and strategic objectives.
3. Why is strategic planning important for contemporary local governments?
4. Describe policies, procedures, and rules and their hierarchical relationship.
5. What is human resource planning?
    a. Briefly describe three techniques for forecasting demand for human resources.
    b. Briefly describe three techniques for assessing the supply of human resources.
6. Why is it necessary to analyze trends in the labor market?
7. What are the major purposes of an HRIS? How can an HRIS help a local government achieve its strategic objectives?

ENDNOTES

[1] Evan M. Berman and Jonathan P. West, "Productivity Enhancement Efforts in Public and Nonprofit Organizations," *Public Productivity & Management Review* 22, no. 2 (1999), 207–219.

[2] Unless otherwise cited, this section is based on Colm O'Gorman and Roslyn Doran, "Mission Statements in Small and Medium-Sized Businesses," *Journal of Small Business Management* 37, no. 4 (1999), 59–66; James C. Collins and Jerry I. Porras, *Build to Last* (New York: HarperCollins, 1997); and Arthur G. Bedeian, *Management*, 3d ed. (Chicago: Dryden, 1993), 124–147.

[3] William F. Crittenden and Victoria L. Crittenden, "Relationships Between Organizational Characteristics and Strategic Planning Processes in Nonprofit Organizations," *Journal of Managerial Issues* 12 (Summer 2000), 150–168; and Theodore H. Poister and Gregory D. Streib, "Strategic Management in the Public Sector," *Public Productivity & Management Review* 22 (March 1999), 308–325.

[4] Eugene Bardach, Timothy Deal, and Mary Walther, *North Richmond Gets Its Buses Back: How a Poor Community and an Urban Transit Agency Struck Up a Partnership* (Berkeley: University of California Press, June 1999).

[5] Jeffrey L. Pressman and Aaron Wildavsky, *Implementation*, 3d ed. (Berkeley: University of California Press, 1984), 143–144, 183, 189, and 201–205.

[6] Poister and Streib, 308–325.

[7] Kathie Brooks, "Strategic Planning for Municipal Enterprises," *Government Finance Review* 15, no. 2 (April 1999), 29–34.

[8] Berman and West, 207–219. David Osborne and Ted Gaebler, *Reinventing Government*, 6th ed. (Reading, Mass.: Addison-Wesley, 1992), 19–20.

[9] Gregory D. Foster, "Ethics in Government," *Vital Speeches of the Day* 65, no. 19 (1999), 583–586.

[10] Stephen T. Bajjaly, "Managing Emerging Information Systems in the Public Sector," *Public Productivity & Management Review* 23, no. 1 (September 1999), 40–47.

[11] Bedeian, 129–130.

[12] George Bohlander, Scott Snell, and Arthur Serman, *Managing Human Resources*, 12th ed. (Cincinnati: South-Western, 2001).

[13] Robert L. Mathis and John H. Jackson, *Human Resource Management*, 9th ed. (Cincinnati: South-Western, 2000), 41–42.

[14] Alan H. Kvanli, Robert J. Pavur, and C. Stephen Guynes, *Introduction to Business Statistics: A Computer Integrated Data Analysis Approach*, 5th ed. (Cincinnati: South-Western, 2000), 810.

[15] Wayne F. Cascio, *Applied Psychology in Human Resource Management*, 5th ed. (Upper Saddle River, N.J.: Prentice-Hall, 1998).

[16] Kenneth A. Kovach and Charles E. Cathcart Jr., "Human Resource Information Systems (HRIS): Providing Business with Rapid Data Access, Information Exchange and Strategic Advantage," *Public Personnel Management* 28, no. 2 (Summer 1999), 275–282.

[17] Marc S. Miller, "Great Expectations: Is Your HRIS Meeting Them?" *HR Focus* 75, no. 4 (April 1998), S1–S2.

[18] Bajjaly, 40–47.

[19] Kovach and Cathcart, 275–282.

[20] James Schultz, "Avoid the DDTs of HRIS Implementation" (Baltimore, Md.: The Hunter-Group, 1999).

[21] Victor Y. Haines and Andre Petit, "Conditions for Successful Human Resource Information Systems," *Human Resource Management* (Summer 1997), 261–275.

[22] Miller, 51–52.

PART 3
STAFFING

The productivity of the organization depends on the capabilities of the people performing the work. Having the right people in the right jobs is the outcome of a process that considers the organization's structure and processes, determines appropriate work assignments, and acquires the people who best match these assignments. This part begins with Chapter 6, a discussion of how work is organized into jobs or other units of work. Chapter 7 covers the techniques of job analysis and explains how information from job analysis is used in designing and validating selection tests and other procedures. Chapter 8 describes recruiting, the activity that attracts a pool of qualified candidates, and Chapter 9 provides a detailed examination of the components of a legal and effective selection process.

CHAPTER 6
ORGANIZING AND DESIGNING JOBS

TRAFFIC JAM

Getting to work in the city of Redmond, Washington, just got a little easier thanks to its telecommuting policy. In response to traffic congestion and regional air quality problems in the Puget Sound area, the city of Redmond has developed and implemented comprehensive telecommuting and other job design strategies for selected employees.

The city offers compressed workweek options, flexible work schedules, and telecommuting options for selected full-time jobs with the city. City employees taking advantage of the alternate work schedules include planners, administrative assistants, supervisors, engineers, and department heads. The city's compressed workweek allows employees to eliminate at least one workday every two weeks, resulting in fewer commuting trips by the employee. A typical compressed workweek consists of four 10-hour days or 80 hours over nine workdays. The city's flexible work schedules allow employees flexibility in choosing their start and end time. A typical flexible work schedule would consist of employees coming in early and leaving early or coming in late and leaving late, resulting in less traffic congestion during peak hours.

The city is particularly excited about its telecommuting policy. Telecommuting allows employees to work from their home at least one day a week on writing, reading, telephoning, analysis, programming, data entry, word processing, and other tasks where they can take advantage of information technologies to get work done without coming into the office.

The city's telecommuting policy has resulted in increased employee productivity and morale, and more efficient use of office space. Further, beyond helping solve traffic and air quality problems, the city's job design strategies make it more competitive in attracting and retaining employees. A study of the city's telecommuting policy found employee productivity increased on average 30 percent for the day employees worked at home. Based on the success of its telecommuting program for selected employees, the city is expanding the program to 10 percent of its employees.

Source: Rosemarie M. Ives, "Telecommuting," *http://www.usmayors.org/USCM/best_practices/bp_volume_2/redmond.htm* (September 14, 2000); and city of Redmond, *http://www.ci.redmond.wa.us/* (September 14, 2000).

INTRODUCTION

Organizations are typically divided into divisions, departments, units, sections, and so on, down to individual jobs and positions. This is, of course, part of the organizing function of management, which relates employees and their jobs to each other for accomplishing objectives. In human resource management the focus is on contributing to effective work performance. Understanding the principles and practices involved in the assignment of work to individuals requires consideration of classification, job structure, and departmentalization; fundamental factors in job design; job design considerations and strategies; and choosing a job design strategy.

THE ORGANIZATION OF JOBS AND WORK

In small organizations the allocation and structure of jobs—who does what—may seem intuitively obvious and simple. Even in this kind of situation, however, and of course even more in larger organizations, analysis often will indicate possibilities for improvement. Similarly, there are various ways jobs can be related or grouped into departments for more effective management. The following sections provide a logical and terminological framework for understanding the organization of jobs and work.

CLASSIFICATION AND JOB STRUCTURE

It is essential to know and understand the terms most commonly used in discussions of classification and job structure.[1] The job is the basic building block of all organized undertakings. Every job is composed of duties and responsibilities. Quite often the terms *job* and *position* are used interchangeably; however, there is an important difference. A position is a collection of duties and responsibilities carried out by one person. A **job** can be several **positions** that are identical with respect to their duties and responsibilities. Thus if there are two persons issuing licenses or permits to qualified applicants, there are two positions, but only one job (license clerk). Continuing with this example, a **class** is a group of jobs that are similar in duties and responsibilities, have the same entrance requirements, receive the same rate of pay, and are referred to by the same class title, although they have different job titles. Thus the jobs of license clerk, insurance clerk, file clerk, and recording clerk (possibly extending across departmental lines) may be part of a class identified as Clerk I.

http://stats.bls.gov/
soc/soc_home.htm
The Standard Occupational Classification (SOC) System is used by all federal statistical agencies to classify workers into occupational categories for the purpose of collecting, calculating, or disseminating data.

A **class series** is a vertical grouping of two or more classes on the basis of type of work and level of difficulty. The different levels of responsibility in a class series usually represent the normal line of promotion. For example, a clerical class series might include Clerk I, Clerk II, Clerk III, and Clerk IV. Finally, an **occupational group** may be created by grouping classes according to the general functional nature or character of duties. Typical occupational groups in a city or county might include professional, administrative, clerical, custodial, labor, trades, and protection.

In regard to the use of these terms in this book, positions and jobs are central to all human resource activities. Classes, class series, and occupational groups are used primarily in compensation management and budgeting. In fact, classification is the primary method of establishing pay structures in local government (a topic covered in Chapters 8 and 12).

It has been argued that the duties and responsibilities of traditional jobs are constantly changing and evolving. This presents local government HR managers with a particular challenge. That is, how can jobs that are constantly changing and evolving be designed and described?

THE CHANGING NATURE OF JOBS

One way to address this problem is to think of jobs on a continuum. Some jobs will need to be strictly designed and described, so that employees use specific competencies to perform detailed duties in completing their work. Other jobs will need to be more loosely designed and described, so that employees will have the flexibility to do whatever is necessary to complete the work. The flexibility and competencies necessary to complete work, however, should be documented as part of the job design and description.

Source: Adapted from Caitlin P. Williams, "The End of the Job as We Know It," *Training and Development* 53 (January 1999), 52–54.

DEPARTMENTALIZATION

The grouping of jobs into departments makes it possible to manage an organization. Several types of departmentalization which are applicable to local government:

- **Functional**—Grouping activities based on the work to be done. Street construction, building maintenance, solid waste disposal, and engineering are often grouped under a division of public works.
- **Geographic**—Grouping activities based on location of work. Police precincts are examples of geographic departmentalization.
- **Customer**—Grouping activities based on users of a particular service. A parks and recreation department might have a section to respond to citizens and groups interested in organized team sports, such as a church softball league.
- **Project**—Grouping diverse activities across functional lines to carry out complex tasks or missions. An example would be a task force on drug education composed of representatives from the school system, police department, and the city court.[2]

Most local government organizations use several types and combinations of departmentalization. Such decisions are not normally made by the human resources department; however, departmentalization is a matter of concern because how jobs are organized into work groups must be considered in developing an appropriate classification and pay plan. Also, some types of departmentalization tend to limit the flexibility of management in designing jobs. This is particularly true of the more formal types such as departmentalization by function, which emphasizes an ever-increasing refinement of specialized skills. As the following sections point out, job design is a useful tool for keeping employees satisfied and motivated to do their best in work that is structured appropriately to accomplish objectives.

FUNDAMENTALS OF JOB DESIGN

Over the past 20 years the "reengineering" of jobs has been an important productivity improvement strategy.[3] Further, job design can affect employee performance, job satisfaction, and employee physical and mental health.[4] Human resource practices, such as quality circles, self-managed teams, job rotation, and so forth have become commonplace. These practices have led to changes in job design regarding employee participation, work schedules, breadth and depth of jobs, employee autonomy, and compensation systems.

Job design consists of organizing duties and responsibilities into a unit of work to achieve a particular objective. This includes specifying job content, identifying work methods, and relating the job to other jobs in the organization. A variety of elements such as employee factors, resource availability, technology, legislation or regulation, and managerial philosophy influence job design (see Exhibit 6-1).[5]

INFLUENCING FACTORS

Employee factors include ability and motivation. Jobs should require ability commensurate with that possessed by employees or potential employees. It may therefore be necessary to simplify the duties involved or train employees to meet the minimum skill levels. For example, a job may be designed to require a skilled worker such as a heavy equipment mechanic. However, very few are available in the job market. In this case an automotive mechanic might be hired and trained to perform the additional tasks required. The job could also be separated into simplified elements (removing crawler treads, disassembling tread blocks, etc.) that a qualified automotive mechanic could learn.

In regard to motivation and satisfaction, routine jobs involving simple, repetitive work are usually appropriate for employees who view work as a means to an end

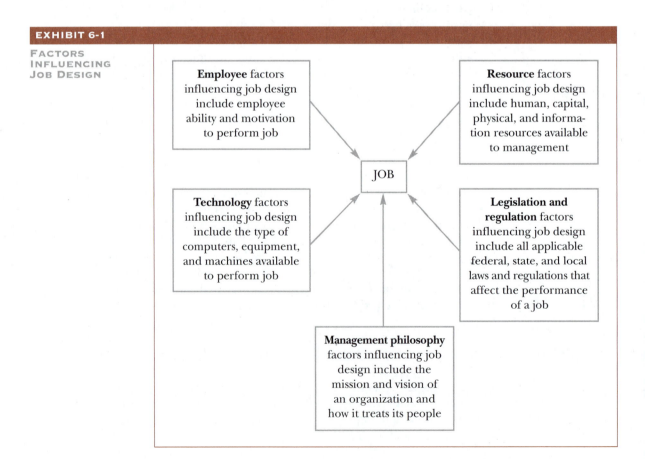

EXHIBIT 6-1

FACTORS
INFLUENCING
JOB DESIGN

Employee factors influencing job design include employee ability and motivation to perform job

Resource factors influencing job design include human, capital, physical, and information resources available to management

Technology factors influencing job design include the type of computers, equipment, and machines available to perform job

Legislation and regulation factors influencing job design include all applicable federal, state, and local laws and regulations that affect the performance of a job

JOB

Management philosophy factors influencing job design include the mission and vision of an organization and how it treats its people (usually, the paycheck). On the other hand, employees who define their personal success in terms of their job performance expect their jobs to be challenging and to provide opportunities for personal growth. (For discussion of these topics, see Chapter 4.)

Resources available to management (economic/financial, physical, human, and information) have a great influence on job design. Many large local government units have considerable resources and the best equipment and working conditions. Small cities and counties must often "make do" with very little. For example, the planning department in a large city would probably use a geographic information system (GIS) in creating plans for a new industrial park or a new residential development. A small rural county, however, might not be able to afford either the GIS system or the services of a professional with the requisite skills to operate such a system. In theory it is usually possible to improve job design. In practice, resources might not be available.

Technology refers to how an organization transforms resources into outputs—in the case of government, services. Technology such as e-mail, digital phones, voice mail, and interactive video conferencing can isolate employees and depersonalize local governments. As shown in the previous example, technology has a major influence on how a job is designed. The more that the design of a job is influenced by technology, the less design flexibility exists. For example, the type of computers, machines, and equipment used in the waterworks is the major factor in the design of a water treatment plant operator job. On the other hand, considerable design flexibility exists in the job of carpenter.

Legislation and regulation in the United States influence job design. The Fair Labor Standards Act, for example, regulates wages, hours of work, and employment relationships. Assume that a city wishes to create a job in which an equipment operator with the public works department performs landscape maintenance on a contract basis outside of regular work hours. Even if the employee requests such an arrangement, the Wage and Hour Division might rule that this violates the special provisions for occasional and sporadic employment.

Safety regulations also influence job design. Even though local government is not covered by the Occupational Safety and Health Act, the manufacturers of machinery and equipment are covered and are required to build in safety features. The safety regulations result in altered characteristics of the machinery and equipment, thus producing a technological influence on job design. Local government must also be concerned with safety from the standpoint of workers' compensation claims. To reduce liability, jobs should be designed to minimize the risk of injuries or illness to employees.

http://www.lni.wa.gov/wisha/ergo/officerg/offergr2.htm
The Washington Department of Labor and Industries provides basic information on designing jobs that take into account ergonomic concerns.

Management philosophy influences job design. Organizations that view employee motivation and satisfaction as major objectives spend considerable time and effort on job design. If these are not matters of concern, jobs are likely to simply evolve, with mixed results. In one case, a dispatcher in a county highway department took on additional responsibilities in records management, right-of-way acquisition, and inventory control, thus redesigning her job to the benefit of the county. Often, however, jobs evolve less efficiently. In a county hospital, it was discovered during a job study that certain activities relating to infection control had not been performed for years. The job of central supply technician had evolved in such a way as to put both patients and staff at risk. Not only employee motivation and satisfaction but efficiency and effectiveness of work performance are put at risk by inattention to job design.

There are a number of possible explanations for the lack of attention to job design. First, many human resource managers in small to medium-sized units of government are hard pressed to keep up with such traditional activities as selection, performance appraisal, compensation, discipline, and legal obligations. Second, the theoretical foundations for job design come from disciplines such as industrial engineering and industrial/organizational psychology. Topics such as work measurement, job enlargement, and job enrichment are not major content areas in typical textbooks and courses in human resource management.

Finally, although job design is an important HR function, little commitment has been made to operationalize the process with practical methods and techniques such as are readily available for job analysis, selection, testing, job evaluation, performance appraisal, and similar traditional activities. This is unfortunate, since (as Chapter 4 shows) in addition to providing efficient and effective services, well-designed work also provides social identity and contributes to self-esteem.

JOB DESIGN CONSIDERATIONS AND STRATEGIES

A historical perspective is useful in understanding job design considerations and strategies. Craft jobs, such as silversmith, potter, and shoemaker predominated until the Industrial Revolution. In these jobs a person makes a whole product. The Industrial Revolution brought a shift toward jobs with a limited number of tasks. These specialized jobs greatly improve worker productivity. But many critics say specialization has gone too far, to the detriment of the human element. Thus there is a move toward jobs in which the number and variety of tasks is increased, along with the influence and control employees have over their jobs. These are called enlarged and/or enriched jobs. Job design strategies, however, are much broader than just job specialization, enlargement, or enrichment. They also include autonomous work groups, job sharing, flextime, compressed work schedules, job rotation, and reengineering. Regardless of the job design strategy followed, all are based on consideration of job characteristics.

JOB CHARACTERISTICS

Variations in job content are accounted for by five characteristics or parameters: skill variety, task identity, task significance, autonomy, and performance feedback.[6]

Skill variety is the extent to which a job demands the performance of a wide range of activities. A job is considered routine if it requires a limited number of activities repeated over and over. A job with high skill variety allows more creativity, requires more education, training, and experience, and typically provides more prestige. For example, it is possible to design the job of insurance clerk so that one employee interviews claimants, another checks the necessary paperwork, and still another processes payments. Such a design would provide little skill variety. The same job could be designed to have one employee handle the entire claim process.

Task identity is the extent to which a job allows employees to perform an entire piece of work and to clearly identify the outcome of their effort. Consider a project that involves painting all offices in the courthouse. This job could be designed so that one painter prepares the surfaces, another paints walls, and a third paints windows and trim. One painter could also do all these tasks for a given office. The latter would constitute a "whole job," with each painter able to clearly identify the results of his or her efforts.

Task significance is the impact of the job on the lives and work of others. For example, workers at a water filtration plant may speak with pride about the fact that their city has an abundant supply of pure drinking water. Feeling that they have accomplished something significant in life is important to many employees.

Autonomy is the extent to which employees are free to schedule their own activities, decide work procedures, and select necessary equipment. Some jobs allow employees to decide what to do, when to do it, and how to do it, as long as the necessary work is done correctly within set time and cost limits. Thus, the employees control their own job pace, tool usage, and other factors, as long as work is completed satisfactorily. The job of city planner would normally be designed with considerable autonomy, as could a craft job such as plumber. On the other hand, jobs can be highly programmed. A sanitation worker, for example, picks up garbage cans and dumps their contents into a packer truck, following the same route, week after week.

http://www.nwlink.com/
~donclark/leader/
jobsurvey.html
The Job Survey provides an on-line survey that is designed to analyze Hackman & Oldman's five dimensions of a job.

Performance feedback provides employees with information about how well they are doing their jobs. It may be systematized, as in formal performance appraisals, or informal. Informal feedback may come from supervisors or from coworkers, clients, or subordinates. Other possible sources include awards and promotions. In many cases, the employee's personal self-evaluation is the major source of feedback. While carrying out a project to design a compensation program for a county government, the author interviewed an employee to determine the nature of the duties being performed. The information was to be used to update the job description so that the job would be properly classified. At the conclusion of the interview the employee remarked, "That's my job, as I see it. I don't know whether I do it right or not. I've worked here for twelve years and nobody has ever said."

SPECIALIZATION

Job specialization (division of labor) originated with the Industrial Revolution. It was refined during the efficiency movement of the early 20th century with Taylor's scientific management and the work simplification approach. Specialization and simplification are powerful tools for improving labor productivity. Few of the goods and services available today would be affordable if they were produced by workers in craft jobs. This is true of government services as well, as in the cases of the insurance clerk whose only job is to check forms, the painter who paints only trim, and the sanitation helper with his daily routine. In each case, specialization results in providing the service at a lower cost. Management consultants and work-study analyses have found that the types of jobs that can benefit from specialization are those that

- have a higher labor content (that is, are time consuming);
- have a large demand (that is, are frequently occurring);
- present quality problems by rejects or rework required;
- are bottlenecks in the system, thus limiting output;
- are unsafe, unpleasant, or fatiguing;
- offer very low or high earnings (including overtime).[7]

Procedures for designing or redesigning jobs to take advantage of work simplification are known by such terms as *methods improvement, time study,* and *work measurement.* An overview of the general process is shown in Exhibit 6-2. Such studies are not normally performed by the HR department.

It should be pointed out, however, that specialization and simplification have a serious downside. Specialized jobs are often monotonous and boring. Many employees try to avoid them entirely or perform them only reluctantly. In fact, specialization carried to extremes can actually lower productivity. Certain jobs, however, must be done, and managers should attempt to make them as satisfying as possible.

EXHIBIT 6-2

STEP 1. Record present method.
Develop a step-by-step procedure describing the present method of work in full detail, beginning with a general sketch of the floor plan, flow of work, etc. Record details of the present method by using a worker-machine chart or a flow process chart.

STEP 2. Critically analyze present method.
Use proven methods of analysis such as the questioning technique, checklist, and/or photographic analysis. The questioning technique is very effective when the analyst asks the questions: What is its purpose? Why is it necessary? Can it be eliminated? Combined with another? Changed in sequence? Simplified in any way?

STEP 3. Develop improved method.
Use information and insights from analysis to produce improvement alternatives. Consider all suggestions, including those from the employees doing the job. Prepare charts of alternative methods for comparison with the existing method. Total time required and number of operations are indicators of improvement. After time, quality, cost, personnel effects, and any other relevant criteria have been considered, select the best method and record it in a summary report.

STEP 4. Install improved method.
Changes must be "sold" to both line management and employees. A major change may involve considerable planning; include management and employee suggestions on implementation. The analyst, supervisor, and employees should all be prepared to spend some effort in overcoming the usual "start-up" problems.

STEP 5. Maintain improved method.
Follow up to ensure that the new method is functioning according to plan. This not only guards against unplanned changes but also provides data and ideas for improvement elsewhere in the system.

Source: Adapted from Richard Metters and Vicente Vargas, "Organizing Work in Service Firms," *Business Horizons* 43 (July/August 2000), 23–32.

Recent efforts in job design have focused on broadening job boundaries by creating generalists rather than specialists.[8] Most jobs in local governments require an employee to be a generalist with a specialty or a specialist who is a generalist. Employees must be able to organize work, manage time, keep a budget, and sell a project. The question is one of degrees and not so much one of either-or.[9] For example, the human resource manager of small city would need to have specialized compensation competencies as well as generalized human resource management competencies in order to carry out her job. The degree to which the human resource manager specializes in compensation would depend on the needs of the city.

JOB ENRICHMENT AND JOB ENLARGEMENT

As noted earlier, the purpose of job design is to increase productivity and employee performance, improve job satisfaction, and ensure the physical and mental well-being of employees by improving the nature of work itself. **Job enrichment** and **enlargement**, shown in Exhibit 6-3, are design strategies used by human resource departments to "improve" the nature of work. It should be pointed out, however, that neither enrichment nor enlargement is necessarily incompatible with special-

EXHIBIT 6-3

JOB ENRICHMENT
OR ENLARGE-
MENT?

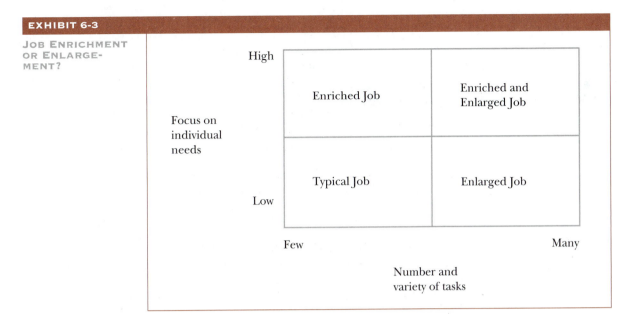

izization. In fact, it is often possible to use enrichment and enlargement strategies in specialized jobs without sacrificing the gains from using improved methods.

Additionally, local government managers should be concerned with job enrichment and job enlargement as well as other job design strategies because of changes in employees' work expectations and training. Employees place a much higher value on intrinsic rewards such as achievement, the work itself, and personal growth. In the workforces of local government, employees can acquire additional skills through **cross-training**. This provides management a degree of flexibility in dealing with downsizing, vacancies, absenteeism, and other situations requiring skills from internal sources. Cross-training also opens additional career opportunities to employees. The first reason is addressed through job enrichment; the second involves job enlargement.

JOB ENRICHMENT

As a design strategy, job enrichment represents a movement back toward craft jobs in which employees perform a larger and more complete segment of work. Job enrichment has been associated with high employee motivation, high-quality performance, high job satisfaction, low absenteeism, and low turnover. Jobs are enriched by allowing employees greater self-direction and the opportunity to perform interesting and challenging work that job enrichment approaches usually include:

- **Increasing skill variety**—combining several jobs into a larger job requiring a broader range of skills
- **Increasing task identity**—giving employees a natural unit of work with which they can clearly identify
- **Increasing task significance**—allowing employees to work on important tasks
- **Increasing autonomy**—giving employees more responsibility for quality control and self-determination of work procedures
- **Increasing performance feedback**—measuring job-related contributions and discussing the results with employees so that they can monitor and self-correct work behavior.[10]

In carrying out a job enrichment program, an organization must make major changes in an employee's duties. Employee acceptance and participation is critical to success. Employees who are satisfied doing essentially the same work for three or five years are not likely to respond positively to job enrichment. On the other hand, an employee who looks forward to more interesting and challenging work is likely to be more productive through job enrichment. Here are eight questions that should be discussed with employees to identify candidates for job enrichment:

WHO WANTS AN ENRICHED JOB?

1. How can your job be designed so that you can control the work situations, methods, and pace?
2. What interdependent tasks can be combined into your job?
3. How can tasks be grouped so that end products or services visibly contribute to organizational goals?
4. Is there a sufficient variety of tasks within your job that include some degree of responsibility and use your competencies?
5. Do you have access to the necessary information to make decisions?
6. Do you receive adequate feedback from the performance of the tasks, customers, and supervisors?
7. Does the achievement of goals result in your obtaining personal goals?
8. Does your job interfere with your personal life?

Source: Adapted from Sharon Parker and Toby Wall, *Job and Work Design: Organizing Work to Promote Well-Being and Effectiveness* (Thousand Oaks, Calif.: Sage, 1998), 20.

Job enrichment increases the depth of a job by allowing the worker to exercise discretion, make decisions, and accept responsibility for a meaningful unit of work.[11] For this reason, job enrichment is often called **vertical job loading**.

JOB ENLARGEMENT

The concept of job enlargement focuses mainly on increasing the number and variety of tasks (of a related nature or at the same level) on which the employee works. It is sometimes called **horizontal job loading**. Job enlargement has been associated with increased job satisfaction and productivity.[12] A maintenance worker's job, performing general vehicle maintenance, could be enlarged by adding additional tasks such as tune-ups, front end alignment, brake repair, and so forth. It can be argued, however, that job enlargement alone does not accomplish very much if employees are merely given more boring tasks to perform. Where possible, job enlargement should be used concurrently with job enrichment.

OTHER JOB DESIGN STRATEGIES

AUTONOMOUS WORK GROUPS

Autonomous work groups are a design strategy that is both an expansion and combination of job enlargement and enrichment principles. As a design strategy, autonomous work groups focus on work performed by a group of employees and not on an individual's job. The idea behind this strategy is to allow the group to control the work from beginning to end. Actual work performed by an individual employee is determined by the group. In addition to carrying out the work, the group is responsible for planning and controlling the work and its associated processes. The focus on group achievements enlarges the number of tasks performed and enriches the job by adding the planning and controlling processes. In addition to building on the motivation effects of job enlargement and enrichment, autonomous work groups increase meaningfulness of jobs and provide a social environment that enhances employee satisfaction.

JOB ROTATION

Job rotation is a form of job enlargement. Job rotation is a design strategy that results in "shifting" employees from one job to another. For example, a library assistant might be assigned one week to work at the circulation desk, the next week to order and receive books and periodicals, and the following week to assist library users. Job rotation has been shown to increase productivity and job satisfaction by reducing job boredom and staleness. It can be argued, however, that rotation alone does not accomplish very much if employees are merely shifted from one boring job to another.

REENGINEERING

Reengineering is a design strategy that focuses on redesigning and rethinking how the employees who hold them interact and carry out their duties.[13] The goal of reengineering is to provide the customer with a better product at a lower cost in a timely manner. The driving force behind reengineering is the assumption that current work processes and organizational structures are not sufficient to meet customer needs. A noted authority and pioneer of the term *reengineering*, Michael Hammer, says that for reengineering to be effective, organizations must make dramatic "go-for-broke" changes in their work processes and organizational structures. Reengineering is not a process that should or can occur in incremental steps. Reengineering incorporates and relies on greater use and dependence on information technology, particularly computers, information systems, and the Internet. As a result of reengineering, greater use of information technology, and more customer focus, jobs, functions, and even departments are often reconstituted or eliminated.

JOB SHARING

Job sharing is a design strategy that allows more than one employee (usually two) to share one position.[14] As a design strategy, job sharing focuses on "partners" creating

---

Following is an example of how a local government "went for broke" in reengineering jobs.

The Montgomery County, Maryland, human resources training team is responsible for all course registration and tuition assistance requests of employees. The team spent most of

GOING FOR BROKE . . . REENGINEERING JOBS

its time handling routine telephone inquiries, processing forms, and manually entering data. There was a need to reduce the time spent on these activities, so the team could focus more on developing and implementing training and development programs. The team drastically reengineered the process by developing and installing a direct-talk voice processing system. With this automatic system employees could register for classes 24 hours a day and receive fax-on-demand information such as training calendars, course bulletins, transcripts, and registration confirmation. As a result of the reengineering process paperwork was cut, phone calls to members of the team were dramatically reduced, and the number of records processed by the team tripled.

Source: Liz Habermann, "Direct-Talk Voice Processing System," in Christine Ulrich, ed., *Ideas in Action: A Guide to Local Government Innovation* 4 (Summer 1998), PRM-12.

a seamless blend of work ethics, personality traits, and egos.[15] Partners work a day or set of hours in common to ensure a seamless work environment. A typical job sharing arrangement would have one partner working mornings and the other afternoons, overlapping between, say 11:00 A.M. and 1:00 P.M. Job sharing provides flexibility to employees whose lifestyles do not allow them to work traditional work schedules. Job sharing has been linked with increased job satisfaction and reduced job stress.[16] Job sharing is just one of three design strategies that require adjustments to the traditional work schedule. The other two are flextime and compressed work schedules.

FLEXTIME

Flextime is a design strategy that allows an individual some flexibility in the hours of work. Most flextime programs (see Exhibit 6-4) have a core period of time that all employees must be present between flexible arrival and departure times. For example, all employees may be required to be at work from 10 A.M. to 3 P.M., but some may arrive at 6 A.M. and leave at 3 P.M.; some may arrive at 8 A.M. and leave at 5 P.M.; and some may arrive at 10 A.M. and leave at 7 P.M. Employees should select one of the flextime options and be required to follow that schedule. Flextime programs have been shown to help reduce employee tardiness and absenteeism and increase productivity and job satisfaction.[17] Flextime programs have also been shown to be an effective recruitment tool. Highly flexible programs tend to be less effective than programs that are more rigid.

COMPRESSED WORK SCHEDULES

Compressed work schedules (see Exhibit 6-4) is a job design strategy that allows the employee flexibility in the number of days worked during a workweek. For example, employees working four days a week may work 10-hour days. In general, the benefits and concerns for compressed work schedules are similar to those of flextime.

TELECOMMUTING

Telecommuting is an emerging job design strategy that allows employees to establish offices and work primarily out of their homes.

JOB DESIGN AND COMPENSATION SYSTEMS

http://www.accel-team. com/work_design/ Accel-Team.com provides in-depth discussion, techniques, and applications for improving productivity through job design.

Job design/redesign is less effective if the accompanying compensation system does not reinforce the design. To have successful work processes and job designs that empower employees and focus on teamwork, local governments must also develop compensation systems tied to such processes and designs. For example, if a city adopts job enrichment as a job design strategy, then an appropriate competency, knowledge, or skill-based compensation program should be the basis for salary increases and promotions. Lack of an appropriate compensation system may induce job redesign. Consider a county's planning director who wants to empower her employees and place a greater emphasis on teamwork. A majority of her employees are civil service employees whose status, pay, and subsequent raises and promotions are largely a result of an impersonal bureaucracy that sits outside of the organization where the work takes place. The likelihood that the planning director can effectively and efficiently implement the new job design will be limited by the bureaucratic constraints of a compensation system not under her control. Thus, the

EXHIBIT 6-4

CREATING JOBS
FOR PEOPLE

The city of Clavemont, California, has flextime and compressed work schedules for its employees. The purpose of the policy to is increase job satisfaction, improve motivation, help with career and professional development, and allow employees to adopt worktimes and schedules that meet the employees' lifestyle choices. Employees are allowed to adopt any worktime or schedule that does not interrupt any essential service provided by their department. The following are based on the city of Clavemont's policy.

Flextime options

Flexible arrival time				Core period of time					Flexible leave time		
7 A.M.	8	9	10	11	12	1	2	3	4	5	6 P.M.

Compressed work schedules

	Option 1[a]	Option 2[b]	Option 3		Option 4
Monday	12 hours	10 hours	9 hours		8 hours
Tuesday	12 hours	10 hours	9 hours		8 hours
Wednesday	12 hours	10 hours	9 hours		8 hours
Thursday	OFF	10 hours	9 hours		8 hours
Friday	OFF	OFF	9 hours[c]	OFF	8 hours

[a] May start workweek Mon., Tues., or Wed.

[b] May start workweek Mon. or Tues.

[c] Every other Fri. off.

Source: Bridget Healy, "Flexible Scheduling Makes Workplace Family-Friendly," in Christine Ulrich, ed., *Ideas in Action: A Guide to Local Government Innovation* 5 (Spring 1999), PRM-2.

civil service employees will likely redesign their jobs according the civil service compensation system.

APPLICATION TO LOCAL GOVERNMENT

Job redesign has been used in the public sector for at least 35 years. At least 65 percent of state and local government employment is knowledge-based work, such as that in education, health, and welfare, dominated by human resource professionals.[18] This mix suggests opportunities to design or redesign jobs that facilitate semi-autonomous performance of work based on knowledge, skill, and motivation rather than by the sequence of tasks listed in the person's position classification.

These efforts in government are inhibited by factors such as classification rules and union resistance.[19] Job redesign in government agencies has been impeded by certain institutional restrictions, most notably the rules and regulations inherent in the classification system of position management. Typically, a request must be made for a job study, and even if it is possible to reclassify the job, the recommendation may be disapproved at higher levels. As Chapter 1 discussed, many local governments have adopted human resource systems patterned after those in the federal and state governments, and the same impediment would apply there also. Job redesign in the public sector has also become a labor relations issue. Traditionally, union bargaining demands centered on economic issues such as wages and benefits. More recently, however, employee representatives have pressed for discussion of changes in civil service regulations applying to work procedures.

CHOOSING A JOB DESIGN STRATEGY

There is no single best job design for a local government, or any organization for that matter.[20] The design approach used by a local government is dependent on a variety of factors including needs, costs, and technology. Additionally, job design strategies are not totally incompatible. As noted, job enlargement is more effective when combined with job enrichment efforts. A city that is having difficulty building a suitable pool of applicants for a secretarial position may wish to consider some combination of job sharing, flextime, and/or compressed workweeks. Regardless of the design strategy used, successful design must be based on a contingency approach that considers the employee(s), management objectives, and the existing work situation and chooses the strategy or the mix of strategies appropriate to the situation.

Unfortunately, successful job design or redesign is easier to talk about than to do. The major problem is the compartmentalization (and specialization) of job design strategies. As has been pointed out, the specialization approach is an area of industrial engineering and applied mainly in manufacturing operations. The local government HR manager will have inherited a workforce featuring more or less specialized jobs but will not likely have received the training to successfully implement a specialization program. On the other hand, job enrichment and enlargement programs are most successfully carried out where human resource departments are large enough to have organizational psychologists.[21]

A concluding example is offered to show how this can work. A supply clerk in a county complained that her job was virtually impossible to carry out and that no one would listen to her suggestions. When she threatened to resign, the county arranged with a local university to analyze the problem and make recommendations.

A graduate student, qualified in production/operations management, identified a large number of activities in the job. These included issuing items to employees, maintaining inventory records, preparing reports, dispensing fuel, and receiving and shelving stock. The student made a study of each activity and recommended improved methods (specialization). The student also recommended that a part-time employee be assigned to assist with receiving and stocking, and to issue supplies and dispense fuel during peak times. This gave the clerk more time to plan and organize her work (job enrichment). The savings from improved inventory control more than offset the cost of the part-time employee. The clerk did not resign, preferring to remain in her present job, which was now much more satisfying and attractive.

While not all job design/redesign efforts have such a happy ending, there seems to be a great potential in this area to the mutual benefit of both employees and managers.

SUMMARY

The job is the basic building block of all organized undertakings. Jobs are grouped into classes, class series, and occupational groups for classification purposes and into departments for management purposes.

Job design focuses on job content and consists of organizing job duties into a unit of work to achieve a particular objective. Job design is influenced by employee factors, resources, technology, legislation, and management philosophy. The effectiveness of job design/redesign is also influenced by a local government's compensation system. Skill variety, task identity, task significance, autonomy, and performance feedback create variations in job content. Design strategies include specialization, job enrichment, job enlargement, autonomous work groups, job rotation, reengineering, job sharing, flextime, and compressed work schedules. Specialization focuses on an ever-increasing refinement of specialized skills and simplification of tasks, while job enlargement and job enrichment move away from specialization. Jobs are enriched by allowing employees greater self-direction and the opportunity to perform interesting and challenging work. Jobs are enlarged by increasing the number of tasks. In the autonomous work group the focus is on work performed by a group of employees and not on an individual's job. Job rotation shifts employees from one job to another. Reengineering involves dramatically redesigning and rethinking how jobs and the employees who hold them interact and carry out their duties. Job sharing focuses on partners dividing the duties of a single position. Flextime provides employees flexibility in daily work hours; compressed work schedules give employees flexibility in number of days worked per week.

All design strategies are useful. Successful job design is based on a contingency approach that considers the employee, management objectives, and the work situation.

QUESTIONS FOR REVIEW AND DISCUSSION

1. Explain the difference between a job and a position.
2. What are four types of departmentalization found in local government?
3. Discuss factors influencing job design.
4. With regard to job characteristics, contrast the job of a city planner with that of a refuse handler.
5. Which types of jobs can benefit from specialization?
6. Discuss how job enlargement and job enrichment can be used to increase the productivity of a title clerk.
7. List five job design strategies (other than job enlargement and job enrichment) and explain how they can be used to increase employee job satisfaction.
8. Imagine you are the HR manager of Montgomery County, Maryland. Based on your success in reengineering the human resource training team, you have been asked to develop a plan for reengineering other county departments. Describe how you will begin the process and what you hope to accomplish.

ENDNOTES

[1] See Sharon Parker and Toby Wall, *Job and Work Design: Organizing Work to Promote Well-Being and Effectiveness* (New York: Sage, 1998).
[2] Arthur G. Bedeian, *Management*, 3d ed. (Chicago: Dryden, 1993), 238–263.
[3] John Garen, "Unions, Incentive Systems, and Job Design," *Journal of Labor Research* 20, no. 4 (Fall 1999), 589–603.
[4] Robert L. Mathis and John H. Jackson, *Human Resource Management*, 9th ed. (Cincinnati: South-Western, 2000), 84–85.

[5] James Colvard, "Restore the Human Touch," *Government Executive* 32, no. 1 (January 2000), 56–58.

[6] J. Richard Hackman and Greg R. Oldham, *Work Redesign* (Reading Mass.: Addison-Wesley, 1980); see also Bedeian, 296–299.

[7] Joseph J. Monks, *Operations Management: Theory and Problems* (New York: McGraw-Hill, 1977), 111.

[8] John M. Usher, "Specialists, Generalists, and Polymorphs: Spatial Advantages of Multiunit Organization in a Single Industry," *Academy of Management Review* 24, no. 1 (January 1999), 143–150.

[9] Barbara Moses, "Career Intelligence: The 12 New Rules for Success," *Futurist* 33, no. 7 (August/September 1999), 28–35.

[10] Kenneth N. Wexley and Gary A. Yuki, *Organizational Behavior and Personnel Psychology*, rev. ed. (Homewood Ill.: Irwin, 1984), 33–34; Hackman and Oldham, 135–142.

[11] Sharon K. Parker, "Enhancing Role Breadth Self-Efficacy: The Roles of Job Enrichment and Other Organizational Interventions," *Journal of Applied Psychology* 83, no. 6 (December 1998), 835–852.

[12] David G. Garson and Michael L. Vasu, "Analysis of Ethical Dynamics in Public Personnel Administration," *Public Personnel Administration* 14, no. 3 (Summer 1994), 75–92.

[13] This section draws on Michael Hammer and James Champy, *Reengineering the Corporation* (New York: HarperCollins, 1994); Michael Hammer, "Reengineering at Net Speed," *Informationweek* 730 (April 1999), 176; and Michael Hammer and Steven Stanton, "How Process Enterprises Really Work," *Harvard Business Review* 77, no. 6 (November/December 1999), 108–118.

[14] Elizabeth Sheley, "Job Sharing Offers Unique Challenges," *HRMagazine* (January 1996), 46–49.

[15] Susan Caminiti, "Fair Shares," *Working Women* 24, no. 10 (November 1999), 52–56.

[16] Bevan Gibbs, "Are Two Heads Better?" *New Zealand Management* 46, no. 11 (December 1999), 110.

[17] Boris B. Baltes, Thomas E. Briggs, Joseph W. Huff, Julie A. Wright, and George A. Neuman, "Flexible and Compressed Workweek Schedules: A Meta-Analysis of Their Effects on Work-Related Criteria," *Journal of Applied Psychology* 84, no. 4 (August 1999), 496–513.

[18] Eugene B. McGregor Jr., "The Public Sector Human Resource Puzzle: Strategic Management of a Strategic Resource," *Public Administration Review* 48 (November/December 1988), 941–950.

[19] Garen, 589–603.

[20] Susan E. Jackson and Randall S. Schuler, *Managing Human Resources: A Partnership Perspective* (Cincinnati: South-Western, 2000), 158–160.

[21] For an excellent discussion of this issue, see Michael A. Campion and Paul W. Thayer, "Job Design Approaches, Outcomes and Trade-offs," *Organizational Dynamics* 15 (Winter 1987), 66–79.

CHAPTER 7
ANALYZING JOBS AND
WRITING JOB DESCRIPTIONS

YOU WANT ME TO DO WHAT?

When Steve and Mary arrived at work on Monday morning they were given a memo from the office manager that contained the following information:

Scioto Township, Ohio, is about to undertake a job analysis project. The purpose of this communication is to explain what job analysis is all about.

Job analysis is an in-depth study of a job and provides information for job descriptions. A human resource consultant has been hired and will be gathering information about jobs by interviewing employees, observing performance of certain tasks, asking employees to fill in questionnaires and worksheets, and collecting information about jobs from secondary sources.

The consultant will write up the results of the analysis and review this material with the job incumbent. The documentation will then be presented to your supervisor for review. The supervisor may add, delete, or modify responsibilities, tasks, knowledge, skills, abilities, and other characteristics. After supervisory approval is obtained, the documentation will be forwarded through channels for final approval. A signed and dated job description will then be prepared. This will become the official record of all aspects of the job.

Next week you will receive a questionnaire and a set of instructions from the consultant. As the person currently employed in this position, you have an important role in this process. The following suggestions should be useful:

- Spend some time thinking about your job. You may wish to make notes or keep a diary of your activities.
- At the outset, fully explain your concept of the job to the analyst.
- Focus on the facts—do not overstate or understate domains, duties, knowledge, skills, abilities, and other characteristics.
- Refrain from side issues. The analyst is concerned with only the job itself. Job performance, wages, complaints, relationships with coworkers, and so forth, are not relevant to this activity.
- Remember that your input is critical; however, establishing the boundaries of the job is a management decision.
- Be aware that there will be no adverse consequences from job analysis. For example, no person's salary will be reduced and no person's job will be

eliminated. The analysts may recommend changes in title or other realignments, subject to management decision.

Thanks for your cooperation! We are looking forward to working with you on this important project.

Mary thought it was a good idea to gather and write up information about her job. She had worked for the township for over 21 years and had never had a job description. Mary was proud of the work she did and felt that if she had a written job description that accurately reflected what she did, her boss would have a greater appreciation for her work.

Steve, on the other hand, thought this whole process was a waste of time. He had worked for the township for over 8 years and received work assignments each morning from his supervisor. Steve was a hard worker who just did not have time to waste talking to a consultant about his job. Besides, Steve thought, "I am not going to get any more money for doing this."

INTRODUCTION

Job analysis is a process by which information about a job is collected and ordered. It is a procedure used to differentiate jobs based on job content, work environment, and human capital.[1] Job content is concerned with what responsibilities and tasks employees perform. Work environment is concerned with where and under what conditions work is performed. Human capital is concerned with the necessary competencies needed by employees to perform their jobs. Job analysis is the most basic activity in human resource management. Individual jobs combine to move the organization toward accomplishment of its strategic goals. Without accurate information on all jobs performed by the organization's workers, management cannot efficiently direct or control the organization's operations and may be vulnerable to damaging lawsuits. Comprehensive job descriptions developed from job analyses are used in selection, training, performance appraisal, and compensation. This chapter include covers the need for job analysis, information required for job analysis, methods of analysis, development of job descriptions, and practical considerations in job analysis.

THE NEED FOR JOB ANALYSIS

Two forces have made job analysis a mandatory organizational consideration: competition and equal employment opportunity legislation.[2] The first major force is competition among organizations for the right to use resources, including human resources, to produce a product or deliver a service. If the product or service is not produced efficiently, the organization will fail. While local government does not normally compete directly against other organizations, it does compete in the job market, and job analysis is an important factor in recruiting and retaining competent workers. Further, local government services must meet standards of efficiency expected by taxpayers. While these standards are not always spelled out, they are nevertheless real. If the standards are not met, taxpayers will complain and eventually take action against the inefficiency or against those they believe to be responsible.

In all organizations, jobs have a life cycle. They are created, reach maturity, become obsolete, and finally die.[3] Because employees have more job protection in government, and because worker efficiency is not so closely tied to organizational survival (governments do not experience business failure), the obsolescence phase of the cycle is usually more prolonged in government than in the private sector. That is, a job may continue to exist long after the purpose for which it was created diminishes or disappears. Close monitoring of jobs—that is, systematic job analysis—is therefore essential to local government efficiency, especially since human resources typically represent the largest cost item in the government budget.

The second major force that makes job analysis essential is the myriad of laws, guidelines, and court decisions that define equal employment opportunity.[4] Since the now-famous 1971 *Griggs v. Duke Power Company* case,[5] employers, including governmental units, have been vulnerable on the issue of discrimination in employment practices. As discussed in Chapter 3, if any employment practice has a disparate impact on a protected group, the employer must produce evidence of job relatedness to a compliance agency or a court. In order to produce such evidence, selection instruments such as work sample tests should be derived directly from job analysis. If paper-and-pencil "ability tests" are used, they must be correlated with performance measures also derived from job analysis. For example, one court stated: "The cornerstone of the construction of a content-valid examination (an examination of qualifications really needed on the job) is the job analysis."[6] Another court, finding that an employer had violated EEO requirements, said "no attempt was made to analyze jobs in terms of the particular skills they might require."[7]

The 1978 "Uniform Guidelines on Employee Selection Procedures," which has the force of law in employment discrimination cases, states:

> There should be a job analysis which includes an analysis of the important work behavior(s) required for successful performance and their relative importance, and, if the behavior results in work product(s), an analysis of work product(s).[8]

While major EEO concerns focus mainly on selection and performance appraisal, information from job analysis is used in virtually all HR activities, as shown in Exhibit 7-1. Job analysis contributes especially to job evaluation, the process by which an organization determines the relative worth of various jobs. Job evaluation requires that information be collected on compensable factors, the elements that differentiate among jobs. Universal compensable factors, such as knowledge (skill), effort, and responsibility, are often adequately described by the categories of information commonly collected in job analysis.

http://www.pstc.com/
Personnel Systems and Technology Corporation (PSTC) provides an on-line survey that compares job tasks and requirements with personality types and compensation potential.

Besides the consideration of universal factors, job evaluation may also require information on a variety of other factors. Depending on the job evaluation system used, it may be necessary to investigate such factors as controls and guidelines, job complexity, scope and effect, nature and purpose of contacts, problem solving, positions supervised, programs and functions supervised, tools and equipment used, accountability, responsibility, consequence of error, decision making, mental demands, physical demands, and work environment. There are a number of job evaluation systems based on compensable factors, typically using from three to ten factors. An organization should decide which method fits its needs before undertaking a job analysis project.

The conclusion is inescapable—a job analysis must be conducted. An effective and thorough job analysis will ensure not only that the organization has the best possible knowledge of its jobs and therefore the best chance of achieving job performance, but also that it has a legal basis upon which to develop employment practices.

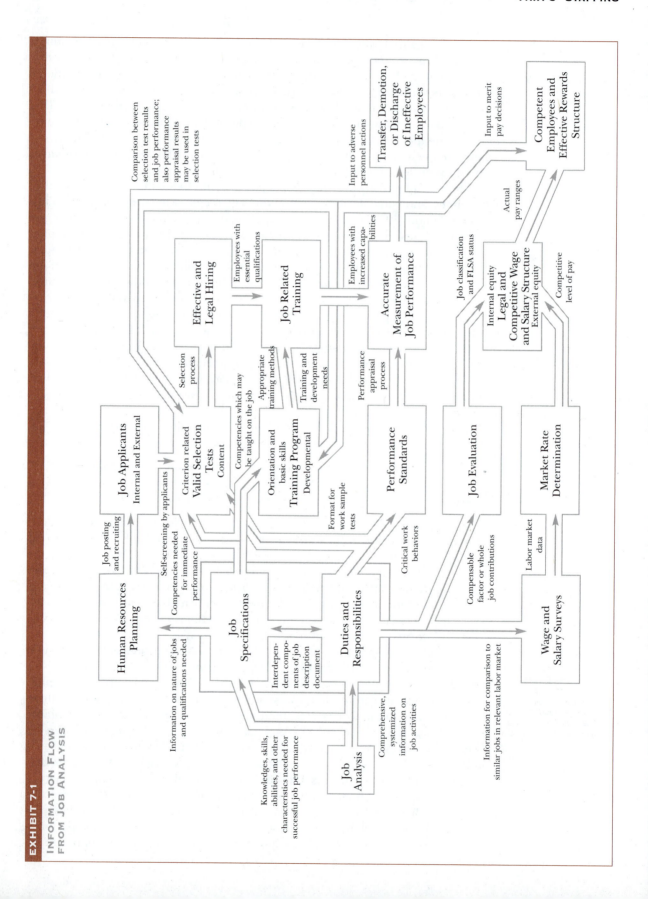

INFORMATION ESSENTIAL TO JOB ANALYSIS

Analysis can be defined as reducing or breaking down a complex whole into its basic parts to discover its true nature or inner relationships. To use a familiar example, consider how an automobile engine is presented in a repair manual. The engine is shown in an exploded view, showing how each part relates to other parts and to its overall function. The process of job analysis produces a fundamentally similar result. Exhibit 7-2 is a highly simplified example of a job analysis for an administrative assistant position in a city manager's office.

Job analysis is a complex process, and different authorities suggest various methods.[9] Whatever approach is selected, certain types of information must be collected. This information can be broken down into work-related information and worker requirements. Work-related information includes job tasks (sometimes referred to as job duties) and job responsibilities (referred to as work behaviors in the EEOC "Guidelines"). Worker requirements include knowledge, skills, abilities, credentials and experience, and other special requirements needed to perform a job.

JOB TASKS

A **task** is a single identifiable job activity. An example of an HR clerk task is "Maintains and updates employee records to document personnel actions and changes in employee status." In job analysis, a task statement must include enough information for a person unfamiliar with the job to understand the nature of the task and the competencies needed to perform the duty. The task statement should clearly describe the operation performed. Also, it is sometimes useful to indicate from whom the assignment or data is obtained and to whom the completed work is given.

Following are typical task statements developed in job analysis work for a county government:

- Diagnoses reason for equipment malfunction and enters commands to correct error or stoppage and resume operations. (Computer Operator)
- Analyzes compensation policies, government regulations, and prevailing wage rates to develop competitive compensation plan. (Human Resources Manager)
- Develops and submits to county commission long-range plans for efficient and economical collection routes and disposal sites. (Solid Waste Control Supervisor)
- Analyzes accounting books and records to determine appropriateness of accounting methods employed and compliance with statutory provisions. (Tax Examiner)
- Answers telephone and gives information to callers, takes messages, or transfers calls to appropriate individuals. (Receptionist)
- Operates a motor grader in digging ditches, grading shoulders, shaping back slopes, shaping driveways, mixing base course, spreading gravel, scarifying, and leveling surfaces. (Equipment Operator)

The job analyst must also make judgments concerning the relative significance of a task. Tasks should be rated as to their importance to the job. A good way to make this determination is to consider the consequence of error. What happens if the task is not performed or is performed poorly? If this would cause a major problem, then the task is probably critical. If poor performance or nonperformance

EXHIBIT 7-2

SIMPLIFIED
EXAMPLE OF A
JOB ANALYSIS
FOR AN
ADMINISTRATIVE
ASSISTANT
POSITION

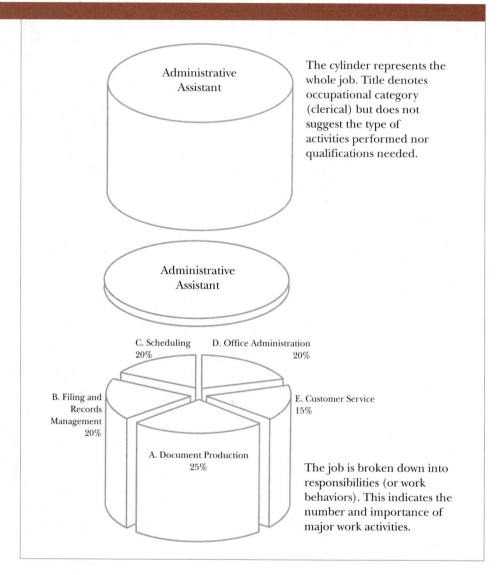

The cylinder represents the whole job. Title denotes occupational category (clerical) but does not suggest the type of activities performed nor qualifications needed.

Administrative Assistant

Administrative Assistant

C. Scheduling 20%   D. Office Administration 20%

B. Filing and Records Management 20%

E. Customer Service 15%

A. Document Production 25%

The job is broken down into responsibilities (or work behaviors). This indicates the number and importance of major work activities.

causes only an inconvenience, then the task is less important. Other factors that should be considered include frequency, complexity, proportion of time spent, and level of difficulty. Actual formats for rating scales normally recognize from two to five degrees of importance. The following example is typical:

1. Of little importance
2. Moderately important
3. Highly important
4. Critical

JOB RESPONSIBILITIES

A job is a collection of related tasks that, when taken together, make up a major part of the job. Job **responsibilities** or **work behaviors** organize and classify duties under

EXHIBIT 7-2 (CONTINUED)

SIMPLIFIED
EXAMPLE OF A
JOB ANALYSIS
FOR AN
ADMINISTRATIVE
ASSISTANT
POSITION

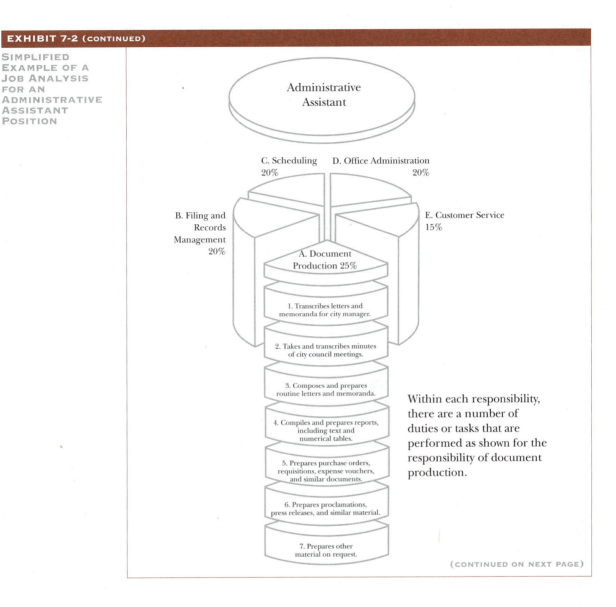

Administrative Assistant

C. Scheduling 20%   D. Office Administration 20%

B. Filing and Records Management 20%

E. Customer Service 15%

A. Document Production 25%

1. Transcribes letters and memoranda for city manager.

2. Takes and transcribes minutes of city council meetings.

3. Composes and prepares routine letters and memoranda.

4. Compiles and prepares reports, including text and numerical tables.

5. Prepares purchase orders, requisitions, expense vouchers, and similar documents.

6. Prepares proclamations, press releases, and similar material.

7. Prepares other material on request.

Within each responsibility, there are a number of duties or tasks that are performed as shown for the responsibility of document production.

(CONTINUED ON NEXT PAGE)

logical headings. Continuing with the example given above, an administrative assistant probably prepares a wide variety of documents from a number of sources. Therefore, the responsibility for these related tasks is "Document Production." A general rule to follow is that jobs have three to eight responsibilities. It is also useful to develop a summary statement describing the responsibility. When these statements include a definition of acceptable job performance, they can be used as performance criteria (see Chapter 11). Shown below is a job responsibility for a supervisor in the public works department of a local government:

Daily Preparation—*Meeting with director, receiving area assignment and special instructions, reviewing work orders, inspecting equipment, tools and supplies, and transporting crew to worksite.*

Another example is one of the responsibilities of a property clerk in the revenue department of a county government:

EXHIBIT 7-2 (CONTINUED)

SIMPLIFIED
EXAMPLE OF A
JOB ANALYSIS
FOR AN
ADMINISTRATIVE
ASSISTANT
POSITION

Credentials

Graduation from post-high school program in secretarial administration or closely related field.

Experience

Office experience with heavy word processing responsibility.

Each task is *linked* to appropriate knowledges, skills, abilities, and other characteristics. Credentials and experience may serve as a substitute mechanism for groups of KSAOs. The process is repeated for all responsibilities.

Knowledges

- Knowledge of modern business communications including style and format of letters, memoranda, minutes, and reports.
- Knowledge of style and format of special purpose documents such as proclamations, legal documents, news releases, and related material.

Skills

- Skill to process verbally transmitted information from original and recorded sources and transcribe accurately.
- Skill to keyboard text material at 60 wpm.
- Skill to use word processing, spreadsheet, and desktop publishing software to produce standard and specially formatted documents.
- Skill in using four-function desk calculator.

Abilities

- Ability to produce neat, accurate properly formatted documents in a timely manner.
- Ability to write in a clear, concise business style using correct grammar and spelling.

Other Characteristics

- Willingness to work overtime and non-standard hours.

A. Document Production 25%

1. Transcribes letters and memoranda for city manager.

2. Takes and transcribes minutes of city council meetings.

3. Composes and prepares routine letters and memoranda.

4. Compiles and prepares reports, including text and numerical tables.

5. Prepares purchase orders, requisitions, expense vouchers, and similar documents.

6. Prepares proclamations, press releases, and similar material.

7. Prepares other material on request.

Business Property Assessment—Mailing forms to county business owners, logging in returned forms, reviewing forms for proper completion, assessing the value of items reported, and entering information into the computer.

A final example is a responsibility for deputy assessor in the same department:

Supervision—Making work assignments, issuing instructions, establishing work goals, leading and directing employees, counseling employees, rating performance, and administering discipline.

The analyst must use proper judgment in establishing and defining responsibilities. A general rule to follow is that a responsibility should account for at least 10 percent of the total job and can be logically defined in a reasonable, unitary sense. This information should be reported as a percentage on the job description. The following are job responsibilities for a representative group of jobs:

- Document production, records management, scheduling, office administration, customer service. (Administrative Assistant)
- Surveying, inspection services, drafting, and computations. (Engineering Assistant)
- Planning and budgeting, organizing, staffing, operations management, and controlling and reporting. (Solid Waste Control Supervisor)
- Preventive patrol, traffic enforcement, apprehension and arrest, records and reports, legal proceedings, community relations. (Police Officer)
- Report preparation, records management, employee services, payroll services, special projects, and public relations. (HR Clerk)

KNOWLEDGES, SKILLS, AND ABILITIES

A person must possess certain knowledges, skills, and abilities (KSAs) to competently perform the various duties that a job requires. Knowledges, skills, and abilities that affect a major part of a job are also referred to as **competencies**.[10] Competencies, therefore, establish the requirements needed to perform a job or a group of activities. Data collected on what competencies are needed to perform a job are used to build a competency model. A **competency model** is a validated decision tool, correlated to job activities, that describes key knowledge, skills, and abilities for performing a specific job. These terms are defined in the "Uniform Guidelines." The definitions of these words are restrictive and more exact than the definitions found in common usage or even in some professional literature:

Knowledge—A body of information applied directly to the performance of a function.
Skill—A present, observable competence to perform a learned psychomotor act.
Ability—A present competence to perform an observable behavior or a behavior which results in an observable product.[11]

It is essential that these definitions be kept in mind when KSAs are identified. Referring again to the HR clerk example, it is useful to set forth the KSAs that are necessary to perform the following duty: "Maintains and updates employee records to document personnel actions and changes in employee status." Knowledge is restricted to information that is directly applied to the work; therefore, it is important to distinguish between what is "nice-to-know" and what is actually needed. For the administrative assistant duty described above, it would be appropriate to specify "Knowledge of policies and practices involved in personnel/human resource activities. This includes recruitment, selection, training, and promotion regulations and procedures; pay programs and benefits packages; labor relations and negotiation strategies; and HR information systems." Skills are work behaviors associated with the actual performance of a job duty. Therefore, we can specify "Skill to organize information by finding ways to structure or classify multiple pieces of information" and "Skill at finding and identifying essential information." Finally, ability is the competence to do a specific task. Thus, "Ability to listen to and understand information and ideas presented through spoken words and sentences" is a legitimate requirement.

Each KSA must be linked to one or more duties. The following are other examples of KSAs that meet the definitions contained in the "Guidelines," beginning with knowledges:

- Knowledge of modern business communications including style and format of letters, memoranda, minutes, and reports. (Administrative Assistant)
- Knowledge of water filtration and treatment including processes, operation of machinery and equipment, and laboratory procedures. (Water Treatment Operator)
- Knowledge of electrical technology including electrical circuits, related accessories and controls, tools and equipment, testing instruments, and safety procedures. (Electrician)
- Knowledge of theories, concepts and methods of comprehensive and regulatory planning including relevant principles of landscape architecture, engineering, building construction, and transportation. (City Planner)

The next examples illustrate skills:

- Skill in the use of surveying equipment such as a level and theodolite to run lines, elevations, and grades. (Engineering Assistant)
- Skill in operating radial arm saw to produce a wide variety of cuts used in cabinet work. (Carpenter)
- Skill in operating an electric arc welder for repairs and fabrication work in different types of metals. (Welder)

The final examples are abilities:

- Ability to plan meals with emphasis on principles of nutrition, management of time, and food budget constraints. (Food Service Supervisor)
- Ability to organize a comprehensive team sports program including leagues and tournaments for all age groups of both genders. (Athletic Supervisor)
- Ability to perform cardiopulmonary resuscitation. (Emergency Medical Technician)

There are other KSAs needed for successful job performance but they cannot be operationally defined like those mentioned previously. These are known as constructs—unobservable traits or characteristics related to work behavior.

- Ability to motivate, communicate with, and lead subordinates in the accomplishment of objectives. (Foreman)
- Ability to learn additions to the tax code relating to the treatment of land use classifications. (Chief Clerk, Tax Assessor's Office)
- Ability to deal with customer complaints. (Administrative Assistant, Solid Waste Department)

It is permissible and desirable to identify constructs in job analysis work. However, the use of constructs in selection tests and other decision areas is subject to further validation.

In describing KSAs, it is important to establish the appropriate level or degree that is needed for successful job performance. Quantitative measures are best, such as "Skill to enter data on a calculator keypad at 6,000 nph (numerals per hour)" or "Skill to keyboard text at 60 wpm with 95 percent accuracy." But this exactness is not always possible, and words such as *substantial knowledge* or *basic skills* are sometimes used. When inexact words are unavoidable, they should be defined and consistently applied. For example, "Substantial knowledge of accounting principles, including the accounting cycle and preparation and analysis of accounting statements" might be defined as knowledge obtained by taking college-level courses. It is often better, however, for the KSA to reflect the nature of the task(s) for which it is intended. For example, "Skill in the use of engine analyzer for diagnosing problems in the electrical systems of automobiles and small trucks."

Finally, KSAs must be rated for importance. The methods used are similar to those used for assessing the importance of tasks. Typical examples are shown below:

How important is this KSA for acceptable job performance?

1. Minimum qualification
2. Desirable qualification; may train on the job
3. Will train on the job

To what degree does this KSA distinguish between superior and adequate performance?

1. Little to none
2. Moderately
3. Considerably
4. Greatly

Can the KSA be learned in a brief orientation period?

1. Yes
2. No

OTHER WORKER REQUIREMENTS

In referring to the entire list of qualifications needed for a job, the abbreviation KSAO is sometimes used, the "O" standing for "Other," including any required work behaviors that do not meet the definition of knowledge, skill, or ability.

The "O" category includes job responsibilities regarding legal requirements, availability requirements, character requirements, and credentials and experience.[12] Legal requirements would include requirements such as potential employees' authority to work in the United States, security clearance to work on certain projects, and/or residency status. Some local governments require employees to live within their jurisdiction. Availability requirements would include willingness to travel, starting date, work schedules, and willingness to work overtime. Character requirements would include background investigations, preemployment drug testing, and work ethic.

The "O" category also includes any degrees, diplomas, certification, and licensure necessary for job performance. These requirements, such as "Possess valid driver's license," should be linked where possible to specific tasks. Quite often, however, they apply to the job as a whole, such as "Graduation from police academy."

A word of caution is in order here, particularly regarding diplomas and degrees. As these requirements are imposed, the number of minority applicants who can qualify for the job decreases. For example, in some situations the requirement of a high school diploma may screen out minority applicants at a disproportionate rate. The requirement of a high school diploma might be justified if:

- There would be serious health or safety consequences if an unqualified applicant was hired.
- There is good, objective documentation that supports the claim that a high school diploma is necessary.
- Qualified applicants are provided with other ways of demonstrating their competence.[13]

If there is no health or safety risk, but merely subjective judgments concerning the need for a diploma, the requirement is not justified.

Much of what has been said about high school diplomas also applies to college degrees. As a general rule, a degree requirement can be justified on the basis of the following factors:

- The job requires knowledge of technical or professional subject matter.
- It is difficult to make a valid assessment of an applicant's absolute qualification, and the degree requirement provides an adequate substitute mechanism.
- The job requires significant exercise of judgment.
- The consequences of hiring an unqualified applicant on the job are severe, especially where public health and safety are involved.[14]

A similar analysis should be made for all types of credentials, and only those that are clearly job related should be included. Some examples: registration as a professional engineer (County Engineer); degree in criminal justice with specialization in youth services from an accredited, four-year institution (Juvenile Probation Officer); magistrate license (Court Clerk).

Experience requirements, particularly when expressed as a certain number of years, also tend to adversely affect minority and female applicants. As with credentials, these requirements must be job related. The following general guidelines are useful when establishing experience requirements:

- The more complex the job, the more reasonable it is to have an experience requirement.
- When recent or extensive experience is a critical measure of competence, such as for attorneys or pilots, the experience requirement may be used more freely.
- Experience requirements should be expressed in terms of type and content, rather than in number of years.[15]

METHODS OF ANALYZING JOBS

Job analysis is not complicated, but it must be done in a systematic, logical manner. Gathering information about jobs can be done in several ways. Four common methods include interviewing employees, observing performance of certain tasks, asking employees to fill in questionnaires and worksheets, and collecting information about a job from secondary sources.[16] Most studies use some elements of each method.[17]

INTERVIEWS

The interview method requires the job analyst to visit the jobsite and talk with the employee who is performing the job. A structured interview form is normally used to record the information. To obtain a complete understanding of the job, it is usually necessary to interview both the employee and the supervisor (often called **subject matter experts** or **SMEs**). The job analyst must decide which information to include as well as its degree of importance. In using this method, the interviewer should be polite and courteous but should not become involved with side issues such as wage classifications, grievances, and alternative work methods. The supervisor should be kept informed and asked to review and verify all information.

http://www.job-analysis.net/
The Job Analysis.Network provides comprehensive information on and forms for conducting job analysis and preparing job descriptions.

Interviewing is time consuming, especially with managerial and professional jobs. During job analysis work for a county government, interviews with entry-level employees (clerk, equipment operator, custodian, etc.) may take no more than 30 minutes; for certain complicated professional jobs (county engineer, tax appraiser), the interviews may take more than one hour. It is usually appropriate to combine the interview with one of the other three methods, both to save time and to provide a check on the information obtained. In many cases, the interview is used as a follow-up in conjunction with a questionnaire or worksheet.

OBSERVATION

In observation, the job analyst watches the individual performing the job and takes notes to describe the duties that are performed. Observation is most appropriate for lower-level, manual labor jobs that have complete, easily observed work cycles. For some types of jobs, this method is impractical. If elements of the work cycle occur at infrequent or unpredictable intervals, the analyst cannot sufficiently record the necessary information, and time becomes a significant factor. This method is not appropriate for professional and managerial jobs because such processes as planning, analyzing, and organizing involve conceptual thinking and cannot be observed.

QUESTIONNAIRES AND WORKSHEETS

Questionnaires and worksheets are probably the least costly and most frequently used methods of collecting job analysis information. A survey instrument is developed and given to employees to complete. Survey instruments may range from standardized to customized questionnaires, depending on the need of the organization. Standardized questionnaires tend to be less expensive to develop and use than customized ones. Customized questionnaires, however, are more useful in gathering detailed information about a job's specific tasks.

There are several specialized questionnaires available. The most widely used is the Position Analysis Questionnaire (PAQ), which consists of a 194-item checklist of job elements that characterize employees' work behaviors and attributes.[18] Another commonly used questionnaire is the Management Position Description Questionnaire (MPDQ).[19] This instrument provides information about managerial activities, responsibilities, demands, and restrictions. Task Analysis, developed by the U.S. Department of Labor, studies workers' traits, functions, and work areas.[20]

A questionnaire method that specifically addresses the requirements of the "Uniform Guidelines" is known as GOJA, an acronym for Guidelines Oriented Job Analysis.[21] This method was developed in 1974 by Richard E. Biddle and has been periodically refined and updated. The GOJA method has been successfully used with numerous public and private employees.

There are two problems associated with questionnaires and worksheets. One is that many survey instruments are often ambiguous and difficult for a typical employee

Job analysis, although one of the most powerful and useful of HR exercises, often comes out flawed because the process is poorly carried out. Here are 10 of the most frequently occurring wrong ways to go about analyzing jobs.

<table>
<tr><td>

WHAT GOES WRONG/RIGHT IN JOB ANALYSIS?

</td><td>

1. No training and motivation for subjects.
2. Employees not allowed enough time to complete analysis.
3. Using a single means and source for gathering data.

</td></tr>
</table>

4. Top management support is missing.
5. Supervisor and subordinate do not participate in the design of the job analysis exercise.
6. Focus on what is rather than what should be.
7. Activities distorted for self-interest.
8. Data not tested for reliability and validity.
9. Weak format for data collection.
10. Job analysis not built into manager's or employee's job descriptions.

The right ways, of course, are the converse of each wrong way. An overall approach to job analysis that may have considerable payoff is having analysts adopt the methodologies of methods and time study engineers. If the job analysts adopted such methods, they could produce more valid and reliable data. The disciplined statistical methods of the engineer could help move job analysis out of the Dark Ages and establish the process as one of scientific rigor.

Source: Adapted from Phillip C. Grant, "What Use Is a Job Description?" *Personnel Journal* 67 (February 1988), 44–53.

to complete. Another problem is that employees may be unwilling or unable to provide accurate responses. Therefore, careful attention must be paid to survey instrument design. Employees who are asked to complete questionnaires and worksheets should receive detailed, item-by-item instructions. Follow-up interviews and observations are usually also necessary. Even with these disadvantages, questionnaires and worksheets are efficient ways to collect a wide variety of information in a short time.

An improved worksheet developed and tested by the authors provides employees with responsibilities that are normally associated with the type of job being analyzed. This procedure alleviates a common problem found in job analysis work—employees often find it very difficult to adequately cover their duties unless a structured format is available. Consider an individual in a secretarial position who is simply asked to provide a list of tasks. In regard to keyboarding, the response may be, "types correspondence, reports, and other documents," followed by other typical duties dealing with different aspects of the job in the same general way. Such information is not particularly useful; perhaps 90 percent of all administrative assistant jobs involve this activity. We still do not know, for example:

- What is the source material for correspondence—dictation, handwritten notes, or standard formats?
- Does the administrative assistant compose any correspondence?
- What is the nature of the correspondence?
- What kinds of reports are prepared?
- Does the administrative assistant compile the reports?
- Do the reports contain numerical tables?
- What are the other documents?
- How important are the various keyboarding duties?
- How often are the various keyboarding duties performed?

In fact, as many as 10 task statements might be needed to adequately cover just the responsibility of keyboarding. By providing a format with responsibility definitions identified, the analyst is much more likely to get a comprehensive and useful response. Exhibit 7-3 shows sections of a job analysis worksheet for clerical classifications. The same approach is used for other categories such as labor, trades and crafts, law enforcement, fire protection, managerial, and so forth.

The use of questionnaires and worksheets can minimize the involvement of a professional analyst and reduce the cost of job analysis. As described previously, established formats for designing questionnaires and worksheets are available. However, after responses have been collected, translating the information into an acceptable written job description is a time-consuming task, requiring the attention of trained personnel. In the interview and observation methods of job analysis, the translation task is much less difficult. The job analyst can record information as it will appear on the job description, thereby simplifying its later use.

SECONDARY DATA

http://www.doleta.gov/ programs/onet/
The Occupational Information Network (O*NET) contains comprehensive information on job requirements and worker competencies.

The three methods described previously depend on contact with a person who actually performs the job. Often, however, it may be necessary to conduct a job analysis before establishing a position or to analyze a vacant position. One approach is to use one or more of the three methods to analyze a similar job in another organization. Another possibility is to establish the responsibilities of the job and list the tasks that are typically performed. The KSAOs requirements are then logically decided. It is also useful to review the Occupational Information Network or O*NET. The U.S. Department of Labor's O*NET provides a comprehensive database system for collecting, organizing, describing, and disseminating data on job tasks and responsibilities.[22] O*Net provides a national benchmark that offers a common language for all users of occupational information. O*NET is intended to replace the Dictionary of Occupational Titles (DOT) which will no longer be published.[23] O*NET's content model for describing jobs, depicted in Exhibit 7-4 on page 145, includes worker requirements, worker characteristics, occupation characteristics, occupation-specific requirements, occupational requirements, and experience requirements.

http://www.oalj.dol.gov/ libdot.htm
The Dictionary of Occupational Titles (DOT) provides basic occupational information for both public and private sectors of the U.S. economy.

An example of an O*NET listing for Human Resources Manager is shown in Exhibit 7-5 on page 146.

DEVELOPING JOB DESCRIPTIONS

Job descriptions, derived from job analysis, provide comprehensive information on the various jobs within an organization. If job descriptions are not based on job analysis, the documents will provide only a general idea of the nature of various jobs, and they will be of limited use in such important areas as selection and promotion. Unfortunately, many organizations fail to do the basic analytical work that is essential for good job descriptions. These organizations run two risks. The first is that the efficiency and effectiveness of the organization will be impaired. The second is that systemic discrimination, inherent in non-job-related employment practices, will result in EEO liability. The point is this: if the organization is not willing to invest time and resources in job analysis, the writing of job descriptions may be futile.

NATURE OF JOB DESCRIPTIONS

Job descriptions provide identifying information about the job, summarize the nature of the job, outline the major duties and responsibilities involved, and define

EXHIBIT 7-3

**SECTIONS OF A
JOB ANALYSIS
WORKSHEET FOR
CLERICAL
CLASSIFICATIONS**

Part I: IDENTIFICATION
[Incumbent provides name, job title, department, etc.]

Part II: RESPONSIBILITIES
Listed below are responsibilities (major areas of work) normally associated with your type of job. A general description of each responsibility is included. Not all responsibilities may be part of your job while others not listed may. Blank spaces are provided for you to identify and describe responsibilities that are not listed. Check responsibilities which apply to your job and indicate the percentage of your job accounted for by each responsibility checked.

( ) **Office Management**—Planning and coordinating office systems and procedures such as personnel, budgets, data processing and workflow and/or the supervision of other employees.   ____%
( ) **Document Production**—Taking material from a variety of sources and producing documents using a computer and various software applications.   ____%
( ) **Reception**—Receiving visitors, answering the telephone, and either providing information or routing callers and visitors.   ____%

.   .
.   .
.   .

( ) **Research/Analysis**—Determining the type of information required, obtaining the needed data, performing data reduction, organizing information in the correct format, and reporting findings.   ____%
( ) **Other**— _____
_____   ____%
                                                                 100%

Part III: JOB TASKS
At the top of the forms in this section, write the responsibilities that you identified in Part II. These responsibilties will be identified as A, B, C, etc., with the responsibility accounting for the highest part of your job listed first. Under appropriate responsibility list the tasks you perform. These will be 1, 2, 3, etc. Indicate how frequently each task is performed. Daily = D; Weekly = W; Monthly = M; Quarterly = Q; Semiannually = SA; Annually = A. Write in other intervals if appropriate. Indicate the importance of each task. If failure to perform the task properly would create a severe problem, the task is critical. If failure to perform the task would create an inconvenience, the task is important. Critical = 2; Important = 1.

Responsibility A. _____

List the tasks you perform as part of this responsibility	Freq.	Imp.
1.		
2.		
3.		
4.		
5.		
6.		
continues with 7–10		

Source: Adapted from Richard E. Biddle, *Guidelines Oriented Job Analysis* (Sacramento: Biddle and Associates, 1976).

EXHIBIT 7-4

O*NET CONTENT MODEL

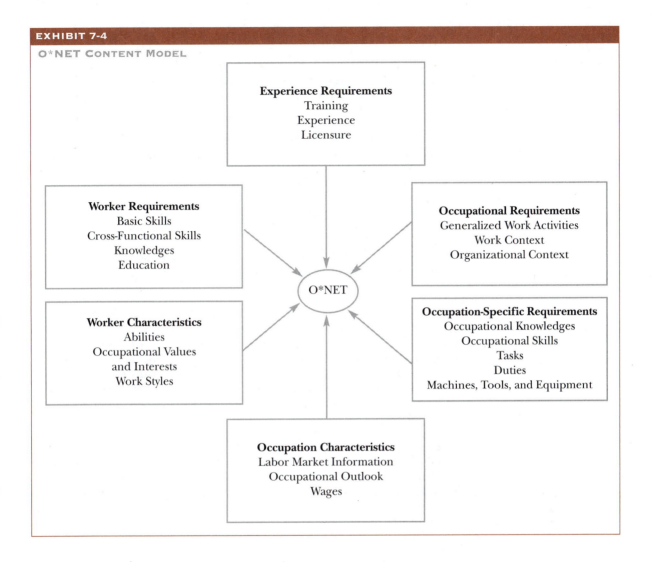

the qualifications required for holding the job. Accurate, complete, and up-to-date job descriptions are critical source documents for designing compensation programs. They are also used to establish performance standards for a job.

Job descriptions should be distinguished from class specifications, which define the tasks and qualifications of a type of job or a group of jobs at the same level in an organization. A sample job description for a Lead Water Treatment Plant Operator is presented in Exhibit 7-6 on page 149.

Job specifications, also referred to as competencies, are an important part of a job description. Instead of describing what an employee does in a particular job, competencies outline what an applicant must be able to do before being hired. In other words, competencies establish the requirements needed to perform a job. Competencies are composed of knowledge, skills, abilities, and others (KSAOs) needed to perform job tasks. Competencies are used in compensation, hiring decisions, orientation and training programs, and information provided to employees who want to upgrade their qualifications for promotion. Competencies are the foundation for competency-based pay systems including knowledge-based and skill-

EXHIBIT 7-5

**O*NET
OCCUPATIONAL
PROFILE: HUMAN
RESOURCES
MANAGERS
(13005A)**

Plan, direct, and coordinate human resource management activities of an organization to maximize the strategic use of human resources and maintain functions such as employee compensation, recruitment, personnel policies, and regulatory compliance.

Abilities

Some of the important abilities for Human Resources Managers include:

- Written Comprehension—The ability to read and understand information and ideas presented in writing
- Oral Comprehension—The ability to listen to and understand information and ideas presented through spoken words and sentences
- Speech Clarity—The ability to speak clearly so that it is understandable to a listener
- Written Expression—The ability to communicate information and ideas in writing so others will understand
- Oral Expression—The ability to communicate information and ideas in speaking so others will understand

Interests

The primary interests of most people who like being Human Resources Managers include:

- Enterprising—Enterprising occupations frequently involve starting up and carrying out projects. These occupations can involve leading people and making many decisions. Sometimes they require risk taking and often deal with business.
- Social—Social occupations frequently involve working with, communicating with, and teaching people. These occupations often involve helping or providing service to others.

Work Values

Some of the work values important to people who like being Human Resources Managers include:

- Achievement—Look for jobs that let you use your best abilities. Look for work where you can see the results of your efforts. Explore jobs where you can get the feeling of accomplishment.
- Independence—Look for jobs where they let you do things on your own initiative. Explore work where you can make decisions on your own.

Skills

Some of the important skills for Human Resources Managers include:

- Management of Personnel Resources—Motivating, developing, and directing people as they work, identifying the best people for the job
- Speaking—Talking to others to effectively convey information
- Writing—Communicating effectively with others in writing as indicated by the needs of audience
- Reading Comprehension—Understanding written sentences and paragraphs in work-related documents
- Problem Identification—Identifying the nature of problems
- Visioning—Developing an image of how a system should work under ideal conditions

Knowledges

Some of the important knowledges for Human Resources Managers include:

- Personnel and Human Resources—Knowledge of policies and practices involved in personnel/human resource functions. This includes recruitment, selection, training, and promotion regulations and procedures; compensation and benefits packages; labor relations and negotiation strategies; and personnel information systems.

EXHIBIT 7-5 (CONTINUED)

O*NET
OCCUPATIONAL
PROFILE: HUMAN
RESOURCES
MANAGERS
(13005A)

- Administration and Management—Knowledge of principles and processes involved in business and organizational planning, coordination, and execution. This includes strategic planning, resource allocation, manpower modeling, leadership techniques, and production methods.
- Mathematics—Knowledge of numbers, their operations, and interrelationships including arithmetic, algebra, geometry, calculus, statistics, and their applications.
- English Language—Knowledge of the structure and content of the English language including the meaning and spelling of words, rules of composition, and grammar.

Job Zone

To help you understand how much preparation is needed to perform this occupation, it has been placed into one of five Job Zones. A Job Zone summarizes the experience, education and training usually required for an occupation.

Human Resources Managers:

Job Zone Four: Considerable Preparation Needed

Overall Experience	A minimum of two to four years of work-related skill, knowledge, or experience is needed for these occupations. For example, an accountant must complete four years of college and work for several years in accounting to be considered qualified.
Education	Most of these occupations require a four-year bachelor's degree, but some do not.
Job Training	Employees in these occupations usually need several years of work-related experience, on-the-job training, and/or vocational training.
Job Zone 4 Examples	Many of these occupations involve coordinating, supervising, managing, or training others. Examples include accountants, chefs and head cooks, computer programmers, historians, pharmacists, and police detectives.

Generalized Work Activities

Some of the important generalized work activities Human Resources Managers may perform include:
- Performing Administrative Activities—Approving requests, handling paperwork, and performing day-to-day administrative tasks.
- Communicating with Other Workers—Providing information to supervisors, fellow workers, and subordinates. This information can be exchanged face-to-face, in writing, or via telephone/electronic transfer.
- Staffing Organizational Units—Recruiting, interviewing, selecting, hiring, and promoting persons for the organization.
- Judging Qualities of Things, Services, People—Making judgments about or assessing the value, importance, or quality of things or people.
- Developing Objectives and Strategies—Establishing long-range objectives and specifying the strategies and actions to achieve these objectives.
- Getting Information Needed to Do the Job—Observing, receiving, and otherwise obtaining information from all relevant sources.
- Resolving Conflict, Negotiating with Others—Handling complaints, arbitrating disputes, and resolving grievances, or otherwise negotiating with others.

EXHIBIT 7-5 (CONTINUED)

O*NET
OCCUPATIONAL
PROFILE: HUMAN
RESOURCES
MANAGERS
(13005A)

- Implementing Ideas, Programs, etc.—Conducting or carrying out work procedures and activities in accord with one's own ideas or information provided through directions/instructions for purposes of installing, modifying, preparing, delivering, constructing, integrating, finishing, or completing programs, systems, structures, or products.
- Analyzing Data or Information—Identifying underlying principles, reasons, or facts by breaking down information or data into separate parts.
- Evaluating Information Against Standards—Evaluating information against a set of standards and verifying that it is correct.

Some of the important occupation-specific tasks Human Resources Managers may perform include:
- Formulates policies and procedures for recruitment, testing, placement, classification, orientation, benefits, and labor and industrial relations.
- Plans, directs, supervises, and coordinates work activities of subordinates and staff relating to employment, compensation, labor relations, and employee relations.
- Directs preparation and distribution of written and verbal information to inform employees of benefits, compensation, and personnel policies.
- Evaluates and modifies benefits policies to establish competitive programs and to ensure compliance with legal requirements.
- Analyzes compensation policies, government regulations, and prevailing wage rates to develop competitive compensation plan.
- Develops methods to improve employment policies, processes, and practices and recommends changes to management.
- Prepares personnel forecast to project employment needs.
- Prepares budget for personnel operations.
- Prepares and delivers presentations and reports to corporate officers or other management regarding human resource management policies and practices and recommendations for change.
- Negotiates bargaining agreements and resolves labor disputes.

Source: Adapted from O*NET, "O*NET Occupational Profile: Human Resources Managers," *http://www. doleta.gov/programs/onet* (December 1, 2000).

based pay. A growing trend in writing job descriptions is to focus exclusively on key competencies for a job.

The usefulness of job descriptions in carrying out various HR activities is indicated in the following examples, listing questions that typically must be answered in order to accomplish the activity satisfactorily. In each case, answers to the questions are either directly available in or derived from the job description.

DESIGNING A SELECTION PLAN FOR A POSITION

- Which competencies (KSAOs) are needed for immediate job performance and thus are minimum qualifications for the job?
- Which competencies (KSAOs) can be learned during orientation or acquired during a training program without having a detrimental effect on job performance?
- Are there competencies (KSAOs) that can be tested or measured by a simulation of the job and thus provide the basis for content validity?

IDENTIFICATION

Job Title: Lead Water Treatment Plant Operator

Department: Utilities

Location: Water Treatment Plant

FLSA Status: Non-exempt

Code: 51-8031.00

Reports to: Division Director

JOB SUMMARY

Performs difficult and complex work in operating and controlling water treatment plant. Monitors control panel, conducts on-site observations, and interprets gauge readings and tests; adjusts gates and valves and starts and stops pumps to regulate water flow; and maintains log of operations. Takes samples of water piped in or collects by hand, performs appropriate laboratory tests according to prescribed procedures, records test results, and submits reports. Performs scheduled maintenance of pumps, generators, and related equipment, repairs or replaces parts using hand or power tools; tests repaired equipment and maintains records. Follows and enforces safety rules and procedures, corrects and reports unsafe behaviors and working conditions, participates on safety committee, administers first aid, implements emergency procedures, and assists in investigations. Attends training and studies technical literature to maintain technical competence, assumes responsibility for operating plant in absence of Division Director, and conducts on-the-job and formal training of lower-level operators. Performs grounds maintenance and housekeeping tasks, maintains vehicles and equipment, performs light building maintenance services, supervises or performs work on distribution system, and performs related tasks as required.

RESPONSIBILITIES AND TASKS

A. Plant Operations (30%)—Monitors control panel, conducts on-site observations, and interprets meter and gauge readings and tests to determine operating conditions. Adjusts gates and valves manually or by remote control and starts and stops pumps to control flow of water from river through temporary storage, chemical feed, rapid mix, flocculator, settling basin, filters, post chemical, clear well, and delivery to water mains and storage tanks. Makes decisions regarding plant operations in unusual/non-routine situations or emergencies. Maintains log of operations and records meter and gauge readings.

B. Laboratory Testing (15%)—Takes samples of water piped in to laboratory or collects by hand. Using laboratory equipment performs alkalinity, pH, carbon dioxide, chlorine, iron, manganese, fluoride, saturation, turbidity, total hardness, calcium hardness, color and phosphate tests of raw , semiprocessed, or processed water according to procedures set forth by state regulations. May assist with or perform tests on wastewater. Records test results, maintains records, and submits reports as required.

C. Equipment Maintenance (15%)—Performs scheduled maintenance of pumps, generators and related water plant equipment. Cleans precipitates, such as grit, sludge and debris from processing tanks and basins. Periodically washes and backwashes filters. Observes/listens to operation of equipment and machinery to locate problems. May disassemble pumps and similar equipment as necessary to diagnose malfunction and gain access to and remove defective parts. May repair or replace parts, using hand and power tools. May remove entire equipment or major assembly for repair by vendor. Starts and tests repaired equipment to ensure proper performance. May initiate requisitions for parts or equipment. Maintains appropriate maintenance records.

EXHIBIT 7-6 (CONTINUED)

JOB DESCRIPTION

D. Safety Management (15%)—Follows safety procedures and rules applying to chemicals, plant machinery and equipment; earth-moving equipment, vehicles, and hand and power tools and equipment. Ensures that lower-level operators are familiar with safety procedures and rules. Ensures that safety posters are displayed in appropriate locations. Monitors safety performance of lower-level operators and ensures that operators wear personal protective equipment (PPE) as required. Corrects unsafe acts as necessary and records nature of act, time and date; may refer serious or repeated violations of safety rules to Director for disciplinary action. Monitors workplace for unsafe working conditions and makes corrections or reports condition as appropriate and shuts down operation if necessary. Follows up to ensure that condition is corrected. Participates in activities of safety committee as required. Administers emergency first aid in case of accident and follows procedures to ensure injured person receives medical care. Participates in investigation of accidents and "near misses;" assists in the preparation of accident reports.

E. Lead Responsibilities (15%)—Maintains and improves knowledge and skills through reading technical literature, self study, attending workshops, and/or taking academic courses. Assumes responsibility for operation of water plant in absence of Division Director. Assists in preparing work schedules. May assign tasks to workers. Conducts on-the-job training of lower-level operators and other employees. May instruct classes in operation and maintenance of plant machines and equipment and safety and laboratory procedures. Assists lower-level operators in preparing for certification exams.

F. Services to Department (10%)—Cuts grass, trims shrubbery, picks up debris, hoses down walkways and performs related grounds maintenance tasks. Sweeps floors, washes and puts away laboratory equipment, and performs related housekeeping tasks. Performs preventive maintenance services on assigned vehicles and equipment. Performs light building maintenance services, including painting and minor electrical and mechanical repairs. Supervises or performs troubleshooting, repair, maintenance, or installation work on water distribution system as required. Performs additional tasks as assigned or upon request.

JOB SPECIFICATIONS

Knowledges, Skills and Abilities
Substantial knowledge of water treatment including processes, operation and maintenance of machinery and equipment, and laboratory testing procedures. Knowledge of organization and operating procedures of Utilities Department. Knowledge of municipal water treatment and distribution system. Knowledge of city procedures and work rules. Knowledge of federal and state regulations. Knowledge of safety management, including safety procedures and rules, protective equipment, inspection techniques, control measures, accident investigation and research, first aid and emergency procedures. Reading skills to comprehend maps, blueprints, procedures, regulations, technical manuals, and related highly complex documents. Writing skills to prepare forms and records, memoranda, reports, schedules, and similar documents. Math skills to solve problems involving percentages, proportions, rates, chemical formulas, and algebraic equations. Mechanical skills to use specialized tools in testing, maintaining, and repairing equipment. Computer skills to keyboard data and use word processing, spreadsheet, database, and specialized water systems programs, including SCAD to prepare documents, manage data, and generate reports. Laboratory skills to perform chemical and physical tests. Verbal communications skills to speak to individuals and small groups, talk on telephone and two-way radio. Instructional skills to conduct

EXHIBIT 7-6 (CONTINUED)

JOB DESCRIPTION

training. Leadership skills to direct and motivate employees. Ability to apply technical knowledge to make correct operational decisions. Ability to work independently.

Credentials and Experience
Have two (2) years of post high school training in water systems technology or equivalent combination of training and experience. Meet certification and experience requirements established by state regulations for high filtration rate operator.

Special Requirements
Be willing to comply with city policies and work rules. Be willing to work during non-duty hours, holidays, and weekends when necessary to achieve goals. Be willing to travel overnight to attend and participate in meetings and activities.

APPROVALS

Kellie Sullivan	Division Director	November 9, 2000
Name	Title	Date

Tom Porter	City Manager	November 11, 2000
Name	Title	

- Which competencies (KSAOs) cannot be tested or measured without further validation?
- How many tests or selection procedures are needed to adequately cover the job?
- Are there physical characteristics listed that can be modified or reduced to make reasonable accommodations for applicants with disabilities?
- Which other characteristics, such as diplomas, licenses, and certifications, are needed for immediate job performance, and which can be acquired on the job?

DESIGNING A PERFORMANCE APPRAISAL SYSTEM FOR A JOB

- What are the major critical work behaviors of the job?
- In writing performance criteria, when is it possible to use quantitative measures and when will it be necessary to use subjective judgment?
- How should various performance criteria be weighted?
- What type of performance appraisal instrument should be developed to best provide consistent, reliable data?

DESIGNING AN ORIENTATION AND TRAINING PROGRAM

- Can the boundaries of the job be explained to a new employee?
- What constitutes an effective orientation program for the job?
- What various kinds of training are needed to provide the necessary competencies (KSAOs) for long-term performance?

MAKING COMPENSATION DECISIONS

- Can the job be evaluated on its content in relation to other jobs in the organization?
- How can the organization be certain that it is collecting valid information on the rates being paid for comparable jobs by other organizations?
- Can the job be properly classified?
- What is the status of the job in regard to the minimum wage and overtime provisions of the Fair Labor Standards Act?
- Can the organization defend its pay practices and decisions to its employees and to third parties?

It is clear that job descriptions must be comprehensively based on job analyses if they are to contribute as they should to selection, performance appraisal, training, and compensation. The common practice, unfortunately, is for organizations to develop job descriptions mainly for use in pay programs. Job analysis data, if it exists at all, is normally maintained separately.

COVERAGE UNDER THE FAIR LABOR STANDARDS ACT

When preparing job descriptions, local governments must now be concerned with the provisions of the Fair Labor Standards Act of 1938 as amended. This act, which includes minimum wage and overtime requirements, is now applicable to units of local government. All employees are covered unless specifically excluded by the law or made exempt from certain provisions.

Many types of workers are not covered under FLSA, although only a few should directly concern state and local governments. If a worker is not covered, the employer need not be concerned about federal minimum wage and overtime laws, nor need the employer keep wage records. However, state laws may still apply.

The FLSA definition of employee excludes any individual who is not subject to civil service laws who holds public office; is selected by a public officeholder to be a member of his or her personal staff; is appointed by an elected public officeholder to serve on a policy-making level; or is an immediate legal advisor to an elected public officeholder.[24]

Other employees may be exempt from certain provisions of the act. The most important exemptions for units of government are executive, administrative, and professional employees.[25] Exemptions are determined by duties actually performed rather than by job descriptions. However, properly written job descriptions based on job analysis provide excellent documentation in justifying various exemptions. When the job description is written, the FLSA status should be indicated as Not Covered, Exempt, Partially Exempt, or Non-Exempt, depending on the situation. For additional information on the FLSA, see Chapter 13.

COVERAGE UNDER THE AMERICANS WITH DISABILITIES ACT

The Americans with Disabilities Act of 1990 (ADA) has had a major impact on job analysis and job descriptions. As Chapter 3 states, ADA prohibits discrimination in employment against a qualified person—in regard to any employment practice or term, condition, and privilege of employment—because that person has a disability that limits one or more of the major life activities, has a record of such impairment, or is regarded as having such an impairment. To comply with ADA, local governments should identify essential and marginal job functions through job analysis and include this information on written job descriptions. Essential job functions are those that are central to the performance of a job—the job could not be performed if these functions did not occur. Marginal job functions are those that are peripheral to the performance of a job—a reasonable accommodation should be provided to persons covered under ADA. This information can prove to be critical in defending against allegations of discrimination and failure to provide a reasonable accommodation.

FORMAT AND STYLE FOR JOB DESCRIPTIONS

There is no universally agreed upon format for job descriptions. Different organizations and different consultants use a wide variety of formats; however, virtually all of them include certain critical data elements.[26]

IDENTIFICATION

The identification section of the job description provides information needed for administrative, record-keeping, and legal functions and logically includes the following elements:

JOB TITLE. The title should describe both the nature and level of the work performed. Titles such as mechanic, clerk, and equipment operator indicate the general nature of the work. Other parts of the title, such as head mechanic, senior clerk, or equipment operator III, indicate the level of skill or responsibility. It is often helpful to include the organizational component in which the job is located, such as tax appraisal clerk. Titles should be acceptable to the worker and not demeaning. Examples of demeaning titles include "common laborer" or "junior forester." It is also important not to use titles that overstate the importance of the work. For example, a janitorial position might be titled building custodian but not sanitation engineer. Job titles that imply the gender of the incumbent, such as copy girl or office boy, should always be avoided. Some authorities recommend a total purge of gen-

---

A recent study found over 132 managerial uses for job descriptions. However, most managers use job descriptions for only 2 or 3 uses, if at all. The most common uses are for recruiting employees, orienting employees, and designing jobs. Listed below are 10 things local governments can do to make job descriptions more useful.

MAKING JOB DESCRIPTIONS MORE USEFUL

1. Train managers how to use job descriptions in managing their human resources.
2. Ensure job descriptions are comprehensive, specific, and detailed.
3. Ensure job descriptions are accurate.
4. Emphasize the utility of job descriptions as a planning tool.
5. Write job descriptions so that they are prescriptive of what should be done, not descriptive of what is done.
6. Structure job descriptions so that tasks are grouped under major responsibilities.
7. Ensure job descriptions are up to date.
8. Use a standardized format for all job descriptions.
9. Collect and bind all job descriptions into one volume or media format.
10. Make job descriptions easily assessable and available.

By following these recommendations, local governments will be better able to realize the benefits of developing and writing job descriptions.

Source: Adapted from Philip C. Grant, "Why Job Descriptions Are Not Used More," *Supervision* 59 (April 1998), 10–13.

der, so that draftsman, for example, becomes drafter; others contend that the suffix -*man* in most cases does not imply gender.

PLACEMENT. This information indicates where the job is placed in the organizational structure. The wording and number of levels needed will depend on the type and size of the organization. In a large unit of government, complete identification might require division, department, and section.

LOCATION. This may include geographical, building, or other physical location; it is usually unwise to include office number or work station, as these are subject to frequent change.

FLSA STATUS. This information is needed in various pay program decisions. Where jobs are exempt, it is useful to state the type of exemption; e.g., Exempt (Administrative).

JOB CODE. This permits the referencing of all jobs. It may consist of letters and numbers in any combination. An example is the O*NET code. The job of Human Resources Manager would be coded as 13500A:

> The structure of O*NET is based on the Occupational Employment Statistics (OES) classification system of the Bureau of Labor Statistics. It has been expanded through O*NET research to provide more detailed information on certain occupations.
>
> O*NET codes are similar to five-digit OES codes with more detailed information on particular occupations indicated by the addition of a sixth alphabetic character.
>
> As the revision of the Standard Occupational Classification (SOC) is implemented, O*NET's classification structure will evolve to reflect that new system.

SALARY OR WAGE CATEGORY. This may indicate the specific salary range or pay grade, as appropriate.

POINTS. If a quantitative job evaluation system is used, this element provides for the number of points assigned.

JOB ANALYST. This is the person who was in charge of collecting and/or verifying the information and who wrote the job description. Because both supervisors and employees may be influenced by personal motives, it is preferable to use independent job analysts.

DATE. This establishes the time when the job was analyzed.

REPORTING RELATIONSHIP. This identifies the supervisor to whom the worker reports. In some formats the title of the immediate supervisor is identified in the job summary.

Other elements that are sometimes found in this section are internal and external contacts, signatories, and date of approval. These should be included if they are not covered in another section. Finally, the organization may need to include a category for EEO/AAP planning, record keeping, and reporting.

JOB SUMMARY

The job summary should be written after other sections of the description have been completed. This section gives the reader a clear picture of the job and differentiates among its major functions. It is useful to preface the job summary with a phrase that indicates the level of supervisory controls,[27] similar to the examples shown below:

- **Under Immediate Supervision**—Work is assigned at frequent intervals and performance is checked regularly.
- **Under General Supervision**—Standard practices enable the employee to proceed alone to other duties, referring questionable cases to a supervisor.
- **Under Direction**—Definite objectives require use of a wide range of procedures; employee plans and organizes own work, referring only unusual cases to supervisor.
- **Under General Direction**—Works from policies and procedures and general direction with little functional guidance, referring only policy issues to superior.
- **Under Guidelines Set by Policy**—Establishes own standard of performance within overall policies and budgetary limits with direct accountability for final results.

The body of the summary should include clear, concise statements that define major responsibilities of the job itself. The job summary must stand alone, since it is used in job posting, evaluation, salary surveys, or wherever a thumbnail sketch of the job is required.

ESSENTIAL RESPONSIBILITIES AND TASKS

Obtained from the job analysis, duties and responsibilities are task or duty statements grouped under appropriate responsibilities. They should be written in the appropriate style and arranged in a logical order, such as sequence of performance, amount of time allotted to each, and relative importance. Job descriptions should indicate which tasks are essential and which are marginal. Because a job description will not always contain a list of all duties performed, an elastic clause should be included in all job descriptions. The following example combines an elastic clause with an essential tasks statement:

> *Essential job tasks unless otherwise indicated as marginal (m). This job description is not intended to be exhaustive, and other closely related or similar tasks within the department may be assigned.*

JOB SPECIFICATIONS

Included in the job specifications section are knowledges, skills, abilities, and other (KSAOs), certification and experience, and special requirements. In writing these items, it is again important to refer to the job analysis. Job qualifications should not be overstated, particularly in regard to education and experience requirements.

This section should also include statements about the job and conditions of work that are used in the organization's evaluation system but that are not explicitly covered elsewhere, such as contacts, supervisory controls, efforts, and working conditions. The number of items that should be included will depend on the particular system.

SIGNATURES

It is a good idea to indicate by signatures that the job description was reviewed and approved by line management and, if appropriate, the HR department. Each signatory should refer to job analysis data to ensure that the job is described adequately and accurately and that the job specifications are realistic and defensible.

WRITING STYLE IN JOB DESCRIPTIONS

Job descriptions should be written in brief and clear sentences. The basic structure for sentences in a job description should be "implied subject/verb/object/explanatory phrase." The implied subject of each sentence is the person or persons occupying the job. The verb is usually present tense. For example, "Develops annual operating budgets for solid waste department." The explanatory phrase tells how, when, or where the tasks are performed. In some cases, explanatory phrases are needed for other purposes, such as indicating from whom or where the assignment is obtained and to whom the completed work is given. The sentence above illustrates telegraphic style, which eliminates unnecessary articles and words.

To enhance the clarity of job descriptions, it is important to define words that may have more than one interpretation, such as *some*, *great*, and *substantial*. It is better to use examples to clarify meanings. Proprietary names should be avoided—they are subject to change, and their inclusion will require frequent rewriting. It is important to avoid any terminology that states or implies the sex of the person or persons assigned to the job.

THE CLASS SPECIFICATION

Rather than describe an individual job, a **class specification** describes a group of jobs that are similar in responsibilities and tasks, have the same entrance requirements, and receive the same rate of pay.[28] For instance, lead operators in the water division of the utilities department might all be in the class entitled "Water Systems Operator IV," shown in Exhibit 7-7. The class specification is used primarily in classification and compensation management. A properly developed class specification serves as an unambiguous criterion against which to compare jobs to establish the class level or grade for pay purposes. Unfortunately, many organizations do not develop job descriptions, and use class specifications as the sole source documents for such activities as selection and appraisal. This is unwise because not enough information is provided to make sound decisions. Moreover, a class specification is

---

Job descriptions should include an elastic clause. An elastic clause states that the employee will perform the duties of the job as outlined in the job description, and other duties as assigned. What happens, however, when duties of a job change so frequently that they entail more of "other duties as assigned" than what is actually described?

FROM JOB DESCRIPTIONS TO ROLE DESCRIPTIONS?

Workforce structures and technology are changing at such a quick pace that by the time job descriptions are written they are often out of date. Traditional job descriptions may lack the flexibility needed to meet today's organizational needs. Many organizations are constantly reinventing themselves in order to stay competitive and to meet the needs of their customers.

Further, many employees are thriving in today's constantly changing organizational climate. Employee flexibility, learning new skills, and taking on new duties is critical to organizational success. According to the Herman Group, a well-known management consulting firm, these changes may result in the demise of the traditional job description. In its place, the Herman Group envisions role descriptions that state in general terms, an employee's job is to help the organization succeed. That is, employees are expected to help out wherever they are needed, to develop a broader set of competencies, and to be diligent in satisfying internal and external customer needs. Will the Herman Group's prediction come true? Only time will tell.

Source: Sharon Leonard, "The Demise of Job Descriptions," *HR Magazine* 45 (August 2000), 184.

EXHIBIT 7-7

CLASS
SPECIFICATION

TITLE: Water System Operator IV

REPORTS TO: Division Director

DEPARTMENT(S): Utilities

DEFINITION: This is very difficult and complex work in the filtration, purification, and distribution of water requiring the highest level of skills. Employees in this class have lead responsibility for plant operations, laboratory testing, equipment maintenance, or major components of the water distribution system and conduct formal and on-the-job training of lower-level operators and other employees. Incumbents operate independently for long periods of time and assume responsibility for operations in the absence of the director. The work requires outstanding judgment to make critical operating decisions.

EXAMPLES OF WORK PERFORMED (Any one position may not include all of the tasks listed, nor do the examples cover all of the tasks which may be performed.)

Operates process to filter, purify, and clarify water for human consumption or industrial use.

Schedules and performs maintenance of pumps, generators, and related equipment.

Sets up, adjusts, and operates laboratory equipment and instruments.

Collects and tests water and wastewater samples, maintains records, and submits reports.

Supervises or performs troubleshooting, repair, maintenance, or installation work on water distribution system.

Implements safety procedures and enforces safety rules.

Maintains and improves knowledge and skills through reading technical literature and attending workshops.

Directs and trains lower-level operators and other employees.

Performs related work as assigned.

REQUIRED KNOWLEDGES, SKILLS, AND ABILITIES

Substantial knowledge of municipal water filtration, purification, storage, and distribution processes and equipment.

Knowledge of federal and state regulations.

Knowledge of city and departmental procedures and rules.

Knowledge of safety procedures and rules.

Reading skills to comprehend technical and highly complex material.

Verbal communication skills to speak to individuals and small groups, talk on telephone and two-way radio.

Writing skills to compose documents and prepare reports.

Mechanical skills to use specialized tools in testing, maintaining, and repairing equipment.

Math skills to calculate rates and proportions and solve algebraic equations.

Computer skills to keyboard data and use word processing, spreadsheet, database, and specialized water systems programs.

Laboratory skills to perform chemical, physical, and bacteriological tests of water and wastewater.

Instructional skills to conduct training.

Leadership skills to direct and motivate employees.

Ability to apply technical knowledge to make correct operational decisions.

Ability to work independently.

QUALIFICATIONS

Two (2) years of post high school training in water systems technology or equivalent combination of training and experience.

CERTIFICATION

Meet state certification and experience requirements for high filtration rate operator.

not an appropriate basis for establishing the job relatedness of employment procedures as required by EEO regulations.

PRACTICAL CONSIDERATIONS IN JOB ANALYSIS

It has been pointed out that conducting job analyses, along with the subsequent
writing of job descriptions, job specifications, and class specifications, is the most
basic work in human resource management. However, most organizations, including units of local government, are poorly equipped to handle this endeavor. This is
not an indictment of the people who manage the HR function, for there are good
reasons why these organizations are not adequately equipped, including:

- Many units of government do not have the resources to employ a full-time, professionally trained human resource manager; thus, the HR function is assigned
  to another official on a part-time basis.
- Job analysis work is not normally a continuing activity.
- Because the person in charge of the HR function is spread too thin, he or
  she does not have the time to keep abreast of the laws, guidelines, and court
  decisions that set forth the type of information required and the format for
  presentation.
- The practical aspects of conducting job analyses and writing job descriptions
  and specifications are not normally taught in college level HR courses.

For these reasons, it is often necessary to obtain professional assistance in job
analysis work. Sources for such help include institutes of government at colleges and
universities, faculty members in schools of business or public administration, and private consultants. In seeking outside help, the organization should ensure that the
necessary expertise is available, along with experience in legal defense, if possible. At
a minimum, the person responsible for the project should carry on intensive preparation, including study and workshop attendance. Although job analysis is necessary
from the viewpoint of management, the process can cause employees and managers
to feel threatened. Among these concerns are the following:

- Some workers fear that formalizing duties and responsibilities will stifle their
  creativity and flexibility.
- People become accustomed to working within established and secure boundaries
  and will often resist changes in a job situation in which they feel comfortable.
- Since job analysis information ultimately influences decisions regarding pay,
  promotion, and training opportunities, people may feel that a detailed examination of their jobs would disadvantage them.

The most effective way to deal with these concerns is to fully explain the purpose
of job analysis and involve members of the organization in the process. Where consultants are used, their time is better spent in organizing and guiding the activities
than in producing a lock-and-key job.

It should be stressed again that jobs change over time—some more rapidly than
others. Jobs in the data processing field may need to be constantly restructured as
new technology is made available. On the other hand, jobs in the area of parks and
recreation evolve much more slowly. For this reason, it is difficult to say how often
an organization should undertake a major job analysis project. Perhaps the best
solution is to schedule a certain amount of time each year for job analysis, with a
view toward covering all jobs over a period of time. Another good practice is to auto-

matically review a job whenever a vacancy occurs. Finally, while the traditional job is most common, work can be organized based on processes, task clusters, skill sets, and other formats to implement various design strategies such as self-directed work teams and job enlargement/enrichment as discussed in Chapter 6, or to structure certain types of pay systems, including skill-based pay and gainsharing (covered in Chapters 12 and 13). The fundamental logic of identifying responsibilities, listing tasks, and linking tasks to KSAOs applies to these formats as well.

In formulating and carrying out a project to analyze jobs or work that is organized on some other basis, local governments should be mindful of the essential nature of this activity and avoid the well-known dilemma expressed by the saying, "There's never time to do it right, but always time to do it over."

SUMMARY

Job analysis is the most fundamental activity in human resource management. Management must have current and systematized information on jobs in order to use its human resources effectively and compete for workers in the labor market. It must also have a logical basis for establishing that selection procedures are job related in order to comply with laws and regulations.

Information collected in job analysis includes work-related data (major job responsibilities and tasks performed in carrying out each responsibility) and worker requirements (job qualifications), including knowledges, skills, abilities, and other requirements (KSAOs), credentials and experience, and special requirements. This information can be collected by interviews, observation, questionnaires, and secondary data. The product of job analysis is a job description, a narrative document stating the duties and responsibilities of the job. A job specification describes the qualifications needed to perform the job. A class specification describes a group of similar jobs and is used in establishing pay levels.

Organizations should continuously monitor and update job information, obtaining professional assistance if internal resources are not available. Job analysis projects should be carried out with a view toward collecting full and complete information while minimizing and alleviating employee concerns that their jobs may be threatened. Some jobs change more rapidly than others; therefore, it is difficult to establish how often job analysis should be conducted.

QUESTIONS FOR REVIEW AND DISCUSSION

1. Why is job analysis considered the most basic activity in human resource management?
2. Select a job with which you are familiar. Identify the major responsibilities of the job. For one responsibility, develop a list of duties.
3. According to the "Uniform Guidelines," how are the terms *knowledge, skill,* and *ability* defined?
4. Describe three things that typically go wrong in job analysis and three things HR managers can do to make job descriptions more useful.
5. Explain the difference between a job description and a class specification.
6. How can secondary data be used in analyzing jobs and writing job descriptions? What are three types of secondary data used in job analysis?

7. Assume that you are working for an organization that employs 180 persons and has 18 managerial/professional jobs and 75 operating jobs. Design a project to analyze all jobs and produce final job descriptions in a period of three months.

8. Give advantages and disadvantages of several job analysis techniques. Which technique would you select if you had sufficient resources?

ENDNOTES

[1] Craig A. Olson, Donald P. Schwab, and Barbara L. Rau, "The Effects of Local Market Conditions on Two Pay-Setting Systems in the Federal Setting," *Industrial and Labor Relations Review* 53, Rev 272 (January 2000).

[2] Robert L. Mathis and John H. Jackson, *Human Resource Management*, 9th ed. (Cincinnati: South-Western, 2000), 214.

[3] Robert N. Ford, *Why Jobs Die and What to Do About It* (New York: American Management Association, 1979), 15.

[4] James P. Clifford, "Job Analysis: Why Do It and How Should It Be Done?" *Public Personnel Management* 23, no. 2 (Summer 1994), 321.

[5] *Griggs v. Duke Power Company*, 401 U.S. 430 (1971).

[6] *Kirkland v. New York State Department of Corrections*, 374 F. Supp. 1361 (S.D.N.Y., 1974).

[7] *Albemarle Paper Company v. Moody*, 422 U.S. 405 (1976).

[8] "Uniform Guidelines on Employee Selection Procedures," 43 *Federal Register* 38,302 (August 25, 1978).

[9] For in-depth coverage of job analysis concepts and methods, see John M. Ivancevich, *Human Resource Management*, 8th ed. (New York: McGraw-Hill, 2001); and Herbert G. Heneman, III, Timothy A. Judge, and Robert Heneman, *Staffing Organizations*, 3d ed. (New York: McGraw-Hill, 2000).

[10] Scott B. Parry, "Just What Is a Competency?" *Training* 35, no. 6 (June 1998), 58–64.

[11] "Uniform Guidelines," 38,307–38,308.

[12] Heneman, Judge, and Heneman.

[13] Robert L. Brady, *Law for Personnel Managers: How to Hire the People You Need Without Discriminating* (Madison, Conn.: Business and Legal Reports, 1987), 30.

[14] Brady, 30–31.

[15] Brady, 32.

[16] For example see Mathis and Jackson, 230–232.

[17] Heneman, Judge, and Heneman.

[18] Ernest J. McCormick, *Job Analysis: Methods and Applications* (New York: American Management Association, 1979), 46, 144–147.

[19] Walter W. Tornow and Patrick R. Pinto, "The Development of a Managerial Job Taxonomy," *Journal of Applied Psychology* 61 (August 1976), 410–418.

[20] U.S. Department of Labor, Manpower Administration, *Handbook for Analyzing Jobs* (Washington, D.C.: Government Printing Office, 1972).

[21] Richard E. Biddle, *Guidelines Oriented Job Analysis* (Sacramento: Biddle and Associates, 1976).

[22] Susan E. Jackson and Randall S. Schuler, *Managing Human Resources: A Partnership Perspective*, 7th ed. (Cincinnati: South-Western, 2000), 229.

[23] Norman G. Peterson, Michael D. Mumford, Walter C. Borman, P. Richard Jeanneret, Edwin A. Fleishman, and Kerry Y. Levin, *O*NET Final Technical Report*, 1 (Utah Department of Workforce Services, 1997).

[24] Fair Labor Standards Act, 29 U.S.C. §213(a)(l) (1938), as amended.

[25] *Executive, Administrative, Professional and Outside Sales Exemptions Under the Fair Labor Standards Act* (U.S. Department of Labor, Employee Standards Administration, Wage and Hour Division, WH Pub. 1363, December 1983).

[26] See, for example, Gary Dessler, *Human Resource Management*, 8th ed. (Upper Saddle River, N.J.: Prentice-Hall, 2000), 98–109.

[27] Based on *Job Evaluation Manual: Clerical, Technical, Engineering, Administrative, Professional, Sales and Supervisory Occupations* (Springfield, Mass.: American Association of Industrial Management, 1998).

[28] *Public Personnel Administration: Policies and Practices* (New York: Prentice-Hall, 1973), 10,021.

CHAPTER 8
PREPARATION FOR STAFFING AND RECRUITING

YOU CAN START TODAY

Michael, a previously unemployed skilled worker, just received the best news he has gotten in six months. He is now a paid employee of the city of Hampton, Virginia. For months Michael searched for the perfect job without luck. He applied over and over for many jobs but never received a job offer for a position that matched his qualifications. Today, however, under Hampton's new recruitment process, an interviewer has successfully matched Michael with a job. Further, the job starts tomorrow.

In the city of Hampton, human resources employees spent long hours, resources, and a vast amount of energy changing their previous methods of recruiting employees. The purpose of the change was to ensure a more efficient standard of keeping positions full and enabling "same day referral and next day start for all high-turnover positions." The new process eliminated 50 redundant or unnecessary steps in the recruiting and hiring process.

The old process involved accepting applications from any interested candidate when a position was vacant. Prompting the change in process was a study done by the city of Hampton. Results showed the same positions were being filled over and over and only a small percentage of applicants were hired.

The new process, which has received a 92 percent "customer delighted rate," is very simple. These are the steps that ensure the process is smooth and accurate:

- Applicant comes to office or calls the "Job Express Line."
- Applicant is directed to an interviewer.
- Questions are asked to ensure applicant has minimal qualifications for the job.
- The applicant is briefed on the city's need.
- Applicant may be selected to submit application and referred for an interview, drug test, and next day start.
- Applicant who is not right for the job will receive information on how to acquire skills and licenses and will be directed to other job opportunities.

Since the new process has been implemented, the city of Hampton has been able to successfully recruit Michael and others into positions throughout the city, including high-turnover positions. They contribute their speedy employment process to the 24-hour job express line, interviews, and the new application process. The city of Hampton's new recruitment policy has resulted in the city being able to recruit and place applicants in a short time, while other organizations struggle to build applicant pools.

Source: Based on Tharon Groone, "City of Hampton's Innovative Recruiting Efforts," *IPMA News* 65 (November 1999), 6.

INTRODUCTION

The development of a legal and effective selection process is a formidable but essential task. The objective is to hire, at least cost, as many best-qualified individuals as needed to fill job openings and to select these individuals in a legal manner. Several important actions must be completed by the HR department before recruitment and selection are initiated. First, as discussed in Chapter 3, legal requirements must be understood and complied with. Second, the department must prepare reliable and valid measurement tools to predict which candidates are likely to be most successful on the job. Finally, the organization must work to recruit only the most capable applicants. Topics addressed in this chapter include EEO requirements affecting selection procedures, the nature and purpose of affirmative action programs, diversity, reliability and validity of selection measures, and key issues in recruiting.

LEGAL ASPECTS OF RECRUITING AND SELECTION

The goals of hiring competent workers and doing that legally are not mutually exclusive. In fact, they reinforce each other. It is quite possible both to comply with the law and to hire only a highly competent workforce. Following equal employment opportunity requirements in the manner described in this and Chapter 9 will result in hiring a more competent workforce. Affirmative action, where required, ensures that an organization avoids legal challenge—and, when combined with a commitment to developing and maintaining a diverse workforce that is representative of the public served, will also result in hiring and retaining a more effective workforce. Further, effective recruiting and selection procedures can reduce exposure to charges of negligent hiring as discussed in Chapters 9 and 16.

EQUAL EMPLOYMENT OPPORTUNITY REQUIREMENTS IN SELECTION

The impact of any selection decision on the individual being considered for a position requires carefully considering the process to ensure that all aspects are free from illegal discrimination. Such discrimination occurs if procedures result in either disparate treatment (intentional) or disparate impact (unintentional).

DISPARATE TREATMENT

Disparate treatment, or intentionally treating protected individuals or groups adversely in the selection process leads to frustration on the part of applicants and contributes nothing to the quality of the selection decision. It is a poor way of doing business. When protected classes (race, color, religion, sex, national origin, age, or physical disability) are involved, such disparate or adverse treatment is also illegal.

Such treatment may or may not be motivated by prejudice or bias. An absolute refusal to consider African Americans for certain types of jobs, for example, is clearly illegal and in most cases results from overt, conscious racial prejudice. Another example of disparate treatment would be rejecting a qualified member of a protected group while continuing to seek applicants with similar qualifications. Disparate treatment, however, often takes more subtle or unconscious forms; for example, allowing a white applicant additional time to submit an application while requiring a nonwhite applicant to meet the posted deadline date. The reason may be innocent enough. Perhaps the white applicant is exceptionally well qualified and explains that she or he has some good reason for needing an extension, and the human resource manager does not want to eliminate this person from consideration. But if the deadline is not extended for all other applicants as well, and the white applicant is selected for the job, the extension maybe viewed by the EEOC or a court as a *pretext* for discrimination. The following are typical examples of incidents that may sustain a charge of disparate treatment:

- Making exceptions regarding application deadlines, interview schedules, documentation required, and other aspects of the selection process to some applicants but not others.
- Selectively pursuing unfavorable information on certain job applicants through reference checks, background investigations, and so on.
- Writing job specifications to favor some candidates and to eliminate others.
- Communicating vacancy announcements only to selected individuals and groups.
- Assisting some individuals in the selection process while not doing that for others; for example, "coaching" certain applicants on desirable responses in the supervisory interview.

When these or similar types of incidents work to the disadvantage of protected class applicants, there is a strong presumption that intentional discrimination occurred. In some cases an employer may find it necessary to deviate from normal practice. For example, a job applicant who is injured in an automobile accident might have his or her interview rescheduled. It is important, however, for the employer to keep these deviations to a minimum and to be able to justify each one with a legitimate nondiscriminatory reason. What is more important is to administer the selection process in a consistent manner and to treat all applicants equally.

DISPARATE IMPACT

Disparate impact, a more pervasive type of selection discrimination, involves selection practices that are not intended to discriminate but have unequal consequences for different protected class member applicants. This type of discrimination disproportionately screens out one or more protected class member with a requirement that on its face seems neutral. The following are examples of practices that often have an adverse effect on members of protected classes:

- Type of military discharge limitations
- Education and experience requirements
- Height and weight standards

Underutilization of protected class members in an organization can make a prima facie case of illegal disparate impact. For example, disparate impact may exist if the percentage of minority employment in an organization is lower than the percentage of qualified minorities in the labor market. The disparate impact of any particular selection practice will be judged illegal if it cannot be shown to be essential to job performance (job related).

There are a number of ways to determine if a selection practice has a disparate impact, all of which involve statistical measures. One quick and easily understood test is the 80 percent, or four-fifths, rule established by the "Uniform Guidelines on Employee Selection Procedures." Generally, disparate impact occurs when the selection rate on a test for protected class applicants is less than 80 percent of the selection rate for majority applicants.[1]

For example, assume that a city requires entry-level police officers to pass an aptitude test. During a certain period 95 white applicants take the test and 60 receive passing scores. The selection rate is 63 percent (60/95). During the same period 50 African-American applicants take the test and 19 pass, a selection rate of 38 percent (19/50) and 25 Hispanic applicants take the test and 15 pass, a selection rate of 60 percent (15/25). Applying the 80 percent rule, $63 \times .8$, or about 50 percent, of the African-American applicants should have passed if the selection procedure was nondiscriminatory. Since only 38 percent did pass, the test has a (presumably unintentional) disparate impact on African-American applicants. As the Hispanic applicants' selection rate (60 percent) was much greater than four-fifths of the most favored group's selection rate, there is no adverse impact on that group of applicants. Note, had the Hispanic selection rate been 20, or 80 percent (20/25), they, not whites, would have been the "most-favored" group for comparison (and African Americans, but not whites, would still have been adversely impacted by the selection procedure).

In the above example, the human resource management department may have exercised great care to ensure that it did *not* intentionally discriminate during any phase of the selection process. Test security was maintained, all applicants were notified regarding location and dates of testing, test procedures were uniformly followed, and tests were graded fairly. However, the overall result creates a real problem for the employer in that it results in a prima facie case of discrimination against a protected race or group. If the test has not been properly validated as a job-related requirement, the human resources department needs to do that. If it does not, it will have to revise the scoring procedures until it does not adversely impact any protected group members making up 2 percent or more of the applicant pool, or eliminate the test entirely. If the test has been used for any length of time, it has probably resulted in underutilization of blacks in the police department.

One approach, and not a good one, would be to continue using the test and wait for any adversely affected class member applicants to file a complaint with the EEOC. Many cities and counties have followed this practice. Another approach would be to develop a voluntary affirmative action program for any such job categories in which there is underutilization of one or more protected class members—until that underutilization has been corrected. As stated above, the best approach would be to concurrently validate that all selection procedures are reliable and job related.

AFFIRMATIVE ACTION PROGRAMS

Affirmative action programs (AAPs) are aimed at ensuring parity between the percentage of qualified protected group members in the organization's relevant labor market and the percentage employed by the organization. Unfortunately, these programs are often seen by elected officials and managers as a set of bureaucratic requirements that cause more problems than they cure. Affirmative action has been misconstrued by both advocates and detractors to mean preferential treatment for selected protected group members by using quota systems unrelated to job qualifications. However, the law requires no preferential treatment.[2] According to Section 703 (j) of the Civil Rights Act:

> *Nothing contained in this title shall be interpreted to require any employer . . . to grant preferential treatment to any individual or to any group because of the race, color, religion, sex or national origin [age and disability were subsequently added] of such individual or group on account of an imbalance which may exist with respect to the total number or percentage of persons of any race, color, religion, sex or national origin in any community, state, section or other area, or in the available workforce in any community, state, section or other area.*

DEFINITION OF AFFIRMATIVE ACTION

http://www.apa.org/ppo/aa.html
The American Psychological Association includes an article, "Affirmative Action: Who Benefits?"

EEO legislation prohibits employment practices that tend to exclude members of protected groups from certain jobs. The underlying premise is that, if practices are job related, then members of all groups will have a fair and equal chance at all jobs. This is a workable premise; job-related tests generally do not have much adverse impact on members of protected groups. On the other hand, the mere replacement of artificial barriers with job-related selection practices cannot be expected to instantly solve the problem of underrepresentation. Under EEO laws, an organization may adopt a position of neutrality and trust that protected groups will be equitably represented in its workforce at some future time. Under **affirmative action**, the organization takes positive action in both recruiting and selection procedures to ensure that equitable representation is achieved as soon as possible.[3]

ELEMENTS OF AN AFFIRMATIVE ACTION PROGRAM

While affirmative action is not required by law, any voluntary AAP that is undertaken should be designed and carried out within the bounds of existing EEO legislation and court case precedent. There are three situations where a company or public entity would adopt an AAP: it is a government contractor, it has lost a discrimination case or entered into a consent degree, or it is attempting to implement a voluntary program.[4] As the first two rarely apply to public sector organizations, only the latter situation is discussed below.

A voluntary AAP (a proactive attempt to increase protected group representation in the workforce), must not violate EEO requirements precluding "preferential treatment to any individual or to any group . . . on account of an imbalance which may exist . . . in any community, state, section or other area, or in the available workforce in any community, state, section or other area." In recognition of this potential conflict, the U.S. Supreme Court, in deciding a challenge to a voluntary AAP established by Kaiser Aluminum and Chemical Corporation and the United Steelworkers of America, provided the guidelines summarized below for a legally acceptable AAP:

- The plan does not unnecessarily trammel the interests of nonprotected employees.
- The plan does not require the discharge of any nonprotected employees and their replacement with minority group employees.
- The plan does not create an absolute bar to the advancement of nonprotected group employees.
- The plan is a temporary measure, not intended to maintain a protected group balance but simply to eliminate a manifest protected group imbalance.[5]

EXHIBIT 8-1

SELF-ANALYSIS REQUIRED FOR AFFIRMATIVE ACTION

Type of Analysis	Description	Purpose
Workforce Analysis	A listing of each job title from the lowest paid to the highest paid with each department or work unit, including the salary range and race and sex of the incumbents.	Provides an overview and identifies potential problems.
Job Group Analysis	The workforce is broken down into job groups with similar content, wage rates and opportunities. A useful grouping method is to use the EEO-4 categories: officials/administrators, professionals, technicians, protective service, para-professionals and office/clerical.	Establishes the basic unit of analysis for determining availability.
Availability Analysis	Considers for the labor market area critical factors relating to minorities and females, including population, unemployment, training institutions, and persons with the requisite skills. The employer also must consider internal promotions and transfers and training programs. These factors are weighted based on importance to the job group.	Makes it possible to establish realistic goals based on women and minorities in the job market holding requisite skills.

Source: Equal Employment Opportunity Commission, "Affirmative Action Appropriate Under Title VII of the Civil Rights Act of 1964, As Amended," 29 C.F.R. 1608 (January 19, 1979), and Office of Federal Contract Compliance Programs, "Affirmative Action Programs," 7 C.F.R. 60-2 (December 18, 1979).

An affirmative action plan should contain three elements: reasonable self-analysis, reasonable basis, and reasonable action.[6]

REASONABLE SELF-ANALYSIS. The objective of a self-analysis is to determine if and to what extent employment practices exclude, disadvantage, restrict, or result in disparate impact or disparate treatment of previously excluded or restricted groups, or leave uncorrected the effects of prior discrimination. If any of these effects are occurring, an attempt should be made to determine why. There is no mandatory method of conducting a self-analysis. The employer may utilize techniques used in order to comply with Executive Order 11246, as amended, and its implementing regulations, or may use an analysis similar to that required under other federal, state, or local laws or regulations prohibiting employment discrimination. The self-analysis includes three parts: workforce analysis, job group analysis, and availability analysis, as shown in Exhibit 8-1.

REASONABLE BASIS. If the self-analysis shows that one or more employment practices (1) have or tend to have a disparate impact on any protected group members, (2) leave uncorrected the effects of prior discrimination, (3) or result in disparate treatment, the employer has a reasonable basis for concluding that action is appropriate. For example, a particular job group of 30 incumbents may include 3 protected group members that equate to 10 percent of the total organization. If this protected group represents 20 percent of the relevant labor market, they are *under-utilized* in this job group. The same kind of analysis should be conducted for all protected group members. It is not necessary that the self-analysis establish a violation of Title VII. This reasonable basis exists without any admission or formal finding that the employer has violated Title VII, and without regard to whether there exist arguable defenses to a Title VII action.

REASONABLE ACTION. The action taken must be reasonable in relation to the problems disclosed by the self-analysis. Such reasonable action may include goals and timetables or other appropriate employment tools that recognize the race, gender, or other protected group member applicants or employees. For example, the job group discussed previously was identified as underutilizing some protected group members by 10 percent. Long-term goals are usually set to equal availability of the qualified protected group members represented in the relevant labor market. The size of the gap determines the length of the timetable and the magnitude of the annual goal. Assume that 10 people will be hired during the year. Then the employer would need to establish a goal of hiring at least $.20 \times 10 = 2$ qualified underutilized protected group members in the job group, which will bring that class representation to 5, or approximately 16.6 percent. The Office of Federal Contract Compliance Programs allows application of the 80 percent rule in determining underutilization; using that standard, the employer would need to have $20 \times .8 = 16$ percent underrepresented protected group representation. Thus the employment of 2 of the underrepresented applicants remedies the underutilization in the job group. If only 5 people were expected to be hired during the year, the goal would still be based on availability; however, only 1 underrepresented protected group worker would be hired during the year and it would take an additional year to bring representation up to 5.

Does a local government have to wait until it is found guilty of discrimination before legally establishing an affirmative action program? That is, in an effort to redress past or present discrimination, should local governments establish affirmative action programs only as a result of court action or should such programs be voluntarily initiated?

DESIGNING A VOLUNTARY AFFIRMATIVE ACTION PLAN

Poorly designed and executed affirmative action programs may result in increased liability for a local government. However, well designed and executed affirmative action programs can help a local government achieve its affirmative action and diversity goals. The following two cases illustrate the need for affirmative action plans to be "carefully designed and meticulously justified if they are to avoid successful challenge."

In the U.S. Supreme Court case of *Johnson v. Transportation Agency*, the Santa Clara County District Board of Supervisors successfully defended their affirmative action program designed to utilize minorities, women, and disabled persons. Their affirmative action program survived challenge because the plan was designed to eliminate agency workforce imbalance in traditionally segregated job categories, did not unnecessarily trammel on the interests of non-minorities and males, did not provide for an absolute entitlement to a job, and was temporary. In *Richmond v. Croson*, the Supreme Court ruled the city of Richmond, Virginia's public contracting set-aside program for minorities unconstitutional. This ruling was based on Court use of the strict scrutiny standard—the city failed to establish a compelling governmental interest.

Source: Carlos R. Gullett, "Reverse Discrimination and Remedial Affirmative Action in Employment: Dealing with the Paradox of Nondiscrimination," *Public Personnel Management* 29 (Spring 2000), 107–118.

Establishing goals and timetables is, however, only the starting point. An effective affirmative action plan should include the following:

- Written affirmative action policy statement
- Senior official to direct the program
- Wide communication of EEO/AA policies
- Expanded recruitment of qualified underrepresented group members
- Redesign of jobs to eliminate underrepresented group barriers
- Development of job-related selection practices
- Training programs for supervisors
- Career counseling for underrepresented group member employees

NEED FOR A COMPREHENSIVE AA PROGRAM

As indicated above, any AAP needs not only expanded recruiting and goals and timetables but also development of and use of reliable and valid job-related selection procedures. Unfortunately, many organizations focus primarily on hiring the supposedly required numbers of underrepresented protected group members. Major emphasis is given to making the statistics look better. As a result, *affirmation action* often means arbitrarily hiring or promoting persons whose major qualifications are membership in a protected group. This causes resentment on the part of *overrepresented* group members, who believe they have been treated unfairly, and on the part of supervisors who are required to hire people who are ill-prepared for the job. It may lead to charges of so-called reverse discrimination—against the majority or overutilized group members.

While it can be argued that the nature of affirmative action involves special attention to underrepresented protected group members, the focus should not be on preferential treatment based on recent Supreme Court cases in the 1990s. One of the most common traps that organizations fall into with voluntary AAPs is continuing to use non-job-related and unreliable selection procedures—those procedures that originally caused the discriminatory disparate impact in the first place. When this happens, preferential treatment, with its associated problems, is almost inevitable. The organization thus will still be vulnerable to legal challenge and will not have an adequately competent workforce. AAPs are effective when they include expanded recruitment efforts, particularly for jobs that have historically been dominated by one race or gender, and rely on selection procedures that measure qualifications actually needed in the job.[7]

DIVERSITY PROGRAMS

http://www.aimd.org
The American Institute for Managing Diversity provides comprehensive information about diversity in the workplace.

As indicated by the above discussion, AAPs are both controversial and constrained by congressional and judicial law.[8] They focus on correcting past problems (manifest imbalances) and generally address only underutilized protected group members (race, sex, color, national origin, religion, age, and disabled). Several Supreme Court cases have focused on the illegality of such programs that continue beyond the point of correcting a manifest imbalance, becoming illegally discriminatory against other protected group members in the process. Although not a selection-related case, of particular interest to municipalities is the U.S. Supreme Court decision in *Richmond v. Croson*. Here, the Court found that a city requirement that prime contractors set aside 30% of the dollar amount of contracts for minority businesses denied equal protection under EEO laws because it discriminated illegally on the basis of race (the minority protected class in this particular case).[9]

Diversity is central to many local governments' strategic objective of better serving customers. One way to ensure a local government is meeting its diversity goals is to periodically take stock of its employees and managers. Local governments may find it useful to develop and implement an organizational questionnaire to aid in establishing diversity goals and reviewing progress toward those goals.

WHAT IS YOUR DIVERSITY SCORE?

The following questions are based on the *Diversity Index*, developed by Allstate Corporation.

1. To what extent does our city deliver quality services to our customers regardless of their differences?
2. How do other city employees treat you with regards to your differences?
3. How do customers treat you with regards to your differences?
4. Do managers in your department value all employee opinions and do they seek to understand problems from a variety of standpoints?
5. Are all city employees treated the same regardless of their differences?
6. Have you observed insensitive behavior toward other employees or customers based on their differences?
7. Has the city created a culture of trust and respect for all employees and customers?

Source: Adapted from Joan Crockett, "Winning Competitive Advantage Through a Diverse Workforce," *HR Focus* (May 1999), 9–10.

Diversity, on the other hand, looks forward, not backward, and goes beyond the legally protected groups covered by Equal Employment Opportunity law and AAPs. The term *diversity* often provokes intense emotional reactions from people who associate the word with affirmative action and hiring quotas.[10] However, **diversity** simply means variety or a point or respect in which things differ.[11] Addressing diversity in the public sector, the term has been defined by management scholars as the systematic and planned commitment by organizations to recruit, retain, reward, and promote a heterogeneous mix of employees.[12] Diversity moves beyond race and gender to include a mix of productive, motivated, and committed workers.[13] For example, the city of Austin, Texas, defines diversity as "a variety of conditions and activities that create an environment where people can achieve their fullest potential, regardless of the many ways they differ from each other."[14]

Local governments need to successfully recruit, select, and train diverse persons to fill organizational requirements in order to receive the benefits of diversity: broader competencies, better decisions based on different perspectives, better services to diverse populations, and increased ability to recruit excellent talent from the entire labor pool.[15] Further, local governments cannot achieve the benefits of diversity without a diverse workforce. Training and commitment to diversity throughout the organization can go a long way toward helping it achieve its strategic objectives.[16]

RELIABILITY AND VALIDITY OF SELECTION PROCEDURES

A selection procedure or "test" is useful only if it is both reliable and valid. These are extremely important concepts and merit further discussion. The concept of **reliability** refers to the stability, consistency, and dependability of a selection measure.[17]

If a test, for example, is reliable, an individual's score should be approximately the same every time the test is taken. Consider, for example, a clerical knowledge test given to candidates for an administrative assistant position. If a person took the test three times and the scores were 73, 71, and 75, then we could say that the test was reliable. The average score of 73 probably represents accurately the individual's ability to answer the questions on that particular test. On the other hand, suppose the scores were 43, 98, and 78. The average score is still 73, but we would have little confidence in the results. If a selection procedure is reliable, as in the first case, we can depend on it. If it is unreliable, we cannot.

Reliability of selection procedures is extremely important, but it is not enough. We must ask the question: What judgments or inferences can we make from scores on a selection measure? **Validity** is the degree to which available evidence supports these inferences or judgments. That is, something is valid if it measures we want it to measure. In the context of a selection test, we need to know how an individual's score on the test predicts future job performance.[18] For example, the clerical knowledge test in the example above was constructed to measure the clerical aspect of an applicant's ability to perform the work of an administrative assistant based on knowledge of certain factual items. Thus, we would expect applicants who made high scores on the test to perform well, those who made low scores to perform poorly. If this prediction proves to be true, then the test is valid. It measures what it was intended to measure; it does what it was intended to do—to predict the applicant's clerical job performance. But this may not be the case. If the adoption of the test was not based on a job analysis and if knowledge of the factual items contained in the test has very little to do with how an administrative assistant performs on the job, the test may be reliable but not valid. It might not measure what it was intended to measure (the applicant's ability to perform the administrative assistant job successfully).

To be useful, a test must be both reliable and valid. Reliability is a necessary but not sufficient prerequisite for validity.[19] That is, one can never make a valid prediction of successful job performance if the predictor test is not stable, consistent, and dependable. The concepts of reliability and validity are illustrated in Exhibit 8-2.

The figure shows the results of clamping three rifles securely on a stationary base and firing five shots with each rifle at the targets shown. The shot group from the rifle fired at target number 1 is considerably scattered, with no particular pattern. We conclude that the rifle is unreliable. The shots from the rifle fired at target number 2 are closely clustered but are located at the upper right portion of the tar-

EXHIBIT 8-2

RELIABILITY
AND VALIDITY

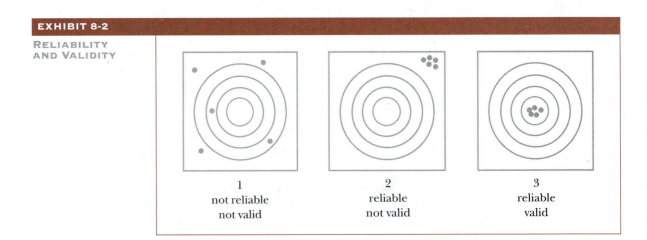

1
not reliable
not valid

2
reliable
not valid

3
reliable
valid

get. The rifle is reliable but not valid. Finally, the shots from the rifle fired at target number 3 are closely clustered in the bulls-eye. This rifle is both reliable and valid.

A number of techniques can be used to determine the reliability and validity of selection procedures. Two cautions are in order: First, the selection of certain applicants for a job is an applied activity, and no selection procedure can approach "scientific" standards of reliability and validity. Second, costs increase as validation requirements become more demanding.[20] Therefore, resources invested in establishing measurement accuracy should be justified by the benefits resulting from better selection decisions and reduced EEO liability.

ESTABLISHING AND MEASURING RELIABILITY

Reliability may be measured by a number of different methods. There are three types of reliability estimates for paper-and-pencil and some types of work-sample tests.[21] A fourth method is used for estimating the reliability of selection interviews done by more than one interviewer.

The first is known as the **test/retest** method and is expressed as the correlation between scores on the same test given to the same people twice. The tests should be given fairly close together so as not to allow learning or practice to influence the results.

The second type of reliability estimate is the **alternate form method**. In this method, two different forms of the same test are developed by drawing random samples of questions from a larger pool. For example, a set of 100 questions could be designed to measure clerical aptitudes. Fifty questions could be drawn as form "A" of the test, while the remaining questions could be form "B." This method is often preferred to test/retest because the same items do not appear on both tests. As with the test-retest method, it is usually used in pre- and post-testing in the development of training program content rather than selection.

The third type of reliability estimate is the **internal consistency method**.[22] Internal consistency can be estimated by calculating Cronbach's alpha using readily available statistical packages. Cronbach's alpha can be used to estimate the internal consistency of question formats that are often used in job performance predictor selection tests such as multiple choice questions and Likert-type scales.

The fourth method of estimating reliability is the inter-rater method. It is used when there may be a problem due to differences in multiple "raters" judging the same person. This could be in performance appraisal results (where, for example, pay decisions are based on ranking employees rated with the same instrument by several different raters); or, as discussed here, where more than one person interviews applicants as part of a selection process. Multiple rating is one of the contributors to the poor validity of the interview in predicting job success. Increasing the reliability of multiple interviewers will increase the validity of a preselection interview by multiple interviewers (such as the HR recruiter or manager initially and, subsequently, the position's immediate supervisor).

As discussed above, interviews are often unreliable and therefore invalid. To increase the reliability and therefore the validity of its interview procedures, an organization must standardize the interview process and train interviewers so that raters are attempting to measure the same thing in the same way. With this standardization, we should expect general agreement among interviewers concerning which candidates are likely to be successful on the job and which are not, and see an increase in their inter-rater reliability and validity.[23]

Selection devices such as application blanks and other forms submitted by

The most important influence on selection in the public sector has been Title VII and subsequent court interpretations. Any selection procedure that has a disparate impact on a protected group must be justified by business necessity. This defense against a charge of discrimination is known as validation. As Joyce D. Ross points out, however, there is another major benefit to the employer:

WHY VALIDATION?

Test validation should be more than a reactive defense to the fear of lawsuits. Validation is an opportunity to develop sound selection devices that ensure quality employees over the long run. For example, a local government in Florida gave all applicants for the position of park maintenance worker an extensive reading test. Between 1968 and 1974, one-third of its applicants were Cuban immigrants, yet there were no Cuban maintenance workers. Since the park maintenance workers received their instructions orally and were shown what to do, the reading test had no relationship to job performance. The test did not distinguish good park maintenance workers from bad ones, it only distinguished between those who could read English well and those who could not.

Source: Excerpted from Joyce D. Ross, "Developments in Recruitment and Selection," in Steven W. Hays and Richard C. Kearney, eds., *Public Personnel Administration*, 2d ed. (Englewood Cliffs, N.J.: Prentice-Hall, 1990), 80–81.

applicants or references should be pretested by having a representative sample of people use the forms to provide the information requested. Responses should then be checked on an item-by-item basis to determine if the information provided is what was intended and the test results' internal consistency measures meet acceptable standards.

In summary, the reliability of a selection device means that the results are stable over time or throughout all of the items. In a paper-and-pencil or work-sample test, we would expect that the test measures whatever it was intended to measure consistently throughout the test. In an interview there would be general agreement among raters concerning which applicants are likely to perform well on the job and which are not.

The reliability of selection procedures must be established before they are used. As stated above, without an acceptable level of reliability, it is difficult or impossible to interpret the value of the selection device in predicting successful job performance. Again, high reliability is no guarantee that a selection procedure will produce good results, but there can be no good results without reliability.

ESTABLISHING AND MEASURING VALIDITY

Recall, the term validity means that something does what it is intended to do. In the context of various selection procedures, we would like to predict the probability of success on the job. In the previous section a number of devices were mentioned that may be able to do that: paper-and-pencil tests, work samples, interviews, and biographical data. Reliability was established as necessary, but not sufficient. The selection procedure must also validly relate to job performance. The results of a paper-and-pencil test may be highly reliable and still unrelated to a candidate's ability to perform on the job. When interviewing applicants for a job, the raters may be in perfect agreement on which candidates are likely to be successful. However, if these predictions are not confirmed by actual job performance, then the interview, while reliable, is not useful as a valid predictor of job success. The same can be said for all selection procedures. If a selection procedure has an adverse impact on a protected group and has not been validated in terms of job performance, it is illegal.

In addition to protecting against EEO liability, validation ensures better selection decisions. There is increasing interest in the HR field in **utility analysis**, or determining how much a valid selection procedure or test improves the quality of applicants selected over that resulting from a procedure that has not been validated.[24] The degree of improvement is known as the *utility* of the test. To the extent utility can be measured in dollars, there is opportunity to justify the expense of validation through benefit-cost analysis. For example, a study of the selection process or computer programmers in the federal government showed an estimated productivity increase of $5.6 million based on one year's use of a validated test. These results are particularly impressive in that they were based on the replacement of a selection procedure that was already producing reasonably satisfactory results.[25] While certain utility analysis techniques must still be refined (for example, measurement of improved quality of work), application of test utility measurements, in terms of dollar payoff, will continue to be a challenge for HR professionals.[26]

Three basic types of validity are recognized by the "Uniform Guidelines on Employee Selection Procedures" and the courts. These are criterion-related validity, content validity, and construct validity.[27] In **criterion-related validation**, a selection procedure is justified by a statistical relationship (correlation) between scores on the test or other selection procedure and measures of job performance.[28] In **content validation**, a selection procedure is justified by showing that it representatively samples "all and only" the significant parts of the job, such as a data entry skills test for a data entry clerk. **Construct validation** identifies a psychological trait (or "construct") that underlies successful performance on the job and then devises or identifies an existing selection procedure that measures the presence and degree of the trait or construct. An example would be a test of "leadership ability." Technical standards and documentation requirements for the application of each of the three approaches are contained in the "Uniform Guidelines."

CRITERION-RELATED VALIDITY

In using this type of validity, we attempt to show that the results of a test accurately predict job success. Numerical test results are the predictor; numerically measured job success, the criterion.

The first step in criterion-related validity is to conduct a job analysis, using appropriate "Subject Matter Experts" (job incumbents and their supervisors). This determines the critical work behaviors of the job—and the knowledge, skills, abilities, and other job-related characteristics (KSAO) necessary for successful job performance. The second step is to measure these KSAOs by administering appropriate tests or predictors to a group of applicants. The test scores are not used in the hiring decisions; in fact, the results are "hidden" from those responsible for selection. After a suitable period of time, the performance of the recently hired applicants is measured. The results of the test are correlated with the group's numerically evaluated job performance. If the coefficient indicates by a statistically significant correlation that those who did well on the test also did well on the job (and those who did not do so well on the test also did not do so well on the job), then we can infer that the test is valid. That is, the test predicted what we intended it to predict—success on the job. The results of the now-validated test can be used in selection decisions.

The method just described is called the predictive model and is the preferred method in terms of statistical purity. Although **predictive validity** is a sound statistical technique, it may be difficult in practice. There may be insufficient applicants to provide an adequate sample size in a reasonable period of time. The organization may have to hire and retain poor performers during the validation period. Thus the model may not be as cost-effective as the concurrent model, discussed below.

In establishing **concurrent validity** the test is given to current employees and the results are correlated with their most recent job performance evaluation results. As with the predictive model, if high scores on the test are associated with high job performance scores, the test is valid. This model provides quicker results and is generally less expensive than the predictive model.

The method actually selected by the organization will depend on time and cost considerations. Although it appears that the predictive model should be preferred, many government units will, for practical considerations, use the concurrent model. If certain precautions are taken, such as random samples of sufficient size, proper test administration, and an accurate performance appraisal system, either method is acceptable.[29]

Exhibit 8-3 shows the relationship between test scores and job performance for a hypothetical group of 30 persons who were hired in secretarial positions. In this example, we will assume that the predictive model was used and applicants were hired without considering their scores on the test.

After a period of six months, each individual's job success was assessed using a weighted performance appraisal instrument.

In our example, it was possible to score 0 to 100 on the selection test. The performance appraisal instrument was a rating scale where poor performance was 1-2-3, satisfactory performance 4-5-6, and outstanding performance 7-8-9. Notice that scores on the test are closely related to actual performance on the job. Thus, it is possible to predict job success from test scores with a reasonable chance of being correct. In the workplace, one would not expect to find a relationship as strong as that shown in the example. This is because most jobs require more than one KSAO and, therefore, need more than one KSAO test to best predict job performance.

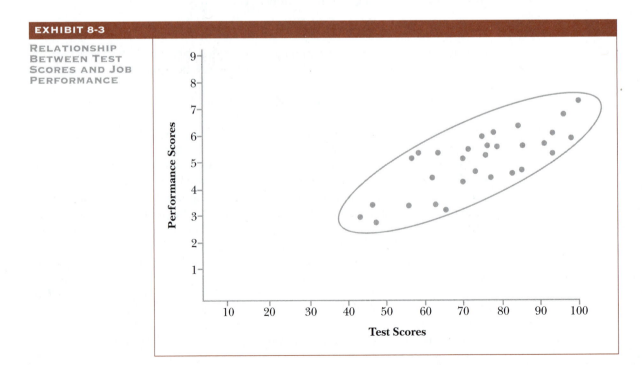

EXHIBIT 8-3

RELATIONSHIP BETWEEN TEST SCORES AND JOB PERFORMANCE

EXHIBIT 8-4

DETERMINATION
OF CUTTING
SCORES

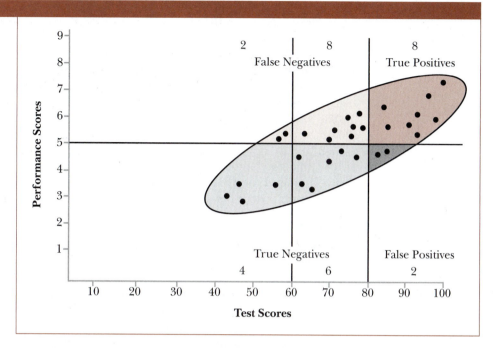

Chapter 9 discusses why multiple linear regression analysis (MRA) of multiple predictor test scores, rather than correlation or simple linear regression of a single score, is usually used to rank-order applicants on the basis of predicted job performance in a combination or MRA "compensatory" method for determining which applicants should be selected for a job.

If this were the sole test being used, after it has been validated, here by the predictive model, a cutting score would be determined for just this test. Applicants who score above this score will be hired (or placed on a list of "eligibles"), while those who score below are considered to be unqualified. As shown in Exhibit 8-4, 5.0 has been established as a minimum acceptable level of job performance. If we wish to have a very high probability of making the correct selection decision, the cutting score on the test would be set at 80. In this case, 8 out of 10 applicants (probability of 0.8) were hired and performed well on the job. These are known as "true positives"—their test scores indicated that they would do well on the job, and they did.

The two applicants who were hired and were not successful on the job are called "false positives"—their test scores indicated that they would do well on the job, but they did not. (Recall that their test score was not used in the hiring process.) The ten applicants who did not meet the cutting score but subsequently did well on the job (performance score above 5.0) are called "false negatives." Finally, all those who scored below the cutting score of 80 and did not perform well on the job (performance score below 5.0) are called "true negatives." As you can see, setting the cutting score lower to 60 increases the true positives and decreases the false negatives—at the cost of also increasing the false positives and decreasing the true negatives.

Setting the cutting score, therefore, is somewhat arbitrary and requires analysis of differential effects on all four sectors. If more selections are needed, for example, you could lower the cutting score. If the score is lowered to 60, a larger number will qualify (true positives); however, at the cost discussed above. The probability of making the correct selection decision is reduced to .67, as only 16 of the 24 applicants performed well on the job. A better approach would be to recruit additional applicants until the number above the cutting score was sufficient to meet job selection requirements.

To establish the "best" cutting score, an organization must consider several factors. These include the desired probability of making the correct selection decision, labor market influences, legal implications, wages paid, number of available applicants, and proportion of present employees performing at an acceptable rate. Good "public relations" may require local governments to establish cutting scores that allow most people to technically "pass" the test and go on the hiring register—even though they do not have a realistic chance of advancing high enough to be hired. This minimizes complaints from applicants, who are also taxpaying citizens who may well remind the HR staff that they pay their salaries. However, if this is done (and the author does not recommend it), final selection still should be made only in terms of those applicants or eligibles who, in fact, are predicted to perform the job well.

Notice also that, even with a very good relationship between test scores and job performance and a cutting score of 60, 33 percent of the people who will not be hired because of low scores on the test would have performed well on the job. These "false negatives" are a concern when the test standard excludes protected class applicants who are capable of doing well on the job.[30] Therefore, the HR department should be prepared to justify the cutting score in job-related terms.

The practical difficulties involved in criterion-related validation of a test can be illustrated with the well-known Correctional Officers Interest Blank. This 40-item assessment device was carefully developed to measure job-related attributes for the jobs of correctional officer, juvenile counselor, and probation officer. One study reported a weak to moderate relationship between test scores and job performance for the dissimilar jobs of correctional officer and juvenile counselor. For the job of probation officer, which is similar to the job of correctional officer, the statistical relationship (correlation) was practically nonexistent.[31]

Criterion validation of any selection test requires the use of only qualified professionals to both establish the reliability of the test and job performance measures and to conduct the validity study. They should also assist in establishing cutting scores and provide guidance on how the tests should be used in the selection process.

CONTENT VALIDITY

Content validity is very different from criterion-related validity. Rather than statistically showing the strength of the relationship between scores on a test and the criterion measure of job performance, validation shows that the content (usually in terms of critical job tasks/behaviors) of the selection procedure or test samples the content of the job.[32] For example, driving a school bus can be shown to be a content-valid measure to use for school bus drivers, because being able to drive a bus is "representative of important aspects of performance on the job for which the candidates are being evaluated."[33]

Though content validity lacks the quantitative rigor of other validation procedures, it is not necessarily inferior. The purpose of all selection tests is to predict an applicant's successful job performance. An appropriate goal of a selection test may be the measurement of an applicant's ability to do the job's tasks rather than to predict future job performance based on the presence or absence of job-related KSAOs. This is recognized by the "Uniform Guidelines on Employee Selection Procedures," which specifically permit use of content validation alone for establishing the job-relatedness of achievement tests.[34]

The first step in establishing content validity is job analysis. The analysis sets forth the critical or important work behaviors of the job (job duties). Then the knowledge, skill, or ability (KSAO) needed to perform each of these duties is identified. For example, consider one of the tasks of a data entry clerk: "Uses a keypad to enter 6,000 numerals into a computer in one hour with no more than 1 percent error rate." We can design a five-minute test based on representative data actually entered by current job holders and measure the applicants' error rates. The test is valid because it accurately samples the content of the job. This concept is behind supplementing a paper-and-pencil driver test of safe driving KSAOs with a work sample test of skills to actually drive a car safely and legally under "real world" driving conditions. Another method of establishing content validity is to have subject matter experts identify the KSAOs needed to perform a job. The more completely the responsibilities of the job are covered, the more content-valid the selection process is.

CONSTRUCT VALIDITY

Construct validity is difficult to establish and, as the least-used method of establishing the validity of a test or other predictor of job performance, will be discussed only briefly. A construct is a trait such as leadership ability, judgment, or personality. Again, job analysis is used to identify any constructs that the subject matter experts (SMEs) believe underlie successful job performance. A selection procedure is developed or, more often, identified from a number of existing construct-measuring tests. The relationship between the construct, as measured by the test, and more or less successful job performance should be supported by empirical evidence from one or more job-related criterion studies. Construct validity is very complex and, as mentioned above, is the least-used approach for validating selection procedures used for initial hiring. A major application of construct validity is in assessment centers (discussed in Chapter 9), where it is used to determine qualifications for managerial jobs. Exhibit 8-5 provides a summary of issues to consider when choosing a selection procedure.

RECRUITING

Recruiting is the process of generating a sufficiently large group of qualified applicants to select the best-qualified individuals for available jobs. If this process is not carried out properly, the organization may not be able to select the best employees. In fact, there may be no selection at all; the organization must either hire those people who are available or allow jobs to go unfilled. This is particularly true for organizations with affirmative action programs. Quite often these programs fail simply because no organized effort is made to develop sources of underrepresented protected class applicants. There is no generally accepted best way to recruit prospective employees for the various jobs in an organization. New employees can be recruited from a number of sources, depending on the type of job. These are usually grouped into two basic source categories—internal and external.

INTERNAL SOURCES

Present employees are an important source of applicants for above-entry-level job vacancies in an organization. Filling vacancies with present employees may involve promotions (upward moves), transfers (lateral moves), or, in the case of downsizing, demotions (downward moves). In general, it is recommended that all vacancies be publicized and that anyone in the organization be allowed to apply for any opening.

EXHIBIT 8-5

SELECTING A TEST

Finding a good employee selection test can be a burgeoning task. With over 3,000 published tests, HR managers should carefully consider the following questions before selecting and using an employee selection test.

- Is the test appropriate for a work setting?
- Is the test reliable?
- Is the test valid?

- Is the test easy to administer?
- Is the test easy to score?
- Are test results easy to interpret?

If you answer no to any of the above questions then the selected test should not be used. If you do not know the answer to any of the above questions, the test should not be used until you can answer yes.

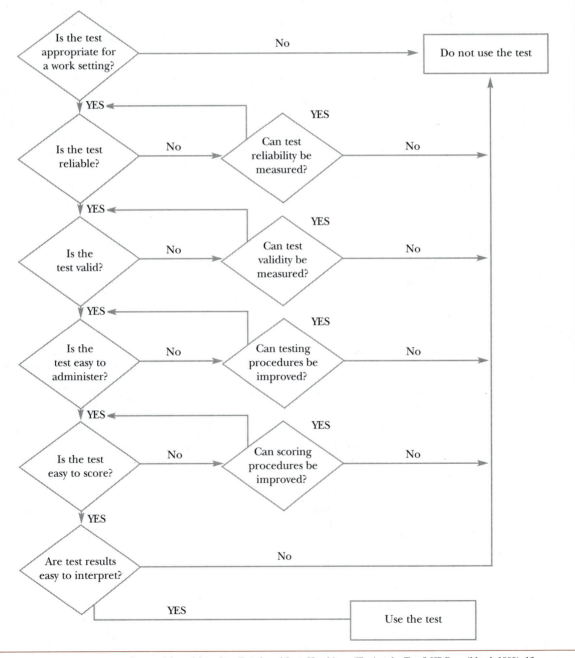

Source: Adapted from Joan Retsch and Scott Hutchison, "Testing the Test," *HR Focus* (March 1999), 13.

Many local governments require jobs to be posted when available. The consensus among experts is that an employee should have been with the organization for at least a year and in his or her present job for six months in order to become eligible to bid for a vacancy.

Job posting traditionally has meant "posting" an announcement or notice of the vacancy on a bulletin board. Now, it often also means "posting" it on the organization's intranet or web page and e-mailing the announcement to supervisors or even the total workforce.[35] Both approaches maximize employee awareness of job openings. The notice should include such items as title, department, job summary, qualifications, and salary. Job posting helps to discover talented, qualified persons within the organization and meet EEO and diversity commitments. Although it is neither necessary nor desirable to give present employees first refusal on all vacancies, a fair and understandable promotion and transfer system will build employee trust and enhance morale. Other advantages include good knowledge of the organization by the employee and good knowledge of the employee by the organization. Also, it is a quick and low-cost way to identify qualified and interested applicants.

The main internal source is present employees, either the applicants themselves or, more often, their immediate supervisors; however, former employees and friends of employees are also a good source of quality referrals. Recently, larger organizations have supplemented the traditional employee referral source by scanning employee information contained in electronic personnel files located in the HRIS. Similar to doing a key KSAO search of disk-filed resumes from outside applicants, the HR department searches its current employee HRIS files.

Employees, especially when they are good performers, are a particularly effective source for job applicants. People usually make friends with people similar to themselves. There are disadvantages to employee referrals, however. Employees might expect that all the people who are referred should receive job offers. Of course, hiring all referrals is usually not possible. A potentially more serious problem is maintaining an existing lack of diversity. Management training programs and internship programs are another source of internal recruiting. Recruiting only internally precludes the infusion of new ideas and methods. The organization can never be more diverse than its entry-level workforce. Thus, although there are important benefits to be gained from employee-related referrals, it is recommended that other sources be developed. Because an organization will not retain its better workers if they perceive the only way to improve themselves is outside their current organization, internal sources should always be used. However, because of the advantages discussed below, they should be supplemented by the use of external sources too.

EXTERNAL SOURCES

One commonly used external recruiting source is advertising, done through mass media such as radio, television, and newspapers, or by posting position announcements in locations where they are likely to be seen by persons seeking jobs. Advertising has the advantage of being selective, in that there is a clear indication of the nature of the job and qualifications needed. Another advantage of advertising is that it can be targeted. To encourage underrepresented protected class applicants, positions can be advertised in class-oriented media and announcements can be sent to grassroots organizations. If an organization is seeking a particular skill, advertising can be placed in trade magazines.

One early survey forecast correctly that recruitment advertising would become increasingly important, using image advertising, four-color ads, sophisticated advertising programs, and advertising research.[36] In some cities, PR firms and advertising agencies have been willing to design advertising campaigns for local government as a community service. These campaigns have been particularly effective in recruiting entry-level police officers. The main disadvantage of advertising, even when the creative work is contributed free of charge, is that it tends to be expensive.

Another external source is walk-ins. This source is relatively inexpensive, and applications can be filed and processed whenever vacancies occur. Walk-ins provide excellent public relations opportunities because applicants who are well treated are likely to share that with their friends and relations. On the other hand, walk-ins occur in a random fashion, and there may be no immediate match with available openings. This is particularly true for jobs requiring specialized skills.

An excellent recruiting source is public employment agencies. These agencies are established to match job openings with listings of job applicants. These agencies will also perform certain classification and screening functions. Most agencies administer work-sample tests, such as typing tests, to applicants. This prescreening of applicants for job-related KSAOs helps decrease the costs and increase the effectiveness of applicant selection. Normally, public employment agencies charge no fees for their services. A limitation of public employment agencies is that professional and technical workers infrequently use them.

Technical colleges, trade schools, and vocational training programs such as those conducted under the Workforce Investment Partnership Act (WIPA) prepare individuals for skilled trades and clerical occupations. Officials of these institutions and programs take a very active role in placing their graduates in suitable jobs. The WIPA is particularly helpful in this regard, since training-related employment for those who enroll in the various courses of study is the major criterion for continuing the program. Another federal program that has proved to provide a dedicated and surprisingly dependable workforce is the Welfare to Work program.[37]

Private employment services and professional search firms (headhunters) are increasingly used to fill professional and executive positions in local governments. Employment agencies represent job applicants, while search firms are hired by the organization. An earlier survey found use of search firms in recruiting for chief executive vacancies was common in jurisdictions of greater than 200,000 population, and the practice extended down to jurisdictions of less than 10,000 population. Search firms are quite expensive, and this method is restricted to units of government with sufficient resources to pay the costs, which, at the time of the survey, ran in the neighborhood of $12,000 plus expenses for a single search.[38]

Potential candidates for entry-level professional positions can be recruited from colleges and universities.[39] Most four-year colleges have placement offices and will set up contacts with seniors and recent graduates. Also, diversity can be increased and specially qualified applicants can be found at specific colleges and universities that graduate high numbers of specific skill program or underrepresented protected class students.

Within the last few years, the Internet has grown exponentially as a cost-effective source of high-quality applicants—especially for the more difficult, technical skill jobs.[40] One recruiting firm's research indicated that 93 percent of organizations surveyed expect to use the Internet more intensively for recruiting in the future, and that recruiting dollars spent on-line will grow tenfold within four years.[41] Driving this growth are a number of advantages to Internet recruiting, including that it is a quick, efficient, and basically paperless process. HR managers perceive that it accesses a large audience and targets qualified applicants with a quick turnaround that is less expensive and easier to manage than printed sources.[42]

Despite this, while most HR managers seem to take the Internet seriously, they struggle with how to use it effectively for recruiting purposes. The very breadth and depth of Internet recruiting activity today deters many local government HR managers from adopting this recruiting strategy.[43] The complexity of on-line recruiting, however, is grossly exaggerated. Sophisticated computer programs, better databases, and smart agent software are all helping on-line recruitment become more user friendly.[44] Smart agents can automatically search the Web for high-quality resumes and then slot them into a database without tying up recruiter or HR personnel time.[45]

http://www.shrm.org/
hrmagazine/articles/
0800cov.htm
HR Magazine provides
an article "Online and
Overwhelmed: Does Using
the Internet for Recruiting
Overwhelm You?"

Internet recruiting is growing worldwide and has been shown to drive down costs, reduce recruiting time, and make everybody feel better about the process.[46] To recruit competitively with private organizations, local governments must understand and use the Internet as a supplement (not a replacement) for the more traditional sources discussed above.

NEED FOR MORE EFFECTIVE RECRUITING

The effectiveness of recruiting varies widely across organizations. The cost of many recruiting techniques limits their use to large organizations with adequate financial resources. Organizational philosophy is also important. One frequently encounters a mindset that asks, "If we already have ten applicants for every opening, why should we recruit?" There are also differences between the public and private sectors. It is very doubtful that any public sector organization conducts the type of recruiting programs that are common in large corporations, particularly the recruiting of high-level executives. On the other hand, there is no real evidence that local governments recruit less effectively than business firms of the same size. It is becoming more common for cities in the 30,000–50,000 population range to conduct extensive searches for applicants when key positions are involved (police chief, city engineer, finance director, city manager) and to pay travel costs of those who are invited for interviews. For smaller cities and counties, such practices are unusual, but that is equally the case with small businesses.

Local governments need to recruit more effectively to compete successfully with their private sector counterparts in the relevant labor market. To be competitive, local governments need to proactively counter the following constraining factors:

• Many people hold negative attitudes about public employment, making government service unattractive.[47]
• Lower pay than private industry for similar jobs causes a shrinking labor pool during periods of full employment.[48]
• Tenured public employees' property and liberty interests in job make it more difficult to terminate poor performers.
• There is often a tendency on the part of hiring officials to request, from current employees, additional names of potential applicants in filling vacancies because of dissatisfaction with applicants on existing registers.[49]
• When the quality of certified applicants is only marginal, there is greater susceptibility to political pressures in making appointments.

In summary, effective recruiting by local governments serves two important purposes. First and most important, the qualification level of the applicant pool is a major factor in obtaining the best job-person match. No selection process can yield productive and competent workers if the applicants identified are marginal at best. Second, recruiting the best rather than marginal or just adequately qualified applicants is necessary to overcome the disadvantages that local governments face in competing with the private sector for quality employees.

SUMMARY

The objective of the selection process is to hire the most competent individuals within existing legal constraints. Before *selection* can take place, several important steps must be taken.

Legal requirements must be understood and complied with. Both disparate treatment and impact discrimination must be avoided. Affirmative action plans can be used to correct the effects of prior discrimination that has resulted in underrepresentation of protected group members in local government employment. Such voluntary AAPs must meet the criteria discussed above—and not become preferential treatment.

Objective, numerical measures of KSAOs tied to successful job performance must be developed. Such measurement plays a vital role in accurately predicting which candidates are likely to be most successful on the job. Reliable and valid selection measures must be used. To be reliable, a procedure must have results that are dependable, stable, and consistent. To be valid, the test or procedure must do what you intend it to do; in other words, it must measure job-related behaviors and KSAOs that predict successful job performance. The "Uniform Guidelines on Employee Selection Procedures" provide guidance in establishing the validity of selection procedures. In criterion-related validity, test results must statistically predict job performance. In content validity, a work sample or similar procedure must measure the job's content; that is, it must be relevant. It must not be contaminated with items that are not important to the job or leave out things that are. In construct validity, traits or constructs that are necessary for successful job performance must be identified, measured, and used to select only the best-qualified applicants.

Recruiting is the process of generating a sufficiently large group of well-qualified applicants to allow selection of only the best-qualified individuals in terms of predicted successful job performance for available jobs. Internal sources, which include qualified applicants in the organization, must be used to retain the best employees. External sources must also be used, choosing the most appropriate for any particular job from the wide variety of sources discussed above.

QUESTIONS FOR REVIEW AND DISCUSSION

1. What options are available to an organization if a selection procedure has a disparate impact on a protected group?
2. Compare the advantages and disadvantages of AAPs and "diversity" initiatives.
3. Define the concepts of reliability and validity.
4. In selecting candidates for a school bus driver job, you would like to administer both a paper-and-pencil test of safety and law knowledge and an actual driving skill and ability work sample test. How should each test be validated; and, if validated differently (hint), why?
5. Develop a policy statement for a city government on how to develop an internal selection (promotions, transfers, and demotions) program.
6. Discuss briefly and defend the use of three external sources of candidates for local government jobs.

7. Compare the advantages and disadvantages of internal versus external sources of recruitment.

ENDNOTES

[1] "Uniform Guidelines on Employee Selection Procedures," 43 *Federal Register* (August 25, 1978), 38,297.

[2] James A. Buford Jr., "Affirmative Action Works," *Commonweal*, 125 (June 1998), 12–15.

[3] Buford, 12.

[4] Robert D. Gatewood and Hubert S. Feild, *Human Resource Selection*, 5th ed. (Chicago: Dryden, 2001), 54–56.

[5] *United Steelworkers of America v. Weber*, 443 U.S. 193 (1979).

[6] Equal Employment Opportunity Commission, "Affirmative Action Appropriate Under Title VII of the Civil Rights Act as Amended," 44 *Federal Register*, 4422–4430 (January 19, 1979).

[7] Carlos R. Gullett, "Reverse Discrimination and Remedial Affirmative Action in Employment: Dealing with the Paradox of Nondiscrimination," *Public Personnel Management* 29 (Spring 2000), 107–118.

[8] Robert J. Grossman, "Is Diversity Working?" *HR Magazine* 45 (March 2000), 46–50.

[9] *Richmond v. Croson Company*, 488 U.S. 469 (1989).

[10] Francis J. Milleken and Luis L. Martins, "Searching for Common Threads: Understanding the Multiple Effects of Diversity in Organizational Groups," *Academy of Management Review* 21 (April 1996), 402–433.

[11] Patricia A. Galagan and Jennifer J. Salopek, "Thinking Differently about Difference," *Training & Development* 54 (May 2000), 52–54.

[12] John M. Ivancevich and Jacqueline A. Gilbert, "Diversity Management: Time for a New Approach," *Public Personnel Management* 29 (Spring 2000), 75–92.

[13] Ivancevich and Gilbert, 75–92.

[14] Milinda Carlton, Philip Hawkey, Douglas Watkins, and William Donahue, "Affirmative Action and Affirming Diversity," *Public Management* 79, no. 1 (January 1997), 19–23.

[15] Audrey Mathews, "Diversity: A Principle of Human Resource Management," *Public Personnel Management* 27 (Summer 1998), 175–185.

[16] Jacqueline A. Gilbert and John M. Ivancevich, "Valuing Diversity: A Tale of Two Organizations," *Academy of Management Executive* 14 (February 2000), 93–105.

[17] Gatewood and Feild, 113–157.

[18] Gatewood and Feild, 161–226.

19 Gatewood and Feild, 161. See Chapters 4 and 5 (113–226) for an in-depth discussion of reliability and validity.

[20] Christopher Daniel, "Science, System or Hunch: Alternative Approaches to Improving Employee Selection," *Public Personnel Management* 15 (Spring 1986), 1–9.

[21] Richard W. Beatty and Craig E. Schneier, *Personnel Administration*, 2d ed. (Reading Mass.: Addison-Wesley, 1982), 282–283.

[22] Gatewood and Feild, 121–138. This is the source of the following discussion of the internal consistency method of estimating reliability.

[23] Elliott D. Pursell, Michael A. Campion, and Sarah R. Gaylord, "Structured Interviewing: Avoiding Selection Problems," *Personnel Journal* 59 (November 1980), 907–912.

[24] Philip L. Roth and Philip Bobko, "A Research Agenda for Multi-attribute Utility Analysis in Human Resource Management," *Human Resource Management Review* 7 (Fall 1997), 341–368.

[25] Frank L. Schmidt, John E. Hunter, Robert C. McKenzie, and Tress W. Muldrow, "Impact of Valid Selection Procedures on Work-Force Productivity," *Journal of Applied Psychology* 64 (December 1979), 609–626.

[26] Gatewood and Feild, 206–211.

[27] "Uniform Guidelines," 38,300–38,303. See also Gatewood and Feild, 164–205.

[28] Alan H. Kvanli, Robert J. Pavur, and C. Stephen Guynes, *Introduction to Business Statistics*, 5th ed. (Cincinnati: South-Western, 2000), 608–672. To determine the relationship between two paired variables, a correlation coefficient is computed. Its range is $+1.00$ (perfect positive correlation) to -1.00 (perfect negative correlation). Zero indicates no correlation.

[29] Gatewood and Feild, 164–171.

[30] Beatty and Schneier, 281.

[31] Bruce A. Sery, "The Concurrent Validity of the Correctional Officers Interest Blank," *Public Personnel Management* 17 (Summer 1988), 135–144.

[32] Part 60-3.5B. Criterion-related, content, and construct validity, "Uniform Guidelines on Employee Selection Procedures" (1978).

[33] Again, see Part 60-3.5B. Criterion-related, content, and construct validity, "Uniform Guidelines on Employee Selection Procedures" (1978).

[34] Dwight R. Norris and James A. Buford Jr., "A Content Valid Writing Test: A Case Study," *Personnel Administrator* 25 (January 1980), 40–43.

[35] John Day, "Online Job Ads with a Human Touch," *HR Magazine* 45 (March 2000), 140–142.

[36] Jo Bredwell, "The Use of Broadcast Advertising for Recruitment," *Personnel Administrator* 26 (February 1981), 45–49.

[37] "Survey Says Welfare-to-Work Program Is a Success," *HR Focus* 77 (June 2000), 8; and A. Jossi, "From Welfare to Work: Filling a Tall Order," *Training* 34 (1997), 44–50.

[38] David N. Ammons and James J. Glass, "Headhunters in Local Government: Use of Executive Search Firms in Managerial Selection," *Public Administration Review* 48 (May/June 1988), 687–693.

[39] Sandra Grabczynski, "Nab New Grads by Building Relationships with Colleges," *Workforce* 79 (May 2000), 98–103.

[40] Steven L. Thomas and Katherine Ray, "Recruiting and the Web: High-Tech Hiring," *Business Horizons* 43 (May/June 2000), 43–52.

[41] Scott Hays, "Hiring on the Web," *Workforce* 78 (August 1999), 76–84.

[42] Hays, 76.

[43] Ruth Thaler-Carter, "Recruiting Through the Web: Better or Just Bigger?" *HRMagazine* 43 (November 1998), 61.

[44] "More Pros and Cons to Internet Recruiting," *HR Focus* 77 (May 2000), 8.

[45] Samuel Greengard, "Putting Online Recruiting to Work," *Workforce* 77 (August 1998), 73.

[46] Thaler-Carter, 68.

[47] H. George Frederickson, "Understanding Attitudes Toward Public Employment," *Public Administration Review* 27 (December 1967), 411–420.

[48] Jay M. Shafritz, Albert C. Hyde, and David H. Rosenbloom, *Personnel Management in Government,* 4th ed. (New York: Dekker, 1992).

[49] Gatewood and Feild, 161.

CHAPTER 9
SELECTING EMPLOYEES

The city of Cheyenne, Wyoming, is known as the "Magic City on the Plains." And recently, according to Rich Abernethy, director of human resources for the city, the HR department has been making "magic" of their own. In today's tight labor market, many organizations are struggling to find and hire qualified employees. Many local governments are finding the struggle particularly challenging because they cannot keep pace with private sector employment practices. In the past, local government jobs were more coveted than today. Over the past few years, Cheyenne, which has a population of approximately 56,000, has overcome these challenges.

Cheyenne's success in finding and hiring highly qualified employees can be attributed to its revamped and improved employee recruitment and selection process. For example, the city, using the Internet and other information technologies, has been successful in recruiting applicants from across the United States. Although Cheyenne's aggressive recruiting efforts have results in large applicant pools, it is their selection process that results in the "best" applicants being hired.

Once a week, the city of Cheyenne posts open positions. The city accepts applications only for positions that are currently open. All applicants for city jobs must complete a standardized application form provided by the HR department. Applications are screened to identify applicants who possess required knowledge, skills, and abilities. Application data for applicants who appear qualified are verified for accuracy. The highest qualified applicants are invited to participate in an interview. A panel of city employees then interviews those applicants. The applicant with the best qualifications is then offered the position contingent on a criminal background check and pre-employment drug and/or alcohol screening. According to Rick Abernethy, this new hiring process has allowed in the city of Cheyenne, Wyoming, not only to recruit large pools of applicants for open positions but also to hire applicants who have the best qualifications for the position.

Source: Rick Abernethy, city of Cheyenne, Wyoming (Personal Communication, October 23, 2000); and city of Cheyenne, Wyoming, *http://www.cheyennecity.org/* (February 14, 2001).

INTRODUCTION

Selecting a competent workforce is one of the most important activities in human resource management. Sound selection helps local governments to find, lawfully and, at least cost, the most competent individuals to fill job openings. Further, selection ensures these competent employees are committed to local government's mission and vision. **Selection** refers to the process whereby job-related information is collected from applicants and offers of employment are given to those applicants who are most likely to be successful.[1]

A strategic approach to selection focuses on both competency and commitment. For example, a city has a strategic objective of maintaining its image, character, and quality of life through historic preservation, controlling commercial development, reducing traffic congestion, and so forth. The city planning department that deals with these issues relies on various information technology (IT) systems and applications. In selection of applicants to fill such jobs as CAD/CAM operator and systems analyst, the city is seeking employees with highly specialized and market-sensitive skills. Employees without the requisite competencies will not be able to perform effectively. On the other hand, employees who view their skills in terms of employment mobility (as opposed to a means to accomplish important planning goals) will continue to pursue opportunities based on the pay rather than the purpose. Thus, to achieve its strategic objectives and "stop the hop," the city must hire both competent and committed employees.

As Chapter 10 discusses, poor selection cannot be overcome with training and development. It is necessary, therefore, for local governments to institute a selection process, based on job analysis, that results in employing the most qualified and committed applicant. The selection process for small local governments is likely to be minimal and simple, involving only a supervisor and/or manager with hiring authority. Larger local governments, on the other hand, are more likely to have larger, more complex selection processes that require numerous people carrying out various tasks. Regardless, the objective of a selection process is to select and hire applicants who will help a local government achieve its strategic objectives.

It is true that legislation and court decisions have limited what an organization can do, particularly with regard to selection.[2] Many previously common practices are now either illegal or questionable. But research has clearly shown that legally defensible practices are also those most likely to result in selecting the person who, in fact, will perform the job the best. In fact, the concepts and techniques presented here would have been recommended in the absence of legal constraints.

In outlining the factors and procedures required for effective employee selection, this chapter addresses the following topics: strategies used in selection, nature of preemployment inquiries, general and job-specific selection procedures, certification and appointment procedures, documentation and record-keeping requirements, and benefits of effective recruiting and job-related selection.

http://www.
monsterboard.com
Monster.com is an on-line
employment search
and employer
recruitment company.

SELECTION STRATEGIES

The selection process consists of the steps that take place between recruitment and job offer. In the public sector this process is also known as examining and includes written and performance tests that require applicants to be present. Examining includes generating ratings of education, training, experience (KSAO), and other job-related achievements described by the applicant. Finally, examining includes the results of background checks such as contacts with references. The selection (or examining) process is typically a combination of these examination types. The sequence of steps used depends on the selection strategy. Two basic job-specific selection strategies are noncompensatory and compensatory approaches.[3]

NONCOMPENSATORY APPROACH TO SELECTION

The **noncompensatory approach** is used when there are minimum qualifications for the job that cannot be "compensated" by high qualifications in other areas. For example, an applicant for a computer specialist position who exceeds the educational requirements for the job, but does not meet the minimum experience levels needed, would not be selected. Under the noncompensatory approach, higher levels of education *cannot* offset (compensate) lack of experience. The noncompensatory approach can be implemented in one of two ways, **multiple-gate** or **multiple-hurdle**. In both methods, applicants face a number of selection procedures, all of which must be cleared before the applicant is determined to be qualified for a job. Thus, both methods identify unqualified applicants prior to tendering any job offer. The difference between the two is in how the selection procedures are applied. When done *all at once*, the procedure is called multiple-gate. Exhibit 9-1 provides an example of the multiple-gate procedure. Referring to our example of a computer specialist position, the applicant would complete an application, undergo preemployment screening, take a work-sample test, be interviewed, and undergo a back-

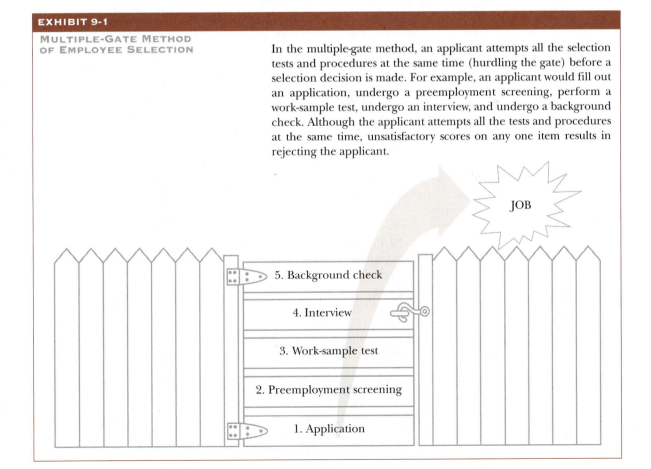

EXHIBIT 9-1

MULTIPLE-GATE METHOD OF EMPLOYEE SELECTION

In the multiple-gate method, an applicant attempts all the selection tests and procedures at the same time (hurdling the gate) before a selection decision is made. For example, an applicant would fill out an application, undergo a preemployment screening, perform a work-sample test, undergo an interview, and undergo a background check. Although the applicant attempts all the tests and procedures at the same time, unsatisfactory scores on any one item results in rejecting the applicant.

JOB

5. Background check

4. Interview

3. Work-sample test

2. Preemployment screening

1. Application

ground check. Regardless of how well the applicant performs on the latter four tests and procedures, lack of experience as indicated on the application form would result in the applicant not being selected.

A *sequential* method, that is, where applicants must successfully pass each element separately before facing the next (like clearing the hurdles in a race), is called multiple-hurdle. Exhibit 9-2 provides an example of the multiple-hurdle method. In our example, the applicant would be rejected upon completing the application and would not be allowed to attempt the remaining selection tests. Most local government positions have some minimum qualifications that can be assessed by the above methods. Further, local governments usually use some form of the multiple-hurdle strategy: for example, discarding some candidates after reviewing their resumes and applications, more candidates after an initial interview, and more after completing reference checks. Both multiple-gate and multiple-hurdle methods result in the same set or pool of minimally qualified applicants. While helpful in eliminating unqualified applicants early in the selection process, they do not help select from that pool the "best" qualified candidate or candidates to which job offers should actually be made.

COMPENSATORY APPROACH TO SELECTION

The **compensatory approach** allows all applicants to progress through the entire selection process. Under the compensatory approach our computer specialist position applicant's high levels of education *would* offset (compensate) lack of experience. Instead of being screened out by any one selection procedure, applicants are evaluated on a composite score of assessments where low scores in certain areas can be offset or "compensated" for by high scores in others areas. This approach provides an opportunity for an applicant to be evaluated for and placed in a variety of jobs. The compensatory approach, thus, provides for a more statistically sound evaluation of each applicant than noncompensatory approaches. The primary compensatory strategy is **multiple-linear regression**. In multiple-linear regression, selection tests and procedures based on KSAOs, tasks, and responsibilities of the job are compared with a single numerical measure of job performance. Exhibit 9-3 provides an example of the multiple-linear regression procedure. This process results in a *predicted job performance* score. Because of the complexity involved in designing and carrying out multiple-linear regression analysis, most local governments use noncompensatory approaches at best or simply hire employees without any evaluation at worst.

The two approaches can, however, be used together. For example, a local government could use a multiple-hurdle method to screen out unqualified applicants and multiple-linear regression to rank-order the remaining applicants on their test and selection procedure scores. Such a combination of the two basic strategies would provide for a more complete evaluation of each applicant and rank-ordering (as discussed in the remainder of the chapter) on the "best and legal" selection criteria of predicted job performance.

All selection procedures or hurdles that have an adverse effect on members of protected groups must be validated as job-related regardless of the selection strategy used.[4] Compensatory or combination selection methods that have not been validated (see Chapter 8 discussion) cannot be used to overcome discriminatory disparate impact (that is, disparate impact that results from selection procedures that are not job related).[5] Since most local governments do not have a variety of vacancies at any one time, the compensatory strategy usually offers no significant advantage of efficiency in filling vacancies. On the other hand, it is much easier to manage the selection process and track the applicant flow data needed for EEO

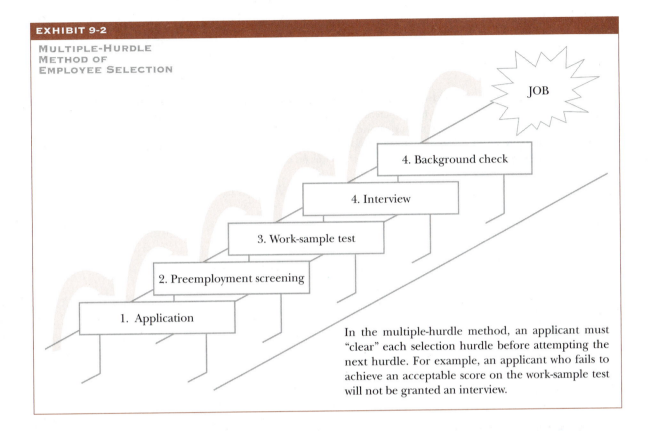

EXHIBIT 9-2

MULTIPLE-HURDLE
METHOD OF
EMPLOYEE SELECTION

JOB

4. Background check

4. Interview

3. Work-sample test

2. Preemployment screening

1. Application

In the multiple-hurdle method, an applicant must "clear" each selection hurdle before attempting the next hurdle. For example, an applicant who fails to achieve an acceptable score on the work-sample test will not be granted an interview.

documentation when a noncompensatory approach is used. Noncompensatory approaches, therefore, offer the most cost-effective approach for small to medium-sized organizations.

NATURE OF PREEMPLOYMENT INQUIRIES

A certain amount of information is needed on all applicants so that the organization will be able to manage the selection process in an orderly and systematic manner. This information is developed through preemployment inquiries and falls into two basic categories. The first category is general information to be used for such things as identification, classification, and record keeping. The second kind of information relates to the suitability of an applicant for a particular job.

Since all selection practices are "tests" within the meaning of EEO laws and regulations, even the preliminary information requested must be job related. At this stage, inquiries should be limited to obvious items, and resulting decisions must be those that can be justified in job-related terms. For example, assume that an applicant is asked to indicate educational attainment and areas of study. No one would question declining to refer an applicant who had completed only the tenth grade for the position of county engineer. On the other hand, if a decision were made to reject the same applicant for a janitorial position because of an arbitrary high school diploma requirement, it would be difficult to establish job relatedness.

It is usually illegal to request data that directly reveal protected class characteristics (except for EEO reporting requirements, discussed later), and one can only

EXHIBIT 9-3

MULTIPLE-LINEAR REGRESSIONAL METHOD OF EMPLOYEE SELECTION

In the multiple-linear regressional method, an applicant attempts all the selection tests and procedures and a potential employee's performance is predicted. For example, an applicant would perform a work-sample test, undergo an interview, and undergo a background check to apply for a job. Each "predictor" variable is weighted and all the variables are added to compute an employee predictor score. An applicant can, therefore, "compensate" for low scores on a test or procedure with high scores on others.

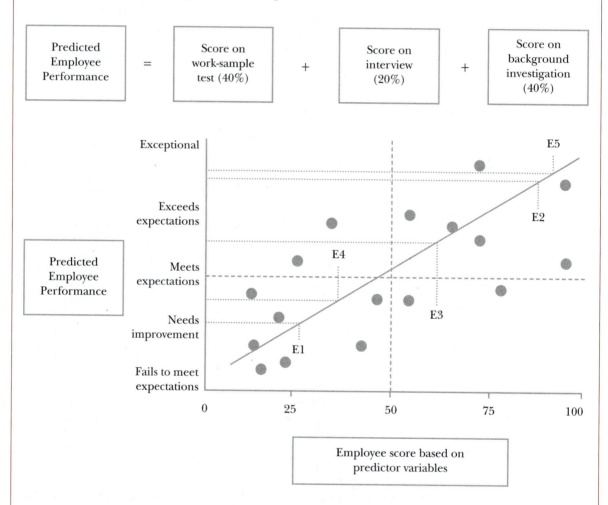

In this example, the minimum acceptable employee score be considered for employment is 50 (based on predictor variables). That is, the predicted employee score for an employee who meets expectations is 50. Note that in this example, employees 2, 3, and 5 would be predicted to exceed performance expectations, but, employee 3 would actually "need improvement." Further, employees 1 and 4 would not be considered employable under the model even though 4's performance would exceed expectations.

question why an employer would want this information in the first place—at least for any kind of selection decision. It is also difficult to believe that an organization can benefit from a standard that has a disparate impact on minorities. The variety of areas in which discrimination can occur is very broad. Exhibit 9-4 contains general guidelines for preemployment inquiries. This guide, although not exhaustive, illustrates the care that organizations must exercise to avoid both the appearance and the actual fact of discrimination.

Most local governments use some form of preemployment inquiry, an inexpensive and relatively easy technique for gathering basic information about a potential applicant. Such inquiries, however, are a poor technique for gathering information about a potential applicant's competencies and commitment to the organization. As long as preemployment inquiries are structured and consistent, they can be a useful initial decision-making tool.

SELECTION PROCEDURES: GENERAL METHODS

As discussed earlier, selection procedures or "hurdles" through which all applicants normally pass typically include the application form, background investigation, and initial screening interview. Prior to passage of the Americans with Disabilities Act (ADA) in 1990, a physical examination would also have been included in that list. Since then, such examinations, while still an important preemployment requirement, should be scheduled only after a provisional job offer has been tendered. While the preceding procedures should be job related, they are not necessarily job specific. For that reason, the selection interview is discussed in a later section.

APPLICATION FORMS

The application form is the most widely used preselection device. A completed form is the dated record of a candidate's interest in a position with the organization. Additionally, it serves as a profile of the applicant for classification, initial screening, and record keeping. If the candidate is subsequently hired, the information becomes the basic personnel record for the employee. There is a tendency for organizations to request too much information on the application form, often including items that are not job related. For example, questions about an applicant's hobbies, extracurricular activities, marital status, emergency contact information, community activities, club memberships, and other non-job-related or potentially illegal questions should not be included on a local government's application form. Although the form is normally standardized, the jobs in an organization vary greatly; thus, items that relate to one job may be irrelevant for others. Because of this, many organizations' existing application forms may not fully comply with current equal opportunity law.[6] Major divisions of an application form typically include identification, employment status, employment record, education record, specialized training, military record, and references. When possible, application forms should be adapted for each job opening.

IDENTIFICATION. Most application forms begin with a request for personal data, usually including name, address, telephone number, e-mail address, and additional contacts for messages. This information is used to establish a file and to contact the applicant.

EXHIBIT 9-4

GUIDELINES FOR PREEMPLOYMENT INQUIRIES

Subject	Acceptable Inquiries	Unacceptable Inquiries
Name	Full name; whether applicant has worked under different name.	Inquiries that would indicate national origin; previous name; preferred courtesy title (Mr., Ms., Mrs.).
Residence	Address	Length of time at that address; inquiry into foreign address that would indicate national origin; name sand relationships of persons with whom applicant resides; whether home is owned or rented.
Race, color, or ethnicity	Race and national origin for purpose of record keeping may be requested on a form to be kept separate from the application.	Race as an employment criteria under any circumstances; color of skin, eyes, hair, etc.; national origin as employment criteria except for BFOQ; requirement that applicant submit a photograph.
Sex	Sex for purposes of record keeping may be requested on a form to be kept separate from the application.	Sex as an employment criteria except for BFOQ; indirect inquiry such as pregnancy, height, or weight to establish sex; requirement that applicant submit a photograph.
Age	Whether applicant can submit legal proof of age upon employment; whether applicant is at least 18 years old.	Age or date of birth.
Marital and family status	Whether applicant can meet work schedules.	Marital status; number and age of children; inquiries related to pregnancy, family planning, child care arrangements, etc.
Religion	Whether applicant can meet work schedules.	Church affiliation; religious holidays observed.
Citizenship	Whether applicant is U.S. citizen or on visa; whether applicant can be lawfully employed.	In what country applicant holds citizenship; whether a natural born or naturalized citizen; citizenship of parents or spouse; birthplace.
Education	Academic, vocational, or professional institutions; areas of study; degrees, diplomas, or certificates awarded.	Racial, ethnic, or religious information about institutions; grade point average; class standing; dates of enrollment used to elicit age.
Organizations	Memberships in trade or professional organizations, including unions, that relate to the job or area of work.	Social clubs, fraternities, lodges, etc.
Health and physical characteristics	Whether applicant can perform job tasks with or without accommodations.	General health and physical status; nature of disability; height, weight.
Financial status	Salary requirements.	Credit rating, garnishments, debts, or assets.
Arrest, conviction, and court record	Convictions related to job or area of work.	Any inquiry into arrests; any inquiry not related to specific job or areas of work.

EXHIBIT 9-4 (CONTINUED)

GUIDELINES FOR PREEMPLOYMENT
INQUIRIES

Subject	Acceptable Inquiries	Unacceptable Inquiries
Reference	Names or personal or professional references; by whom referred.	Name of pastor or religious leader.
Military status	Arm or branch of service, date of discharge, rank; training and experience related to job or area of work.	Type of discharge; dates of service used to elicit age.
Type of job sought	Specific position or nature of work desired; whether applicant can meet work schedules.	Preferences regarding race or sex of workforce; child care arrangements.
Experience	Work experience, including names and addresses of previous employers and dates worked; type of position held; reason for leaving; salary history.	Inquiries that focus on experience not required for the job.
Emergency contact	Name and contact information of person to be notified in an emergency.	Name and contact information of nearest relative to be contacted in an emergency.
Non-job-related conduct	None.	Inquiries that focus on conduct not associated with the job; whether applicant rides motorcycles or likes bluegrass music.

Source: Robert D. Gatewood and Hubert S. Feild, *Human Resource Selection*, 5th ed. (Chicago: Dryden, 2001), 11–420; and Arthur H. Bell, "Handling the Fatal Five Hiring Questions," *Credit Union Executive Journal*, 40 (May/June 2000), 27. James A. Buford Jr., Arthur G. Bedeian, and James R. Lindner, *Management in Extension*, 3d ed. (Columbus, OH: Ohio State University Extension, 1995), 150–152.

EMPLOYMENT STATUS. These items relate to the applicant's work objective and availability. Information that should be requested includes type of work or specific job sought, date available for work, previous applications or employment, and how the applicant was referred. This information assists the HR department in matching the applicant's work objective and qualifications with jobs available in the organization. It is also used to monitor the effectiveness of various recruitment sources.

EMPLOYMENT RECORD. Applicants should list their previous jobs, accounting for all elapsed time in the workforce. The HR department can tell from this information if a person is a "job-hopper" or a prospective long-term employee. This section also identifies periods of unemployment that should be checked out. Reviewing the type of jobs held also indicates what types of knowledge, skills, and abilities the candidate has gained through work experience.

EDUCATION. An important factor in evaluating applicants for various jobs, the educational record indicates the applicant's ability to read and write and the type and level of knowledge and skills acquired through formal study. In this section the applicant should provide specific information on the subject matter studied and diplomas, degrees, or other credentials received.

SPECIALIZED TRAINING AND SKILLS. Many job-related skills and aptitudes are acquired outside the classroom. For this reason the applicant should provide information on specific competencies resulting from on-the-job training, military service, self-study, and other types of experiential learning.

MILITARY RECORD. Questions about military service should include branch of service, date of discharge, rank, and military occupation specialty (MOS). This information is used in the same manner as employment history. It also provides an indication of how the applicant has been able to function in a structured environment and whether or not the candidate is a veteran.

REFERENCES. Applicants are often asked to list persons who can attest to their character, work habits, job performance, qualifications, and so on. Additional "reference" information can and should be obtained from other sections of the application form for use in conducting necessary background investigations.

SIGNATURE. Applicants should be required to sign and date their application. It is important for the signature line to provide that the applicant affirms that the information is true and that falsification may be grounds for discharge. Blanket authorization allowing the employer to contact references, verify employment and education data, and undertake other necessary investigations should also be included.

Some organizations have successfully weighted various items on the application form to predict job success rather than just screen out the unqualified. When this is done, the content and weights assigned to items on the form must be based on a job analysis.[7] It would usually not be appropriate to use a weighted application form as the sole instrument to predict job performance. Other devices (such as the supplemental application form) are even more appropriate for collecting job-specific information. Several of these are discussed below.

Information on race, sex, and other characteristics is also needed for use in computing and reporting appropriate EEOC-required statistics. The EEOC allows a detachable or separate survey form requesting data regarding race, religion, sex, national origin, and age. The form should indicate that the data is kept solely for EEO purposes and will be kept separate from other application materials. No employment decision can be made on any information provided on this form. Although collecting this information many seem paradoxical in view of the previous discussion, the fact is that lacking the data is not considered a valid excuse for failing to provide required reports.

Ease in use, low cost, and the need to gather basic applicant information contributes to the wide use of application forms by nearly all local governments. Application forms, however, often request information from applicants that is not directly related to an applicant's ability to perform a job. Application forms should be designed to gather information about an applicant's knowledge, skills, and abilities.

INITIAL SCREENING INTERVIEWS

In some cases an interview may be held shortly before or after an individual has completed an application. This brief interview, called an initial screening interview, helps to find out whether the individual's qualifications are likely to match any of the present or projected job openings in the organization and determines if there is any advantage to be gained by either the applicant or the organization in maintaining contact.[8] It can also be used to determine an individual's knowledge of the organization's mission and vision. Initial screening interviews have moderate use in local governments and are relatively easy to develop and implement. Typically, areas covered include job interests, career goals, location desired, salary expectations, and availability for work.

A structured interview is much more reliable and valid for selection than the more traditional open-ended interview. The interviewer should be supplied with a list of general employment or job-related items that require short answers. Even this type of interview has EEO implications; therefore, if the response to an item is one that might affect protected classes differentially, the interviewer should not use it.

BACKGROUND INVESTIGATIONS

Background investigations involve collecting and using information concerning an applicant's past performance, credit, health, character, personal activities, and education. Other persons than the applicant supply this information. The principal sources of such information are reference checks. Background investigations and reference checks are used extensively by local governments but can increase legal risks.[9] Checking backgrounds and references of potential employees is time consuming and costly. Such information, however, is useful in confirming information previously provided by the candidate and for gaining a broader perspective on the candidate's competencies. Background investigations are also important in reducing exposure to charges of **negligent hiring**. Employers have a common law duty not to hire persons who are likely to engage in discriminatory conduct or injure others (also discussed in Chapter 16). Certain types of jobs require the exercise of a *heightened duty of care.* Such positions include those in which employees have access to master keys (custodians), cash (customer service representatives), narcotics (health care professionals), children (day care workers), patients (health care professionals), weapons (police officers), and dangerous materials (water treatment plant operator). The duty is increased when such employees must work without direct supervision.

http://www.corporate-screening.com/employment_screening.htm
Corporate Screening Services provides examples of types of employee background information that can be investigated.

Following a structured format and recording information on a standardized form can improve the effectiveness of background investigations and reference checks and reduces the complexity in administering and analyzing information. Many local governments require extensive background investigations for potential public safety employees and those who interact with children.

The investigation process is both systematic and intuitive and includes a wide range of job-related issues such as performance on previous jobs and the ability to work with people. Reference checking may appear to be a simple matter, but it is one of the least understood aspects of the selection process. The contacts that should be made depend on the nature of the job; in some cases, the references listed on the application are not useful. It is only natural for an applicant to list those people who are likely to praise his or her job performance. The best references are obtained in person, where there is a chance to see whether nonverbal behavior (body language) matches what is said. If such a meeting cannot be arranged, then the telephone is the next best method. HR professionals report the following information may be obtained by reference checking:

- Dates of employment
- Eligibility for rehire
- Prospective qualifications for specific jobs
- Overall impression of employability
- Driving record
- Work habits
- Human relations skills
- Credit history
- Personality traits[10]

Checking applicant references, conducting background investigation on potential employees, and submitting applicants to medical exams, drug tests, and polygraph tests are commonly used employment screening devices. The purpose of such screening devices is to identify applicants who will best help an organization achieve its objectives. Cities are particularly vulnerable targets of litigation. Of the five employee screening devices listed, reference checking and medical/physical exams were more likely to be challenged in federal court than background investigations and drug tests.

WILL YOUR EMPLOYMENT SCREENING DEVICES WITHSTAND LEGAL CHALLENGE?

Polygraph tests were the least likely of the five to be challenged. When legally challenged, use of polygraph tests and background investigations resulted in the highest percentage of lost cases for organizations, followed by reference checks, medical/physical exams, and drug tests. Of the five employee selection devices listed, background investigations and reference checking are the most legally risky procedures and, not surprisingly, least valid and reliable procedures used. In light of this information, cities should carefully consider whether such selection devices are necessary and/or whether alternate devices, such as letters of reference, biographical information blanks, weighted application blanks, honesty tests, and so on are more appropriate and legally sound. Regardless of the selection device used, cities can take steps to reduce their liability and stave off litigation by ensuring that all employee selection devices are reliable, valid, and job-related.

Source: David E. Terpstra et al., "The Nature of Litigation Surrounding Five Screening Devices," *Public Personnel Management* 29 (Spring 2000), 43–54.

For references to serve as indicators of future performance, the people who give them must be knowledgeable about the applicant and his or her job-related activities, experience, or KSAO. It is rare that one person can provide a complete picture of the applicant's job-related strengths and weaknesses. One person may know why a person quit a job, another about work habits, and yet another about academic performance. The key point to remember is that when questionable job-related information surfaces, the investigation should be pursued until the issue is resolved, one way or the other. Background investigations must comply with the Fair Credit Reporting Act (FCRA). FCRA requires employers who use outside agencies to conduct such background investigations to notify applicants that an outside agency is being used. If an applicant is not hired, he or she must be notified that rejection was because of adverse information resulting from the background investigation.

Reference checking is a type of selection test and, therefore, the information sought must, as stated several times above, be job related. Standards of information should be applied uniformly within any job classification. If one item is grounds for denial of a job to one person, it should be the same for any other person who applies for the same job. Reference checks and background investigations should be documented to prove that decisions were based on relevant, job-related information. Both can increase legal risks, and city governments are increasingly vulnerable to litigation.[11]

MEDICAL EVALUATION/PHYSICAL EXAMINATION

Many cities and counties require a medical examination, particularly for public safety jobs such as police officers, firefighters, and solid waste handlers, where physical exertion and stamina are job related. Medical evaluations and physical examinations are expensive and complex selection tools. As stated before, since passage of the Americans with Disabilities Act in 1990, the examination should not be scheduled until after a provisional job offer has been tendered and accepted. This is because the ADA specifically prohibits preemployment inquiries that would provide information about a person's disability.[12] Typically, the applicant is asked to complete a health questionnaire, often supplemented with a physical examination by a nurse or physician, after a provisional job offer. Like other procedures, this evaluation should be related to requirements of the type of job for which the candidate is being considered. Organizations must be careful not to use the information to screen out protected class members—including disabled applicants. Purposes of the medical evaluation and physical examination include

- Ensuring that prospective employees are physically and mentally capable of performing the essential functions of the job (with reasonable accommodation that does not cause undue hardship on the organization),
- Establishing a record of the applicant's health for obtaining lower group insurance rates,
- Complying with state and local laws regarding communicable diseases, particularly in food handling operations, and
- Protecting the organization against workers' compensation claims for preexisting conditions.

JOB-SPECIFIC SELECTION PROCEDURES

Job selection techniques that are job specific rather than general should include supplemental application forms, employment tests, and structured interviews. The key to designing job-related selection procedures is job analysis. Recall from Chapter 8 that job analysis is the systematic process of gathering, understanding, and reporting information about a job. There is considerable evidence that selection procedures based on job analysis are more valid and less biased against protected class members than procedures developed without the benefit of job analysis. Use of job analysis ensures that "the only discrimination that occurs is that of the best applicant from the others and the process is fair to all."[13] If the job analysis has been properly conducted, the resulting job specifications will contain a unique set of knowledge, skills, abilities and, other characteristics (KSAO); any special requirements; and credentials and experience needed for job performance. Each of these factors should be properly linked to one or more job duties. Selection techniques then "test" whether or not applicants have the necessary KSAO, physical characteristics, special requirements, credentials, and experience.

Exhibit 9-5 shows the complete specifications for the job of Park Maintenance Foreman, focusing on KSAO. Each KSAO that is needed for immediate job performance is identified as a minimum qualification (MQ). Those that are desirable are identified as "may train" (MT). Those that will be acquired during a brief orientation period or during on-the-job training are identified as "will train" (WT). The choice of tests or other selection measures to be used depends on determination of the relative importance of KSAOs that they are intended to measure. In the example shown, the KSAOs that are minimum qualifications would receive the highest weights, those that are desirable considerably less weight, and those that are to be acquired on the job no weight.

In this particular case, the decision was made that those KSAOs relating to oral communications, reading, writing, mathematics, landscape and grounds maintenance, simple construction, and supervisory management would be minimum qualifications. Those KSAOs involving building maintenance were established as desirable qualifications. Other KSAOs would be taught or acquired on the job. Had

SPECIFICATIONS FOR JOB OF PARK MAINTENANCE FOREMAN

Knowledge, Skills, and Abilities

1. Knowledge of principles of landscaping, including care and maintenance of ornamental plants and landscaping construction.	MQ
2. Knowledge of construction and maintenance of shelters, fences, decks, and related park structures.	MQ
3. Knowledge of basic maintenance of buildings, including minor wiring and plumbing.	MT
4. Knowledge of safety rules and procedures.	WT
5. Knowledge of city and department policies, procedures, and work rules.	WT
6. Verbal skills to communicate information to subordinates, vendors, supervisors, and the general public.	MQ
7. Writing skills to clearly and neatly complete forms and records.	MQ
8. Reading skills to comprehend directives, policies, procedures, operator manuals, landscape plans, and similar written documents.	MQ
9. Math skills to add columns of figures and multiply and divide using decimals.	MQ
10. Estimating skills to compute bills of material for construction projects using primarily lumber and concrete.	MQ
11. Skills to operate and/or demonstrate the use of hand and power tools used in rough carpentry.	MQ
12. Skills to maintain, operate, and/or demonstrate the use of power mowers, tillers, tractors, loaders, and light earthmoving equipment.	MQ
13. Skills in estimating, forming, mixing, pouring, and finishing concrete.	MT
14. Skills in planning and scheduling construction and maintenance work.	MQ
15. Ability to communicate with, lead, and motivate subordinates.	MQ
16. Ability to work independently to accomplish objectives.	MQ

Other Requirements

1. Be willing to attend training programs as required.	MQ
2. Be willing to work overtime and weekends when needed.	MQ
3. Be willing to wear appropriate attire and personal protective equipment.	MQ

Credentials and Experience

1. Graduation from high school or equivalent.	MQ
2. Three to five years experience in landscape construction and maintenance or equivalent combination of training or experience.	MQ
3. Commercial driver's license (CDL).	

management believed that sufficient qualified applicants were available, desirable qualifications could have been changed to minimum qualifications. On the other hand, the nature of the applicant pool might have been such that even fewer KSAOs could have been established as minimum qualifications.

SUPPLEMENTAL APPLICATION FORMS

A supplemental application form (SAF) is a selection device that has survived the test of time. Essentially, it is a structured resume. It is one of the products of the Guidelines Oriented Job Analysis (GOJA) system described in Chapter 7.[14] Other terms used include *self-crediting questionnaire* and *biographical questionnaire*. The SAF is so named because it supplements the organization's general application form. It is designed as an application form for one job classification. As such, many items can be in-clu-ded that would not otherwise be appropriate. A number of advantages are gained by using the SAF as a selection device. One of the most important is job-related self-screening of applicants. A person is a candidate only after completing the SAF; thus, the applicant-flow statistics collected will be more reliable and probably more favorable, because they will not include individuals who are obviously not qualified.

Another positive feature of the SAF is that education and experience are evaluated in terms of type and content. This evaluation is much easier to defend than the traditional method of requiring a minimum number of years of experience or education and accomplishes the same legitimate objective. Finally, the SAF provides a basis for determining whether an applicant can perform the requirements of the job without discriminating against otherwise qualified applicants on the basis of sex and disability.

Exhibit 9-6 shows an SAF for the position of Park Foreman. Notice that there are sets of KSAOs relating to landscape and grounds maintenance, basic structures, and supervisory management that were established as minimum qualifications. These KSAOs are addressed in Part I. Part II addresses those KSAOs related to building maintenance and concrete finishings, which are desirable qualifications. Part III merely informs the applicants of which KSAOs will definitely be taught on the job.

In evaluating the completed SAF, it is not necessary to weight the responses or to establish numerical cutting scores. It is better to carefully examine the responses to Part I (minimum qualifications) and decide if the applicant's qualifications on each item are reasonable and consistent with normal expectations of proficiency. Keep in mind, however, that failure to satisfy any item that has been identified as a minimum qualification disqualifies the applicant. It is not proper then to evaluate responses to Parts II and III and allow one or more desirable qualifications to "compensate" for any qualification that has been determined to be essential for job performance.

Most local governments do not use SAFs even though they represent a more valid and reliable approach to job selection than standardized application forms. SAFs are slightly more costly and complex than traditional application forms. SAFs can be particularly useful in identifying a potential job/person match.

EMPLOYMENT TESTS

Employment tests are selection devices that attempt to measure the probable match between applicants and factors required in the job. Such tests can be classified as aptitude tests or achievement tests. Aptitude tests measure employees' ability to learn, while achievement tests measure employees' performance. Two types of the most used tests are **ability tests** and **work-sample tests**. Drug, honesty, and personality testing are additional employment tests used by local governments.

ABILITY TESTS

Ability tests are almost always paper-and-pencil tests that are administered in a standardized manner to groups of applicants. They are not often used in local governments even though they are relatively inexpensive to administer. Legal concerns, discussed below, and complexity in use, analysis, and validation contributes to low usage rates. Tests have been developed for a wide range of employment uses; however, each type of test has a specific purpose. Exhibit 9-7 identifies and gives examples of the major types. Ability tests are useful in identifying a potential job/person match.

For a first-level supervisory job such as Park Maintenance Foreman, a general mental ability test has a high validity coefficient, as would be expected, since the job requires verbal, mathematical, memory, and reasoning abilities. Other types of tests would be used for different types of jobs. In general, ability tests are among the most valid for a large number of different jobs.[15]

Ability tests have some limitations. As Chapter 3 pointed out, court decisions in a number of important EEO cases focused on these types of tests and, in some cases,

EXHIBIT 9-6

SUPPLEMENTAL
APPLICATION
FORM (SAF)

A. Typical SAF coversheet, with instructions

SUPPLEMENTAL APPLICATION FORM

Position _____

Names   _____

This organization is an equal employment opportunity employer. As such, we comply with all relevant laws and guidelines. This application form may appear quite different from others you have seen; but is has been designed so that we can comply with equal opportunity laws and guidelines, be fair to all applicants, and select the best qualified people for the job.

This form must be filled out as completely as possible. Include the most relevant qualifications that you possess. Your answers on this form will determine your eligibility for the position.

The Supplemental Application Form contains:

Part I—Factors that are **minimum qualifications** (MQ). Applicants **must** have all the MQs listed. These MQs will not be taught or acquired on the job.

Part II—Factors that may be taught on the job (MTs). We are hoping to find applicants who now have some or all of these MTs; but such people may not be among those who apply. So, if you have all the MQs but only some or none of the MTs, you may apply.

Part III—Factors that will be taught on the job (WTs). Applicants are not expected to have the WTs listed in this section. They will be acquired on the job.

Directions for Completing the Supplemental Application Form

In the space provided below each question, explain how your education and/or experience have prepared you to use the required knowledge or skills to perform the tasks of the job. In your answers to MQ and MT questions, the number of years of your experience and education will not be evaluated. We are interested in quality, not quantity, of experience and education as they relate to job requirements. Level and degree of responsibility, frequency of performance, past performance appraisals, etc., are more relevant than lengths of time.

---

found them to be discriminatory. For example, Duke Power Company's use of the Wonderlic Personnel Test shown in Exhibit 9-7 was found to have adverse impact on black employees. Further, Duke Power failed to provide sufficient evidence that the test was job related. Limitations of such tests include difficulties in evaluating practical usefulness of available tests, variations in psychometric qualities of tests, selection factors in which better information is obtained from other measures, and improper test administration.

Well-designed ability tests, applied by qualified professionals, are useful in selection provided the particular test is matched to the factor being measured, and that

EXHIBIT 9-6 (CONTINUED)

SUPPLEMENTAL
APPLICATION
FORM (SAF)

B. Typical SAF items (for job of Park Maintenance Foreman)
Ample space should be provided for answers; SAFs are usually 6 to 8 pages long.

Part I. Factors that are minimum qualifications (MQs).

Please respond yes or no to the following questions and then provide a detailed descriptive explanation of your answer.

1. Do you know how to select, install, and maintain ornamental plants? _____
Explanation:

2. Do you know the basic principles of landscaping, including knowledge of landscape plans and specifications, landscape construction, man-made features (fences, retaining walls, etc.), and irrigation systems? _____
Explanation:

3. Do you have the skills to maintain, operate, and/or demonstrate the use of power mowers, tillers, tractors, loaders, and light earthmoving equipment? _____
Explanation:

4. Do you have skills to operate and/or demonstrate the use of hand and power tools used in rough carpentry? _____
Explanation:

5. Can you establish priorities, work independently, and proceed with objectives without supervision? _____
Explanation:

Part II. Factors that may be taught on the job (MTs).

Please respond yes or no to the following questions and then provide a detailed descriptive explanation of your answer.

1. Do you know how to maintain buildings, including minor wiring and plumbing? _____
Explanation:

2. Do you have skills in estimating, forming, mixing, pouring, and finishing concrete? _____
Explanation:

Part III. The following factors will be taught on the job (WTs).

No response is needed.

1. Knowledge of safety rules, including causes and prevention of accidents.
2. Knowledge of first aid procedures.
3. Knowledge of departmental policies and procedures.

Note: For an excellent source on the use of standardized and supplemental application forms see city of Broomfield, Colorado, *http://www.ci.broomfield.co.us/jobs/index.shtml* (October 25, 2000).

EXHIBIT 9-7

ABILITY TESTS USED
IN SELECTION

Type of Test	Measures	Example
Mental ability	Verbal, conceptual, visualization, memory, numerical, fluency, semantic relations, logical evaluation, and general reasoning abilities.	Wonderlic Personnel Test (entry and first-level supervisor jobs)
Mechanical ability	General and specific abilities associated with success in work with machines and equipment such as the ability to perceive and understand the relationship of physical forces and mechanical elements in job settings.	Bennett Mechanical Comprehension Test and MacQuarie Test for Mechanical Ability
Physical ability	Muscular strength, cardiovascular endurance, and movement quality related to physical performance of job-related tasks.	Joyce Hogan's Physical Abilities Tests
Clerical ability	Speed of reading, spelling, group measures of intelligence, mathematical abilities.	Minnesota Clerical Test

Source: Robert D. Gatewood and Hubert S. Feild, *Human Resource Selection*, 5th ed. (Chicago: Dryden, 2001), 567–588.

factor can be shown to be job related. Organizations using these tests may want to conduct their own reliability and validity studies. At a minimum, they should review any reliability and validation results furnished by the test publisher or reported in the professional literature.

WORK-SAMPLE TESTS

The previous chapter indicated that work-sample tests must be content valid and neither contaminated by tasks unimportant to job success nor deficient in those that are. Applicants should perform only activities that are as closely as possible the same as those they will actually perform on the job. An appropriate work-sample test should address a representative sample of a set of skills necessary to perform a critical work behavior; should closely approximate an observable work product; and should as far as possible replicate the actual work situation. Development and use of such a test involves several steps. The task or activity to be focused on should be identified from job analysis data developed by appropriate subject matter experts (SMEs), including job incumbents, supervisors, instructors, and others who have a high level of proficiency. A test must also be designed to measure any KSAOs needed to carry out each task. The raters (judges) who will score the performance must be trained, and the test must be tried out on a sample of individuals before being used in the selection process.

Work-sample tests may be administered in a classroom, at a worksite, or in a job simulation setting, as appropriate. An applicant's performance on the test is assumed to represent his or her performance in an actual job situation. Examples of types of work-sample tests are shown in Exhibit 9-8. Exhibit 9-9 illustrates a work-sample test for the job of Park Maintenance Foreman. The job specifications for this position identify a certain proficiency in writing, reading, mathematics, and estimating skills necessary for simple construction projects, a critical work behavior. In taking the test, the applicant produces a typical observable work product, a least-cost list of materials. The test replicates an actual work situation (pencil-and-paper calculation from given information).

A number of different approaches could be used to evaluate the results of this test. One way would be to pass all of the candidates who obtained the correct answer and fail those who did not. Another alternative would be to consider first whether the candidate worked the problem in an acceptable manner, and discount simple errors, as in multiplication or misplaced decimal points. Finally, a formal grading system could be established to count off a certain number of points for each type of error and set a cutting score. The actual procedure should be based on the judgment of people with knowledge of the job, and the scoring should be done in a consistent manner.

In regard to work-sample tests in general, several cautions are in order. While these tests are inherently reliable and valid, they can be misused. Consider a timed test designed to determine the data entry skills of a data entry clerk. If the five-minute test is designed to measure skill in entering complex data with 95 percent accuracy, but the job requires only entry of much simpler data, the test would not be appropriate. On the other hand, if the job requires a person to enter the more complex data as a major task, then the test would measure needed skills. Thus, basing ability tests on effective and thorough job analysis cannot be overemphasized.

Another misuse of work-sample tests is using the scores to rank applicants without empirical evidence that higher scores are associated with better job performance. The result of such a test does not imply a prediction of future job performance; rather, it indicates whether or not an applicant has a job-related KSAO. For example, if the required data entry skill has been established to be 99 percent accurate, we would not normally consider an applicant who entered data with 100 percent accuracy on that particular test to be significantly better qualified. In most cases, all applicants who pass the test would be considered to have sufficient skill to perform the job, and decisions as to which to hire would be made on some other basis. The data entry test would be a "noncompensatory hurdle" that must be

EXHIBIT 9-8		
WORK SAMPLE TESTS	**Example**	**Job**
	Word processing	Administrative assistant
	Repairing a gearbox	Mechanic
	Exercising judgment at crime scene (video)	Police officer
	Demonstrating leadership skills through role-playing	Fire lieutenant
	Reading and interpreting recorder-controller chart	Central supply technician
	Computing a bill of materials	Park maintenance foreman
	Grading to specifications established by reference stakes	Motor grader operator
	Reading and understanding safety and work procedures	Water treatment plant operator

EXHIBIT 9-9

WORK-SAMPLE
TEST FOR PARK
MAINTENANCE
FOREMAN

Situation

Your plan of work calls for a decorative fence to be built according to the design shown in the figure below. The fence is to be 48 feet long. Posts will be six feet high; boards will be two inches off the ground and extend two inches above the top rail. Boards will be 1 × 6, spaced one-half inch apart. Posts will be set two feet in the ground. Using the most economical lengths, compute the total lumber cost of the fence.

Given

Item	Price
4 × 4 × 10	9.69
4 × 4 × 8	5.48
2 × 4 × 8	2.68
2 × 4 × 12	4.05
2 × 4 × 16	6.69
1 × 6 × 10	3.55
1 × 6 × 12	4.80

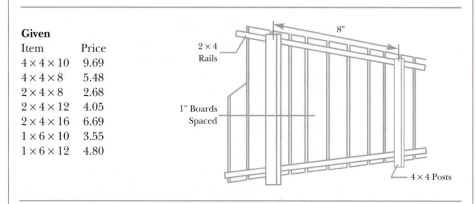

Computations
(Show all work)

ANSWER $ _____

passed to narrow the pool of applicants to only those who meet minimum job qualifications. Final selection would be based on the ranking of the qualified applicants on their predicted job performance—usually by use of multiple-linear regression of all predictor test scores against a numerical job performance criterion.

Local governments are more likely to use work-sample tests than ability tests, but, overall usage is low compared with other selection techniques. Work-sample tests tend to be expensive and moderately complex. Well-designed work-sample tests are a powerful selection tool in identifying an applicant's competencies related to the job.

ADDITIONAL EMPLOYMENT TESTS

Drug tests, personality tests, and honesty tests are additional notable employment tests used by local governments. The desire for drug-free workplaces has driven many local governments to test applicants for drug use. Because employee drug use significantly affects workplace safety, productivity, and profitability, screening applicants provides local governments with a effective means of combating the problem.[16] **Drug testing** typically takes place during background investigations to screen out applicants or during a postselection medical examination. In establishing drug testing policies and procedures, local governments need to ensure they are not infringing an applicants' or employees' protected rights under the Americans with Disabilities Act or their constitutional rights regarding illegal search and seizure. While the use of applicant drug testing is increasing, currently there is low usage among small local governments and moderate usage by medium and large local governments. The cost of drug testing is a major inhibiting factor in adoption. Individuals applying for jobs working with children and in public safety are more likely than others to be required to submit to drug testing.

Personality tests are used to identify employee characteristics or traits that may be associated with an employee's job performance.[17] One of the most widely used personality tests is the Myers-Briggs Type Indicator. With Myers-Briggs, people are classified on four dimensions: introvert or extrovert, sensor or intuition, thinker or feeler, and judger or perceiver. The predictive validity of personality tests is typically low. Therefore, demonstrating job relatedness of personality tests is difficult and may result in unintentional discrimination. Personality testing is limited in local governments even though it is an inexpensive and moderately easy test to administer and score. As Chapter 10 discusses, the personality test is more appropriate for employee training and development purposes than as an employment test.

Assessing applicant **honesty** is the final type of selection test discussed in this section. Two ways of assessing applicant honesty are **polygraph tests** and **paper-and-pencil tests**. Polygraph tests are costly and complex. Paper-and-pencil tests are inexpensive and moderately complex. Although local governments are exempt from the Employee Polygraph Protection Act, negative reactions by employees and other legal and constitutional concerns have limited the use of polygraphs. The paper-and-pencil test is a widely available alternative. Honesty tests are most likely to be used for police, fire, and other protective services positions. The purpose of honesty testing in selection is to identify and eliminate from consideration, potentially dishonest people. Honesty tests, like any selection test, should be validated and shown to be job related if they are used.[18]

INTERVIEWS

http://www.job-interview.net/
Job.Interview.net provides an employer resource link that includes employer tips on interviewing applicants.

The final hurdle for most local government applicants is a selection interview. The selection interview is often the last opportunity to verify an individual's KSAOs related to the job and commitment to the organization's mission and vision. While traditional informal interviews are less costly and complex, the structured interview is a stronger predictor of employee performance. Selection interviews should measure job-related factors, such as interpersonal skills and personality characteristics. Interviews are normally conducted between a single interviewer and the applicant; however, this is not always the case. Group interviews are often used for managerial selection or in situations where the person selected will report to more than one superior. The interview, like a pencil-and-paper test and other selection procedures, is a type of "test" and must meet job-relatedness and nondiscrimination standards. In the typical informal interview the discussion often spills over into areas that are either not job related or questionable from an EEO standpoint.

Traditional interviews have several weaknesses other than just legal problems.[19] Research over the last 80 years has resulted in pessimistic conclusions regarding their reliability, validity, and usefulness in selection. Recent examinations of interview techniques, however, have provided positive results.[20] This is fortunate, as employment interviews are obviously here to stay. One of the corrections is use of a "structured" interview format. It increases reliability and accuracy by reducing the subjectivity and inconsistency inherent in traditional, informal interviews.

STRUCTURED INTERVIEWS

If different questions are asked of several applicants, there can be no consistent basis for evaluating applicants against job-related standards. A structured interview avoids this problem by using a set of standardized, job-related questions prepared in advance and a standardized interview evaluation form using a numerical rating scale. It is advisable also to develop sample answers to the interview questions. For example, a 5-point answer rating scale can be constructed, including for each question a sample "good" answer (a 5 rating), a "marginal" answer (a 3 rating), and a "poor" answer (a 1 rating). Completion of such a form also provides valuable documentation for EEO purposes.

Although an interview should be structured, it should not be rigid. The interviewer should avoid simply reading a list and should encourage the applicant to clearly explain until the answers are adequately understood in each area to be examined. Exhibit 9-10 shows sample structured interview questions for the position of Park Maintenance Foreman.

EFFECTIVE INTERVIEWING

The purpose of the selection interview is to gather information about the applicant's job-related qualifications and evaluate this information relative to an objective standard, based on job-related requirements. A properly developed and implemented interview is a valuable selection instrument, as it provides direct observation of the applicant's appearance, demeanor, and, particularly, interpersonal communications skills. This information can then be integrated with information previously obtained from the application, tests, supplemental application forms, and reference checks. The interviewer, then, needs to obtain as much job-related information about the applicant as possible during the limited interview time. The interviewer can (and should) also give the applicant realistic information about the job so that the applicant can accurately evaluate his or her own qualifications and expectations.

There are so many variables in an interview situation that it would be difficult to cover them all. The following guidelines are a summary of findings and conclusions concerning the interview.

- Interviews should be the "final hurdle" in the selection process and should never be the only method used to assess job suitability.
- The knowledge, skills, abilities, and other characteristics (competencies) needed for successful job performance should be identified and defined.
- A structured interview should be designed. For each competency area, behavioral questions should be developed to elicit examples of past accomplishment and performance.
- Interviewers should be provided with guidelines on what to look for in an applicant's responses to key questions. This is particularly important in group or panel interviews where different interviewers may use different standards.
- Only those questions that have been previously developed should be used. Questions should not be changed during an interview. Good questioning depends on the use of job-related, open-ended questions. Questions that are leading, illegal, obvious, non-job-related, and those that result in canned responses, should be avoided.
- Immediately after the interview, observations and information should be documented for future reference. Comments need to be concise, understandable, job related, and free from bias.

EXHIBIT 9-10	
STRUCTURED INTERVIEW QUESTIONS FOR PARK MAINTENANCE FOREMAN	**Situational Questions** 1. What would you do if a herbicide such as Roundup® were accidentally sprayed on ornamental plants? 2. If a landscape plan specified pine bark mulch for a bed of shrubbery and the material was not available locally, what action would you take? 3. How would you handle a situation where an employee reported to work with alcohol on his breath? 4. You have an integrated work crew. A crew member tells a racial joke that offends a minority worker. What action will you take? **Job Knowledge Questions** 1. Can you describe the basic procedures used in constructing a French drain? 2. What type of irrigation system should be used for azalea beds? 3. You plan to construct a retaining wall of crossties. The wall is 50 feet long and 4 feet high against a bank of clay. Can you describe what should be done to prevent static pressure from tilting the wall? 4. Can you explain the important aspects of supervisory leadership in terms of your own experience? **Worker Requirements Questions** 1. Are you willing to work overtime and on weekends during the Azalea Festival in April and approximately one Saturday or Sunday each month? 2. Are you willing to travel and spend approximately 10 nights away from home each year attending workshops, taking pesticide applicator examinations, and performing similar activities?

- Applicants should be evaluated on each competency area against job standards, not against one another. Rating scales should be used to assess applicants.
- Interviewers should be aware of the "Guidelines" and other legal restrictions concerning certain types of questions, particularly those that are likely to have an adverse effect on protected groups.[21]

ASSESSMENT CENTERS

The assessment center, pioneered in industry by AT&T, is rapidly gaining in popularity, although its use as a selection tool in local governments is low. Assessment centers are expensive and complex but can be an excellent predictor of employee performance and commitment. While the term suggests a place, an assessment center is actually a procedure for measuring job-related KSAOs and is used to make internal promotion decisions.[22] Assessment centers simulate key parts of various managerial jobs. A typical assessment lasts several days, with groups of candidates participating in a variety of exercises. Most centers include "in-basket" tests of decision-making skills and group exercises to access interpersonal skills. Other exercises include speaking, problem analysis, role-playing, in-depth interviews, and various tests. Several observers, often including managers from several levels above the job for which candidates are being considered, assess candidates. The assessors pool judgments on candidates' performance and an overall evaluation is made of each candidate.

Cities and counties apply the assessment center to the selection of candidates for promotion in police and fire departments and as a developmental tool for other types of managerial positions.[23] Research has shown that assessment centers are quite effective in evaluating the potential of individuals for managerial jobs. They have also been shown to be generally fair in terms of race and gender. Such findings of general validity and lack of adverse impact do not mean that their use is without some criticism, however. Unless designed by qualified professionals, assessment results are no more accurate than those of other methods. The cost can also be quite high.

CERTIFICATION AND APPOINTMENT

When the selection process has been completed, an employment or hiring register of all remaining applicants, based on results, should be prepared (some probably will have withdrawn), and the names of qualified applicants should be certified to the appointing authority. The HR department normally administers hiring registers. In general, the smaller the number of applicants certified, the more control the HR department has over the ultimate appointment. A decision rule establishes the actual number. The most rigid rule is for the HR department to certify only the one "best qualified" applicant. The least rigid is for the appointing authority to review and select from the entire hiring register.

THE RULE OF THREE

http://www.
governmentexecutive.
com/dailyfed/0699/
062299k1.htm
Government Executive Magazine includes an article that questions the usefulness of the "rule of three."

Many local government selection systems follow the "rule of three," which permits the appointing authority to select from among the three highest-scoring applicants. There are good arguments for using the rule of three and similar "short" lists. First, human resource selection is not an exact science, and it is unrealistic to assume that the selection process will always be reliable and valid. Second, operating managers have an obvious stake in the selection decisions, since the successful applicants will report to them. One problem with the rule of three is that top-ranked applicants are often separated by only fractions of points. If, for example, scores of the five highest-ranked applicants are 94.5, 94.4, 94.2, 94.1 and 94.0, it is unrealistic to assume that any of the applicants is really less qualified than the others.

Use of the rule of three can also have legal implications. One district court found that county officials used the rule to avoid hiring black applicants in both professional and clerical positions.[24] In another case a decision by an affirmative action officer to appoint a woman to the previously all-male classification of road dispatcher led to a reverse discrimination lawsuit by a male applicant who had a slightly higher score.[25]

OTHER DECISION RULES

An alternative practice is certifying only the highest-ranking applicant, sometimes known as the "rule of one." The argument for this rule is that HR professionals are best able to manage the complexities of the selection process. The main disadvantage is that the only input into the selection decision left to operating managers is to terminate poor performers during the probationary period. Another "rule" is category rating, recommended by the Hoover Commission in 1949. Under this rule, applicants are grouped into categories such as "outstanding," "well qualified," "qualified," and "unqualified." All candidates in each category except "unqualified" are considered in descending order until the required number of applicants is appointed. Most government HR professionals prefer category rating.

Finally, any decision rule may be altered by selective certification. This allows appointing authorities to impose special qualifications that applicants would not normally have to meet. For example, the head of the Finance Department might request certification of a clerical candidate who was not originally referred but had prior experience in using an electronic spreadsheet in budget analysis. Selective certification should always be made on job-related factors.

Whatever decision rule is used, it is the job of the HR department to ensure that selection decisions are job related.[26] For example, if certain procedures warrant a heavy weight because of their importance (for example, work-sample tests), the department must consider this in ranking applicants on the hiring register. As discussed earlier, the department should also develop guidelines and train operating managers in conducting and documenting the results of all selection interviews.

VETERANS' PREFERENCE

Many local governments give special preference to veterans in the selection decision. This is seen as an aid to the veteran in adjusting to civilian life, or as a continuing reward for having served the country.[27] Both are value judgments, and the practice is somewhat controversial. For an otherwise qualified veteran to receive several additional points (perhaps more for disability or wartime service) for an entry-level job is well accepted. Practices such as continuing entitlement, not requiring minimum qualifications, and automatic placement at the top of eligible registers generate more objections. One practice that is particularly inappropriate is appointment of retired military personnel, particularly officers, to high-paying government jobs for which they are not necessarily the best qualified. This and the fact that they already have attractive retirement annuities lead to accusations of "double dipping."

DOCUMENTATION AND RECORD KEEPING

The entire selection process should be documented. If a job-related system has been developed, documentation is a relatively simple matter. At a minimum, the documentation for each position must consist of the following.

1. Job analysis data, including job descriptions, and job specifications if developed separately.
2. Complete descriptions and examples of all selection procedures including application forms, paper-and-pencil tests, work-sample tests, and structured interviews, indicating the required correspondence between the selection procedure and the job, and a description of how the procedure is to be used. The rationale for any cut-off scores should be provided.
3. Adverse impact information on each selection "test" and on the selection process as a whole. Any steps taken to reduce adverse impact on protected groups should be included.
4. A description of the method used to arrive at the final numerical ranking of candidates on the hiring register, including weights assigned to various procedures and rules of combination.
5. A description of the decision rule used to refer eligible applicants to appointing authorities.

In addition, whenever a position is filled, a documented summary of all actions taken, including reasons for selection or nonselection, should be maintained in a

In an effort to improve employee testing procedures, the California State Personnel Board partnered with local, state, and federal governments as well as private and nonprofit organizations to create more effective and efficient employee testing procedures. Specifically, the

FROM PAPER AND PENCIL TO CYBERSPACE

goals were to make the exam easier to take; make the testing format more flexible and increase access to employment information; make testing available 24/7; reduce testing costs; increase test reliability; and increase test validity. To achieve its goals, the California State Personnel Board redesigned its civil service recruitment and examinations procedures. Three key features of the redesigned process include (1) a new examination based on job analysis that evaluates applicants' relevant education and experience related to competencies correlated with job performance; (2) use of information technologies that allows for access to information and testing on-line (24/7/365); and use of Telephone Application Process to allow for access to information and testing via the telephone (24/7/365).

Source: Karen Coffee, Jim Pearce, and Roberta Nishimura, "State of California: Civil Service Testing Moves Into Cyberspace," *Public Personnel Management* 28 (Summer 1999), 283–300; and California State Civil Service On-Line Exam System, available *http://exams.spb.ca.gov/* (October 27, 2000).

separate case file. In general, the organization is required to maintain the case file for a period of six months unless a charge of discrimination has been filed. Then, all records relevant to the charge must be preserved until final disposition. Records on overall selection and utilization needed to complete form EEO-4 (protected class information) should be retained for three years.[28] These are federal requirements and subject to change. Amendments will appear in such services as the Federal Register. The organization is also subject to the record retention requirements of the state, city, and county.

SUMMARY

The basic objective of selection is to hire candidates with a high probability for job success. All selection procedures are "tests" within the meaning of EEO laws and regulations and must be job related. A combination of noncompensatory and compensatory selection approaches provides for a more complete evaluation of applicants than either one alone. Most local governments, however, use noncompensatory approaches because of ease in use and cost-effectiveness. General selection procedures used for all applicants include application forms, initial screening interviews, background investigations, and, after a provisional job offer, medical evaluations. Job-related selection procedures include supplemental application forms; work-sample, ability, and personality tests; structured interviews; and assessment centers. When the selection process has been completed, a hiring register should be prepared and the names of qualified applicants certified to the appointing authority. Many local government HR departments use the "rule of three" to determine the number of applicants to certify. However, many HR professionals prefer an evaluative category rating. The entire selection process should be documented and retained for at least six months as a defense against any charge of illegal discrimination.

QUESTIONS FOR REVIEW AND DISCUSSION

1. Compare and contrast the noncompensatory and compensatory approaches to selection.
2. Describe three general selection methods.
3. List and discuss three types of employment tests.
4. Why should ability and personality tests be validated?
5. Select a job with which you are familiar and design a work-sample test.
6. What are some of the problems with traditional informal and unstructured interviews?
7. Discuss the nature and uses of an assessment center.

ENDNOTES

1 Robert D. Gatewood and Hubert S. Feild, *Human Resource Selection*, 5th ed. (Chicago: Dryden, 2001), 4–5.

2 *Griggs v. Duke Power Company*, 401 U.S. 430 (1972).

3 The following discussion of compensatory and noncompensatory selection methods draws heavily from Gatewood and Feild's discussion of "Strategies for Combining Predictor Scores," 242–248.

4 Carol Hacker, "Profiling Job Candidates," *Security Management* 41 (May 1997), 25–27.

5 *Connecticut v. Teal*, 645F.2d.133 (1982).

6 Gatewood and Feild, 407–426. Also see Jeffrey A. Mello, "Ethics in Employment Law: The Americans with Disabilities Act and the Employee with HIV," *Journal of Business Ethics* 20 (May 1999), 67–83.

7 Gatewood and Feild, 471–513. Also see Christopher Orpen, "The Use of Psychological Tests: A Guide for Management," *Management Services* 42 (March, 1998), 14.

8 Jill H. Maxwell, "Of Resumes and Rap Sheets," *Inc.* 22 (June 2000), 27.

9 David E. Terpstra, R. Bryan Kethley, Richard F. Foley and Wanthauee Limpaphayom, "The Nature of Litigation Surrounding Five Screening Devices," *Public Personnel Management* 29 (Spring 2000), 43–54.

10 Gatewood and Feild, 444–465.

11 Terpstra et al., 43–54.

12 Robert L. Mathis and John H. Jackson, *Human Resource Management*, 9th ed. (Cincinnati: South-Western, 2000), 189–192.

13 Richard Sisley, "The Recruitment Gamble—Improving the Odds," *Management-Auckland* 44 (May 1997), 22–24.

14 Richard E. Biddle, *Guidelines Oriented Job Analysis* (Sacramento, Calif.: Biddle & Associates, 1976).

15 Gatewood and Feild, 549.

16 Eugene F. Ferraro, "Is Drug Testing a Good Policy?" *Security Management* 44 (January 2000), 166.

17 Seth A. Berr and Janine Waclawski, "The Right Relationship Is Everything: Linking Personality Preferences to Managerial Behaviors," *Human Resource Development Quarterly* 11 (Summer 2000), 133–157.

18 José M. Cortina, Nancy B. Goldstein, Stephanie C. Payne, H. Davison, and Stephen W. Gilliland, "The Incremental Validity of Interview Scores Over and Above Cognitive Ability and Conscientiousness Scores," *Personnel Psychology* 53 (Summer 2000), 325–351.

19 Arthur H. Bell, "Handling the Fatal Five Hiring Questions," *Credit Union Executive Journal* 40 (May/June 2000), 27.

20 Allen I. Huffcutt and David J. Woehr, "Further Analysis of Employment Interview Validity: A Quantitative Evaluation of Interviewer-Related Structuring Methods," *Journal of Organizational Behavior* 20 (July 1999), 549–560.

21 William G. Kirkwood and Steven M. Ralston, "Inviting Meaningful Performances in Employee Interviews," *Journal of Business Communication* 36 (January 1999), 55–76; and Mathis and Jackson, 300.

22 Gatewood and Feild, 648–664.

23 For a more detailed discussion of the use of assessment centers for police and fire departments, see Charles D. Hale, *Assessment Center Handbook for Police and Fire Personnel* (Springfield, Ill.: Charles C. Thomas, 1999).

[24] *Strain v. Philpott*, CA 840-E, MDA (1971).

[25] *Johnson v. Santa Clara Transportation Authority*, 480 U.S. 616 (1987).

[26] George Bohlander, Scott Snell, and Arthur Sherman, *Managing Human Resources*, 12th ed. (Cincinnati: South-Western, 2001), 200–203.

[27] Bonnie G. Mani, "Challenges and Opportunities for Women to Advance in the Federal Civil Service: Veterans' Preference and Promotions," *Public Administration Review* 59 (November/December 1999), 523–534.

[28] Bradley E. Heard, "How to Survive an EEOC Commissioner Charge," *Human Resource Professional* 13 (March/April 2000), 8–10.

PART 4
DEVELOPING EMPLOYEES AND MEASURING WORK CONTRIBUTIONS

People in the organization can be considered as assets that grow in value as their capabilities increase. By periodically assessing their performance, the organization both facilitates their development and measures their contributions. Chapter 10 covers orientation, skills training, and development, including evaluation of these activities. Chapter 11 examines the nature and uses of performance appraisal and describes how appraisal systems are designed and implemented to accurately measure the extent to which employees have demonstrated expected behaviors and achieved desired results.

CHAPTER 10
ORIENTATION, TRAINING, AND DEVELOPMENT

To ensure its new employees get off to a great start, the city of Concord, California, has designed and implemented a comprehensive organizational training and development program. The program's strategic objectives are designed to support and promote the city's mission, vision, and values.

Key to the success of Concord's organizational training program is its new employee orientation program. Beginning on their first day of work, new employees at Concord begin an orientation program that lasts up to 18 months. Two orientation objectives that support Concord's mission, vision, and values are facilitating the transition of new employees into the organization and its culture and helping employees to quickly become productive and contributing members of Concord's team.

The orientation program consists of three parts. Before the formal orientation program begins, however, new employees are sent a welcome letter and orientation itinerary. The first part of the training is intended to introduce new employees to the city and begin their transition into the organization. During the first two days, the new employee completes necessary paperwork; reviews Concord's mission, vision, values, and organizational structures; receives initial safety training; tours facilities and departments; and begins on-the-job training. The second part of the program lasts approximately four months and consists of the employee working closely with a departmental sponsor to ensure that the new employee understands the city's mission, vision, and values and has become a productive and contributing member of the work team. Part three of the program consists of a new employee meeting to confirm that employees understand and are committed to Concord's mission, vision, and values, and to ensure that they understand their role in achieving strategic objectives. This part also contains ongoing orientation and continued contact with the departmental sponsor.

In addition to the city's new employee orientation program, Concord has designed and implemented a variety of training programs and policies that support employee training and development. The city's "Gateway to Organizational Achievement and Learning" program is designed to help employees strengthen competencies and obtain new ones needed to help attain the city strategic objectives. The program is composed of approximately

30 competency-based workshops. Concord's "Innovative Methods for Performance and Achievement by Concord Teams" program is designed to help work teams in analyzing existing work processes, identifying alternate approaches and processes, choosing the best alternative, implementing the new work processes, and evaluating the results. Concord's tuition reimbursement program supports its commitment to employee excellence. The program allows employees to advance their educational goals and provides tuition reimbursement for eligible full-time employees. The city also has a training and development library from which employees can access over 250 books, videos, and audiotapes. Collectively, Concord's organizational training program ensures its new employees are getting off to a great start!

Source: City of Concord, California, *http://www.ci.concord.ca.us/hr/org-train-dev.htm* (February 15, 2001).

INTRODUCTION

Recruitment and selection of employees are important and costly HR procedures. Each local government employee represents a considerable investment for the organization even before the employee reports for work. In order to protect that investment and attract, recruit, and retain competent employees, the HR department should be involved in developing, implementing, and evaluating orientation, training, and development programs. Some benefits of orientation, training, and development programs include increasing production, reducing errors, reducing turnover, empowering employees, enhancing employee competencies, developing new competencies, and creating a culture of change.[1] Training, however, is expensive. Effective training is an investment that justifies its cost. Poor training, on the other hand, increases costs without realizing the potential benefits. In addition to wages and benefits, facilities and equipment, and lost productivity, organizations spend over $62 billion a year on formal orientation and training programs.[2] These funds do not account for the spending on informal training programs that account for 70–80 percent of total training time.[3]

Despite the benefits of orientation and training programs, concern over costs or return on investment (ROI) has contributed to make training and development one of the most neglected HR activities.[4] Training needs are seldom carefully analyzed, and efforts are devoted mainly to improving employees' abilities to perform specific jobs. It is unusual for organizations to provide opportunities for employees to reach their full potential. One reason for this in local government probably is that many local officials face elections every two to four years, giving them incentive to promote programs that produce immediate and obvious results. Training and especially development programs rarely fit this prescription. Gradually, however, training and development activities of governments are becoming more systematic and comprehensive. A caveat to all local government leaders and managers: learning will occur in the *presence* or *absence* of formally planned and controlled orientation, training, and development programs. In the *absence* of formal training, learners are more likely to be subjected to informal and potentially counterproductive training practices such as hazing and harassment. In the presence of *formal* training, learners are more likely to gain competencies needed to fulfill strategic objectives. This chapter shows how the HR department, working with line management, can improve contributions of employees to organizational goals. The key objectives are to orient new employees to the organization and their jobs, to train employees to improve performance in present jobs and to maintain performance levels as their jobs change, and develop employees to handle new responsibilities in future jobs.

ORIENTATION

New employees presumably arrive with knowledges, abilities, and skills needed by the organization. In order to meet the expectations of the organization, however, new employees must learn both the nuts and bolts of their assigned jobs and the cogs and wheels of the organizational process they are becoming part of. New hires also have needs and expectations—to be welcomed into the organizational "family," to settle into their new work with a minimum of stress and anxiety, to find satisfaction in the exercise of their talents and in relationships with co-workers. An effective orientation program brings these various needs and interests together. By appropriately introducing new employees to their jobs, coworkers, superiors, and the organization, **orientation** ensures that they will get up to speed on their new jobs as soon as possible, and also begins the socialization process whereby employees come to identify with the organization's values, beliefs, and traditions. Orientation programs in local governments should make new employees feel welcomed and help them understand the organization in general and specifics in key areas.[5]

http://www.
orientxpress.com/
IVID Communications
provides an example of an
intranet application for
employee orientation.

BENEFITS OF AN ORIENTATION PROGRAM

In the absence of a planned orientation program, new employees usually will make some attempt to figure out the system for themselves. Within a month most employees will have already figured out how things work or at least their perception of "how things work."[6] This kind of impromptu orientation is likely to be long, drawn out, and stressful for everyone, and costly to the organization. By controlling the orientation process through a structured program, an organization demonstrates commitment to its employees, reduces start-up costs, reduces employee anxiety and hazing, reduces employee turnover, and increases productivity.[7]

DEMONSTRATING COMMITMENT

An orientation program should send a clear message to new employees that they are valued and the organization has a vested interest in them. Employees who feel valued by their organization are more likely to stay.[8] Further, employees who attend orientation programs are more likely to demonstrate **organizational commitment** than those who do not attend.[9]

REDUCING START-UP COSTS

Few new workers are able to hit the ground running; many of those who do run in the wrong direction. New employees are generally unfamiliar with the specifics of their job, how the organization functions, and whom to see on different matters. Thus, at least for a time, new employees will be less efficient or effective than their experienced coworkers. This period of relative incompetence obviously will be prolonged if getting the needed information is left to the chance that coworkers or superiors will think to provide needed information at the right time and/or that the new worker will ask the right questions of the right people. An uncontrolled orientation process thus wastes everyone's time. By helping new employees learn the ropes, an effective orientation program can save everyone's time and reduce costs.

REDUCING ANXIETY AND HAZING

In its worst form, **hazing** is illegal. The negative consequences associated with hazing have resulted in many local governments prohibiting such behavior. It is the HR department's responsibility to promote a positive organizational culture and ensure hazing does not occur. Hazing can interfere with the new employee's (and others') work and greatly add to the anxiety a new employee normally feels about being able to perform as expected. By providing immediate and systematic information about the new employee's job and about the organization, orientation reduces the likelihood that hazing will occur. Assuring new employees that hazing will not be tolerated reduces employee anxiety and increases productivity.

REDUCING TURNOVER

If new employees judge themselves ineffective, unwanted, or unneeded, and therefore experience negative feelings, they may seek to deal with these feelings by quitting. **Turnover** is typically high during the "break-in" period, when employees who could have turned out to be valued long-timers quit in frustration. A new employee's first few months of a job are critical to his or her identification with the organization and development of healthy work attitudes. By helping new employees establish realistic job expectations and a sense of belonging, effective orientation can greatly reduce costly turnover.

INCREASING PRODUCTIVITY

Oriented employees are more likely to contribute sooner to a local government's goals and be more productive than employees who are not oriented. Oriented employees are more likely to learn how to perform their first jobs correctly and require less supervision. Orientation saves time for line managers and peers by having the HR department provide organizational information, thereby allowing line managers and peers to focus on helping the new employees learn their job and achieve departmental goals.

DESIGNING AN ORIENTATION PROGRAM

The nature and design of orientation programs varies among organizations and even from job to job, and from informal to highly structured and formal. Whatever the type and size of the organization, there are two levels of orientation, organizational and departmental. **Organizational orientation** covers matters of relevance to all employees. **Departmental orientation** covers topics unique to the new employee's department and job.[10]

Since there are two levels of orientation, responsibility is shared by the HR department and the employee's immediate supervisor. The HR department's share of orientation includes such areas as history, operations, mission, vision, and policies, as well as employee services. As orientation becomes more technical, the immediate supervisor takes over and covers topics relating to the job itself, procedures and rules, and other specific departmental matters. Exhibit 10-1 provides a list of topics commonly covered in both levels of orientation.

The actual orientation program selected should be based on the needs of the organization and its employees. The following are elements of a successful orientation program:

- Representatives of both management and employees are involved in development of orientation plans and policies.
- Adequate funds are budgeted for the orientation program.

EXHIBIT 10-1	
TYPICAL INFORMATION COVERED IN FORMAL ORIENTATION PROGRAM	**Organization-wide** 1. Welcome by top official. 2. Overview of the organization, including its mission, vision, and values. 3. Organizational chart. 4. General review of key policies and procedures. 5. Explanation of the compensation and benefits program. 6. Discussion of safety and accident prevention. 7. Review of important aspects of employee relations and communications, including disciplinary procedures and union relations (if applicable). 8. Tour of physical facilities. 9. Distribution of employee handbook and other information. **Departmental** 1. Explanation of departmental strategic objectives, functions, priorities, and relationship with other units. 2. Detailed explanation of job duties and responsibilities, tools, hours of work, performance expectations, and type of assistance available. 3. Detailed explanation of procedures and rules unique to the job or department. 4. Explanation on acquisition and use of office equipment and tools. 5. Tour of department. 6. Introduction to coworkers. 7. Assignment to mentor. 8. Emergency procedures.

- Specific orientation responsibilities are assigned to the HR department and the employee's supervisor.
- HR representatives and supervisors participate in training programs to develop orientation proficiency.
- The program strikes a reasonable balance between providing only a sketchy overview and overwhelming the employee with information.
- Checklists can be used to ensure all aspects of orientation are covered (see Exhibit 10-2).

The orientation program should be continually monitored. It will probably be necessary to periodically remind supervisors to carry out their part and furnish the HR department with a "check-off" report. There should also be an official and comprehensive year-end evaluation of the program, conducted by the HR department with help from supervisors. Feedback from employees should be obtained from unsigned questionnaires, interviews of randomly selected employees, and group discussions.

TRAINING

Like a number of other HR activities, **training** can be viewed as a process. Exhibit 10-3 illustrates the sequence of events that should be followed. Training needs should first be assessed. These needs consist to a large degree of performance deficiencies that can be corrected with training. With these needs established, it is then possible to design and implement an effective training program, setting instructional objectives, determining program content and training techniques, and

EXHIBIT 10-2

Employee Name _____   Department _____

Job Title _____   Supervisor _____

Preeble Township is happy to welcome you to our team. We have developed the following checklist to help introduce you to the Township, your job, and Township employees. Please check (✓) each item once completed. Upon completion of the orientation program and after consultation with your supervisor, you and your supervisor should sign this document and return it to the HR department.

HR Department (First Day on Job)
_____ Probationary employment
_____ Personnel record
_____ I-9 documentation
_____ Payroll and benefit forms
_____ Employee handbook

Departmental Orientation (First Day on Job)
_____ Tour of department and introduction to coworkers
_____ Work hours and procedures for documenting time
_____ Appropriate dress
_____ Emergency procedures
_____ Job description (including major tasks and responsibilities)

Departmental Orientation (First Week on Job)
_____ Review job description (including major tasks and responsibilities)
_____ Safety training
_____ Sexual harassment training
_____ EEOC and affirmative action training
_____ Discussion between supervisor and employee on "How Things are Going"

Departmental Orientation (First Month on Job)
_____ Review job description (including major tasks and responsibilities)
_____ Check with HR department to ensure paperwork has been processed
_____ Ensure employee has acquired and is properly using office equipment
_____ Review departmental policies and procedures
_____ Supervisor and employee orientation consultation

Employee Signature _____   Date _____

Supervisor Signature _____   Date_____

choosing appropriate training sources. After implementation, evaluation provides feedback to the HR department and supervisors as a tool to modify and improve the training program. Finally, as shown in Exhibit 10-3, training should be built around adult learning principles.

ADULT LEARNING PRINCIPLES

http://www.astd.org/
The American Society for Training & Development provides comprehensive training and development information and research tools through its learning communities using discussion boards, hot topics, links, and other tools.

The more **adult learning principles** are included in training the more effective the training is likely to be. Further, the authors believe that local governments should take advantage of the self-directed nature of local government employees by placing them in charge of their own learning. Toward this end, the authors recommend that training should incorporate the adult learning principles pioneered by Malcolm Knowles, a leading scholar in adult learning.[11] These adult learning principles are referred to as andragogy and include the following. Exhibit 10-4 is a tool to help trainers evaluate their training programs with respect to adult learning.

LEARNER'S NEED TO KNOW. Learners need to know why they need to learn something before training begins. Trainers should help learners identify gaps between what they know and what they need to know. Structured events that guide learners to self-assess such gaps are particularly useful.

SELF-CONCEPT OF THE LEARNER. Learners want to be in control of their lives. They do not want to be dependent on trainers to "teach" them. Training programs should focus on the self-directed nature of learners.

PRIOR EXPERIENCE OF THE LEARNER. Learners have vast and differing experiences that affect training. They want to be trained in a manner consistent with their experiences. That is, they want to use their life experiences to facilitate learning. Training, when possible, should focus on activities that use a learner's experience.

READINESS TO LEARN. Learners learn best when the information to be learned can be directly applied to solving a problem or filling an identified gap. Training should focus on information that can be directly applied to a learner's job.

EXHIBIT 10-3

TRAINING
PROCESS

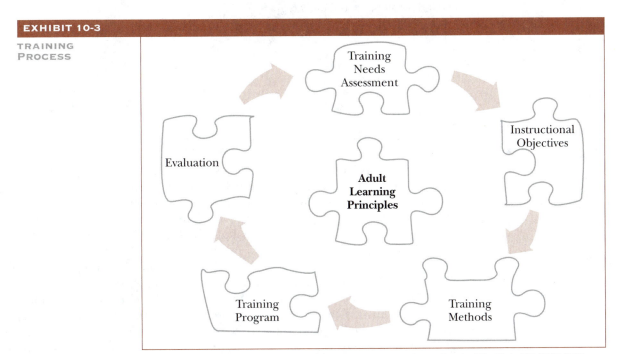

Source: Sheila W. Furjanic and Laurie A. Trotman, *Turning Training into Learning* (New York: AMACOM, 2000).

EXHIBIT 10-4

The following questionnaire is designed to help local government trainers develop programs that take advantage of basic principles of adult learning. Read each statement and place a ✓ in the box that most represents your training program.

	Rarely	Sometimes	Always
1. Training includes structured activities that allow employees to identify their competency levels.	☐	☐	☐
2. Employees understand the purpose of the training activity and why they are participating.	☐	☐	☐
3. Training program takes advantage of self-directed nature of learners.	☐	☐	☐
4. Training program allows learners to be active participants and not passive observers.	☐	☐	☐
5. Training program incorporates real-life examples based on employee experiences.	☐	☐	☐
6. The content of the training program closely matches the content of trainees' job.	☐	☐	☐
7. Participation in training program will directly help employees solve work-related problems.	☐	☐	☐
8. Training allows employees to use their competencies to solve real problems.	☐	☐	☐
9. Training program is designed to increase employee job satisfaction.	☐	☐	☐
10. Trainees are willing participants in the training program.	☐	☐	☐

It is not likely that any one training program will be able to take advantage of all adult learning principles. However, the degree to which they can be incorporated into training will result in better training programs.

ORIENTATION TO LEARNING. Learners learn better when training occurs in the context of real-life situations. Learners are task oriented in their approach to learning. That is, they want to be able to use acquired competencies to solve real problems. Training should be people centered not topic centered.

MOTIVATION TO LEARN. Learners want to increase their competencies. Learners are motivated by internal motivators such as job satisfaction, self-esteem, and quality of life, and to a lesser degree external motivators such as higher pay, better jobs, and advancement opportunities. Training programs should be developed to take advantage of learners' internal motivators. Ideally, application of the learning principles should be maximized in training; however, this is not usually possible. Factors that must be considered in selecting a training technique include cost, content, capabilities of trainers, qualification and skills of trainees, place and time constraints, available facilities and equipment, and class size.[12] Trade-offs must be made depending on the situation and the priority assigned to the training; for example, cost would not be a major factor in selecting a technique to train firefighters in procedures at a fire scene, but would be a factor in public relations training.

ASSESSING TRAINING NEEDS

The **training needs assessment (TNA)** is the basic building block of an effective training and development program. The major arguments for conducting a TNA are as follows:

- The TNA promotes a process view of training and development. The components of the process include assessment, design, and evaluation.
- The TNA provides a database to support and enhance other HR activities; for example, refer to the discussion of human resource planning in Chapter 5.
- The TNA provides a bottom-line empirical measure for HR operations. Justification of resources allocated to training and development as well as other HR activities is an ever-increasing necessity.[13]

Each TNA should be adapted to fit the unique organizational culture and intended uses. The following is an overview of the process.[14]

The first step is to outline the TNA project in terms of scope, methods, staff, budget, timetables, and so forth. For example, the project may cover the entire organization (city government), a job family (clerical), a department or unit (public works), or an organizational level (first-line supervisors). The resources required and time needed to complete the project will depend on how much has been previously accomplished in such areas as job analysis, human resource information systems (HRISs), and performance appraisal.

The second step is to establish an advisory group of key members of each organizational unit. These individuals are valuable both for their direct input and assistance and also for their credibility and ability to "market" the TNA project in the organization when it is completed. The advisory group should be kept informed via memos, progress reports, and meetings.

The next step is job analysis, particularly the identification of knowledges, skills, and abilities and other characteristics (KSAOs) needed for effective job performance. The process of job analysis is covered in detail in Chapter 7. From job analysis information, a set of KSAO lists is obtained. For example, referring to Exhibit 9-5 in the previous chapter, the job of Park Maintenance Foreman contains 20 KSAOs. Obviously, many of these KSAOs are common to other first-level supervisory jobs. In other words, it is possible to identify common KSAO areas for this and other job families. Through such data reduction a manageable list of relevant and important KSAOs is developed.

Following this step it is necessary to determine KSAO deficiencies. This analysis is based largely on performance appraisal results (see Chapter 11).[15] Individuals

Did anyone train you to do your job? Probably not; if you were like most people you worked it out by yourself. You observed the good and bad practices of others doing similar work, read what you could find, got some good coaching, and may have learned something useful in school. The point is this: You weren't "trained" by your employer. You learned to do your job by your own initiative, which is the way it happens in most organizations. The amount of useful information that takes place as a result of "training" is minor compared to the amount picked up by employees themselves. We don't really train employees; they learn in spite of us.

LET'S HEAR IT FOR TRAINING!

Source: David W. Brown, "Is Your Training Department Working on the Wrong Problem?" *Training and Development Journal* 17 (May 1969), 17.

with low appraisal scores in certain areas can be assumed to be deficient on certain KSAOs. These individuals then develop performance improvement plans that spell out how they are to reach appropriate levels of job performance. Aggregated information, drawn from the improvement plans of all ratees within the selected category, defines the employee training needs. For example, an excessive number of lost time accidents might relate to an appraisal criteria of "safety management" and lead to the conclusion that first-line supervisors are deficient in a KSAO relating to accident causation, occupational health hazards, and methods of prevention. The direct, unambiguous linkage of the training effort to performance appraisal establishes legitimacy, provides economies of scale in conducting training activities, and focuses managerial attention on improvement of employee capacity.

Many cities and counties do not have the resources to carry out a TNA using the process described above. Regardless of the situation, however, organizations should assess training needs. One alternative approach would be to partially implement the process. For example, the HR department could evaluate existing job descriptions or class specifications to identify critical tasks. With an understanding of those tasks, plans can be developed to provide the necessary training.

Another approach is supervisory recommendations. Supervisors must closely and continually observe job performance and are an excellent source of recommendations for training. Supervisory recommendations should be carefully reviewed, however. Supervisors may "play favorites" or improperly use training as a reward for good performance. On the other hand, supervisors can gain a temporary respite from having to deal with a difficult employee by sending him or her to a training session. Finally, supervisors may fail to recommend an employee for needed training for various personal and other non-job-related reasons.

Employees may be allowed to nominate themselves for training. The idea behind this approach is that trainees are likely to be more receptive to employee-initiated training. This approach assumes that employees know what training they need, which may not be the case. Self-nomination is probably more useful for developmental training, in which the employee is attempting to gain KSAOs for career development opportunities.

The HR department should always be alert for other sources of information that may indicate a need for various types of training. Typical sources include accident reports, EEO complaints and grievances, absenteeism reports, turnover statistics, employee surveys, cost records, and exit interviews. Information gained from these sources may indicate both problems and opportunities that can be addressed through appropriate training activities.

DETERMINING INSTRUCTIONAL OBJECTIVES

Once a TNA is conducted, the organization should establish instructional objectives. Objectives should be based on **gap analysis**, which identifies a gap between the baseline of where employees are now and the benchmark for where employees should be in the future. Gap analysis is also useful in establishing training priorities. These objectives contain a statement of desired performance, conditions under which the performance is to take place, and a criterion for measurement. The focus of the objectives may be on knowledges, skills/abilities, attitudes, behaviors, and results. Exhibit 10-5 shows how each type of objective could be stated for a supervisory training program on safety management.

As Exhibit 10-5 implies, a training program usually includes several instructional objectives. Note also that in regard to knowledges, attitudes, and skills/abilities,

	EXHIBIT 10-5

Type Objective	Example
Knowledge	All trainees will be able to obtain a grade of 60 on a test designed to measure knowledge of accident causation and prevention.
Attitude	All trainees will believe that both the organization and employees benefit from a safe working environment as measured by their statements in class and behavior on the job.
Skills/Abilities	All trainees will (1) learn to identify unsafe working conditions, (2) investigate an accident, (3) complete an accident report. All trainees will satisfactorily complete a practical exercise in each topic.
Behavior	All trainees will conduct a safety investigation, establish a safety committee, and hold weekly safety meetings.
Results	All trainee work groups will have a reduction of 10 percent in work-related injuries.

accomplishment of objectives can be measured during or immediately after the training. Changes in job behaviors cannot be observed until trainees return to work. Measuring actual results achieved by training is a long-term process.

DETERMINING TRAINING METHODS

Once instructional objectives have been determined, then training methods and approaches must be selected. There are a wide variety of training methods and approaches that depend on a local governments' needs and available resources.[16] Training methods can be grouped into three categories: on the job, off the job, and distance learning. Additionally, information technologies such as computer-based training, web-based training, and other synchronous and asynchronous technologies are affecting how training is carried out and what methods are selected.[17] The remainder of this section considers the nature and uses of each of the categories of training. Also included are a number of examples of specific training methods.[18]

ON-THE-JOB METHODS

On-the-job training methods include any training an employee receives on the job while under direct supervision. The training may be formal or informal and is done by both managers and supervisors.

JOB INSTRUCTION TRAINING

Perhaps the most widely used method of training is also the oldest. **Job instruction training (JIT)** consists of assigning a new employee to an experienced supervisor or senior coworker. Typically, the supervisor or coworker is told to "break in this trainee" or "teach Bob your job." The trainee is expected to learn by observing the supervisor or coworker and working with the actual equipment and materials that will be used once JIT is completed. Apprenticeship combines JIT with classroom instruction. At work the trainee is assigned to an experienced journeyman for a fixed period of time. During off-duty hours, he or she is required to complete a program of classroom instruction. This method is used to train employees in skilled crafts such as line repairer for a city light and power department. The advantages of JIT are that no special facilities are required and trainees are immediately engaged in productive work. However, if JIT is improperly handled, the expense of damaged machinery, wasted materials, dissatisfied customers, and poorly trained employees can be high. To avoid such problems, trainers must be carefully chosen and rewarded for doing a good job. Exhibit 10-6 summarizes the basic steps in applying JIT.

JOB ROTATION

A second frequently used on-the-job training method is job rotation. This method consists of periodically shifting employees from one job to another. The supervisors of the units in which the jobs are located provide training. The advantages of job rotation include:

- **Flexible assignments**—Employees learn other jobs so they can cover for one another during vacations or illness.
- **Employee development**—Employees acquire additional skills, knowledge, and abilities, thus creating a larger pool of qualified candidates for promotion.
- **Easier staffing**—Jobs that require extensive physical exertion or exposure to disagreeable working conditions may be difficult to staff. Rotation allows employees to "share" such jobs.
- **Less boredom**—Jobs that require a narrow range of skills can easily become boring. As noted in Chapters 3 and 5, boredom can lead to low motivation, low-quality performance, low job satisfaction, high turnover, and high absenteeism. Rotation provides skill variety and offsets boredom.

EXHIBIT 10-6

STEPS IN APPLYING JIT

Preparing for Training

Step 1.   Decide what the trainee must be taught in order to do the job efficiently, safely, and economically.

Step 2.   Have the right tools, equipment, and supplies ready.

Step 3.   Have the workplace properly arranged, just as the trainee will be expected to keep it.

Conducting Training

Step 1.   Prepare the trainee: Put the trainee at ease. Find out what the trainee already knows about the job. Get the trainee interested and desirous of learning the job.

Step 2.   Present the knowledge and/or operations to be learned: Tell, show, illustrate, and question in order to put over the new knowledge and operations. Instruct slowly, clearly, completely and patiently, one point at a time. Check, question, and repeat.

Step 3.   Give performance tryout: Test by having the trainee perform the job. Ask questions beginning with why, how, who, when, or where. Observe performance, correct errors, and repeat instructions if necessary. Continue until you know the trainee knows.

Step 4.   Follow up: Allow the trainee to work independently. Check frequently to be sure the trainee follows instructions. Taper off extra supervision and close follow-up until the trainee is qualified to work with normal supervision.

Source: Adapted from War Manpower Commission, *The Training within Industry Report* 1940–1945 (Washington, D.C.: Government Printing Office, 1945), 195.

As is true with JIT, the effectiveness of job rotation depends on competent and interested trainers.

MENTORING

Mentoring is one of the more informal methods of training.[19] A **mentor** is an experienced supervisor or coworker who helps with day-to-day coaching, counseling, and monitoring of an employee or coworker (protégé). Mentoring is most effective when the mentor and protégé build a strong relationship based on mutual confidence, trust, and respect. As the protégé becomes more effective and efficient in their job, the role of the mentor should diminish. Mentoring is particularly useful in helping new employees understand a local government's culture.

OFF-THE-JOB METHODS

Off-the-job training methods include any training an employee receives on the job site but not on the actual job and any training an employee receives at a location other than the job site. This type of training is typically more formal than on-the-job training.

CLASSROOM

When instructional objectives focus on the attainment of knowledge, information presentation methods are used. They are a relatively efficient and inexpensive way to organize and present factual material to groups of people. The most commonly used information presentation technique is the **classroom type lecture**, which may be supplemented with videos, group discussions, computer-generated slide presentations, and the like. The lecture method would be appropriate for training situations such as explaining amendments to the tax code to employees in the revenue office, communicating features of the benefits program to groups of operating employees, or teaching a group of supervisors how to recognize the early symptoms of employee stress.

As anyone who has been in a classroom knows, however, lectures can become dull and dry. Lectures should be reinforced by other types of training to accommodate individual differences in knowledge, motivation, attitudes, and interests.

GROUP DISCUSSION

Information processing techniques are designed to involve groups of trainees in the generation and discussion of material to be learned. In a **group discussion**, a leader or facilitator provides guidance and feedback and keeps the discussion on track. An application of this approach would be for a group of supervisors who had attended a lecture on performance appraisal to exchange information on dealing with various types of performance problems.

SIMULATION METHODS

Simulation methods are designed to duplicate the work situation and environment as much as possible. These methods approximate on-the-job methods except that the work is simulated, not real. The most important simulation technique is the case method, first developed and used at the Harvard Business School in the 1880s. In using this method trainees are given a well-researched case, taken from a real situation. A major goal of the case method is for trainees to see the "big picture," the relationship between events, the internal and external forces at work, the role of personality in decision making, and so on. Trainees listen to the divergent views of the group and try to find the "best" solution.

The case method can be used effectively to involve trainees in solving problems such as redesigning an undesirable job (sanitation helper, for example), dealing with sexual harassment, enforcing work rules (for example, employees caught gambling), allocating discretionary funds in a department budget, responding to a charge from the EEOC, or deciding which applicant to hire.

ROLE-PLAYING

Role-playing requires trainees to assume different identities. For example, a male supervisor and a female worker might reverse roles and be placed in a typical work situation. The result is that the players see themselves as others see them. Role-playing develops interpersonal skills and may create empathy and greater tolerance.

Behavior modeling is a form of role-playing and is a process by which a trainee observes some other individual and imitates his or her behavior. For example, the trainee may be shown the negative consequences when the wrong behavior is used to handle an incident, and then the correct way to handle such an incident. The trainee then practices what he or she has seen. For behavior modeling to be successful it should be reinforced on the job.

DISTANCE LEARNING

Distance learning methods include any training an employee receives where the trainer and the employee are separated by location and/or time. This type of training relies on the trainee's ability to be self-directing and internally motivated. This type of training is particularly appealing to employees whose lifestyle (time and distance constraints) does not allow them to take advantage of other types of training. Distance learning takes advantage of a local government's need to quickly and continually update its employees' skills by providing training when, where, and how the employee will best respond to the training.[20]

INTERACTIVE VIDEO

Interactive video or **videoconferencing training** allows trainers and trainees at different sites to see and hear each other in real time. It facilitates local government assess to subject matter experts who may not be able or willing to make an on-site presentation, but may be willing to train via videoconferencing. Videoconferencing is particularly useful when trainee and trainer interaction is necessary, but time, cost, and physical space considerations prohibit a centralized training location.

WEB-BASED TRAINING

Web-based training provides a platform from which employees can individually plan and take advantage of training at a convenient time and location (asynchronous learning). It provides an active learning environment for employees and expands computer-assisted training through forums, on-line chat sessions, threaded discussion boards, and real-time interactivity. The technical aspects of developing and implementing web-based training are burgeoning.[21] Additionally, local governments must also contend with hosting and maintaining the website. See Exhibit 10-7 on page 230 for a comparison between traditional versus on-line training methods.

COMPUTER-ASSISTED TRAINING

Computer-assisted training provides a quick, easy, and efficient training method for delivering information to large groups of employees.[22] It has been shown to be effec-

In order to meet public demands for quality services at reasonable sources, local governments will need employees who constantly learn. Learning new knowledge and skills and transferring information is faster, cheaper, and better on the Internet. Following are 10 reasons that e-training is better than traditional training methods.

LET'S HEAR IT FOR E-TRAINING!

- Employees can receive training when they are prepared to learn.
- Employees can control the pace of training.
- Employees can accelerate the pace of training.
- Employees can have more interaction with trainers.
- Employees can participate more in training discussions on-line.
- All employees can participate in training programs.
- Trainees can learn from experts from around the world.
- E-training is less expensive than traditional training methods.
- E-training provides vast assess to information from primary sources.
- Employees will be able to create a learning environment in which they control the learning process.

Source: Adapted from William A. Draves, *Teaching Online* (River Falls, Wis.: LERN Books, 2000), 11–14.

tive for drill and practice, problem solving, simulation, gaming, and tutoring. Some advantages of computer-assisted training include:

- It puts employees in control of learning.
- It provides opportunities for training in any location where a computer can be setup.
- Training can be interactive.
- Training can occur asynchronously.
- It can be designed to assess employee competencies and adjust training accordingly.
- It can be used to deliver training to large numbers of employees quickly and inexpensively.
- It can be developed to maintain training records and be linked to a local government's HRIS.
- Training materials can be updated relatively easily.
- It can provide trainee with immediate feedback.[23]

SELECTING TRAINING SOURCES

A local government organization may institute its own in-house training program, or send its people to outside sources for training, or use a mix of the two approaches. An in-house training program can, of course, be more closely controlled by the organization, ensuring its relevance and applicability. Certain kinds of training that would be impractical or too expensive for the organization to offer may be affordably available from external sources.

IN-HOUSE TRAINING SOURCES

In-house programs are convenient, easy to attend, and can be designed to meet specific objectives. Potential trainers for in-house programs can be recruited from a

EXHIBIT 10-7

WHAT'S
DIFFERENT
ABOUT ON-LINE
TRAINING?

On-line training is in its infancy and very few local governments take full advantage of on-line training methods. Most local governments continue to use traditional classroom training methods as their primary means for training their employees. As local government leaders and HR managers weigh the strengths and weaknesses of traditional versus on-line training methods, the following information may be useful.

Traditional Classroom Training	On-line Training
Most training is delivered through lecture.	Training contents are delivered through e-learning methods: e-mail, threaded discussion boards, chats, interactive videoconferencing, audio and video streaming, tests, and exams.
Learner preparation for training begins when the training session begins.	Preparation for training must occur in advance of on-line training sessions.
Training occurs at specific times and places.	Training occurs anytime/anyplace (24/7/365).
Trainees *do not* have to be self-directed.	Trainees *must* be self-directed.
Training takes *more* time.	Training takes *less* time.
Trainees can be *passive* participants.	Trainees must be *active* participants.
Training objectives are *process* oriented.	Training objectives are *results* oriented.
Trainees usually get free coffee and jelly donuts.	No free coffee or donuts.
Training does not support basic principles of adult learning.	Training supports basic principles of adult learning.

Source: Adapted from William A. Draves, *Teaching Online* (River Falls, Wis.: LERN Books, 2000), 29–41.

number of sources, both within and outside the organization. In selecting trainers, major emphasis should be given to obtaining a "match" between the trainer's expertise, style, behavior, and credibility and the training situation. Selecting the right trainer is a major key to results in the form of trainee interest, retention, and on-the-job application. The following examples illustrate some appropriate trainer selections:

- Explanation of benefits program—HR representative
- Executive briefing on EEO liability—Attorney
- Employee wellness program—Physician
- Class on safety and accident prevention—Risk manager
- Management case studies workshop—Management professor
- Class on supervisory communications—Training specialist

Ideally, a trainer should have both subject matter knowledge and appropriate training skills, but this combination is not always possible. As shown above, an attorney would be an appropriate choice to train department heads on legal matters. He or she would be selected because of technical expertise and credibility, but it would be highly unusual to find an attorney who was also a "training professional." On the other hand, in the training on supervisory communications the presentation skills of the instructor are as important as the subject matter. Finally, while line managers

The city of Chillicothe has lagged behind in training due, for the most part, to a lack of resources. Further complicating the problem is a large seasonal and temporary workforce that must be trained each year.

A BETTER WAY TO TRAIN?

To address these problems the city's new HR director decided to totally redesign Chillicothe's training program using distance learning methods. The new program included CD-ROM based training that included interactive video clips and multimedia graphics. Further, job sites throughout the city were equipped with new computer workstations. Training programs were developed to be self-paced with competency testing at various intervals. Employees could start and stop at will; however, they could not receive credit for the training module until at least an 80 percent mastery was achieved on all items. Once this was achieved, the COMPLETED button would become active. By pressing the button, the file would be saved with the employee's identification number and uploaded to the master employee file in the HR Department.

Once implemented, the city discovered many benefits it had not considered: (1) ability to reach more of the workforce, (2) savings of time, cost and travel, (3) flexibility and adaptability of the delivery modality, (4) ability to reach large numbers of employees at one time, (5) just-in-time training, (6) collaboration of teams that did not exist before, (7) increased communication channels, (8) greater access by both management and labor, (9) ability to utilize technical experts efficiently and effectively, and (10) a higher-quality training program.

The introduction of the CD-ROM training also had a very important side effect: the city's management team became more comfortable with the technology and decided to try other modalities of distance learning, such as videoconferencing. They quickly found the additional benefits of videoconferencing for such applications as conferencing, continuing education, administrative applications, association meetings, and task force meetings. They also found that they could save considerable amounts of money by using distance learning to deliver their training needs.

Source: Adapted from Larry M. Dooley, Kim E. Dooley, and Keith Byrom, "Unanticipated Attitudinal Change: The Progression Toward Self-Directed Distance Training at H. B. Zachry," in *Distance Training: How Innovative Organizations Are Using Technology to Maximize Learning and Meet Business Objectives*, Deborah A. Schreiber and Zane L. Berge, eds. (1998), 351–368.

may lack both academic credentials and training expertise, they can be very effective in bringing a "real-world" dimension and serving as role models in various types of mining.

EXTERNAL TRAINING SOURCES

An excellent outside source for local government training may be nearby universities, which often have centers or institutes of government providing training in a variety of areas. Auburn University's Center for Governmental Services, for example, offers courses such as Fundamentals of Real Property Appraisal, Income Approaches to Valuation, Property Tax Administration and Laws, and Basic and Advanced Mapping. University courses are conducted by highly qualified instructors and targeted to specific needs of local governments. They are also very cost-effective. For example, the content of a course in property appraisal would be essentially the same for all counties in a particular state. The cost of developing and conducting an appropriate training program for a few employees in the revenue department would be prohibitive for a single county. Sending the employees to an external training course accomplishes the objective for a fraction of the cost.

Land-grant universities also conduct programs in local government education through the Cooperative Extension Service. Other colleges and universities usually offer continuing education programs and will work with local governments to design appropriate training courses.

State government departments often assist their local government counterparts with training. For example, the state highway department might offer training conferences for county engineers. City and county law enforcement officers are typically trained at the state police academy.

A *Certified Public Manager* training program is available, usually through either universities or state government departments, or both, with supervision by the national Certified Public Manager Program Board. The program includes a mix of one- or two-week intensive training sessions, on-the-job projects, and university-level public administration courses. Successful completion of a written examination is required for certification.

Various associations such as state affiliates of the National League of Cities and the National Association of Counties either sponsor or conduct training. For example, the League held a number of workshops for city officials when the provisions of the Fair Labor Standards Act were extended to local governments. Training activities of these associations are usually highly relevant and timely.

Finally, such organizations as the American Management Association (AMA), the Society for Human Resource Management (SHRM), and the International Personnel Management Association (IPMA) offer excellent training programs.

EVALUATING THE TRAINING PROGRAM

Evaluation of the training program is essential. Evaluation measures outcomes against stated objectives. The cost of training, both in funds expended and time spent by trainees and in-house trainers, is too high to risk on a gamble that the program is helpful. The organization must have assurance that training is producing the intended benefits. Lack of evaluation is a major shortcoming of most training efforts.

Evaluation begins with the establishment of instructional objectives (refer to Exhibit 10-4). A number of constructs are expected to change as a result of training. Training should produce, in order, changes in attitude, knowledge, behavior, and ability to apply training (results or performance). This suggests that evaluation should take place at four levels:

- **Level 1**—Participant reaction (trainees' attitudes and feelings)
- **Level 2**—Knowledge (application of concepts in the classroom)
- **Level 3**—Behavior (performance on the job)
- **Level 4**—Impact (productivity increases)[24]

As evaluation moves from level 1 to level 4, the evaluation data become more meaningful but also more difficult to obtain. The ideal training evaluation approach would be to use both trainees and a control group to measure attitude, knowledge, behavior, and results before and immediately after training, and again six months later. Management must, however, be sensitive to the costs involved in evaluating training. These include staff time, the time of employees who are interviewed and complete questionnaires, and time required to analyze results.

The following sections discuss the nature of evaluation at the four levels.

PARTICIPANT REACTION

Participant reaction data are usually assessed immediately following the training program. The normal practice is for participants to complete an evaluation form. The form usually provides a rating scale for such things as content of instruction,

Although research has shown that training benefits organizations through increased productivity, reduced absenteeism costs, and lower workers' compensation claims, many leaders and managers fail to draw a parallel between training outcomes and attainment of organizational objectives.

THE BOTTOM LINE OF EVALUATION

A new approach to evaluating training programs allows leaders and managers to place a monetary benefit on investments in training programs. This approach is called return on investment (ROI). ROI can be used not only to justify organizational investments in training, but also to evaluate the effectiveness of training. The following outlines a process for determining ROI for training programs.

Step One:	Calculate all direct costs associated with the training program.
Step Two:	Calculate lost productivity while trainees are in the program.
Step Three:	Calculate the total cost of the program.
Step Four:	Estimate expected hourly, weekly, or monthly productivity benefits per trainee. Methods may range from establishing control groups to using a standard linear regression formula.
Step Five:	Estimate the actual quality benefit from the training.
Step Six:	Using a standard discount rate formula, estimate the time length of the training's effect.
Step Seven:	Calculate profit per trainee.
Step Eight:	Calculate benefits of the total training program.
Step Nine:	Calculate return on investment.

Source: From Edward E. Gorden, "Training ROI: Answering the Return-on-Investment Puzzle," *SHRM White Paper* (August 1999), *http://www.shrm.org/whitepapers/documents/61313.asp* (October 3, 2000).

quality of presentation, aspects that facilitated or retarded learning, most and least useful topics covered, and whether or not individual objectives were met. Since participant reactions are easy and economical to gather, they are the most frequently used approach to training evaluation. Results can be very useful to trainers, particularly in eliminating major deficiencies and as a guide to program improvement. The major weakness of the participant reaction approach is that it reports only attitudes and feelings, not "hard" data. Thus there is no solid indication of whether or not any learning or behavioral change occurred. Finally, if behaviors and results change, attitudes will generally follow. For these reasons, participant reaction, while useful, should never be the only method used to evaluate training.

KNOWLEDGE GAINED IN THE CLASSROOM

A better measurement of training effectiveness is the actual learning that has taken place in the classroom. In this approach we find out not only what participants feel, think, or believe, but also what they now can do differently as a result of the training. This can be accomplished in several ways.

- **Observation**—It is possible to note differences in performance levels when participants engage in before and after activities such as writing, speaking, role-playing, problem solving, and so on.
- **Action plans**—Commitments to engage in a new behavior can indicate the degree to which the training has been internalized.
- **Attitude surveys**—Although changes in attitude obviously are not as definitive as changes in performance or behavior, they do indicate that a change has taken place.

CHANGE IN ON-THE-JOB BEHAVIOR

Change in observable behavior in the classroom, as previously described, is a good indicator that the new learning may be carried over to the job. But this is not conclusive evidence, because the workplace structure may not support the use of the skill. What is needed is data about actual on-the-job performance, such as implementation of action plans producing measurable or observable change, supervisors' day-to-day observations concerning behavioral changes, or employee reports concerning behavior change in their superiors.

MEASURABLE IMPACT OF THE TRAINING ON THE ORGANIZATION

As the name suggests, "measurable impact" is the bottom line or payoff level of evaluation. It is the most important level of evaluation, since it provides data for benefit-cost analysis. Unlike other kinds of evaluation, measuring the actual impact of training requires "hard" data such as actual productivity increases, evidence of better service to customers, and reductions in key indicators of performance deficiency (waste, errors, complaints, accidents, etc.). Information for this level of evaluation is obtained from records and reports, including those that are already being generated.

What Goes Wrong with Training

Regardless of whether a local government uses in-house or external training sources, problems associated with trainers can and will occur. The effectiveness of training can be improved to the extent a local government can identify and deal with the following delivery problems on the part of the trainer:

- Fear of teaching and training
- Lack of credibility
- Lack of personal experiences from which to relate
- Lack of ability to deal with difficult learners
- Difficulty in engaging trainees
- Difficulty with timing and passing of presentation
- Not adapting material during presentation based on learner needs
- Difficulty in asking and responding to questions
- Lack of ability to make formative evaluations of trainees and make appropriate adjustments
- Inadequately prepared media, materials, and facilities, including contingencies
- Failure to use openings and introductions and concise summaries and closings
- Failure to effectively use notes and practice presentation[25]

DEVELOPMENT OF HUMAN RESOURCES

Although the terms are often used synonymously, **development** has a different focus than training. A training program aims at eliminating deficiencies in workers' performance in their current jobs. Through a human resource **development program**, management attempts to prepare individuals for future responsibilities. A well-designed development program assists management in addressing many organizational issues. An advantage is that the development program can be built to a great extent on the training program already in place.

BENEFITS OF A DEVELOPMENT PROGRAM

The major benefits of a development program are that it can reduce the organization's dependence on the external market in hiring new workers and can provide significant assistance in addressing the issues of skill obsolescence, worker productivity, affirmative action, staffing managerial jobs, and career growth/management.

OVERCOMING SKILL OBSOLESCENCE

Human capital is a major investment for all units of government. In many cases, however, skills that an organization has worked hard to develop are no longer needed: **skill obsolescence**. The increased rate of change of technology in the workplace will require creative and proactive HR planning. Development activities are becoming increasingly important. An employee may need to have his or her skills retooled 10 times or more during the course of a career. Thus job retraining is an essential element of a development program.

A classic example of the pervasiveness of changing technology is the area of office automation. During the past 10 years the advent of the desktop computer has revolutionized office procedures with word processing, electronic filing and retrieval, and computer software programs to accomplish virtually every administrative task (inventory control, payroll, licenses, billing, and the like). Clerical employees trained in conventional typewriting, stenography, and manual procedures had to develop an entire new set of competencies to remain productive.

IMPROVING WORKER PRODUCTIVITY

A governmental organization's efficiency, the ratio of services to inputs (Chapter 1), depends to a great extent on worker productivity. Pressure to increase worker productivity can take various forms. Employee turnover, for example, is a problem faced by all units of government. During the time that it takes to fill a vacancy, the work must go on, but efficiency will suffer unless ways can be found to maintain services with remaining employees. A similar problem exists when budget problems result in hiring freezes or even layoffs. Typically the total workload is at least temporarily spread over fewer people. There is also a renewed interest, spurred by taxpayer demand for increased efficiency, in increasing worker productivity as an end itself. Once an almost exclusive concern of the private sector, productivity improvement is now recognized as one of the most critical issues facing government managers.[26]

http://www. trainingsupersite.com
The Training Supersite provides comprehensive information on training and human resource productivity.

Development programs address these issues through cross-training. Cross-training provides management a degree of flexibility in dealing with downsizing, vacancies, absenteeism, and other situations requiring reallocation of skills from internal sources. Cross-training is closely related to the concepts of job enlargement and job enrichment discussed in Chapter 6 and the same methods are used. The most common method is job rotation.

It is intuitively obvious that cross-training provides a reserve force of employees able to meet various staffing needs, but there are other positive benefits. One, discussed in Chapter 6, is increased job satisfaction, although there is insufficient "cause and effect" research in this area. The same is true regarding measurable productivity gains from cross-training. Results do appear to indicate a great potential. In a compilation of research by the National Cooperative Transit Research and Development Program, one study showed cross-training clerical employees and their supervisors in five specialized areas resulted in a 30 percent increase in workload with no new staff, reduced turnover, and increased morale.[27]

FACILITATING AFFIRMATIVE ACTION

Many cities and counties have developed affirmative action plans to improve employment opportunities of minorities and women, particularly in areas where these groups are underutilized. For example, such plans often establish goals for the hiring of women in skilled craft and other "outside" jobs. Affirmative action plans attempt to improve the selection of both minorities and women in such job categories as administrators, professionals, technicians, and protective services. For such plans to be successful, development programs should be in place to help less-qualified applicants acquire KSAOs necessary for available vacancies. Development programs are an effective means of assuring qualified applicants are selected for open positions.

STAFFING MANAGERIAL JOBS

Most first-level management jobs in local governments (foreman, supervisor, chief clerk) are filled from within. Thus a journeyman lineman in the city light and power department becomes a line supervisor. While this individual can climb a 60-foot pole and safely and correctly install complex hardware, he or she may not be familiar with even the major functions of the new job (planning, organizing, etc.). The fact is, this situation is typical. Most so-called management development is actually management training.

If operating employees are properly developed for first-level management positions, the organization will realize immediate benefits in efficiency and effectiveness. First-level managers typically spend a large part of their time in directly supervising the work of operating employees. If, prior to being promoted to the management job, these individuals acquire "people skills" such as motivation, leadership, and communications, both the employees who report to them and the organization will be well served. If not, they will have to learn through experience—usually with mixed results.

Generally, technical skills are present or the employee would never have been promoted to a first-level management job. As managers become more experienced and move up in the hierarchy, development activities should focus on maintaining people skills, and becoming familiar with skills from other disciplines. For persons who have senior management potential, development activities should emphasize conceptual skills, intellectual challenges, and dealing with emerging technologies.[28]

CAREER GROWTH/MANAGEMENT

A **career** is a profession or occupation that an employee trains for and pursues as a normal life activity. From an employer's perspective, **career growth** is concerned with an employee's progressive acceptance of new roles and responsibilities within the same organization. Thus, an organization seeks to maximize its return on investment. From an employee's perspective, career growth is typically associated with promotions and wage increases either within or outside the same organization. An employee, therefore, seeks to maximize job satisfaction and motivation. Regardless, the results of career growth are the same—improved productivity, higher job satisfaction, and more career rewards.[29]

In developing and implementing a career growth/management program, local governments must be concerned with both organizational and employee career development objectives. Failure of a local government to consider an employee's career development objectives may result in negative outcomes such as employee turnover. The need for local governments to develop and implement career growth/management programs has been tempered by the fact that changing jobs has become com-

http://www.keirsey.com/cgi-bin/newkts.cgi
The Keirsey Temperament Sorter is an assessment tool that helps individuals identify their personality types.

monplace. Concern over this is paradoxical. On one side organizations benefit from employee career development, on the other side organizations often help employees develop competencies that make them more attractive to other organizations. This paradox has resulted in a greater emphasis on employees taking charge of their own career development. Some important tools for assessing and understanding an employee's career needs include Myers-Briggs Type Indicator tests, assessment centers, and 360-degree performance appraisals (discussed in Chapter 11).

DEVELOPMENT CONCEPTS AND METHODS

The process of human resource development is essentially the same as that for training, as presented in Exhibit 10-3. There are, however, several important distinctions. Development activities concentrate more on the goals and potential of the individual employee and less on the immediate needs of the organization. As noted earlier, local governments have a considerable investment in its employees and must be concerned with expanding employees' capabilities on a systematic basis.[30] Accomplishing this requires a commitment from line managers, HR professionals, and employees.[31] Line managers in particular are in an excellent position to help people develop. They can help employees determine what skills and talents are needed for success in jobs at various organizational levels, assess employees' past performance and current strengths and weaknesses through performance appraisal, and assist employees in planning to achieve career goals.

The HR department also plays a critical role. What line managers must have is a prescreened, edited, tested, and quality-controlled set of developmental options for their people. Providing this is the responsibility of the HR department. It is a continuing responsibility and requires the ability to analyze trends and make critical judgments.

For development programs to be successful, employees must identify their own training and development needs and take control of and be responsible for their own learning and development.

Evaluation of development activities is also essential. In addition to the types and levels of evaluation discussed previously, the assessment center (covered in Chapter 9) is an excellent tool both for evaluating the results of development and for identifying further developmental needs.

SUMMARY

Orientation introduces new employees to their jobs, coworkers, superiors, and the organization. It teaches the basics of the job and begins the socialization process, in which the employee comes to identify with the organization's values, beliefs, and traditions. Orientation demonstrates organizational commitment, reduces start-up costs, reduces anxiety and hazing, reduces turnover, and increases productivity.

After workers are oriented they may still lack the necessary knowledges, skills, abilities, and other characteristics (KSAOs) to perform successfully. A training needs assessment (TNA) focusing on KSAO deficiencies is the basic building block of an effective training program. The TNA should be linked to performance appraisal results. Training programs should begin with instructional objectives. Trainers can then plan the program content, select appropriate methods, and incorporate as many learning principles as feasible. Training should be evaluated based on previously established instructional objectives. Evaluation should not be limited to participant reactions. Follow-up evaluation is necessary to determine if learning was ultimately transferred to the job.

Human resource development prepares employees for future job responsibilities. At the same time, development programs address such issues as obsolescence, worker productivity, affirmative action, staffing managerial jobs, and career growth/management.

QUESTIONS FOR REVIEW AND DISCUSSION

1. Briefly explain the purposes and benefits of an orientation program.
2. Discuss how the HR department and the employee's immediate supervisors share responsibility for orientation.
3. Describe the training process. Why is training needs assessment essential to the training process?
4. Develop instructional objectives that focus on a knowledge, a skill, and an ability needed by a license clerk to upload local files to the county's mainframe.
5. What are the six basic principles of adult learning? How can these be incorporated into training and development?
6. What are the three categories of training methods? Give an example of each.
7. Describe two methods for evaluating training. What are the strengths and weaknesses of each method?
8. Explain the differences between training and development.
9. Explain how development programs can address the following situations:
   a. An electronic engine analyzer is installed in a county maintenance shop.
   b. Financial exigency results in laying off three employees in the probate office.
   c. Citizens complain about inefficiencies in the city street department.
   d. A goal is established to promote three minority employees from custodial work to building maintenance.
   e. During the next three years, several equipment operators will be promoted to supervisory jobs.
   f. The chief clerk in the revenue office has a goal of becoming county administrator in 10 years.

ENDNOTES

[1] Robert L. Mathis and John H. Jackson, *Human Resource Management*, 9th ed. (Cincinnati: South-Western, 2000), 316–317.

[2] "Industry Report, 1999," *Training* 36 (October 1999), 37–81.

[3] Kevin Dobbs, "Simple Moments of Learning," *Training* 37 (January 2000), 52–58; and George Benson, "Informal Training Takes Off," *Training & Development* 51 (May 1997), 93–94.

[4] Daniel P. McMurrer, Mark E. Van Buren, and William H. Woodwell, Jr., "Making the Commitment," *Training & Development* 54 (January 2000), 41–48; and George R. Gray, McKenzie E. Hall, Marianne Miller, and Charles Shasky, "Training Practices in State Government Agencies," *Public Personnel Management* 26 (Summer 1997), 187–202.

[5] Sabrina Hicks, "Successful Orientation Programs," *Training & Development* 54 (April 2000), 59–60.

[6] Kathryn Tyler, "Take New Employee Orientation Off the Back Burner," *HRMagazine* 43 (May 1998), 49–57.

[7] Arthur G. Bedeian, *Management*, 3d ed. (Chicago: Dryden, 1993), 370–371.

[8] Tyler, 49–57.

[9] Howard J. Klein and Natasha A. Weaver, "The Effectiveness of an Organizational-Level Orientation Training Program in the Socialization of New Hires," *Personnel Psychology* 53 (Spring 2000), 47–66.

[10] Mathis and Jackson, 324.

[11] For an advanced discussion of adult learning principles, see Malcolm S. Knowles, Elwood F. Holton III, and Richard A. Swanson, *The Adult Learner*, 5th ed. (Houston: Gulf Publishing, 1998).

[12] Julius E. Eitington, *The Winning Trainer*, 3d ed. (Houston: Gulf Publishing, 1996), 441.

[13] Craig E. Schneier, James P. Guthrie, and Judy D. Olian, "A Practical Approach to Conducting and Using the Training Needs Assessment," *Public Personnel Management* 17 (Summer 1988), 191–205.

[14] Schneier, Guthrie, and Olian, 191–205; and William B. Werther and Keith Davis, *Personnel Management and Human Resources*, 2d ed. (New York: McGraw-Hill, 1985), 234–237.

[15] Charles Nanry, "Performance Linked Training," *Public Personnel Management* 17 (Winter 1988), 457–463.

[16] For example, see Susan E. Jackson and Randall S. Schuler, *Managing Human Resources: A Partnership Perspective*, 7th ed. (Cincinnati: South-Western, 2000), 367–374; Mathis and Jackson, 334–339.

[17] Carol Auerbach, "Matching Group Needs to Training Methods," *SHRM White Paper* (June 6, 2000). *http://www.shrm.org/whitepapers/documents/61315.asp*.

[18] Unless otherwise cited, the material in this section draws on Julius E. Eitington, *The Winning Trainer*, 3d ed. (Houston: Gulf Publishing, 1996); and Jackson and Schuler, 367–374.

[19] Jackson and Schuler, 370; and Brenda Seevers, Donna Graham, Julia Gamon, and Nikki Conklin, *Education Through Cooperative Extension* (Albany, N.Y.: Delmar, 1997), 58.

[20] Amy S. Glenn, "Designing a Distance Learning Course That Can Do It All," *The 7th Annual Distance Education Conference* (Austin: College of Education, Texas A&M University, 2000), 63–67.

[21] Blake Haggerty and Atsusi Hiumi, "Being Realistic About Web-Based Instruction: A Web-Developer's Perspective," *The 7th Annual Distance Education Conference* (Austin: College of Education, Texas A&M University, 2000), 79–84.

[22] Auerbach.

[23] George Bohlander, Scott Snell, and Arthur Sherman, *Managing Human Resources*, 12th ed. (Cincinnati: South-Western, 2001), 232.

[24] This section is based on Eitington, 402–415.

[25] Richard A. Swanson and Sandra K. Falkman, "Training Delivery Problems and Solutions: Identification of Novice Trainer Problems and Expert Trainer Solutions," *Human Resource Development Quarterly* 8 (Winter 1997), 305–314.

[26] Evan M. Berman and Jonathan P. West, "Career Risk and Reward from Productivity," *Public Personnel Management* 28 (Fall 1999), 453–471.

[27] Ron Zemke, "French Bank Trains for Work-Group Autonomy," *Training/HRD* 18 (October 1981), 76.

[28] David E. Ripley, "Trends in Management Development," *Personnel Administrator* 34 (May 1989), 93–96.

[29] Berman and West, 453–471.

[30] George R. Gray, McKenzie E. Hall, Marianne Miller, and Charles Shasky, "Training Practices in State Government Agencies," *Public Personnel Management* 26 (Summer 1997), 187–202.

[31] Jackson and Schuler, 353–355.

CHAPTER 11
PERFORMANCE APPRAISAL

IRVING GAUGES PERFORMANCE

The city of Irving, Texas, is recognized for its innovative leadership, excellent customer service, cultural diversity, and superior quality of life. According to City Manager Steve McCullough, "the city's competitive advantage rests with the creativity and expertise of its employees." The city's commitment to developing its talent base is enhanced through its performance management system, GAUGE© (Guide to Achievement, Understanding, Growth and Excellence).

Prior to GAUGE©, many departments did not appraise performance or used measures that did not incorporate the importance of competencies. According to Director of Human Resources Jo-Ann F. Bresowar, "Success in performance cannot be left to project results alone. It is the 'how' that can make the difference if the city wants continued success. In order to sustain a good working environment, employees must demonstrate behaviors (competencies) that support such an environment."

All city jobs share competencies that relate to the core values of the city. These competencies are customer service, ethics and integrity, job knowledge and skills, professionalism, and self-management. Other competencies relate to the nature of the work. The city's skill groups—including clerical, maintenance/trades, technical, professional, supervisory, and executive management—have different sets of competencies that contribute to success.

The four phases of GAUGE© include performance planning, performance execution, performance assessment, and performance review. While supervisors are required to conduct GAUGE© after the first six months of employment, supervisors recognize that the system may be used as an ongoing tool to provide both formal and informal feedback.

The successful implementation of GAUGE© was brought about through top management support, employee focus groups, and ongoing communication through newsletters, payroll inserts, the intranet, and partnering with departmental leaders to train and educate supervisors. As more employees and supervisors work together with GAUGE©, benefits are realized throughout the organization. For example, Parks and Recreation Specialist Medeanna Ferttoloso says, "GAUGE© creates a record of my successes and opportunities for improvement. It also helps me understand how my work supports the city's mission and values."

INTRODUCTION

Performance appraisal is a formal, written assessment of employee work contributions and the communication that takes place with employees before, during, and after the assessment. As the Irving example indicates, this process is of great importance to both em-ployees and the organization and should be done well. Other terms are often used in referring to this general area of activity. Performance management suggests a process aligned with strategic objectives, and might better represent the approach presented in this chapter. For that part of the process in which job performance is measured and rated, performance appraisal has become the preferred term in the professional literature. The authors suggest that the term *evaluation* should especially be avoided because it refers to methods used to establish the internal worth of jobs (it should be noted, however, that many excellent articles cited in this chapter use this term).

Researchers, writers, consultants, HR professionals and practicing managers see performance appraisal as an important tool in managing resources. It should, theoretically, provide a number of positive benefits. It should improve the quality of administrative decisions in such areas as merit pay, promotion, and termination. For employees the feedback reinforces good performance and suggests areas needing improvement. Performance ratings can be used to identify training needs and validate selection tests. In practice, however, most performance appraisal systems fail to achieve these benefits. Studies have indicated that up to 90 percent of appraisal systems are ineffective and 40 percent of employees say that their performance is not appraised at all.[1] Disappointing results from performance appraisal can be attributed to a number of factors.[2] Often performance appraisal systems are not aligned with the organization's mission and strategic plan. When this is the case, performance appraisal contributes little to the accomplishment of objectives. Lack of support by top management is one of the most important causes of poor implementation. When raters are not held accountable they are unlikely to invest the necessary time and effort in setting expectations, counseling employees, providing feedback, and accurately rating performance. Many supervisors find confronting performance issues to be very difficult, particularly when they have to criticize an employee. Performance appraisal is often threatening to employees, especially if they do not understand the rating criteria or if they view the process as unfair. Administrative and developmental purposes may conflict with each other. For example, if an employee knows the ratings will be used to set merit pay in the upcoming budget, he or she will be less concerned with goal setting, skill building, and performance improvement, which do not have immediate implications. Finally, performance ratings used for administrative purposes can result in legal liability under fair employment laws and regulations.

http://www.performance-appraisal.com
Archer North's Complete Online Guide to Performance Appraisal provides extensive information on the theory and practice of performance appraisal.

However, these and other problems are attributable mainly to shortcomings in how performance appraisal systems are designed and administered, not because of inherent deficiencies in either the concept itself or in the techniques described in the professional literature, some now over 50 years old. One writer suggests that for many organizations, using these techniques would amount to a significant improvement over what they are doing now.[3] Moreover the new focus on strategic HRM has resulted in the development of improved methods and approaches. Interestingly, most successful examples of these "best practices" are found in the public sector.[4] It should also be pointed out that legal compliance focuses on job-related performance measures and fair administration, conditions that are necessary to gain the benefits mentioned above even if legal liability were not a consideration.

PURPOSES OF PERFORMANCE APPRAISAL

Performance appraisal systems should support an organization's HR strategies. For example, if one such strategy is to reward individual contributions, performance ratings can be used to determine merit pay. On the other hand, traditional job-based performance appraisal may not be compatible with the objective of building work teams. Or, as mentioned earlier, strategies may conflict with each other and trade-offs become necessary. Therefore it is important for organizations to review their strategies and develop clear policies on how performance ratings will be used. For administrative purposes, ratings can be used as input to decisions involving pay, promotion, reassignment, and dismissal. For developmental purposes ratings can be used in counseling, training, and development. Last, ratings can be used to validate selection requirements.

ADMINISTRATIVE PURPOSES

Research has shown that the major use of performance appraisal in organizations is for pay decisions.[5] This is not surprising. As a society we are committed to the idea that hard work and achievement should be rewarded. There is also a perception that things do not operate this way in the public sector as evidenced by the pejoratives "government worker" and "bureaucrat." Another reason concerns employee motivation. Chapter 4 points out that a clear link between performance and pay has been shown to generate more effort and increased work contributions. As was noted, there is a concern that basing pay increases on performance minimizes the developmental aspects of appraisal, but the opposite case can also be made. Employees may feel that if ratings have no influence on pay, then the organization is not serious about performance appraisal. Moreover, the effectiveness of such approaches as merit and incentive pay requires that certain conditions exist. These include a climate of mutual trust, fair and accurate ratings, and consistent administration, conditions that also promote employee development. These and other aspects of performance-based pay systems are discussed in Chapter 13.

Performance ratings can provide input to a number of placement decisions

---

Dick Grote, a nationally recognized authority on performance appraisal whose work is cited extensively in this chapter, is decidedly optimistic about the potential benefits of well-designed performance appraisal systems. He especially likes what he sees happening in the public sector.

**PERFORMANCE APPRAISAL:
WHERE'S THE ACTION?**

Innovative performance management systems are no longer found exclusively in private sector organizations. The evidence is clear—America's cities, states, and federal agencies, and other public sector organizations are taking a leading role in creating novel and highly effective approaches to managing people on the job. . . . If this trend continues, it won't be long before private sector senior managers start saying, "We need some fresh thinking around here. Let's call City Hall and see what fresh ideas we can swipe."

A review of recent literature in performance appraisal tends to confirm this observation. Examples of "best practices" increasingly come from state agencies and local governments.

Source: Dick Grote, "Public Sector Organizations: Today's Innovative Leaders in Performance Management," *Public Personnel Management* 29 (Spring 2000), 19.

including promotion, reassignment, and dismissal. Deliberations over which candidates will be chosen for promotions should always begin by matching the requirements of the job with the applicant's qualifications. Even so, good performance in the employee's present assignment should be a minimum requirement for consideration. Moreover it is usually possible to identify certain aspects of performance on a present job that can be useful in predicting performance in a different assignment. For example, if a supervisor receives high ratings in planning and scheduling work, such ratings should be a major consideration in a possible promotion to department head. On the other hand, a person who is essentially a good performer, but has difficulty in completely and accurately filling out forms and records, is a poor prospect for a job involving much paperwork.

There are many situations other than promotion where decisions involve changing an employee's work assignment. These include lateral transfers, job redesign, reorganizations, and poor performance. Performance ratings that identify both strengths and weaknesses can provide information about the type of work that best utilizes the employee's strengths. There will also be cases where, regardless of the best efforts of the organization, an employee is either unwilling or unable to meet reasonable expectations for job performance. In these cases, the ratings provide a basis for such adverse actions as demotion, suspension, probation, and, ultimately, discharge.

DEVELOPMENTAL PURPOSES

Many HR professionals view performance appraisal as an effective setting for counseling and employee development. In counseling, the approach is on problem solving while development deals with capacity building.

The counseling aspect occurs in "real time." At the beginning of the work cycle employees and supervisors can reach an understanding regarding performance expectations. Employees can be encouraged to set both performance and personal improvement goals. During the work cycle a two-way exchange between the employee and supervisor can be used to correct shortcomings before they result in a poor rating and later to identify and mutually resolve significant problems.

The development aspect identifies opportunities for employees to improve performance and acquire potential for growth. Low performance ratings for individual employees are often the results of a deficit in knowledge or skills. Patterns of performance problems in certain areas across groups of employees almost always indicate a need for training. Finally, performance ratings can be used by employees in career planning.

Both counseling and employee development depend on feedback, usually provided by the superior as a performance manager or "coach" during the work cycle and as a facilitator of strategies to enhance personal goals and future contributions. Even when performance ratings are used for administrative decisions, the feedback from performance appraisal benefits both the employee and the organization.

VALIDATION OF SELECTION REQUIREMENTS

Title VII of the Civil Rights Act of 1964 and a series of court decisions have required organizations to justify selection requirements, including traditional paper-and-pencil tests that purport to measure intelligence, aptitude, ability, and so on. To validate such a test, the employer must demonstrate a relationship between scores on the selection test and performance on the job. This process is known as criterion-related validity, in which performance ratings are the criteria. If it can be shown that selection tests are predictors of performance (high test scores are associated with good performance and low scores are associated with poor performance), the test is considered valid (refer to Chapter 8). Performance ratings therefore can be extremely useful in validating a variety of selection procedures.

Obviously, the criterion measures (performance ratings) must accurately measure performance for the results of a validity study to be useful. Further, performance ratings, when used to justify decisions on such matters as promotion, pay, and dismissal, are considered to be tests themselves and subject to the same laws and regulations. For these reasons performance appraisal systems should be validated, usually through a content validity approach, also discussed in Chapter 7 and in a following section.

LEGAL ASPECTS OF PERFORMANCE APPRAISAL

As is the case with selection, using performance ratings for administrative purposes can cause legal exposure under Title VII, based on both disparate treatment and disparate impact theories of discrimination discussed in Chapter 3. Employers must also be concerned with the contractual and constitutional rights of employees in administering a performance appraisal program.

DISPARATE TREATMENT

Disparate treatment in performance appraisal involves procedures and decision rules with a sexual, racial, or other prohibited premise. Because of this, disparate treatment is also known as intentional discrimination. It is a frequent cause of complaints, but also the most obvious and most easily avoided legal risk of performance appraisal. Examples of disparate treatment include:

- A black and a white employee receive different ratings when there is no observable difference in job performance.
- Male employees receive day-to-day counseling to improve their performance ratings. Female employees do not.
- Written procedures providing for a hearing are not followed when a black employee is discharged for poor performance.
- A female employee receives a poor performance rating after making a sexual harassment charge against a male coworker.

Such incidents can form a basis for a prima facie case of discrimination, which triggers the EEO liability process described in Chapter 3. The employer is then required to produce a legitimate, nondiscriminatory reason for the action to an enforcement agency or to a court. The plaintiff must then prove that the employer's reasons were a pretext for discrimination. Although disparate treatment claims are difficult to prove, they create the appearance of unfairness and cause employees to mistrust the process.

DISPARATE IMPACT

Disparate impact occurs when procedures that appear to be neutral have an adverse effect on members of protected groups. Disparate impact, also referred to as unintentional or systemic discrimination, focuses on the effect of practices and procedures rather than the causes. There may be no intent to discriminate or evidence that one group or individual is actually treated differently from another. Examples include:

- A statistical analysis reveals that blacks receive significantly lower performance ratings than whites.
- Performance ratings lead to differential promotions and training opportunities for minorities or women.
- Pay disparities between males and females are based on performance ratings.

While disparate treatment can involve either individuals or groups of people, disparate impact always involves groups. The EEOC and many courts have adopted the **80 percent rule** for such cases. The rule states that any selection ratio (such as number promoted vs. number eligible) for members of protected groups must be at least 80 percent of the majority selection ratio.[6]

As with disparate treatment, disparate impact can be used by plaintiffs to prove a prima facie case of discrimination. The employer must then show to an enforcement agency or court that the practice or procedure is valid or job related according to the "Uniform Guidelines." There are variants and combinations of these defenses, but the important point to remember is that, once a prima facie case has been established, the burden shifts to the employer to justify the practice resulting in disparate impact. Unlike cases alleging disparate treatment, this is a burden of proof.

The legal principles for disparate impact cases were established in *Griggs v. Duke Power Company* (discussed in Chapter 3). The following important court cases involving disparate impact in performance appraisal are instructive in showing most of the ways that employers lose such cases.

BRITO V. ZIA COMPANY. A U.S. circuit court ruled that the organization had violated Title VII when, on the basis of poor performance ratings, it laid off a number of employees. The Court said the practice was illegal because (1) a disproportionate number of Hispanic workers were laid off and (2) the performance appraisal instrument was not related to important elements of work behavior but was based on "the best judgments and opinions of supervisors" and was not administered and scored under controlled and standardized conditions. The decision also clearly established that performance ratings were employment "tests."[7]

WADE V. MISSISSIPPI COOPERATIVE EXTENSION SERVICE. A U.S. district court noted that what the organization had called an "objective appraisal of performance" of county extension agents actually was based on supervisory ratings of traits such as leadership, public acceptance, attitude, grooming, personal conduct, outlook on life, resourcefulness, and loyalty. The court ruled that such ratings prevented blacks from being promoted to the position of county director and could not be used as selection standards. The court ordered the Mississippi Cooperative Extension Service to develop an appraisal system that would meet the requirements of the EEOC "Guidelines."[8]

ALBEMARLE PAPER COMPANY V. MOODY. The U.S. Supreme Court found that performance ratings were based on subjective standards not related to tasks workers performed. The Court ruled that because job analysis had not been conducted, the company could not use such ratings to validate selection requirements that eliminated a disproportionate number of black applicants.[9]

ROWE V. GENERAL MOTORS. A U.S. circuit court of appeals found that subjective appraisals of traits such as ability, merit, and capacity had an adverse effect on black employees. The court ruled that basing promotion decisions on these ratings violated Title VII.[10]

On the other hand, studies examining the effects of 13 appraisal system characteristics in 66 federal court cases involving discrimination found the following characteristics to correlate strongly with judgments for employers:

- Deriving the content of the appraisal from job analysis,
- Basing the appraisal criteria on observable job behaviors rather than traits,
- Providing written instructions to raters, and
- Reviewing the results of the appraisal with the employee.[11]

Although the case law on performance appraisal was developed almost 20 years ago, the principles apply equally today. Clearly, comprehensive, on-site job analysis and establishment of job-related criteria are the major keys to minimizing legal liability in performance appraisal. The job relatedness aspect can be addressed through a strategy of content validity, as discussed in Chapter 7. The procedures are basically the same; however, instead of developing a measure of employee potential, the organization develops a measure of actual performance. Such items as written instructions to raters, review of results with employees, and other administrative matters should be covered by policies and procedures as discussed in Chapter 5.

OTHER SOURCES OF LIABILITY

As Chapter 3 discussed, the common-law doctrine of employment at will has been significantly eroded by the courts. Employers may encounter legal liability where they attempt to discharge employees for poor performance, even if the employees are not members of a protected class. Representations made in employee handbooks, policies, procedures, and even oral statements can be construed as implied contracts. Once a contract has been found to exist, either by fact or implication, the employee has a legal claim if its terms are not followed. The common claim of breach of contract occurs when employers fail to follow their own specified procedures when discharging employees. Even when procedures are followed, arbitrary, capricious, or malicious actions may be seen by the courts as violations of the implied covenant of "good faith and fair dealing."[12] Finally, permanent employees of local government with liberty and property interests in their jobs have due process rights guaranteed by the Fourteenth Amendment to the U.S. Constitution.

ISSUES IN PERFORMANCE MEASUREMENT

In designing a performance appraisal system attention must be given to a number of aspects that impact on how effectively the system actually measures employee contributions in a work setting. These include reliability and validity, what is to be measured (criteria), sources of appraisal information, timing of appraisals, and control of rater errors.

RELIABILITY AND VALIDITY

Both reliability and validity are major considerations in performance appraisal. As Chapter 8 stated, reliability refers to the stability and consistency of performance ratings and validity is concerned with how well the ratings actually measure work contributions.[13]

Reliability is an important property for performance measures. Reliability is present when the ratings made by a single rater are stable over several performance periods, or when there is close agreement between two or more raters during a single performance period. Reliability can be improved when performance measures are more job related as discussed below. For a number of reasons, however, reliability of performance ratings is not likely to be as high as for other measures such as ability and work-sample tests. Improvement during the next performance period is one of the desirable outcomes of performance appraisal. Achieving this outcome, however, decreases reliability. Another point that must be considered is that different raters observe and measure different dimensions of performance. While this is important information to have, it is intuitive that the greater the number of raters, the greater the amount of variation that can be expected in the ratings. Other factors that may reduce reliability are timing and rater errors. These issues are discussed in a later section.

Validity is indicated when a "test," in this case a performance appraisal instrument, measures what it was intended to measure, such as behaviors or results related to job performance. Although there are several strategies or procedures for establishing validity, content validity as discussed in Chapter 8 is the most appropriate. Content validity is present when the content of the measure samples the content of the job and the manner and setting of the procedure closely approximates the work situation. It would be difficult to exactly meet these conditions with a performance appraisal instrument. Both accepted professional practice and rulings by enforcement agencies and courts support a more realistic standard, often called job relatedness. In order to meet this standard, a job analysis must be conducted to identify the performance dimensions of the job, also called responsibilities, accountabilities, and work behaviors (the term used in the "Uniform Guidelines"). Once the performance dimensions have been identified, there are a number of formats and methods that can be used to measure and rate performance. These are discussed in a following section.

A final aspect of validity involves the relevance of measures or *criteria* used to rate performance. Generally criteria are relevant when they sample the important performance dimensions of a job. For example, "enforces traffic laws" is likely to be a performance dimension for a police officer and should be assessed in performance appraisal. If a criterion measures the officer's performance in the task of patrolling streets and pulling over motorists who exceed the speed limit, make improper turns, fail to stop at traffic signals, and so on, then that particular criterion seems to be relevant. On the other hand, if the criteria leave out other tasks such as administering field sobriety tests to drivers who appear to be intoxicated, the criteria are *deficient*. Finally, criteria may measure dimensions not related to job performance or factors beyond the employee's control. This is known as *criterion contamination*. An appraisal of police officers on the dimension of "conducts crime prevention activities" should not be contaminated by the fact that an inner-city neighborhood containing public housing is likely to have a higher crime rate than a subdivision of single family homes. The type of criteria that are measured has a major influence on reliability, validity, and relevance as discussed below.

PERFORMANCE APPRAISAL CRITERIA

The three types of criteria most frequently measured are traits, behaviors, and outcomes. The nature of each of these measures is discussed below. The following section examines how they are incorporated in various appraisal methods and formats.

TRAIT-BASED CRITERIA

Traits are personal characteristics or attributes of individuals. The basic premise of appraisal on **trait-based criteria** is that certain traits such as leadership, judgment, dependability, and initiative are positively correlated with job performance. For example, a mechanic who completes an assigned task of tuning an engine and decides to clean the shop without being directed could be considered to have a high degree of initiative. Trait-based appraisals are widely used for two reasons. First, certain traits such as those listed above are seen as desirable, and it is not difficult to infer that employees who exhibit these traits will perform well (and conversely). Second, trait-based appraisals are simple and inexpensive to develop.

However, trait-based rating has a number of disadvantages. Traits are difficult to measure because they mean different things to different people. To one supervisor a dependable employee may be one who has a good attendance record. To another it may mean one who completes work assignments correctly. Many employees feel that trait ratings are based on personality characteristics and personal relationships rather than job performance.[14] Traits may apply to some jobs and not to others. For example, the trait of leadership would be relevant to the job of construction supervisor, but less so for a heavy equipment operator. No useful purpose is served by informing the supervisor that he or she is "weak in leadership" even if the assessment is accurate. Most importantly, however, the "Uniform Guidelines" explicitly state that content validity is not appropriate for validation of procedures based on traits and constructs.[15]

BEHAVIORALLY-BASED CRITERIA

Behaviorally-based criteria focus on how tasks are performed. In the job of construction supervisor a job dimension such as "manages construction operations" could be defined and used as an item on a rating form. The rater would rate the supervisor on the degree to which he or she carried out various expected behaviors such as efficiently planning and scheduling the work, using the right equipment, and enforcing safety rules. An emerging development using behavioral criteria is known as **competency-based appraisal.**[16] A competency is a set of knowledge, skills, and abilities (KSAs) necessary to accomplish a work activity. The organization identifies a number of "core" competencies needed by all employees and other competencies related to the job or kind of work as illustrated in the city of Irving case. Performance criteria are written in terms of observable behaviors that indicate ineffective to exceptional performance in applying the competency. A major advantage is that clearly identified behaviors are very useful in setting expectations and providing feedback (refer to expectancy and goal-setting theories of motivation discussed in Chapter 4). Behavioral criteria can also be validated using a content validity strategy.

As will be shown in the following section, performance appraisal instruments based on behaviors are more difficult to develop. Perhaps the major shortcoming of behavioral criteria is that carrying out all the expected behaviors does not necessarily lead to success on the job. For example, the construction foreman may do all the "right things" and still not complete projects on time or within budget.

OUTCOME-BASED CRITERIA

Outcome-based criteria focus on measurable results. Using the construction supervisor example, the objective might be to complete the site preparation for an athletic field in 30 days at a cost of $80,000. In that outcomes ultimately determine whether an organization succeeds or fails, this type of criterion can be very useful in performance appraisal. There are a number of disadvantages, however, such as external factors over which the employee has no control and critical aspects of the job that are difficult to quantify. For example, rain may shut down construction operations for a week, causing the project to take longer than expected. The supervisor may meet the deadline by allowing equipment to be operated in an unsafe manner. Outcome-based criteria are more fully covered in the discussion of management by objectives in the following section.

SOURCES OF APPRAISAL INFORMATION

Successful performance appraisal requires judgment by a knowledgeable individual who has directly observed the employee's work (or work products) and who can rate performance without error or bias, relying on acceptable quantitative and qualitative measures. Such data must be incorporated into the rating, no matter who is selected to conduct the performance appraisal. In many cases performance appraisal is conducted by the immediate superior, who can integrate both types of measures. In some cases, however, responsibility for appraisal may best be assigned to other persons. In addition, other sources of appraisal judgment may be taken into consideration by whoever is assigned final responsibility for the appraisal. This section provides a brief description of the various sources that are currently accepted within organizations.

SUPERVISORY APPRAISAL

Supervisory appraisal is appropriate for several reasons. An organizational superior or "boss" has both a right and a duty to make both administrative and developmental decisions regarding subordinates. In addition, the superior normally assigns and observes the work and is responsible for giving rewards and/or sanctions in accordance with job behaviors and outcomes. The disadvantages of supervisory appraisal include the familiar objection to "playing God" as well as a possible lack of interpersonal skills needed to maintain positive relationships with subordinates. Moreover, the superior may commit rater errors or allow personal considerations unrelated to performance to influence the ratings.

MEASURING OUTPUTS AND OUTCOMES IN DeKALB COUNTY

In an effort to operate more effectively, local governments are reassessing how they measure the performance of their employees. In 1996 DeKalb County, Georgia, set out to establish a performance management system that would focus on the county's goals and those of its "customers." Early efforts produced a large set of output indicators such as efficiency and productivity, many of which had little to do with service quality. Departments then refined and narrowed the lists of indicators, each assuming the role of internal customers. The final set of performance measures also incorporated customer service outcomes. For example:

- The Animal Control Division established goals for responding to priority 1 calls (dog attacks, etc.) as well as general calls.
- The Emergency Medical Services Division set a goal of responding to life support calls within eight minutes.

All of the county's departments factor such measures into performance appraisal in order to assess both outputs and outcomes. The result has been an increase in both efficiency and customer satisfaction.

Source: Liane Levetan, "Implementing Performance Measures," *American City & County* 115 (September 2000), 40–44.

SUBORDINATE APPRAISAL

Subordinate appraisal has been used in organizations for some time. One of the most familiar applications (at least to the authors) is where students rate the performance of their instructors. A major advantage is that the feedback from such appraisals can be very useful for development purposes. It can also cause superiors to be more responsive to legitimate concerns of their employees. This type of appraisal also has a number of disadvantages. It may be resented by superiors if they believe that it undermines their authority or threatens their self-esteem. It may lead superiors to make decisions that ensure good ratings rather than decisions that accomplish objectives. Finally, even without a formal system, a superior is already being appraised by subordinates, albeit indirectly. The superior's rating is usually influenced by how well or poorly the subordinates perform their work.

PEER/TEAM APPRAISAL

Peer or team appraisal is very useful because work group members see various aspects of their coworkers' performance that may not be observed by the superior. For example, an employee may "cut corners" in carrying out a task if the poor workmanship is not obvious in the finished job. Another employee may take pains to ensure all tasks are performed properly, even if the superior is not present. However, peer appraisals have a competitive aspect and can be disruptive. Conflicts may arise between making objective appraisals and maintaining good relationships with coworkers. Also, peers may form cliques and agree among themselves to base ratings on who is "in" or "out" rather than on job performance. Appraisal of team performance as a whole typically involves cost and/or productivity standards as discussed in Chapter 13.

SELF-APPRAISAL

In some situations employees rate their own performance. This could be appropriate if a job is so unique and highly specialized that the employee is the only person who understands it. This is sometimes the situation when new technologies (such as GIS) are first introduced. In most cases, however, self-appraisal is combined with supervisory appraisal. Self-appraisals are useful in development because they emphasize personal growth, intrinsic motivation, and goal setting. They also communicate to the superior how the subordinate perceives his or her performance and provide insights not otherwise available. However, the standards that an employee uses to rate his or her performance may be different than those established by the organization. Moreover, an employee who has a personal stake in the outcome of the appraisal cannot be expected to take an objective, dispassionate approach. Therefore self-appraisal has limited value as input to decisions in administrative areas such as promotion and merit pay.

APPRAISAL BY OUTSIDERS

Appraisal by outsiders is useful in several situations. There may be a need for someone with specialized expertise but without a vested interest in the appraisal results. An example is retaining a CPA firm to conduct an audit of a financial statement. Another application is the assessment center, where candidates for managerial positions participate in a variety of situational exercises and are assessed on their performance by several trained observers. The customers or clients of an organization are important sources of information on service quality. For jobs that involve contact with citizens, such as customer service representatives, police officers, and recreation workers, the citizens who interact with these employees are in the best position to observe and rate certain important job behaviors.

MULTI-RATER APPRAISAL

Many organizations are combining the various sources of appraisal information to create what is called multi-rater or 360-degree appraisal and feedback systems. This approach to appraisal recognizes the advantages and limitations of the sources of information discussed above. As has been shown, there are aspects of how an employee performs his or her job that cannot be captured or even observed by a single rater. It is intuitive, therefore, that 360-degree appraisal and feedback should be more fair and balanced.

There are, however, a number of significant problems with 360-degree appraisal. Effective performance appraisal is difficult to carry out, even with simple methods and single raters. Developing the systems needed, training the raters, managing the process, and combining multiple sources of information is a vastly more complex task. Using multiple raters tends to lower reliability, even though each rater's assessment may be accurate from his or her perspective. Inaccurate or unfair ratings resulting from rater errors, bias, favoritism, and personal vendettas are equally as likely from coworkers, subordinates, and customers as from a superior. In fact, there is an increased opportunity for collusion among raters to advance their own agendas, having little relation to job performance. The concern is whether 360-degree appraisal improves the process or simply multiplies the problems by the number of raters.[17]

http://www. performanceappraisal. com/ Grote Consulting provides information on creating and implementing performance appraisal systems and numerous articles on performance appraisal.

Even so, 360-degree appraisal appears to be a tool with significant potential. A review of research and practice provides several points that can guide organizations in successfully implementing the process.[18] First, 360-degree appraisal should be thoughtfully and carefully introduced. Each component requires the same attention to design, development, and administration that would be appropriate for a single method. Ratings should be collected anonymously and treated confidentially. Because individuals may be uncomfortable with negative feedback, as well as legal risk, there is a strong consensus that ratings should be used for developmental purposes only. However, employees should be encouraged to share feedback with superiors without revealing specific ratings or comments in order to set development goals.

TIMING OF PERFORMANCE APPRAISALS

Practices vary widely not only in the types and methods of appraisals but also in their frequency. Timing should be consistent with the appraisal method used and should support strategic objectives. The major approaches are focal point, anniversary, and natural time span of the job.[19]

FOCAL POINT TIMING

In focal point timing, appraisals are conducted at regular intervals such as quarterly, semi-annually or annually. Annual/fiscal year appraisals are best for programs using actual-versus-budget results as one measure of performance, and for programs in which it is important to know how the performances of several employees compare at a particular time. Semiannual or quarterly appraisals are often conducted, usually on an informal basis. This helps to ensure that employees receive timely feedback, especially in areas that need to be improved. The main disadvantage of this approach is that all appraisals are due at the same time. Focal point appraisals cause a major workload for a concentrated period, which can be very burdensome.

ANNIVERSARY TIMING

Annual anniversary date of hire appraisals give the appraisal a personal characteristic that is important in employee development. This approach also distributes the workload across the year. However, this approach is extremely difficult to use if actual-versus-budget results are measured, since the budget cycle rarely coincides with the anniversary dates of employees. Also, research suggests that ratings given to employees earlier in the year are higher than ratings given later.[20]

NATURAL TIME SPAN OF THE JOB

In this approach, the appraisal is conducted when it is possible to determine how well an employee performed on the job. The basis for using time span is that performance is assessed at the point when it can be measured, which may occur either before or after an arbitrary date. This is useful in project work, especially when a performance standards or management-by-objectives format is used. This kind of timing is dictated by the critical incident approach because examples of good and bad behavior occur at random over a continuum of time. The major problem with this approach occurs when time spans run longer than administrative cycles, such as annual salary adjustments. Feedback also may be delayed, which impedes employee development.

SOURCES OF ERROR IN PERFORMANCE APPRAISAL

There are several common sources of error in performance appraisal. **Common rater errors** include recency, first impression, halo, central tendency, rater patterns, similar-to-me effect, contrast effects, and stereotyping.[21] Some of these errors can be controlled by good methods and techniques and others by rater training. Because rater errors are well-entrenched habits that are difficult to break, rater training is extremely important. It is possible to develop systems that are resistant to errors, but only after raters are trained can the rating system be most effective. However, no system can be made error free, and results always require careful assessment and monitoring.

RECENCY

Recency errors occur when raters remember events that occurred most recently instead of remembering an employee's performance during the entire appraisal period. Employees contribute to the problem by becoming more concerned about job performance as appraisal time approaches. This error is understandably common, and the attitude of "Yes, but what have you done for me lately?" enters most situations. To overcome the recency problem, there should be continuing communication between the supervisor and subordinate throughout the appraisal period. Another solution is for the supervisor to keep accurate written records concerning the employee's performance.

FIRST IMPRESSION

First impression errors occur when a supervisor makes an initial judgment (favorable or unfavorable) about an employee and then ignores information that fails to support that judgment. This type of error is most common when employees are hired or promoted. To overcome this problem, the rater should concentrate on systematically observed performance during the period of time that the working relationship is being established. In this way, performance appraisal and counseling can be based on a representative sample of behavior.

HALO

Halo error occurs when supervisors allow their rating of an employee on one item to influence ratings on all other items. The halo error is not, as commonly believed, necessarily associated with good performance. It is also likely that a poor rating may carry through on all items. An appraisal that shows the same rating on all items should be closely examined for halo error. Clearly specifying the categories to be rated and training raters are the best ways to deal with halo error.

CENTRAL TENDENCY

Central tendency describes the reluctance of some supervisors to rate an individual as either very good or very poor. Consequently, all employees receive a rating of "average," or "meets standards." This error usually occurs when a superior does not critically observe job performance and at appraisal time is not in a position to make distinctions. Another reason the error occurs is that the supervisor may be asked to explain very good or very poor ratings. To overcome this problem, management must make it clear to the rater that the performance appraisal is an important part of the managerial job and that it is worth the time and effort needed to do it right.

RATER PATTERNS

Rater pattern errors occur because of the range of individual differences among managers. This is analogous to the situation faced by college students when a course is taught by several professors. One professor might turn out to be an easy grader, another is a middle-of-the-road grader, and maybe one is so tough that students delay taking the course until another professor is teaching it. It is the same with raters, who display patterns ranging from leniency to strictness. These patterns create problems when comparing the performance of individuals working under different supervisors. Some organizations use a statistical technique that standardizes the ratings. A better application of performance criteria and counseling with individual supervisors who have fallen into specific patterns can help overcome this kind of error.

SIMILAR-TO-ME EFFECT

This is the tendency to favor employees who resemble the rater. The error develops when raters feel that certain aspects of their background or experience are especially noteworthy. Then they consciously or unconsciously reward employees for having these attributes with higher ratings than are justified by their performance. A supervisor who has served in the military may exhibit this error when rating employees who are veterans. A female supervisor may identify with single mothers and single them out for favorable treatment. Rater training is useful in overcoming this error; however, raters must be motivated to conduct self-analysis to identify and confront this tendency and not allow it to influence their ratings.

CONTRAST EFFECTS

Contrast effects are present when a rater compares a person's performance with that of others although the instrument is designed to measure performance against standards. These errors are troublesome because many raters assume performance is distributed on a normal curve with a certain number of excellent, good, fair, and poor performers. Such reasoning is self-defeating, since one of the objectives of a performance appraisal system is to motivate individuals to meet performance standards.

STEREOTYPING

Stereotyping is the tendency to judge individuals on the basis of perceptions about the group to which they belong. Stereotypes are often associated with race, ethnicity, gender, and age. A rater who has a positive stereotype, such as that Asians are hard-working and conscientious, will tend to rate members of this group more favorably (as in the similar-to-me effect discussed above). What is more troubling is when raters penalize employees based on negative stereotypes such as that older employees have less energy and a woman's place is in the home (or in the secretarial pool). Overcoming this error requires rater training of the type discussed for the similar-to-me effect.

PERFORMANCE APPRAISAL FORMATS AND METHODS

This section is organized based on various formats used to rate performance. Several points should be noted, however. Certain measurement devices (such as the absolute or "Thurstone" rating scale) are used in more than one method. Others (such as the behavioral frequency or "Likert" scale) are associated with a particular method. Finally, several formats (such as rating scales and essays) are often combined in a single rating instrument. The formats described in this section are those that are most common. They include graphic rating scales, essay appraisals, comparative methods, checklist methods, critical incidents, performance standards, behavioral scales, and management by objectives.[22]

GRAPHIC RATING SCALES

The **graphic rating scale**, which was introduced in 1922, is the oldest and most commonly used performance appraisal format. In this format, an absolute scale (similar to a ruler or thermometer) is used to rate performance on several items. Each item is rated on a continuum of scale points typically ranging from three to nine.

The advantages of graphic rating scales are that they are relatively simple to develop, easy to understand, and less time-consuming to administer than other formats. They can be highly job related and can be combined with other methods such as behaviorally phrased essays.[23] Graphic rating scales are most useful when the items represent major responsibilities established by job analysis and are weighted in accordance with their importance to overall job performance. Also it is important that scale points representing various levels of performance be defined in unambiguous terms. Exhibit 11-1 is an example of this format for the job of lead water treatment operator (note the correspondence between the work behaviors identified on the job description illustrated in Chapter 7 and the rating factors). In general, the more items that are job specific and can be either quantitatively measured or at least observed, the higher the degree of reliability and validity that can be obtained. To make ratings more useful, the rater, along with completing the scale,

---

Although it is the process, not the form, that is important in performance appraisal, the form is the most visible manifestation of the process. It serves as a report card for organization members. Just as we can gain some insights into the approach to education that different

FORM AND SUBSTANCE

schools may take by examining the report cards they use to evaluate student achievement, so we can learn about the processes and behaviors and results an organization considers important by looking at its report card: the performance appraisal form it has chosen to use.

Source: Excerpted and condensed from Dick Grote, *The Complete Guide to Performance Appraisal* (New York: American Management Association, 1996), 36.

is asked or required to justify the rating and to discuss suggestions for improvement in space provided for written comments.

Graphic rating scales actually in use tend to have serious flaws. In many cases they are designed to measure personal traits such as "leadership" and "initiative" or "judgment," or global factors such as "quality of work." Ratings from such items provide little meaningful feedback or assistance in setting goals. Scale points that indicate different levels of performance are subject to different interpretations by different raters. Items are usually not weighted based on importance to the job. Graphic rating scales are also subject to a number of rater errors including halo, recency, and central tendency, discussed earlier. Finally, some versions of this format (particularly trait-based scales) do not meet the validity requirements of the "Uniform Guidelines" and the courts.

ESSAY APPRAISALS

The narrative **essay appraisal** is a discussion of an employee's job performance in the rater's own words. Often, guidelines are provided. For example, the rater may be asked to describe such things as strengths, weaknesses, and potential and to make suggestions for improvement as shown in Exhibit 11-2 on page 258. The essay approach to performance appraisal assumes that a candid and honest expression from a knowledgeable rater is just as accurate as more formal and quantitative methods. Narrative essays can provide detailed feedback regarding job performance, particularly if the rater uses an accurate job description to ensure that all areas are covered.

There are several problems with essay appraisals, however. They may be unfocused such that some performance dimensions are overemphasized while others are not covered at all. Another problem with essay appraisals is that the employee's rating may depend more on the writing skills of the superior than on the employee's performance. Finally, this method is highly subjective, time consuming, difficult to administer, and impractical for large groups. For these reasons the essay is best used as a supplement to a more structured method such as the graphic rating scale.

COMPARATIVE APPRAISAL METHODS

Comparative appraisal methods measure individuals against each other rather than against standards. Individuals may be compared on measures relating to overall job performance or, less frequently, on several traits or work characteristics. Comparative methods produce a listing of individuals from first to last in order of performance. Several formats are used.

http://work911.com/
performance/
index.htm
Bascal and Associates
provides articles on
and forms for
performance appraisals.

Paired comparison, illustrated in Exhibit 11-3 on page 259, is an example of this approach. In paired comparison individuals are compared one at a time with every other individual; the final rank is determined by the number of times the comparison resulted in a higher rating. One of the better applications of paired comparison is the Judgment Quotient Assessment method. As in paired comparison, workers are compared with each other, but multiple raters are used and workers are compared on several job-related performance dimensions. The results are tabulated for each performance dimension, as shown in Exhibit 11-4 on page 260.

Another comparative format is the *forced distribution*, in which the rater assigns a specific proportion of individuals to predetermined performance categories, as shown in Exhibit 11-5 on page 261. This is somewhat analogous to an instructor "grading on the curve," resulting in a few As and Fs, slightly more Bs and Ds, and a large number of Cs.

A major problem with comparative methods, particularly the forced distribu-

EXHIBIT 11-1

Name _____

Title _Lead Water Treatment Plant Operator_____

Rating Period : From _____ To _____

Rater Name _____

Rater Title _____

Department _Utilities_____

Rating Scale Key

5. **Exceptional**—Exceeds job requirements

4. **Very Good**—Meets job requirements with distinction

3. **Acceptable**—Fully meets job requirements

2. **Marginal**—Barely meets job requirement

1. **Unacceptable**—Fails to meet job requirements

PART I RATING SCALES FOR MAJOR RESPONSIBILITIES

A. Plant Operations PCT. 30%	**RATING**	1 ☐	2 ☐	3 ☐	4 ☐	5 ☐

Monitors control panel, conducts on-site observations, interprets gauge readings and tests, adjusts gates and valves, starts and stops pumps to regulate water flow, and maintains log of operations	**Comments:**

B. Laboratory Testing PCT. 15%	**RATING**	1 ☐	2 ☐	3 ☐	4 ☐	5 ☐

Takes samples of water piped in or collects by hand, performs appropriate laboratory tests according to prescribed procedures, records test results, and submits reports.	**Comments:**

C Equipment Maintenance PCT. 15%	**RATING**	1 ☐	2 ☐	3 ☐	4 ☐	5 ☐

Performs scheduled maintenance of pumps, generators, and related equipment, repairs or replaces parts using hand or power tools, tests repaired equipment, and maintains records.	**Comments:**

D. Safety Management PCT. 15%	**RATING**	1 ☐	2 ☐	3 ☐	4 ☐	5 ☐

Follows and enforces safety rules and procedures, corrects and reports unsafe behaviors and working conditions, participates on safety committee, administers first aid, implements emergency procedures, and assists in investigations.	**Comments:**

E. Lead Responsibilities PCT. 15%	**RATING**	1 ☐	2 ☐	3 ☐	4 ☐	5 ☐

Attends training and studies technical literature to maintain technical competence, assumes responsibility for operating plant in absence of division director, and conducts on-the-job and formal training of lower-level operators.	**Comments:**

F. Services to Department PCT. 10%	**RATING**	1 ☐	2 ☐	3 ☐	4 ☐	5 ☐

Performs grounds maintenance and housekeeping tasks, maintains vehicles and equipment, performs light maintenance and building maintenance services, supervises or performs work on distribution system, and performs related tasks as required.	**Comments:**

PART II PERFORMANCE DISCUSSION AND SUMMARY

Does the employee have knowledge, skills, abilities, and other qualifications needed for successful job performance?　　[　] yes　[　] no　　If no, please explain.

Describe any specific actions employee needs to take to improve job performance.

Summarize this employee's overall job performance.

PART III SIGNATURES

This report is based on my observation and knowledge of both the employee and the job.

My signature indicates that I have reviewed this appraisal. It does not mean that I agree with the results.

_____   _____
Supervisor   Date

_____   _____   _____   _____
Reviewer   Date   Employee   Date

EXHIBIT 11-2

**PORTION OF
AN ESSAY
APPRAISAL
FORM**

Make a clear and concise statement describing the employee's performance on each of the factors below.

Productivity: Volume of work and major accomplishments.

_____

_____

_____

_____

_____

_____

Accuracy: Meeting quality standards.

_____

_____

_____

_____

_____

Coordination: Planning and organizing work and supervising employees.

_____

_____

_____

_____

_____

_____

tion, is that they assume that performance is distributed "normally," with a certain proportion of good, fair, and poor performers in the population under consideration. In order to make such an inference, 30 to 50 observations are needed; thus many work groups are too small. In most applications, individuals are compared in terms of overall job performance. This kind of comparison limits the usefulness of the appraisal for providing feedback to the individual on which aspects of job performance are acceptable and which need improvement. Therefore, the results of comparative methods are likely to be meaningless and may be damaging to morale, since someone must be last. To illustrate how comparative methods can distort reality, consider that there is a slowest runner on the U.S. Olympic gold medal relay team and a fastest runner among 45- to 55-year-old finishers in a local "fun run."

EXHIBIT 11-3

RANKING WITH PAIRED COMPARISON

Persons Rated	As compared to:										SCORE	RANK
	SB	WB	WC	WF	HL	RL	JM	DS	JS	SW		
Sam Burton		X		X	X	X	X	X	X	X	8	2
William Buford				X	X	X	X			X	5	5
Warren Clark	X	X		X	X	X	X	X	X	X	9	1
William Fowler					X	X	X			X	4	6
Harry Larkin						X		X			2	8
Robert Lee								X			1	9
John McCord											0	10
Deborah Stinson		X		X	X	X	X			X	6	4
James Strawn		X		X	X	X	X	X		X	7	3
Sylvia Watt					X	X	X				3	7

Note: X means that the person's performance is better than the person with whom he/she was paired. For example, Clark's performance is better than any of the others. Lee's is only better than McCord's.

Finally, if raters compare employees on the basis of subjective judgments—personality traits and similar factors—the ratings are no more likely to measure job performance than other methods.

One point can be made in defense of comparative methods. An organization may need to determine rankings for administrative purposes, such as a validity check on another method. A supervisor who has rated 10 employees on a graphic rating scale may be asked later to list the individuals from first to last in order of performance. A strong positive rank correlation would be expected.

CHECKLIST APPRAISALS

Checklist appraisals attempt to provide the rater with a wide range of performance indicators that are designed to cover all aspects of the job. Raters are required to check items that are most representative of the employee's characteristics and work contributions.

To overcome the problem of lenient ratings, the checklist format known as *forced choice* was developed by the U.S. Army for use in rating the performance of noncommissioned officers. Although there are a number of variations, the procedure usually requires raters to select from a group of statements those that are related to the individual's behavior. A group of statements is shown in Exhibit 11-6 on page 262. The rater is usually required to pick one statement that is most descriptive and one that is least descriptive of the individual. The statements are designed so that only one of the favorable and one of the unfavorable statements is associated with job performance. This information is not provided to the rater; thus, the results of the rating are known only to the HR department, which has the key. The authors' experience with forced choice appraisal in both military and civilian orga-

EXHIBIT 11-4

OVERVIEW OF
THE JUDGMENT
QUOTIENT
ASSESSMENT
PERFORMANCE
APPRAISAL
TECHNIQUE

1. Job-related performance criteria are determined for each job. Similar jobs are then aggregated into performance groups.

2. Observable behavioral illustrations are identified for each performance criterion such as shown below:

   Criterion: Organization and Planning
   * Setting objectives
   * Developing contingency plans
   * Scheduling activities and agendas
   * Setting priorities
   * Using a "To Do" list

3. Each assessee chooses five to eight raters, who must include his or her supervisor. Each assessor rates performance on a scaled comparison rating format:

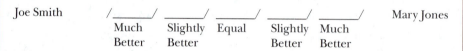

Joe Smith   /_____/ _____/ _____/ _____/ _____/   Mary Jones
              Much   Slightly Equal   Slightly Much
              Better   Better   Better   Better

4. A talent profile is provided to each assessee:

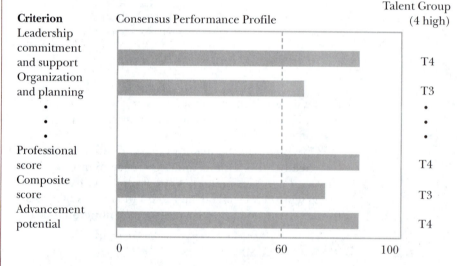

Criterion	Consensus Performance Profile	Talent Group (4 high)
Leadership commitment and support		T4
Organization and planning		T3
•		•
•		•
•		•
Professional score		T4
Composite score		T3
Advancement potential		T4

0   60   100

The length of the bar graph indicates the assessee's relative position in the group. Score range is 60 to 100, which minimizes negative motivation to poor performers.

Source: Adapted from Mark R. Edwards, "OJQ Offers Alternative to Assessment Center," *Public Personnel Management Journal* 12 (January 1983), 146–155.

nizational settings has not been positive. The ratings were resented by both employees and supervisors. Feedback is, of course, impossible.

A better application of this format is the *weighted checklist*. In this method a comprehensive list of behavioral statements is developed. HR analysts, with the assistance of supervisors and experienced job incumbents, then evaluate these statements and assign weights based on the importance of the behavior in question and on how well the statement distinguishes between good and poor performance. To appraise the employee, the supervisor checks those statements that best describe the employee's

EXHIBIT 11-5	

RATING BY
FORCED
DISTRIBUTION

Instructions: Assign the employees in your department to the appropriate categories using the following distribution as a guide:

Outstanding (10%)	Above Average (20%)	Average (40%)	Below Average (20%)	Un-Satisfactory (10%)
W. Clark	S. Burton	D. Stinson	H. Larkin	J. McCord
_____	J. Strawn	W. Buford	R. Lee	_____
	_____	W. Fowler	_____	
	_____	S. Watt	_____	
		_____		
		_____		
		_____		
		_____		

Note: Employee forced distributions take various forms. In the example shown above, five categories are used to approximate the bell-shaped curve of the "normal" distribution. A similar result is obtained when raters are instructed to place an equal number of employees in four quartiles. The second and third quartiles are then combined into an "average" category containing 50 percent of the employees rated. Still another variation is to divide employees evenly into upper, middle, and lower thirds. The key feature of the forced distribution method is that the number of employees assigned to each category is predetermined; thus "forced" on the rater.

performance and leaves the rest blank. The overall rating is computed by adding the weights of the items checked. An example is shown in Exhibit 11-7 on page 263.

CRITICAL INCIDENTS

Critical incidents are reports made by knowledgeable observers of action taken by individuals who were especially effective or ineffective in accomplishing their jobs. The critical incident technique, or CIT, was developed in 1954 by John C. Flanagan.[24] Critical incidents are recorded by superiors as they happen; they are short and to the point, and they normally consist of a single sentence. The following are examples of critical incidents that illustrate effective performance:

- Located $800 error in final settlement report (clerk, tax assessor's office).
- Developed spreadsheet for analysis of budget requests (administrative assistant).
- Saved engine of packer by stopping vehicle when low oil pressure indicator light came on (driver, sanitation department).

Critical incidents also describe ineffective or poor performance, such as the following:

- Neglected to relay relevant information to patrol unit after receiving report of wreck on Highway 78 (police dispatcher).
- Became irate and overbearing when individual requested explanation of why sales tax was collected on used car (cashier, tax collector's office).

EXHIBIT 11-6

FORCED
CHOICE
APPRAISAL

From each group of statements below, mark M beside the statement that is most descriptive of the employee's behavior and mark L beside the statement that is least descriptive.

A. _____ Inclined to avoid responsibility.
   _____ Takes pride in the job.
   _____ Shows poor leadership.
   _____ Open to suggestions.

B. _____ Exercises good judgment.
   _____ Tends to resist change.
   _____ Treats subordinates with respect.
   _____ Has gaps in job knowledge.

C. _____ Fails to establish priorities.
   _____ Complies with policies and procedures.
   _____ Pays attention to details.
   _____ Does not meet deadlines.

D. _____ Excessively criticizes subordinates.
   _____ Operates on a crisis basis.
   _____ Sets high goals.
   _____ Encourages subordinates to express ideas.

E. _____ Often misses deadlines.
   _____ Works well under pressure.
   _____ Leads by example.
   _____ Fails to deal with poor performers.

- Failed to post stock record cards, resulting in wheel cylinders not being reordered (parts clerk).

Critical incidents provide useful information, particularly when they are collected and placed in appropriate categories. For example, a person whose critical incidents reveal a pattern of innovation, such as developing a budget spreadsheet, might be considered for a promotion to a position where this characteristic could be more fully utilized. The main disadvantage of the critical incident method is that it is time consuming and burdensome and may be neglected by supervisors.

PERFORMANCE STANDARDS

Performance standards are statements of what is considered acceptable and attainable on a particular job.[25] This approach is similar to management by objectives (discussed below); however performance standards focus more on behaviors than results. Many organizations have implied performance standards, but these are not spelled out in accordance with job tasks. In a formal system using performance standards, a job analysis sets forth what is to be done. Performance standards describe how much is expected or how well the tasks are to be performed. Shown below are examples of performance standards for two jobs. Typically the set of statements is prefaced by the phrase "performance meets standards when:"

EXHIBIT 11-7	
EXCERPT FROM WEIGHTED CHECKLIST	

Employee's Name _____ Department _____

Rater's Name _____ Date _____

Weight[a]	Behavioral Statement	Yes	No
4.5	1. Employee takes extra work during peak time.		
4.0	2. Employee stays at work station when not on break.		
3.7	3. Employee follows instructions and procedures.		
3.6	4. Employee usually meets deadlines.		
·	· · · · · · · · · · · · · · ·	·	·
·	· · · · · · · · · · · · · · ·	·	·
2.5	30. Employee keeps workplace clean and neat.		
100.0			

[a]Weight is usually omitted from form used by rater

- **Financial Technician** (financial controls)—Standard bookkeeping procedures are followed; all checking accounts, ledgers, and journals are balanced; bank statements are reconciled; errors are identified and corrected; audit trail is maintained for receipts and expenditures.
- **Automotive Mechanic** (major repairs)—Appropriate diagnostic techniques are used to determine need to repair engines and other major assemblies; after disassembly, all critical parts are checked for possible repair/replacement; units are reassembled to correct tolerances and appropriate tests are performed; after being placed in operation, repaired units stay in service without problems for appropriate number of miles/hours.

Standards should be established through negotiations between the individual or group of subordinates and the superior. Advocates of performance standards recommend that they be written in quantitative terms when possible. However, as the examples show, some job aspects are difficult to reduce to quantitative terms; therefore, behavioral statements must be made.

Performance standards have many advantages and one major shortcoming. The participative approach provides the opportunity for an interchange of thoughts between the superior and subordinate regarding performance responsibilities, priorities, and expected results. It helps facilitate the subordinate's agreement to achieve standards and the superior's commitment to provide the necessary support. Since standards are known in advance, there is sufficient time to correct performance deficiencies as they develop. Performance ratings can be more objective and feedback interviews more productive.

The major disadvantage of the performance standards approach is the amount of time and effort required by both the superior and the subordinate. Developing realistic and comprehensive standards, negotiating performance expectations, and defining them in clear and measurable terms is a major undertaking.

BEHAVIORAL SCALES

Behavioral scales are an extension of both the item-based graphic rating scale and the critical incident technique and are designed to assess the various behaviors that can be observed when an employee is performing a job. Such formats reduce the amount of judgment required by the rater in item-based scales. They also quantify the level of performance represented by observed behaviors, an aspect missing from the critical incident approach. The formats used most frequently are *behaviorally anchored rating scales* (BARS) and *behavioral observation scales* (BOS).

BARS is the most complex and sophisticated format as well as the most expensive to develop. The construction of BARS generally follows procedures developed by Smith and Kendall.[26] The first step is to collect critical incidents that describe a wide range of behaviors. The critical incidents are then placed in broad categories that serve as performance dimensions. A group of supervisors and possibly experienced job incumbents known as subject matter experts (SMEs) are given the set of critical incidents and categories and asked to match each incident to the category that they believe the incident illustrates (known as retranslation). Incidents that are not assigned to the same category by a high percentage of the SMEs and those that fall frequently into two or more categories are discarded. Another group of SMEs is given the retranslated list and asked to rate each incident on a 5- to 9-point scale, representing a continuum of job performance from outstanding to poor. The only items retained are those on which the ratings are closely "clustered" (do not vary excessively around the group mean). These incidents are used as anchors on the rating scale; hence the term *behaviorally anchored*. An example of BARS for a supervisory job dimension of "resolving employee problems" is shown in Exhibit 11-8.

http://doleta.wdsc.org/jobs/prfguide.html
The U.S. Department of Labor's *Performance Management Appraisal Guide* provides comprehensive information on the performance appraisal process, including developing and writing performance standards.

While BARS is highly job related, there are several disadvantages.[27] The most obvious problem is that raters may have difficulty in matching actual observed behaviors with the examples used as scale anchors. There are many more critical incidents that describe performance under the dimension of "resolving employee problems" than the seven items provided on the scale. As with the critical incident technique, the process requires the rater to keep extensive behavioral records, and few managers have the discipline to do this. Another problem is that scale anchors may overlap such that the same behavior can be rated high in one category and low in another. The rater might observe both "good" and "bad" performance on the same dimension. For example, a supervisor who calms down frustrated employees might also cover up drinking on the job. Finally, there is no research that shows that BARS is more accurate and valid than a well-designed graphic rating scale.

A procedure that overcomes these limitations of BARS is called behavioral observation scales (BOS), as set forth by Latham and Wexley.[28] The primary difference is that BOS is developed by attaching a 5-point behavioral frequency scale to each behavioral item, as shown in Exhibit 11-9 for the dimension of "safety and accident prevention," which would apply to a number of jobs in public works, building maintenance, water/wastewater, and others. The major advantage of BOS is that raters are forced to make a more complete appraisal of the individual's performance, rather than emphasize only those items they can recall at the time of the rating and are able to match with one of the scale anchors. A major disadvantage of the BOS format is that behavioral frequencies are not always true measures of performance. For example, the scale in Exhibit 11-9 allows employees 13 working days a year to not use safety equipment and still receive a rating of 5 (almost always).

A competency-based behavioral scale contains features of both BARS and BOS. Like BARS, an absolute rating scale is used to define various levels of performance in behavioral terms; however, more complete coverage is provided, similar to the BOS format. This type of instrument is constructed by considering groups of related tasks associated with a particular competency (made up of various knowledges, skills, and abilities). Core competencies applying to all jobs might be cus-

EXHIBIT 11-8

A BEHAVIORALLY
ANCHORED
RATING SCALE

Performance Category: Resolving Employee Problems
Assisting employees in coping with on- and off-the-job stress and related problems by recognizing early signs, counseling employees, taking other corrective actions, and/or making appropriate referrals.

Extremely Outstanding Performance	7	You can expect this supervisor to recognize and deal effectively with the symptoms of excessive amounts of employee stress.
Good Performance	6	You can expect this supervisor to calm down frustrated employees.
Fairly Good Performance	5	You can expect this supervisor to use discretion when employees confide in him or her about personal matters.
Acceptable Performance	4	You can expect this supervisor to be flexible in rearranging work assignments for troubled employees.
Fairly Poor Performance	3	You can expect this supervisor to refer most employees with problems to the HR Department.
Poor Performance	2	You can expect this supervisor to cover for an employee who drinks on the job.
Extremely Poor Performance	1	You can expect this supervisor to ridicule an employee who cannot adjust to a new work procedure.

tomer service and ethics. Job-specific competencies could be employee counseling (supervisor), safety (equipment operator), and community relations (police officer). Written statements or critical incidents are used to describe levels of performance in that competency ranging from ineffective to exceptional. SMEs may assist with scaling the behavioral examples, which are not usually "anchored" as in BARS. The number of levels of performance depends on the number of scale points. The rater selects the behavioral statement that "best fits." An example of this format for a police officer is shown in Exhibit 11-10.

All behaviorally based scales have several general advantages over other methods. Superiors and subordinates usually are involved in their development. The feedback provided is highly job related, and performance appraisal sessions focus on behaviors that contribute to successful job performance. However, these formats require considerable time and effort to develop. BARS in particular is extremely

EXHIBIT 11-9

A BEHAVIORAL
OBSERVATION
SCALE AND
RATING KEY

Safety and Accident Prevention

1. Uses the safety equipment that has been provided in performing daily work assignments.

    Almost Never   1   2   3   4   5   Almost Always

2. Wears the prescribed uniform and safety shoes as required.

    Almost Never   1   2   3   4   5   Almost Always

3. Operates equipment or uses tools only for which training or orientation has been received.

    Almost Never   1   2   3   4   5   Almost Always

4. Warns coworkers of unsafe conditions or practices they are engaged in that could lead to or cause an accident.

    Almost Never   1   2   3   4   5   Almost Always

5. Immediately reports defective equipment to a supervisor.

    Almost Never   1   2   3   4   5   Almost Always

6. Reports dangerous or unsafe conditions that exist in the workplace as well as throughout the city.

    Almost Never   1   2   3   4   5   Almost Always

7. Reports injuries and accidents regardless of severity.

    Almost Never   1   2   3   4   5   Almost Always

8. Protects unsafe conditions resulting from city work that present a hazard to the public.

    Almost Never   1   2   3   4   5   Almost Always

Rating Scale Key

5 Represents almost always (95–100% of the time)
4 Represents frequently (85–94% of the time)
3 Represents sometimes (75–84% of the time)
2 Represents seldom (65–74% of the time)
1 Represents almost never (0–64% of the time)

Source: Critical incidents are from Jimmy R. Glisson, *Safety Program Development:Fundamental Loss Control Programs for Local Governments* (Looseleaf notebook, 1990), section 3.

complex. The development procedures must be repeated for each job, which may not be cost-effective for jobs with few incumbents.

MANAGEMENT BY OBJECTIVES

Although the comparison of results achieved against plans has always been used by managers, **management by objectives (MBO)** was first proposed by Peter Drucker in 1954.[29] As a formal performance appraisal system, MBO consists of the following steps:

1. Organizational goals are established during the planning process and commitment to these goals is established at all managerial levels.

2. The key results areas of the job are identified. These are highly selective areas in which the employee must achieve an acceptable level of performance to be successful.

3. The superior and subordinate mutually agree on several objectives within key results areas that coincide with or support organizational or departmental goals. Performance requirements and timetables are established and the subordinate is allocated the necessary resources.

4. The superior and subordinate hold interim progress reviews. These reviews provide feedback to the subordinate and may involve corrective action needed to stay on target or revision of objectives in the face of unforeseen problems.

5. At the end of the period, actual accomplishments are measured against performance requirements, and objectives for the next period are established.[30]

For MBO to be effective, a distinction must be made between objectives and performance requirements. Unless this distinction is made, there probably will be no basis for determining if the objective was accomplished. Exhibit 11-11 illustrates this

---

EXHIBIT 11-10

COMPETENCY-BASED BEHAVIORAL SCALE FOR POLICE OFFICER

COMMUNITY RELATIONS

Participation

(5) Outstanding	Presents an extremely positive image of the department. Seeks out ways to make contributions to the community. His or her sense of service extends to off-duty hours.
(4) Excellent	Deliberately and consistently works to present a positive image of the department.
(3) Good	Is a willing representative of the department. Takes care to present a positive image.
(2) Marginal	Presents a somewhat negative image of the department. Grudgingly participates in community relations activities.
(1) Unsatisfactory	Presents a very negative image of the department; often refuses to participate in community relations activities.

Assistance

(5) Outstanding	Is constantly on the alert for opportunities to assist citizens. Is often commended by citizens.
(4) Excellent	Goes out of his or her way to assist citizens.
(3) Good	Willingly assist citizens.
(2) Marginal	Rarely does more than answer direct questions from citizens.
(1) Unsatisfactory	Is often rude or abusive to citizens. Never offers assistance. Citizens complain to department about this officer.

Intervention

(5) Outstanding	Almost always achieves positive results from conflict situations.
(4) Excellent	Is usually able to resolve conflict situations in a way that is seen to be fair by all parties.
(3) Good	Conscientiously mediates conflict situations.
(2) Marginal	Avoids conflict situations rather than try to mediate them.
(1) Unsatisfactory	When this officer becomes involved in a conflict situation, he or she makes it worse.

Source: City of Selma, Alabama.

EXHIBIT 11-11

OBJECTIVES AND PERFORMANCE
REQUIREMENTS

Position	Objective	Requirements
Solid Waste Manager	Increase participation in rural house-to-house collection services.	125 new customers will be signed up by June 15.
County Engineer	Reduce flooding in District 4.	Construction and installation of 3 culverts on County Road 37 will be completed by second quarter.
Laboratory Supervisor	Improve timeliness of reports.	Monthly report of test results will be submitted by the fifth working day of following month.

point. MBO has many attractive features and is especially appropriate for management jobs. Performance appraisals are job related because the objectives define the most important aspects of job performance. Where objectives are mutually agreed to and performance requirements can be objectively measured, employees are likely to be motivated to achieve the desired level of performance. Interim progress reviews allow employees to adjust their efforts periodically to ensure that objectives will be attained. MBO is adaptable to any type of organization with a mission to be carried out.

Like other appraisal methods, MBO has its disadvantages. Emphasis is placed primarily on results that can measured. Consequently, there is often a failure to appraise behavioral aspects of the job that cannot be measured in quantitative terms. Even when results can be objectively measured, an individual's performance usually is affected by factors beyond his or her control. The exclusive use of MBO can promote the attitude that ends justify means, which discourages teamwork and can lead to ethical problems. Finally, and most important, performance outcomes alone do not tell employees what they need to do to maintain or increase productivity. For example, merely telling the solid waste supervisor that the department failed to sign up 125 new customers is not constructive. He or she needs to know what to do to achieve the desired result and how the organization can help. For example, the supervisor's presentation to explain the advantages of garbage service to homeowners may need improvement. Perhaps the service is too expensive and the county should lower its fees. These are the reasons authorities emphasize the need to combine MBO with other measures of job behavior.

IMPLEMENTING THE PERFORMANCE APPRAISAL SYSTEM

Effectively implementing the performance appraisal system involves establishing appraisal policies and procedures; training raters; testing the system; initiating the appraisal process through familiarization, observation and counseling; rating performance; conducting appraisal interviews; and reviewing results.[31]

ESTABLISHING POLICIES AND PROCEDURES

Written policies are essential to ensure that performance appraisal contributes to organizational objectives. The policy statement should cover such areas as the purposes for which the system is intended (pay, promotion, etc.), integration with EEO policies, and the responsibilities and obligations of management to ensure fairness to employees.

Procedures should be developed to cover how the policy is to be implemented. Detailed procedures should cover such areas as scheduling of performance appraisals, who will conduct appraisals, guidelines for conducting the appraisal interview, completion of necessary forms, reviews by higher levels of management, right of appeal, and documentation.

Performance appraisal policies and procedures should be clearly communicated to both managers and employees. It is also a good practice to include a section on performance appraisal in the employee handbook. Fully informing everyone will minimize uncertainty and resistance and will increase the probability of positive results.

TRAINING RATERS

Clearly established objectives supported by policies and procedures and a well-designed performance appraisal instrument are necessary components of a performance appraisal program. However, it is the raters who will ultimately determine whether or not the program accomplishes its purposes. Training should be conducted to develop rater competencies in three areas: implementing administrative procedures, managing performance, and counseling.[32]

The policies and administrative procedures are critical to success. Raters need to know how ratings will be used, the forms and records required, and exactly what they are supposed to do and when. They must become familiar with every step in the performance appraisal process. This type of training is particularly important when a new system is implemented.

As performance managers, raters must be able to set expectations, observe job behaviors, correct shortcomings, and accurately rate performance. These tasks include:

- Helping subordinates understand the key accountabilities of their jobs,
- Establishing reasonable goals and measures of performance,
- Coaching subordinates before and after important events,
- Adjusting expectations where appropriate,
- Observing and recognizing various levels of performance,
- Overcoming common rater errors,
- Keeping consistent performance records, and
- Accurately and consistently appraising performance.

Training in performance management should include instructional techniques that provide trainees with opportunities to deal with realistic situations. The traditional classroom lecture is usually not sufficient. Case studies are particularly effective in this phase of training.

As counselors and feedback providers, raters should develop interpersonal skills needed to deal with the human relations aspects of performance appraisal. Attributes and behaviors displayed by effective raters include:

While well-designed, job-related formats and rating scales facilitate effective appraisal of job performance and reduce legal liability, they are no guarantee of good results. In fact, the development of better methods has not greatly improved the process. The greatest improvement in accuracy of measurement comes from rater training. The focus areas include:

RATER TRAINING IS THE KEY

1. **Rater error training**—Raters learn to identify and avoid common rater errors. Example: Assessing each factor independently to control halo error; observing performance during entire period so that ratings will not be excessively influenced by recent events.
2. **Performance dimension training**—Raters learn to recognize and use appropriate performance dimensions on which ratings will be required. Example: Assessing a secretary's performance in such areas as *keyboarding, document production,* and *filing,* rather than on a global factor such as *quality of work.*
3. **Frame-of-reference training**—Raters develop a common understanding of standards against which performance will be measured. Example: Arriving at a consensus among raters about what is acceptable performance in the dimension of *safety* among jobs that involve operation of equipment.
4. **Behavioral observation training**—Raters develop skills in recognizing and recording events and behaviors that influence performance. Example: Identifying key behavioral indicators of performance in the area of *customer service* for cashiers, license clerks, and others.

Integrating these areas in rater training has been shown to improve the accuracy and quality of performance ratings. It should be noted that rater error training that presents "correct" distributions of ratings tends to decrease rating accuracy.

Source: David J. Woehr and Allen I. Huffcutt, "Rater Training for Performance Appraisal: A Quantitative Review," *Journal of Occupational and Organizational Psychology* 67 (September 1994), 189–208.

- Listening effectively,
- Recognizing different emotional reactions and responding accordingly,
- Anticipating sensitive issues and dealing with them effectively,
- Giving timely or present-tense feedback,
- Focusing on observable behaviors and describing specific examples to support their assessments,
- Describing performance shortcomings without resorting to generalizations, judgments, or attitudinal concerns,
- Displaying the courage to confront performance problems in a straightforward and unapologetic way, and
- Gaining employees' agreement to meeting acceptable standards of performance.[33]

Training should be conducted by individuals who are competent in the field of human behavior. Carefully observing and correctly rating performance is one thing; handling the uncomfortable situation that results when a rater must justifiably criticize an employee's performance is another matter. The training program should focus on improving rater effectiveness in interacting with employees in difficult situations, particularly those where the rater must give negative feedback. As with training in performance management, an experiential approach is best. For example, having trainees view videotapes on how to conduct counseling sessions and hold appraisal interviews, followed by role-playing and critiques, is very useful.

TESTING THE SYSTEM

Before full implementation of a performance appraisal system, it should be tested in a trial administration. As stated from experience by a public administrator:

> *No matter how competent and professional the team that developed the program, or how high the level of management support, or how deeply involved were supervisors and employees, there will be problems in implementation. Employees and supervisors who were involved in job analysis will point out that the factors to be rated do not match work assignments. Performance criteria that were clear and concise when written will suddenly become vague and ambiguous. Errors that were fully covered during rater training sessions will proliferate and several new ones will emerge. Carefully designed weighting systems will come apart. When the dust settles, it will be discovered that the problems are not that serious and can be corrected without making fundamental changes.*[34]

The organization should anticipate these problems and conduct a "shakedown administration." Another approach would be to establish a demonstration project in a unit that is receptive to performance appraisal.[35] In either case, problems should be worked out before ratings are used for administrative purposes.

INITIATING THE APPRAISAL PROCESS

A number of preparatory activities should be carried out to lay the groundwork for ultimate rating of performance. Even if the organization has developed a job-related performance appraisal system, the results will be disappointing if the focus is only on getting together with employees once or twice a year to rate performance. Employees must be familiarized with the performance appraisal system at the outset. A commitment to performance measures must be obtained. Then, a continuing process of performance observation and measurement must be carried out, including giving feedback and coaching to employees.

The first step in performance appraisal counseling should be to review with the employee the performance appraisal system used by the organization, including the purposes, instructions, forms, and other information. The employee should then gain a clear understanding of the factors that will be rated (performance standards, objectives, behaviors, etc.). It is also important that very early in the performance cycle the employee and his or her supervisor reach a mutual understanding regarding what is expected in terms of performance levels. For example, if a behaviorally based system has a 5-point scale, which behaviors on a given factor will be awarded a 3 rating? Does a 3 rating meet the organization's standards, or should the employee attempt to achieve a 4 or 5? The more the system is job related, the easier it will be to answer such questions. But even the most carefully written factors are subject to interpretation.

The next step is continuing observation and measurement of performance, with informal, day-to-day appraisals. Employees must have continuing feedback on how well they are doing. Properly carried out, day-to-day observation and counseling will vastly improve the effectiveness of the performance appraisal interview.

Most important, the employee will have had an opportunity to bring performance up to desired levels. But even if certain problems still exist, he or she can anticipate those areas in which the ratings will be low.

RATING PERFORMANCE

At the end of the performance period it is necessary to rate performance and prepare the appropriate supporting documentation (justification of ratings, discussion of factors that influenced performance, identification of training needs, general summary, etc.). The rater should review expectations established in each performance dimension; consider objective data, critical incidents, and observed behaviors; and rate each dimension independently. Raters should be aware of and avoid rater errors, the most common of which are recency and contrast effects.[36] If the appraisal process has been effectively carried out, most ratings should be positive, but it may also be necessary to deal with negative aspects of performance. High or low ratings should be justified with written comments. Raters should neither inflate ratings nor give lenient ratings to avoid hurt feelings and arguments. Finally, the completed appraisal should support the message that will be given to the employee in the interview.

HOLDING THE APPRAISAL INTERVIEW

The formal performance appraisal interview is an important step in the appraisal process. The structure of the interview can take a number of forms depending on the appraisal system, the purpose, and the amount of day-to-day performance counseling that has been accomplished. Before the interview, the supervisor should carefully review all relevant information such as previous counseling sessions, critical incidents, and performance expectations. The supervisor should be particularly aware of problem areas such as aspects of performance still below standards, unfavorable critical incidents, and objectives that have not been achieved. In conducting the appraisal interview, there are three basic approaches.[37]

A traditional approach is known as *tell and sell*, in which the superior dominates the interview, tells employees where they fell short of expectations, and attempts to persuade the employee to make the necessary improvements. This type of interview has overtones of the "Theory X" style of leadership discussed in Chapter 4. It can cause defensive reactions and creates a face-saving situation for the supervisor once the subordinate questions his or her ratings.

In the *tell and listen* approach the superior is less dominating. He or she listens carefully to what subordinates think and lets them know that their concerns are understood. In this approach the focus mainly is on allowing the employee to "vent" excuses, frustrations, and similar defensive reactions. Employees tend to be better satisfied with this approach, but there is no real effort to deal with underlying issues; consequently any subsequent improvement in performance will be slight.

The *problem-solving* approach allows employee participation, identifies needed improvements, and sets specific goals. As such, this approach contains the best features of "tell and sell" and "tell and listen." In the problem-solving interview the supervisor clearly explains the purpose of the meeting, which is to recognize areas in which performance is meeting or exceeding expectations and to identify where deficiencies exist. After the superior recognizes and reinforces examples of good performance, the subordinate is given the opportunity to identify problem areas. If there are problems and the subordinate does not bring them up, the supervisor should point out no

Why do performance appraisal systems that are virtually identical succeed in one organization and fail in another? If an organization's culture lacks a solid foundation in open communication, managers fail to establish expectations, and employees are rated on vague measures that

EFFECTIVE PERFORMANCE APPRAISAL IN LAKELAND

they do not understand, the system is destined to fail. For performance appraisal to be successful there must be an environment where there are ego-less exchanges of ideas, a high degree of trust and mutual respect, and a commitment by supervisors and managers to carry out the full process. An example of where this works is the city of Lakeland, Florida. The employees enjoy the consistency and fairness of a system that was developed nearly five years ago in the Electric and Water Department. The system has largely eliminated such obstacles as unclear performance expectations, rater biases and inconsistencies, and lack of understanding and agreement about the process. The system provides measurable performance standards, has increased communications, and created a smooth process. It requires managers to be realistic and fair in their appraisals and provide informative, narrative statements that support ratings and give guidance on how performance can be improved.

Source: Excerpted and condensed from Michael DePaoli, "Culture Determines Success of Performance Review," *IPMA News* 65 (August 1999), 18–19.

more than one or two areas where improvement is needed. After a mutual discussion the superior and subordinate should come to agreement on steps to be taken by both to improve performance. Finally, they should agree on a follow-up date for determining the extent to which the employee's and supervisor's concerns have been eliminated and to determine if progress has been made on the expectations that were set.

REVIEWING RESULTS

The performance appraisal process does not end with the completion of rating forms and interview. Ratings should be reviewed by the next higher level of management, and the supervisor's superior should determine whether the ratings accurately reflect job performance and that the procedure was handled correctly.

Provisions should be made so that employees can appeal ratings that they believe are unfair. This can be made part of the regular grievance procedure or a separate procedure can be established. The employee should have access to all records relating to his or her appraisal. This builds confidence in the system's basic fairness, provides an additional means of communicating results, and protects employee rights.

Performance ratings should be analyzed periodically for evidence of discrepancies and adverse impact.[38] Statistical tests do not prove that raters are making errors or showing bias. However, properly designed analysis can highlight certain patterns that might not be found merely by reviewing a list of ratings. When such patterns appear, management should determine the cause and, if necessary, correct the problem—particularly when members of protected groups such as blacks and females receive significantly lower ratings.

SUMMARY

After an employee has been selected, oriented, and trained, his or her job performance should be appraised. While numerous problems are associated with performance appraisal, the organization really has no choice. Performance ratings serve as a basis for administrative decisions such as promotion and pay and should be used in employee training and development. Although most of the attention in the EEO area has focused on selection, the performance appraisal process is subject to the same laws and guidelines. To meet legal requirements, performance ratings must be based on job-related criteria and the appraisal program must be fairly administered under standardized and controlled conditions.

In designing a performance appraisal system, attention must be given to a number of aspects that impact on how effectively the system actually measures employee contributions in a work setting. These include reliability and validity, what is to be measured (criteria), sources of appraisal information, timing of appraisals, and control of rater errors.

The most commonly used performance appraisal techniques include graphic rating scales, essay appraisals, comparative methods, checklist methods, critical incidents, behavioral scales, and management by objectives. No method alone can be expected to accomplish all the objectives of performance appraisal, and all have advantages and disadvantages.

When the purposes for which the performance appraisal system is intended have been determined and the appropriate method selected, the organization implements the performance appraisal system. This includes establishing appraisal policies and procedures, training raters, testing the system, familiarizing employees and obtaining their commitment, periodically counseling employees and providing feedback, rating performance, conducting the appraisal interview, providing an appeal procedure, and periodically analyzing ratings for evidence of discrepancies or adverse impact.

QUESTIONS FOR REVIEW AND DISCUSSION

1. What are some of the reasons for dissatisfaction with performance appraisal in general?
2. Give an example of how one use of performance ratings might conflict with another.
3. List three potential legal problems with performance appraisal.
4. Which performance appraisal method do you think would be most effective in appraising employees in the following city jobs?
   a. Finance director
   b. City planner
   c. Sewer maintenance supervisor
   d. Water treatment plant operator
   e. Patrol officer
   f. Custodian
5. Why is the employee's superior usually the individual who rates performance? List three other sources of appraisal data.
6. What are the advantages of multi-rater or 360-degree appraisal?
7. Rating employees on an annual/fiscal year basis takes advantage of the cycle in which the organization's work is normally performed. Under what circumstances would timing appraisals based on project completion be better?
8. Name five rater errors and explain what can be done to reduce or eliminate them.
9. Why is it necessary to train raters?
10. Why should an appraisal system be tested in a "dry run" before ratings are used in administrative decisions?
11. Briefly describe three approaches to holding a performance appraisal interview.

12. What are the benefits of establishing a procedure for employees to appeal ratings they believe are unfair?

ENDNOTES

[1] Bob Nelson. "Are Performance Appraisals Obsolete?" *Compensation and Benefits Review* (May/June 2000), 39–42.

[2] For a review of five major studies on the effectiveness of performance appraisal see Dick Grote, *The Complete Guide to Performance Appraisal* (New York: American Management Association, 1996), 5–14. See also Gary E. Roberts, "Perspectives on Enduring and Emerging Issues in Performance Appraisal," *Public Personnel Management* 27 (Fall 1998), 301–322.

[3] Grote, *The Complete Guide to Performance Appraisal*, 15.

[4] Dick Grote, "Performance Appraisal Reappraised," *Harvard Business Review* 78 (January 2000), 21–23.

[5] Jeanette N. Cleveland, Kevin R. Murphy, and Richard E. Williams, "Multiple Uses of Performance Appraisal: Prevalence and Correlates," *Journal of Applied Psychology* 74 (February 1989), 130–135.

[6] "Uniform Guidelines on Employee Selection Procedures," 43 *Federal Register* (August 25, 1978), 38,297–38,298.

[7] *Brito v. Zia Company*, 478 F.2d 1200 (1973).

[8] *Wade v. Mississippi Cooperative Extension Service*, 372 F. Supp. 126, 7EPD 9186 (1974).

[9] *Albemarle Paper Company v. Moody*, 422 U.S. 405 (1976).

[10] *Rowe v. General Motors Corporation*, 457 F.2d 348 (1972).

[11] Hubert S. Feild Jr. and William H. Holley, "The Relationship of Performance Appraisal Characteristics to Verdicts in Selected Performance Appraisal Cases," *Academy of Management Journal* 25 (June 1982), 392–406, and Hubert S. Feild and D. T. Thompson, "Study of Court Decisions Involving Employee Performance Appraisal Systems," Bureau of National Affairs, *Daily Labor Report* (December 26, 1984), E1–E5.

[12] See Roger L. Miller and Gaylord A. Jentz, *Business Law Today*, 5th ed. (Cincinnati: West, 2000), 570–571.

[13] For a more complete discussion of performance appraisal reliability and validity see Frank J. Landy and James L. Farr, *The Measurement of Work Performance* (Orlando: Academic Press, 1983), 8–25.

[14] James P. Clifford, "The Collective Wisdom of the Workforce: Conversations with Employees Regarding Performance Evaluation," *Public Personnel Management* 28 (Spring 1999), 119–156.

[15] "Uniform Guidelines," 38,302.

[16] See Les Pickett, "Competencies and Managerial Effectiveness: Putting Competencies to Work," *Public Personnel Management* 27 (Spring 1998), 103–115, and Maureen Smith, "Competency-Based Performance Appraisal Systems," *IPMA News* 65 (August 1999), 16.

[17] Robert L. Mathis and John H. Jackson, *Human Resource Management* 9th ed. (Cincinnati: South-Western, 2000), 92.

[18] See Leanne Atwater and David Waldman, "Accountability in 360-Degree Feedback," *HRMagazine* 43 (May 1998), 96-104, and Susan J. Wells, "A New Road: Traveling Beyond 360-Degree Evaluation," *HR Magazine* 44 (September 1999), 83–89.

[19] Susan E. Jackson and Randall S. Schuler, *Managing Human Resources*, 7th ed. (Cincinnati: South-Western, 2000), 460–461.

[20] Jackson and Schuler, 462.

[21] A similar discussion of rater errors can be found in most HR texts; for example, Jackson and Schuler, 476. For in-depth coverage consult a performance appraisal text such as Grote, *The Complete Guide to Performance Appraisal*, 137–141.

[22] Unless otherwise cited, this discussion draws on Grote, *The Complete Guide to Performance Appraisal*, 36–81.

[23] James A. Buford Jr., Bettye B. Burkhalter, and Grover T. Jacobs, "Link Job Descriptions to Performance Appraisal Forms," *Personnel Journal* 67 (June 1988), 132–140.

[24] John C. Flanagan, "The Critical Incident Technique," *Psychological Bulletin* 61 (July 1954), 327–358.

[25] Wendell L. French, *Human Resources Management*, 4th ed. (Boston: Houghton Mifflin, 1998), 174–175.

[26] Patricia C. Smith and Lorne N. Kendall, "Retranslation of Expectations: An Approach to the Construction of Unambiguous Anchors for Rating Scales," *Journal of Applied Psychology* 47 (April 1963), 149–155. For a simplified approach to the development of behaviorally anchored rating scales see Grote, *The Complete Guide to Performance Appraisal*, 46–50.

[27] Grote, *The Complete Guide to Performance Appraisal*, 52–54.

[28] Gary P. Latham and Kenneth N. Wexley, "Behavioral Observation Scales for Performance Appraisal Purposes," *Personnel Psychology* 30 (Summer 1977), 255–268, and *Increasing Productivity Through*

Performance Appraisal (Reading, Mass.: Addison-Wesley, 1994). The textbook contains a number of examples and case studies of behavioral observation scales.

[29] Peter F. Drucker, *The Practice of Management* (New York: Harper and Row, 1954).

[30] Based on Dale D. McConkey, *How to Manage by Results* (New York: American Management Association, 1983), 89–160. See also Grote, *The Complete Guide to Performance Appraisal*, 61–77.

[31] See David C. Martin and Kathryn M. Bartol, "Performance Appraisal: Maintaining System Effectiveness," *Public Personnel Journal* 27 (Summer 1998), 223–231.

[32] This section draws on Grote, *The Complete Guide to Performance Appraisal*, 270–277.

[33] Grote, *The Complete Guide to Performance Appraisal*, 275, and John F. Kikoski, "Effective Communication in the Performance Appraisal Interview," *Public Personnel Management* 28 (Summer 1999), 301–323.

[34] Condensed and paraphrased from a quote by Richard J. Federinko in James A. Buford Jr, *Personnel Management and Human Resources* (Auburn University: Center for Governmental Services, 1991), 255.

[35] Clifford, 126.

[36] Grote, *The Complete Guide to Performance Appraisal*, 137–138.

[37] Norman R. F. Maier, *The Appraisal Interview—Three Basic Approaches* (La Jolla, Calif.: University Associates, 1976).

[38] Martin and Bartol, 227.

PART 5
COMPENSATING
EMPLOYEES

An adequate and fair compensation program is necessary for attracting and retaining employees and motivating them to achieve the organization's goals. Chapter 11 focuses on the design of a pay system that supports the organization's strategic objectives and is internally consistent and externally competitive. Chapter 12 continues with a discussion of individual pay systems and the factors used to reward employees for their service, skills, and work contributions, and considerations in the development of a benefits package. This chapter also covers how the compensation program should be administered to ensure compliance with legal requirements and policy guidelines.

CHAPTER 12
COMPENSATION: STRATEGIES AND STRUCTURE

Compensation management is considered to be one of the most challenging HR responsibilities. This is especially true today as local governments strive to become more efficient and cost-effect while attracting and retaining a competent and motivated workforce in a highly competitive labor market. These pressures are forcing elected officials and managers to look seriously at how people get paid. One of the most basic issues is the pay structure. Traditional classification systems are being questioned, and many local governments are considering or have implemented systems that replace grades with broad bands. Systems that reward employees based on their knowledge and skills rather than their job assignments are gaining increasing acceptance. Which approach is best?

"There is no simple answer," says Floyd Decker, president of Yarger, Decker & McDonald, Inc., in Boise, Idaho, a leading public sector human resources consulting firm. It depends on the HR and compensation strategies that the organization would like to implement, financial resources available, and the culture that the organization is attempting to create." Decker points out that many cities and counties are organized in a hierarchical model with staff sections and functional departments. Job-based classification systems with centralized control by the HR staff facilitate this type of operation. Others are changing to a more egalitarian organization and focusing on cross-functional work teams. For these organizations such approaches as broad-banding and decentralization of compensation decisions to line managers may be appropriate, or broad bands may be used in certain departments to structure skill-based pay.

Organizations should also be aware that all approaches have advantages and disadvantages. "Traditional systems that are bureaucratic and reactive are a constant source of frustration to line managers who want to retain and properly reward employees who are contributing to objectives," he says. On the other hand, Decker notes that using broad bands and shifting decision-making authority to line managers can also cause problems. "Line managers are advocates for their occupational areas and employees, but not necessarily for organization-wide internal equity. This can lead to misalignment of pay for jobs requiring equal skill, effort, and responsibility and an increase in payroll costs."

In Decker's view the "best" pay structure is the one that matches up with what the organization is about and is competently developed to achieve desired outcomes. "In the final analysis, there are no universal solutions," he comments "Both new developments and established approaches can be appropriate depending on the situation."

INTRODUCTION

Compensation is one of the most challenging areas in HR management. As Floyd Decker points out, there are a number of established practices and emerging models available but no approach is clearly superior in all situations. Moreover, HR professionals are generally less prepared to analyze the various alternatives and make sound decisions in compensation than in other HR areas. George T. Milkovich, one of the most respected authorities in the field, suggests that research information in compensation is shared mainly among academics and consultants, while organizations build their compensation programs through trial and error.[1] Finally, public jurisdictions have, in the past, tended to reject potentially useful concepts and techniques that are identified with the private sector, although this attitude appears to be changing.[2] Clearly, however, it is necessary to do a better job in applying the considerable knowledge that is available.

The first task is to design a pay system that supports the organization's strategic objectives and is internally consistent and externally competitive. The pay system is the centerpiece of the compensation program, but there are additional tasks. Procedures must be developed to reward employee contributions fairly and equitably. The program must be competently administered to comply with laws and regulation and carry out the organization's compensation policies. Finally it is necessary to design and offer employees a package of services and programs known as employee benefits. This chapter examines the forms of compensation, discusses policy issues, and covers the development of various types of pay structures.

FORMS OF COMPENSATION

Compensation includes all types of financial and nonfinancial returns that employees receive as part of the employment relationship. In this and the following chapter it will often be necessary to refer to forms of compensation before they are discussed in detail; therefore it will be useful to begin by discussing concepts relating to direct, indirect, and intrinsic compensation and defining key terms.

DIRECT COMPENSATION

Direct compensation is the cash contribution that an employer pays for the work performed and includes base and variable pay. **Base pay** that is computed on hours actually worked is known as wages, while salaries are computed on some other basis such as monthly or annually. The second type of direct compensation is **variable pay,** which is linked to factors such as performance, seniority, and skills. Examples include merit pay (an addition to the base wage or salary of an individual as a reward for past contributions) and incentive pay (a one-time payment offered as an inducement for future contributions for both individuals and work groups or teams). Variable pay that is added to the base wage or salary is permanent and therefore not "at risk." Incentive pay, because it is tied to a productivity goal for a time period, is considered to be "at risk." The most common forms of direct compensation are illustrated in Exhibit 12-1. The major part of this chapter will be concerned with building structures to administer this form of pay.

INDIRECT COMPENSATION

http://erieri.com/codes/
The Economic Research Institute provides a comprehensive listing with definition of compensation terms. It also provides information on U.S. and state compensation laws.

Indirect compensation or benefits are offered to employees for their membership in the organization. These include legally required benefits and discretionary benefits. Legally required benefits are benefits that employers are required to provide by state and federal laws. They include the employer contributions to Social Security, unemployment compensation, and unpaid leave for family emergencies that are mandated in federal law. In addition, workers' compensation is compulsory in 47 states. Discretionary benefits are those that the employer has the option of providing. This group of benefits includes retirement and savings plan payments, health care benefits, payment for time not worked, and various other benefits and services. Both types of benefits are covered in Chapter 13.

INTRINSIC COMPENSATION

Intrinsic compensation represents the nonmonetary rewards that employees derive from their jobs. Compensation programs are more effective when they connect with or take advantage of rewards associated with affiliation, work content, and personal development.[3] These rewards, discussed more fully in Chapter 4, include satisfaction and motivation. In the area of compensation, satisfaction relates mainly to the *level* of pay. To the extent an employee feels that the pay is adequate based on the value of his or her skills in the external market, the employee will be satisfied. While increased satisfaction does not necessarily lead to higher performance, employees who are *dissatisfied* with their level of pay are likely to seek other work.

Motivation is an employee's predisposition to engage in a behavior to fill a *need*. Compensation is motivational to the extent that it is associated, directly or indirectly, with filling a need. Both merit and incentive pay are motivating if there is a clear relationship between desirable behavior and a pay increase and also to the extent that they are attached to the need for achievement, recognition, and approval.

STRATEGIC COMPENSATION

As Chapter 5 discussed, strategic planning forms a vision of what an organization should be about. Strategic objectives convert this vision into performance outcomes. Strategies are selected and policies are developed in all HR areas to ensure that various activities contribute to these outcomes. How this should work in compensation is discussed below.

COMPENSATION STRATEGIES

In theory, compensation programs are designed to implement strategies that support the organization mission and strategic objectives. Such strategies might include being competitive in the market, improving productivity, reducing costs, building teams, promoting customer satisfaction, rewarding individual performance, providing upward mobility, encouraging employees to expand job boundaries, developing employee potential, and complying with laws and regulations. In practice, however, pay programs

EXHIBIT 12-1

Base Wage—The cash contribution that an employer pays for time actually worked, computed on an hourly basis. (For example, a heavy equipment operator earns $12.65 per hour.) This is also called the *regular rate*. Under provisions of the Fair Labor Standards Act (FLSA), employees who earn wages must be paid one and one-half times their regular rate for overtime work.

Base Salary—The cash contribution that an employer pays for work performed, computed on some other basis, commonly weekly, monthly, or yearly. (For example, an office manager earns $30,000 per year.) A salaried employee is not necessarily expected to be present and working during specific hours. Certain salaried employees may be exempt from the overtime provisions of the FLSA.

Merit Pay—An addition to base wage or salary in recognition of *past* contributions, usually computed as a percentage of the base. (For example, the office manager above receives an 8 percent merit raise for outstanding performance, resulting in a new salary of $30,000 + $2,400 = $32,400. Even if performance declines during the following period, and there is no merit raise, pay remains at $32,400.)

Seniority Pay—An addition to base wage or salary based on length of service, usually computed as a percentage of the base, often referred to as an annual increase or "step raise." The calculations are the same as for merit pay.

Cost-of-Living Adjustment (COLA)—An addition to base wage or salary, often indexed to a measure of inflation such as the Consumer Price Index. The calculations are the same as for merit pay.

Skill-Based Pay—A form of pay in which additions are made to the base wage as employees master additional skills in a "skill block." (For example, the heavy equipment operator above receives an additional $2.05 per hour resulting in a new wage of $2.05 + $12.65 = $14.70 for passing a proficiency test on grading to reference stakes using a motor grader. The operator will continue to receive this rate even when assigned to perform other, less difficult tasks.)

Individual Incentive Pay—A one-time payment offered to an employee as an inducement for *future* contributions. (For example, the office manager above receives a bonus of $2,400 for achieving a prescribed goal.) If the goal is not achieved during the next period, the bonus will be decreased or possibly not paid at all; therefore incentive pay is "at risk."

Group Incentive Pay—A one-time payment offered to a group or team as an inducement for *future* contributions. (For example, the Solid Waste Department achieves a savings of $5,000 in the labor budget, of which 50 percent or $2,500 is distributed among the employees.) The Scanlon plan is probably the most widely used group incentive plan. Group incentive pay is also "at risk."

are typically a set of techniques and procedures put in place with little if any regard for strategy implications. When properly carried out, a technique or procedure accomplishes its intended purpose, which may or may not implement a strategy.

In some cases they actually prevent strategies from being implemented. For example, a pay structure with a large number of narrowly defined grades discourages employees from taking on additional responsibilities without a grade promotion. This also illustrates the point that certain strategies are mutually exclusive. The organization must decide which strategy is more appropriate (encouraging employees to expand job boundaries or providing upward mobility). In any case a clearly articulated pay strategy is necessary if the program is to match the unique characteristics, culture, and objectives of the organization.[4]

COMPENSATION POLICIES

Effective compensation programs are guided by pay policies. Policies lead compensation managers to examine the various techniques available and choose those that facilitate the implementation of strategies. These policies form the building blocks or foundation for the pay system and ultimately for the compensation program. In formulating policies, organizations consider internal consistency, external competitiveness, individual contributions, and benefits.[5]

INTERNAL CONSISTENCY

Internal consistency (or equity) is achieved when an organization establishes a hierarchy that corresponds to the internal "worth" of each job or skill level. For example, consider three jobs found in a county probate office. How does the work of a file clerk compare to the work of a recording clerk and that of a recording clerk to the chief clerk of the county probate office? It is such relationships among jobs that result in the structure or levels of work in an organization. The job of chief clerk is quite different from the jobs of subordinate clerks; moreover the contribution of the chief clerk who designs the procedures for recording and filing documents is greater than that of the clerks who carry out the procedures.

The example given illustrates content and value, the two aspects of internal consistency. Content refers to the tasks performed and the skills required for the job. Value refers to relative contribution of the job to the organization's goals. Internal consistency is operationalized in pay systems through the process of job evaluation, which is discussed later in this chapter. Through various methods of job evaluation the organization systematically measures the relative worth of jobs based on a combination of content and value. Organizations conduct separate evaluations for various job "families" as shown above for clerical positions, or they may elect to use a method that compares unlike jobs such as clerks and mechanics. If jobs that are similar in content and value are paid similarly, and dissimilar jobs are paid less or more in accordance with the job hierarchy, then the criterion of internal consistency has been met.

EXTERNAL COMPETITIVENESS

External competitiveness (or equity) requires that an employer provide a rate of pay that corresponds to rates paid for similar jobs or skill levels in the relevant external market. In establishing a policy in this area the organization has a certain amount of flexibility. Small differences may not matter at all, and for various reasons the organization may decide to pay wages and salaries that lead, lag, or match those paid by other employers.

Obviously, however, if rates are too low, many employees will leave for higher-paying jobs. For example, the chief clerk mentioned above has a good idea of the pay for similar jobs in other agencies and in firms in the private sector. The clerk who is being paid $5,000 less than the going market rate is probably scanning the want ads for job openings as administrative assistant, office manager, and so forth. On the other hand, if the chief clerk is paid $5,000 more than the going rate for similar work, the county may not be using its financial resources wisely.

In deciding what pay rates to establish, the employer will typically conduct a compensation survey. Such a survey discovers what other employers in the same labor market are paying for key jobs as well as information on related compensation practices (rate ranges, frequency of pay adjustments, merit/incentive pay, and employee benefits). After analyzing data from the survey, the organization is in a position to establish actual pay rates for its jobs and also to determine an appropriate benefits package (discussed in the following chapter).

EMPLOYEE CONTRIBUTIONS

Fairness in rewarding employee contributions requires that pay differences among employees doing the same or similar work reflect actual differences in work-related contributions and/or personal qualifications. This fairness criterion is also known as individual equity. For example, it is appropriate that one file clerk be paid more than another if one has more seniority or has received higher performance ratings. Other factors might include experience on another job, training and education, and job-related skills. Especially important in this regard are pay outcomes related to job performance. Both expectancy and reinforcement theories of motivation (discussed in Chapter 4) emphasize that employee behavior is strongly influenced by rewards if employees believe that good performance will result in a pay increase. However, employees also want to be treated fairly. Equity theory (also discussed in Chapter 4) holds that if employees believe that rewards are not proportional to actual contributions, then the motivational value of merit pay is greatly reduced. The following chapter discusses how organizations develop procedures and administer pay to employees.

BENEFITS

Benefits, some of which are required by law, must be considered part of the total compensation program. Once viewed as "fringes," benefits are now a major and increasing cost of compensation and considered by employees as a right of employment. The challenge is to design a benefits package that is both motivational and cost-effective.

POLICY DEVELOPMENT AND ADMINISTRATION

To provide effective guidance, written policies should be developed. They should implement strategic objectives and cover such points as:

- How responsibility for the compensation program is to be allocated among the executive leadership, the HR department, and line management
- The commitment of management to comply with laws and regulations
- Whether to have single or multiple job evaluation systems and resulting pay structures
- Whether to lead, lag, or match pay rates in the relevant labor market
- How seniority, skills, and performance (individual and/or group) are to be rewarded in determining employee pay
- How total compensation dollars will be split between pay and benefits
- Types of benefits and services to be offered
- The degree of access to pay data granted to employees (openness vs. secrecy)
- What general type of control process will be used to ensure that allocations to pay will be within budget guidelines

The policy structure provides a framework for administration of the compensation program by ensuring that decisions support strategic objectives. Exhibit 5-3 (Chapter 5) is an example of compensation policy for a small city. Policies, however, must provide a degree of latitude in their interpretation and application. As is probably obvious, it is very difficult if not impossible to achieve an optimum state in all policy areas and certain compromises and trade-offs have to be made or policies may need to be realigned.[6]

For example, a city is preparing to hire a technician in the planning department to implement the Geographic Information System (GIS). However, the salary required to attract a qualified candidate is considerably higher than the starting rate for the grade. Offering the higher amount would result in several employees with several years of service in that grade being paid less than a new hire. The city could avoid this situation by arbitrarily reclassifying the job to a higher grade. Either approach would probably cause dissatisfaction and might even bring on a lawsuit. On the other hand, not making a high enough offer may mean that the city will not be able to fill the position. While there is no simple answer to this problem, the city's strategic objectives should be reviewed. Perhaps the city is committed to becoming a technological leader in providing services. In this case the city might decide to document its reasons and make the offer.

DETERMINING THE INTERNAL WORTH OF JOBS

Differences in the relative worth of jobs in an organization are assessed through a process known as **job evaluation.** Although there are various methods of job evaluation, each one considers, explicitly or implicitly, a set of compensable factors. These are job attributes that provide the basis for determining the worth of jobs within an organization. Compensation professionals typically work with the "universal" factors of skill, effort, responsibility, and working conditions (factors also identified in the Equal Pay Act for determining whether jobs are "equal"). Recall that the term *skill* in job analysis was defined as the capability to perform a psychomotor act. In job evaluation the term refers to the full range of competencies needed to perform a job, including education, training, certifications, experience, and so on.

In some job evaluation methods these factors are considered together, hence these are called "whole job" or nonquantitative methods. Other methods consider each factor separately and usually break each universal factor into more specific subfactors. These are called quantitative methods. Although there are a number of job evaluation methods, most are variants and combinations of the nonquantitative methods of ranking and classification and the point method, which follows a quantitative approach.

http://hr-guide.com
HR-Guide.Com provides comprehensive information on compensation, job evaluation, and links to additional resources.

Whatever method is selected, organizations must decide whether a single job evaluation plan is adequate to cover the diverse group of jobs found in a local government. While some plans attempt to do this, many compensation authorities would suggest that except for very small organizations, it is better to use separate plans for different types of work. There are two important reasons: First, the work content is too varied to be compared on the same factors. Factors that distinguish among levels of equipment operators include manual dexterity, physical effort, and working conditions. These factors are not important at all in clerical and administrative support jobs. Rather, other factors such as knowledge of office technology, public contacts, and access to confidential data are more relevant. The second reason relates to the need to address market conditions (external competitiveness) in subsequently establishing pay levels. Job "families" that can be evaluated on the same set of factors are also likely to be in the same labor market. On the other hand, using multiple market-based plans conflicts with the standard of providing equal pay for work of equal value, which is a major concern in the public sector (the "comparable worth" debate will be covered in the next chapter).

A final consideration is whether job evaluation should be performed by the HR department or a committee. Although using a committee takes longer and costs more, this approach is likely to be more acceptable to employees, who have a major stake in the results. The committee should include experienced and respected employees representing the full range of jobs being evaluated. It is also important that the committee be properly trained and participate in a "dry run" where the members evaluate enough sample jobs to become proficient.

The following sections will discuss ranking, classification, and the point system, which are the most common job evaluation methods. It will be assumed that job analysis has been conducted and that accurate job descriptions are available.

WHOLE JOB RANKING

Whole job ranking is the oldest and simplest job evaluation method and is used primarily by small organizations.[7] Ranking orders jobs from highest to lowest based on an overall definition of content and/or value. The most widely used ranking techniques are card sorting, alternation ranking, and paired comparison. In card sorting, job descriptions are written on cards and the evaluator places the cards in the proper order. While most evaluators are able to determine which have the least value and which have the most, it is difficult to differentiate among middle-level jobs. This problem is overcome to some extent by alternation ranking and paired comparison.

In alternation ranking the evaluator selects the most and least valued job, and then the next most and least valued, and so on until all jobs have been ranked. In paired comparison, a matrix is used to compare each job against all other jobs. The job valued more than all other jobs will receive the highest score and the highest overall rank. The job receiving the next highest score will receive the next highest rank and so on until all jobs are evaluated. For example, assume that the organization wants to rank the following jobs: administrative secretary, clerk, drafter, heavy equipment operator, juvenile probation officer, and mechanic helper. Exhibit 12-2 gives examples of comparisons that could be made among these jobs.

The ranking method is highly subjective and is not favored by compensation professionals. A major disadvantage is that the person who ranks the jobs must be completely knowledgeable about every job under study. This knowledge is usually found only in small organizations. The evaluation criteria are subjective and often poorly defined, and decisions are difficult to explain in work-related terms. Another problem with ranking is that it does not establish how much more valuable one job is compared to another. Finally, as the number of jobs increases arithmetically, the number of comparison decisions increases geometrically. When ranking six jobs, as shown in Exhibit 12-2, the evaluator makes 15 comparisons. If the number of jobs is 50, the number of comparison decisions increases to 1,225.[8]

THE CLASSIFICATION METHOD

As has been pointed out, the **classification method** is widely used in the public sector. Classification systems in local government may follow the approach used by the U.S. Office of Personnel Management that assigns federal jobs to one of 15 pay grades (known as the General Service or GS schedule).[9] An approach that has been considered somewhat as a standard in the public sector is set forth by Prentice-Hall.[10] This discussion is a simplified overview of the Prentice-Hall approach.

EXHIBIT 12-2

PAIRED COMPARISON RANKING

Job Title	JPO	HEO	AS	D	MH	C	Score	Rank
Juvenile probation officer		X	X	X	X	X	5	1
Heavy equipment operator			X	X	X	X	4	2
Administrative assistant				X	X	X	3	3
Drafter					X	X	2	4
Mechanic helper						X	1	5
Clerk							0	6

Classification differentiates jobs horizontally by kind of work performed and vertically by level of difficulty and responsibility. In this method all jobs are first subdivided into occupational categories. The result will be broad groups of jobs in such areas as executive, administrative, professional, clerical, service maintenance, and protection. The next step is to subdivide these broad groups of jobs into finer groups based on more specific characteristics. For example, service maintenance jobs in a city could be subdivided into water filtration and distribution, wastewater collection and treatment, building maintenance, automotive and equipment maintenance, equipment operation, labor, and supervisory work. Each of these groups becomes a *class series*.

The next step is to arrange the class series into a descending order of jobs based on their value to the organization. This can be based on professional judgment, or a point system (discussed in the following section) can be used. Levels are established based on how the jobs fall into "clusters" based on the criteria used. Each level is known as a class. Each class series in the plan is related to every other class series with a grade structure. Exhibit 12-3 illustrates a classification plan for service maintenance jobs in a small city. The final step is to document the distinguishing features of each class in the series. In some cases tasks from a representative sample of jobs in the class are added to the class description on a separate document called a class specification, discussed in Chapter 7. Exhibit 12-4 shows the class descriptions for a four-class water system operator series.

The major advantage of the classification method is that it is conceptually sound, simple to use, and easy for employees to understand. The actual development of an acceptable plan is a different matter, and standard compensation texts do not typically cover the process. The example presented is deceptively simple and straightforward. The full methodology is much more complex, and decisions regarding occupational groupings, class series, and levels required in each series require expert judgment. Class descriptions must be carefully written so that descriptions of work performed and qualifications clearly distinguish one class from another.

THE POINT METHOD

The **point method** is a widely used and easily understandable method that is based on numerically scaled and weighted **compensable factors**.[11] Although a wide variety of factors is used in standard plans, the factors tend to measure *skill, effort, responsibility,* and *working conditions*. These four factors are the basis for the "classic" plans

EXHIBIT 12-3

CLASSIFICATION PLAN FOR SERVICE
MAINTENANCE JOBS IN SMALL CITY

Grade	Water Filtration and Distribution	Wastewater Collection and Disposal	Building Maintenance	Automotive and Equipment Maintenance	Equipment Operation	Labor	Supervisory
SM-6	Water System Operator IV	Wastewater System Operator IV					
SM-5	Water System Operator III	Wastewater System Operator III	Building Maintenance Technician III	Automotive and Equipment Technician III			Supervisor III
SM-4	Water System Operator II	Wastewater System Operator II	Building Maintenance Technician II	Automotive and Equipment Technician II	Equipment Operator II		Supervisor II
SM-3	Water System Operator I	Wastewater System Operator I	Building Maintenance Technician I	Automotive and Equipment Technician I	Equipment Operator I		Supervisor I
SM-2						Service Maintenance Worker II	
SM-1						Service Maintenance Worker I	

developed over 50 years ago, such as the National Metal Trades Association plan for manufacturing and office jobs. The NMTA plan, now published by the American Association of Industrial Management (AAIM) with only slight changes from the original, is still widely used (and imitated).[12] Some local governments use the Factor Evaluation System (FES) of the U.S. Office of Personnel Management. It should be pointed out, however, that the FES is designed to establish "benchmark" jobs in the GS classification system discussed above and not as a stand-alone point plan. This section covers the steps in the design and use of a point plan.

Depending on the type of jobs and the complexity of the plan, the universal factors are usually divided into two or more subfactors. A point plan begins with the selection of subfactors that are relevant to the work and that support the organization's strategic objectives. For example, a city that emphasizes customer satisfaction would probably consider "interpersonal skills" to be an important subfactor for clerical and administrate support jobs because certain jobs such as license clerk, cus-

---

EXHIBIT 12-4

EXAMPLE OF CLASS
DESCRIPTIONS IN WATER SYSTEM
OPERATOR SERIES

Grade	Description
SM-6	**Water System Operator IV.** This is very difficult and complex work in the filtration, purification, and distribution of water requiring the highest level of skills. Employees in this class have lead responsibility for plant operations, laboratory testing, equipment maintenance, or major components of the water distribution system, and conduct formal and on-the-job training of lower-level operators. Incumbents operate independently for long periods of time and assume responsibility for operations in the absence of the director. The work requires outstanding judgment to make critical operating decisions. **Benchmark Job: Lead Water Plant Operator.**
SM-5	**Water System Operator III.** This is difficult work in the filtration, purification, and distribution of water requiring a high level of skills. Employees in this class perform a variety of tasks in plant operations, laboratory testing, equipment maintenance, and maintenance of the water distribution, and conduct on-the-job training of lower-level operators. The work requires considerable judgment in carrying out assignments, referring unfamiliar situations and advanced technical problems to higher-level operators for assistance. **Benchmark Job: Water Plant Operator.**
SM-4	**Water System Operator II.** This is moderately difficult work in the distribution of water, requiring a variety of intermediate skills. Employees in this class operate and maintain pumping stations, storage tanks, and other major components of the water distribution system and may perform treatment and purification tasks in a training status. The work requires moderate judgment in carrying out assignments, and referring technical problems to higher-level operators or supervisors. **Benchmark Job: Pumping Station Operator.**
SM-3	**Water System Operator I.** This is somewhat difficult work in the installation and maintenance of water lines and appurtenances in the water distribution system requiring equipment operation and pipefitting skills. Employees in this class use equipment such as small backhoes and trenchers and pipefitting tools and equipment to excavate and backfill trenches and install, maintain, and repair lines and perform limited street repairs. Employees may perform similar work in wastewater collection system. The work requires some judgment in carrying out standard practices. **Benchmark Job: Water Line Installer/Repairer.**

Note: Operator helpers (semiskilled) are classified in the labor series. Employees who operate additional pieces of earthmoving equipment such as bulldozers, loaders, large backhoes, graders, and so forth, as a primary function are classified in the equipment operator series. The entry-level class in this series is coextensive with Wastewater System Operator I in the wastewater collection and disposal series.

tomer service representative, cashier, and similar jobs involve public contacts. Increasing levels or degrees of job worth are defined within each subfactor and a point value is assigned to each degree.

Weights must be assigned to each subfactor based on its relative importance. It is intuitively obvious that most organizations would be willing to pay more for skill needed to perform the job and responsibility assigned than for effort expended and willingness to work under unpleasant conditions. Therefore the group of subfactors that measure skill and responsibility are typically weighted at 70 to 90 percent of the value of the plan. Exhibit 12-5 is an example of a point factor plan for clerical and administrative support jobs.

A point manual is then developed. The manual contains definitions for each degree of the various subfactors, as shown in Exhibit 12-6 for the subfactors of "education" and "confidential data." When the point plan and manual are ready, the point value of each job can be determined. The process requires that job descriptions be compared with the manual. The match between the job description and the subfactor degree definition determines the number of points assigned. The points for each subfactor are totaled as shown in Exhibit 12-7 on page 293 for the job of revenue clerk.

A major advantage of the point method is that the final evaluation is determined by decisions made on each factor rather than on one decision. As with classification and ranking, the decisions are still subjective, but errors tend to cancel each other. For example, there is a chance that for a particular job the degree selected for a skill subfactor might be on the high side. There is an equal chance that a responsibility or other subfactor might be rated too low. Another advantage of the point method is that there are a number of accepted plans available, some of which are in the public domain and others that may require payment of a modest royalty fee. These plans can be adapted if necessary to meet the specific needs of an organization.

Since the point method is more accurate in differentiating jobs than ranking or classification, it is often seen as being more objective and "scientific." This is not necessarily true. What is measured depends on the subfactors used and weights assigned; these are subjective decisions of the creators of the particular plan. Even point plans designed for specific occupational groups tend to produce slightly different results.

RELIABILITY AND VALIDITY OF JOB EVALUATION

Reliability refers to stability and consistency of results. Reliability can be increased by using evaluators who are familiar with the jobs and the job evaluation method that is used. A useful test of reliability is a version of the "test-retest" method. After a committee has evaluated a group of jobs, the committee could be reconvened at a later date and asked to reevaluate a small sample (5 to 10 percent). Close agreement with the original results would indicate that the evaluation was reliable.

Validity means that a procedure measures what it purports to measure, in this case job worth. There are two major problems in establishing the validity of job evaluation. First, an evaluation method measures what it is designed to measure, and different methods produce different results. Second, to establish validity it is necessary to compare the results to some benchmark of job worth. If such a benchmark were available it would not have been necessary to evaluate jobs in the first place. Some authorities suggest that evaluating a group of jobs with a different system and comparing the results provides a validity estimate, but that seems to be circular reasoning. Possibly the best estimate of job worth that can be used for comparison is provided by the labor market (discussed in the following section).

EXHIBIT 12-5

EXAMPLE OF A POINT PLAN
FOR CLERICAL AND
ADMINISTRATIVE JOBS

Factor	Degrees and Points				
	1	2	3	4	5
Skill (420 points)					
1. Education	30	60	90	120	150
2. Experience	30	60	90	120	150
3. Complexity	15	30	45	60	
4. Supervisory Controls	30	40	60	50	
Responsibility (300 points)					
5. Confidential Data	15	30	45	60	
6. Contacts	15	30	45	60	
7. Consequence of Error	20	40	60	80	
8. Work of Others	25	50	75	100	
Effort (75 points)					
9. Physical Demand	10	20	30		
10. Mental/Visual Demand	15	30	45		
Working Conditions (75 points)					
11. Job Stress	15	30	45		
12. Physical Environment	10	20	30		

ASSESSING THE EXTERNAL MARKET

To establish a competitive pay structure, organizations must determine the rates being paid by other employers in the relevant labor market. This is accomplished with a **compensation survey**. There are several important steps in conducting a survey, including selecting jobs to be surveyed, defining the relevant labor market, selecting employers, designing and administering the survey, and analyzing the data.[13]

SELECTING JOBS TO INCLUDE

Even if the job evaluation process included all jobs, it is neither necessary nor desirable to obtain survey information on all jobs. Because of the wide variety of jobs in a local government, it is important to identify a sample of **benchmark jobs**. The content of these jobs is well understood and they can be found in other organizations. For exam-

EXHIBIT 12-6

1. EDUCATION

> This factor measures the competencies required at *entry level*. The competencies are usually obtained through formal education, but may, in some cases be obtained by experience on lesser jobs, by outside study or combinations of these approaches.

1st Degree   **30 points**

Knowledge of simple, routine, or repetitive clerical tasks. Skill to read and comprehend simple instructions, look up information in alphabetic listings, enter simple information on forms, write simple comments, and perform basic arithmetic computations using decimals such as adding a column of figures and calculating a percentage. Familiarity with office machines such as phone, fax, copier, and microcomputer. Equivalent to high school education.

2nd Degree   **60 points**

Knowledge of basic clerical procedures and rules. Skill to read and comprehend material of moderate complexity, complete forms, compose short paragraphs, file and retrieve material and perform slightly advanced arithmetic computations such as balancing, converting units of measurement, and calculating proportions. Skills in using office machines. Basic keyboarding and clerical microcomputer skills. Equivalent to high school education with additional specialized training.

3rd Degree   **90 points**

Knowledge of a body of standardized rules, procedures, and operations requiring proficiency in areas of business/office technology. Skill in selecting and performing appropriate procedures from prescribed options in area of assignment. Advanced clerical microcomputer skills. Equivalent to one-year post high school training.

4th Degree   **120 points**

Knowledge of a specialized or technical field such as office administration, business management, or information technology. Skill in determining and performing procedures from interrelated or nonstandard options covering several areas. Equivalent to an associate degree.

5th Degree   **150 points**

Knowledge of a professional or administrative occupation such as accounting, finance, and business administration. Skills in analyzing situation and designing and implementing administrative systems using principles and concepts of the occupation. Equivalent to a bachelor's degree.

6. CONFIDENTIAL DATA

> This factor measures the access to confidential and sensitive information, the effect on the organization if the information were divulged and the realistic opportunity to divulge information.

1st Degree   **15 points**

Little or no access to sensitive or confidential material.

2nd Degree   **30 points**

Access to sensitive information such as work assignments, schedules, reports, and administrative actions where unauthorized disclosure could result in embarrassment or misunderstandings confined mainly within the department or work group.

EXHIBIT 12-6 (CONTINUED)

3rd Degree   **45 points**
Access to confidential information such as employee data, financial transactions, and material available on a "need to know" basis where unauthorized disclosure could result in invasion of personal or organizational privacy.

4th Degree   **60 points**
Access to highly confidential information such as investigations, audits, pending reorganizations and layoffs, and material protected by attorney-client privilege where unauthorized disclosure could result in adverse internal consequences, loss of customers/clients, negative publicity, or legal exposure.

ple, Water Treatment Operator, Patrol Officer, Firefighter and Administrative Assistant might be benchmark jobs in a municipality. The jobs should be those in which a sizable proportion of the workforce is employed and should represent the entire job structure under study. Finally, the market for these jobs should be relatively stable.

DEFINING THE RELEVANT LABOR MARKET

Labor markets may be local, regional, or national. A local labor market is within convenient commuting distance. Most trades and clerical jobs are filled from the local labor market. The boundaries of the local labor market are basically defined by residential addresses of employees. Technical, administrative, and professional jobs tend to have labor markets that are broader than local markets. Accountants, planners, professional engineers, police and fire officials, and many technicians will be recruited from outside the local labor market. Recruiting experience and interviews with departing employees will help to place the boundaries on regional markets. National markets exist for some jobs. These usually are jobs for highly skilled

EXHIBIT 12-7

Subfactor		Degree	Points
1.	Knowledge	2	60
2.	Experience	2	60
3.	Complexity	2	30
4.	Supervisory Controls	2	40
5.	Confidential Data	2	30
6.	Consequence of Error	2	40
7.	Contacts	2	30
8.	Work of Others	1	25
9.	Physical Demand	1	10
10.	Mental/Visual Demand	2	30
11.	Job Stress	1	15
12.	Physical Environment	1	10
	Total Points		380

professionals and managers, such as physicians, high-level administrators, and engineers. In dealing with national markets, management normally relies on data collected by others rather than on a wage survey.

SELECTING EMPLOYERS TO BE SURVEYED

Having determined the relevant labor market, management must then decide which employers within the area will be surveyed. Some employers chosen for the survey will likely be other units of local government, since wages within the same "industry" are likely to be comparable. The survey should also include organizations in the private sector that have similar jobs. If the market is small, or if there are only a few major employers, five to ten organizations may provide all the information needed. In larger local markets, the survey might require dozens of organizations, especially if the government unit is seeking information on a large number of key jobs.

DESIGNING AND CONDUCTING THE SURVEY

The survey should be designed to collect several types of data. The first is general information about the employer such as name, nature of business, and number of employees. The pay data collected should include the grade range (minimum, midpoint, and maximum), average rate paid, and number of incumbents in the job that matches the benchmark job. Finally, the survey should collect information on the nature of the benefit program.

Three methods of collecting wage and salary data include telephone interviews, mailed questionnaire, and on-site interviews. Telephone interviews can be useful within informal professional networks, especially in collecting small amounts of information or as a follow-up to other methods. The mailed questionnaire is the most common method for compensation surveys. It allows for a structured format that will elicit comparable information from all surveyed organizations. Because of the convenience of the form, more information can be requested. A disadvantage of the questionnaire method is that respondents may ignore or delay in returning the form or be careless in providing the information requested. The best method is for a compensation analyst to conduct on-site interviews because the analyst can be expected to ensure proper job "matches" and collect accurate data. Unfortunately, this method is also very expensive.

The specific structure of the survey is determined by the data collection method chosen and the information needed. The administrative techniques used for a mail survey, however, also generally apply to other kinds of surveys. Before initiating the survey itself, employers to be surveyed should be contacted to explain the purpose of the survey, outline the kinds of requested information, and obtain commitments for cooperation. The confidentiality of individual survey responses must be guaranteed; this means that only compiled or anonymous data can be published. Each surveyed employer should be provided a copy of the survey results. This practice encourages those contacted to cooperate, since the information may as helpful to them as it is to the organization conducting the survey.

ANALYZING THE DATA

In order to effectively use information from compensation surveys, it is necessary to make accurate comparisons among employers that furnished the data. The survey results should first be reviewed to ensure that pay data were collected on jobs that closely match those found in the organization. Then it is necessary to compute an estimate of market pay. It is important to note that some employers have many incumbents in these jobs while others have only a few. For example, a large construction firm may employ 25 equipment operators at an average rate of $15 per hour while a small landscape contractor may employ two at $10 per hour. A simple average ($12.50 per hour) does not take this into account. An average weighted by the number of job incumbents ($14.63 per hour) provides a better estimate. Other statistical techniques may be used if necessary to account for variations in time-in-grade, qualifications, and other factors.

USING OUTSIDE WAGE AND SALARY SURVEYS AND SECONDARY DATA

http://www.acinet.org/ acinet/
America's Career Info Net provides comprehensive information on wages and occupations trends in the United States.

Many organizations lack the resources, expertise, or time to conduct in-house surveys. There are a number of possible outside sources of wage and salary data. The Bureau of Labor Statistics (BLS) conducts and publishes area wage surveys for 90 metropolitan areas, industry wage surveys, and the National Survey of Professional, Administrative, Technical and Clerical Pay. The BLS also publishes the Employee Benefits Survey. These surveys may be ordered from the federal government and can be found in larger public and university libraries. Such associations as the National League of Cities, National Association of Counties, and other similar groups have affiliated state associations that collect labor market data. Most states conduct surveys on a city, county, or standard metropolitan statistical area (SMSA) basis. SHRM chapters often conduct local surveys that are shared among their members. Many major universities have a bureau of business research, institute of government, or both. In many cases, these organizations conduct compensation surveys. Many surveys conducted by governmental agencies (such as the BLS) can be accessed on the Internet. National compensation consulting firms such as Hay, Wyatt, Mercer-Medlinger-Hanson, and Yarger, Decker & McDonald provide salary data for a fee and/or conduct surveys for clients. Two problems with all published surveys are that (1) they are not necessarily compatible with the organization's jobs and (2) the organization cannot specify what data to collect.[14]

http://stats.bls.gov/ blshome.htm
The Bureau of Labor Statistics (BLS) collects, processes, analyzes, and disseminates essential statistical data to the American public, the U.S. Congress, other federal agencies, state and local governments, business, and labor.

DEVELOPING THE PAY STRUCTURE

It is now necessary to build a pay structure that is internally consistent and externally competitive. This is accomplished by merging the external pay based on market data with the internal work structure based on job evaluation. One aspect of the structure is the market line, which is adjusted based on whether the policy is to match, lead, or lag the market. The other aspect is pay grades and ranges, which provide a basis to administer individual pay.

THE PAY POLICY LINE

Once market data have been obtained for benchmark jobs, the rates are plotted against job evaluation data in a "scattergram." Note that how well these rates are correlated with the evaluation data is a validity check of the evaluation results. A trend line is established through the points by using an ocular estimate (eyeballing) or by using a statistical technique called least squares regression. The latter technique is preferred and both the scattergram and trend line (market line) can be graphed on a spreadsheet program as shown in Exhibit 12-8.

EXHIBIT 12-8

PAY SCATTERGRAM
AND MARKET LINE

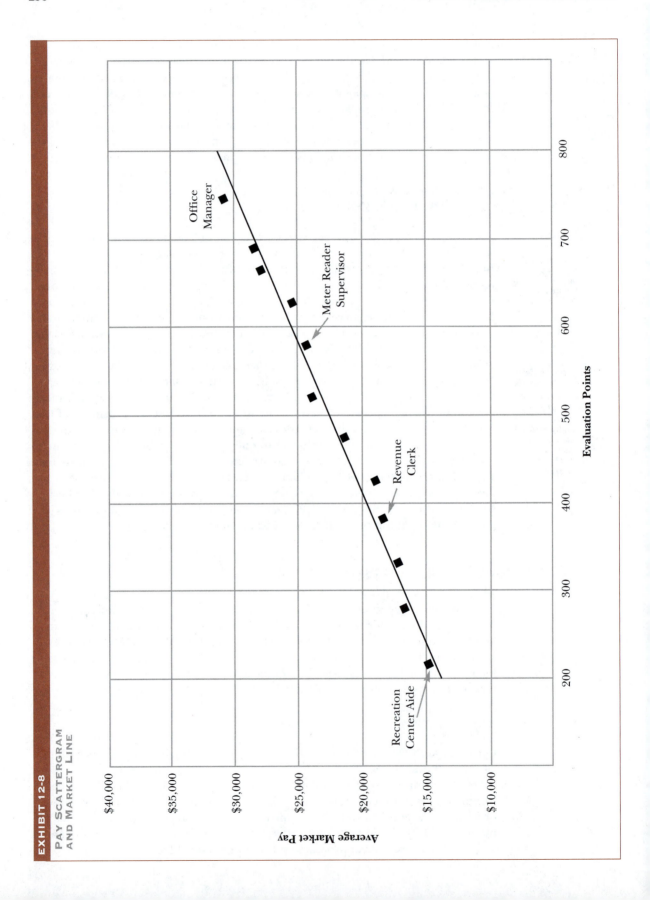

It is now necessary to consult organization policy, which may be to match, lead, or lag the market. If the organization offers a good benefits program, it may be possible to establish pay rates slightly below market levels and still attract and retain employees. Or the organization may decide to match the market. Most local governments would encounter considerable political resistance to a policy of leading the market.[15] In deciding where to place the **pay policy line**, note that during the time that the pay structure is in place, rates paid in the external market will probably increase. Therefore, building the pay structure around the market line has the effect of lagging the market. If the organization wishes to match the market and estimates that pay rates in the labor market will increase by 10 percent before the structure will be adjusted, the pay policy line should be set at 5 percent above the market line. For simplicity the examples shown will be based on the market line.

PAY GRADES AND RANGES

A **grade** is composed of a group of jobs that are considered to be substantially equal for pay purposes. There is no accepted rule for the number of grades in a structure. The AAIM plans discussed above provide 12 grades for service maintenance jobs and 20 grades for clerical, technical, administrative, and supervisory jobs.[16] The General Service or GS schedule covers hundreds of these kinds of jobs with 15 grades.[17] These examples do not necessarily represent current practice, which is to use fewer grades in all types of structures. The number of grades in a structure should be based on policy guidance. Career paths, a high degree of position control, and work specialization are facilitated by structures with many narrow grades. Lateral mobility, decentralization, and growth within jobs are best achieved with structures containing relatively few grades.

A **pay range** for each grade must be established. The point where the pay policy line crosses each grade becomes the grade midpoint. The midpoint is the control point for each grade because it is the target rate of pay for a fully trained employee performing at a satisfactory level. Maximum and minimum rates of pay are generally set as a percentage above and below the midpoint. The difference between the maximum and the minimum is the range spread, which provides latitude in recognizing differences in qualifications, seniority, and performance among individual employees.[18] Range spreads can vary from 10 to 50 percent above and below the midpoint with 15 to 30 percent being fairly common.

Most pay structures provide for grades to overlap to allow an experienced employee to earn as much as another employee with less experience in a higher grade. A high degree of overlap (4 to 5 grades) would indicate small differences in job value among grades and promotions with little increase in pay. A slight overlap (one to two grades) indicates greater differences in job value and promotion increases.[19] There is no consensus among compensation professionals regarding the degree of overlap, but a two- to three-grade overlap is typical.

With the pay structure established, all jobs are placed in appropriate grades as shown in Exhibit 12-9. In certain situations, jobs may be evaluated so that assigned points place them above the maximum for the grade. These jobs have *red circle rates* indicating that the organization is paying too much for the work performed. Jobs that are paid below the minimum have *green circle rates*. In dealing with red circle rates, the organization can freeze the pay or award smaller increases until the rate range catches up. Another alternative is to assign additional responsibilities to the job and move it into a higher range. Actual pay reductions are not recommended. As for green circle rates, an increase should be given, at least to the grade minimum. Ideally this should

EXHIBIT 12-9
PAY STRUCTURE FOR CLERICAL,
ADMINISTRATIVE SUPPORT,
AND SUPERVISORY JOBS

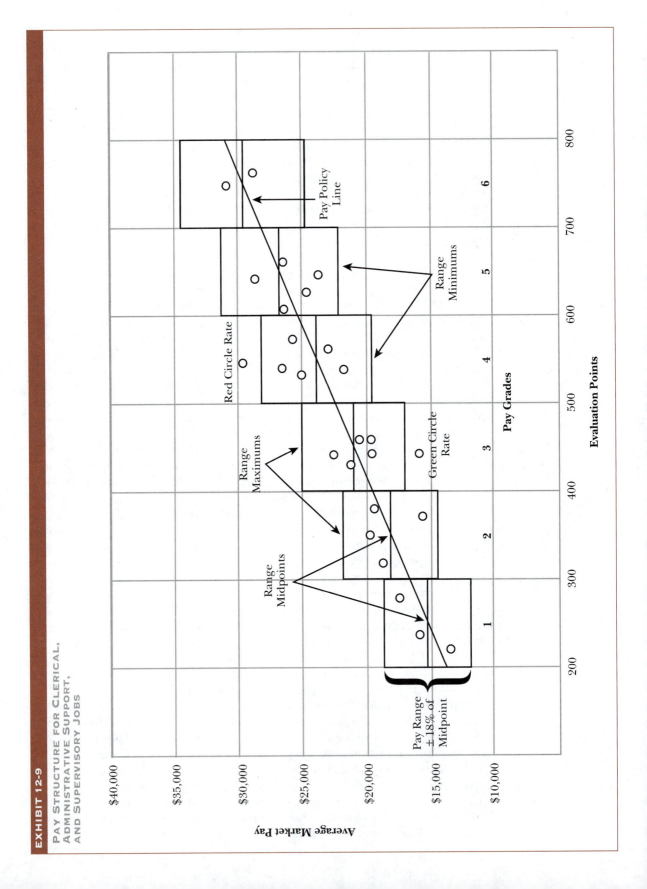

A NEW PAY STRUCTURE FOR MONTGOMERY COUNTY

In 1996 in the Montgomery County, Alabama, the personnel department was spending an inordinate amount of time dealing with pay issues. The problem was that the pay structure contained 44 grades, making it difficult to determine if jobs were properly classified. Additionally, because pay for certain jobs was not at market levels, there was pressure to reclassify jobs to avoid losing key employees. The county established a compensation committee to study the problem. A facilitator with knowledge and experience in compensation was retained to work with the committee.

The committee developed a point factor plan and used the plan to evaluate every job in the county. The personnel department and county administration accepted the results of the evaluation with only slight modifications. The committee then proposed a market-based pay structure with 13 grades. When the county commission implemented the structure in 1997 there were only two appeals, both of which were resolved. According to Personnel Director Barbara Montoya, the new pay structure is a major improvement. "It is much more logical in terms of natural groupings of jobs and career paths, which makes administration more efficient and cost effective. Because employees can understand how it works they are confident that their jobs are classified properly and that their pay is in line with the market value of their skills," she says.

be done immediately, but certainly no later than the next scheduled pay increase (administration of pay to employees is discussed in the next chapter).

ALTERNATIVES TO TRADITIONAL PAY STRUCTURES

The job-based systems discussed above are still the major approaches to pay in local government. Such systems, however, are coming under increasing criticism. Rather than build flexibility, participation, and contribution to objectives ("I want to help our team succeed"), they seem to reinforce bureaucracy, individual agendas, and entitlement ("It's not in my job description"). In recent years approaches such as skill-based pay and broadbanding have begun to generate considerable interest.[20]

SKILL-BASED PAY

Skill-based structures pay employees based on the number of skills that they have mastered rather than the task they are assigned to perform; in fact, these structures essentially do away with job boundaries. Although the concept is at least 70 years old, **skill-based pay** was not widely used until the results achieved by innovative companies such as Northern Telecom in the late 1980s attracted the attention of compensation professionals.[21]

The steps in building a skill-based structure are related to those discussed in building a job-based structure.[22] Rather than focus on individual jobs, the organization considers all work behaviors and tasks of a group or team and identifies the complete set of knowledges and skills required to perform the work (this is often called a skills analysis). The next step is to divide the set into units called *skill blocks*. There are no rules or conventions regarding how skill blocks should be determined, except that the skill block should be linked to a logical set of tasks. How many skill blocks are needed will also vary depending on the type of work. Plans typically contain a block of basic skills, a number of blocks of "core" or required skills, and additional blocks of optional skills. Exhibit 12-10 illustrates a skill-based structure for grounds maintenance work. Typically training and certification systems are established to ensure that employees have adequately learned the skills for which they are being paid and that these skills are maintained as discussed in Chapter 13.

The value of the skills is determined by using a skill evaluation plan, usually a variation of the point method of job evaluation. Finally, the skills are priced based on a survey of the relevant labor market. The resulting range would begin at the approximate minimum of a job-based structure containing the same skills but could be higher than the maximum of the grade containing the highest-value jobs. The reason is that a building maintenance technician who has journeyman-level skills in both electrical wiring and plumbing can perform a wider range of tasks than either a journeyman plumber or electrician.

EXHIBIT 12-10

SKILL-BASED PAY PLAN FOR GROUNDS MAINTENANCE WORK

Foundation (no points)
1. Orientation
2. Safety
3. Basic grounds maintenance

Basic Core Electives (10 points each)
1. Horticultural practices I
2. Tree surgery
3. Park and field maintenance
4. Irrigation system techniques I

Advanced Core Electives (15 points each)
1. Horticultural practices II
2. Irrigation system techniques II
3. Landscape construction
4. Greenhouse operations

Optional Electives (20 points each)
1. Training
2. Supervisory management
3. Landscape design
4. Administration and logistics

Level	Requirements	Points	Total Points	Hourly Rate Increase	Total Hourly Rate
Trainee	All foundation skills	NA	NA	NA	$ 7.50
Technician I	Requirements for Trainee 2 basic core electives	20	20	$1.30	$ 8.80
Technician II	Requirements for Technician I 2 basic core electives	20	40	$1.30	$10.10
Technician III	Requirements for Technician II 2 advanced core electives	30	70	$1.95	$12.05
Technician IV	Requirements for Technician III 1 advanced core elective 1 optional elective	35	105	$2.28	$14.33
Technician V	Requirements for Technician IV 1 advanced core elective 1 optional elective	35	140	$2.28	$16.61
Technician VI	Requirements for Technician V 2 optional electives	40	180	$2.60	$19.21

These kinds of structures are used mainly in hourly trade and craft work. **Competency-based pay** and pay-for-knowledge systems extend this approach to clerical, administrative, and technical work, and the design features are essentially the same as for the skill-based structures discussed above. However, the term *competency* covers a wider range of employee attributes. For example, the competency to use a specialized computer software package such as TRANSPLAN for stated applications in planning is similar to a skill in that it can be unambiguously defined and measured. On the other hand, the competency to "make effective and timely decisions" would be more difficult to build into a structure.

Benefits attributed to skill- or competency-based pay include greater employee commitment and satisfaction, productivity increases, and a higher degree of flexibility in assigning work.[23] There are also several disadvantages.[24] Implementing these kinds of structures will likely increase payroll and training costs, at least initially. Also worker productivity declines as employees shift from tasks in which they are proficient into a "learning curve" mode. Developing the skill blocks and arranging them into an appropriate progression is a difficult task. Finally the structure must be continuously reviewed and skill blocks added or deleted as work group requirements and technology change.[25]

BROADBANDING

In **broadbanding** a number of traditional grades are consolidated into a single band with one maximum and one minimum rate of pay.[26] Broadbanding is often used to structure pay rates for employees using the skill- and competency-based systems discussed above. But the concept extends beyond skill-based pay. Broadbanding is compatible with the flatter, more egalitarian, organization structures that are associated with self-directed work teams, employee empowerment, continuous quality improvement, customer service orientation, and other features of the process-centered organization.

In implementing this method it is first necessary to establish the number of bands. Most organizations use four to eight bands set at major "breaks" in skill/competency requirements. Consider a 12-grade structure in which grades 1–3 are clerical jobs, 4–6 are supervisory and administrative support jobs, 7–9 are adminis-

---

Englewood, California, decided to address the question of how to reward employees for performing tasks that were not necessarily part of their job descriptions. The answer was a skill-based pay plan entitled "Creating Opportunities to Excel" in which employees who accept

SKILL-BASED PAY IN ENGLEWOOD

additional responsibilities or acquire skills that have a potential benefit to the city receive additional pay. In developing the plan the city priced skill blocks without regard to job boundaries. The skill blocks were then divided into two categories: those essential to the job and those associated with licensing and certification programs or tasks outside their normal work assignments.

"At the outset we said that if the plan works, then it will pay for itself in both direct and indirect costs," said Randie Bartholeme, director of Administrative Services. And the plan did just that. For example, the city saved more than $10,000 on a brochure that was produced by an employee with desktop publishing skills, and almost $250,000 when employees in one division completed projects that were previously outsourced. The city also benefited from increased productivity, higher morale, and reduced turnover.

Source: Bill Leonard, "Creating Opportunities to Excel," *HRMagazine* 40 (February 1995), 47–51.

trative and professional jobs, and 10–12 are senior professional and executive jobs. These grades could be replaced with four bands as shown in Exhibit 12-11. During the past several years a small but growing number of local governments have replaced traditional grade structures with broadbands.[27]

Within each band are a number of functions with different market rates; for example, the administrative/professional band might contain the functions of planning, engineering, and finance. Reference rates or zones based on market survey data may be provided for each of these functions. These are often known as "shadow grades," since they serve much the same purpose as traditional grades in administration of pay to individuals as discussed in Chapter 13.

Administration of pay to individuals follows a within-range approach (discussed in the following chapter). Under banding, however, employees are encouraged to move cross-functionally; for example from engineering to planning. Career moves under banding emphasize lateral rather than upward mobility.

Because broadbanding removes many of the control mechanisms of traditional pay structures (for example, the range midpoint) and decentralizes pay decisions, some critics have suggested that the method could lead to increased costs, legal liability, and a disconnection with the labor market. However, these problems have apparently not materialized. In a recent American Compensation Association/ Hewitt Associates study of 200 companies using broadbanding, reviews were generally positive regarding cost containment, legal compliance, and the ability to maintain market competitiveness.[28] On the other hand, benefits in the area of career planning and development were less than expected (somewhat ironic in that this is one of the purported advantages of broadbanding). The emerging consensus is that broadbanding can be an effective approach, especially if organizations give more attention to support mechanisms including implementation plans, ongoing communication, formal programs for skill and career development, and objective evaluation of overall effectiveness.

Broadbanding is not necessarily appropriate for every organization. Most local governments still operate with a traditional hierarchical structure. Moreover,

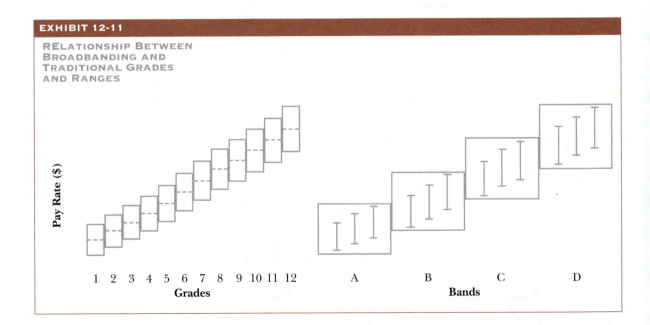

EXHIBIT 12-11

RELATIONSHIP BETWEEN
BROADBANDING AND
TRADITIONAL GRADES
AND RANGES

Pay Rate ($)

1 2 3 4 5 6 7 8 9 10 11 12   A   B   C   D

Grades   **Bands**

The city of Charlotte, North Carolina, is one of the early leaders in adopting the philosophy and techniques of what has been called the "new pay" approach. The framework for this approach is broadbanding. The city replaced its structure containing multiple pay grades with six bands as shown below:

BROADBANDING IN CHARLOTTE

Band	Group	Minimum	Maximum
A	Support/Clerical/Labor	$12,360	$ 30,900
B	Technical/Administrative	$20,860	$ 41,720
C	Professional/Supervisory	$28,160	$ 56,320
D	Senior Professional/Manager	$38,020	$ 76,020
E	Middle Management	$51,130	$102,640
F	Top Management	$69,280	$138,560

The bands are defined to encompass career ladders, and except for the lowest band, are 100 percent in width. Labor market data are a guide in administering pay within bands. Authority for pay decisions has been largely delegated to line managers and supervisors. The new system is compatible with the city's strategy of deemphasizing traditional hierarchies and creating a team environment and is described as "very much a success."

Source: Howard Risher, "Emerging Model for Salary Management," *Public Management* 79 (April 1997), 10–14 and "Are Public Employers Ready for a "New Pay" Program?" *Public Personnel Management* 28 (Fall 1999), 323–344.

employees continue to value the outward and visible signs of career advancement. Undoubtedly becoming more versatile, being on a "winning team," and contributing to objectives are motivational to employees because they address higher level "needs." But so does a grade promotion—possibly more so. It should be noted here that both traditional pay structures and broadbanding are relative terms, and that pay systems can contain features of both. Many of the advantages of broadbanding can be gained simply by combining two or three grades while retaining ranges and midpoints to keep the structure intact.

SUMMARY

Compensation includes all types of financial and nonfinancial returns that employees receive as part of the employment relationship and include direct, indirect, and intrinsic forms of pay. Designing a compensation program that attracts qualified employees, motivates them to perform on the job, and is cost-effective is no simple matter. The first task is to design a pay system that supports the organization's strategic objectives and is internally consistent and externally competitive. Internal consistency requires that employers establish an internal hierarchy of job worth. External competitiveness focuses on pay rates that are responsive to those in the external labor market. Written compensation policies help ensure that decisions support the organization's strategic objectives in designing the pay system as well as in other areas of compensation administration.

Differences in the relative worth of jobs in an organization are assessed through a process known as job evaluation. Although there are various methods of job evaluation, each one considers, explicitly or implicitly, a set of compensable factors. These are job attributes that provide the basis for determining the worth of jobs within an organization. Compensation professionals typically work with the "universal" factors of skill, effort, responsibility, and working conditions. The three basic job evaluation methodologies are whole job ranking, classification, and the point system. The job evaluation process involves selecting an appropriate method, appointing a job evaluation committee, conducting the evaluation, and documenting the results.

To establish a competitive pay structure, organizations conduct a compensation survey to determine the rates being paid by other employers in the relevant labor market. There are several important steps in conducting a survey, including selecting jobs to be surveyed, defining the relevant labor market and selecting employers, designing and administering the survey, and analyzing the data.

Job-based systems are still the major approaches to pay in local government. Such systems, however, are coming under increasing criticism. Rather than build flexibility, participation, and contribution to objectives, they seem to reinforce bureaucracy, individual agendas, and entitlement. In recent years, approaches such as skill- and-competency based pay and broadbanding have become increasingly popular. Skill-based structures pay employees based on the number of skills that they have mastered rather than the task they are assigned to perform; in fact these structures essentially do away with job boundaries. In broadbanding a number of traditional grades are consolidated into a single band with one maximum and one minimum rate of pay.

QUESTIONS FOR REVIEW AND DISCUSSION

1. Select a local government with which you are familiar and review (or infer) its strategic objectives. Does its pay system appear to support these objectives?
2. Briefly define the concepts of internal consistency and external competitiveness and how they are addressed in compensation policies.
3. Identify the three most common methods of job evaluation. Which method is used most often in local government?
4. Is the point method of job evaluation a "scientific" method of establishing job worth?
5. Review how a pay structure was developed by combining job evaluation data from a point plan with pay data from the external market. How could market data have been linked to the pay structure if the classification method had been used?
6. What are some of the major criticisms of job-based pay structures?
7. Explain the essential features of skill- and competency-based pay structures.
8. How does broadbanding support self-directed work teams, lateral mobility, customer service, and other features of the process-centered organization?

ENDNOTES

[1] George T. Milkovich and Jennifer Stevens, "From Pay to Rewards: 100 Years of Change," *ACA Journal* 9 (First Quarter, 2000), 6–17.

[2] Howard Risher, "The Search for a New Model for Salary Management: Is There Support for Private Sector Practices?" *Public Personnel Management* 27 (Spring 1998), 431–439; and "Are Public Employees Ready for a New Pay Program?" *Public Personnel Management* 28 (Fall 1999), 323–343.

[3] Paul W. Mulvey, Gerald E. Ledford Jr. and Peter V. LeBlanc, "Rewards of Work: How They Drive Performance, Retention and Satisfaction," *WorldatWork Journal* 9 (Third Quarter 2000), 6–27.

[4] Gerald E. Ledford Jr. and Elizabeth J. Hawk, "Compensation Strategy: A Guide for Senior Managers," *ACA Journal* 9 (First Quarter 2000), 19–27. See also Terry R. Satterfield, "A Step by Step Approach to Developing an Effective Pay Philosophy," *ACA News* (September 1999), 22–27.

[5] This section draws on Marc J. Wallace Jr. and Charles H. Fay, *Compensation Theory and Practice*, 2d ed. (Boston: Kent, 1988), 16–19; and George T. Milkovich and Jerry M. Newman, *Compensation*, 6th ed., (Boston: Irwin/McGraw-Hill, 1999), 22–27.

[6] Milkovich and Newman, 37.

[7] Milkovich and Newman, 112–114; and Joseph T. Martocchio, *Strategic Compensation* (Upper Saddle River, N.J.: Prentice-Hall, 1998), 181–182.

[8] Milkovich and Newman, 114.

[9] U.S. Office of Personnel Management, *Draft Classification, Job Grading and Classification Standards*, *http://www.gov/fedclass/html/draft.htm* (October 2000).

[10] *Public Personnel Administration: Policies and Practices for Personnel* (Englewood Cliffs, N.J.: Prentice-Hall, 1973), 10,001–10,509.

[11] H. G. Dogett, *Advancing Management Excellence: A Report on Improving the Performance Management and Recognition System* (Washington D.C.: U.S. Office of Personnel Management, 1994); and Milkovich and Newman, 117–118.

[12] American Association of Industrial Management, *Job Evaluation Handbook* (Springfield, Mass.: AAIM, 1997).

[13] This section draws on Wallace and Fay, 152–163. See also Milkovich and Newman, 219–240.

[14] Arthur Sherman, George Bohlander, and Scott Snell, *Managing Human Resources*, 11th ed. (Cincinnati: South-Western, 1998), 364.

[15] See, for example, James B. Katz and John C. Morris, "The 'Overpaid Bureaucrat': Comparing Public and Private Wages in Mississippi," *Public Personnel Management* 29 (Spring 2000), 129–144.

[16] American Association of Industrial Management, Parts 2 and 3.

[17] U.S. Office of Personnel Management, *General Service Pay Scale* (1999).

[18] Milkovich and Newman, 249–252.

[19] Milkovich and Newman, 252–253.

[20] Howard Risher, "Emerging Model for Salary Management," *Public Management* 79 (April 1997), 10–14.

[21] See Gerald D. Ledford Jr., "Three Cases of Skill-Based Pay: An Overview," *Compensation and Benefits Review* (March/April 1991), 11–77.

[22] C. Douglas Jenkins Jr., Gerald D. Ledford Jr., Nina Caputa, and D. Harold Doty, *Skill-Based Pay* (Scottsdale, Ariz.: American Compensation Association, 1992); and Milkovich and Newman, 145–152.

[23] Martocchio, 147–148.

[24] Martocchio, 148.

[25] Karen Pavlinsky, "Compensation Design in College Station: Skill and Competency Based Pay," *IPMA News* 65 (February 1999), 10–11.

[26] Kenan S. Abosch and Janice H. Hand, *Broadbanding Models* (Scottsdale, Ariz.: American Compensation Association, 1994).

[27] Risher, "Emerging Model," 12–13.

[28] Kenan S. Abosch, "Confronting Six Myths about Broadbanding," *ACA Journal* 7 (Autumn 1998), 28–36.

CHAPTER 13
COMPENSATION: PAY AND BENEFITS

CAN WE HIRE THIS GUY?

In about a month Reginald "Reggie" Jackson will graduate from Calhoun State Community College with an associate degree in engineering technology with emphasis on drafting. During his studies he has taken several courses in computer-aided design and mapping and is especially interested in working with the Geographic Information System (GIS). As a student he worked part-time for Tri-County Electric Membership Corporation, assisting in converting their system maps. The company was very well satisfied with his work, and Hall Green, the assistant general manager, told him to check with them when he graduated.

As Reggie began to think seriously about full-time employment, he discovered that his skills were in high demand and that a number of attractive jobs were available. This was especially pleasing to him because he and his wife were ready to start a family. Although he had always intended to find work in industry, he noticed that the city of Greenville had an opening for a GIS Technician in the Planning Department. While the salary is not quite as high as many jobs in industry, the location is quite attractive and he decided to follow up. He is going for an interview this week where he will visit with Alice Green, the HR manager, and Gregg Glass, head of the Planning Department.

Several questions are in his mind: Along with outstanding technical skills he has a strong work ethic and is interested in a job where pay increases are based on performance. He also wants to know about benefits, especially the medical and retirement plans. Also, since he is in the National Guard he needs to find out if the city provides military leave. Somehow Reggie has never thought of himself as a government employee, but this might be the opportunity he has been looking for. Both Alice and Gregg hope that this turns out to be the case.

INTRODUCTION

Developing a pay structure that is compatible with the organization's HR strategies is an important task. However, local governments do not usually offer the highest pay in their labor market. But it is still possible to attract and retain people like Reggie Jackson by rewarding performance and providing attractive benefits. Therefore it is necessary to design pay systems for employees and to determine benefits and services to be offered. Compensation, like many other HR functions, is subject to external influences. Therefore it will be necessary to first discuss the major aspects of the legal environment and the role of labor unions. Once in place, the compensation program, including pay and employee benefits and services, should be managed to achieve compensation strategies and comply with policy guidance. This requires procedures for maintenance and periodic auditing.

LEGAL ASPECTS OF COMPENSATION

Employee compensation is heavily influenced by public policies that emphasize fairness, sufficiency, and protection. Legislation provides comprehensive regulation of minimum wages, maximum hours, equal pay for equal work, and, more recently, discrimination based on race, gender, and age. Most of these laws implement policies by constraining pay practices that are exploitative or discriminatory. In compensation management, one must be able to recognize and operate under these constraints while meeting efficiency and effectiveness objectives for both the organization and the employee.

THE FAIR LABOR STANDARDS ACT OF 1938

The major law on compensation is the Fair Labor Standards Act (FLSA), which establishes minimum wages, maximum hours, overtime pay, restrictions on child labor and record-keeping requirements.[1] The FLSA originally applied only to the private sector, but in 1985 the U.S. Supreme Court decision in *Garcia v. San Antonio Metropolitan Transit Authority* extended coverage to virtually all functions of state and local government.[2] The following is an overview of the most important provisions of the FLSA.[3]

COVERAGE

http://www.dol.gov/dol/ esa/public/whd_org.htm
The U.S. Department of Labor Wage and Hour Division enforces federal minimum wage, overtime pay, record keeping, and child labor requirements of the Fair Labor Standards Act.

An employee covered under FLSA must be paid a **minimum wage** and **overtime pay** of not less than one and one-half times his or her regular rate of pay for all hours worked in excess of 40 in a workweek unless the employee is specifically exempt. Certain employment records must also be maintained. Most local government employees are covered, but there are some important exceptions. The FLSA excludes any individual who is not subject to civil service laws and who holds public office, is selected by a public officeholder to be a member of his or her personal staff, is appointed by an elected public officeholder to serve on a policy-making level, or is an immediate legal advisor to an elected public officeholder.

In addition to employees not covered at all by the FLSA, **exempt employees** are not subject to the minimum wage and overtime provisions. The main exemptions of concern relate to *executives*, *administrative*, and *professional* employees, otherwise known as the EAP or white-collar exemptions. First, these employees must be paid a set salary on a regular basis, regardless of the time actually worked, as opposed to hourly wages. The employees also must meet certain FLSA tests regarding their primary duty, as well as other requirements. For example, the primary duty of an executive employee is management of a department. In what is called the FLSA "long test," a fairly low minimum salary is required, but 80 percent of the employee's time must be devoted to the primary duty, and other detailed requirements must be met. In the "short test," the minimum salary is higher, 50 percent of the employee's time must be devoted to the primary duty and there are fewer requirements. Exemptions are based on actual job duties rather than position or class title. For more details on EAP exemptions, see Exhibit 13-1.

Other specific exemptions provided in the act also apply to local government. Seasonal employees of recreational establishments are exempt in most cases. This exemp-

---

EXHIBIT 13-1

EAP EXEMPTION STATUS OF SELECTED LOCAL GOVERNMENT TITLES

The proper classification of many local government jobs will qualify them for one of the EAP exemptions. As shown below, each exemption contains a primary duty and other requirements. A review of recent rulings indicates the general status of various titles.

Category of Exemption	Usually Exempt	May Be Exempt	Usually Nonexempt*
Executive Primary duty must be management. Must regularly supervise two or more employees.	Department head Fire battalion chief Police captain	Fire captain Superintendent	Working supervisor Police sergeant Fire lieutenant
Administrative Primary duty must be nonmanual work directly related to management policies or general business operations. Must regularly exercise discretion and independent judgment.	Risk manager HR administrator	Executive/administrative assistant Chief clerk Police desk sergeant Fire training lieutenant	Probation Officer Building inspector
Professional Primary duty must require prolonged course of specialized instruction. Must regularly exercise discretion and independent judgment.	City/county engineer Accountant Registered nurse Systems analyst	Project engineer Computer programmer	Engineering technician Bookkeeper Licensed practical nurse

*Certain jobs that are nonexempt under the category indicated may be exempt under other categories.

Note: Exemptions are determined based on *actual job duties* rather than titles. In general, an employee being paid at least $250 per week on a salary basis will qualify for the exemption by spending 50 percent of worktime on the primary duty. For questionable cases, the organization should request an opinion letter from the Wage and Hour Division and/or advice from a field office. There are *substantial* costs associated with classifying an employee incorrectly.

Source: *Fair Labor Standards Handbook for States, Local Governments and Schools* (Washington, D.C.: Thompson, October 2000, as updated), Tab 200; *Executive, Administrative and Outside Sales Exemptions Under the Fair Labor Standards Act* (U.S. Department of Labor, Employment Standards Administration, Wage and Hour Division, WH Publication 1363 (December 1983), various WH opinion letters and court rulings, and 29 C.F.R. 541.

tion would include employees of golf courses, swimming pools, parks, zoos, and museums. If the governmental unit has fewer than five full- or part-time law enforcement officers or firefighters, the act excludes these employees from the overtime provisions.

Individuals are not considered employees if they volunteer their services to an organization and receive no pay other than reimbursement for incidental expenses. Volunteer police officers and firefighters who are not considered employees of the police or fire department may receive benefits from a retirement fund, relief fund, worker's compensation plan, life insurance policy, or health insurance plan.

MINIMUM WAGE

http://www.flsa.com/
The FLSA home page provides information, resources, and links regarding the Fair Labor Standards Act, as Amended.

The FLSA minimum wage is $5.15 per hour for all covered employees except full-time students, apprentices, and a few other categories. Some jurisdictions also have "living wage" ordinances, which apply to local government and firms with service contracts. In 2000, minimum wages required by these ordinances ranged from $6.25 to $10.75 per hour.[4]

OVERTIME

The FLSA generally requires that employees who work more than 40 hours in a workweek must be compensated for the overtime at one and one-half times their regular rate. A workweek is defined as a regularly recurring seven consecutive days (168 hours). It may begin on any day of the week and at any hour of the day. Hours worked includes all time that an employee is required to be on duty, on the employer's premises, or at a workplace for the employer. Hours worked also includes all time that the employee is suffered or permitted to work. The regular rate is the hourly rate if this is the basis of pay. If not, the regular rate is the salary divided by the number of hours the salary is intended to compensate. A special overtime rule known as "halftime" applies to employees who work a fluctuating work period for a fixed salary. Exhibit 13-2 provides details on calculating overtime pay in various situations.

Regulations also provide that local governments (unlike private firms) can award **compensatory time** for overtime in lieu of overtime pay. Compensatory time must be awarded at one and one half times the overtime hours worked. Employees must be permitted to use compensatory time in a manner similar to leave. Compensatory time can be accumulated up to 240 hours for most employees and up to 480 hours for police and fire employees. At separation the employer must pay the employee for accumulated time.

The law provides a partial overtime exemption for public agency employees engaged in fire protection and law enforcement, including security personnel in correctional institutions. Under this provision, an employer can establish a work period of 7 to 28 consecutive days for the purpose of providing overtime pay. If certain conditions are met, this exemption can be used for ambulance and rescue squad workers but not for civilian employees of police and fire departments. The maximum number of hours during a 28-day work period is 212 for fire protection employees and 171 for law enforcement employees.

CHILD LABOR

The FLSA protects children (persons under 18) from performing hazardous work, working excessive hours, and having work interfere with their education. Persons 16 and 17 do not have hourly restrictions; however, they are not permitted to work in hazardous jobs, such as in electrical distribution or heavy construction. Regulations prohibit persons aged 14–15 from cooking in food establishments, operating power-

EXHIBIT 13-2

COMPUTING
OVERTIME
PAY

Section 207 of the FLSA requires the payment of overtime at one and one-half times the regular rate for all hours over 40 in a workweek for fixed workweeks of 40 hours (see 1, 2, and 3 below) or one-half the regular rate for fluctuating workweeks (see 4 below). In these typical examples it is assumed that a nonexempt employee worked 47 hours.

1. Wage of $7.60 per hour
   Regular rate: $7.60
   Overtime rate: $7.60 × 1.5 = $11.40/hr
   Total pay: ($7.60 × 40) + ($11.40 × 7) = $304.00 + $79.80 = $383.80

2. Salary of $300 per week for fixed workweek of 40 hours
   Regular rate: $300/40hrs = $7.50/hr
   Overtime rate: $7.50 × 1.5 = $11.25/hr
   Total pay: ($7.50 × 40) + ($11.25 × 7) = $300.00 + $78.75 = $378.75

3. Salary of $1,200 per month for fixed workweek of 40 hours
   Regular rate: ($1,200 × 12) / 2,080 hrs = $14,400/ 2,080 hrs = $6.92/hr
   Overtime rate: $6.92 × 1.5 = $10.38/ hr
   Total pay: ($6.92 × 40) + (10.38 × 7) = $276.80 + $72.76 = $349.56

Note: If salary is semimonthly, regular rate is salary times 24 divided by 2,080. If salary is annual, regular rate is salary divided by 2,080.

4. Salary of $300 per week for all hours worked
   Regular rate: $300/47 hrs = $6.38/ hr
   Overtime rate: $ 6.38 × 0.5 = $3.19/hr
   Total pay: $300.00 + ($3.19 × 7) = $300.00 + $22.33 = $322.33

Note: With straight time already compensated in the salary, only one-half the basic rate must be paid for overtime. This is a "half-time" plan and is appropriate only if employee understands salary covers all hours worked; salary will not be reduced (in this case from $300) if hours worked falls below 40; hours worked fluctuates above and below 40; and average hourly wage does not fall below the minimum wage.

Source: *Fair Labor Standards Handbook for States, Local Governments and Schools* (Washington, D.C.: Thompson, 2000, as updated), Tab 500; and 29 C.F.R. 778.

driven machinery, working in freezers and coolers, working past 9:00 P.M., working more than 40 hours a week or working during school hours. Most problems in local government involve "summer youth" employment, especially in parks and recreation activities. Teenagers often work at events such as summer league softball games or at municipal golf courses. Common violations involve underage persons assigned as short-order cooks at concession stands and not being released from duty when events last beyond 9:00 P.M.

RECORD KEEPING AND ENFORCEMENT

The FLSA requires that employers keep certain records for all covered employees. This requirement includes those who are exempt from minimum wage and overtime provisions. Mandatory information includes personal data on employees and detailed records on time and wages. Special records must be kept in certain situations. Records must be maintained for two or three years, depending on the records involved. The FLSA is enforced by the Wage and Hour Division of the U.S. Department of Labor. Inspectors from the division investigate complaints filed by employees or may initiate investigations based on patterns of violations noted in local governments. Penalties for violation of the FLSA typically include awards of back pay for affected current and former employees for up to two years. Willful violations subject the employer to liquidated (double) damages.

THE FAMILY AND MEDICAL LEAVE ACT OF 1993

The Family and Medical Leave Act (FMLA) is designed to provide employees with job protection in cases of family or medical emergencies.[5] An eligible employee is entitled to 12 weeks of unpaid leave for birth or adoption; serious health condition of a spouse, parent, or child; or the employee's own serious health condition. To be eligible an employee must have been employed for at least 12 months and worked at least 1,250 hours during that period. An employer may require, or the employee may elect, to use accumulated sick and annual leave prior to being placed on unpaid leave. While on leave employees retain all previously earned seniority and employment benefits. Upon returning to work the employee must be assigned to his or her previous job. If this is not possible, the employee must be placed in a job with equivalent pay, benefits, and other terms and conditions of employment. The FMLA is enforced by the Wage and Hour Division with penalties as prescribed under the FLSA discussed above.

THE EQUAL PAY ACT OF 1963

The Equal Pay Act (EPA) was the first federal law to address sex-based wage discrimination.[6] This act is an amendment to the Fair Labor Standards Act and requires employers to provide equal pay for equal work. The equal pay for equal work standard prohibits an employer from paying male and female employees differently for doing the same work within the same establishment. Equal work is defined as that which requires equal skill, effort, and responsibility and is performed under similar working conditions. A plaintiff must establish that the jobs being compared meet each of these conditions before a possible violation may be found. Jobs need not be identical, but substantially equal. Actual job content, rather than job title, is the basis for comparison.

However, even where the equal work standard is satisfied, an employer can compensate males and females differently in four specific situations. These *affirmative defenses* or exceptions authorize pay differentials where they are the result of a seniority system, a merit system, a system that measures earnings by quantity or quality of production, or where pay differentials are based on any factor other than sex.

In a wage discrimination action under the Equal Pay Act, the plaintiff must first establish that an employer pays its male and female employees differently for doing substantially equal jobs. The employer's defense is to show that the jobs in question are unequal or, where the jobs are equal, that one of the four affirmative defenses apply. The legislative history of the act makes it clear that Congress endorsed the equal work standard of comparison. On the other hand, in considering what obligation should be imposed on employers, Congress expressly rejected the idea that pay comparison could be made between dissimilar jobs.

The act is enforced by the EEOC, but remedial provisions are the same as for the Fair Labor Standards Act, discussed above. An employer who unlawfully differentiates wages based on gender may not reduce the wage of any employee to equalize pay.

THE AGE DISCRIMINATION IN EMPLOYMENT ACT OF 1967

The Age Discrimination in Employment Act (ADEA) prohibits employment discrimination against individuals over 40 years of age.[7] The ADEA prohibits employers from paying employees in the protected age class less than younger employees and sets limits on mandatory retirement. An employer who unlawfully pays a younger employee more than an older employee may not reduce the wage rate of the higher paid employee to achieve equity. The major ADEA issues facing local governments involve maximum hiring age and mandatory retirement provisions for public safety employees.

Employers charged with violations of the ADEA have two defenses. The bona fide occupational qualification defense (BFOQ) applies to mandatory retirement based on the idea that capability to perform essential tasks (pursuing a fleeing suspect, using a weapon, etc.) diminishes with age. Therefore a city might use the BFOQ defense to justify requiring police officers to retire at age 60. Or the city might establish a maximum hiring age of 35 for entry-level police jobs in order to ensure that the employee will be able to work a sufficient number of years to recover the considerable investment required for training. Federal appeals courts have often upheld the BFOQ defense when applied to these practices, based on precedents set by federal law enforcement agencies. The other defense is reasonable factor other than age (RFOA), which is similar to one of the affirmative defenses provided by the EPA. Rather than require police officers to retire at age 60, the city could require its police officers to undergo an annual performance test. Those who passed, regardless of age, would continue their employment while those who failed would be separated. The ADEA is enforced by the EEOC. Remedial provisions for violations of the ADEA are the same as those under the FLSA, FMLA, and EPA, discussed above.

http://www.eeoc.gov/
laws/adea.html
The U.S. Equal Employment
Opportunity Commission
provides full text of the
Age Discrimination in
Employment Act.

TITLE VII OF THE CIVIL RIGHTS ACT OF 1964

Amended in 1972 to cover state and local governments, Title VII prohibits discrimination against any individual with respect to compensation, terms, conditions, or privileges of employment because of such individual's race, color, religion, sex, or national origin.[8] Title VII also provides in the Bennett Amendment that sex-related pay differentials are not unlawful if such differences are authorized by the Equal Pay Act.

Title VII is much broader than the EPA, and a key issue has been the precise interpretation of the Bennett Amendment, namely if the provision incorporates the equal work standard along with the four affirmative defenses. Court decisions make it clear that Title VII claims of wage discrimination are not necessarily limited by the equal work standard. Penalties for violating Title VII are substantial, as discussed in Chapter 3.

THE COMPARABLE WORTH ISSUE

The relative pay of men and women and the various approaches used by employers to determine pay have become major concerns. The basic issue involves the persistent gap between the earnings of men and women, and the question of whether (and how) this disparity should be eliminated. One view is that the labor market is discriminatory and therefore pay should be determined by using internal criteria designed to establish pay structures based on work of equal value or **comparable worth**.

THE EARNINGS GAP

In 1996 white women working full-time earned approximately 75 percent of the wages paid to men. For black women the ratio was 60 percent.[9] This earnings gap, although not as great as in past years (in 1985 the ratio for white women was 64 percent), began to widen again in 1990 and has always favored white men. Although there may not be pay disparities within job categories, there are large pay differences between female-dominated and male-dominated jobs. Billing clerks earn less than plumbers, administrative assistants earn less than water treatment operators, and (in at least one case) nurses earn less than tree trimmers.

http://www.epf.org/
pay_equity.htm
The Employment Policy Foundation provides a variety of articles on pay equity and comparable worth.

There are, of course, a number of possible explanations for this shortfall. Among these are that women, as a group, drop out of the workforce to have children, and they accumulate less seniority than men; women prefer to work only in certain types of jobs, and the resulting surplus of available workers depresses the pay; couples migrate geographically to maximize the earnings of the husband; women have less education and training, particularly in fields with good income potential; and women are less likely to be represented by unions.[10] These and other "legitimate" factors, taken together, tend to explain about 40 percent of the earnings gap.[11]

An opposing view is that whole groups of jobs, such as those in clerical and nursing work, are traditionally underpaid because they are held by women and that these lower wage rates constitute sex discrimination under Title VII. Proponents of this view maintain that women have historically been channeled into certain occupations through discriminatory practices in society, and that the labor market reflects this by undervaluing female-dominated jobs. Thus it is argued that pay systems based on the labor market reflect present and past discrimination.

THE DOCTRINE OF COMPARABLE WORTH

Because the current legal standard, **equal pay for equal work**, has not eliminated the earnings gap, some advocate replacing it with another standard, known as comparable worth, pay equity, or equal pay for work of equal value. Various definitions of comparable worth have been suggested; however, the basic premise is that the rate of pay for a job should be based on its intrinsic "value" or "worth" in relation to other jobs. This relates to the criterion of internal consistency discussed earlier, but with the additional condition that the scale of comparison be applied across all jobs. In other words, comparable worth goes beyond the relationship between a file clerk and a recording clerk—it concerns relationships between clerks and mechanics. Exhibit 13-3 illustrates the typical result when the wages of female-dominated office jobs and male-dominated service maintenance jobs are compared on a common scale. The vertical scale is the wage rate, while the horizontal scale represents the value of the job established by an evaluation study. The figure shows that male-dominated jobs, on average, receive higher pay than female-dominated jobs with the same number of evaluation points. Advocates of comparable worth suggest that the pay of female-dominated jobs should be raised to the male rate to eliminate the disparity caused by the market.

There are several problems with comparable worth. It assumes the existence of some common scale on which the relative amounts of intrinsic worth in dissimilar jobs can be objectively measured and compared. As was shown in Chapter 12, job evaluation involves a substantial amount of subjective judgment, even for similar jobs. Another problem is that whether the market discriminates against women has not been established. If the market correctly allocates labor resources, ignoring the market results in a surplus of candidates for certain jobs and shortages in others; moreover, Title VII already provides job mobility, a proven means of improving the economic sta-

PAY LINES
FOR MALE-
AND FEMALE-
DOMINATED
JOBS

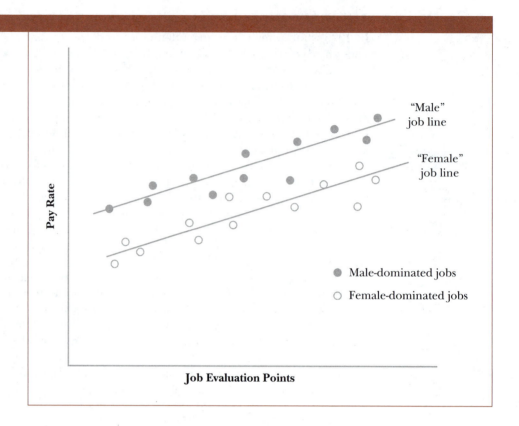

tus of women. In other words, women are now attaining high-paying jobs once available only to men. Finally, equal work and comparable worth represent very different standards on which to base pay. Equal work has a reasonably well accepted interpretation in labor management relations, within the judicial system, and among compensation professionals; however, comparable worth has yet to be operationally defined. It can be compared with such terms as fair price, quality education, and compassionate conservatism. All of these phrases mean different things to different people.

In the private sector, comparable worth is essentially a management issue. Although a number of major corporations are experimenting with pay equity initiatives, they do not usually support the idea of comparable worth as a legal standard of pay. Moreover, the mainstream of professional opinion advocates that the external market should be a major factor in wage determination. This is not necessarily the case in the public sector. In 1998 all but five states were involved in some level of pay equity activity and eight states have enacted pay equity laws.[12] Generally such laws apply to the state civil service system, but there is a trend to include local governments. Minnesota, for example, requires each political subdivision to establish equitable compensation relationships between female-dominated, male-dominated, and balanced classes of employees based on "comparable work value." Additionally, compensation philosophy in the public sector tends to emphasize the importance of pay equity. Public sector literature reflects this philosophy; professional articles on compensation often focus more on how pay equity programs can be implemented rather than whether or not the concept has merit.

LEGAL STATUS OF COMPARABLE WORTH

Even if the work is different, employers can encounter legal liability for sex-based pay disparities. As was shown above, a number of states have, or are considering, pay equity laws that may apply to local government. In regard to Title VII the following cases provide an overview of the more significant decisions.

LEMONS V. CITY AND COUNTY OF DENVER. Nurses employed by the city of Denver challenged the government's practice of basing their pay on the pay received by other nurses in the community. They alleged that nurses were underpaid by the city and in the community in comparison with nonnursing jobs that were of equal or less value to the city (for example, sign painter and tree trimmer). The court noted that the only allegation against the employer was that it paid the market rate, not that it discriminated in hiring and assigning females. Because the jobs in question were not substantially equal, the court rejected the claim.[13]

GUNTHER V. COUNTY OF WASHINGTON. Female jail matrons alleged that the county had undertaken its own objective evaluation of the worth of their jobs compared to the male position of guard and determined that the females should be compensated at 95 percent of the male rate. Disregarding its own evaluation, the county set the female wage rate at only 70 percent of the male rate. The plaintiffs contended that this action discriminated against women. The district court denied the claim on the basis that the work was not equal. The case ultimately reached the U.S. Supreme Court, which ruled that a Title VII pay case was not limited by the equal work standard and instructed the trial court to consider additional evidence of discrimination. The Court emphasized, however, that in reaching its decision it did not endorse the concept of comparable worth.[14]

TAYLOR V. CHARLEY BROTHERS. The court found that the company had engaged in a number of sexually discriminatory practices, including maintaining sexually segregated job classifications; channeling women to women's jobs and men to men's jobs; classifying women employees as temporary or part time for disproportionately long periods of time, resulting in less company seniority for women; and violations of the Equal Pay Act. Based on the evidence of sex discrimination in almost all aspects of employment, the court concluded that the company was also discriminating in the establishment of wage rates for female-dominated jobs.[15]

BRIGGS V. CITY OF MADISON. The court found the jobs of health nurse (female) and sanitarian (male) were substantially equal in skill, effort, and responsibility. However, the wage differential was still justified by the higher rate required to attract and retain those in the male-dominated job. The court noted that there was nothing in Title VII holding an employer responsible for market conditions.[16]

AFSCME V. WASHINGTON. A job evaluation study commissioned by the state found significant differences in salary treatment between predominantly male and predominantly female classifications, and that females were earning an average of 20 percent less than men who were performing jobs of equal value. A district court ruled that by failing to correct this disparity, the state had violated Title VII, and the court appointed a master to determine new pay scales for approximately 15,000 women's jobs. The decision was overturned on appeal, but the plaintiffs gained a substantial victory in a settlement with the state.[17]

AVOIDING PAY DISCRIMINATION LIABILITY

As the cases above show, intentionally paying women less than men (disparate treatment) is clearly illegal, even though the work is substantially different. Statistics showing sex-based pay disparities resulting from a facially neutral practice (disparate impact) are not usually sufficient, however, to prove a prima facie case of wage discrimination. As case law presently stands, it would be difficult to state with certainty what is permissible and what is not. However, some general observations can be made. Employers should be aware that certain employment practices, some only indirectly related to pay, have been viewed by the courts as evidence of disparate treatment. These practices are "smoking guns" and can result in legal liability even when the jobs in question are not equal. Exhibit 13-4 lists specific steps organizations can take to minimize liability.

THE ROLE OF LABOR UNIONS IN COMPENSATION

Some states have laws that require local governments to bargain collectively with unions that are certified to represent groups of employees. Compensation is one of the most important issues in collective bargaining. Even in a nonunion organization the decisions of compensation managers are influenced by external union activities. Reflecting the classic adversarial nature of collective bargaining, the employer's goal (controlling compensation costs) typically conflicts with the union's goal (higher income and better benefits for members). For this reason, the role of the union must be considered in all phases of compensation management.

The union will be concerned with how jobs are grouped for classification and pay and the general level of pay (discussed in Chapter 12). The union may also take

---

EXHIBIT 13-4

GUIDELINES FOR MINIMIZING WAGE DISCRIMINATION LIABILITY

- Eliminate, where possible, job classifications filled predominately by members of one sex; above all, do not channel females into clerical or similar work.
- Do not undertake a job evaluation study covering dissimilar classifications and then fail to correct sex-based inequities identified by the study.
- If labor market data are used in establishing pay rates, attempt if possible to isolate historical sex bias from the market comparison.
- Do not fill jobs previously held by men with women at a lower pay rate except when there are authorized reasons; for example, seniority.
- Validate employment practices that impact women, such as performance appraisal systems used to establish merit pay, and selection requirements that tend to screen out women for certain types of jobs.
- Refrain from making statements, orally or in writing, that lead to a conclusion that the employer values the work of women less than that of men.
- Once a compensation policy has been established, follow the policy for all job classes. Avoid, for example, meeting market rates for male-dominated jobs and lagging market rates for female-dominated jobs.
- Combine into one classification male- and female-dominated jobs having a common core of responsibilities, even though these jobs may not meet the technical definition of equal work.
- Restructure or reclassify female-dominated jobs where job content has increased; for example, typist to word processor.

Source: Adapted from materials developed by Dwight R. Norris, Auburn University.

a position on such matters as pay equity. In addition to the Washington State case discussed earlier, the American Federation of State, County, and Municipal Employees (AFSCME) has been in the forefront of comparable worth initiatives throughout the nation. Unions, led by AFSCME, have negotiated settlements in Chicago, Los Angeles, and San Jose.

In regard to employee pay the union will typically favor automatic pay increases such as cost-of-living adjustments and other types of annual increases based on seniority. They will be less favorable to pay-for-performance systems (such as merit pay) and nontraditional approaches such as skill-based pay and group incentive systems. Unions often negotiate overtime pay agreements that go beyond requirements of the FLSA such as time and one-half for hours worked over eight in a day and double time for holidays and weekends. Unions have always promoted attractive benefits packages for their members, especially defined benefit retirement plans (pensions) and comprehensive health and medical insurance.

In summary, when a local government is unionized it can expect the union to take a position on virtually every aspect of the compensation program. Because management is required to negotiate an agreement with the union, the compensation program is less likely to achieve all the strategies that were intended. A more complete discussion of labor unions and their activities with local governments is contained in Chapter 15.

DETERMINING PAY FOR EMPLOYEES

To this point the discussion has focused on two components of the compensation program. Jobs were evaluated and placed in a hierarchy of internal worth to the organization. A compensation survey was conducted to determine pay rates of key jobs in the relevant labor market. Job evaluation and market data were combined in a pay structure. The next task is to develop employee pay systems, considering attributes employees bring to the job and performance on the job. Employee attributes that can be rewarded include seniority, performance (individual or group), and job-related skills. Rewards for performance include merit pay and individual and group incentive pay. Compensation systems for executives should also be considered.

ADMINISTRATION OF INDIVIDUAL PAY WITHIN GRADES OR BANDS

In traditional job-based structures, the pay of an employee is administered within the minimum and maximum for the grade. The control mechanism is the **midpoint**, which represents the target level of pay for a fully trained employee performing at a satisfactory level. Exhibit 13-5 illustrates the basic approaches for a salary grade with a midpoint of $22,000 and a range of plus and minus 18 percent. In panel A the grade is divided into quartiles. Pay adjustments are designed to set pay at a level appropriate to an employee's length of service, job performance, qualifications, and so forth. A recently hired employee would likely be paid in the first quartile while the pay of a long-term, high-performing employee would be in the fourth quartile. In panel B the grade is divided into 13 steps. Each step represents a 3 percent increase from the previous step. Note that the steps become wider as they increase. The actual midpoint is between steps 7 and 8, and step 13 is set higher than the planned maximum in order to accommodate a 3 percent increase. In panel C (12 steps), each step represents 3 percent of the midpoint rate. Since steps are equal amounts, the per-

EXHIBIT 13-5

APPROACHES TO
MANAGING PAY
WITHIN GRADES

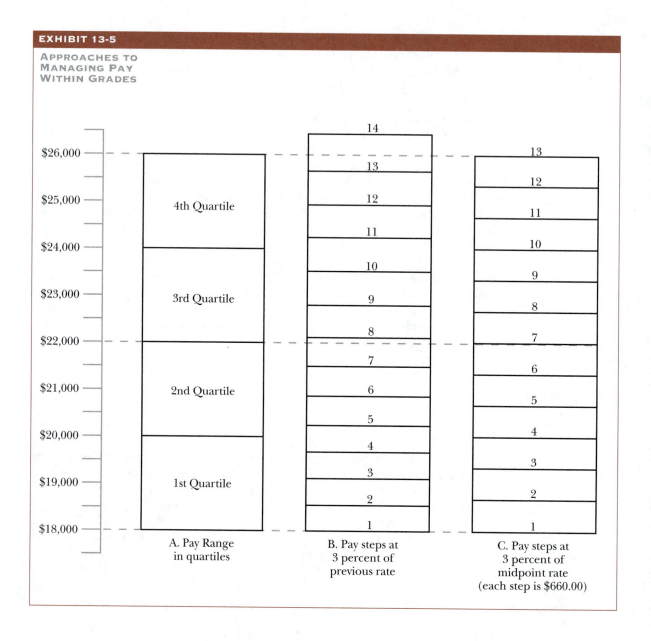

A. Pay Range
in quartiles

B. Pay steps at
3 percent of
previous rate

C. Pay steps at
3 percent of
midpoint rate
(each step is $660.00)

centage of the base rate declines with each step. In this approach step 7 is the midpoint rate. When steps are used, organizations typically adjust pay by awarding "step increases" to employees based on the factors noted above.

In the approach described above, the guidelines and controls are designed into the pay system. As discussed in Chapter 12, however, some organizations use broad bands instead of pay grades. Under bands, line managers have more flexibility and are limited only by the total pay increase budget. However, as experience with bands has increased, many organizations have begun to establish guidelines such as zones or "shadow grades." Where this is the case, within-band pay increases are treated much the same as within-grade pay increases except that zones are more flexible regarding maximum rates of pay and do not contain midpoints.[18]

SENIORITY-BASED PAY

In seniority systems, employees are placed in and advance through rate ranges based on length of service. While there is no evidence that paying employees for their length of service provides any motivation other than to remain on the job, there are good arguments that seniority should be considered. Recall from Chapter 12 that grade midpoints are typically established at market rates. The entry-level rate of pay is often the grade minimum, which is considerably lower than the midpoint. For example, assume that a water treatment operator job is assigned to the pay grade illustrated in Exhibit 13-5. Steps within grade are set at 3 percent of the midpoint rate as shown in Panel C. In a typical situation a new employee would be hired at the minimum rate of $18,040 and given a one-step raise of $660 after successfully completing the probationary period. Note that the employee is, by definition, "performing at a satisfactory level." Assume that an employee with the basic qualifications would be expected to become "fully trained" in five years. At the end of that time the employee will have been given five more step raises and will be earning the midpoint rate of $22,000.

Recall from Chapter 4 that a pay rate significantly below what similar skills are paid in the relevant labor market is a source of dissatisfaction, and dissatisfied employees can be expected to seek other work. Without the automatic step increases, the organization might well lose an employee it trained and would like to keep. Thus in this case rewarding seniority serves a useful purpose. But as was also pointed out in Chapter 4, the level of pay is a hygiene factor. Once an employee is earning the market rate (is not dissatisfied), additional automatic raises have little or no motivational value. Therefore there is no longer any reason to reward seniority for satisfactory performance.

Even so, organizations typically do reward seniority, even for employees wh are already being paid in the upper ranges of their grades, for several reasons. In the first place, length of service and/or time in grade can be objectively measured; hence it is "fair." Second, not to recognize seniority at all suggests that employees gain nothing from experience on the job. Third, employees have come to believe that an annual increase is an entitlement. Although not generally favored by management, which would rather reward performance, seniority to some extent is and will continue to be a part of most employee pay systems. Finally as discussed in Chapter 11, management is often not willing to invest the time and effort necessary to accurately measure performance; thus seniority may be all that is left. Thus we cannot "bury" seniority; we can only damn it with faint praise.

PERFORMANCE-BASED PAY

As noted in Chapter 3, expectancy theory suggests that performance levels of employees are related to their ability and motivation. It was shown that an employee must have the ability to do the job, must see a link between the desired behavior and the reward, and must value the reward. A major factor in how pay influences motivation is the actual relationship between pay and performance. Increasingly, local governments are using job performance ratings as a factor in determining employee pay.[19] The major applications are merit pay and financial incentive programs. For a performance-based pay system to work in practice, a number of necessary conditions must exist, as illustrated in Exhibit 13-6.

EXHIBIT 13-6

- The level of trust between employees and managers must be high. Pay is a very sensitive issue with employees. If they do not have complete confidence that they will be treated fairly, most will reject any pay-for-performance system. The key to building trust is to involve employees in all phases of decision making.
- The system must consider intrinsic as well as extrinsic rewards. There is a wide range of intrinsic rewards (the work itself, pride of accomplishment, etc.) that also motivate performance.
- Employees must have some control over their performance. A gate guard at the sanitary landfill, for example, controls his or her performance only to the extent of showing up for work on time and following instructions. A carpenter, on the other hand, has continuous opportunities to perform better or worse.
- The performance differential must be important to the organization. A building custodian performs such tasks as cleaning floors, dusting furniture, and emptying wastebaskets. Performance is assessed mainly on whether rather than how well these tasks are carried out. However, quality performance by a line repairer is very important because citizens depend on a continuous supply of electrical energy.
- The organization must conduct valid and reliable performance appraisal. This is the most difficult condition for local government organizations to meet; adequate performance appraisal, as discussed in detail in Chapter 11, is essential.
- The organization must be both able and willing to reward performance. The organization must have sufficient resources to make meaningful adjustments in pay, and it must "bite the bullet." This means high performance is well rewarded, mediocre performance is rewarded less well, and poor performance is not rewarded at all. If the salary adjustment guidelines call for a 4 percent across-the-board adjustment with only an extra 1 percent for "merit," the organization should save itself the trouble.

Source: Marc J. Wallace and Charles H. Fay, *Compensation Theory and Practice*, 2d ed. (Boston: Kent, 1988), 235–236; and Merlin MacReynold and Janet Hopkins, "Breaking the Step-and-COLA Cycle," *Public Management* 80 (December 1998), 10–14.

MERIT PAY

A merit pay system provides periodic pay adjustments based on measures of past performance, typically an increase in the employee's base rate of pay. For example, a water treatment plant operator earning $22,000 per year received a two-step or 6 percent increase ($1,320) for excellent performance during 1999, for a new pay rate of $23,320. While it is desirable to reward high performance, merit pay has two disadvantages. First, the increase is "locked in" and will be paid even if job performance decreases. Assume that the employee performs poorly during 2000 (numerous safety violations were committed; also results of several required chemical tests were not recorded). The employee will (obviously) not be recommended for a merit increase; however his or her pay remains at $23,320. In other words, merit pay is not "at risk." The other disadvantage is that merit increases (as well as other adjustments to the base rate) have a compounding effect. Because of this a high-performing employee could earn or exceed the grade maximum (the limit of what the job is worth as discussed in Chapter 12) in a short period of time.

A merit increase matrix, such as shown in Exhibit 13-7, is designed to address this problem. The idea is that the increase should be based on both performance and existing level of pay. For example, suppose our water treatment operator with a pay rate of $23,320 did not really perform poorly during 2000 but received another rating of excellent. A coworker earning only $19,500 received the same rating. The employee earning $23,320 is paid in the fourth quartile and is eligible for a merit increase of 5 percent. The coworker whose pay rate is in the first quartile will receive an increase of 8 percent. If grades are divided into steps, a somewhat similar result is obtained by establishing steps at a percentage of the midpoint rate as was the case with the seniority example above. Assume that the organization rewards performance by granting one or more steps for merit. For the employee earning $23,320, each step of $660 represents 2.83 percent of his or her base pay. The increase for the employee earning $19,500 is 3.38 percent.

INDIVIDUAL INCENTIVE PAY

Unlike merit pay discussed above, individual incentive pay is provided as an inducement to future performance. An example of incentive pay is the familiar "piecework" plan. Used mainly in manufacturing industries, piecework plans reward employees based on a base rate and an incentive rate. For example, an employee has a base rate of $12.00 per hour and an incentive rate of $2.00 per unit. The standard is 40 units per 8-hour shift. If the employee produced 45 units he or she would receive the base rate for eight hours, or $96, and incentive pay of $10 for the five units, for a total of $106. If production fell below 40 units the employee would still earn the base rate of $12 per hour. An example with more applications to local government is a variation known as the standard hour plan. Assume a mechanic also earns $12 per hour and it is expected to take four hours to replace a transmission in a light truck. Therefore the expected labor cost is $48. If the mechanic takes only three hours to replace the transmission, he or she still earns $48, or an effective rate of $16 per hour. As in straight piecework, the mechanic would still earn the base rate if the task required more than four hours to complete. Other types of individual incentives include bonuses for achieving goals related to productivity, quality, customer service, and so forth. For example, an office manager in the utilities department might receive a cash award for implementing a new billing system, or a clerk could earn a bonus for reducing the error rate. Employees can receive bonuses for recruiting successful job applicants. Standards for incentive awards can be established by supervisors or programs can be based on a nomination and judging process involving coworkers. Note that unlike merit pay, the employee's pay reverts to the base rate during any period in which output does not exceed the standard or other criteria are not met. Therefore, incentive pay is "at risk."

Pay-for-performance approaches such as merit and incentive pay are generating

EXHIBIT 13-7

MERIT GUIDELINES CHART

Position in Range	Performance Rating				
	Unsatisfactory	Marginal	Satisfactory	Good	Excellent
4th Quartile	0%	0%	3%	4%	5%
3rd Quartile	0%	0%	4%	5%	6%
2nd Quartile	0%	0%	5%	6%	7%
1st Quartile	0%	2%	6%	7%	8%

increasing interest in the public sector.[20] As has often been the case, the federal government served as the original model.[21] The merit pay provisions of the Civil Service Reform Act of 1978 proved to be ineffective, however, and the Performance Management Recognition and Improvement System (PMRS) was created in 1984. New regulations dealing with performance management and incentive awards became effective in 1995. It is generally agreed that there has been improvement; however, federal agencies are still dealing with differing philosophies of performance appraisal and how to link contributions to rewards.[22] A major problem with performance-based pay is that it can promote unhealthy competition and a "me first" attitude among employees. It can also threaten the self-esteem of low performers and decrease their productivity.[23] A disadvantage of even well-designed programs is that they tend to pull employees further and further apart and discourage teamwork.

Even given these problems, performance-based pay is seen to have significant potential in local government because of the evidence that it motivates and sustains high performance.[24] One useful approach to the problem of negative motivation of poor performers might be to recognize that even though these employees might not be competitive, they may be effective "group" workers. Thus some provision for rewarding the entire work group (discussed below) might reduce the distress of those who receive low individual ratings.

GROUP INCENTIVE PAY

The pay-for-performance systems discussed above are designed to reward individual performance. However, work processes have changed and teams have increasingly become the basic unit of work. Group incentive pay is designed to reward employees for working together to achieve goals. Private sector group incentives are often

---

Merit pay can work if organizations are willing to establish performance expectations, accurately measure performance, and reward work contributions. This is easier said than done, but organizations that are willing to invest the time and effort required to develop an effective merit pay system have achieved good results. In 1996 the city of Normandy Park, Washington, determined that its established step-and-COLA plan was inadequate and decided to develop a

CAN MERIT PAY SYSTEMS WORK?[0]

pay program in which pay increases would be based on performance. An *ad hoc* committee of the city council was appointed to work with the city administration on developing the program. The committee conducted a wage comparability study to ensure that pay was aligned with the market and worked with employees and managers to develop a formal, job-related performance review process.

After more than eight months, many meetings, and over 250 hours of employee involvement, the committee took its recommendation to the city council. The comparability study and the performance-based pay system was approved by a 6-1 council vote. The system, which was implemented in 1997, provides performance-based pay increases from 2 percent to almost 7 percent. Employees whose performance is rated below standard receive no increases. To date the feedback from employees has been positive. As with any new program, some changes have been suggested, and the standing employee committee will be given the task of reviewing the appraisal form and distribution methodology and making recommendations for future consideration.

Source: Merlin MacReynold and Janet Hopkins, "Breaking the Step-and-COLA Cycle," *Public Management* 80 (December 1998), 10–14.

linked to profit, which would be difficult to define and measure in a unit of local government. However, the concept of profit or "bottom line" is a useful paradigm for structuring a plan that can apply in local government. Consider the function of solid waste collection and disposal. This function is often "privatized," which means the firm with the contract hopes to earn a profit. The firm's profit is the difference between its revenue from collection fees and the cost of operation. The firm can increase profits in two ways: it can increase revenues or reduce costs. If the function is performed by a city government there is no "profit" as such, but the objective of the city would be to either generate net income (possibly to subsidize another service) or at least to break even. Moreover, the government would undoubtedly wish to keep collection fees in line with what a private firm might charge.

A team-based form of incentive pay that applies in this situation is known as **gainsharing**. Gainsharing plans in local government typically focus on the cost components of providing the service, of which one of the most important is labor costs. If the labor costs of solid waste collection are less than expected, the saving is a "gain." As the name suggests, employees share in the gain. The most widely used gainsharing approach is based on the "Scanlon Plan," conceived by union leader Joe Scanlon at Lincoln Electric Company during the 1930s. During the past 10 years a number of local governments have adopted gainsharing plans as parts of broader strategies to build team performance.[25] There are several considerations involved in designing a gainsharing plan.[26] The most important is the productivity standard, which is established using a combination of work measurement techniques and historical "benchmark" data and expressed as a projected budgeted expenditure for labor. Assume that for a particular month the labor cost standard for solid waste collection is $50,000. The actual labor cost for that month is $45,000, resulting in a gain of $5,000. The second consideration involves how the gain is distributed. One common approach would be to pay 50 percent, or $2,500, to the work group, return 25 percent, or $1,250, to the city government, and hold the remaining 25 percent in reserve for months in which labor costs were more than projected.

The design and implementation of a gainsharing plan is much more complex than the above example suggests. If employees are expected to "buy in," the productivity standard must be linked to factors that they have some control over. In one local government employees felt that they had very little control over labor costs, which was the major element in the standard.[27] Possibly the savings described above were the result of people taking vacations, which meant that there was less waste to collect. A month in which costs were higher than the standard may have seen street construction interfere with collection routes. Factoring out environmental influences, not controllable by plan participants, is very difficult.

There are also a number of inherent disadvantages in gainsharing plans. The computations used to develop the productivity standard are very involved and may be so complex that the plan is virtually incomprehensible to employees. Group incentive plans may reward employees who do not carry their share of the load. Service quality may decline; for example, waste handlers, in an effort to complete their routes as quickly as possible, may fail to replace tops on cans or spill garbage on citizens' lawns. FLSA regulations require that whenever a nondiscretionary bonus is awarded, the amount must be figured into nonexempt employees' regular rate and any overtime hours worked must be compensated at time and one-half. The Society for Human Resource Management (SHRM) contends that the difficulty in calculating overtime pay is a major impediment to the adoption of gainsharing plans.[28] Finally, any type of reward or bonus distributed to government employees may be seen as a waste of taxpayers' money.

Excellent execution is the key to making group incentive plans effective, according to the most recent research by the Consortium for Alternative Reward Strategies (CARS). Three aspects in particular are critical to success:

FEATURES OF EFFECTIVE GROUP INCENTIVE PLANS

- **The strength of local management support**—Management should have high expectations and believe in their employees.
- **Employee understanding and ability to influence plan measures**—Employees must know how the plan works and how their efforts should be focused to affect the payout.
- **Consistent communication**—In successful plans, managers communicate at all times, especially during times of poor performance and small or no payouts.

Based on experience with incentives it is also clear that "families of measures" such as productivity, cost, and customer satisfaction are better than single measures. It is also important that group incentive plans be aligned with other HR systems; for example, stressing teamwork and paying people for individual performance can send a mixed message.

Source: Jerry McAdams and Elizabeth J. Hawk, "Making Group Incentive Plans Work," *WordatWork Journal* 9 (Third Quarter 2000), 28–34.

PAYING FOR SKILLS

Skills acquisition by employees has a number of dimensions, depending on the objectives of the organization. Relatively few employees have the full set of skills needed for maximum effectiveness when they are first hired for a job. Organizations typically offer some combination of on-the-job and formal training so that employees will learn these skills. Other organizations seek to build a more flexible workforce by cross-training employees on skills needed in other jobs. In some cases a work group may be structured in such a way that job boundaries are replaced by skill levels. In all cases as employees acquire new skills they become more valuable; therefore it is intuitive that skills should be addressed in both the design of the pay program and in the administration of pay to individuals.

There are a number of ways that this can be accomplished. As employees learn additional skills in their present job, performance is expected to improve; thus merit and incentive pay (discussed above) implicitly reward employees for learning these skills. In some cases skills can be associated with job grades. For example, a water treatment operator might receive a grade promotion (along with a pay increase) for each level of certification because he or she would be capable of performing more difficult tasks and assuming greater responsibility. Cross-training employees on jobs closely related to their own facilitates teamwork and cooperation. For example, a billing clerk in a municipal utility department who can cover for a cashier or customer service representative is more valuable than one who can only process and mail statements. It is logical that the billing clerk should be rewarded for learning the necessary skills. Recall from Chapter 5 that failure to integrate cross-training programs with pay has been given as a reason for unsatisfactory results.

In skill-based pay structures (discussed in Chapter 12), skill is the major factor in individual pay. For this approach to be effective the organization should establish a method of certifying that an employee has learned the skill and knows how to apply it in a work situation. Because skill-based pay is an evolving approach, there are no commonly accepted methods and techniques (as there are for job-based pay). One practice is similar to the work-sample test described in Chapter 8. For example, an equipment operator in a skill-based plan earns $12.65 per hour, the result of having become certified in various skills such as scarifying, trenching, rough grading, and so on. The skill of finish grading is valued at $2.05 per hour; therefore if the employee becomes certified, the pay increases to $14.70 per hour. The test might require driving a motor grader in successive passes over a working area, adjusting height and angle of the blade to level the surface to specified grade established by reference stakes. Test performance would be graded by subject matter experts (SMEs) who may be experienced employees, supervisors, or outside evaluators from other organizations. Another practice would be to require the employee to complete a formal training course in finished grading and spend a period of time performing construction tasks where the skill was required.

EXECUTIVE COMPENSATION

The term *executive* is typically used to describe the two top levels in an organization. In local government this may include elected officials such as mayor, sheriff, and revenue commissioner. In these cases pay is typically set by state law or local ordinance. In other cases executive-level positions are appointed, such as city manager, county administrator, and director of public safety. In smaller jurisdictions these types of jobs are often included in the classified structure even though some or all do not have merit system protection. In larger jurisdictions pay is often established and administered by the governing body (city council, county commission, etc.). Executives may be included in a separate structure where pay levels are significantly higher and ranges are much wider. Base pay may also be set at a level the governing body believes is necessary to recruit a desirable candidate or to retain an incumbent that it would like to keep. Increases (and possibly continued employment) are often tied to the achievement of short- and long-term objectives.

The purpose of executive compensation is to encourage high-level staff to meet strategic goals, not simply complete tasks.[29] Because of the nature of the work and lack of job security, executive pay administration tends to follow a "high-risk, high-reward" philosophy, which is both legitimate in terms of strategic management and ethical in regard to merit principles. In the public sector, however, many aspects of executive compensation, such as profit-sharing, stock options, and "golden parachutes" are not available. Others, such as six-figure salaries, performance and retention bonuses, and executive perquisites (or "perks") such as membership in country clubs and personal automobiles may be subject to political considerations. Because of these factors, local governments do not have as much flexibility in executive compensation as their counterparts in the private sector.

DETERMINING EMPLOYEE BENEFITS AND SERVICES

The major part of the compensation task is the development of a wage or salary structure with policies for placing individuals in the structure based on criteria such as seniority or merit. The creation of a benefits package is the final step in designing the compensation program. Benefits are rewards to employees for membership in the organization. Once called "fringes," benefits are now an important form of compensation involving substantial costs. In 1998 benefits in state and local government accounted for 29.7 percent of compensation costs compared to 27.1 percent for private industry.[30] This part will cover considerations in designing a benefits package and the major categories and costs of benefits.

CONSIDERATIONS IN DESIGNING A BENEFITS PACKAGE

The benefit package should be designed so that it effectively contributes to the compensation program. This requires the organization to consider strategic objectives and policies, allow employee input, and address several key administrative issues.

STRATEGIC OBJECTIVES AND POLICIES

As was the case with pay, strategic objectives and policies play a major role. Perhaps the most important policy question involves how compensation costs are to be divided between pay and benefits. To some extent the answer to that question is influenced by the nature of local government. Firms in the private sector are established to make a profit from their products and services. Some succeed and some do not, forcing them to lay off workers, shut down a division, or even disband the entire company. Although job security in local government can be similarly affected by developments such as reduced revenues and privatization of services, the likelihood of suddenly becoming unemployed is much less. Since it is not as necessary to offset this risk with higher pay and also because of political considerations, local governments often lag the market. Moreover, their objective is to retain employees for long periods of time. Thus they must offer reasonably attractive benefits packages.

EMPLOYEE INPUT

What is "attractive" depends on the needs and preferences of employees. Even if the decision is made to offer a uniform plan (as opposed to flexible benefits, discussed below), employees should be consulted. Some organizations establish committees of employees and managers to assess these needs and preferences and suggest "trade-offs." For example, a defined benefit retirement plan such as a pension and a traditional health insurance plan (discussed below) would likely be preferred by employees, but a local government might not have the resources to offer both. The committee might recommend that if a pension plan were offered, a less costly managed care plan for health coverage (also discussed below) would be acceptable.

ADMINISTRATIVE ISSUES

The first major issue to be addressed is deciding who is to be covered (employees, of course). But there are different kinds of employees—probationary, continuing, temporary, part-time, full-time, and so on. There are also dependents of employees such as spouses and children. Although the idea is controversial, benefits may be extended to live-in companions and same-sex "domestic partners."[31]

The second issue is how benefits are to be financed. Under a noncontributory alternative the employer pays all the costs. In the contributory alternative the employer and employee share in the costs. In general employers prefer the contributory alternative, because of the idea that anything that is "free" is less valuable.

The third issue involves the choices that employees should have in selecting benefits. Many benefits packages are structured based on the preferences of the "average" employee and do not accommodate varying needs. Increasingly, local government employers are offering "flex benefits," also known as "cafeteria" plans, that allow employees various choices. The payment of employee contributions on a pretax basis is one of the simplest forms. A more complex version is a program in which employers allocate credits up to a set amount, which employees can use to purchase selected benefits or receive additional pay.[32]

CATEGORIES OF BENEFITS

Major categories of benefits include legally mandated benefits, retirement and savings plans, health and welfare benefits, and payment for time not worked. These four categories, which will be discussed in some detail, account for over 90 percent of employer expenditures for benefits. Various other types of benefits will be covered briefly.

LEGALLY MANDATED BENEFITS

Although almost every benefit is affected by laws and regulations, an employer typically has the option of whether to offer the benefit or not. However, there are certain benefits that employers are required to provide. These benefits include workers' compensation, unemployment compensation, and Social Security.

WORKERS' COMPENSATION. **Workers' compensation** is insurance that provides a percentage of lost wages and medical and rehabilitation expenses resulting from on-the-job accidents and illnesses. Employees are eligible to receive this benefit even if they are at fault. Workers' compensation is covered by state rather than federal laws. Programs vary by state; however, premiums are paid by the employer, based on the employer's classification and individual safety record. Some employers elect to be self-insured.

UNEMPLOYMENT COMPENSATION. Job security has been a traditional benefit of public employment; however, this has changed somewhat in recent years. Perhaps the most dramatic example was when the federal government cut back or eliminated domestic programs (for example, revenue sharing) and state and local governments were forced to lay off employees. More recently, privatization of government services has resulted in layoffs. In 1976, Congress amended the **unemployment compensation** law to cover state, city, and county workers. Employees laid off through no fault of their own who are seeking work and are willing to accept a similar job have been entitled to this benefit.

SOCIAL SECURITY. Since 1950, when public jurisdictions were first allowed to participate in **Social Security**, coverage has been extended to approximately 80 percent of state and local government employees. Governments that do not participate are required by law to provide a comparable retirement benefit (known as a 457 plan). Should Social Security reform become a reality, it is likely that all local governments will be required to participate.[33] Since the Social Security Act was passed in 1935, the program has evolved to the extent that it is seen as a retirement benefits "floor" to be integrated with other plans. Employees pay 7.65 percent of their wage income up to a maximum of $60,000 and 1.45 percent (Medicare) on the remaining amount. Employers are required to match the employee contribution. Benefits are determined by the amount and duration of the employee's earnings. In addition to retirement income, Social Security provides disability, death, survivor, and health insurance benefits (Medicare).

RETIREMENT AND SAVINGS PLANS

These benefits enhance the employees' retirement income. The two types of retirement plans discussed in this section are defined benefit plans and defined contribution plans.

DEFINED BENEFIT PLANS. In a **defined benefit plan** an employer agrees to provide a specific level of retirement income, typically a percentage of earnings based on age and length of service. A major feature of a pension system is "vesting," which is a provision giving rights to retirement benefits after a specified number of years of service, even if the employee quits before retirement. Most plans are contributory, requiring both the employer and employee to pay part of the cost. Some local governments participate in state retirement plans while others offer their own plans.

The cost to local governments of pension benefits began to escalate in the 1970s. For example, periods of high inflation dramatically increase pension costs when benefits are tied to the Consumer Price Index (CPI). Providing early retirement, "grandfathering" noncontributing groups, and changing the earnings formula (for example from "high-five" to "high-three") can also increase the cost. Finally, advances in medical care mean that people are living longer. A major aspect of this problem is that local officials have, in the past, offered or extended this benefit without following an actuarially determined formula to establish the current payments needed to provide the funds needed in the future. In many cases a different set of officials are discovering that the future has now arrived. Because of these factors, employers are shifting away from defined benefit plans. Although this trend is more evident in the private sector, local governments are also examining retirement and savings plan alternatives that will reduce the cost and uncertainty.

DEFINED CONTRIBUTION PLANS. In **defined contribution plans** the costs to the employer are known, but the final benefit received by the employee is unknown, depending on the yield of the funds that are invested. An example is the well-known 401(k) plan, named for the section of the Internal Revenue Code describing the requirements. Although local governments generally cannot offer 401(k) plans, they can offer a similar plan known as 403(b), which features matching contributions by employers and vesting schedules.[34] Another alternative is setting up a 457 plan as a voluntary plan to supplement other retirement benefits. Employers can "supercharge" their 457 plan, which typically consists of employee earnings only, by providing matching dollars with a 401(a) plan.[35]

There are a number of advantages with defined contribution plans.[36] They avoid the uncertain funding liabilities and high administrative costs of defined benefit plans. Portability offers an advantage to the employees who separate before retirement, because plan assets remain invested or can be transferred to an individual retirement account (IRA) or other qualified plan. Finally, these plans offer employees the opportunities to manage their own investments.

HEALTH AND MEDICAL BENEFITS

A wide variety of benefits may be included in this category. The most common benefits are traditional insurance coverage, managed care, and preferred provider organizations.[37] This section will also cover medical savings accounts and other health benefits.

The idea of managing one's own retirement account and watching the assets grow is widely regarded as an attractive feature of defined contribution (DC) retirement plans, especially with younger employees. For example, over 70 percent of those in the 20–24 age group pre-

WHAT KIND OF RETIREMENT
PLAN DO EMPLOYEES WANT?

fer DC plans over the more traditional defined benefit (DB) plans. But the idea of having an annuity for life becomes increasingly attractive as retirement approaches. Preferences of employees aged 35–44 are almost evenly split, and those in the 55–64 age group favor the DB plan by over 70 percent. Almost 95 percent of employees who are age 65 and older want a DB plan.

In other words, the possibility of having $200,000 (give or take) at some time in the future is a pleasant thought when the future is decades away. As it begins to loom large on the horizon, $1,500 per month looks better and better.

Source: R. Evan Englis, "Defined Benefit Plans Still Measure Up," *HRMagazine* 42 (June 1997), 123–138.

TRADITIONAL COVERAGE. Under traditional insurance coverage, the employee can select a health care provider (physician, hospital, clinic, etc.) of his or her choice. Regular checkups and preventive services not usually covered, but diagnostic tests and all or most of hospitalization expenses are covered under major medical provisions. By the early1990s the premiums for traditional coverage had increased to such levels that employers began intensive efforts to control costs. These efforts included increasing the employee's share of the premiums, requiring copayments, instituting "wellness" programs, and establishing maximum benefits. Other approaches used by employers to contain health care costs fundamentally change the nature of health care delivery.

MANAGED CARE. An alternative to traditional insurance is **managed care** through **health maintenance organizations** or **HMOs**. HMOs operate on the same principle as group insurance, but employees receive comprehensive health care from designated providers that have negotiated a flat rate contract with the employer. Since the HMO works on a flat fee basis (no matter how many or how few employees require medical attention), it has an incentive to promote wellness rather than to simply respond to costly medical emergencies. But employees are generally less satisfied with HMOs for several reasons. Most people want to choose a physician who will act completely in their interests (for example, order an expensive diagnostic test when there is a very small probability that a condition is present). Under managed care the patient must see a physician designated by the plan. Moreover, the physician has a responsibility to provide cost-effective care (order the test only under specified conditions). The standard of care and length of stay is also based on cost-effectiveness, not necessarily on the needs of the patient.

PREFERRED PROVIDER ORGANIZATIONS. A middle ground approach is the **preferred provider organization (PPO)**. Under a PPO various health care providers contract with the employer to provide services at competitive rates. Employees can select among these providers or choose other providers and pay the differences in costs. Some traditional insurance plans also have features of a PPO, except that the doctor-patient relationship is not changed.

IMAGE PROBLEMS FOR MANAGED CARE

While managed care plans have been effective in reducing health care costs of employers, they tend to be perceived negatively. The public tends to regard managed care as a system that is driven by business considerations rather than the needs of patients. Such issues as HMOs purchasing formerly not-for-profit hospitals, reducing qualification levels of staff (such as replacing RNs with LPNs), and allowing physicians to become shareholders have contributed to this perception. Incidents such as individuals being put at risk because of limited diagnostic and treatment options or mandatory limits on hospital stays typically receive wide publicity. As a result many states including California and Texas have passed patients' rights legislation and others such as Massachusetts are actively considering such initiatives. On the national level both houses of Congress have passed bills designed to regulate managed care plans.

Source: "Patients' Rights Progressing at State Level," *ACA News* 43 (January 2000), 14.

MEDICAL SAVING ACCOUNTS. Another aspect of health cost containment is the **medical savings account** or **MSA**, which may apply to any of the approaches discussed above.[38] Typically the employer offers a comprehensive health care plan with high deductibles, for example, $2,500 per employee. The employer deposits all or some of the premium savings into a personalized MSA for the employee. The funds in this account may be used to pay the employee's out-of-pocket costs. If the employee does not spend all of the money in his or her MSA, the remainder is returned as a cash reward. The advantages of MSAs include lower premium costs and an incentive for the employee to carefully use the MSA balance.

OTHER HEALTH BENEFITS. Dental care plans are designed to promote dental health through regular examination and to help pay for the cost of various dental procedures. Vision insurance also encourages preventive care and screening for diseases such as glaucoma and may pay all or part of the costs of lenses and frames. Salary continuation and long-term disability insurance are a form of income protection when an employee is no longer able to work but not eligible to retire. They are designed to become operative when benefits provided by workers' compensation and sick leave run out. All of these benefits may be combined with traditional or managed care approaches discussed above.

PAYMENT FOR TIME NOT WORKED

This category is exactly what it seems; the employee is paid for a period ranging from as little as a few minutes to as long as several months but is not present for duty. Representative examples include paid holidays and paid leaves of absence.

PAID HOLIDAYS AND LEAVE. Governments at all levels usually give more days off than their counterparts in the private sector. Many state and local governments follow the lead of the federal government and allow New Year's Day, Presidents' Day, Martin Luther King's Birthday, Memorial Day, Independence Day, Labor Day, Thanksgiving Day, and Christmas Day. Local governments generally follow the lead of state governments in granting additional paid holidays. Such holidays normally have a statewide or regional religious or historical significance. Typical examples include Columbus Day, Good Friday, and Mardi Gras. In addition, many local governments release employees for all or part of election day.

Most local governments provide various forms of paid leave. The length of vacation or annual leave that may be earned is normally a function of years of service; for example, an employee with less than 10 years of service might accrue 12 days per year while an employee with 10 or more years can accrue up to 18 days. Sick leave operates in a separate, but similar, fashion. Restrictions are normally imposed on the amount of annual leave that may be accrued; however, some jurisdictions allow unlimited accumulation of sick leave. It should be pointed out that accumulated annual and sick leave must be paid on separation or retirement. Leave is also granted for military duty (usually 14 days), jury duty, and for "personal" reasons such as attending a funeral.

Other examples of this benefit, not all of which are officially sanctioned, include coffee breaks; conventions and travel; civic, educational, or religious work during duty hours; nonproductive activities such as making coffee, watering plants, and various "rituals" having little or nothing to do with the work to be done. Time spent by employees making personal calls, writing personal letters, computing their taxes, and running errands can cut deeply into the time left for work-related activities. Taking personal time during official work hours is sometimes called "slick leave."

OTHER BENEFITS AND SERVICES

LIFE INSURANCE. Local governments often arrange with a private carrier for group term life insurance for their employees. The premium may be paid by the employer, or the employee may be required to contribute. The amount of coverage is usually based on some multiple of the employee's base salary.

MISCELLANEOUS SERVICES. Miscellaneous services represent a wide range of employer-sponsored activities such as social events and morale-building activities. One county in Alabama, for example, gives its sanitation workers a day off every year while department managers and elected officials collect garbage. Other examples of such services include employee assistance programs (discussed in Chapter 13), tuition refund programs, credit unions, home-to-work use of vehicles, off-duty access to shops for personal work, clothing allowances, and employee picnics and parties.

Some of these benefits are questionable; for example, the home-to-work use of vehicles causes public criticism, and if the employee transports coworkers, the commuting time can be interpreted as compensable time under the FLSA. Other benefits may not be available to all employees; personal use of shops, for example, is probably limited to those engaged in particular trades. Like some forms of payment for time not worked, some of these services may not be officially sanctioned. Administrators may simply "look the other way." Nevertheless, they are benefits and represent a significant cost to the government.

COMMUNICATION OF BENEFITS

Benefits and services make up a significant part of the payroll costs of an organization. In order to realize any motivational value from the cost of benefits and services, management must ensure that employees are aware of what they are receiving.

Organizations should classify and place a value on benefits and services and provide employees with this information. Employees should also be informed of the benefits for which they pay only part of the cost. Many employees, for example, do not know how large the employer contribution to their medical insurance is and may believe that such protection could be acquired in the open market for an amount similar to their payroll deduction. Some organizations provide information on the type and cost of benefits and services on the stub of the payroll check. Benefits information can be included in employee handbooks, using straightforward language and avoiding highly technical material and jargon. It is also useful to hold meetings with groups of employees to provide additional information and to answer questions about the program.

MANAGEMENT OF THE COMPENSATION PROGRAM

The methods and procedures discussed thus far relate to legal aspects, employee pay systems, and the benefits package. Once in place, the compensation program should be managed to achieve strategic objectives and comply with policy guidance. This requires procedures for maintenance and periodic auditing.

MAINTENANCE PROCEDURES

The first element of compensation management is to establish maintenance procedures to ensure that actions taken are in accordance with the compensation policy (discussed in Chapter 11). These procedures and how they are communicated relate to the "nuts and bolts" of the compensation program. Maintenance procedures should be put in writing and incorporated into a compensation administration manual. Key items include:

- **Timing of Pay Adjustments**—Adjustments should be made at some predetermined point during the fiscal year. Annual wage and salary reviews are consistent with general practice.
- **Approval Levels**—A determination should be made concerning which levels of management will serve as the final authority on salary adjustments, performance ratings, job evaluations, and grade placements.
- **Communications**—Employees should receive current information about how their jobs were evaluated, their pay grade and rate range, appeals of classification, how individual pay adjustments are determined, and inputs to their pay (performance ratings, seniority, credit for skills, etc.).
- **Adjustments to Pay Structures**—Pay structures that were completely adequate when they were designed and implemented tend to become obsolete over time because of both internal and external factors that were not anticipated. Procedures should be developed to revise the structure as needed to respond to changing conditions.
- **Dealing with Pay Inequities**—Inequities can develop in a number of areas and for various reasons. How extensive they are can be determined by periodic audits (see below). While inequities are inevitable, procedures should be developed to correct those inequities that conflict with compensation policy or violate the law.

Responsibility for the ongoing maintenance of the salary administration program is usually assigned to the HR department, but the executive leadership should continue to stay involved to provide guidance.

COMPENSATION AUDITS

In order to ensure that the compensation management is carried out in accordance with organizational policies, the program should be periodically audited. The policy areas of internal consistency, external contributions, and employee contributions discussed in Chapter 12 provide a useful framework.

Periodic analysis of rates is necessary to determine if jobs are paid relative to their internal value. This includes an examination of midpoint separations (the percentage difference between the midpoint rates of adjacent rate ranges). The analyst should consider whether the progression as an employee moves from one rate range to the next is correct in terms of job evaluation results. Next, the analyst must consider the spread between the maximum and minimum range for each rate range and the overlap between adjacent ranges. The need to recognize individual differences in such determinants as seniority and merit must be balanced against the need to maintain a significant difference in rate ranges.

Another consideration regarding internal consistency involves clusters of jobs that tend to be dominated by one sex (or race). Where multiple pay structures are used, the organization should guard against creating rate ranges that unnecessarily suppress the pay of certain types of jobs. One example is the so called pink-collar ghetto that may result when a clerical pay structure adequately reflects differences in related jobs but the overall pay levels compare unfavorably with service/maintenance jobs. Multiple structures are both legal and useful, but they are individually market driven. The pay dissatisfaction brought about by real or perceived inequities requires the attention of management. The added cost of moving certain structures somewhat above the market rate may be offset by gains in productivity and satisfaction.

Finally, pay structures should be audited for differences in salaries paid to men and women (or blacks and whites) in equal jobs. Differences that cannot be attributed to seniority, merit, performance, grade, or other factors not based on sex (or race) must be corrected. Regression analysis is a useful tool for auditing pay structures for disparities based on impermissible classifications such as race and gender.[39]

In regard to external consistency, recall that the midpoint represents the organization's policy relative to the external market (lead, lag, or match). To assess the actual pay of employees relative to the competition a **compa-ratio** is calculated.[40] Compa-ratios are calculated as follows:

$$\frac{\text{Average rate paid}}{\text{Range midpoint}}$$

A compa-ratio of 1.00 indicates that the average pay rate is correct with regard to policy guidelines. A compa-ratio of less than 1.00 means that actual pay is less than intended policy. This may be due to a number of reasons: Possibly most employees were recently hired, or they are poor performers, or promotions are so rapid that they do not stay in grade for any length of time. A compa-ratio of greater than 1.00 means that average pay is greater than intended policy. This would likely be caused for the opposite reasons, such as high seniority, good performance, or slow promotions. In any case, management should analyze the reasons and take the action necessary to bring employee pay in line with policy.

In auditing internal consistency and external competitiveness, the analyst is concerned with groups of employees; however, what is true for the group is not necessarily true for the individual. Assume that an employee holds the job of equipment operator. The rate range for the job may be correct with regard to the local labor market. The range may also be correct in relationship to other ranges in the pay structure. An individual employee, however, may be in an inequitable situation. For example, a scheduled step increase may not have been granted while the employee was on family leave without pay, or the pay rate may not adequately reflect his or her performance ratings. Thus, pay rates must be examined on an individual basis to identify these kinds of inequities.

SUMMARY

Employee compensation is heavily influenced by public policies that emphasize fairness, sufficiency, and protection. Legislation provides comprehensive regulation of minimum wages, maximum hours, equal pay for equal work, and, more recently, discrimination based on race, gender, and age. Most of these laws implement policies by constraining pay practices that are exploitative or discriminatory. In compensation management, one must be able to recognize and operate under these constraints while meeting efficiency and effectiveness objectives for both the organization and the employee.

Some states have laws that require local governments to bargain collectively with unions that are certified to represent groups of employees. Compensation is one of the most important issues in collective bargaining. Even in a nonunion organization the decisions of compensation managers are influenced by external union activities. Reflecting the classic adversarial nature of collective bargaining, the employer's goal (controlling compensation costs) typically conflicts with the union's goal (higher income and better benefits for members). For this reason, the role of the union must be considered in all phases of compensation management.

Fairness in recognizing individual contributions is achieved by developing employee pay systems and considering attributes employees bring to the job and their performance on the job. Employee attributes that can be rewarded include seniority, performance (individual or group), and job-related skills. Rewards for performance include merit pay and individual and group incentive pay. Executive compensation is designed to reward high-level staff for achieving strategic objectives.

The creation of a benefits package completes the compensation program. Benefits are rewards received by employees for membership in the organization. Once called "fringes," benefits are now an important form of compensation involving substantial costs to local governments. Major categories of benefits include legally mandated benefits, retirement and savings plans, health and medical benefits, and payment for time not worked. These four categories account for over 90 percent of employer expenditures for benefits.

Compensation management is based on a compensation policy, with procedures established regarding timing of adjustments, approval levels, communications, revisions to pay structures, participation, and dealing with pay inequities. Finally, the structure should be periodically audited to ensure that internal consistency, external competitiveness, and fairness in rewarding individual contributions are addressed in accordance with compensation policy and laws and regulations.

QUESTIONS FOR REVIEW AND DISCUSSION

1. Identify the major federal laws regulating compensation.

2. Compare and contrast equal pay for equal work and equal pay for work of equal value (comparable worth).

3. Give the arguments for and against considering seniority in individual pay decisions.

4. Compare and contrast merit and incentive pay.

5. Your organization has a well-developed merit pay plan. What is at least one negative consequence you can expect when the plan is implemented?

6. Identify an individual incentive plan applicable to local government employees.

7. Briefly explain the Scanlon Plan. What are its advantages and disadvantages in local government?

8. Why do both individual and group incentive plans involve "pay at risk?"

9. List the major categories of employee benefits and services and give two examples of each.

10. In auditing employee pay the compa-ratio for a job category was calculated to be 1.05. What does that mean in terms of policy guidelines?

ENDNOTES

[1] Fair Labor Standards Act, 29 U.S.C. §§201–216. Interpretations issued by the U.S. Department of Labor include 29 C.F.R. Parts 511–800.

[2] *Garcia v. Metropolitan Transit Authority*, 469 U.S. 528, 105 S. Ct. 1005 (1985).

[3] This explanation of the FLSA is based on *Fair Labor Standards Handbook for States, Local Governments and Schools* (Washington, D.C.: Thompson, 2000, as updated).

[4] Carolyn Hirschman, "Paying Up," *HR Magazine* 45 (July 2000), 34–41.

[5] Family and Medical Leave Act, 29 U.S.C. §2601 et seq.

[6] Equal Pay Act, 29 U.S.C. §206 (d).

[7] Age Discrimination in Employment Act, 29 U.S.C. §621 et seq.

[8] Civil Rights Act, 42 U.S.C. §2000 (e).

[9] U.S. Department of Labor, Bureau of Labor Statistics, *Employment and Earnings* (Washington, D.C., January 1998).

[10] Reviews of 20 articles and studies dealing with factors contributing to the earnings gap are in George T. Milkovich and Jerry T. Newman, *Compensation*, 6th ed. (Boston: Irwin/McGraw-Hill, 1999), 557–567.

[11] See, for example, June O'Neil and Solomon Polachek, "Why the Gender Gap in Wages Narrowed in the 1980s," *Journal of Labor Economics* 11 (January 1993), 205–228.

[12] Susan E. Gardner and Christopher Daniel, "Implementing Comparable Worth/Pay Equity: Experiences of Cutting-Edge States," *Public Personnel Management* 27 (Winter 1998), 475–489.

[13] *Lemons v. City and County of Denver*, FEP Cases 906 (D. Colo. 1978), aff'd, 620 F.2d 228, 22 FEP Cases 959 (10th Cir. 1980).

[14] *Gunther v. County of Washington*, 452 U.S. 161 (1981).

[15] *Taylor v. Charley Brothers*, FEP Cases 602, (E.D. Pa. 1981); analysis by Dwight R. Norris.

[16] *Briggs v. City of Madison*, 536 F. Supp. 435 (W.D. Wisc. 1982); analysis by Dwight R. Norris.

[17] *AFSCME v. Washington*, 770 F.2d 1401 (1985).

[18] Milkovich and Newman, 254–256.

[19] Merlin MacReynold and Janet Hopkins, "Breaking the Step-and-COLA Cycle," *Public Management* 80 (December1998), 10–14.

[20] Howard Risher, "The Search for a New Model for Salary Management: Is There Support for Private Sector Practices?" *Public Personnel Management* 26 (Winter 1977), 431–439.

[21] James L. Perry and Beth Ann Petrakis, "Can Pay for Performance Succeed in Government?" *Public Personnel Management* 17 (Winter 1988), 359–367.

[22] Current developments on performance management and incentive programs in the federal government can be accessed at *http://www.opm.gov/*.

[23] Paul J. Taylor and Jon L. Price, "Effects of Introducing a Performance Management System on Employees' Subsequent Attitudes and Efforts," *Public Personnel Management* (Fall 1999), 424–453.

[24] Risher, "The Search for a New Model," 432.

[25] Howard Risher, "Can Gain Sharing Help to Reinvent Government?" *Public Management* 80 (May 1998), 17–21.

[26] This section draws on Milkovich and Newman, 311–316.

[27] Kevin R. Patton and Dennis M. Daley, "Gainsharing in Zebulon: What Do Workers Want? *Public Personnel Management* 27 (Spring 1998), 117–131.

[28] Robert W. Thompson, "FLSA Discourages Bonus Pay, SHRM Witness Tells Congress," *HR News* 18 (May 1999).

[29] More information on executive compensation is in Milkovich and Newman, 458–462. For a public sector perspective see Eleanor Trice, "Executive Compensation Elements," *IPMA News* 65 (February 1999), 14–15.

[30] U.S. Department of Labor, Bureau of Labor Statistics, *Employer Costs for Compensation* (Washington, D.C., 1998).

[31] Milkovich and Newman, 400–401, and Kim I. Mills, "Domestic Partner Benefits Slowly Gaining Acceptance," *Workspan* 43 (August 2000), 32–35.

[32] Don Heilman, "Flex Benefits Plans Can Save Money," *American City and County* (January 1998), 6. See also Ronald W. Perry and N. Joseph Cayer, "Cafeteria Style Health Plans in Municipal Government," *Public Personnel Management* 28 (Spring 1999), 107–117.

[33] Irene Khavari, "Choices for a Secure Retirement," *American City and County* (August 1998), 41–47.

[34] Khavari, 42.

[35] Duane Meek, "Selecting the Right Pension Program," *American City and County* (March 1999), 8.

[36] Joseph J. Jankowski Jr., "Defined Contribution Plans Can Be Win-Win Solutions for the Public Sector," *Public Management* 79 (February 1997), 14–17.

[37] This discussion draws on Milkovich and Newman, 436–440.

[38] Michael T. Bond, Brian P. Heshizer, and Mary W. Hrivnak, "Medical Savings Accounts: A Health Insurance Option for the Public Sector?" *Public Personnel Management* 26 (Winter 1997), 535–542.

[39] See James A. Buford Jr. and Dwight R. Norris, "A Salary Equalization Model: Identifying and Correcting Sex-Based Salary Differences," *Employee Relations Law Journal* 6 (Winter 1980–81), 406-421. See also U.S. Department of Labor, Employment Standards Administration, Office of Federal Contract Compliance Programs, "Analyzing Compensation Data," *http://www.dol.gov/dol/esa/public/regs/compliance/ofccp/compdata.htm* (January 19, 2001).

[40] Milkovich and Newman, 586–587.

PART 6
ENHANCING EMPLOYEE RELATIONS AND PROVIDING SECURITY

To ensure the continuing contribution of the workforce to strategic objectives, the organization must create a satisfying work environment and attend to the physical and mental health and safety of the workforce. Chapter 14 discusses how organizations can build effective relationships between management and employees by anticipating typical problems and having programs in place to deal with issues when they arise. Chapter 15 addresses labor relations in local government and covers the collective bargaining process as it is carried out in states that have legislation based on the federal model. This part concludes with Chapter 16, which is a general overview of safety, health, and security programs.

CHAPTER 14
IDENTIFYING AND RESOLVING WORKPLACE PROBLEMS

Tommy Barnes has been the human resource director for Jackson County since 1995. Peggy Bridges, the county administrator, selected him shortly after obtaining approval from the County Commission for a full-time position. During the past five years, Tommy has worked hard to improve HR management in the county and has had a number of successes. The recruiting and selection process has been revamped to better match applicants with jobs and increase opportunities for minorities and women. For example, recruiting efforts have been expanded, hiring and promotion standards are job-related, and the "rule of three" system of supervisors picking the applicant they liked was replaced with structured oral interviews. Two years ago the county authorized an additional analyst position and also funded an expanded training program. All supervisors have completed courses in basic management and a number of them have reported that the material presented has been helpful in their work. Skills training programs have been established in almost all areas and arrangements have been made with a local community college to offer additional training opportunities. After considerable discussion, the county commission agreed last year to undertake a wage and salary comparability study, to replace the old classification plan with one that was more flexible, and to increase pay to market levels. Not only has the county gained a reputation as a good place to work; the HR program is beginning to receive attention in professional circles. Tommy realizes that much of what has been accomplished can be attributed to Peggy's support, both with managers and with the County Commission. He is planning to nominate her for the outstanding achievement award presented annually by the state association of public administrators.

But not today. In a few minutes he is scheduled to meet with Mary Green, an equipment operator, who is upset with several coworkers for telling off-color jokes and displaying pinups in the break room. He notes that this is the third sexual harassment complaint this year. Joe Phillips, the county finance director, has asked him to mediate a situation in his department. Two people had, in his words, "gotten crossed up over something," and relationships in the office were very hostile. He said that "it may be a racial thing." And then he has to hold several exit interviews. He was particularly unhappy that Bill

Lankford, an engineering technician, had just resigned. Bill was a good performer and had received a significant pay increase when the new compensation program was implemented. It also occurs to Tommy that reducing turnover was one of the major selling points that he and Peggy used to convince the County Commission to fund the project, and the turnover rate is still too high. Bill sighs and thinks to himself, "If this is such a good place to work, why are we having all these problems?"

INTRODUCTION

Maintaining the good health of his or her patients is the ultimate goal of a physician; however, periodic evaluations are necessary. In these situations the physician will stress such measures as balanced diet, exercise, and so forth, but will also be alert for symptoms that might indicate a condition that requires intervention and treatment. It is the same way with organizations, which benefit from good employee relations. Enlightened leadership, a motivational work climate, and HR systems that employ competent employees, develop talent, and reward performance have been stressed throughout this book. Additional proactive approaches are covered in this chapter. But, as Tommy Barnes has discovered, in spite of the best efforts of organizations to provide an environment where employees can flourish, workplace problems can still arise. Employees may have personality characteristics or other attributes that are associated with negative behaviors. The work setting can create conditions that bring out and reinforce these behaviors. Finally, there are aspects of the "high performance" organization such as flexible assignments, employee empowerment, and merit or incentive pay that can frustrate employees who would be more comfortable with performing the same set of tasks, referring all problems to the supervisor, and receiving an annual step raise. Therefore both HR and line managers must be alert for problems that are negative indicators regarding the state of employee relations, understand the likely sources of these problems, and be prepared to take appropriate measures. In maintaining both human and organizational health, preventive measures are always desirable, but intervention and treatment are sometimes necessary.

DYSFUNCTIONAL SIGNS AND SYMPTOMS

It is useful to begin by identifying and discussing a number of workplace behaviors and conditions that are typically considered dysfunctional. These include poor work relationships, substance abuse and violence, employee revenge, and employee dishonesty. Excessive absenteeism and turnover, also considered dysfunctional, are linked to several of these problems. For example, employees may quit because of conflicts with coworkers or supervisors. Employees who drink excessively or abuse drugs are more likely to be late or stay away from work. Attendance can be expected to decline sharply for several days after a violent incident. On the other hand, employee revenge and dishonesty are concerns mainly because of the direct consequences of such behaviors. All of the behaviors mentioned above are triggered by a variety of underlying causes as shown in Exhibit 14-1. Organizations must ultimately identify and deal with the causes as explained in the following sections. First, however, it is necessary to recognize the symptoms.

EXHIBIT 14-1

SYMPTOMS OF WORKPLACE
DYSFUNCTION

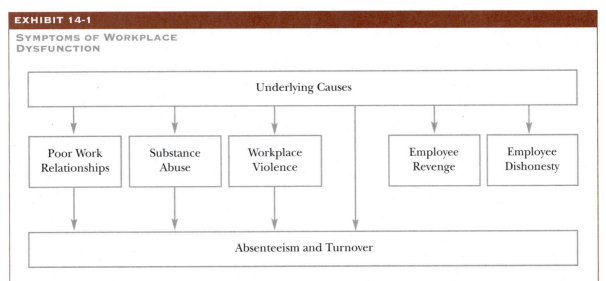

Absenteeism and turnover rates are general indicators of the state of employee relations. Excessive rates are considered symptoms of underlying conditions or causes. Certain other problems such as poor work relationships, substance abuse, and workplace violence contribute (along with other factors) to absenteeism and turnover and are both symptoms and intermediate causes. Employee revenge and dishonesty are not necessarily linked to absenteeism and turnover.

POOR WORK RELATIONSHIPS

Employees spend more than one third of their time at work. Their relationships with supervisors and coworkers are an important and influential part of their lives. The quality of these relationships can deteriorate and lead to diminished organizational performance. Common symptoms of poor work relationships include organizational politics, workplace conflicts, and unhealthy competition.[1]

"Politics" is a particularly unattractive aspect of organizational life. Basically, organizational politics occurs when people use gamesmanship, strategies, ploys, status, trade-offs, and other mechanisms to obtain benefits, get ahead, or even survive. Politicking exists in any organization. In some forms it is relatively harmless, but it always detracts from contributions to objectives. For example, in the public works department a certain worker is continually assigned to deliver equipment to various worksites in an air-conditioned truck. Others, less favored—and less prone to pay compliments to the supervisor—cut brush along the right-of-way in 100-degree heat. In another case the police chief has a sideline of arranging for traffic control and parking by off-duty officers at private functions. In order to be promoted, officers are expected to "volunteer" for such duty. The connotation of organizational politics is almost always negative. Rewarding individuals based on connections rather than contributions is unethical in any organizational setting.[2] In local government these kinds of behaviors are a vestige of spoils patronage and violate merit system principles.

To some extent workplace conflicts are a natural outcome of people working in groups and can even be a positive force. However, when conflicts have a negative impact on group performance they become dysfunctional.[3] The manager may intervene and attempt to settle the issue or let the employees "fight it out." In either case, conflicts are damaging to productivity and morale. A certain amount of interpersonal conflict is inevitable. Differences in personality types—the ways in which individuals view the world and make decisions—can cause serious problems.[4] Conflicts can arise over such issues as gender, race, and ethnicity. They may be caused by deliberate acts such as employees using racial or ethnic epithets. In many cases, however, employees may not be aware that their behavior may be insensitive or even provocative. For example, a remark intended as a compliment by a male may be offensive to a female coworker. Certain "innocent" expressions by a white person may be seen as degrading and insulting to Hispanics or African Americans. Also, the usual human conflicts can be intensified by conditions such as inequity in work responsibilities and pay, favoritism, jealousies, and social cliques, to name a few. Interpersonal conflict becomes a serious problem when employees (or management) allow disagreements and personality clashes to consume an inordinate amount of time and effort, coworkers choose up sides, and adversarial relationships become the norm.

http://nadm.org/
The National Association for Diversity Management (NADM) provides information with regards to diversity in education, human resources, the public sector, health care, and people.

Employee competition in a supportive workplace environment stimulates innovation and productivity. But competition between employees and groups can become pathological and cause conflicts, lower morale, and destroy teamwork. Competition is unhealthy when it sets up win/lose situations, tears down employee self-esteem, reduces communication and supportive interaction, or fosters a "results-at-all-costs" mentality. Even such innocuous programs as "employee-of-the-month" and "best crew" contests can get out of hand. In one situation, a solid waste supervisor established a program to recognize the best-maintained packer truck every month. The winning crew displayed a sign on the truck, and employees received a letter of commendation. The award was based on appearance, cleanliness, maintenance, and so forth, of assigned equipment. The crews went to extreme lengths, including waxing the undercarriages of packer trucks. Winning the monthly contests became more important than picking up waste along the routes. Complaints from customers increased because in their haste to complete their routes and get back to the motor pool, workers spilled garbage. There were heated arguments over access to the pressure hose, and cleaning supplies were hoarded. Unhealthy competition can quickly create an atmosphere of selfishness and mistrust and cause employees to lose sight of legitimate objectives.

SUBSTANCE ABUSE

Substance abuse is another broad issue with many legal, health, safety, and ethical implications. Substance abuse is defined as the illegal and/or socially destructive use of alcohol, prescription drugs, and other controlled substances. Studies have indicated that alcohol is the most used (and abused) drug. Marijuana is the illicit drug of choice, followed by cocaine. Tranquilizers and painkillers are the most widely abused prescription drugs.[5] The negative impact of drugs in the workplace is a matter of some debate. Some estimates suggest that 10 percent of the workforce is affected. Other authorities contend, however, that most casual users of drugs confine their use to evenings and weekends, like their coworkers who use alcohol, and that the figure is considerably lower.[6] Even so the U.S. Department of Labor estimates that drug use in the workplace costs employers $75 to $100 billion annually in lost time, accidents, health care, and workers' compensation costs.[7]

WORKPLACE VIOLENCE

In an earlier time, acts of violence were associated with unskilled jobs involving manual labor. Disagreements between workers turned into shouting matches that occasionally escalated into fistfights. Sometimes the fights took place on the job, or possibly the foreman required the protagonists to settle the matter after work. Other than a black eye or split lip, nobody really got hurt, and the behavior was tolerated (and sometimes encouraged) as a reality of working-class life.

Although this attitude has changed, workplace violence of a more serious nature is increasing at an alarming rate.[8] Most incidents still involve physical altercations, but shootings, stabbings, and sexual assaults are becoming much more common. Homicide is now the second leading cause of work-related deaths in the United States and the first leading cause among women because domestic violence is often brought to the workplace.[9] Casualties are not necessarily limited to victims. Acts of violence can be so debilitating to other employees that they are not willing to return to work for fear that a deadly act will occur.[10] In local governments high-risk areas for murder and assault include law enforcement and work involving contact with clients and customers (social workers, customer service representatives, cashiers, etc.). However, violence and assault may occur in any type of work setting and in any occupational group, and few organizations have programs in place to deal with the problem.[11] Violence prevention and workplace security programs are discussed in Chapter 16.

EMPLOYEE REVENGE

As Chapter 4 pointed out, employees who believe they have been treated inequitably will seek to redress the balance. One way is to "get even" with the organization for real or imagined injustices. Employee revenge takes a number of forms. An employee who is dissatisfied with his or her rate of pay may engage in a work slowdown or deliberately lower the quality of his or her work. Another who was passed over for a promotion may deliberately damage a piece of equipment. Actions that in themselves may be legitimate and justifiable, such as "whistle-blowing" or union organizing, may be motivated by revenge. An inspector for a county highway department who felt that he had been unfairly disciplined reported that he had been told to alter the results of asphalt, concrete, and soil tests.

EMPLOYEE DISHONESTY

Employee dishonesty causes even more negative consequences. The problem of theft is widespread and costly, and management is often at a loss to do anything about it.[12] Most selection techniques are inadequate as predictors of employee dishonesty, such as theft and white-collar crime. Traditional administrative procedures are designed for such purposes as restocking, financial management, and generation of reports, and do little to pinpoint theft and related activities. Employees may have character deficiencies, addictions, or economic needs, all of which increase the likelihood of dishonesty.

Theft can take a variety of forms, from pilfering office supplies to taking materials, tools, and equipment. For example, employees of a county road department took fuel from 50-gallon drums at a worksite on weekends. So-called white-collar crime is committed by nonphysical means and uses concealment or guile. Types of white-collar crime include bribery of employees and elected officials, embezzlement, and fraud. A clerk in the HR department of a city altered leave records of employees who resigned or retired. The "cut" was a percentage of the payout for accumulated leave. Few organizations recognize the complexity of employee dishonesty or acknowledge the management role in discouraging it. Many accept employee dishonesty as a cost of doing business or wash their hands of the matter by turning the problem over to security personnel.

ABSENTEEISM

Absenteeism is generally defined as the failure to report for work at scheduled times. Some absenteeism is to be expected because of illness, family emergencies, and legitimate personal reasons. Organizations typically provide for these types of absences with various types of paid and unpaid leave as was discussed in Chapter 13. However, unnecessary absenteeism is a major concern in both the public and private sectors. During 1999 absence rates for all employers averaged 1.7 percent of scheduled workdays.[13] A major contributing factor is use of sick leave for minor discomforts, personal business, and recreation.[14] Absenteeism also takes more subtle forms. Tardiness in particular has a significant and cumulative effect. If an employee is late to work by an average of 10 minutes per day, this amounts to over four days over the course of a year. The same is true of extended breaks. The employee uses up approximately the same amount of time by taking 5 extra minutes on each authorized 10-minute break. In all cases, work is delayed, not completed, or done by coworkers or supervisors. Absenteeism in the United States represents a cost of approximately $505 per employee per year.[15]

As Chapter 4 pointed out, absenteeism is associated with job dissatisfaction, but it can also be associated with other symptoms such as workplace conflicts and violence. It is often related to the workplace culture. Absenteeism can become what is called a "norm," which is a standard of behavior that is accepted by the members of a work group or department.[16] Once a norm has been established, it has the power to enforce a certain degree of conformity among group members. In some situations a person who attempts to comply with the official rules can be subjected to ostracism and even physical coercion. Attitudes such as, "They expect us to come in late occasionally," and "If I'm not there, someone will cover for me," and "If I need to go shopping, I'll take a sick day" are symptoms of the absenteeism culture. Employers accept and reinforce the absenteeism culture by making allowances for it. They build it into leave policies, work assignments, and schedules, and even budget for it in the form of temporary workers and overtime.

TURNOVER

Employee turnover is permanent separation from the organization. It may occur from voluntary employee actions such as resignations and retirements or from organizational actions such as layoffs and discharges. The turnover rate, like absenteeism, may be influenced by other problems and is not a perfectly straightforward barometer of organizational health. Some amount of turnover is normal, as when a given employee finds a better paying or more attractive job. Moreover, turnover may actually be advantageous to the organization. For example, turnover can renew an organization by introducing fresh ideas and experiences. Turnover can rid the organization of poorly performing, ill suited, hostile, or troublemaking employees. It can allow the organization to replace higher paid employees with new employees at entry-level rates. In many cases, however, turnover is dysfunctional. Replacing an employee is costly (see below) and there is still a loss of organizational "memory." Moreover, the employees who are able to find other jobs are not usually poor performers or troublemakers; rather they are the ones that the employer would like to keep.

There is no real agreement as to how much turnover is considered "normal." The monthly separation rate during the 1990s tended to fluctuate around 1.0 percent of employers' workforces. During 1999 the rate was 1.2 percent, the highest level in almost 20 years.[17] A higher rate may indicate problems, particularly if separations involve key employees and/or good performers, or if it is associated with other dysfunctional conditions and behaviors. In any case, significant costs result from excessive turnover. These include costs of recruitment, hiring, and orientation and training of replacement workers, in addition to reduced productivity while the new employees learn the job. Costs incurred for departing employees include pay for accumulated leave and compensatory time. Also, in many types of retirement plans employees who quit are allowed to "cash out" both the employee and employer contributions. One study estimates that the direct and indirect cost of turnover is approximately 33 percent of the employee's direct rate of pay.[18] Using this factor, replacing a clerk being paid $17,000 would cost $5,610. For a planner with a salary of $40,000 the figure is $13,200.

SOURCES OF WORKPLACE PROBLEMS

Problems such as those discussed above are outward and visible signs of much deeper underlying conditions. Programs designed to prevent or resolve these problems will be more effective when they address the sources of problems rather than merely treating symptoms. Understanding of the root causes of these problems requires consideration of workforce demographics, how employees form their basic value systems, and how they are affected by stress.

WORKFORCE DEMOGRAPHICS

The racial, gender, and age composition of the workforce have important managerial implications. Until recently, the U.S. workforce was considerably more homogeneous. Even after Title VII of the Civil Rights Act was passed in 1964, different demographic groups tended to remain segregated by organizational level and occupational category. For example, executive and professional (white-collar) jobs were mainly held by white men. Clerical and administrative support (pink-collar) work was performed by women (mostly white). Service/maintenance (blue-collar) jobs were male dominated. To some extent whites tended to be in the skilled trades and African Americans and other minorities were relegated to unskilled and semiskilled work. It should be pointed out, however, that African Americans have always worked in skilled trades (such as the building trades), especially when represented by unions. Also, lack of education and poverty, along with race, have always been barriers to job mobility. Many whites also held unskilled and semiskilled jobs.

In recent years, however, the workforce has changed dramatically.[19] Although African Americans are still the largest minority group, the percentage of Asian and Hispanic workers is growing more rapidly. It is estimated that by 2006 approximately 28 percent of workers will be nonwhite. More women are working, increasingly in jobs formerly held by men, and both women and minorities have been advancing to higher-level jobs. Another important demographic is age. In the United States and other developed countries people are living longer, and families are having fewer children. The median age will increase from 31 in 1986 to 40 by 2006. This is reflected in the age distribution of the workforce, with people over age 45 showing the greatest increase. The number of dual career couples and working single parents is increasing. The educational level of workers has continued to rise, even though at the lower end of the spectrum, HR professionals and writers point out that many workers are still not able to read, write, and solve simple math

Increasingly people are encountering problems that diminish their capacity to function effectively. They may have psychological symptoms or even become physically ill. These problems appear in the workplace as behavioral symptoms, causing disruptions and a loss of productivity. Where did all these problems come from?

WORKPLACE PROBLEMS: A THERAPIST'S VIEW

They came from individuals, each of whom has his or her own style, preferences and ways of facing life's challenges. One person's sense of humor comes across to another person as a lack of sensitivity. Someone's need to observe a religious custom offends someone else whose beliefs are different. An individual with a mental or emotional disorder has performance problems and clashes with coworkers. Or he or she misses work, which causes more difficulties.

They are driven by demographics. More women are working, the average age is increasing and the workplace is much more diverse with respect to race, ethnicity and cultural background. Single parents and dual career couples are not able to balance work and family. Generation X is facing simultaneous child care and elder care needs.

They are related to organizational conditions, management practices and the pace of change. Employees have increasingly less job security. Skills can become inadequate almost as soon as they are acquired. Add to this stress created at work with pressure to do more with less by supervisors who are feeling the heat from their bosses. Everything seems to be changing—technology, language, values, jobs, even who we are.

As a consequence of all this a variety of organizational illnesses appear, from personality clashes to protracted conflicts and from alcoholism to absenteeism. Does this mean that the workplace is suddenly coming apart? Not at all. Organizations have always been faced with these kinds of difficulties, including many that are very successful. The fact that we identify these problems and bring them out into the open (rather than ignoring them or covering them up) is very positive. At the least it sends a message to employees that the organization is aware and concerned. But more importantly it is the careful observation of conditions and analysis of trends that lays a foundation for determining the underlying causes and taking appropriate action.

Source: Excerpted from Johnna Flowers, LPC, LMFT, "Causes and Consequences of Employee Problems," Unpublished essay (October 2000). Used by permission. (Ms. Flowers is a marriage and family therapist whose clients include referrals from businesses and public organizations.)

problems.[20] While barriers to job mobility still exist, there is no question that the workforce has become much more diverse.

Although workplace diversity is a positive outcome of fair employment legislation, better education and health care, and changing attitudes, it creates its own challenges. Many of the approaches currently used for organizing and managing the workforce were developed when groups of employees tended to be much more homogeneous.[21] When issues arise or incidents occur, the management response often fails to solve the problem or even makes things worse.

For example, a certain amount of sexuality is a normal part of the workplace culture; however, certain behaviors that may be generally acceptable to men are not acceptable to women.[22] Thus when women are employed in a work group formerly dominated by men, sexually oriented comments, physical touching, and visual displays are often offensive to female employees as shown in Exhibit 14-2. A supervisor may fail to notice or may even tell a woman who complains that she is being oversensitive. This can result in a "hostile work environment," which lowers morale and productivity and causes legal liability under Title VII (see Chapter 3).

Although significant progress has been made in hiring and promoting minorities, many authorities contend that subtle racism continues to persist in organiza-

EXHIBIT 14-2

ACCEPTABLE AND OFFENSIVE
SEXUAL BEHAVIORS

Category	Generally Acceptable Behaviors	Behaviors Often Found to Be Offensive
Touching and other physical behaviors	• Gentle, nonsexual touching in appropriate situation (pat on the back, friendly hug). • Touching related to social customs and courtesies (shaking hands, assisting coworker out of vehicle).	• Deliberate or gratuitous touching (cupping hands behind neck, placing arm around shoulder). • Forceful, coercive, or unexpected touching (pushing, shoving, reaching over).
Verbal Behaviors	• Compliments on attire referring to style, color, or fashion ("That color looks good on you"). • Conversation about popular culture or social issues with sexual dimension but without sexual details (literary merit of romance novel, problem of teenage pregnancies). • Addressing or referring to persons using courtesy titles, first names or nonsexual nicknames and references (Mr., Ms., Dr., John, J.B., Elizabeth, Liz, Doc, etc.).	• Sexually oriented compliments on attire ("That's a sexy outfit you're wearing"). • Conversations that focus on sexual details ("steamy" passage in novel, sexual activities of teenagers). • Addressing or referring to persons using gender-based "slang" (honey, sweetie, babe, stud, etc.).
Visual displays	• Photographs (implication is spouse, boyfriend, girlfriend) that depict men or women appropriate to setting on desk, in locker, or other personal space (photograph of woman in swimsuit at beach, man in shorts in road race). • Posters or pictures of men or women as part of larger, nonsexual theme (poster of band with majorettes).	• Photographs intended to be provocative or prominently displayed (posed picture of woman in swimsuit or man in body-building contest). • Posters or pictures that depict persons as sex objects ("cheesecake" poster showing woman in revealing swimsuit posing next to car).

Source: Developed from Brenda Ryan, "Hostile Environment Sexual Harassment and Attitudes of Offensiveness Toward Workplace Behaviors as Measured by the Hostile Environment Sexual Harassment Inventory," Unpublished M.S. Thesis, Auburn University, 1996, and additional research by James A. Buford Jr. and Dwight R. Norris.

tions and may even be increasing. Poor-quality supervision is cited as one of several reasons that multicultural professionals (MCPs) do not see themselves as valuable resources and are leaving their employers.[23] While concerns and sensitivities involving race and gender receive the most attention, similar workplace issues can arise over sexual orientation, religion, language, and age.

CONTEMPORARY EMPLOYEE VALUES

An understanding of how employee values evolve over time helps to explain and predict their behavior.[24] The baby boom generation began to enter the American workforce in the mid-1960s and is still the largest identifiable group in most organizations. They came of age during the period including the sexual revolution, the civil rights movement, and the assassination of national leaders such as President

John F. Kennedy and Dr. Martin Luther King. Finally, they shared, in one form or another, the Vietnam experience. As the baby boomers came into their own, the traditional assumptions that had shaped employer-employee relations for decades no longer applied. The traditional "work ethic" that emphasized hard work, respect for authority, and material success began to be replaced by a concern for quality of life and autonomy. The accumulation of money and possessions was much less important. Individuals who entered the workforce in the 1970s through the late 1980s reflected a return to more traditional values.

The newest cohort, born between 1963 and 1981, known as Generation X, now composes about 20 percent of the U.S. workforce. While continuing to view money as an indicator of success, GenXers tend to be more like the baby boomers in seeking personal fulfillment. Bruce Tulgan, a noted authority on this cohort, points out that they are also different from the baby boomers in several ways.[25] Many spent a great deal of time alone as the result of the high divorce rates during the '60s, '70s, and '80s, the increase in dual career couples, and more permissive parenting. They grew up during the information revolution. This has made them more independent and better suited to assimilate and process information and deal with technology. They tend to view themselves as sole proprietors of their skills. Where the baby boomers were often viewed as arrogant children determined to reshape organizations, GenXers are more flexible and self-reliant and ready to reinvent themselves and their roles.[26]

"Having a job" is no longer an end in itself; in fact the concept of "a job" is less relevant now. Developments such as contingent workers, reengineering, information technology, work teams, skill- and competency-based pay systems (to name a few) all tend to deemphasize the job as a way of organizing work. In regard to employment status, an individual may tend to think more in terms of his or her "work situation."[27] This can be positive if it reinforces teamwork and cooperation and builds commitment to achieving the goals of the work group and carrying out the mission of the organization. On the other hand, performing a set of tasks at a given location during a specific time (characteristics of a traditional job) also provides an identity with the organization that is diminished when job boundaries give way to teams and work is performed at other places (for example, at home) and during times that are not "normal business hours."

Related to this has been the decline of company loyalty. In this context, "company" refers to one's employer. In the years following the Depression and World War II, men and women anxious for job security sought situations in which they could spend their working lives with one organization. The relationship was based on a parent-child model where the company served as a parent, taking care of its employees in many areas of their lives. Employees who remembered when being out of work was associated with breadlines and homelessness viewed jobs more at that basic level of need. There was an informal social contract between employers and employees that provided security in return for faithful performance of duties, and loyalty was strong.

In recent years, however, the terms of that contract have changed, for both employers and employees.[28] The "new social contract" focuses on customer/client needs as a driving force for employer actions, employee responsibility for maintaining skills useful to the employer and/or readily marketable if the need arises, and employment relationships where employees are seen as contractors or "business partners," with relationships built on adult-adult attitudes and responsibilities. While company loyalty as traditionally understood has probably declined, this does not necessarily mean that employees are not keeping their side of the agreement. The nonpermanent and nonfamilial environment in many organizations has also contributed to the decline of loyalty.[29]

Once upon a time, life was simpler. Virtually all "office work" was done where it belonged—in the office. Certainly people took work home and spread it out on the kitchen table. The engineering assistant computed a survey from field notes and the finance director worked on

HOW SOON WE FORGET

the city budget. Analysis pads, hand calculators, and sharp pencils were very much in evidence. A trusted secretary took the "homework" the next morning, deciphered it, and typed the necessary documents. Telephone tag was played with a stack of pink "while you were out" slips. The computer was in an air-conditioned, double-locked room. It mostly crunched numbers; however there was this thing called "word processing" that seemed to offer potential benefits. Occasionally one of the more brainy types would acquire a personal computer and could be seen plugging numbers into Visicalc. That scenario from the dark ages is not as ancient as we might think. In fact it is a fairly accurate description of worklife in the early eighties.

As we know, things are different now. We have seen dramatic, unprecedented, and (to some) unsettling changes in the nature of work, workers, and where they do their work. The idea of a full-time, permanent job is fading. Technology has created new work processes and altered roles. But it is the change in work location that may be the most profound. This is the first time in the history of the workplace that we can separate activity from location. In the agricultural and industrial ages we had no choice but to bring the workers to the workplace; that was where the dirt or the machinery was. But in the information age we have the option of separating what people do from where they do it. The good news is that the new workplace, has, in most places, changed things for the better. The less good news is that many of our workplace systems, policies, and practices have not kept up with the changes.

Source: Condensed and adapted from Gil Gordon, "Compensating the Workplace of the Future," *ACA Journal* 7 (Winter 1998), 8–11.

EMPLOYEE STRESS

Stress affects the physical and emotional health of employees as well as their job behaviors and productivity. **Stress** may be defined as a condition in which an individual is confronted with opportunities, constraints, and demands and the outcome is both important and uncertain.[30] For example, an employee who is having a performance appraisal would like to get a high rating, which could lead to a merit raise or a promotion. On the other hand, a poor rating could result in denial of merit pay or even termination (note from Chapter 11 that such uncertainty over ratings is preventable when supervisors carry out their responsibilities). While stress is usually discussed in a negative context, it is not necessarily bad. High-performing individuals often use stress positively to rise to the occasion, especially in critical situations. Potential sources of stress include environmental, organizational, and individual factors.

ENVIRONMENTAL FACTORS

Environmental factors arise because of uncertainties outside the work environment. As was pointed out in previous chapters, these uncertainties influence how local governments are organized and managed, including all HR activities. Similar economic, political, and technological uncertainties influence stress levels of employees.

Fluctuations in business conditions create economic uncertainties. A downturn in the economy could mean less tax revenue for a local government, leading to lack of funds for pay improvement, increased workloads due to hiring freezes, possible layoffs, and so forth. Political threats and changes can induce stress. For example, a new city administration that campaigned on a platform to privatize solid waste collection would cause a great deal of stress among employees and managers assigned to that function. Technological uncertainty is an important cause of stress. Innovations can make an employee's competencies obsolete in a short time. Recall, for example, how microcomputer-based word processing, spreadsheet, and database programs quickly changed the nature of skills needed in an administrative office. More recently, geographic information system (GIS) technology has had a similar impact in such functions as planning and engineering. To suddenly realize that one's knowledges and skills are completely inadequate for the work is highly distressing.

ORGANIZATIONAL FACTORS

Organizational factors are present within the work environment. A typical employee spends 40 hours at work every week and experiences a number of factors that cause stress. These include aspects such as job characteristics, role demands, work relationships, and organization policies.[31]

Task demands are related to an employee's job. They include design considerations such as autonomy, interaction with others, task variety, and working conditions. Being able to set priorities and make decisions, along with performing an interesting variety of tasks, is seen to be desirable and less stressful. On the other hand, performing one task under constant deadline pressure from other individuals and departments can be very stressful. Undesirable working conditions such as exposure to extremes of temperature, noise, and close confinement can increase stress levels.

Role demands are pressures based on the nature of the assignment. Role ambiguity occurs when the worker feels unclear about job duties and responsibilities or other aspects of the job. Role conflict is a condition in which the worker knows what is expected but feels unable to reconcile work priorities, supervisors' demands, or perhaps moral/ethical considerations related to job requirements. Work overload is experienced when the worker routinely has more to do than can be reasonably accomplished during a normal workweek.

Work relationships involve pressures created by employees and supervisors. The worker may have a negative relationship with one or more coworkers or with the supervisor. There may be lack of social support from members of the work group, or the worker may feel that he or she is "out of the loop" because of being excluded from the clique that has access to information. The supervisor may be overbearing, play favorites, fail to show appreciation, or engage in any number of behaviors that create anxiety. In fact, one survey suggested that the lack of a trusting relationship with the supervisor was the primary reason that employees decided to leave their organizations.[32] Note from an earlier discussion that poor work relationships are both an observable symptom of dysfunction and likely a contributing cause to absenteeism and turnover.

Organization policies include such factors as culture, organizational structure, and managerial style. The executive leadership may create a culture characterized by tension and fear (recall from Chapter 4 the "Theory X" assumptions). Such a culture is likely to feature centralized decision making, top-down communications, extensive regulations and control procedures, and strict discipline. Supervisors and managers, who are afraid for their own jobs, put undue pressure on employees to meet expectations placed on them even if they are unrealistic or even counterproductive.

Recall from Chapter 4 that the stressors discussed above are similar to Herzberg's hygiene factors. When these factors are negative, the outcome is job dissatisfaction, which is linked to a number of problems discussed earlier. For example, studies have shown that job dissatisfaction is related to excessive turnover. Other undesirable consequences of job dissatisfaction include absenteeism, defensive behaviors, and poor performance.[33]

External and internal factors are not independent of each other. Stress often occurs as a result of interaction between the two—as in the case of an anticipated budget cut on an employee whose job responsibilities are unclear. Role ambiguity coupled with job uncertainty can compound the stress this person experiences. The effects of these kinds of stresses are further compounded by individual factors.

INDIVIDUAL FACTORS

While the typical individual may work a 40-hour week, there are many sources of stress that originate in the other 128 hours. While management would prefer that they not be brought to work, most would agree that this is unrealistic. They often spill over into the work environment. These factors come from family issues, financial problems, and personality characteristics.

Family/work conflict is consistently identified as a major area of concern for employees.[34] Problems include work schedules not being compatible with family obligations, lack of balance between work time and family time, economic insecurity, and loss of mental and physical effectiveness, often attributable to poor eating habits and not getting enough sleep. A major factor is the increase in dual career couples. In these situations it is often difficult to find a work situation that accommodates the career goals of both partners. Also one or both of the partners may find it difficult to continually adjust from the role of spouse to the role of employee. Working single parents feel the need to be involved with their children's educational and recreational activities as well as have "quality time" with them at home. However, inflexible work schedules and fatigue are barriers that prevent them from fulfilling their parental responsibilities. While the struggles of working women have been well documented, the issue of trying to balance work and family increasingly impacts on men.[35]

http://www.
jobstresshelp.com/
Job Stress Help provides news, articles, and other information regarding job stress.

Stress in the workplace affects everyone, from top managers to entry-level workers. Regardless of demographics, the causes are largely the same. Janet Cahill, professor of psychiatry at Rowan University, cites the following three major factors causing stress:

WHY ARE WORKERS STRESSED?

- The degree of control over work
- Demands on employees (too many or too few)
- Lack of support from coworkers and supervisors

According to the American Institute of Stress, other important stressors include:

- Responsibility without authority
- Inability to voice complaints
- Prejudice because of age, gender, race, or religion
- Poor working conditions
- Inability to work with others because of basic differences in goals and values
- Inadequate recognition
- Inability to use personal talents to their full potential
- Lack of a clear job description and chain of command
- Fear, uncertainty, and doubt

Source: Maureen Smith, "Coping with Employee Stress," *IPMA News* 65 (January 1999), 17.

A typical employee has multiple family relationships including those with parents, siblings, spouses, in-laws, and children. These relationships are very important and, at certain times, cause employees to expend vast amounts of emotional energy. Caring for aging parents, going through a divorce, and experiencing discipline problems with children are examples of relationship problems that almost always have a negative impact on behavior and job performance.

Regardless of income level, people in this country have difficulty in handling personal finances. Those who were brought up during the Depression (parents of the baby boomers discussed in a previous section) tended to be very conservative about money and had a philosophy of "pay as you go." But they are barely represented in today's workforce. Since the end of World War II, the way people have taken care of their wants is "buy now, pay later." Many employees are overextended with short-term debt (especially credit card debt). Periodic financial crises, often leading to bankruptcies, can create stress and divert employees' attention from work.

The familiar Type A/Type B theory of personality suggests the existence of two basic personality types as they relate to pressures of work, life, and stress.[36] Type A individuals are characterized by extremes of competitiveness, aggressiveness, impatience, restlessness, and the feeling of being under pressure of time and responsibility. Work activities are especially important to Type A people, and they seek out stressful jobs, work long hours, and meet difficult and recurring deadlines. The Type B personality is far more relaxed, easygoing, satisfied, and unhurried. Naturally, extremes of these types will react to all types of stress very differently because of their different stress thresholds. In addition to experiencing stress as a result of external and internal factors such as those discussed above, these types might also feel stress from interactions with coworkers and supervisors of types different from themselves. For example, a division director of a water board, who was responsible for implementing new testing procedures mandated by the state environmental management department, experienced extreme frustration with what he perceived to be a laboratory manager's lack of a sense of urgency. (Interestingly, the HR director described this situation to one of the authors using the Type A/B descriptors.) Other personality theories may also be useful in understanding differences in perceptions of issued problems and in choosing approaches for dealing with them. For example, the Myers-Briggs Type Indicator (MBTI) discussed earlier can identify personality types for which stress is likely to be a serious problem.

From a management standpoint, low to moderate amounts of stress are not necessarily a major concern. Recall from the earlier discussion that such levels (so-called good stress) may be functional and lead to higher job performance. On the other hand, excessive stress is associated with a number of undesirable consequences including increased smoking, alcohol, and/or drug abuse, sleep disorders, absenteeism, and aberrational job behaviors. In all cases, job performance is negatively affected.

The stress-performance relationship is often depicted as illustrated in Exhibit 14-3. Note that stress initially improves job performance, presumably by stimulating the body and increasing its ability to react. However, as stress continues to increase, there is less improvement, and further increases cause performance to decline as the stress wears down the individual and uses up his or her energy resources. At some point continued high stress levels, or the accumulated stress, may cause a precipitous drop in job performance often known as **"burnout."** The relationship is very similar to an agricultural production function in which additions of a plant nutrient first increase the yield and later become toxic. While the model is useful as a general explanation and may explain why individuals in certain jobs such as police

EXHIBIT 14-3

RELATIONSHIP
BETWEEN
STRESS
AND JOB
PERFORMANCE

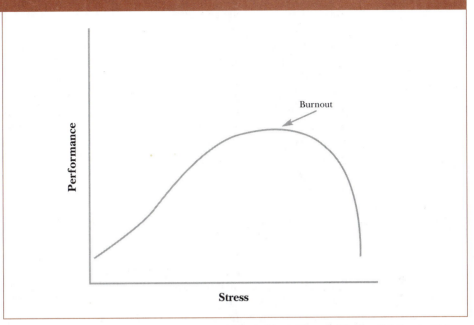

Source: Based on Stephen S. Robbins, *Organizational Behavior,* 8th ed. (Upper Saddle River, N.J.: Prentice-Hall, 1998), 660.

officer or detention nurse sometimes experience career burnout, it has never been empirically tested. It also fails to address the fact that burnout is also associated with boring, nonchallenging jobs that produce little stress. In any case what we do know is that excessive stress can affect the physical and mental health of employees and contribute to absenteeism and turnover discussed earlier. It also leads to increased medical costs, workers' compensation and legal costs, reduced productivity, and accidents.[37]

RESOLVING WORKPLACE PROBLEMS

In designing programs to resolve workplace problems, emphasis should be given to addressing the underlying conditions. The "quick fix," as exemplified by the failure of many drug control programs, is an illusion. However, it will not always be possible to alter the underlying conditions. The attitudes and values of the generational cohorts that make up the present workforce will be with us for some time. To the extent that these attitudes and values result in problems, time may be the only solution; in other words, "this too shall pass." Yet a variety of approaches have met with some success. The following sections examine how the HR department, working with managers and supervisors, can reduce and manage many of the problems that have been discussed.

Proactive measures include the preventive strategies crucial at the recruitment, selection, and socialization stages of the individual-organizational relationship. These stages are covered in depth in previous chapters, and their importance cannot be overemphasized. Other proactive efforts would include the establishment of policies for dealing with specific problems of a disciplinary nature. If policies have been established prior to a problem's occurrence, and employees know of the consequences, these can serve as deterrents to the negative behavior. Of course, it is difficult to have an established policy for every possible occurrence. Reactive measures are, as the word implies, responses to circumstances as they arise. Ideally, HR managers should strive to be proactive in their approach rather than reactive.

Another concern of managers is how much intervention is appropriate, especially in cases of substance abuse or when employees' personal problems impact the workplace. There can be legal considerations, especially concerning testing and treating for substance abuse. Managers must remember that their concern with employee problems is legitimate only as the behavior is affecting the workplace. However, this effect can be in the area of performance, attendance, worker relationships, customer relations, and/or safety and health. Approaches to resolving employee problems include both interpersonal and workplace activities.

INTERPERSONAL APPROACHES

The focus of interpersonal approaches is on intervention with the individual employee. The intervention begins when the supervisor becomes aware of a problem and counsels the employee. If the problem cannot be resolved at this level, the employee is referred for more specialized counseling. Some organizations have developed employee assistance programs (EAPs) to deal systematically with a wide range of employee problems. Another interpersonal activity is discipline.

SUPERVISORY COUNSELING

In this type of intervention supervisors serve as counselors and feedback providers as discussed in Chapter 11, except that the feedback is usually negative and the issues are more sensitive. An effective supervisor who is in touch with his or her employees should be aware of problems at their earliest stages. Key terms in this statement are "effective," "in touch," and "aware." Not all supervisors have these qualities or abilities. Training is required to ensure that supervisors are prepared and comfortable with this personal aspect of managing. A major responsibility of HR management is to provide this training. A supervisor's daily contact with employees can provide the foundation for resolving problems or determining the need for further intervention.[38]

A higher level of communications skills is required for counseling than for other supervisory activities. Training should be provided in such skills as active listening and nonverbal communication. Active listening generally means paying attention to details, understanding the picture from the employee's perspective and responding accurately and constructively. The process begins with the listener giving the speaker his or her undivided attention. This builds rapport and indicates to the speaker that the listener values what is being said. Other ways to listen effectively include allowing enough time and avoiding distractions, searching for common ground or areas of agreement, offering encouragement, and rephrasing or summarizing the speaker's statements to gain clarity. In addition to verbal messages, consideration must be given to the nonverbal aspects of communication, which are often more decisive signals than spoken words. These messages are many times contrary to what is said in words, and even contrary to the person's conscious intention. Therefore, it is important that supervisors send positive, accurate nonverbal cues. Some simple guidelines that will enhance the process include eye contact and a relaxed, reassuring manner. They should also avoid nonverbal cues that send negative messages.[39]

Supervisory counseling is usually the first step in dealing with employee problems. It is important to note, however, that the focus of the discussion is on the impact of the personal problem on job performance. A supervisor should avoid the role of a therapist and not attempt to solve personal problems. If the employee shares the source of the problem and expresses a need for help, referral is in order.

REFERRALS

HR professionals are often more skilled than supervisors and may be able to offer additional assistance to troubled employees. In many cases, however, further referral will be required. Larger organizations often have employee assistance programs (EAPs), which include combinations of in-house and outside counseling services. These programs are discussed in a following section. Smaller organizations without professional counselors refer most problems to various community agencies. Every HR manager should develop a comprehensive list of public and private referral organizations and agencies. Rather than refer employees to individual therapists, it is best to refer to the local association of therapists who can then recommend particular specialists. This practice will ensure privacy and prevent the manager from seeming to have something to gain by recommending one therapist over another. Because there may be instances that require immediate assistance, the HR manager should be prepared with necessary emergency numbers.

In regard to referrals, one point should be stressed. Many supervisors feel that simply referring employees with problems to the HR department is their only responsibility. This sends a subtle message to employees that the supervisor does not care much about helping them. All supervisors should have a basic awareness of the referral programs available to aid employees. When making referrals, supervisors should tell the employee what to expect and express a continued interest in a positive resolution of the problem.

EMPLOYEE ASSISTANCE PROGRAMS

An **employee assistance program (EAP)** is a worksite-based program designed to assist in the identification and resolution of productivity problems associated with employees impaired by health, marital, family, financial, alcohol, drug, legal, emotional, and other concerns that adversely affect job performance.[40] Core activities of the typical EAP include:[41]

- Expert consultation and training to appropriate persons (e.g., supervisors) regarding their role in dealing with employee issues related to the above
- Confidential, appropriate, and timely problem assessment
- Referrals for appropriate diagnosis, treatment, and assistance
- The formation of linkages between the workplace and community organizations that provide specialized services
- Provision of follow-up activities for employees who use these services

Counseling and other services are paid for by the employer, either in total or up to an established limit. EAPs are also useful as part of a comprehensive violence prevention program (see Chapter 16).[42] In recent years EAPs have been begun to focus more proactively on programs and services designed to deal with conflicts faced by employees in balancing the demands of their jobs with concerns for personal health and family responsibilities as part of a workplace approach known as work/life (discussed in the following section). Wellness programs and child care services are major examples of this focus. Exhibit 14-4 illustrates the range of services offered by EAPs.

EXHIBIT 14-4

SERVICES
PROVIDED BY
EMPLOYEE
ASSISTANCE
PROGRAMS

Typical Services (provided by more than 70 percent of EAPs)

Health education and wellness programs—Classes and seminars on diet, exercise, and lifestyle issues, medical examinations, on-site and sponsored fitness programs, cessation of smoking programs.

Counseling and referral services—Assistance with personal problems relating to drug and alcohol abuse, marital/family problems and emotional or mental disorders, addictions such as gambling, and debt and financial difficulties; may include referral to community-based providers for in-depth assistance or rehabilitation.

Other Services

Child care services—Workshops and seminars on parenting, children with special needs, etc., provision of information resources, child care referrals, emergency back-up child care, and on-site child care center.

Elder care services—Workshops and seminars on problems related to aging, age-related diseases such as Alzheimer's, and care alternatives for elderly persons; information resources, elder care referrals, and support services (see below).

Time and stress management programs—Workshops and seminars on establishing priorities, planning and organizing work activities, and reducing stress.

Legal services—Access to qualified advice regarding situations and issues with legal implications such interpretation of contracts, recovery of damages, dispute resolution, bankruptcy, etc.; does not normally include representation.

Crisis line—Access to 24-hour service providing qualified counselors to assist employees who are facing personal exigency; purpose is to "talk out" the problem and avert negative outcomes such as hopelessness, violence, or even suicide.

Loans and financial assistance—Provision of small loans in certain emergency situations such as eviction, repossession of vehicle; not designed to provide normal services of bank or credit union; may involve in-depth financial/credit/debt counseling (see counseling and referral services above).

Termination and outplacement assistance—Assistance to separated employees in preparing resume, locating employment opportunities and preparing for job interviews.

Support group facilitation—Assistance in forming groups of employees confronting particular problems such as going through divorce, caring for aging parents, undergoing treatment for disease, etc.; employer may also provide meeting facilities, information, and resource persons.

Source: Compiled from multiple sources including Bureau of National Affairs, *Services and Assistance for Employees*, Personnel Practices Forum Survey No. 54 (June 1996); SHRM Information Center and Library, *http://www.shrm.org/*; and contacts with selected employers.

While EAPs benefit both the employer and the employee, they can create legal risks.[43] Because they are often connected to disciplinary procedures (see below), employees may view the referral as punishment. If the employee is ultimately terminated and files a charge, enforcement agencies and courts will review the program for evidence of discriminatory treatment. Other legal problems involve violation of privacy, improper assessment of substance abuse, failure to obtain informed consent, conflicts of interest, and failure to use relevant research in making treatment decisions. To minimize the legal risk involved, local governments should develop clear policies, carefully design the program, use trained, licensed professionals as service providers, and continuously monitor EAP activities including contracted services.

According to recent survey by the IPMA, approximately 12,000 employers in the United States have EPAs, including most corporations, states, and large cities as well

http://www.eap-association.com/
The home page of the Employees Assistance Professionals Association.

as a large number of independent businesses and medium-sized to small public organizations.[44] Cost-effectiveness data indicate that each dollar invested returns from $2 to $8 in funds that would have otherwise been lost to poor quality work, absenteeism, medical benefits, and work-related accidents.[45] Many cities and counties, ranging from small jurisdictions such as Madison County, Alabama, to large ones such as Phoenix and Los Angeles, have used such programs successfully.

WORKPLACE APPROACHES

Not all workplace problems can be resolved through interpersonal activities. Moreover, proactive HR management can prevent many problems from occurring in the first place. Diversity management, work restructuring, work/life initiatives, and quality of work life (QWL) programs are approaches designed to build satisfaction and create a motivational workplace environment. Workplace approaches designed to prevent or, if necessary, respond to workplace violence are covered in Chapter 16.

Employee opinions can be used to both uncover specific areas of dissatisfaction and identify needs of employees. As discussed in Chapter 4, a climate or **attitude survey** can be used to measure employees' perceptions in various dimensions such as pay, promotional opportunities, task clarity and significance, skills utilization, organizational commitment, and relationships with supervisors and coworkers.[46] The HR department may design a questionnaire or use a commercially available instrument. The IPMA Center for Personnel Research has sample surveys collected from various organizations available to members.[47] Such surveys are a useful starting point when undertaking the activities discussed below.

ORGANIZATIONAL COMMUNICATIONS

Communication can be defined as the transference of understood information among individuals. Within organizations, communication serves four major functions: control, information, motivation, and emotional expression.[48] As a control mechanism, communication is needed so that employees understand and follow policies and rules. Communication provides employees with the information they need to make informed decisions. Motivation is increased when employees understand what is expected of them and receive feedback on how well they are doing. Within their work groups employees socialize with each other and show feelings ranging from satisfaction to frustration. In this way communication provides emotional expression. For organizations to perform well, all four functions are important. The effectiveness of the motivation and emotional expression functions are influenced mainly by how well line managers perform their responsibilities. HR contributes to these functions in a supporting role. For the control and information functions, however, HR should take the leadership. Important tools include policy manuals, employee handbooks, and newsletters.

As Chapter 5 discussed, organizations should develop written policies in all HR activity areas such as staffing, training, performance appraisal, compensation, employee relations, health, safety and security, along with procedures to cover specific situations. Having these policies and procedures "on file" in the HR department does very little to facilitate the purpose for which they were written, namely to provide a guide for managerial decisions. They are much more useful when they are organized into a manual and provided to managers.[49] By doing this the organization reinforces the idea that policy guidance applies continuously and that all decisions should implement HR strategies. HR policy manuals help ensure that managers are active partners in HR activities. They are also the basis for employee handbooks, a closely related HR communications tool.

While the HR policy manual contains detailed, technical information and administrative procedures for managers, employee handbooks are developed for employees and their families.[50] They are written in a more informal, positive style and format. Employee handbooks often include general information on the organization (history, size, mission, etc.). They should include summary information on all HR policies as well as specific information on such topics as pay, benefits, probationary period, work rules, and disciplinary procedures. Since employee handbooks have sometimes been interpreted by courts as implied contracts, they should be carefully reviewed by legal counsel for appropriate language (for example, describing an employee who has completed a probationary period as a "regular" rather than "permanent" employee) and disclaimers.

Newsletters are a very useful HR communications tool. They can provide a forum to highlight specific policies, address areas of concern, spotlight employees, recognize achievements of individuals and groups, and promote events and activities.[51] Newsletters should be short so that employees can review them easily, and they should contain bullet points, graphics, and cartoons to reinforce points. It is recommended that newsletters be produced in print (hard copy) version and use intranet and e-mail as a supplement. Newsletters reinforce both the information and control functions of organizational communication and market HR to employees and line managers.

DIVERSITY MANAGEMENT

As was discussed in an earlier section, workplace diversity has a number of positive consequences for both individuals and local government such as increased job mobility, an expanded talent pool, and better reflection of the demographics of citizens. On the other hand, diversity can lead to tensions and conflicts over issues related to race, gender, age, sexual orientation, religion, language, culture, ethnicity, and other dimensions of diversity that employees bring to work every day. Diversity management is an emerging field that integrates diversity into virtually all organizational processes. The major initiative for most organizations is training, an activity in which HR typically assumes the leadership role. But diversity management also extends to a number of other areas. According to the American Institute for Managing Diversity (AIMD), the major responsibilities in diversity management include the following:

- **Research and policy development**—This includes maintaining current information on diversity trends, determining organizational requirements and opportunities, and addressing diversity objectives in both general and HR policies and procedures.
- **Diversity training**—Performing this responsibility begins with the training needs assessment (TNA) and follows the process discussed in Chapter 10.
- **Communication**—The focus should be on creating and maintaining awareness of diversity issues and initiatives and should emphasize where possible the relationship between diversity and organizational success; i.e., the "business case."
- **Oversight**—Diversity initiatives should be continuously monitored with the idea of moving diversity beyond a schedule of events and activities and into the culture of the organization.
- **Evaluation**—This involves developing and using instruments and other accountability measures to assess the results of various diversity initiatives and using the data to modify and improve programs.[52]

There is a growing consensus that the positive benefits of workforce diversity far outweigh the tensions and conflicts that may be initially experienced. Rather than something that is "nice to have" and "politically correct," diversity is related to productivity, effectiveness, and, possibly, to survival. It is important that HR managers translate the need for and worth of diversity management into measurable outcomes. As line managers come to recognize the importance of diversity management to their overall business strategy, the necessary competencies will come to be seen as essential as those related to other, more traditional job functions (e.g., planning, financial management, and safety). Moreover, diversity should become a key results area in appraising managerial performance.[53]

WORK RESTRUCTURING

The concepts and methods of **job design** and redesign discussed in Chapter 6 are very useful in developing a healthy workplace environment. One strategy that deserves another mention is job enrichment. As a design strategy, job enrichment represents a movement back toward craft jobs in which employees perform a larger and more complete segment of work. Job enrichment has been associated with high employee motivation, high-quality performance, high job satisfaction, low absenteeism, and low turnover. Jobs are enriched by allowing employees greater self-direction and the opportunity to perform interesting and challenging work. Job enrichment usually includes increasing skill variety, task identity, human interaction, autonomy, and performance feedback.

Much of what has been written about job enrichment contains undocumented claims about its advantages. Job enrichment is certainly no panacea. It is costly and not applicable to all work situations; moreover, some employees do not want enriched jobs. Recall, however, from Chapter 4 that for some employees work provides social identity and a sense of self-esteem, a characteristic that job enrichment can certainly reinforce.

WORK/LIFE INITIATIVES

An area that is receiving increased emphasis is known as **work/life initiatives**. As pointed out earlier, many employees find it difficult to balance the demands of work with their personal lives. The area originated with child care benefits and evolved into a variety of programs designed to promote personal health and deal with related family concerns such as elder care and financial planning, often as part of an EAP, discussed above. However the most basic issue faced by employees is expressed by the familiar saying, "You can't be in two places at once." Approaches available to employers in dealing with this issue include developing policies that provide employees with additional options in using paid leave to handle personal needs and providing more flexibility in work assignments.[54]

Under a traditional sick leave policy, an employee has to invent a last-minute "emergency" to take a half day off to attend a play at her child's school. One approach that has proven to be effective is to combine sick and annual leave to give each employee a bank of paid time that can be drawn on for any reason. This benefits the employee, who can attend the play without misusing sick leave, and the employer, who can plan for the absence. Another work/life initiative involves taking a more flexible approach to how work is organized. Flextime, compressed workweeks, job sharing, and telecommuting/work-at-home are all effective measures to help employees balance demands on their time as well as become more productive.

Where professional counseling, employee assistance programs, diversity management, and work/life initiatives were once seen as "cutting edge" approaches to enhancing employee relations, they have become increasingly essential in maintaining a healthful, satisfying work environment and retaining valued employees. In other words, such activities and programs are implemented because it is believed that they positively impact the core success of the organization. They also represent a significant investment, and unless HR builds the "business case," it is not possible to know whether they are an effective use of the organization's resources. The following measurement and evaluation techniques have been found to be useful:

- **Pretesting/posttesting**—The question is whether the program changed employee behaviors and/or results. Organizational records provide data on such indicators as performance, attendance, grievances (HR records), level of satisfaction (employee surveys), productivity, and costs (financial/accounting records) before and after implementation.
- **Focus groups**—The organization needs to know how employees perceive specific features of programs and activities (highly preferred, indifferent, negative). This information is useful both in developing the program and assessing effectiveness after implementation.
- **Case studies**—It is often possible to "pilot test" an approach in one or more work groups to determine the effect on work relationships and productivity before implementing it throughout the organization. If "hard" data can be obtained, studies of test group vs. control groups can also be conducted.
- **Interviews**—These can uncover information relating to recruitment, retention, and turnover. Newly hired employees should be asked what attracted them to the organization. Interviews with valued employees should concentrate on what part the programs play in their ability to maintain a high level of performance. Exit interviews should determine reasons for leaving. Aggregate data can be analyzed to identify key indicators and trends.

Source: Barbara Parus, "Measuring the ROI of Work/Life Initiatives," *Workspan* 43 (September 2000), 50–54.

Gaining the support of line managers in offering such options is also important, particularly those who equate presence at work and long hours with productivity.

THE QUALITY OF WORKLIFE APPROACH

Quality of Worklife (QWL) is a concept that originated in the 1970s and focused on improving product and service quality by involving employees in decisions that had previously been made by management. These early programs often featured **quality circles (QCs)**, which were small groups of employees from the same group or department who met regularly to identify a wide range of work problems, attempted to determine the causes, and recommended solutions. Results were somewhat disappointing, and QC activity has declined in recent years.[55] During this time, however, QWL has become identified with almost all management activities seen as "progressive" or "enlightened," and writers have broadened the concept to include a variety of initiatives that promote fairness, respect, meaningful work, employee empowerment, development opportunities, safety, and a balance between family and worklife.[56] Exhibit 14-5 is a compilation of basic criteria. Activities included in QWL are not particularly new or different; in fact, QWL incorporates theories, concepts, approaches, and methods discussed both in this chapter (interpersonal and workplace approaches) and throughout this book. Some of the major elements included are the following:

- Fair employment and constitutional rights (Chapter 3)
- Content and process theories of motivation (Chapter 4)
- Job design, particularly job enrichment and work teams (Chapter 6)
- Skills training and employee development (Chapter 10)
- Job-related performance appraisal (Chapter 11)
- Pay structures that promote expanding job boundaries (Chapters 12 and 13)
- Merit and skills pay, group incentives, and flexible benefits (Chapter 13)
- Employee health, safety, and security (Chapter 16)

Many of these elements have both a developmental and an employee relations dimension. For example, training in a new technology builds the capacity of an employee. It can also reduce the stress of an employee who feels threatened because the technology requires skills that he or she does not have. A basic thrust of QWL is that rather than implement various criteria on a piecemeal basis (for example, job enrichment or work/life initiatives), the organization takes action in all possible areas. The objective is to replace the hierarchical or "top down" approach with one of employee involvement and self-direction in which employees can be expected to commit themselves to organizational goals and eagerly involve themselves in their work. QWL usually involves changing the organizational culture; therefore it is essential that both elected officials and the executive leadership be committed to

---

EXHIBIT 14-5

BASIC CRITERIA FOR QUALITY OF WORKLIFE

Sufficient and Equitable Compensation—Income is adequate to support socially acceptable standard of living and rewards system is administered fairly.

Safe and Healthful Work Environment—Employees are protected from injuries, occupational diseases, and workplace violence.

Meaningful Work—Jobs and work assignments allow employees to complete work products rather than merely perform tasks, and employees are granted considerable autonomy.

Opportunities for Development—Employees are provided with opportunities to build their capacity by maintaining and updating skills needed on current assignment and to acquire new skills needed for advancement.

Job Security—Employees have a reasonable expectation that their jobs will continue or that the organization will take appropriate measures to minimize the effect of actions that impact on their employment status.

Sense of Community—The organization provides a friendly and accepting workplace, free from bias and conflict, with an atmosphere of mutual support.

Constitutionalism—The organization provides workplace rights such as due process, respect for privacy, and free speech (note that employees of local governments have these and other rights as a matter of law).

Work/Life Balance—Employees are provided the necessary flexibility to handle personal and family responsibilities and still contribute effectively to the objectives of the organization.

Socially Responsible Work—The organization exists to provide a product or service that contributes to the greater good and operates in accordance with ethical principles.

Source: Adapted from Richard E. Walton, "Criteria for Quality of Working Life," in Louis E. Davis and Albert B. Cherns, eds., *The Quality of Working Life* (New York: Free Press, 1975); and Wendell L. French, *Human Resource Management*, 4th ed. (Boston: Houghton Mifflin, 1998), 57–58.

the program. The best way to ensure that efforts are coordinated and that projects and activities are implemented is to incorporate QWL into strategic objectives and functional policies as discussed in Chapter 5.

EMPLOYEE DISCIPLINE

The last-resort measure for resolving workplace problems is **discipline**. Simply defined, discipline is action taken against an individual for misconduct that the employee has the capacity and ability to correct. Many managers are uncomfortable as disciplinarians, even though they are aware that discipline is occasionally necessary for maintaining employee performance. In general, the best discipline is self-discipline. Once people understand what is expected of them, they will often perform satisfactorily. In other cases, supervisory counseling and referral to employee assistance programs may be necessary to alleviate the problem. Work restructuring and quality of worklife programs can also improve performance. Yet the possibility of having to use discipline always exists. To provide for effective discipline, an organization must establish a well-publicized and unambiguous disciplinary process. Practice has shown that the eight-step process outlined in Exhibit 14-6 is quite effective.

Most organizations adopt a policy of progressive discipline. The purpose is to give the employee a clear warning of the consequences of repeated misconduct. Progressive disciplinary sanctions normally applied include oral reprimand, written reprimand, suspension, and discharge. Certain types of misconduct, such as being late to work, would typically be handled with the full range of sanctions. Other offenses, such as employee theft, might justify immediate suspension or discharge. The organization should establish in advance a list of disciplinary responses appropriate to specific misconduct.

Exhibit 14-7 illustrates a unique approach to providing an accurate measurement of specific degrees of workplace misconduct and linking the misconduct to an appropriate disciplinary response, known as Behaviorally Anchored Disciplinary Scales (BADS).[57] The acronym BADS is appropriate, but it is not a pun. BADS is based on the approach taken in developing Behaviorally Anchored Rating Scales (Chapter 11). This approach employs three types of scales: Misconduct, Repeat Offense, and Discipline. In the example shown, an employee who was absent from his or her work station less than 30 minutes would receive 3 points; if this were the second offense (previous offense of a lesser degree), 5 points would be added, for a total of 8 points. The discipline scale then calls for either a written reprimand or a one- to five-day suspension. (This approach, in the opinion of the authors, seems to be a more useful application of behavioral anchors than performance appraisal.)

In unionized organizations, disciplinary procedures are usually part of the collective bargaining agreement. The objective of the union is to ensure that any disciplinary action taken against an employee is fully warranted. Grievance procedures, discussed in Chapter 15, are normally established for that purpose, and disciplinary actions are often subject to arbitration by neutral third parties.

Finally, in regard to suspension and discharge, local government employees have additional constitutional protections, as discussed in Chapter 3. These employees can acquire property and liberty interests in their jobs, and the Fourteenth Amendment prohibits cities and counties from depriving such employees of these rights without organizational due process.

http://www.joe.org/joe/
1987winter/a5.html
The *Journal of Extension*
includes an article
"Refining Performance
Appraisal," which has an
excellent application of
a behaviorally anchored
disciplinary scale.

EXHIBIT 14-6

STEPS IN
DISCIPLINARY
PROCESS

Step 1. Determine what occurred. In some situations, the supervisor will have observed what happened. More commonly, the offense is reported and must be investigated. It is essential to collect specific information beginning with the date, time, location, and exact nature of the behavior in question. The objective is to verify the alleged incident of misconduct.

Step 2. Seek advice on the case. Normally, no disciplinary sanction should be applied until the manager has consulted with the HR department and if necessary with labor relations authorities. Although management should act promptly to avoid the appearance of condoning the offense, it is sufficient to inform the employee that disciplinary action may be taken and that an investigation of the matter is under way.

Step 3. Conduct the discipline hearing. This hearing is management's opportunity to explain the alleged misconduct and the employee's opportunity to respond to the evidence of misconduct. It is a key step in the investigation of the case. Once management has presented and clarified its evidence, the responsibility shifts to the employee. The employee's (or union's) explanation should be recorded.

Step 4. Investigate the employee's explanation and attempt to verify the employee's defense. This investigation may involve questioning supervisors, coworkers, or others. Documentation related to the offense, such as work schedules, overtime claims, and sick leave applications, should also be reviewed.

Step 5. Consider mitigating factors. These are factors that might indicate no disciplinary action, or a lesser disciplinary sanction, be taken. Common mitigating considerations include length of service, previous work record, awareness of rules violated, and impact of conduct and of handling of the offense on operations.

Step 6. Record the results of the investigation. All steps should be thoroughly documented. At the beginning, the employee misconduct and disciplinary action may be clear in the supervisor's mind, but with the passage of time the manager might forget critical evidence. If the case goes to arbitration or becomes a legal matter, the burden is on management to prove that discipline was warranted. For that reason, the importance of accurate and complete information cannot be overemphasized.

Step 7. Give management's decision. In meeting with the employee (the union steward may be present), the supervisor should cover the following points:

* What occurred and when
* The employee's explanation
* The results of the investigation
* The disciplinary decision
* Requirements for future conduct
* The consequences of further misconduct

These points should be summarized in writing with a copy given to the employee. The employee (or union) that disputes the decision should be informed that grievance action is the appropriate recourse. Management must remain calm throughout, even if the employee or union representative becomes abusive. If necessary, the meeting can be adjourned to a later time. Management must make clear that the matter can be discussed only in a rational environment.

Step 8. Conduct the discipline review. The supervisor should meet with the employee at a later date to review work performance. At that time, he or she should acknowledge the employee's progress in achieving the correct behavior. This type of review can serve as an incentive for improved performance.

Source: Based on Don Cameron, "The When, Why and How of Discipline," *Personnel Journal* 37 (July 1984), 77–78.

EXHIBIT 14-7	
BEHAVIORALLY ANCHORED DISCIPLINARY SCALES FOR ABSENTEEISM	

Misconduct Scale
Nature of the Offense: Absenteeism

Points	Anchors
1	Reporting for scheduled work time or returning from lunch break less than 15 minutes late without authorization or satisfactory excuse.
3	Reporting for scheduled work time or returning from lunch break 15 or more minutes late without authorization or satisfactory excuse. Reporting for scheduled work time or returning from lunch break late, without authorization or satisfactory excuse, resulting in a documented decrease in productivity. Leaving work station without permission for less than 30 minutes, without authorization or satisfactory excuse, resulting in a loss of productivity.
4	Leaving the work station without permission for a period of time greater than or equal to 30 minutes without authorization or satisfactory excuse.
6	Failure to report for work without appropriate authorization or satisfactory excuse.
8	Leaving the work station without authorization or satisfactory excuse resulting in physical harm to other employees.

Reckoning Period: One Year

Repeat Offense Scale

Points	Anchors
0	First offense
5	Second offense—previous offense of lesser degree
7	Second offense—previous offense of equal or greater degree
13	Third offense

Discipline Scale*

Points	Anchors
1	Oral reprimand without official documentation
3	Oral reprimand with official documentation
6	Written reprimand
9	1–5 day suspension
12	5–15 day suspension
21	Dismissal

*When the discipline factor falls between two points, the supervisor is allowed discretion in determining the greater or lesser penalty.

Source: Richard C. Kearney and Frank Whitaker, "Behaviorally Anchored Disciplinary Scales," *Public Personnel Management* 17 (Fall 1988), 345–347. Used by permission. Reproduced by permission of International Personnel Management Association, 1617 Duke Street, Alexandria, VA 22314.

SUMMARY

In spite of the best efforts of organizations to provide a workplace where employees can flourish, problems can still arise. These dysfunctional symptoms include poor work relationships, substance abuse, workplace violence, and employee revenge and dishonesty. Excessive absenteeism and turnover, also considered dysfunctional, can be associated with these problems.

Problems such as these are outward and visible signs of much deeper underlying conditions. Programs designed to resolve workplace problems will be more effective when they attempt to address the sources of the problems than when they merely treat the symptoms. Two sources of interest are the changing nature of employee values and employee stress. In regard to employee values, there has been a decline both in the work ethic and in company loyalty. Another problem source is stress, which has varied consequences depending on the individual and the organization.

In designing programs to resolve these problems, emphasis should be given to addressing the underlying conditions. The "quick fix" is an illusion. However, it will not always be possible to alter the underlying conditions. Interpersonal approaches include counseling, referrals, and employee assistance programs. Major workplace approaches include organizational communications, diversity management, work restructuring, and work/life initiatives. Quality of worklife (QWL) is an approach designed to integrate a wide range of measures including interpersonal and workplace approaches along with practices from various HR areas. A last resort for resolving employee problems is a disciplinary process, featuring progressive sanctions and organizational due process.

QUESTIONS FOR REVIEW AND DISCUSSION

1. This chapter discusses a number of employee workplace problems. Rank these problems in order of importance, based on your opinion of their negative impact on productivity.
2. Can you think of other problems that should have been mentioned?
3. How do the values and attitudes of the baby boom generation differ from those of earlier generations of American workers and from Generation X?
4. Discuss the concept of "company loyalty." Is loyalty a two-way street? Do organizations deserve loyalty from their employees?
5. In designing programs to resolve employee problems, should a problem such as absenteeism be treated in isolation? Why or why not?
6. Discuss the components of a comprehensive diversity management program.
7. Define the term quality of worklife (QWL). Why might an organization develop a QWL program?
8. The director of Parks and Recreation has just informed you that Bill Jones, a park foreman with a spotless record, has begun to drink on the job. How would you handle the situation?
9. Bill is still drinking on the job and has slipped badly. Your city has an Employee Assistance Program (EAP). What might you expect from this program in salvaging Bill's job? What are the legal risks in referring Bill to the EAP?
10. Unfortunately, nothing seemed to work in Bill's case. You just learned that while driving under the influence of alcohol, Bill wrecked a city truck and the Parks and recreation director has recommended that he be discharged. What steps should be followed?

ENDNOTES

[1] The incidents and cases described in this section are based on actual situations observed in local government and other public sector organizations. Names and locations have been withheld.
[2] See John R. Boatright, *Business Ethics*, 2d ed. (Upper Saddle River, N.J.: Prentice-Hall, 1997).
[3] Stephen P. Robbins, *Organizational Behavior*, 8th ed. (Upper Saddle River, N.J.: Prentice-Hall, 1998), 434–437.
[4] Isabel Briggs Myers and Peter B. Myers, *Gifts Differing* (Palo Alto, Calif.: Consulting Psychologists Press, 1980), 205–208. See also David Kearsey, *Please Understand Me II: Temperament, Character, Intelligence* (New York: Prometheus Nemesis, 1998).

[5] Jane Easter Bahls, "Drugs in the Workplace," *HRMagazine* 43 (February 1998), 81–87. See also Donald Klinger and Gary Roberts, "The Miami Coalition Surveys of Employee Drug Use and Attitudes: A Five-Year Retrospective (1989–1993)," *Public Personnel Management* 27 (Summer 1998), 201–223.

[6] Lewis Maltby, "Drug Testing May Not Be Worth the Cost," *HRMagazine* 43 (March 1998), 112.

[7] Bahls, 82.

[8] Errol Chenier, "The Workplace: A Battleground for Violence," *Public Personnel Management* 27 (Winter 1998), 557–568. See also *Workplace Violence Survey* (Alexandria, Va.: Society for Human Resource Management, 1999) (SHRM).

[9] J. R. Slosser, "Combatting Workplace Violence," *ACA News* 43 (January 2000), 44–47.

[10] Arthur Sherman, George Bohlander, and Scott Snell, *Managing Human Resources*, 11th ed. (Cincinnati: South-Western, 1998), 488.

[11] Chenier, 557–558.

[12] Robert R. Taylor, "Your Role in the Prevention of Employee Theft," *Management Solutions* 31 (August 1986), 20–25. See also Samuel Greengard, "Theft Control Starts with HR Strategies," *Personnel Journal* 72 (April 1993), 81–91.

[13] Bureau of National Affairs, "BNA's Quarterly Report on Job Absence," *Bulletin to Management* (Fourth Quarter 1999).

[14] Rolf E. Rogers and Stephen R. Herring, "Patterns of Absenteeism Among Government Employees," *Public Personnel Management* 22 (Summer 1993), 215–236.

[15] "1998 CCH Unscheduled Absence Survey," *IPMA News* 65 (June 1999), 18–19.

[16] Robert F. Allen and Michael Higgins, "The Absenteeism Culture: Becoming Attendance Oriented," *Personnel* 5 (January–February 1979), 30–37.

[17] Bureau of National Affairs, "BNA's Quarterly Report on Employee Turnover," *Bulletin to Management* (Fourth Quarter 1999).

[18] Laura Michaud, "Turn the Tables on Employee Turnover," *IPMA News* 66 (August 2000), 20.

[19] Demographic statistics and trends are based on U.S. Department of Labor, Bureau of Labor Statistics, *Employment Projections 1996–2006*.

[20] Sherman, Bohlander, and Snell, 24–25.

[21] Susan E. Jackson and Randall S. Schuler, *Managing Human Resources* (Cincinnati: South-Western, 2000), 32.

[22] Brenda Allen, "Hostile Environment Sexual Harassment and Attitudes of Offensiveness toward Workplace Behaviors as Measured by the Hostile Environment Sexual Harassment Inventory," (Unpublished Master's Thesis, Auburn University, 1996).

[23] Robert J. Grossman, "Race in the Workplace," *HR Magazine* 45 (March 2000), 40–45. See also Vanessa J. Weaver, "If Your Organization Values Diversity, Why Are *They* Leaving?" *Mosaics* 5 (May/June 1999), 1–4.

[24] This discussion is based on Robbins, 136–137, and Carole Jurkiewicz, "Generation X and the Public Employee," *Public Personnel Management* 29 (Spring 2000), 55–74.

[25] Bruce Tulgan, "Raised on Chaos, Xers Thrive in New Economy," *USA Today* (September 18, 1997), 15A.

[26] For a review of 15 recent works on Generation X, see Bruce Tulgan and Robert J. Green, "Generation X–Compatible Rewards and Strategies," *ACA Journal* 8 (First Quarter 1999), 21–26.

[27] Jackson and Schuler, 244.

[28] For more coverage see Denise M. Rousseau, *Psychological Contracts in Organizations* (Thousand Oaks, Calif.: Sage, 1995). See also Sylva Pate, "New 'Psychological Contract' Sets Goals, Not Boundaries," *Dallas Business Journal* 20 (June 27, 1997), B9.

[29] Larry T. Davidson, "Loyalty Is a Two-Way Street," *ACA News* (April 2000), 8–10.

[30] Unless otherwise cited this discussion is based on Robbins, 652–661.

[31] Maureen Smith, "Coping with Employee Stress," *IPMA News* 65 (January 1999), 17.

[32] Caela Farren, "Survey Finds Employee Retention Dependent on Relationship with Manager," *IPMA News* 65 (November 1999), 22.

[33] Robbins, 155–156, and French, 111.

[34] *Life's Work: Generational Attitudes Toward Work Life and Integration* (Boston: Radcliffe Public Policy Center and FleetBoston Financial, 2000). See also George T. Milkovich and John Boudreau, *Human Resource Management*, 7th ed. (Burr Ridge, Ill.: Irwin, 1994), 716.

[35] Andrea C. Poe, "The Daddy Track," *HR Magazine* 44 (July 1999), 83–100.

[36] John M. Ivancevich and Michael T. Matteson, "A Type A-B Person Work Environment Attraction Model for Examining Occupational Stress and Consequences," *Human Relations* (July 1984), 496.

[37] Smith, "Coping," 17.

[38] For more coverage on supervisory intervention see Arlene Darick, "Clinical Practices and Procedures," in James M. Oher, ed., *Employee Assistance Handbook* (New York: Wiley, 1999), 3–13.

[39] Kittie W. Watson, *Managing by Listening Around* (New Orleans: Spectra, 1993) and Margaret Fitch-Hauser, *Coaching Manual* (Auburn, Ala.: Leadership Communications Group, 2000).

[40] Based on definition adopted by the Employee Assistance Professionals Association (EAPA).

[41] Maureen Smith, "Employee Assistance Programs: Promoting a Healthy Work Environment," *IPMA News* 65 (May 1999), 13.

[42] Robert L. Mathis and John H. Jackson, *Human Resource Management*, 9th ed. (Cincinnati: South-Western, 1999), 555.

[43] Taryn F. Goldstein, "Employee Assistance Programs and the Law," *IPMA News* 65 (May 1999), 12–14.

[44] International Personnel Management Association, Center for Personnel Research, "Personnel Program Inventory Survey" (1997).

[45] Goldstein, 12.

[46] Yaun Ting, "Determinants of Job Satisfaction of Federal Government Employees," *Public Personnel Management* 26 (Fall 1997), 311–335.

[47] Maureen Smith, "Measuring Employee Satisfaction," *IPMA News* 65 (March 1999), 15–16.

[48] Robbins, 310–311.

[49] For more coverage see Joseph W. R. Lawson II, *How to Develop a Personnel Policy Manual*, 6th ed. (New York: American Management Association, 1998).

[50] For more coverage see Lawson, *How to Develop an Employee Handbook*, 2d ed. (New York: American Management Association, 1998).

[51] Eleanor Trice, "Market and Communicate via Employee Newsletters," *IPMA News* 65 (May 1999), 16.

[52] Patricia Dingh, "Do You Have What It Takes?" *Mosaics* 4 (May/June 1998), 1–4.

[53] Audrey Mathews, "Diversity: A Principle of Human Resource Management," *Public Personnel Management* 27 (Summer 1998), 175–186.

[54] Paul C. Gibson, "Reducing Absenteeism Costs Through Effective Work/Life Programs," *ACA Journal* 8 (Second Quarter 1999), 6–12. For more details and additional work/life initiatives see *ACA Journal* 7, Special Edition (Winter 1998).

[55] Thomas Li-Ping Tang and Edie Aguilar, "Attribution of Quality Circles' Problem-Solving Failure: Differences Among Management, Supporting Staff and Quality Circle Members," *Public Personnel Management* 26 (Summer 1997), 203–226.

[56] Wendell L. French, *Human Resources Management*, 4th ed. (Boston: Houghton Mifflin, 1998), 57–58.

[57] Richard C. Kearney and Frank Whitaker, "Behaviorally Anchored Disciplinary Scales (BADS): A New Approach to Discipline," *Public Personnel Management* 17 (Fall 1988), 341–349.

CHAPTER 15
LABOR RELATIONS

THE UNIONS AND THE CITIES*

More than 40 percent of local government employees are now represented by unions, and how the labor relations process is evolving is a matter of considerable interest to HR management. Recent events and developments provide some indication as to where things might be headed if we can interpret what they mean. Consider the following examples:

On July 25, 2000, negotiators for the city of Philadelphia and District Councils 33 and 47 of the American Federation of State, County, and Municipal Employees (AFSCME), representing slightly more than 14,000 municipal workers, reached tentative agreement on a four-year contract. By settling the dispute, the city was able to avoid a strike and a potentially embarrassing disruption of services during the Republican National Convention.

Source: "City, Unions Reach Deals, Avoid Strike," *Philadelphia Inquirer* (July 26, 2000), A1.

An arbitrator ruled that the city of Memphis violated a collective bargaining agreement when it refused to pay the health care coverage of two police officers who were injured in the line of duty. The officers had changed physicians without submitting a written request and receiving permission to do so. However, the agreement provides that the city will pay all costs of on-the-job injuries, with the qualification that an employee will assign recoveries from third parties to the city.

Source: "State and Local Arbitration Notes," Bureau of National Affairs, *Government Employee Relations* 38 (August 8, 2000), 913.

In 1994 relations between labor and management in Detroit were adversarial and the city was not making notable progress in such areas as economic development, efficiency of services, and quality of life. Detroit mayor Dennis Archer is proud of the city's successes in recent years, including billions of dollars in development, workforce training initiatives, improvements in service delivery, and renovations to the infrastructure. Mayor Archer credits the turnaround to labor-management cooperation.

Source: "The Power of Partnership," *IPMA News* 65 (June 1999), 6.

In Philadelphia, some would say that the union used the Republican National Convention as leverage to negotiate a more favorable contract than could have been obtained under normal circumstances—in effect, holding the city hostage to its demands. Others might argue, however, that such tactics are justified because management will use technicalities to avoid complying with a contract, as illustrated in Memphis. Then again, maybe both views are wrong. As Detroit has demonstrated, the solution is for unions and management to replace confrontation with cooperation and work together for the greater good.

Actually, all the views expressed above can be supported to some degree, but mainly to the extent that anecdotal evidence tends to support previously held perceptions. Some workers in Philadelphia felt that the city used a "divide and conquer" strategy in negotiating with the two district councils. The fact that the dispute over health benefits for police officers in Memphis went to arbitration could indicate that the city was seeking clarification of an issue with broader implications. And while the Detroit experience is positive, participative decision making (PDM) is an emerging development in labor relations. Even its advocates point out that PDM is not necessarily appropriate in all situations and that more information is needed on implementation strategies and results.

*The title of this vignette is borrowed from Harry J. Wellington and Ralph K. Winter Jr., whose 1971 book with that title is a classic in labor relations.

INTRODUCTION

As the opening vignette suggests, there are widely different views regarding labor unions in local government. It is clear, however, that unionization has important implications for HR management. Membership in public employee unions began to grow dramatically during the 1960s and 1970s, particularly at the state and local level, even as union membership in the private sector declined as a percentage of the total labor force. As this development has taken place, a framework for labor relations has evolved in local government centered on the unique process known as collective bargaining. This subject, while very important to unionized organizations, obviously does not apply in many local governments. Moreover, labor relations is a specialized and complex area covered by a number of books,[1] and an in-depth analysis is beyond the scope of this chapter. As an overview of the area, the chapter covers the evolution of labor-management relations, issues of labor relations in local government, the legal framework, unionization and collective bargaining, and trends in labor relations.

EVOLUTION OF LABOR-MANAGEMENT RELATIONS

The history of labor-management relations in the United States is long and complex, and labor relations at the local government level has been influenced by a number of key developments in both public and private sectors. The local government manager will be confronted with difficult labor relations issues, an understanding of which is greatly aided by knowledge of the historical background and of recent trends in the union movement.

The American Trade Union Movement

Developments in the private sector have had a major influence on labor relations in government, particularly at the state and local level. It is therefore important to review the history of the American trade union movement.[2]

Unions, as they are known today, did not exist before 1800. There were organizations known as guilds, or joint associations of workers and employers in such crafts as shoemaking, masonry, and printing. True unions developed when workers began to realize that their skills gave them bargaining power, usually over wages, with their employers. These early unions, which had no legal right to exist, faced a hostile public policy environment. Unionizing attempts were prosecuted for restraint of trade under the criminal conspiracy doctrine of common law. It was not until 1842 that they first gained limited legal recognition, when a Massachusetts court held in *Commonwealth v. Hunt* that organized labor activities were lawful. However, full legal support (federal or state) for activities such as collective bargaining and strikes would not come until almost a hundred years later.

Unions experienced rapid growth throughout the 1800s, although they were still strongly opposed by management and government. Heavy industrialization during the mid 1800s provided a new and rapidly growing industrial labor force of nonskilled and semiskilled workers. This segment of the workforce was organized on a national basis by the Knights of Labor (KOL), which became involved in strike actions during the 1880s. The union lost control of its members and was blamed for unauthorized strikes, sabotage, and acts of violence including the famous Haymarket Riot in Chicago in 1886. By the late 1890s the KOL had failed.

The labor organization that gained dominance in the late 19th century was the American Federation of Labor (AFL), a federation of craft and skilled trade unions. Less confrontational than the KOL, the AFL grew steadily, surviving the depression of 1893–96, scientific management, yellow dog contracts, court injunctions against strikes, and the Great Depression of the 1930s. Throughout this time, the AFL refused to admit unskilled workers. During the early 1900s, the Industrial Workers of the World (IWW) attempted to organize these workers, along with the skilled, into one large union, but like the KOL before it the IWW soon failed. Interest in union representation for industrial workers remained alive, however. In 1938, seven national unions that had been expelled from the AFL formed the Congress of Industrial Organizations (CIO). Unlike the AFL unions, which organized on a craft basis, the CIO unions organized on an industry basis.

The 1930s were characterized by a great deal of labor unrest. Employers' denial of employees' rights to organize and refusal to bargain with unions led to strikes and other conflicts that often escalated into violence. This struggle also affected the flow of commerce and further aggravated the already dismal economic conditions. The situation changed dramatically with the passage of the Wagner Act of 1935. This act gave employees the right to form unions and bargain collectively with management, as well as to engage in activities such as strikes, picketing, and boycotts. The act also established the National Labor Relations Board (NLRB), an administrative agency, to conduct representation elections and adjudicate unfair labor practices of employers. The act was modified in 1947 by the Taft-Hartley Act (adding unfair labor practices of unions) and in 1959 by the Landrum-Griffin Act (adding rights of union members), but its fundamental provisions are still intact. The act is important because it provides the model for public sector labor legislation at the state level (discussed in a following section).

By the onset of World War II, organized labor was steadily increasing in membership. An intense rivalry developed between the CIO and AFL, which began organizing production workers. In 1955 the two organizations merged into one major national federation, the AFL-CIO. This was probably the high-water mark of the American trade union movement. Unions still represent a large number of employees, and their success has had a spillover effect, with many nonunion shops granting workers pay and benefits comparable to those gained by unions through collective bargaining. Organized labor is still a minority movement, however. Moreover, the relative proportion of unionized labor force participants has shown a steady decline over the last 40 years. Although membership in unions increased slightly during the 1990s, unions in 1999 represented only about 9.4 percent of the private sector workforce.[3]

THE EVOLUTION OF UNIONISM IN GOVERNMENT

Unionism in government has followed two evolutionary tracks, developing somewhat differently in regard to federal employees than for workers in state and local governments.[4]

UNIONISM IN THE FEDERAL GOVERNMENT

Public employee organizations first became active during the early 1800s, mainly in federal shipyards. The first major labor dispute affecting the operations of the federal government occurred in Philadelphia in 1839 when workers in the Naval Shipyard went out on strike. The confrontation ended when President Andrew Jackson personally granted the federal employees a 10-hour day. The first federal employee organization of any significant national consequence was created by New York letter carriers in 1863. In the late 1880s, postal workers began to organize with the Knights of Labor, and the National Association of Letter Carriers was established in 1890. The National Federation of Postal Clerks, affiliated with the AFL, was formed in 1906.

The pressure exerted by postal worker unions on Congress for wage increases and improvements in working conditions drew strong reactions from the federal government, culminating in President Theodore Roosevelt's "gag rule" forbidding all lobbying activities of federal employees. Postal workers campaigned against the anti-gag rule and secured enough congressional support to pass the Lloyd-LaFollette Act of 1912, which guaranteed the right of federal employees to join unions and petition Congress either individually or through their organizations. A number of other organizational efforts were made, including most civil service occupations. In 1917, the National Federation of Federal Employees (NFFE) was formed as the first "umbrella" organization for all federal employees, followed in 1932 by the American Federation of Government Employees (AFGE) and shortly thereafter by the National Association of Government Employees (NAGE). These unions had no statutory basis for collective bargaining, and attempts to pass a federal law failed repeatedly. Employer-employee relationships continued to be determined unilaterally by management.

In 1962 President John F. Kennedy issued Executive Order 10988, establishing for the first time the principle that federal workers had the right to form unions and bargain collectively (but no right to strike). This order had major significance in public sector labor relations, even though it applied only to federal employees. The order gave a degree of respectability to public employee unions and stimulated state legislatures to give state and local employees the right to organize and bargain collectively. While Kennedy's order had great symbolic importance, there were a number of practical problems with its implementation, involving form of recognition, individual agency control over labor relations, bargaining unit determination, and impasse resolution. Many provisions were modified by subsequent executive orders of Presidents Nixon and Ford.

Postal workers gained full bargaining rights under the Postal Reorganization Act of 1970. A statutory basis for labor-management relations for federal employees was achieved with the passage of the Civil Service Reform Act of 1978. The act established the Federal Labor Relations Authority (FLRA) to monitor labor-management relations and requires arbitration of unresolved grievances. Strikes by federal employees are still prohibited. This fact was forcefully pointed out by President Ronald Reagan to the striking Professional Air Traffic Controllers Organization (PATCO) in 1981. The president broke the strike (and the union) by dismissing 11,000 controllers.

In 1993, President Bill Clinton attempted to generate increased cooperation between labor and management with Executive Order 12871. This order is limited to the federal sector of labor but can serve as an example for the other sectors. It provides the path for management and labor to reach this "higher-echelon partnership" through the use of committees and councils to identify and solve problems. In 1999, President Clinton sent a memorandum to the heads of executive departments and agencies reaffirming the executive order. He noted that benefits had resulted from increased labor-management cooperation but urged both sides to "do more."[5]

UNIONISM IN STATE AND LOCAL GOVERNMENT

The drive for unionization in state and local government began in the 1800s with police and firefighters. In 1919, Boston police officers went on strike. While there were many grievances, the major issue was the right of police officers to form a union and affiliate with the American Federation of Labor. The violence surrounding the strike assumed major national significance, and Governor Calvin Coolidge subsequently called in the Massachusetts National Guard to restore order. The political fallout from the Boston police strike was a major setback to public sector unionism at all levels and helped lead to the selection of Coolidge as the nominee for vice president on the Republican ticket in 1920. Coolidge became president in 1923 when Warren G. Harding died in office.

Until the 1960s, state and local organizations tended to be separated into organizations of teachers, firefighters, and police and were not strongly influential. The largest state and local union today, the American Federation of State, County, and Municipal Employees (AFSCME), originated in Wisconsin in 1932, but because of its conservative approach it did not become a major force until the 1960s. During that time it adopted a more aggressive style, which led to substantial gains in membership.[7] Today the AFSCME, with its strong national office and network of "intermediary" councils and locals, is the most dominant and visible union representing local government employees.

http://www.afscme.org/
The American Federation of State, County, and Municipal Employees (AFSCME) is the largest state and local union.

Several factors contributed to the continuing growth of unionization in state and local governments during the 1970s.[8] The number of government employees increased, with most of the growth occurring in state and local government. Private sector unions saw the rapidly expanding government workforce as a prime source for new members. Public employees had noticed the private sector experience, in which unions had gained improved working conditions and wage and fringe benefit increases for their members. The legal environment became more favorable

AFSCME: NO SHRINKING VIOLET

The American Federation of State, County, and Municipal Workers (AFSCME) is one of the most prominent unions representing local government employees. International president Gerald W. McEntee and International secretary treasurer William Lucy suggest that AFSCME is the "best union in America." Other unions and local government officials might disagree with that assessment, but McEntee and Lucy do make a case, citing its large membership, aggressive staff, effective programs, and record of winning nearly 90 percent of its representation elections. There is little room for misunderstanding in the statement of the union's purpose, which is "to make sure that each and every member of the AFSCME gets a fair deal from the boss and from the politicians."

Source: "About AFSCME," *http://www.afscme.org* (October 2000).

when the domination of state legislatures by rural, predominately antiunion interests changed under U.S. Supreme Court–ordered reapportionment of Congress and the 50 state legislatures on the basis of "one person, one vote." Finally, young people and minorities, who tended to be distrustful of the "establishment" and favorably disposed toward unions, began to enter the workforce in large numbers.

In 1999, 37.3 percent of public sector workers belonged to unions. Within this group, local government workers had the highest unionization rate, at 42.9 percent.[9] These workers are represented by both local organizations and national unions, as shown in Exhibit 15-1. Much unionization in state and local government is still functionally specific and structured on divisions of professionals, such as educators, police and fire protection employees, and miscellaneous government professions. Union strength varies from region to region and from state to state because of fundamental differences in the determinants of unionization. A major determinant is the state's collective bargaining legislation. There tends to be a reciprocal relationship between a permissive legal environment, which allows collective bargaining (discussed in a following section), and high state and local government union membership levels.[10]

http://www.nea.org/
The National Education Association (NEA) has more than 2.5 million union members at schools and colleges throughout the United States.

WHY DO GOVERNMENT EMPLOYEES JOIN UNIONS?

While factors underlying union membership in the private sector have been researched for 50 years, the determinants of public employee union membership are not well understood. A study of 12,557 state and local government workers provides useful insight.

- Males and nonwhites are more likely to join unions than females and whites.
- Private sector union density has a strong, positive relationship to membership probability, especially at the local (municipal) level.
- Individuals with jobs that require occupation-specific training and have limited opportunities for exit to the private sector, such as teachers, police, and firefighters, are more likely to join unions.
- Collective bargaining provisions in state law increase the probability of union membership.
- Union security provisions have a substantial positive effect, particularly the mandatory agency shop with dues checkoff.
- Provisions for resolving bargaining impasses through compulsory arbitration significantly increase the probability of union membership.

Source: Based on Greg Hundley, "Who Joins Unions in the Public Sector? The Effects of Individual Characteristics and the Law," *Journal of Labor Research* 4 (Fall 1988), 301–321.

EXHIBIT 15-1

NATIONAL UNIONS
REPRESENTING
LOCAL
GOVERNMENT
EMPLOYEES, 2000

Name of Union	No. of Members
National Education Association (NEA)	2,500,000
American Federation of State, County, and Municipal Employees (AFSCME)	1,300,000
American Federation of Teachers (AFT)	800,000
Service Employees International Union (SEIU)	585,000
Fraternal Order of Police (FOP)	280,000
International Association of Fire Fighters (IAFF)	237,542
Teamsters (IBT)	170,000
Communication Workers of America (CWA)	125,000
Laborers' International Union of North America (LIUNA)	85,000
American Nurses Association (ANA)	25,000

Source: Compiled by Margaret Nanson, Auburn University, from the following: Information or links to NEA, AFSCME, AFT, SEIU, IAFF, LIUNA and CWA: *http://www.aflcio.org/*; FOP: *http://www.fop.org/*; IDT: *http://www.teamster.org/*; ANA: *http://www.ana.org/*.

Following the example set in the federal government, labor-management relations in state and local government have become less adversarial in recent years (see concluding section). Some authorities have suggested that the continued success of unions in both sectors depends on working with management to create a cooperative atmosphere.[11]

ISSUES OF LABOR RELATIONS IN LOCAL GOVERNMENT

A number of significant issues arise in a government's relationship with organized employees. Probably the leading issue in the field of public sector labor relations is the legitimacy of a union strike. The major reason employees organize is to bargain collectively for terms and conditions of employment that they could not achieve individually. When parties cannot agree on these terms and conditions, the ultimate union bargaining chip is the threat of a strike. The legitimacy of bargaining itself can be called into question, however, when one of the parties is a democratically chosen government. Consideration of these and other government-labor issues all in one way or another depend on interpretation or valuation of three interrelated elements: the concept of sovereignty, the practical matter of the nature of government services, and the principles of democratic process.[12]

The concept of sovereignty has its origins in English common law. English kings (or queens) received their mandate from God and their will was law. In the United States the citizenry as a whole exercises sovereignty, with an elected government carrying out the will of the people. Through most of the history of the United States, interpretation of this concept has held that the government at any level is "sovereign" and has sole power to establish conditions under which public employees must work. From this perspective, government bargaining with a group of employees, in which the government yields part of its power to a nonrepresentative group, would violate the concept of sovereignty.

The special nature of government services also tends to make labor relations in government very different from those of the private sector. To a great extent, a unit of government has a monopoly on its services, which are felt to be essential or at least highly important. Therefore union actions that disrupt such services can represent a threat to the public welfare. Local government employees who provide such services, particularly "essential" services such as law enforcement and fire protection, can hold the public welfare hostage to their demands. Even where local governments provide a service that can more readily be privatized, such as solid waste collection or public transportation, contracting the service is rarely an immediate option. Moreover, providing the service usually takes precedence over making a profit. A private company would have to pay all its costs and make a reasonable profit, given the price that people would be willing to pay for a particular service. It would not accede to any demand that might drive it out of business. In government this check on the bargaining power of a group of employees is not necessarily present. Governments can, and often do, subsidize various services.

The status and power of public employee unions can also be questioned from the standpoint of maintaining the democratic process. Even if the concept of sovereignty is less strictly interpreted, public employee organizations are political forces partly inside and partly outside government, and thus in a special position to influence public policy. As mentioned above, the threat of a possible strike or slowdown (lawful or not) in performance of public services can be a very powerful weapon. A public employee union may also be in a position to manipulate the government decision-making process. If the union is unsuccessful at the bargaining table, it can circumvent the process and appeal directly to elected officials, whose reelection may depend on the efficient and timely provision of government services. The basic question is whether institutionalizing the power of public employee unions can leave the public, or competing groups in the political process, at a permanent and substantial disadvantage.

Possible violation of the concept or process of democratic majority rule and the threat of interruption of services for which there are no market-based substitutes are serious issues. For local governments, state laws provide a legal framework for dealing with these and other important policy questions.

THE LEGAL FRAMEWORK FOR LABOR RELATIONS

At present there is no federal law governing public sector labor relations at the state and local level. Until recently the U.S. Supreme Court had held in *National League of Cities v. Usery* that the Tenth Amendment grants a substantial measure of sovereignty to the states in employment matters. This, however, changed dramatically in 1985 when the Court reversed itself in *Garcia v. San Antonio Metropolitan Transit Authority*. In deciding that the commerce clause permitted states and local governments to be covered by the provisions of the Fair Labor Standards Act, the Court opened the door for such a law. In fact, the proposed Fire Fighters Labor Act of 1987 was the prototype of a national law.[13] The latest attempt to mandate state bargaining legislation is the Public Safety Employer-Employee Cooperation Bill introduced in the U.S. Senate on May 12, 2000 by Sen. Mike DeWine (R-Ohio).[14] Each state, however, now has the flexibility to adopt its own labor relations practices, and most states have well-developed programs, although some, such as Alabama and Mississippi, have little or no legislation. State labor relations can be divided into the **meet and confer** and the **collective bargaining** approaches.

Federal legislation now being considered would require the Federal Labor Relations Authority (FLRA) to determine whether each of the 50 states provides collective bargaining rights to
state and local public safety employees. For states without formal procedures the FLRA would
issue regulations establishing such procedures.

**SHOULD STATES BE REQUIRED
TO ESTABLISH COLLECTIVE
BARGAINING PROCEDURES?**

Unions including the Fraternal Order of Police and International Association of Fire Fighters support such legislation, not-
ing that they are aware of the federalism issues involved and,
rather than have the federal government mandate a law, the leg-
islation instead seeks to encourage the development of 50 state laws administered by state
agencies and enforced by state courts. Since only two states (Virginia and North Carolina)
currently bar public safety employees from engaging in collective bargaining, they suggest
that the legislation will require little more federal intervention than already exists. Gilbert G.
Gallegos, national president of the FOP, stated that the legislation would be "a modest, but
crucial effort" that "merely establishes a framework" for collective bargaining.

The National League of Cities, National Association of Counties, U.S. Conference of May-
ors, and other employer groups oppose the legislation on the basis that it would require most
states to substantially modify their current laws or face regulation by the FLRA. In addition,
they contend that Congress does not have the authority to abrogate the Eleventh Amendment
immunity of states under the Commerce Clause of the U.S. Constitution. According to attorney R. Theodore Clark, who represents several employer groups, the legislation would be a
mistake. "The needs of state and local government in employer-employee relations can best be
determined on a local basis rather than by resort to federal legislation," he said.

Source: "Police, Firefighters Urge Senate Support of Bill Setting State Bargaining Standards," Bureau of National Affairs,
Government Employee Relations 38 (August 1, 2000), 873–874.

THE MEET AND CONFER APPROACH

In the meet and confer approach the employer consents to a discussion with representatives of an employee organization regarding terms and conditions of employment.
This approach to labor relations is philosophically compatible with a strict construction
of sovereignty. The meet and confer approach has the following characteristics:

- The partners (labor and management) are not equal.
- The employer has no duty to bargain.
- The employer establishes the agenda for discussion.
- Outcomes ultimately depend on management's viewpoint.
- Management retains almost all rights.
- Management exercises final authority.
- Labor laws are enforced by state courts rather than specialized agencies.[15]

The meet and confer approach is useful to the extent that it provides a mechanism for the union to raise issues with management and make a case for its proposal. On the other hand, it does not ensure that its proposal will be considered or
even taken seriously. The union may achieve all or part of what it is seeking, but this
depends mainly on such factors as having accurate data and making a convincing
argument rather than management's obligation to agree, offer a counterproposal
or explain why it is not willing to agree. This approach is sometimes viewed as a
"middle ground" between formal collective bargaining (discussed below) and the
lack of any process at all. One authority suggests, however, that meet and confer,
with its emphasis on employer control of rule making and administration, is a "baby
step" in the direction of full bargaining rights for unions.[16]

THE COLLECTIVE BARGAINING APPROACH

http://www.nlrb.gov/
index.html
The National Labor Relations Board (NLRB) is an independent federal agency created in 1935 to enforce the National Labor Relations Act.

The majority of states having comprehensive labor laws follow the negotiations, or collective bargaining, approach.[17] This approach is modeled after National Labor Relations Board (NLRB) procedures that have applied to the private sector since the Wagner Act was passed in 1935. This model includes:

- The right of employees to form unions for purpose of collective bargaining
- An administrative agency to determine the bargaining unit and administer procedures
- Exclusive recognition of any union winning majority support
- The employer's compulsory duty to bargain with the union
- Management rights clause excluding certain matters from negotiations
- Impasse resolution procedures
- Union security provisions
- Codes of unfair labor practices

Before moving to an examination of the sequence of events during the collective bargaining process, it is necessary to discuss two aspects of the model that impact on the process at all stages. These are union security provisions and unfair labor practices.

UNION SECURITY PROVISIONS

Certain arrangements are intended to strengthen and stabilize the position of the union. These provisions may be negotiated in the contract or set forth in the state laws that cover labor-management relations, or both. The following are typical **union security provisions**:

- **Closed shop.** Individual must become a member of the representing union prior to employment (provision is illegal but continues to exist *de facto* in a few settings).
- **Union shop**. Individual must become a member of the representing union after a period of time as specified by the collective bargaining agreement, usually 30 days.
- **Agency shop**. Individual need not become a member of the representing union but must pay a service charge for representation in collective bargaining, grievances, arbitration, and so on.
- **Maintenance-of-membership**. Individual must remain a member of the representing union after joining.
- **Checkoff**. Individual may request payroll deduction of union dues, to be remitted to the representing union.[18]

http://www.nrtw.org/
The National Right to Work Legal Defense Foundation provides news, issue briefs, and comprehensive information regarding "right-to-work."

The use of union security provisions has steadily increased since the mid-1960s. Such provisions are desirable for unions because they guarantee a high rate of dues payment and ensure steady membership and a financially sound organization. It may also be argued that union security is desirable for the employer, who gains labor peace from dealing with a stable union. A final point regarding union security involves state "right to work" laws. The Taft-Hartley Act, which prohibits the closed shop (individual must be a member of the union before being hired), permits states to enact **"right-to-work" laws** forbidding employers and unions from agreeing to union and agency shops. Such laws, which greatly diminish the strength of unions, are found mainly in Sunbelt states and are uncommon in states with a strong union tradition.

UNFAIR LABOR PRACTICES

Following the example of the National Labor Relations Board (NLRB), most comprehensive state laws set forth codes of unfair practices that apply to both employers and unions. Some of the commonly prohibited practices are shown in Exhibit 15-2. Upon the filing of a complaint, the administrative agency investigates complaints of unfair practices by either the union or the employer. Usually the agency has the authority to issue cease and desist orders on its own or to seek a court injunction. An allegation of an unfair practice may arise at any time, including during organization of the union, representation elections, contract negotiations, resolution of an impasse, or administration of the contract.

UNIONIZATION AND COLLECTIVE BARGAINING

Collective bargaining is a unique process that identifies and resolves conflicts between labor and management. This section examines unit determination, election and certification of the union, the conduct of contract negotiations, and impasse resolution.

EXHIBIT 15-2

EXAMPLES OF
UNFAIR LABOR
PRACTICES IN
GOVERNMENT

Unfair Employer Practices

- Interfering, restraining, or coercing public employees in the exercise of statutory rights
- Interfering or assisting in formation or operation of an employee organization
- Encouraging or discouraging membership in any labor organization through employment actions
- Discharging or discriminating against an employee because of filing charges, giving testimony, forming or joining an employee organization
- Denying rights of exclusive representation to the legally designated bargaining agent
- Refusing to follow statutory impasse procedures
- Instituting a lockout
- Dealing directly with employees rather than with their bargaining representatives on bargaining issues
- Violating the terms of a contract

Unfair Union Practices

- Interfering with, restraining, or coercing public employees in regard to protecting the exercise of statutory rights
- Interfering with, restraining, or coercing a public employer in regard to protecting the exercise of employee rights or selecting a bargaining representative
- Refusing to meet and bargain in good faith
- Refusing to follow statutory impasse procedures
- Engaging in or instigating a strike
- Interfering with an employee's work performance or productivity

Source: Based on Richard C. Kearney with David G. Carnevale, *Labor Relations in Public Sector*, 3d ed. (New York: Marcel Dekker, 2001), 76–77.

ORGANIZING AND DETERMINING THE BARGAINING UNIT

Before a union can obtain the legal right to represent employees of a local government, a majority of employees must support the union. Typically the union will conduct an organizing campaign. Activities include distributing flyers, holding meetings with groups of employees, and obtaining signatures on petitions by members of what the union envisions as a **bargaining unit**. The bargaining unit is the specific group of operating employees determined to be eligible for union representation, such as police, fire, labor and trades, clerical, and so forth. Those states which authorize collective bargaining for public employees typically invest a public employee relations board or commission with the power to determine bargaining units in local government. The criteria used in determining the makeup of a bargaining unit vary by states but are similar to those used by the NLRB. They generally include the following:

- **Community of Interest**. This is determined by a number of factors, including similarity of duties, skills, working conditions, job classification, promotional ladders, and supervision.
- **Bargaining History**. This refers to previous relationships between labor and management in the jurisdiction, including patterns of negotiation and representation.
- **Efficiency of Operations**. This factor must be considered when a bargaining structure imposed over traditional administrative groupings might disrupt personnel policies and practices.
- **Unit Size**. The group must be large enough to negotiate effectively with the government; a large number of small bargaining units can create serious administrative problems for the government and shortchange the unions by spreading the time and attention of both parties' representatives too thin.
- **Exclusion of Supervisory Employees**. The operating assumption is that such employees are part of management and should not be permitted to bargain alongside their subordinates.[19]

In regard to these criteria, two points should be mentioned. The criterion of community of interest is the most widely used in that a local government has diverse groups of employees (labor, trades, transportation, clerical, police, fire, etc.). The number of bargaining units that would be established differs among state agencies. Supervisory exclusion is less rigidly interpreted in the public sector. Some states exclude all supervisors while others include classifications of "working supervisors" (for example, police sergeant and fire lieutenant). Some states allow supervisors to be represented in autonomous bargaining units.

ELECTION AND CERTIFICATION

When the bargaining unit has been determined, the next step is to determine if the union will be allowed to represent the unit in collective bargaining. This may occur through voluntary recognition of the union by the employer, but more typically through a representation election. The election may be requested by the employer or by the union, depending on state law. Normally the union must produce evidence indicating that a significant proportion of employees in the unit wish to be represented. Most state laws prohibit management from using force, threats, or promises of benefits in an attempt to defeat the union. If any union receives at least 50 percent of the votes in an election, that union is generally recognized as the exclusive bargaining agent for all employees in the unit.

Certification by the state or local labor relations agency normally stands for at least one year. The status of the union may be challenged by another union or by employees. If this happens, a **decertification** election procedure similar to the above is used to determine whether the union will continue as the bargaining agent. If the union loses, it is decertified and a new election may then be held to decide whether to select another union. If a majority votes against, the collective status of the bargaining unit is dissolved.

CONTRACT NEGOTIATIONS

The negotiation of a contract between the union and management is the heart of collective bargaining. When a collective bargaining relationship has been established, the scope of bargaining issues is extremely important. These issues fall into three categories.[20] **Mandatory bargaining issues** almost always include wages, hours, and other terms and conditions of employment. In this regard, states tend to follow the NLRB model (federal employees cannot bargain over wages and hours). **Prohibited issues** are usually those which are covered by civil service regulations, related to the organizational "mission," and set forth in state legislation as **management rights**. Rights reserved to management in public sector contracts are usually much broader than in the private sector. **Permissive issues** are those that fall in between. The phrase "other terms and conditions of employment" has led to disputes over which issues are negotiable and which are not.

Collective bargaining involves several mutual obligations of labor and management. These are to meet at reasonable times, confer and negotiate in good faith, and execute a written agreement. The term *reasonable times* has been determined by several NLRB decisions that have been carried over into the public sector and used as guidelines. For example, meetings on Sunday or late at night are unreasonable times. If contract negotiations are held during regular working hours, the union negotiators are usually compensated at their regular rate of pay.

The laws of the individual states require that bargaining be carried out in good faith, although this term has not been precisely defined. In general it is the duty to approach negotiations with an open mind and with a sincere purpose to reach an agreement. Most decisions that provide guidance in this area were made by the NLRB and the courts in regard to the private sector. It can, however, be reasonably assumed that the understanding of good faith would be essentially the same in both sectors. Exhibit 15-3 illustrates union and management obligations.

All states require that a written agreement (contract) must be executed with regard to wages, hours, and other conditions of employment. In this way both employers and the union are prevented from attempting to circumvent each other by construing verbal agreements. In addition to the mandatory issues of wages and hours, the contract may cover virtually any issue, including benefits, control over work scheduling, overtime and holiday pay, work rules, disciplinary procedures, and pay equity (comparable worth).

CONDUCTING NEGOTIATIONS

Before negotiations actually begin, both sides will typically attempt to gain a public relations advantage. The official position of the employer may be that agreeing to the union demands will financially cripple the government and can only result in a tax increase. The union perhaps counters this by alleging that management is hiding discretionary funds in secret budget categories and has a record of wasting

EXHIBIT 15-3

Mutual Obligations

- Make serious attempt to resolve differences and reach common ground.
- Offer counterproposal when other party's proposal is rejected.
- Do not constantly shift positions with regard to contract terms.
- Do not engage in evasive behavior during negotiations.
- Be willing to incorporate oral agreements into written contract.

Examples of Employer Bad Faith

- Engaging in "take it or leave it" approach while attempting to bypass the union.
- Refusing to furnish wage information pertaining to nonunion employees.
- Granting a wage increase over union protest before bargaining to impasse.
- Refusing to compensate union representatives for bargaining during nonworking hours.
- Refusing to divulge names of chemical substances used and employee medical records when bargaining over health and safety issues.

Examples of Union Bad Faith

- Forbidding union members to work overtime in violation of agreement.
- Refusing to bargain without merger of historically separate bargaining units.
- Forbidding union members to accept temporary supervisory assignments in violation of agreement.
- Insisting that persons designated as stewards be hired by employer.

Source: Based on Benjamin J. Taylor and Fred Whitney, *Labor Relations Law*, 6th ed. (Englewood Cliffs, N.J.: Prentice-Hall, 1992), 182–184.

funds on unnecessary items (for example, high salaries and "perks" for government executives, unnecessary facilities, etc.). Much of this verbiage is an attempt to gain leverage and does not represent the bargaining position of either side.

It is important that the employer understand that the negotiations are bilateral. The paternalistic system exemplified by the meet and confer approach is replaced by an adversarial perspective (but with due consideration for the rights and responsibilities of both parties). Management negotiations should focus on carrying the management position, not on what might be best for employees. For that reason it is often useful to use labor relations experts as negotiators, rather than elected officials or managers.

Although the process varies among jurisdictions, traditional collective bargaining tends to exhibit recognizable strategies and patterns of behavior.[21] In the negotiations process, a large number of proposals and counterproposals are offered. Whatever agreement is reached, the employer will pay all or part of the cost. It is important that management be able to accurately evaluate these proposals and make a rational decision. For example, the union may agree on the employer's latest offer on wages and benefits if the employer will agree to pay employees for skills learned through cross-training, regardless of the job they are performing at the time. Determining the cost requires a fairly complex analysis. A practical tool that expands management's decision-making capacity is a computer-based decision support system (DSS).[22] A DSS can interact with the organization's human resource information system (HRIS), which is described in Chapter 5, and make appropriate calculations quickly and efficiently.

Neither the employer nor the union is compelled to agree to a proposal or grant a concession. However, each party must continue to bargain in good faith and to offer counterproposals until an agreement has been reached or an impasse has occurred.

IMPASSE RESOLUTION

An impasse occurs when negotiators for labor and management are not able to reach an agreement on their own and either refuse to continue bargaining or conclude that further bargaining would yield no agreement. A number of procedures are available for resolving impasses. The major procedures include mediation, fact-finding, and interest arbitration.[23]

MEDIATION

In **mediation**, a third neutral party facilitates communication and uses powers of persuasion to assist the two parties in reaching an agreement. The mediator may hold a joint meeting to clarify the most recent proposal on unresolved bargaining issues. Then the mediator meets with the parties separately to assess how much each is willing to negotiate. Moving back and forth between the two sides, the negotiator attempts to close the gap. If the parties can be brought close together, the mediator will likely hold a joint meeting to finalize an agreement.

FACT-FINDING

Fact-finding is a more structured form of third-party intervention, used when impasse is reached or when mediation fails. The fact finder usually holds a hearing at which the positions of both sides are presented, together with all arguments and supporting evidence. When the hearing has been completed, the fact finder evaluates all of the facts and arguments and submits a report and recommendation for settlement. The recommendations are nonbinding and may be rejected by either or both parties. When fact-finding is successful in resolving an impasse it is usually because both parties feel that the recommendations are as favorable as they are going to get. Prospects for a settlement are also enhanced where public opinion swings behind the fact finder's recommendation.

INTEREST ARBITRATION

Interest arbitration is a judicial type of proceeding in which the arbitrator holds hearings at which each party submits evidence. These hearings can involve testimony and cross-examination. The arbitrator's decision, called an award, sets forth what action is to be taken with regard to each of the issues in the dispute. In binding arbitration, compliance with the award is mandatory. In advisory or nonbinding arbitration, each party considers the award and makes a decision on whether or not to accept it. Even nonbinding arbitration is powerful because of public pressure for a settlement. A special type of arbitration that should be mentioned is final-offer arbitration, in which the arbitrator chooses the more appropriate final offer of one of the parties (labor or management). The arbitrator may select the final offer of one party on all issues in dispute or make decisions on an issue-by-issue basis.

STRIKES BY GOVERNMENT EMPLOYEES

In the private sector the **strike** is an accepted alternative for resolving impasses and reaching agreement. This is not necessarily the case in the public sector. As has been

previously discussed, strikes by federal employees and postal workers are prohibited. In addition, strikes by public employees are illegal in a majority of states. However, this situation continues to evolve. In the first place, work stoppages, illegal or
not, occur with increasing frequency. Second, more and more states are granting
the right to strike for some public employees in certain situations. This section discusses the nature of public employee strikes, typical conditions surrounding the
statutory right to strike, and management responses to a strike.

THE NATURE AND USES OF THE STRIKE

The most straightforward use of a strike is as simply another mechanism for resolving a bargaining impasse. Negotiations in collective bargaining break down, third-
party intervention does not produce a settlement, and a work stoppage is the next
logical alternative for the union. The goal of a strike is to pressure management to
agree to union demands by ceasing performance of government services. This is
basically a public sector parallel to the private sector model.

   The above scenario is not typical, however. In many states strikes are illegal, and
work stoppages take other forms. Perhaps the most well known is the "blue flu," in
which police officers involved in a labor dispute call in sick. Other job actions accomplish the same purpose.[24] For example, in a work slowdown, production is reduced,
but workers remain at their jobs. Work slowdowns can evolve into "malicious obedi-
ence" (sometimes known as work-to-the-rule), by which employees follow procedures to the letter. Both tactics create a backlog of work. There is a developing consensus in public sector management that outlawing strikes does not necessarily
prevent them. Although strikes in government do not happen frequently, outlawing
them only makes them more unpredictable, changes their form, and leaves the government without an acceptable policy alternative when they occur.

STRIKE STATUTES

The current trend in dealing with strikes by state and local employees is to move
toward the private sector model but to prohibit strikes that endanger public health,
safety, or welfare (such as a police strike).[25] Since 1970, a number of states have
granted public sector employees the statutory right to strike. The rationale is well
stated by B. V. H. Schneider:

> [The right to strike is based] . . . on a belief that bargaining will thereby be strengthened
> along with a belief that true essentiality of certain types of employees can be defined, and
> should be, to protect the interests of both public employees and the public. It is the latter objec-
> tive which has most strongly marked these statutes. In no case is the right to strike unfet-
> tered. In all cases, a threat to the public health, safety, and/or welfare triggers a "no-strike"
> mechanism. In most cases, certain prestrike impasse procedures must be complied with.[26]

   This line of reasoning concludes that if public employees are to have bargaining
rights, the possibility of a strike (or threat of a strike) must be accepted. This is not
really a matter of preference; rather it is an acknowledgment of fact. For example,
in the negotiations in Philadelphia (refer to the opening vignette), the AFSCME
district councils represented nonuniformed workers with a legal right to strike.[27]
The focus is on how to guard against strikes and, if that fails, how to deal with them
effectively when they occur.

MANAGEMENT PLANNING FOR STRIKES

Whether legal or not, strikes by government employees are not uncommon. Strike
planning in government is essential both to maintain critical services and to ensure

a strong bargaining position. Local governments should develop strike contingency plans similar to other plans for emergency procedures. The plan should focus on maintaining services during the strike, gaining public support for the employer position, and seeking legal recourse.[28]

In maintaining services, priorities should be established with a view toward providing for essential needs. Skills inventories can be used as an aid in assigning supervisory personnel to operating tasks. Other sources of personnel include nonstriking workers, citizen volunteers, assistance from other jurisdictions or from state and federal government, and private contractors. During the strike the employer should attempt to gain public support for the management position. The objective is to use public opinion to pressure unions to return to work. This requires effective use of television, radio, and print media.

Legal action should be anticipated. If the strike is unlawful, the first action is to seek a court injunction. If strikers delay back-to-work orders or carry out other illegal actions, it may be necessary to invoke sanctions such as fines, suspensions, or terminations against union members or officials. More extreme penalties might be necessary, such as imprisonment for law violators or decertification of the union.

When a strike occurs, a command post should be established, with communications links to operations personnel, elected officials, the media, and the union. A strike task force composed of the executive leadership and staff and key department heads can be used to assess problems on a day-to-day basis and make necessary decisions.

ADMINISTERING THE CONTRACT

The collective bargaining agreement is a document that has a major impact on the daily working lives of union members and officials and of government supervisors and managers. The task now is effective implementation. This statement by Richard C. Kearney seems particularly appropriate:

> A collective bargaining agreement may be effectively administered by each party or it may be poorly administered. The union, like an unruly child, may attempt to tilt interpretation of the contract to its advantage by picketing, walkouts, or job slowdowns. An immature management may ignore the terms of the agreement and attempt [to impose] terms and conditions of employment unilaterally. . . . Conflict and controversy are inherent in any labor-management relationship. The key to a healthy and stable employment relationship, however, is to manage conflict and controversy over the implementation of the contract in a peaceful manner, with due consideration of the rights and responsibilities of each party.[29]

NATURE OF THE CONTRACT

Typically, contract provisions are classified as fixed, contingent, or related to dispute resolution. Fixed provisions usually remain unchanged during the life of a contract and relate to such topics as duration, wages, hours, benefits, union security, and union and management rights. Contingent provisions govern management or union actions resulting from a changing environment. These provisions address layoffs, recalls, discipline, work assignment, and similar topics. Dispute resolution procedures are designed to resolve conflicts arising in interpretation and application of provisions, particularly contingent provisions.

While it has been stated that the basic purpose of a contract is to clearly specify the relationships that will exist between the parties, most contracts are difficult to read and understand. They are often poorly drafted with long sentences, multisyllable words, and legal jargon.[30] For this and other reasons, situations can and do arise in which decisions made by management or actions taken by the unions appear to breach the terms of the contract. Grievance procedures are a means of resolving these questions in an orderly and timely fashion.

PROCESSING GRIEVANCES

Most grievance plans involve three steps, with a view toward settling the grievance at the lowest possible level.[31]

STEP 1—SUPERVISORY LEVEL. During this phase the complaint is raised and responded to at the supervisory level. The process is very informal. The supervisor should collect all facts, consult with the union steward if necessary, and make a decision. While it is hoped that the matter can be resolved at the supervisory level, this may not be possible. Therefore, the reasons for the decision should be documented in anticipation of an employee appeal.

STEP 2—UNION INTERVENTION. This phase begins a "formal" grievance. The complaint is reviewed by a union committee, reduced to writing, and forwarded to the next management level. The responsibility of management is to review the grievance in view of relevant contract language and other significant information and try to determine grounds for resolving the matter. In some cases a number of higher managerial levels may become involved. The designated level of management reviews the case and makes a decision.

STEP 3—BINDING ARBITRATION. Most negotiated public sector grievance procedures are settled through binding arbitration by a neutral third party. This process obviously cuts into such traditional management prerogatives as assigning work and disciplining employees. The union member, however, has nothing to lose at this stage and may succeed in having the management decision set aside. In contracts not calling for arbitration, mediation is sometimes used, or management may make a unilateral decision.

Although most issues are raised by the union, management also protects its interests under the contract. For example, management might complain that union activities such as excessive release time for union stewards, dissemination of unauthorized information, work stoppages, or certain political activities violate the terms of the contract. These disputes are typically settled by binding arbitration. It is clear that both management and the union have a major stake in effective contract administration. As Kearney stresses:

> Labor and management alike share responsibilities in ensuring that they and their constituencies live with the contract in a reasonably efficacious manner. . . they eschew "brinksmanship, constantly pushing grievance procedures to the final step in order to make the other side blink. . . . [They] seek to keep communications channels open and clear, and resolve grievances at the lowest possible level.[32]

TRENDS IN LABOR RELATIONS

Although the relationship between labor and management in the United States has traditionally been adversarial, there is a growing support among writers, business and government executives, and union leaders and their membership for a more cooperative approach as exemplified by the city of Detroit in the opening vignette.[33] For the union this involves giving up its traditional focus on workplace issues in return for more input into the decision processes of employers. For management it involves allowing the union to share authority, or exercise to some extent what have been known as "management prerogatives." The principle that "management acts and workers grieve" gives way to joint planning and cooperation.[34] This approach is known as labor management cooperation or **participative decision making (PDM)**.[35]

Although this approach is beginning to gain acceptance in both the public and private sectors, the major momentum for change has been with cities, counties, and states.[36] The impetus was provided by a task force appointed by former Secretary of Labor Robert Reich. The report of this task force in 1996 illustrated 47 examples of how state and local governments had greatly improved service quality and productivity through labor-management cooperation.[37] There are three major components in this approach. The first is education and training to facilitate teamwork and communication between management and workers. The second is mitigating conflict, which requires creating a better initial contract and reducing grievances. The final component is cost-efficient and improved service delivery. Exhibit 15-4 contains local government examples of benefits gained by labor management cooperation.

This approach is facilitated by labor-management committees or LMCs, which may represent several organizations and unions in a community. Recently LMCs from 27 counties, cities, and states participated in a two-and-a-half-day program at the Harvard University School of Government. Teams made up of union members and government administrators learned how to create and sustain cooperative labor-management initiatives through problem-solving and team-building methods.[38]

Participative decision making seems to offer an opportunity to further democratic processes by bringing unions and management together to recognize and define their interests and the public's interest, rather than narrow self-interests. The traditional approach that relies heavily on restrictive on contract language and grievance procedures appears to be increasingly out of step with the needs of competent and, particularly, high-performing organizations. Public employee unions and management have made considerable progress in recent years, and further innovation and experimentation holds the prospect of gaining improved delivery of government services while enhancing the dignity, morale, and quality of worklife for employees.[39]

An important aspect of labor management cooperation is interest-based bargaining (IBB), also called "mutual gains" bargaining or "win-win" bargaining. This is a form of negotiating where the parties look for common ground and attempt to satisfy mutual interests through the bargaining process. Whereas traditional bargaining focuses on

INTEREST-BASED BARGAINING

taking and defending positions, in IBB the emphasis is on exploring the interests of the parties and how they can be reconciled. IBB is an effort to look behind positions to determine the needs of the parties and whether there are mutually acceptable ways that labor and management can satisfy those needs.

IBB differs substantially from traditional negotiating techniques in its reliance upon a variety of techniques to promote open communication, such as brainstorming, facilitation, and information sharing. The purpose of exchanging ideas and information is to develop options. Those options are then evaluated in terms of both their effectiveness in resolving the problem and their acceptability to the parties. The objective of the entire process is to reach agreement by consensus. In consensus decision making, the intent is to achieve a resolution that everyone can accept and support even though that course of action might not be their first choice.

Source: U.S. Department of the Interior, "Interest Based Bargaining," *http://www.doi.gov/hrm* (November 18, 1998).

EXAMPLES
OF LABOR-
MANAGEMENT
COOPERATION
IN LOCAL
GOVERNMENT

Mercer Island, Washington. Working closely with maintenance workers and their union, the city established self-directed work teams to reengineer virtually all aspects of their department including the mission, operational procedures, and worker and management responsibilities. The labor contract was transformed from a long, cumbersome legalistic document into a simpler, service-focused agreement. Accomplishments have included a reduction in full-time positions by attrition from 42 to 35, demonstrated improvements in productivity, customer satisfaction and morale, improved record keeping, and enhanced community and political acceptability of the department's efforts.

Multnomah County, Oregon. In 1993 the leadership of the county sought ways to improve services and increase efficiency. What has emerged is a plan called Reaching Excellent Services Using Leadership & Team Strategies (RESULTS). Since then the county has engaged in a serious and effective labor-management partnership that produced a savings of $160,000 in its first round of projects from a workforce already credited with being hard working and productive. Both county and union officials stress the importance of a core of people with skills in team building, communication, and facilitation to work through changes in historic relationships and workplace culture.

Peoria, Illinois. In 1994 health care costs were climbing annually at a rate of 9 to 14 percent and the city's revenues were declining. The solution appeared to be to bargain with its six unions for lesser benefits or higher deductibles. Instead, the issue was taken off the bargaining table and referred to a labor-management committee. Through collaborative efforts the city was able to save $1.2 million and continue to offer health care benefits acceptable to employees. In the past, impasses over health care almost always occurred and were ultimately arbitrated. Since the committees have been involved, no health care decisions have been arbitrated.

Portland, Maine. The benefits of labor-management cooperation became apparent in 1993 when the city wanted to build a baseball stadium to attract a minor league team but did not have the $8 to $10 million that the project was expected to cost. Management challenged workers to build it themselves, which they did—in record time, and at a cost of only $2.5 million. After the stadium project demonstrated the ability to accomplish construction projects in-house at a lower cost, a city construction company was established. The company develops written plans for projects and checks them against expected or actual bids. In one example the company built a brick sidewalk in a historic district for 42 percent of the estimated cost of contracting with a private construction firm.

Source: U.S. Department of Labor, *Working Together for Public Service*, Report of the Secretary of Labor's Task Force on Excellence in State and Local Government Through Labor Management Cooperation (May 28, 1996).

SUMMARY

Key developments in both public and private sectors have influenced labor relations in local government. Only since the 1930s (Wagner Act, 1935) have labor unions gained large membership and a legal basis for collective bargaining. A legal framework for labor relations in the federal government was provided by legislation and presidential executive orders in the 1960s and 1970s. Police, firefighters, and teachers began organizing at state and local levels in the 1900s but did not have major influence. With increased acceptance of unionism and enabling state laws, strong unions began to emerge in the 1960s.

Currently there is no federal labor law for state and local government. State laws are conditioned by attitudes on such issues as sovereignty of elected government, the essential nature of government services, and application of democratic principles. The "meet and confer" approach to labor relations is based on a strict construction of sovereignty. The collective bargaining approach, used in a majority of states, is modeled after procedures used in the private sector, based on the Wagner Act.

If state law authorizes a union, an agency usually regulates bargaining unit determination, election, and certification of the union. The collective bargaining process identifies and resolves conflicts between labor and management. This process includes conduct of contract negotiations to determine wages and other terms and conditions of employment. If an impasse occurs, resolution procedures include mediation, fact-finding, and arbitration. The strike is well accepted in the private sector, but not in the public sector. Strikes by federal employees are prohibited. Strikes by public employees are illegal in a majority of states, but there is a trend toward more acceptance of strikes in state and local government.

Contract administration focuses on implementing and interpreting the contract and handling disputes. Grievance procedures are used to handle union claims of contract violations. Unresolved disputes are typically settled by arbitration.

Although the relationship between labor and management in the United States has traditionally been adversarial, there is a growing belief among writers, business and government executives, and union leaders and their membership that a more cooperative approach is needed. Although this approach is beginning to gain acceptance in both the public and private sectors, the major momentum for change has been with cities, counties, and states.

QUESTIONS FOR REVIEW AND DISCUSSION

1. What was the major influence of the American trade union movement on labor relations in local government?
2. Given the fact that Executive Order 10988 did not provide a substantive framework for labor relations, what was its significance?
3. Discuss briefly the major issues concerning labor relations in government.
4. Compare and contrast the meet and confer approach to labor relations with the collective bargaining approach.
5. Briefly describe the following steps in the collective bargaining process:
   a. Unit determination
   b. Election and certification
   c. Contract negotiations
6. What is meant by the duty to "bargain in good faith"?
7. Discuss three approaches used to resolve a bargaining impasse.
8. What are the important issues surrounding the right to strike by public employees?
9. Describe the mechanism used to resolve grievances that arise during the term of a contract.
10. Think of a city government with which you are familiar and a local manufacturing firm with approximately the same number of employees. Explain how they differ in terms of:
    a. Nature of services
    b. Bargaining structure
    c. Negotiable issues
    d. Right to strike
11. Discuss recent developments in labor relations in government. What have been the benefits of increased cooperation between labor and management?

ENDNOTES

[1] See especially Richard C. Kearney with David G. Carnevale, *Labor Relations in the Public Sector*, 3d ed. (New York: Marcel Dekker, 2001), which is a major source of information for this chapter. See also Jay M. Shafritz, Norma M. Riccucci, David H. Rosenbloom, and Albert C. Hyde, *Personnel Management in Government*, 4th ed. (New York Marcel Dekker, 1992), 319–405.

[2] This section draws on William H. Holley and Roger S. Wolters, *The Labor Relations Process*, 7th ed. (Homewood, Ill.: Dryden, 2001, forthcoming).

[3] U.S. Department of Labor, Bureau of Labor Statistics, "Union Members Summary," (January 19, 2000).

[4] This section is based on Kearney, 12–15, 49–50.

[5] Edward L. Suntrup and Darold T. Barnum, "Reinventing the Federal Government: Forging New Labor Management Partnerships," in Bruce Nissen, ed., *Unions and Workplace Reorganization* (Detroit: Wayne State, 1997), 145–155.

[6] Kearney, 14. See also Shafritz et al., 319–320.

[7] Kearney, 15.

[8] Kearney, 16–20.

[9] U.S. Department of Labor, Bureau of Labor Statistics, "Union Member Summary" (January 19, 2000).

[10] Kearney, 28–29.

[11] Joseph B. Mosca and Steven Pressman, "Unions in the 21st Century," *Public Personnel Management* 24 (Summer 1995), 159–167.

[12] Kearney, 230–234. See also Harry J. Wellington and Ralph K. Winter Jr., *The Unions and the Cities* (Washington, D.C.: The Brookings Institution, 1972), 12–32, Ronald D. Sylvia, *Public Personnel Administration* (Belmont, Calif.: Wadsworth, 1994), 241–252, and Shafritz et al., 335–341.

[13] Leo Troy, "State and Local Government Employee Relations After Garcia," and "The Proposed Fire Fighters Labor Act of 1987: An Analysis and Critique," *Government Union Review* 7 (Summer 1986), 1–37, 38–76.

[14] Bureau of National Affairs, "Police, Firefighters Urge Senate Support of Bill Setting State Bargaining Standards," *Government Employee Relations News* 38 (August 1, 2000), 873.

[15] Kearney, 67.

[16] Personal conversation with Roger Wolters, professor of labor relations at Auburn University.

[17] For more coverage see Kearney, 68–79, B. V. H. Schneider, "Public Sector Labor Legislation—An Evolutionary Analysis," in Benjamin Aaron, Joyce M. Najita and James L. Stern, *Public Sector Bargaining*, 2d ed. (Washington, D.C.: Bureau of National Affairs, 1988), 189–228, and John Lund and Cheryl L. Moranto, "Public Sector Law: An Update," in *Public Sector Employment* (Madison: University of Wisconsin, Industrial Relations Research Association, 1996).

[18] Kearney, 72–73.

[19] Kearney, 86–94.

[20] Kearney, 71–72.

[21] Kearney, 117–119.

[22] R. M. Patterson Jr., "Decision Support Systems in Collective Bargaining: A Capacity Building Measure for the Public Manager," *Public Personnel Management* 9 (Fall 1987), 269. See also Bill Roberts, "Making Employee Data Pay," *HR Magazine* (November 1999), 86–89, and Kenneth A. Kovach and Charles Cathcart Jr., "Human Resource Systems (HRIS): Providing Business with Rapid Access, Information Exchange and Strategic Advantage," *Public Personnel Management* 28 (Summer 1999), 275–383.

[23] This section was developed by William H. Holley. See also Holley and Wolters, forthcoming, and Kearney, 263–284.

[24] Holley and Wolters, forthcoming.

[25] For more coverage see Dane M. Patridge, "Public Policy and Public Sector Strikes: A Review of the Literature," *Journal of Collective Negotiations in the Public Sector* 23 (Spring 1994), 1–14.

[26] Schneider, 201.

[27] Bureau of National Affairs, "Tentative Pacts Avert City Workers' Strike as Philadelphia Prepares for Convention," *Government Employee Labor Relations* 38 (August 1, 2000), 874.

[28] Kearney, 249–254.

[29] Kearney, 293.

[30] Clyde Scott and James Suchan, "Public Sector Collective Bargaining Agreements: How Readable Are They?" *Public Personnel Management* 16 (Spring 1987), 15–23.

[31] Kearney, 302–305.

[32] Kearney, 322–323.

[33] Martin M. Perline, "Union Views of Managerial Prerogatives Revisited: The Prospects for Labor-Management Cooperation," *Journal of Labor Research* 20 (Winter 1999), 147–154.

[34] Thomas A. Kochan, Harry A. Katz and Robert B. McKersie in Perline, 147.

[35] Kearney, 338–344.

[36] Jon Brock, "Cooperative Labor-Management Relations as a Strategy for Change: The Critical Role and Opportunity for the Human Resource Profession," *Public Personnel Management* 27 (Spring 1998), 1–10. See entire issue 27.

[37] U.S. Department of Labor, "Report of the Secretary's Task Force on Labor-Management Cooperation," (1996).

[38] "State and Local Government Labor Management Teams Attend First Joint SLG-LMC/Harvard Executive Program," *IPMA News* 65 (July 1999), 7–8.

[39] Kearney, 345.

CHAPTER 16
SAFETY, HEALTH, AND SECURITY

Although Bill Sims, the HR director for the city of Jonesboro, does not have a background in the technical aspects of health, safety, and security, he believes that the work environment is acceptable in all of these areas. The accident rate is lower than the average for municipalities and the workers' compensation premium has been reduced. There have been no serious work-related injuries or illnesses in recent years, and the city has never had an incident of workplace violence. To determine if his assessment is accurate he has requested assistance from Dan Mims, a safety consultant. He asked Dan to visit the worksites of five employees whose names were selected at random from a workforce of approximately 500 employees. During these visits Dan interviewed the employees and their supervisors and made observations as appropriate. What he discovered on these visits is summarized below:

- Jack Green is a CAD/CAM operator in the city engineer's office. He likes his work space, an attractive cubical in an air-conditioned building. Occasionally he experiences eye irritation, a scratchy throat, and headaches. He is not inclined to complain about these minor discomforts.
- Carol Warner works in an office environment similar to Jack's except that it is in an older building. She is a billing clerk for the Utilities Department and spends most of her workday entering data on a keyboard. Lately she has felt some pain and numbness in her fingers and weakness in her hands. She doesn't think that it is anything serious.
- Dena McAllister is employed in the Codes Enforcement Department. Her job of building inspector requires her to spend considerable time at construction sites examining work in progress and ensuring that procedures and materials conform to codes. Dena is very careful to follow all safety procedures and has never been injured or had an accident.
- Joan Lowe, the activities director at the Ridge Road Community Center, says that her job "is like being in a health club, except you get paid." The only problem in her life involves a man she broke up with when he hit her during an argument. He calls her frequently and insists that they should get back together. Sometimes he parks near her house and watches her activities.

- Al Bush is Joan's coworker in Parks and Recreation. During May through August he is in charge of maintenance for all city pools. One of his tasks is to measure and pour granules of calcium hypochlorite into a hopper connected to the water filtration and purification system. He is required to wear a respirator, apron, and gloves when performing this task.

In reviewing this information Bill saw no cause for concern but was interested in what Dan might have to say. It was somewhat disquieting when Dan began the discussion by saying, "Bill, we have some problems."

- Based on Dan's analysis, Jack Green's "minor discomforts" may be caused by poor indoor air quality (IAQ). Indoor pollution attributed to faulty heating, ventilation, and air-conditioning systems in energy efficient buildings has been linked to health problems ranging from discomfort to life-threatening illnesses.
- Repetitively using the same muscles to perform tasks can result in muscular and skeletal injuries. Carol's symptoms are often associated with carpal tunnel syndrome, a debilitating condition affecting the tendons in the wrist.
- While it is commendable that Dena follows safety procedures at construction sites, she does not fasten her seat belt when driving to these locations. This greatly increases her risk of being injured or killed in an accident.
- The hitting incident and current behavior of Joan's former boyfriend are signs that he may be a stalker. Violence by a former intimate is the leading cause of death of women in the workplace.
- Requiring Al to wear personal protective equipment (PPE), although essential, is *last* in the hierarchy of control measures used to protect worker health and safety. Calcium hypochlorite is available in both granule and tablet form, with tablets involving considerably less risk. Substitution is *first* in the hierarchy of control measures.

During his meeting with Dan it becomes apparent to Bill that in each of these cases the city is either causing or ignoring conditions that subject employees to unacceptable risk of injury and illness, and that similar situations likely exist throughout the workforce. It is also clear to Dan that everyone from the city manager to the lowest operating employee is part of the problem. The city has been fortunate to have a good record in safety, health, and security, and if this record is to continue they will have to be part of the solution.

INTRODUCTION

Local governments, like all employers, have an obligation to provide their employees with a safe, healthful, and secure work environment. Accidents and illnesses result in both organizational and human costs. For example, they reduce both the employee's level of job performance and attendance record. Disabling accidents and illnesses may jeopardize the employee's ability to earn a living. Although the terms **safety** and **health** are often used interchangeably, some distinctions should be made. Safety refers to the avoidance of injury-causing accidents. Health is a broader term and includes both the prevention of illness and maintaining the overall well-being of employees. **Security** involves protection of facilities from unauthorized access and the protection of employees at the worksite or while they are on assignment.[1] Safety, health, and security are complex topics and a complete discussion is beyond the scope of a text in HR management. This chapter is designed to provide an overview of basic principles and concepts.[2]

LAWS AND REGULATIONS

The legal framework for safety and health involves state workers' compensation laws (discussed in Chapter 13), which provide benefits to employees who have suffered a work-related accident or illness, and the federal Occupational Safety and Health Act, which seeks to improve the physical security of employees. Workers' compensation is an after-the-fact effort to deal with problems that have already occurred. The Occupational Safety and Health Act and similar state laws are proactive in that they seek to prevent the occurrence of accidents and illnesses.

WORKERS' COMPENSATION

http://www.osha.gov/
The United States Occupational Safety and Health Administration (OSHA) provides comprehensive information on the Occupational Safety and Health Act and guidelines for compliance.

Work-related accidents and illnesses are a major threat to an employee's ability to earn a living. Less than 100 years ago, the only recourse available to a disabled employee was to sue the employer. In 1902 the state of Maryland passed the first workers' compensation (WC) law in the United States.[3] It was declared unconstitutional by the U.S. Supreme Court, but in 1911 the Court reversed itself and held constitutional a number of state laws requiring employers to pay for lost time and injuries resulting from occupational accidents and illnesses. Today every state has laws requiring such payments. Such laws vary from state to state; however, all laws have certain common features.

http://gopher.law.
cornell.edu/topics/
workers_compensation.
html
The Legal Information Institute provides a comprehensive overview of worker compensation laws with links to federal statutes, regulations, and judicial decisions.

WC laws typically provide three types of benefits. Death benefits are a lump sum payment to survivors of employees killed on the job. Medical benefits include payment of bills for physicians, hospitals, physical therapy, drugs, and related items. Partial replacement of earnings is also provided until employees are able to return to work. WC is basically an insurance program financed by premiums paid by the employer; the amount of the premium is determined by the safety record of the "industry." Some states permit employers to be self-insured. WC insurance rates declined during much of the 1990s, and the combined ratio of the industry (ratio of funds paid out to premiums) dropped below 100 in 1995. However, the ratio began to increase in 1996, and the long-term trend is for continued upward pressure on WC insurance premium rates.[4]

THE OCCUPATIONAL SAFETY AND HEALTH ACT

The major shortcoming of WC is that it deals only with the effects of unsafe working conditions and health hazards: injuries and illnesses. The Occupational Safety and Health Act addresses the causes of these problems.[5] It was passed in 1970 ". . . to assure so far as possible every working man and woman in the Nation safe and healthful working conditions and to preserve our human resources." The act is administered by the Occupational Safety and Health Administration (OSHA). The act also established the National Institute of Occupational Safety and Health (NIOSH) to conduct research and develop standards and the Occupational Safety and Health Review Commission (OSHR) to review enforcement actions and resolve disputes between OSHA and employers who have been cited for violations.

Major provisions of the act include publication and enforcement by OSHA of safety and health standards.[6] Where OSHA has not promulgated specific standards, employers are responsible for following the act's general duty clause. The general duty clause of the act states that each employer "shall furnish a place of employment which is free from recognized hazards that are causing or are likely to cause death or serious physical harm to employees." Employers are required to develop and communicate safety and health procedures and rules, correct hazards, provide safe tools and equipment, train employees, and maintain appropriate records. OSHA inspections are made by compliance officers who will review possible violations with the employer. After such inspections the OSHA area director determines what citations will be issued, what civil penalties will be imposed, and a proposed time period for abatement. Criminal penalties may be levied in serious cases. Exhibit 16-1 contains an overview of the provisions of the act.

OSHA provisions do not apply to state and local governments in their role as employers. However, the act does provide that any state desiring to gain OSHA approval for its private sector occupational safety and health programs must provide a program that covers its state and local government workers and is at least as effective as its program for private employees. To date, 23 states, along with Puerto Rico and the Virgin Islands, have developed such programs (see Exhibit 16-2).

Local governments in states without comprehensive safety and health regulations might find it beneficial to voluntarily comply with OSHA. In the first place, federal laws are expressions of national policy, which is to provide safe and healthful working conditions. Second, there are benefits in terms of lower costs for medical insurance and WC contributions. Third, efficiency is increased when employees are at work

EXHIBIT 16-1

OVERVIEW OF PROVISIONS OF THE OCCUPATIONAL SAFETY AND HEALTH ACT

- Requires employers to meet general duty responsibility to provide a workplace free of safety and health hazards and comply with rules and standards issued by the Occupational Health and Safety Administration (OSHA).
- Requires employers to disseminate information (including OSHA- and state-approved poster), establish operating procedures, provide medical examinations, conduct training, and maintain records in accordance with OSHA regulations.
- Requires employers to provide employees and/or their representatives with access to medical and exposure records and organizational data regarding work-related injuries and illnesses.
- Provides that employees or their representatives may file a complaint with the nearest OSHA office requesting an inspection of conditions they believe are unsafe or unhealthful; protects employees from retaliation for filing a complaint.
- Provides that OSHA representatives may inspect the workplace and issue citations to employers who have violated the act; requires employers to cooperate with the investigation by furnishing a designated representative to accompany the investigator.
- Provides for mandatory civil penalties of up to $7,000 for violations and up to $7,000 per day for failure to correct violations; also provides criminal penalties of up to $250,000 ($500,000 for corporations) for willful violations resulting in death of an employee.
- Encourages voluntary efforts by labor and management to reduce workplace hazards and to develop or improve safety and health programs; provides assistance to employers in conducting these activities at no cost.

Source: U.S. Department of Labor, *All About OSHA* (1995) and additional information at *http://www.osha.gov* (November 2000).

EXHIBIT 16-2 STATES WITH APPROVED OCCUPATIONAL SAFETY AND HEALTH PLANS	Section 18 of the Occupational Safety and Health Act encourages states to develop and operate their own plans. The following states have approved plans:

Alaska	Indiana	Minnesota	Oregon	Virginia
Arizona	Iowa	Nevada	South Carolina	Washington
California	Kentucky	New Mexico	Tennessee	Wyoming
Connecticut*	Maryland	New York*	Utah	
Hawaii	Michigan	North Carolina	Vermont	

*The Connecticut and New York plans cover state and local government employment only.

Source: Occupational Health and Safety Administration, U.S. Department of Labor (2000).

rather than recovering from work-related accidents or illnesses. Finally, the coverage of federal regulation of the HR function is usually, in time, extended to local governments, the most recent example being the Fair Labor Standards Act. Those jurisdictions that were already in voluntary compliance had a great advantage.

ORGANIZATIONAL RESPONSIBILITY FOR SAFETY AND HEALTH

Providing a safe, healthful, and secure workplace is an organizational function demanding the same executive direction and control as other responsibilities; moreover, health, safety, and security are part of every job, and employees are also responsible. While they may seem to be simple, commonsense matters, the design and implementation of effective programs raise complex issues, and certain activities require special skills. Thus a staff position or department is needed to provide expertise, advice, and other support to line managers.[7]

LINE RESPONSIBILITIES

In order for safety and health programs to work, elected officials, managers, supervisors, and employees must meet certain responsibilities. The executive leadership of the government must demonstrate a commitment to health and safety by authorizing necessary expenditures, approving safety policies, and generally being involved. This might include making safety tours, reviewing reports, praising safe and healthy practices, and appraising supervisors on their safety records. The supervisor or manager plays a critical role in maintaining safe and healthful working conditions. For example, a supervisor should remind employees to wear appropriate safety equipment and should observe his or her employees to see if any of them show symptoms of illness or of alcohol, drug, or emotional problems. The supervisor is also responsible for advising higher management of the need to take care of potentially unsafe working conditions, such as installing a guard or railing.

Employees are also responsible. No matter how well safety is built into a job or how well managers carry out their responsibilities, much of the safety and health of employees depends on their own conduct. Some people work safely in dangerous surroundings, while others have accidents on jobs that appear to be safe. Employees' attitudes about safety and health are extremely important. Many problems are caused by employees simply being careless or negligent. Some, particularly younger and less experienced employees, may be "accident prone." Employees must work in accordance with accepted practices, observe safety rules, report accidents and illnesses, and point out unsafe or unhealthy conditions.

STAFF RESPONSIBILITIES

While the responsibility for health and safety rests ultimately with line managers and employees, these issues are quite complex. In carrying out their responsibilities, line management needs the assistance of the staff. Staff specialists are used as internal consultants on health and safety matters. They provide support such as conducting safety training for employees and supervisors, measuring incidence rates, and keeping records. The staff also represents top management in developing, implementing, and evaluating policies and programs. Note that this involves the advisory, service, and control roles of staff, as discussed in Chapter 1.

Many organizations require a staff unit to take the lead in developing and carrying out safety and health programs. There are a number of reasons why this might logically be the HR department. First, safety and health issues have a direct effect on the human resources of the organization. Second, the necessary training of employees and supervisors is typically a responsibility of HR management. Finally, the record keeping and reporting aspects of health and safety are components of the human resource information system (HRIS). In any case, even if the leadership for safety and health programs is assigned to another individual or department (for example, risk management), the HR department will always be involved to a significant extent.

DESIGNING OCCUPATIONAL HEALTH AND SAFETY PROGRAMS

A safe and healthy work environment is the result of programs that focus on prevention. The alternative is to react to incidents as they occur, sometimes called the

---

While all HR areas involve partnership roles and responsibilities among the executive leadership, staff specialists, line managers and employees, workplace safety and health is arguably the best example of an activity where all roles are vital. The leadership must understand and communicate the strategic importance of a safe and healthful workplace and hold line managers accountable, or efforts will be reactive in nature. Unless staff specialists develop effective strategies, design creative programs and make the "business case" people in the organization will see safety and health as matters that someone else is taking care of. Unless supervisors and managers deal effectively with workplace conditions and worker behaviors, programs will exist mainly on paper. Finally, this is an area in which the behavior of an individual employee has major consequences because it is not possible to recover the loss when an employee is injured or contracts an occupational disease. Strategic direction, accountability, well designed programs and effective supervision always matter. But if employees themselves do not take personal responsibility these things won't matter very much.

SAFETY AND HEALTH: IT'S EVERYBODY'S BUSINESS

Source: Excerpted from unpublished essay prepared by Steve Reeves, HR director, city of Auburn, Alabama. Used by permission.

"body count" method because no improvement takes place until something happens. A proactive type of program operates at three levels:

1. **Building a general level of health and safety consciousness.** Employees, who are experts on their own work, must be aware that health and safety have a top priority.
2. **Capturing and understanding unplanned events, regardless of whether an injury or illness occurs.** These "near misses" can provide critical information on the effectiveness of safety and health procedures.
3. **Investigating and analyzing all accidents and incidents as well as significant near misses to determine the root cause.** Discovering the root cause of an event can lead to fundamental changes in work design, management, and programs.[8]

Although health, safety, and security programs are structured differently, they are related to each other in various ways. It is useful therefore to take an overall approach in formulating policy guidance and assessing needs. After this has been accomplished the necessary programs can be designed and evaluated.

FORMULATING THE ORGANIZATIONAL POLICY

The organizational policy provides guidance for designing programs. A major policy issue involves the amount of risk that the organization is willing to take. OSHA standards in the area of safety are generally based on risk levels of one event (accident) in one thousand. The Environmental Protection Agency and other public health organizations are more conservative, with acceptable levels of risk set at one event (contracting a disease) in ten thousand to one million. These levels of risk should be considered legal and ethical minimums. More conservative levels of risk require a higher investment, which may possibly be offset by lower insurance premiums and higher productivity.[9] The policy should provide overall guidance in the areas of safety, health, and security and should assign responsibilities to staff, line managers, and employees. Either the policy itself or key nontechnical excerpts should be disseminated to all employees to indicate the organization's commitment to a safe, healthy, and secure workplace and to promote awareness and involvement.

http://infoventures.com/osh/

OSH-Link provides information on occupational-related studies and links to other occupational safety and health resources on the Internet.

ASSESSING PROGRAM NEEDS

A complete evaluation of environmental, health, safety, and security risks should be conducted. The inventory should include the following:

• Risks of chemical exposure through inhalation, skin contact, and ingestion
• Safety risks including walking/working surfaces, fire hazards, materials handling, equipment, machines, tools, welding equipment, electrical systems in buildings (110–220v), electrical distribution systems (high voltage), water, wastewater, gas, solid waste, and transportation
• Biological risks including bloodborne pathogens, molds and bacteria, and other infectious diseases
• Risks that increase the probabilities of developing an injury or disease resulting from factors such as repetitive motion, unnatural body positioning and movement, lifting and carrying, and vibration
• Security risks including unauthorized access to facilities, crime in surrounding neighborhood, and potentially violent employees[10]

These types of risks are largely independent of each other and quite complex. The type of analysis required for program development requires input from specialists such as safety engineers, occupational physicians, industrial hygienists, and security professionals. Local governments typically have more in-house expertise than the typical private firm (police, fire and emergency rescue personnel, engineering and health professionals); however, it may also be necessary to retain outside consultants. A competent and professional analysis and assessment is essential for the development of effective programs.

MONITORING INCIDENCE RATES

Employers should keep accurate records of work-related accidents and illnesses. From these records they can compute their **incidence rate**, which is the number of injuries and illnesses per 100 full-time employees during a given period, typically one year. The standard formula is shown below:

Incidence rate = $N/EH \times 200,000$

where

N = Number of experiences (injuries/illnesses, fatalities, etc.).

EH = Total employee hours worked in year

200,000 = Equivalent of 100 full-time employees (each working 40 hours per week, 50 weeks per year)

Other statistics include frequency and severity rates, which use one million hours rather than one year. Such rates can be compared with experience in previous years and with "industry" (local government) standards. However, they are less useful as measures of the effectiveness of safety and health programs, especially in small- to medium-sized organizations. Recall from the opening vignette that low incidence rates in Jonesboro indicated only that the city had been lucky.

SAFETY PROGRAMS

The major objective of a safety program is accident reduction. Accomplishing this objective has direct benefits in terms of employees' job performance and attendance. Another benefit involves reduction of legal liability exposure from personal injuries and property damage occurring in the process of providing government services. This emerging area is known as risk management. Components of a safety program include safety procedures and rules, safety committees, safety training, accident investigation, and safety publicity. In general these components also apply to health and security programs discussed in following sections.[11]

SAFETY PROCEDURES AND RULES

The safety program should include procedures to define, identify, and correct unsafe conditions and rules that identify what employees must do to ensure safe practices are followed. Although staff specialists will be involved, it should be stressed that this aspect of safety is a line responsibility and should have the same priority as responsibilities related to productivity, cost, and quality. In the past, occupational accidents were attributed to unsafe acts, unsafe working conditions, or both. Present thinking holds supervisors and managers more accountable, especially if they did nothing to enforce safety rules or eliminate unsafe conditions.

In determining technical requirements, applicable OSHA standards are useful. Other sources include manuals dealing with safety and risk management.[12] Supervisors and managers should make periodic inspections to identify unsafe conditions. After unsafe conditions are identified, corrective action should be taken, including effective interim measures if the full corrective action cannot be implemented immediately. Follow-up activities are very important. It is also important to update procedures when new machinery or equipment is purchased.

In developing safety procedures and rules, the first step is job analysis (see Chapter 7) to identify work behaviors and tasks for each job. For each work behavior (one or more tasks) possible safety hazards are identified. For those that cannot be eliminated, safety control procedures and rules are established. Exhibit 16-3 is an example of safety procedures for a loader operator. Aggregated information drawn from groups of jobs provides the basis for various departmental procedures. How many departmental procedures are needed and how much detail should be involved for a particular unit of government would depend on the size and complexity of the organization.

SAFETY COMMITTEES

As discussed previously, the organizational responsibility for safety is shared by the staff, line management, and employees themselves. Safety programs, however, are often coordinated by safety committees that may perform a wide range of functions, as shown in Exhibit 16-4. Staff specialists, managers, and employees should serve as committee members. Managers demonstrate the organizational commitment to safety, staff specialists provide expertise, and employee representation helps employees to "buy in" to the program. Committees that are properly organized and used can generate a spirit of open communication and cooperation in resolving safety issues.[13] Safety committees do, however, have inherent limitations. Accountability is compromised when supervisors can refer problems to the safety committees that they should be handling themselves. Other limitations include insufficient employee representation, irregular meetings, and lack of expertise.

SAFETY TRAINING

Organizations typically conduct training for both employees and supervisors. As with all types of training, what is taught must be reinforced on the job. Objectives of safety training for employees include creating safety awareness, motivating employees to accept their safety responsibilities, developing a knowledge base in accident causation and prevention, building skills in hazard recognition and methods of corrective action, and bringing about desired behaviors when trainees return to the workplace. Supervisory training has the same general objectives, but it should include more information on the technical aspects of safety management and should emphasize the role of the supervisor in monitoring the workplace and ensuring that safety procedures and rules are enforced.

Like a number of other HR activities, training can be viewed as a process. Exhibit 10-2 in Chapter 10 illustrates the sequence of events that should be followed. The chapter also includes specific examples related to safety training. First, training needs should be assessed. These needs consist to a large degree of performance deficiencies that can be corrected with training. With these needs established, it is possible to set instructional objectives and conduct appropriate training (Exhibit 10-3, Chapter 10, contains objectives for supervisory training in safety). Evaluation is the

EXHIBIT 16-3

SAFETY PROCEDURES FOR
LOADER OPERATOR

General Procedures

OPERATOR:
1. It's YOUR job to do everything reasonable to prevent an accident.
2. Don't take chances.
3. ALWAYS LOOK where you are going.
4. Check clearances before moving.
5. Don't rush the job.
6. CONCENTRATE on what you are doing.
7. READ manufacturer's instructions.
8. INSPECT equipment **before** operating.
9. NEVER HORSE AROUND with machines.
10. Operate SMOOTHLY; don't jerk.
11. Take **extra care** getting in and out of the machine.
12. DON'T CARRY PASSENGERS.
13. Lower bucket to ground when parked.

PROCEDURES:
1. Keep load or bucket LOW when moving.
2. Use EXTRA CAUTION when working on SLOPES.
3. LOADERS are **unstable** on SLOPES.
4. **USE LIGHTS** when driving or working the dark.
5. If working on or near a road, use a flashing light on top.
6. Dig into a pile with the bucket cutting blade in a HORIZONTAL position to prevent excessive stress.

CAPACITY:
- KNOW the equipment CAPACITY.
- Capacity includes operator and fuel.
- Attachments will reduce capacity.

HAZARDS:
WATCH OUT for hidden objects, such as:

| manholes | wires | curbs | pipes |
| bumps | junk | stakes | people |

Pile Dynamics

It is dangerous to work on product piles higher than the height of the cab of a loader.

Do not allow the product pile to become a hazard; knock it down *before* it falls on the equipment.

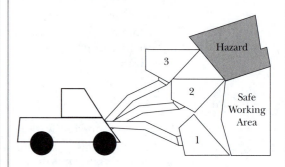

Material stacked piled higher than the top of the loader may slide onto the loader cab.

Source: John R. Webber, *Safety Technician's Handbook,* 2d ed. (Sherwood Park, Alta: Pacific Safety Institute, 1999), 247–248. Reproduced by permission of Pacific Safety Institute, 12 Merryvale Circle, Sherwood Park, Alberta, Canada T8A ON3, 780-467-9822.

EXHIBIT 16-4

RESPONSIBILITIES
OF SAFETY
COMMITTEE

- Become informed about safety, including regulations, technical material and organization policies, procedures, and rules.
- Participate in formulation of safety policies and procedures, design of safety programs, and evaluation of safety efforts.
- Serve as a safety resource center/clearinghouse for organization members by providing information, receiving concerns and suggestions, and communicating with management.
- Coordinate or perform periodic formal safety inspections, prepare reports, and communicate findings and recommendations to management.
- On a continuous basis, observe workplace behavior and identify unsafe acts and unsafe working conditions.
- Review accident and injury reports including near misses to determine causes; initiate necessary action and conduct follow-up activities.
- Conduct safety promotion activities including posters, newsletter items, awards, and recognition programs.

Source: Based on John R. Webber, *Safety Technician's Handbook*, 2d ed. (Sherwood Park, Alta: Pacific Safety Institute, 1999), 578.

---

final step in the process. The results of evaluation are used as feedback to the human resource department and supervisors as a tool to modify and improve the training program. A safety training program can now be created by a computer with the knowledge-based safety training system, which gives the supervisor the ability to identify the training needs, plan training, and evaluate the performance.[14]

ACCIDENT INVESTIGATION AND ANALYSIS

Investigation and analysis concern both injury and noninjury accidents; the term *accident* is used here in its broadest sense (an occurrence that may lead to injuries and property damage). There should be a thorough investigation of every accident that results in a disabling injury or lost workdays to determine contributing circumstances. Accidents that do not result in personal injury are warnings and should not be ignored. Accident investigation and analysis is a defense against a hazard or hazards that were previously overlooked, often were not obvious, and may possibly involve a combination of unforeseen circumstances. Investigation and analysis produce information, which leads to conclusions, which lead to action, which prevents or reduces future incidents of like or similar causes(s). The investigation should be fact-finding rather than fault-finding. If human error has played a role, investigation fixes responsibility but neither accuses nor excuses. The investigation is impersonal, factual, and, to the degree possible, free of involvement with any possible disciplinary action.[15]

SAFETY COMMUNICATION AND MOTIVATION

Without reinforcement, employees will not keep safety standards in mind and may even resist following rules and procedures that they find bothersome. This is especially true in regard to wearing personal protective equipment (PPE) such as safety shoes, gloves, and goggles. In addition to safety training discussed above, continuous communication to maintain consciousness is necessary. As discussed earlier, supervisors should continually stress safety issues. Posting safety policies and rules is essential. Safety contests, recognition programs, and individual and group incentives are additional ways of promoting awareness and encouraging employees to work safely. Such actions as changing safety posters, continually updating bulletin boards, and posting attractive company safety information signs in high-traffic areas are also recommended.

EVALUATION OF SAFETY EFFORTS

Organizations must evaluate their safety program. Statistics such as incidence rates are useful, but they are only "downstream" measures of performance. Safety should be viewed as an integral element of organizational culture. The determinants of safety performance include culture/systems, behavior, safety programs, and learning/growth.[16] Measurements in these areas are "upstream" indicators and drivers of safety performance (as well as performance in health and security). Evaluation is often a responsibility of the safety committee. However, the executive leadership, operating managers, and staff specialists should continually examine and evaluate the organization's progress in developing a safe environment for its employees.

OCCUPATIONAL HEALTH PROGRAMS

Organizational health programs seek to reduce or prevent the occurrence of work-related illnesses (also known as occupational diseases). Health programs involve identifying health hazards, adopting preventive measures, and conducting health promotion activities.

SAFETY INCENTIVES IN ROLLING MEADOWS

The city of Rolling Meadows, Illinois, conducts regular team safety sessions, displays safety posters in the workplace, provides ongoing safety training, holds managers accountable for safety, and emphasizes the safety responsibility of each employee. While these are all sound techniques, the city decided that there was a need to forge an even stronger partnership among employees in the campaign to lower risks.

The Safe Team Award Recognition System (STARS) program was implemented to provide an incentive to employees to conduct themselves in a safe manner. Employees and work teams are awarded points for avoiding work-related medical injuries or preventable accidents. Points earned are converted to dollar bonuses at the end of the year. The maximum number of points that can be earned is 100 for field-unit employees who work out-of-doors and 50 for employees who work in an office environment.

The STARS program was implemented in 1997. The number of workers' compensation claims declined from 31 in 1996 to 16 in 1999, a reduction of 48.4 percent. Liability claims were reduced by 32.3 percent, from 59 in 1996 to 40 in 1997. According to William Barlow, city manager, the community as a whole benefits from the STARS program. "Lower incidences of workers' compensation and general liability claims result in lower operating costs, which can translate into reduced demand on limited resources," he says. He also points out that the ability of the city to continue important programs and services is enhanced because fewer employees miss work because of injuries.

Source: William P. Barlow, "Safe Team Award Recognition System (STARS)," *IPMA News* 66 (September 2000), 14–16.

IDENTIFICATION AND CONTROL OF OCCUPATIONAL HEALTH HAZARDS

Many types of jobs in local government involve health hazards known to cause occupational diseases. Some of the more pervasive hazards include exposure to toxic chemicals, poor indoor air quality, deficient work systems, and infectious diseases. This section briefly discusses the nature of these hazards, kinds of jobs impacted, and types of control measures that organizations should use to eliminate these hazards or reduce their severity.

EXPOSURE TO TOXIC CHEMICALS

There are thousands of industrial chemicals in use today with which employees may come in contact. Many of these are potentially harmful, and while accidental contact through spills is addressed in safety programs, a major problem is the effect of cumulative exposure. Examples in local government include jobs involving herbicides and pesticides (grounds maintenance workers), cleaning materials (custodians), contaminated waste (sanitation workers), and chemicals in the purification of water (water system operators and pool maintenance workers).

Control measures follow a four-level hierarchy.[17] The first and most desirable level is to explore the alternative of substituting a nontoxic or less toxic material that accomplishes the same purpose. Second in order of desirability is to limit the exposure through enclosure, isolation, and ventilation. The third level is to modify behavior. For example, all types of potentially hazardous chemicals are required to have detailed information on containers that identify the contents and contain appropriate hazard warnings. Risk can be minimized by establishing and enforcing rules that require employees using these chemicals to read and follow label directions. The last level is to require the use of **personal protective equipment (PPE)**. In most circumstances several levels of control are used.

POOR INDOOR AIR QUALITY

Many employees of local government spend virtually all of their worklife indoors breathing air that makes them sick or uncomfortable.[18] Symptoms include headaches, eye, nose, and throat irritations, tightness in the chest, skin irritations, nausea, loss of memory, and a lethargic feeling. The general trend of sealing office buildings for better energy efficiency reduces outside air and has been identified as a major cause of the problem. Individuals with **sick building syndrome (SBS)** experience health and comfort problems that appear to be associated with working in a building, but the specific cause cannot be identified. In another condition known as **building-related illness (BRI)**, the symptoms can be clinically diagnosed and linked to a source. Both conditions result from inadequate air distribution systems that allow chemical contaminants, mold, fungi, and bacteria to remain in the air and be inhaled by occupants. These same symptoms have been attributed to passive inhalation of tobacco smoke.[19] While most cases involve discomfort and annoyance, poor indoor air quality (IAQ) has been linked to asthma, heart disease, lung cancer, Legionnaire's disease, tuberculosis (see below), and radon poisoning.

Organizations face a dilemma in dealing with this issue. The worst case scenario is for management to assess the problem and either dismiss it or undertake "further studies." Employees, who are convinced that something in the air is making them sick, become polarized, and an "us" vs. "them" attitude prevails. The effective HR response is to take complaints seriously, build a file for analysis purposes, and begin investigating. In the interim it is important to demonstrate a concern for employees

According to both the Occupational Safety and Health Administration (OSHA) and the Environmental Protection Agency (EPA) poor indoor air quality (IAQ) is one of the most serious environmental problems in the United States. Contrary to the conventional wisdom the

SICK BUILDINGS COME IN ALL AGES

problem is not limited to buildings that were constructed after the OPEC oil embargo of the early 1970s. In many cases, *particularly in the public sector*, buildings that date from the WPA era of the 1930s and 40s are still being used. These buildings had high ceilings and large windows that were opened in the summer for air circulation, but now most of them are air conditioned. Often the ceilings have been dropped and the windows sealed to make them more energy efficient. In most cases, however, the original ductwork and control mechanisms are still in place. In that deficiencies in air distribution systems cause 50 percent of the problems with IAQ, it would not be surprising if the situation with older buildings is even worse and there is considerable anecdotal evidence that this may be true [emphasis added].

Source: Carol K. Woolbright, "Indoor Air Quality Issues in Local Governments and Schools," unnumbered technical paper, The Center for Local Government Studies, Boise, ID, *http://www.clgsonline.com* (February 2001). Used by permission.

by taking immediate steps. These can range from relocating work stations, allowing employees with severe problems to work at home, or even evacuating the building. At the same time the underlying problems have to be corrected.

There are two basic approaches to alleviating indoor air quality problems. The first is improving the heating, air-conditioning, and ventilation (HVAC) system through upgrading, better maintenance, or replacement if necessary. A system that works properly should be free of system contaminants and should remove outdoor air contaminants such as fumes, smoke, and dust. The second is to remove indoor air contaminants such as solvent vapors and dust. A related measure is to ban smoking entirely (most effective) or to permit smoking only in designated areas. According to one authority, IAQ problems can usually be attributed to air distribution and the first step should be air monitoring. Often the problem can be identified and addressed without major expense. But he also cautions that organizations may be required to "drill down deeper and deeper. Each time you do so, of course, it's more costly."[20]

DEFICIENT WORK SYSTEMS

The human body is capable of performing a large range of activities, some of them quite strenuous and/or sustained, without damage. However, certain types of jobs create physical stresses that can cause damage to vital systems (the muscular and skeletal systems are especially vulnerable). A number of these jobs are found in local government. For example, office jobs (clerk, CAD/CAM operator) that involve use of computers and video display terminals (VDTs) are associated with visual difficulties, radiation hazards, and muscular aches and pains. Jobs requiring workers to repetitively use the same muscles to perform tasks (painter, keyboard operator) can cause **cumulative trauma disorders (CTDs)** including inflammation of the tendons in the carpal tunnel area of the wrist. Pressure on the median nerve causes debilitating pain and numbness in the fingers, a condition known as carpal tunnel syndrome. Jobs that involve lifting and carrying (warehouse worker) or subject the worker to vibration in a sitting position (heavy equipment operator) can cause chronic back problems.

Although these and other jobs and tasks have inherent characteristics that can lead to problems, it is possible to greatly reduce the risk of occupational disease by improving workplace design and worker techniques.[21] A work system consists of the interaction between workers and their occupations, tools and equipment, and working environment such as atmosphere, heat, light, vibration, and sound. **Ergonomics** is a body of knowledge about human abilities, human limitations, and other human characteristics that are relevant to the work system. Ergonomic design is the application of this knowledge in work settings so that jobs can be made to match the capabilities of the workers.

Ergonomic design addresses a number of factors including workspace layout, motion, body position, task duration, task mix, and technique, based on the work being performed. A recent application involves workstations where operators work with personal computers (PCs) or video display terminals (VDTs) as illustrated in Exhibit 16-5. Note that the level of the work surface, vision level of the screen, and chair height are designed to minimize eyestrain, properly position the wrists, and provide back support. In addition, the worker could be taught stretching exercises to alleviate muscle fatigue.

In jobs requiring physical exertion, a major emphasis has been on worker technique to reduce the risk of spinal degeneration related to lifting. One way to

---

EXHIBIT 16-5

ERGONOMICALLY DESIGNED
WORKSPACE FOR
PC/VDT OPERATOR

1. Keep **feet** comfortably and flat on floor.
2. **Knees** should be lower than hip level.
3. **Keyboard** flat and close to level of elbow.
4. **Wrists are relaxed** and straight.
5. The **screen top** is at eye level or slightly lower.
6. **Head** about ¾ to 1 arm's length from screen.
7. **Neck and shoulders relaxed.**
8. **Head and neck straight.**
9. Use an ergonomic keyboard.
10. Elbow relaxes, between 70° and 135°.
11. Keep **back straight**, sit upright.
12. **Seat** and back should be adjustable.
13. **Seat** should be large enough and comfortable.
14. **Seat back** must include a lumbar support.
15. Anti-static pad below **chair** wheels on floor.
16. **Seat** has a **separate** back support, if possible.
17. **Seat** arm rest should support arm while working.
18. Ensure chair/seat can move easily.
19. **Chair legs** should prevent tipping over.
20. **Seat back support** should be shoulder height.
21. Use a **track-ball** or touch-pad to move cursor.
22. Keep phone within ¾ arm length.
23. Ensure work surface doesn't interfere with movement.
24. Ensure work area **heating is adequate**.
25. Keep reflective light off the computer screen.

Source: John R. Webber, *Safety Technician's Handbook,* 2d ed. (Sherwood Park, Atla: Pacific Safety Institute, 1999), 260. Reproduced by permission of Pacific Safety Institute, 12 Merryvale Circle, Sherwood Park, Alberta, Canada T8A ON3, 780-467-9822.

minimize the load generated by the object being lifted is to shorten the horizontal distance between the spine and the center of gravity of the object. Different jobs (solid waste handler, mechanic, grounds maintenance worker) involve different lifting requirements. Contrary to popular belief, the traditional deep squat position is not always appropriate. There are various safe lifting techniques based on the size, weight, and configuration of the object.

INFECTIOUS DISEASES

Employers are increasingly confronted with problems associated with **infectious diseases** caused by viruses or bacteria.[22] The two major viral diseases that impact the workplace are hepatitis B, which causes liver inflammation, and the human immunodeficiency virus (HIV), which usually leads to acquired immune deficiency syndrome (AIDS). Both of these viruses are called **bloodborne pathogens** because they have their highest viral load in the blood of infected people. Jobs that involve contact with viral-infected blood or other fluids have a significantly higher risk of infection. This includes police officers, firefighters, EMTs, paramedics, custodians, housekeepers, jailers, laundry workers, and sanitation workers. Tuberculosis is caused by a bacterium that attacks the lungs, causing chronic or acute infection. Although it was originally believed that tuberculosis could be eliminated by 2000, tuberculosis cases began to increase in 1985, especially among persons with HIV. Bacteria are carried in airborne particles (from speech, sneeze, or cough) of those infected and spreads to others who inhale the contaminated air.

Control measures for viral exposure include requiring employees to take "universal" precautions (which assume all blood and body fluid is contaminated) such as washing hands after exposure, providing biohazard devices, and using PPE such as goggles, masks, and gloves. Control measures for occupational exposure to tuberculosis include identification and isolation of infected persons, exhaust ventilation, and PPE such as filtration masks.

HEALTH PROMOTION

Workplace safety and health hazard control programs reduce the risks of an employee being injured or contracting an industrial disease. However, the major risk to an employee's health and safety comes from the employee's lifestyle and habits rather than from the work environment. For example, the organization may stress the use of safety devices on earthmoving equipment used in construction, but the equipment operator fails to fasten his or her seat belt for the drive home from work and is seriously injured in an automobile accident. Although appropriate measures are taken to improve air quality in the office, a secretary who smokes may still contract lung cancer. A warehouse worker who is out of shape and overweight is likely to have back problems in spite of the fact that his or her job is designed in accordance with ergonomic principles.

Health promotion or "wellness" activities are designed to encourage employees to access health knowledge, develop good habits, and take responsibility for their own health and safety.[23] This is more than a noble idea—benefits to the organization include lower WC and health benefit costs, fewer accidents, and illnesses and faster recovery, less absenteeism, improved employee attitudes, and productivity gains. Employer approaches to health promotion include measures to deal with emotional and mental issues such as counseling, stress management, and employee assistance programs (discussed in Chapter 14), medical screening and health education and awareness programs.

MEDICAL SCREENING AND SURVEILLANCE

Screening is a method for detecting disease or body dysfunction before an individual would normally seek treatment. Screening tests are administered to individuals without symptoms who might be at high risk for certain adverse health outcomes. Surveillance is the analysis of health information to look for problems with individuals and groups that may be occurring in the workplace and require targeted prevention. Physical examinations (post-offer/baseline, periodic, fitness-for-duty, exit, etc.) are the basis for medical screening and surveillance. Data are used in placement decisions (including accommodations for disabilities) to lower work-related health risks for employees. Data are also used in connection with fitness and health education programs discussed below. It should be noted that physical examinations raise legal issues. They should be carried out in accordance with requirements of the Americans with Disabilities Act and other laws and regulations.

HEALTH EDUCATION AND AWARENESS ACTIVITIES

Health education initiatives focus on regular exercise, proper nutrition, weight control, avoidance of harmful substances (especially tobacco), abstinence or moderation in the use of alcohol, defensive driving, and similar aspects of a healthy lifestyle. The worksite is an excellent setting for these activities. Since employees spend most of their waking hours at work, there can be a relatively heavy "dose" of preventive medicine. Other advantages include more efficient use of employee time and travel, peer support (and peer pressure), and a stable target population. Many local governments have both facilities and in-house expertise for worksite-based programs in their parks and recreation departments. Another alternative is to make arrangements with community-based facilities such as gyms and fitness centers. The local extension (county agent) office has information on all aspects of nutrition and health and will schedule programs during off-duty hours.

http://eapage.com/
EAPage.com provides resource articles and information links regarding employee assistance programs.

PROGRAM ADMINISTRATION

Health programs are somewhat less structured than safety programs; however, many of the same elements apply. An organizational health policy should be developed (it may be part of a health, safety, and security policy), and all activities should be designed to implement the policy. Procedures and rules should cover health hazards in the workplace; however, these can also be combined with safety procedures and rules. Administration should also include training, periodic inspection, and health publicity. Health programs should be evaluated. In addition to using incidence statistics, WC and health benefit claim records can be compared to previous patterns to determine if progress is being made. Other indicators might include changes in absenteeism, modification of lifestyle, and participation in health education and awareness programs.

WORKPLACE SECURITY PROGRAMS

Security is an important aspect of employee health and safety mainly because of the increase in workplace violence. Most of the jobs that have been associated with an elevated risk of violence are found in local government.[24] These include jobs that involve receiving and disbursing money (cashier), delivering passengers (bus driver), delivering services (utility service technician), working in criminal settings other than sworn officers (jailer, court therapist), and jobs performed alone (meter reader) or in small groups (survey party). Workplace security programs include a comprehensive assessment of risk factors (discussed earlier), proper screening of applicants, security hazard prevention and control, and postincident response.[25]

SECURITY HAZARD PREVENTION AND CONTROL

After assessing the risk factors, security procedures and rules (similar to safety procedures and rules discussed earlier) should be developed. They involve measures to increase the security of facilities and measures designed to regulate employee workplace behaviors.[26]

SECURITY OF BUILDINGS AND GROUNDS

There are a number of proactive measures that will substantially reduce the risk of violence to employees. Increased lighting and trimming trees and bushes near buildings and around parking lots will increase the safety of employees entering or leaving the workplace. In some cases this can be supplemented with security escorts or group travel to parked cars, especially at night. Access to certain areas such as detention centers and locations where cash is handled should be controlled with access codes, key cards, ID badges, and security guards.

WORK PRACTICES SECURITY

Work practice rules (also similar to safety rules) should be established and communicated. These might include checking security cameras, reducing the amount of currency in cash drawers, and using drop safes. Procedures should be developed for off-site work such as home visits, delivery of services, or community work. Finally, emergency procedures should be developed to handle incidents such as holdups, security breaches, and acts of violence. These should include providing communications devices and backup means of calling for assistance. As with safety and health, a vital component is open communications and employee reporting of situations that are potential threats to security. Security training should be integrated into

---

Although violence has always been pervasive in our society, until recent years the workplace was considered relatively safe. This is no longer the case. Workplace violence can be experienced in the commission of a crime such as robbery, assaults from angry customers, disgruntled employees, and stalkers or the spillover from domestic violence. While some writers contend that the problem has been sensationalized and overstated, research indicates otherwise.

WORKPLACE SECURITY: AN AREA OF GROWING CONCERN

Homicide, the most easily studied, has been identified as the leading cause of workplace death among women and is the first, second or third leading cause of death in some states for all workers. Still, many employers view workplace violence in terms of incidents that occur at random, rather than as a risk to be managed as in other safety and health areas. More than half of all victimizations are not reported and incidents are often considered to be minor if there is no injury requiring medical treatment. As is the case in safety management such "near misses" are predictive of more serious and even fatal occurrences. This kind of approach exposes workers to unacceptable levels of both physical and psychological risk. Clearly any comprehensive safety and health program must include a carefully conceived and proactive component dealing with workplace security.

Source: Condensed from Joyce A. Simonowitz, "Employee Safety and Security Programs," in Marci C. Balge and Gary R. Krieger, eds., *Occupational Health & Safety* (Washington, D.C.: National Safety Council, 2000), 31.

health and safety training, but it will probably be necessary to include additional instruction in certain safety-sensitive jobs such as those identified earlier. Safety committees covering these jobs should also be involved in security issues.

VIOLENCE PREVENTION

Violence prevention programs tend to focus on three major areas. These are screening out, where possible, applicants with work histories of violent acts; training line managers on how to recognize and deal with the warning signs and characteristics of a potentially violent employee; and developing procedures to diffuse hostile situations and if necessary respond to incidents of violence.[27]

IDENTIFYING POTENTIALLY VIOLENT EMPLOYEES

As Chapter 9 pointed out, the HR department should attempt to gain as much information as possible on new employees. This may be accomplished by the HR staff or referred to investigative services that perform background checks for a fee. Employers are often reluctant to furnish needed information on former employees because of the fear of defamation lawsuits, but many states have passed laws granting qualified immunity to employers who disclose this kind of information.

In general, background investigations are designed to determine if an individual has a history of violence, which is the most valid predictor of who will become violent.[28] However, it is not always possible to uncover all incidents in an applicant's past and some will likely be hired. Also certain other possible indicators may not be grounds for refusal to hire or are difficult to investigate. Employees who are not potentially violent may have relationships with nonemployees who are, such as former intimates. Finally, an employee's personal situation can change over time. Therefore it is necessary to continually monitor indicators in the workforce. Most workplace violence is predictable and preventable if managers and supervisors are sensitive to their employees. Although they may appear to occur randomly, most episodes of violence are preceded by numerous warning signs as illustrated in Exhibit 16-6. Managers and supervisors should be trained to recognize these and other signals and intervene as appropriate (counseling, referral to the HR department or EAP as discussed in Chapter 14).

CRISIS MANAGEMENT

Finally, management must be prepared to deal with situations of potential or actual violence. Crisis management teams composed of HR representatives, managers, and operating employees should perform risk assessments, develop action plans to diffuse explosive situations, and respond to incidents. Violence prevention programs should be integrated with other approaches contained in this chapter and with certain key HR activities including recruitment and selection, training, performance appraisal, and employee relations programs discussed in previous chapters.

POSTINCIDENT RESPONSE

Once an incident has occurred, rapid recovery and corrective action is essential for the employee(s) and the organization. Standard procedures for management and employees should include prompt first aid and medical treatment of the victim and other follow-up care as necessary. Law enforcement (police or sheriff department) should be notified and the premises secured to safeguard evidence.

EXHIBIT 16-6

Psychological dysfunction. Examples include changes in personality, withdrawal, depression, chemical imbalances, paranoia, low self-esteem, and similar disorders.

Personal exigency. These can be work-related (conflicts with coworkers or supervisors, disciplinary action, termination) or involve life and family issues (financial crisis, relationship problems, divorce).

Antisocial or extremist tendencies. Potentially violent individuals are often "loners" who resent authority, hold extremist views, and believe conspiracy theories.

Aggression. This includes a tendency to use profanity, verbally or psychologically abuse other people, make threats, abuse property, or engage in sexual harassment.

Lack of support system. In many cases the individual may not have family or friends to empathize, offer assistance, and so on, may not have access to personal counseling, or may reject such support.

Fixation with weapons. This characteristic is significant to the extent it is associated with characteristics listed above. Individuals who are hunters, gun collectors, and so forth are not seen as violent.

Source: Based on Jim Merrill, "Violence in the Workplace: A Complex Issue with Multiple Causes," Society for Human Resource Management White Paper at *http://www.shrm.org* (December 2000); and Joyce A Simonowitz, "Employee Safety and Security Programs," in Marci C. Balge and Gary R. Krieger, eds., *Occupational Health & Safety*, 3d ed. (Washington, D.C.: National Safety Council, 2000), 315–323.

In addition to physical injuries, victimized employees may suffer mental trauma. Postincident counseling and/or referral to the employee assistance program (see Chapter 14) may be necessary. Restoring the facility to its original clean and orderly state after any investigation is also important to restore normal functioning. As was the case with other types of incidences such as accidents or illnesses, a complete investigation should be conducted and a report prepared. Analysis of the results should be used to modify and improve security measures.

SUMMARY

Local governments, like all employers, have an obligation to provide their employees with a safe, healthful, and secure work environment. Safety refers to the avoidance of injury-causing accidents. Health is a broader term and includes both the prevention of illness and maintaining the overall well-being of employees. Security involves protection of facilities from unauthorized access and the protection of employees at the worksite or while they are on assignment.

The legal framework for safety and health includes state workers' compensation laws and the federal Occupational Safety and Health Act. WC deals with problems that have already occurred. OSHA and similar state laws are proactive in that they seek to prevent the occurrence of accidents and illnesses. Safety and health efforts are enhanced when accurate and consistent data are obtained to identify causes of accidents and illnesses and focus attention on the severity of problems. Baseline figures on incidence rates are needed to establish goals and facilitate the evaluation of safety and health programs.

The major objective of a safety program is accident reduction. Accomplishing this objective has direct benefits in terms of employees' job performance and attendance. Another benefit involves reduction of legal liability exposure from personal injuries and property damage occurring in the process of providing government services. This emerging area is known as risk management. Components of a safety program include safety procedures and rules, safety training, safety committees, safety publicity, and accident investigation.

Organizational health programs seek to reduce or prevent the occurrence of work-related illnesses (also known as occupational diseases). Health programs involve identifying health hazards, adopting preventive measures, and conducting health promotion activities.

Security is an important aspect of employee health and safety mainly because of the increase in workplace violence. Most of the jobs that have been associated with an elevated risk of violence are found in local government. Workplace security programs include a comprehensive assessment of risk factors, screening of applicants, identification and referral of potentially violent employees, hazard prevention and control, and postincident response

QUESTIONS FOR REVIEW AND DISCUSSION

1. Differentiate among safety, health, and security as organizational activities.
2. Briefly describe the responsibilities of the following positions in maintaining a safe and healthful work environment.
   a. Mayor
   b. City manager
   c. Head of public works department
   d. Sewer maintenance supervisor
   e. Sewer operator
3. Describe the nature and purpose of the Occupational Safety and Health Act (OSHA).
4. Why is adequate measurement of incidence rates a prerequisite to effective safety and health programs?
5. Outline the components of a safety program.
6. Give examples of health risks faced by employees of local government.
7. Why do local governments, particularly municipalities, have an advantage over private firms in offering worksite-based health education and awareness programs?
8. How would you evaluate the effectiveness of the following:
   a. a safety training program for supervisors
   b. a health promotion program for all employees
9. Give examples of several local government jobs that are exposed to an elevated risk of violence.
10. How can workplace security activities be integrated with the safety and health program?

ENDNOTES

[1] Robert L. Mathis and John H. Jackson, *Human Resource Management*, 9th ed. (Cincinnati: South-Western, 1999), 530.

[2] This chapter draws on Marci Z. Balge and Gary R. Krieger, eds., *Occupational Health & Safety*, 3d ed. (Washington, D.C.: National Safety Council, 2000).

[3] Wendell L. French, *Human Resources Management*, 4th ed. (Boston: Houghton Mifflin, 1998), 35.

[4] Mary Ann Godbout, "Heading for Trouble," *Occupational Health and Safety* 68 (August 1999), 76–79.

[5] The Occupational Safety and Health Act at 29 U.S.C.§§564 et seq.

[6] Condensed from U.S. Department of Labor, Occupational Safety and Health Administration, OSHA Fact Sheet 93-01 (1993) and *All About OSHA*, revised edition (1995).

[7] This section draws on Jimmy R.. Glisson, *Safety Program Development: Fundamental Loss Control Programs for Local Governments* (Tallahassee, Fla.: Crawford, 1990, as updated).

[8] Michael Larsen, "Health and Safety Program Design," in Balge and Krieger, 109–116.

[9] Larsen, 113.

[10] Larsen.

[11] Based on Dan Peterson, "Safety Programs," in Balge and Krieger, 153–156, and John R. Webber, *Safety Technician's Handbook*, 2d ed. (Sherwood Park, Alta: Pacific Safety Institute, 1999).

[12] See, for example, Dan Peterson, *Techniques of Safety Management*, 3d ed. (Des Plaines, Ill.: American Society of Safety Engineers, 1998).

[13] Dennis Zimet, "A Comprehensive Safety and Health Program for the Small Employer," *Occupational Health and Safety* 67 (August 1999), 129.

[14] Janicak, Christopher, "Computer-based Training: Developing Programs with the Knowledge-based Safety Training System," *Professional Safety* 44 (June 1999), 34–36.

[15] Peterson, 162, and Glisson, Sec. 2.

[16] Theodore S. Ingalls Jr. "Using Scorecards to Measure Safety Performance," *Professional Safety* 44 (December 1999), 23–28.

[17] Douglas P. Fowler, "Industrial Hygiene Profession," in Balge and Krieger, 101–104.

[18] This section draws on Robert J. Grossman, "Out with the Bad Air," *HR Magazine* 45 (October 2000), 37–45.

[19] Paul H. Marshall, "Addressing Indoor Air Quality Concerns," *Occupational Hazards* 58 (January 1996), 83–85.

[20] Grossman, 43.

[21] Ira Janowitz and David Thompson, "Ergonomics Programs," in Balge and Krieger, 277–314.

[22] Connie Lawson, Nita Drolet, Regina M. Cambridge, Kenneth R. Pelletier, Thomas J. Coats, Edwin B. Fisher Jr., and Joan M. Heins, "Occupational Health Nursing Programs," in Balge and Krieger, 127–151, especially 143–146.

[23] Lawson et al., 128–135.

[24] Stephen C. Yohay and Melissa L. Peppe, "Workplace Violence: Employer Responsibilities and Liabilities," *Occupational Hazards* 58 (July 1996), 21–26.

[25] Joyce A. Simonowitz, "Employee Safety and Security Programs," in Balge and Krieger, 315–323.

[26] See, for example, Richard A. Gardiner and Richard A. Grassie, "A Comprehensive Approach to Workplace Safety," *Security Management* 38 (July 1994), 97–102; and "Employers Should Take Workplace Security Measures," *Capital District Business Review* 26 (September 1999), 25–27.

[27] This section is based on Chenier and James F. Bowman and Christopher J. Zigmund, "State Government Response to Workplace Violence," *Public Personnel Management* 26 (Summer 1997), 289–301.

[28] Simonowitz, 318.

To best utilize the human resources of a local government the executive leadership, line managers, and HR practitioners must deal with key organizational, management, and professional issues. This final part consists of Chapter 17, which first examines the state of HR management in local government and recommends how these issues can be addressed most effectively. The chapter concludes with a discussion of the direction in which HR management is expected to move during the next few years based on current challenges and emerging trends.

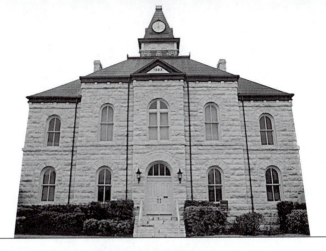

CHAPTER 17
LOOKING AHEAD IN
HUMAN RESOURCE MANAGEMENT

WHERE DO WE GO FROM HERE?

Hugh Allen, SPHR, has lived in McLemore County since taking the position of vice president for human resources at Apex Corporation, one of the county's largest employers, almost 10 years ago. Hugh holds a master's degree in HR management and is past president of the local chapter of the Society for Human Resource Management (SHRM). Hugh has built a very strong HR program at Apex that has contributed greatly to making the corporation an industry leader.

Hugh was not active in local politics until last year, when he agreed to become part of a slate of mainly businesspersons who ran for the county commission on a platform of increasing efficiency and improving service quality. Much to everyone's surprise, the slate was elected and took office in January of this year. With the assistance of the institute of government at the state university, the new administration undertook its first initiative, which was to develop a strategic plan. During the process, Hugh became familiar with the operations of the county HR department, which consists of the director, John Andrews, an assistant director, a personnel analyst, and two clerks. John has completed three years toward a degree in administrative science and is the only member of the department who has had college training. The department serves a county workforce of approximately 650 employees.

Based on Hugh's observations, the HR operation seems to be well managed, but focused mainly on implementing established procedures and enforcing rules. John is open-minded, but not really clear about what Hugh means by a "strategic role" for the HR management. He also points out that with only five employees, the department is hard-pressed to keep up with routine activities. The department holds membership in the International Personnel Management Association (IPMA), and John occasionally reads *Public Personnel Management*. However, Hugh does not recall ever seeing him at SHRM meetings, although other public sector professionals participate regularly (there is no local IPMA chapter). John has not given much thought to becoming certified. On the bookshelf in John's office, Hugh noticed a copy of a 1985 edition of a public personnel text.

Hugh believes very strongly that the HR department could make a major contribution in implementing the county's strategic goals, but several things have to happen first. It is obvious that the county government needs to consider providing additional resources to the department. Since he has been successful in adding staff and increasing funding in his corporate office, he was confident that he can sell the idea to his fellow commissioners. At the same time, the county HR effort needs to take on a strategic focus and become more proactive. Finally, John and his staff have to take more responsibility for their own professional development if they are going to be up to the challenges that lie ahead.

INTRODUCTION

Throughout this book it has been stressed that local governments have a great opportunity to manage their human resources in such a way that people contribute willingly and harmoniously to the achievement of productivity and quality goals. To this point the discussion has included the history, legal environment, behavioral foundations, and various activity areas of HR. It is now useful to consider the HR function as a whole and to suggest approaches that offer the greatest potential for success.

The effectiveness of HR management in a local government setting depends on a number of factors. Because cities and counties are diverse in size, political organization, and financial resources, it would be a mistake to suggest that there is "one best way" to organize and manage the HR function and that HR practitioners must have certain prescribed attributes. There are, however, organizational, management, and professional issues in which clear indicators and trends have emerged. This chapter proposes a way of addressing these issues and concludes with a projection of future directions in HR management.

ORGANIZATIONAL ISSUES: HR MANAGEMENT STATUS AND RESOURCES

In order to make an effective contribution, the HR function in local government must have organizational status commensurate with its importance and sufficient resources to make its maximum contribution. The organization addresses these issues by determining the reporting relationship of HR, the staffing of the HR unit, and the funding of HR programs and activities.

ESTABLISHING AN APPROPRIATE REPORTING RELATIONSHIP FOR HR MANAGEMENT

Two important trends in local government with implications for HR management are the continued movement toward the executive responsibility model and an increasing focus on strategic management. Many local governments have abolished boards and commissions, or limit them to an advisory role.[1] The executive responsibility model facilitates managerial innovation and accountability by allowing the chief executive to exercise substantial influence over how the HR function is managed. The strategic approach is designed to ensure that HR decisions contribute to the accomplishment of the government's mission and objectives.

The involvement of the HR leader and staff is crucial in deciding appropriate HR strategies. Because of the vital nature of HR management and its impact on the organization, the authors believe that HR management should report to the chief executive officer of the jurisdiction. The model suggests that this will be a city manager or county administrator but would also apply to other arrangements like a "strong mayor." Although it is not unusual for HR to report to another executive (such as the finance director), this relegates the HR function to a status that emphasizes procedures and record keeping and filters HR input through an additional level of administration.

Providing Adequate HR Staffing and Funding

The resources allocated to the HR function have a major impact on the quality of HR management. In small organizations particularly, the HR leader and staff are spread too thin. In 2000, the median HR staff per 100 employees was 0.8 for education and government (and probably lower for local government) compared with 1.0 for all employers. In transportation, communications, and utilities, a group that has basic similarities to local government, the ratio was 1.1.[2] A related area of concern is the budget for HR activities. In 2000, the median funding for HR as a percentage of the total operating budget for government and education was 0.4 (also probably less than that in local government). By contrast, the level was 0.9 for all employers.[3]

HR units with low staffing levels and insufficient funding are hard-pressed to keep up with the organization's day-to-day needs. They can carry out a limited number of activities, such as posting vacancies, certifying and referring applicants, dealing with classification issues, keeping records, monitoring legal compliance, and submitting reports. Less attention can be given to support activities such as planning, analyzing jobs and work, and maintaining internally equitable and externally competitive pay structures. Many of the proactive approaches discussed in this book (developmental training, measuring and rewarding performance, designing various initiatives to enhance employee relations, etc.) may never be implemented at all.

Recall from Chapter 1 that the success of an organization depends on how well its resources are managed. These include financial, physical, information, and human resources. In the final analysis the wise use of these resources and the productivity of the organization as a whole depend on effective and efficient functioning of human resources. This, however, comes at a cost. Having proactive HR management that contributes to objectives and adds value requires a commitment of people and money. Demonstrating on a continuing basis that HR activities are linked to organizational performance is the way to make this an attractive investment.

Michael J. Lottio, the first nonpractitioner chair of SHRM, suggests that HR, often underappreciated, is the foundation of business and is poised to become a major player in the affairs of organizations:

HR Management: A Major Player

HR has traditionally been seen as the soft side of business, but I submit that attracting and retaining the right people for your organization is the hard side of business because that is the foundation on which everything is based. I think that HR should be repositioning itself as a key profit center within this fight for talent. I also believe that HR should see itself as the implementer of the vision, mission and core values of the organization. And I think that is an awesome responsibility.

Source: Bill Leonard, "Our Horizons Are Limitless," *HR Magazine* 45 (January 2000), 45–49.

MANAGEMENT ISSUES: HR ACTIVITIES AND PROGRAMS

The previous chapters have focused on individual components of HR management, such as analyzing jobs and work, staffing the organization, developing employees and measuring their work contributions, designing compensation programs, enhancing employee relations, and providing security. There have been several recurring themes. First, these activities are related to each other. Second, they should collectively contribute to the accomplishment of strategic objectives. Finally, although the HR department has important roles to play, it shares many with line managers who are ultimately responsible for managing the people in the organization. It would be useful to reinforce each of these themes.

TAKING AN INTEGRATED APPROACH

It is important to recognize that HR activities are interrelated. For example, a merit or incentive pay plan should be connected to a system designed to measure performance, which relates back to work behaviors and competencies identified and documented in job analysis. In designing training programs it is necessary to assess the output of "upstream" activities such as the selection process, which may not produce new hires with all the requisite skills needed in their work assignments, and "downstream" indicators such as performance ratings that identify problem areas. In other words, HR activities should be viewed not as a linear series they but as a network. Each activity receives input from or is influenced by several other activities.

Taking an integrated approach recognizes that performance is strongly influenced by these interactions and that two or more HR activities can achieve results of which either is incapable. The creation of a whole that is greater than the sum of its parts is called **synergy**, sometimes referred to as "2 + 2 = 5." In other words, the sum of benefits of the combined operations in HR is more than if they remained separate. A related advantage is that HR performance is more efficient when all possible impacts are considered. For example, in conducting a job analysis project for classification purposes, it would be useful to also collect information needed to support test validation, determine training needs, and establish safety procedures.

CONTRIBUTING TO STRATEGIC OBJECTIVES

Having the pieces fit together is a necessary but not sufficient condition. A well-designed, integrated, and smoothly functioning HR system does not necessarily facilitate the achievement of the organization's goals and may even be detrimental.[4] It is also necessary to determine what strategies are to be implemented by the various HR activities that make up the system.[5] As we have continually pointed out, there are within each area a number of practices that have been shown to be effective. Some, such as merit pay, are receiving increasingly positive reviews in the literature as part of the "new pay" approach for local governments. It is possible to design a system that properly integrates all necessary HR activities and accurately measures and rewards individual contributions. But is that what the organization wishes to accomplish? If the objective is to have employees work across job boundaries and maximize group performance, other reward systems such as skill-based pay and gainsharing are more appropriate.

http://www.mapnp.org/ library/plan_dec/ str_plan/str_plan.htm

The Management Assistance Program for Nonprofits provides comprehensive information on links to information on strategic planning.

While it might be desirable if every unit of local government carried out strategic planning in accordance with the process described in Chapter 5 (write mission statement, conduct SWOT analysis, establish strategic objectives, etc.), many, espe-

The HR department mission is the answer to the question "What are we about and what are we going to accomplish for our customers?" A well-reasoned mission statement provides both direction and a sense of purpose as shown by the mission statements of the 2000 winners of the IPMA Award for Excellence:

ON A MISSION

- **San Jose, California**—To deliver innovative and timely human resource services and leadership to enable the city, its departments, and employees to provide world-class municipal services to its diverse residents and businesses.
- **Gaithersburg, Maryland**—To provide high-quality services to the city staff, as well as the citizens served, and to bring creative human resource solutions that support the overall mission of the city, as well as the city's strategic plan.
- **City of Baton Rouge/Parish of East Baton Rouge**—To provide the human resources and services that best meet the requirements and expectations of city/parish employees and the public in an efficient, effective, and economical manner.

The statements above are more than words on paper; they define the values and core principles of these departments will uphold as well as the benefits the organization should expect. They communicate meaning, generate enthusiasm, and inspire people to put forth their best efforts. The results, in these cases, speak for themselves.

Source: "2000 Agency Award for Excellence," *IPMA News* 66 (August 2000), 5–7.

cially small organizations, do not. However, strategic planning does not necessarily require a formal, sequential process of the kind described in textbooks. It is more important that managers think and act strategically by linking what they do to the results they wish to accomplish. HR management should work closely with the executive leadership and elected officials to determine or at least impute the strategic objectives. When this has been accomplished, it is necessary to develop and obtain approval for HR policies to guide activities and programs.[6]

ADJUSTING TO SHIFTING ROLES AND RESPONSIBILITIES

The responsibility for many HR activities is divided between the HR department and line management. In selection, for instance, the HR department may screen and refer applicants while a department head recommends which applicant to hire. Establishing performance appraisal procedures and designing forms are tasks in which HR usually takes the lead, but managers almost always rate job performance and hold appraisal interviews. It is intuitive that the effectiveness of HR management depends on how well line managers carry out these and other responsibilities.

Recall from Chapter 1 the service, advisory, policy control, and employee advocacy roles of HR management. Providing technical services and advocating employee concerns are well understood roles that will continue to be performed mainly by the HR unit in much the same way as before. In regard to advisory and policy control roles, the situation is changing. To a great extent HR management has affected outcomes in line departments by performing these roles. As advisors, HR professionals typically interpreted policy and recommended a particular course of action. If a line manager insisted on doing something else, then the HR professional could exercise functional authority and ensure that policy guidelines were followed. Obviously it was better when line management accepted the advice, but HR management still had the final word.

In many organizations, existing HR systems are impediments to accomplishing the organization's strategic purpose. Often they are designed to reduce variability and to standardize behavior, not to promote the flexibility needed to achieve objectives. HR professionals must

A NEW PARADIGM FOR HR MANAGEMENT

direct their efforts away from procedures and rules and deal with the same strategic and operating issues as others who are running the organization. They must have a sound working knowledge of business drivers such as revenue, productivity, and customer satisfaction. They must focus on building organizational capability, coaching and assisting managers, not handling specific people-related activities for them.

Source: Excerpted and adapted from Richard A. Shafer, "Only the Agile Will Survive," *HR Magazine* 44 (December 1999), 50–51.

In many organizations this is no longer how things work, especially in such key HR activity areas as selection and pay. Increasingly, HR policy control is being delegated to line departments, and these departments may also have more influence in policy development. This means that HR management must present itself as a facilitator rather than an enforcer.[7] For a good illustration, consider an organization that decides to replace traditional pay grades with broad pay "bands" as discussed in Chapter 12. A major premise of this approach is that responsibility for establishing ranges and setting pay should be shifted from the HR department to line managers. Of course, the HR unit will continue to be involved by providing labor market data, assisting with the determination of "shadow grades," and counseling on issues related to the administration of individual pay. Ideally this approach provides needed flexibility to line managers to maintain market competitiveness and reward performance without creating problems such as pay inequities, cost overruns, or legal challenges. Policy control is, of course, a means of preventing such problems, but the HR role has been diminished. Moreover, there is less policy to be controlled because such mechanisms as grade ranges, midpoints, and pay increase guidelines no longer exist.

This is only one example of how decentralization of HR activities has made it essential for the HR unit to build strong relationships with line managers. As discussed in the following section, this can be accomplished when HR professionals have a strong knowledge base, inspire confidence, and lead by example.

STAFFING ISSUES: CREDIBILITY OF THE HR STAFF

The HR department in local government does not possess the ability to reward and punish, which are major sources of organizational power. One writer suggests that to be effective the HR professional "must become an effective teacher and molder of ideas."[8] This requires the ability to influence and inspire, and derives from the person rather than the position he or she holds. In HR management, **expert power** and **referent power** are especially important.[9] Expert power is based on the possession of valued knowledge. When HR management has the right answers to questions of line managers and is organized to provide support, it wields expert power. Thus, in a very real sense, "knowledge is power." Referent power attaches to individuals because people identify with them and admire them. When HR management exhibits integrity, adheres to high ethical standards, and sets the example, it wields referent power.

BUILDING CAPABILITIES OF HR PROFESSIONALS

The capabilities of HR professionals in local government have major implications. Clearly, HR management should be viewed less as learning intuitive techniques, following prescribed routines, and enforcing rules and more as drawing on a body of knowledge. HR management must become more like other knowledge-based fields.

A good example is engineering, which has historically been the most well respected profession in local government.[10] Decision makers in a municipality would routinely approve a recommendation by the city engineer to make major repairs when a bridge appears to be sound but technical analysis indicates that serious deterioration has occurred. They would accept both the body of knowledge in civil engineering and the city engineer's mastery of that knowledge. It is less likely that the same decision makers would agree so readily to a recommendation by the HR director to discontinue unstructured interviews that are having an adverse effect on minorities and women in several city departments (possibly including the engineering department). They are more likely to discount the HR body of knowledge (such as literature showing that such interviews are unreliable and create legal risk) as well as the professional expertise of the HR manager. If the city engineer is degreed and certified (highly probable) and the HR director lacks such credentials (as likely as not), such scenarios are quite predictable.

In teaching an accreditation course for city and county HR administrators, one of the authors often hears the following request: "Will you talk to my (city manager, county administrator, mayor, etc.)? They need to hear this from an expert." Unfortunately, this is not the solution. The HR practitioner must *become* the expert. The broad range of issues faced by HR practitioners suggests that knowledge equivalent to a college degree is essential, and certification (discussed below) is highly desirable, especially for the HR leader. In large departments, this also applies to higher-level managers and professional specialists. The HR leader should have a strong foundation in a number of competency areas including organizational management, employment, training and development, compensation, employee and labor relations, health and safety, and employment law. Many writers also suggest that the HR leader should have experience in line management positions.[11] Other HR managers and professionals should have academic credentials in their field of specialization.

Computer literacy has, for some time, been identified as a requirement for HR practitioners at all levels. HR departments in both the public and private sectors heavily use software applications such as word processing, basic spreadsheets, and HRIS. Many organizations, however, do not use the Internet for information retrieval, and do not integrate computer software with HR activities.[12] Unless HR professionals become skilled in information retrieval, there will be a continuing waste of the Internet's potential to provide timely information on virtually any HR topic. Other applications can provide additional benefits. For example, certain HR activities and processes such as validating tests, computing return on investments, projecting trends, modeling the outcome of alternative courses of action, and determining market pay lines require the use of quantitative techniques such as financial and statistical analysis. Such techniques are greatly facilitated by the use of advanced spreadsheet applications and statistical programs.

HR professionals also need to constantly update their knowledge in a field that is constantly changing. Involvement in professional associations is one of the best ways to maintain technical proficiency. The International Personnel Management Association (IPMA) addresses HR issues and concerns unique to the public sector while the Society for Human Resource Management (SHRM) deals with areas of general interest and is more likely to have a local chapter. Both associations have certification programs. SHRM has offered certification through the Human Resource Certification Institute (HRCI) since 1974, and IPMA introduced its public sector certification program in 1999. Both the HR Competency Model established by IPMA and the Content Outline of the HR Body of Knowledge of the Human Resource Certification Institute (HRCI) are shown in the Appendix.

INCREASING DIVERSITY IN THE HR UNIT

In the typical HR department the highest proportion of women and minorities are found at the clerk level. Approximately 70 percent of the professionals are white, 17 percent are Hispanic, and 14 percent are African American. Although HR is an area in which women and minorities are well represented, diversity is reflected mainly in lower to middle ranks of HR units. At senior managerial levels, key positions tend to be held by white males.[13]

While what is true in the aggregate is not necessarily true for a particular HR department in local government, it does raise an important point. HR diversity is an issue of credibility. If an organization is committed to building a diverse workforce, it seems reasonable to expect that the HR staff should exemplify diversity in its own ranks. Wally Bonaparte, who manages recruiting and selection for the city of Detroit, supports this view. "The role that HR plays within an organization has to be a leadership role, indicating to the rest of the organization that what we are asking them to do, we are also doing," he says.[14]

What does it take for an HR professional to move into a strategic position at the top of an organization? This question was posed to a group of eight senior HR executives serving in both the public and private sectors. Here is what they believe are the keys to success:

KEYS TO SUCCESS

- **Solid Foundation of HR Knowledge.** This includes both a mastery of HR competencies and an understanding of how technology and financial issues affect the profession. Many of these individuals held advanced certification (SPHR) and all stressed the need for continuous professional development through active participation in external professional and industry associations.
- **Business Perspective.** There was universal agreement that HR professionals need to understand both business fundamentals and the characteristics of the "industry" (manufacturing, financial, government, etc.) and to view their roles as strategic contributors rather than specialists. Experience *outside* the HR field was considered essential, either through prior service in line management positions or special projects and assignments.
- **Willingness to Take Risks.** Taking on unfamiliar and challenging tasks was seen as an essential element in building HR executive potential. These individuals were clear on the requirement to become proactive, using expressions such as "asking forgiveness, not permission," "pushing the envelope," and "moving out of the HR comfort zone."
- **Communications Skills.** An HR professional must be adept in handling a wide range of interpersonal roles—counseling, negotiating, selling, resolving conflicts, and building consensus were mentioned. While some people are naturally better communicators than others, it was pointed out that the necessary skills can be learned through study, experiential learning, and professional development.

Source: Lin Grensing-Pophal, "Getting to the Top: Advice from Those Who've Made It," *HR Magazine* 45 (December 2000), 96–102.

The methods described in Chapter 9 for developing affirmative action plans (workforce analysis, job group analysis, availability analysis, and goal setting) apply generally. Note that the focus is on identification of *qualified* candidates in areas of underrepresentation based on race, ethnicity, sex, and so forth, rather than on establishing quotas and "hiring by the numbers." Diversity initiatives in HR should also be tied to strategic objectives as discussed in Chapter 14. How various groups should ideally be represented in the HR staff of a local government will likely be different than for other types of organizations, even those in the same labor market.

DEMONSTRATING HIGH ETHICAL STANDARDS

http://www.eoa.org
The Ethics Officer Association is a nonprofit organization that provides programs and links to numerous articles, survey findings, and research on ethics.

Ethics, as defined in Chapter 1, is a system of values that considers business, legal, and moral criteria in making decisions. Therefore, an ethical decision is one that benefits the organization, complies with the law, and follows moral principles. Because virtually all decisions involve people, HR management has a major influence on the organization's social behavior and should be looked to as a role model.[15] The need to be considered a partner with line managers and viewed as a facilitator rather than an enforcer can create pressures to go along with, and possibly cover for, questionable decisions. In such cases the HR manager should stand firm. Being a team player is one thing, but when things are headed down the wrong path, the organization requires the services of a "dedicated dissenter."[16]

Besides adhering to high personal and professional ethical standards, HR professionals should contribute to the development of policies that stress fair treatment, workplace rights, and respect for human dignity. They can also make a strong impact by pointing out the negative consequences of unethical acts and decisions.

FUTURE DIRECTIONS IN HR MANAGEMENT

It is at this point that textbook authors gaze into the future and confidently predict the direction in which HR management will move. Planning horizons for this purpose tend to be five years or the approximate date of the next edition, whichever comes first. This exercise is considerably less speculative now than at certain times in the past. The advent of the new millennium stimulated a concerted effort among noted authorities in the field to identify key issues and emerging trends. These were noted in Chapter 1 and addressed in subsequent discussions of various activity areas. With due respect to noted authorities, much of what has been projected in the way of future challenges has already emerged. The authors should also acknowledge that as they suggested innovative approaches and presented state-of-the-art methods and techniques for dealing with a particular challenge, it was almost always possible to locate an example of a local government where a project had already been implemented. With these qualifiers in mind, it is now useful to briefly review the issues that HR management will be dealing with during the coming years.

THE LEGAL ENVIRONMENT

The next few years will be characterized by increased litigation along with interpretations by courts and action by regulatory agencies involving existing laws. Most rulings will tend to increase both administrative requirements and legal exposure of employers, as did recent court decisions in sexual harassment creating "vicarious liability" and the recent ADA regulations regarding reasonable accommodation.

Rulings that favor employers are less likely. For example, it would be useful if FLSA regulations were reformed to accommodate new pay initiatives such as gainsharing, but reducing administrative burdens on employers has never been a major priority of the Wage and Hour Division. On the other hand, there is no real indication that Congress will enact major employment legislation or that courts are about to create additional workplace rights.

ORGANIZATIONAL MANAGEMENT AND LEADERSHIP

There will be a continued movement toward flatter organization structures and a more participative leadership style. Supervisors and managers will increasingly assume the role of coaches rather than bosses. There will be more emphasis on work teams, group decision making, improved service quality, and better customer relations. Although line managers are responsible for implementing these approaches, HR management will be expected to support these efforts by reviewing (and often redeveloping) HR systems and processes, training managers, and becoming a catalyst for organizational change.

HUMAN RESOURCE PLANNING

Local governments will increasingly use a strategic approach to planning in order to gain a competitive advantage. Larger organizations will follow a formal, sequential process, while small jurisdictions will use an informal approach. HR planning will be linked to the strategic objectives of the organization. The strategic approach also involves an expectation on the part of HR management to make the "business case." Organizations will use various information technologies in the planning process, and human resource information systems (HRISs) will become more sophisticated. Certain metrics accepted as standards of measurement in each activity area will be widely used to demonstrate the value of HR practices to both internal and external stakeholders.

DESIGN AND ANALYSIS OF WORK ACTIVITIES

Ways of organizing work will continue to evolve. While traditional jobs will always exist, in many cases the possible set of responsibilities and tasks will be expanded to allow for more flexibility in work assignments. In some cases job boundaries will disappear with work assignments made and pay structures developed to utilize the qualifications of individual employees. The process of analyzing and documenting work performed and worker requirements will include alternative formats such as task clusters and skill sets. Such formats are necessary for input to other HR systems that are not job based, such as training programs and pay structures used in skill-based pay plans.

RECRUITING AND SELECTION

Because of a tight labor market with few people seeking jobs, intense competition for talent in key areas such as information technology, and the need to build a diverse workforce, recruiting strategies will become increasingly proactive. Organizations will continue to use traditional approaches augmented internally by computerized talent banks and electronic job posting and externally by home pages that list employment opportunities and accept on-line applications. In the selection process, organizations will continue to refine and improve methods and techniques. There will be increased utilization of supplemental application forms, validated work-sample and ability tests, and structured interviews in order to better match applicants with jobs and meet legal requirements. However, organizations will be less successful in hiring workers who can be expected to make long-term commitments to the organization.

TRAINING AND DEVELOPMENT

Rapidly changing technology, skills deficiencies, and difficulties in recruiting external talent will increase the pressure on local governments to develop the capabilities of both operating employees and managers. Accordingly, training and development activities will become more systemized and comprehensive. Increased attention will be given to assessment of needs and establishment of training objectives. Approaches to training will move from pedagogy to andragogy (adult learning). In addition to traditional training methods, there will be an increased use of distance learning technologies such as web-based training, interactive video, and computer-assisted instruction. While additional resources will be allocated to training and development, there will be an expectation that training outcomes be evaluated and that the benefits of training justify the costs.

PERFORMANCE APPRAISAL

Local governments are beginning to place more emphasis on measurement of work contributions, both as a means of improving employee performance and developing potential and also as a basis for administrative decisions involving pay, promotion, and discharge. In general the focus will be on improving the appraisal process, using behavior and outcome-based techniques that have been available for some time. Increasing attention will be given to validation of appraisal instruments and training of raters in setting expectations, counseling employees, and observing and measuring performance. Multisource appraisal or 360-degree feedback will continue to generate interest, but there are concerns about whether this approach can be implemented effectively or such feedback can be used for administrative decisions.

COMPENSATION

Job-based classification and pay systems will continue to be widely used in local government. In recent years, however, approaches such as broadbanding have begun to generate considerable interest. In the area of pay administration there is a move away from granting annual "step" increases toward rewarding individual and team performance and/or skills and competencies. Merit pay will continue to gain acceptance, along with nontraditional approaches such as skill-based pay and gain-sharing at a somewhat slower pace. Benefits programs will become more flexible and organizations will focus on controlling retirement and health care costs.

EMPLOYEE RELATIONS

Local governments will become more proactive in enhancing employee relations. Rather than wait for problems to occur, organizations will develop programs to deal with underlying causes. Increasing attention will be given to identifying and removing stress associated with workplace conditions and assisting employees in coping with other sources of stress. The need to balance work and family for single parents and dual-career couples will be a major concern. Growth is expected in employee assistance programs (EAPs) and work/life initiatives.

LABOR RELATIONS

Union-management relationships have stabilized during recent years. Unions will continue to be strongest in the Northeast and weakest in the Sunbelt. Federal legislation that mandates collective bargaining for state and local employees will continue to be introduced in Congress but is not expected to become law. Although the relationship between labor and management in the United States has traditionally been adversarial, there is a growing movement toward an alternative model known as labor management cooperation or participative decision making (PDM). There will be increasing numbers of programs focusing on employee involvement in productivity, service quality, and related initiatives of interest to both labor and management.

HEALTH, SAFETY, AND SECURITY

The trend for local governments to improve workplace safety and reduce health hazards will continue to be reinforced by projected increases in workers' compensation rates. The emphasis will be on prevention of accidents and illnesses and programs will become more sophisticated. Violence committed at work against employees by coworkers, former employees, and intimates, along with vandalism, theft of organizational property, and robbery will be growing concerns. Local governments will integrate workplace security measures with safety and employee relations activities.

CONCLUDING COMMENT

The theories, principles, and techniques presented in this book, with their supporting research, should provide a framework for HR professionals in local government to deal with contemporary challenges and emerging trends. It should be stressed, however, that there is no science in which everything is known and all relationships are proved. In HR management, which is a social science, theories and principles are even less exact than in the physical and biological sciences. For example, contrary to the predictions of expectancy theory, pay increases based on job performance will actually demotivate some employees. Likewise, the most carefully designed employment test will select some applicants who will perform poorly on the job and reject others who would have succeeded.

However, although there is no "grand unifying theory," the science of HR management does allow us to design practical approaches that improve the contribution of the organization's human resources. Therefore we should not be discouraged by the occasional difficulties and irritations; they come with the job. If we cannot always make things exactly right, we can usually make them better. It has been said, "To look for solutions to the difficult problems is to profoundly misunderstand their natures. The quest is not to solve, but to diminish; not to cure, but to manage . . ."[17]

The term "quest" might be somewhat heroic, in that it suggests an adventurous journey in pursuit of a lofty purpose. It also suggests that one occasionally tilts at windmills. As most of those who practice our profession in local government will attest, HR management is some of both. On with the quest.

QUESTIONS FOR REVIEW AND DISCUSSION

1. Briefly discuss why HR management in local government should report to the chief executive officer of the jurisdiction.

2. What are the negative consequences when HR units in local governments are understaffed and underfunded?

3. Consider the service, advisory, policy control, and employee advocacy roles of HR management. Which roles will be performed as before and which are changing?

4. How does taking an integrated approach to HR management create *synergy*?

5. Select possible strategies in two HR activity areas and identify techniques that best implement these strategies.

6. Briefly discuss why it is important for HR professionals to have *expert* and *referent* power.

7. Why have college degrees and professional certification become so important in HR management?

8. Why is it important for HR professionals to serve as ethical role models?

9. Consider the projections for future directions in HR management. How can HR professionals become prepared to deal with the challenges that lie ahead?

ENDNOTES

[1] Jonathan Tompkins and Aleksandra Stapcznski, "Planning and Paying for Work Done," in Siegrun Fox Freyss, ed., *Human Resource Management in Local Government* (Washington, D.C.: International City/County Management Association, 1999), 1–27.

[2] Bureau of National Affairs, *Bulletin to Management*, "Human Resource Activities, Budgets and Staffs, 1999–2000," SHRM-BNA Survey No. 65, S-13.

[3] Bureau of National Affairs, S-19.

[4] Richard A. Schafer, "Only the Agile Will Survive," *HR Magazine* 44 (December 1999), 50–51.

[5] Tompkins and Stapcznski. See also Carla Joinson, "Public Sector HR: Leaving Bureacracy Behind," *HR Magazine* 45 (June 2000), 78–83.

[6] Tompkins and Stapcznski.

[7] Judith Brown, "Marketing the HR Department," *IPMA News* 66 (August 2000), 15–16.

[8] Allen Saltstein, "Personnel Management in the Local Government Setting," in Steven W. Hays and Richard C. Kearney, eds., *Public Personnel Administration* (Englewood Cliffs: Prentice-Hall, 1995), 50.

[9] See, for example, Arthur G. Bedeian, *Management*, 3d ed. (Fort Worth: Dryden, 1993), 269–270.

[10] Beth Wade, "Q&A with Incoming ICMA President Bruce Romer," *American City and County* 115 (September 2000), 24–28.

[11] Susan E. Jackson and Randall S. Schuler, *Managing Human Resources* (Cincinnati: South-Western, 2000), 24. See also Lin Grensing-Pophal, "Getting to the Top: Advice from Those Who've Made It," *HR Magazine* 45 (December 2000), 96–102.

[12] Robert H. Elliott and Sirwal Tevavichulada, "Computer Literacy and Human Resource Management: A Public/Private Sector Comparison," *Public Personnel Management* 28 (Summer 1999), 259–273.

[13] Lin Grensing-Pophal, "Is Your HR Department Diverse Enough?" *HR Magazine* 45 (September 2000), 46–52.

[14] Grensing-Pophal, 48.

[15] Sharon Leonard, "Walking the Talk," *HR Magazine* 45 (October 2000), 256.

[16] Gordon F. Sea, *Practical Ethics* (New York: American Management Association, 1988), 72.

[17] Leon A. Hargreaves of the University of Georgia attributed this quote to Harry J. Wellington and Ralph J. Winter Jr. in a speech delivered in 1975. No source was given.

QUESTIONS FOR CRITICAL THINKING

CHAPTER 1

1. Are advances in technology likely to increase or decrease the strategic importance of human resources in local governments?
2. Is it realistic to expect that line manages who have traditionally viewed HR procedures and rules as an impediment to operational efficiency will become partners in HR management?
3. What barriers can hinder the evolution of HR management from focusing on administrative activities to being a strategic contributor?
4. What are the implications of the certification program recently established by IPMA? Should HR professionals in local government who are presently certified by the HRIC earn this certification?

CHAPTER 2

1. Is it really necessary to study the history of HR management in order to understand contemporary theory and practice or is this something that is merely "nice to know"?
2. To what extent are current developments in HR management a reaction to the unintended consequences of historical movements such as civil service reform that were seen at the time to be major advances?

CHAPTER 3

1. Federal laws protect individuals and groups from employment discrimination based on such factors as race sex, age, disability, and so on. Is this sufficient, or should additional "protected classes" such as sexual orientation be established?
2. Are affirmative action programs still needed to ensure adequate representation of minorities and woman at all levels of local government organizations, or have these kinds of initiatives outlived their usefulness?
3. Would local governments implement policies that carried out the intent of EEO and other employment laws in the absence of voluminous federal regulations?
4. Which workplace rights of local government employees are based on principles of fairness and justice that HR management should support based on professional considerations and ethical standards even if they were not protected by the Constitution?

CHAPTER 4

1. Are contemporary motivation theories too varied and complex to be useful to managers and supervisors in a work setting?
2. It has been suggested that the factors affecting job satisfaction apply to the workforce in general and remain stable over time. Is this likely to be the case as the workforce becomes more diverse?
3. The managerial philosophy of the executive leadership of a local government, along with the views of elected officials, shape the organizational culture and environment. If the prevailing philosophy is detrimental to effective utilization of human resources, what can HR management do to bring about a more "enlightened" attitude?

CHAPTER 5

1. Given that much of the information gathered in the planning process cannot be used to predict the future with total accuracy, why should it be used at all?
2. Identify the HR interests of various stakeholders inside and outside a local government organization in determining objective measures of success. In what circumstances are these interests likely to conflict? Whose interests should prevail?
3. Do you believe that most HR planning in local government is undertaken to implement strategic objectives or on the basis of "thinking ahead"?

CHAPTER 6

1. In the typical local government, which functions are organized differently than they were probably organized 25 years ago?
2. For jobs considered essential but not "meaningful" on such measures as the job characteristics model, what should HR management do to improve employees' perception that their work is interesting and challenging?

CHAPTER 7

1. What are the implications of changing technology, more egalitarian organizations, and the shift in focus from tasks and skills to roles and competencies on the way work is analyzed and documented?
2. Would the process of analyzing jobs and work be more effective if organizations took an overall approach rather than collect only the information needed to support a specific requirement such as selection testing, performance appraisal, or job evaluation?

3. If traditional job descriptions are becoming obsolete, as some writers suggest, what will take their place?

CHAPTER 8

1. Is the strategic importance of recruiting greater or less for local government than for other organizations (public and private) that compete for applicants with the same skills?
2. Do traditional methods of setting qualifications for vacancies increase or decrease the probability of obtaining the best match between applicants and jobs?
3. What are the implications (positive and negative) of the dramatic increase in online recruiting?
4. Should local governments offer signing bonuses as an inducement to applicants with critical and/or market sensitive skills?

CHAPTER 9

1. How can local government improve the likelihood of hiring applicants who have both the necessary competencies and a commitment to the organization's mission and values?
2. One objective of the selection process is to hire individuals who "fit in" with the organizational culture. If a certain city emphasizes teamwork and consensus building, should otherwise qualified candidates who are loners or have big egos be screened out?
3. In selecting the workforce of the future, which traditional and emerging techniques offer the greatest potential benefits? How can local governments balance efficiency and equity in using these techniques?

CHAPTER 10

1. What changes that are facing local government will increase the importance of training and development?
2. Should an employee who receives training that increases the market value of his or her skills be required to sign an agreement to work the length of time necessary for the organization to recover its investment?
3. Is it really possible to evaluate training when many of its effects are difficult to predict and measure?

CHAPTER 11

1. Is it realistic to believe that performance ratings can be used to make administrative decisions (pay, promotion, discharge) and the appraisal process can still be an effective tool for employee development?
2. According to the literature, up to 90 percent of performance appraisal systems are ineffective and there have been no major advances in theory and methods. Does this suggest that one should be skeptical regarding the local government "success stories" that are now being reported?
3. Performance appraisal techniques such as BARS, BOS, and competency-based appraisals have been shown to improve the accuracy of ratings, but they are quite expensive to develop. Would small- to medium-sized local governments achieve better results by using less sophisticated techniques such as graphic rating scales and investing more in rater training?

CHAPTER 12

1. Give examples of how local government organizations might adopt different compensation policies based on such considerations as organizational culture, external conditions, and strategic objectives.
2. Some writers contend that traditional pay structures are not compatible with lateral mobility, flexible assignments, work teams, and other features associated with high-performance organizations. Do you agree or disagree?
3. Are there functions of local government (for example, law enforcement and fire protection) where broadbanding and/or skill-based pay systems could not be implemented effectively?

CHAPTER 13

1. There are "living wage" ordinances now in effect or under consideration in more than 100 cities and counties. Will this movement help poor workers support themselves and their families, or will it raise wage costs, displace workers, and waste tax dollars?
2. As performance-based pay gains acceptance in local government, do you think that the use of individual and group incentive plans where pay is "at risk" will increase?
3. Defined contribution (DC) retirement plans are becoming more popular in local governments as an alternative to traditional pension plans. Are such plans better because of financial stability, portability, and greater opportunity for participants to manage their assets, as proponents claim, or do they place employees' long-term security at risk, as critics have suggested?

CHAPTER 14

1. Do you believe that dealing proactively with employee relations issues, such as providing employee assistance programs (EAPs), is becoming part of the implicit social contract between local governments and their employees?
2. How can HR management implement "family friendly" policies that are equitable to childless workers?
3. A criticism of progressive discipline is that it is based on the premise that the worse an employer treats an employee the better he or she will become. How can the developmental side of discipline be emphasized to provide a more balanced approach?

CHAPTER 15

1. How would you assess the current state of labor-management relations in local governments?
2. Would it be desirable to have federal legislation mandating collective bargaining for local government employees?
3. If labor relations are "reinvented" along the lines of participative decision making (PDM), does this work to the advantage of labor or management?

CHAPTER 16

1. Can comprehensive workplace safety and health programs be justified for local governments in states that have not implemented regulations patterned after those promulgated by OSHA? If so, discuss the strategic importance of providing a safe and healthful workplace.

2. Do you believe that local governments have a responsibility to help employees with health problems not related to their work environment?

3. Has the potential for workplace violence been exaggerated by the media attention given to isolated events, or is it s serious problem?

CHAPTER 17

1. The premise of this book is that HR management is centralized, and a case was made that the HR leader should report to the chief executive officer of the jurisdiction. Are there other arrangements that may be appropriate, such as decentralizing HR and having it report to line departments? Would this facilitate HR management becoming a strategic business partner?

2. In which HR activity areas would additional HR staff and/or funding provide the greatest return? Can these investments be justified by cost-benefit analysis?

3. How are the roles of HR management likely to evolve over the next 10 years?

4. Some writers suggests that it may be time to implement licensing programs in HR similar to those in other professions such as law, medicine, and accounting. Explain why you agree or disagree.

APPENDIX B

CONTENT OUTLINE OF THE HR BODY OF KNOWLEDGE

APPENDIX B	Content Outline of the HR Body of Knowledge

After each of the major functional sub-areas are the weightings for that sub-area. **The first number in the parentheses is the PHR percentage weighting and the second number is the SPHR percentage weighting.** These weightings should help you allocate your time in preparing for each respective examination.

I. MANAGEMENT PRACTICES (15%, 21%)

  A. Role of HR in Organizations (2.78%, 3.91%)
- 1. HR Roles: Advisory/Counselor, Consultant, Service, Control
- 2. Change Agent Role/Reengineering and Facilitating Both Content & Process
- 3. HR's Role in Strategic Planning
- 4. HR Generalist and HR Specialist Roles
- 5. Effects of Different Organizational Contexts and Industries on HR functions
- 6. HR Policies and Procedures
- 7. Integration and Coordination of HR Functions
- 8. Outsourcing the HR Functions

  B. Human Resource Planning (2.04%, 2.87%)
- 1. Environmental Scanning
- 2. Internal Scanning
- 3. Human Resources Inventory
- 4. Human Resource Information Systems
- 5. Action Plans and Programs
- 6. Evaluation of Human Resource Planning

  C. Organizational Design and Development (.65%, .99%)
- 1. Organizational Structures
- 2. Organizational Development
- 3. Diagnosis and Intervention Strategies: Action Research, Sensing, Team Building, Goal Setting, Survey Feedback, Strategic Planning, Visioning, Sensitivity Training (T-groups), Grid Training
- 4. Role of Organizational Culture in Organizational Development
- 5. Role of International Culture in Organizational Development
- 6. Organizational Development in Response to Technological Change

  D. Budgeting, Controlling, and Measurement (1.08%, 1.56%)
- 1. HR Budgeting Process
- 2. HR Control Process
- 3. Evaluating HR Effectiveness

  E. Motivation (.59%, .77%)
- 1. Motivation Theories
- 2. Applying Motivation Theory in Management

  F. Leadership (.97%, 1.32%)
- 1. Leadership Theories
- 2. Effect of Leadership in Organizations
- 3. Leadership Training

  G. Quality and Performance Management/TQM (1.82%, 2.41%)
- 1. Performance Planning: Identifying Goals/Desired Behaviors
- 2. Setting and Communicating Performance Standards
- 3. Measuring Results and Providing Feedback
- 4. Implementing Performance Improvement Strategies
- 5. Evaluating Results

  H. Employee Involvement Strategies (2.11%, 2.57%)
- 1. Work Teams
- 2. Job Design and Redesign
- 3. Employee Ownership/ESOPs
- 4. Employee Suggestion System
- 5. Participative Management
- 6. Alternative Work Schedules
- 7. Role of HR in Employee Involvement Programs

  I. HR Research (.71%, 1.16%)
- 1. Research Design and Methodology
- 2. Quantitative Analysis
- 3. Qualitative Research

  J. International HR Management (1.49%, 2.48%)
- 1. Cultural Differences
- 2. Legal Aspects of International HR
- 3. Expatriation and Repatriation
- 4. Issues of Multinational Corporations
- 5. Compensation and Benefits for Foreign Nationals and Expatriates
- 6. The Role of HR in International Business

  K. Ethics (.77%, .96%)
- 1. Ethical Issues
- 2. Establishing Ethical Behavior in the Organization

II. GENERAL EMPLOYMENT PRACTICES (19%, 17%)

  A. Legal & Regulatory Factors: Definitions, Requirements, Proscribed Practices, Exemptions, Enforcement, Remedies, & Case Histories (6.38%, 5.29%)
- 1. Title VII of the Civil Rights Act (1964) as Amended (1972, 1991)
- 2. Age Discrimination in Employment Act (1967) as Amended
- 3. Health, Medical, & Rehabilitation Statutes (e.g., Vocational Rehabilitation Act, Pregnancy Discrimination Act, Americans with Disabilities Act, Family & Medical Leave Act, HMO Act, etc.)
- 4. Vietnam-era Veterans Readjustment Act (1986)
- 5. Immigration Reform and Control Act (1986) as Amended (1990)
- 6. Employee Polygraph Protection Act (1988)
- 7. Uniform Guidelines on Employee Selection Procedures
- 8. Worker Adjustment and Retraining Notification Act (1988)
- 9. North American Free Trade Act
- 10. Common Law Tort Theories
- 11. Copyright Statutes
- 12. Compensation Laws and Regulations
- 13. Consumer Credit Protection Act: Wage Garnishment (1968), Fair Credit Reporting (1970)
- 14. Social Security/Retirement Legislation (e.g., ERISA)
- 15. COBRA (Consolidated Omnibus Budget Reconciliation Act (1990)); Omnibus Budget Reconciliation Act (1993)

16. Workers' Compensation and Unemployment Compensation Laws and Regulations
17. Legal and Regulatory Factors Affecting Employee and Labor Relations (e.g., NLRA, Taft-Hartley, Landrum-Griffin, etc.)
18. Federal Health, Safety, and Security Legislation (e.g., OSHA)

B. Job Analysis, Job Description, and Job Specification (2.14%, 1.78%)
1. Methods of Job Analysis
2. Types of Data Gathered in a Job Analysis
3. Uses of Job Analysis
4. Job Descriptions
5. Job/Position Specifications
6. Validity & Reliability of Job Analysis, Job Description, & Job Specification

C. Individual Employment Rights (1.72%, 1.67%)
1. Employment-At-Will Doctrine
2. Exceptions to Employment-At-Will
3. Common Law Tort Theories
4. Job-As-Property Doctrine
5. Non-Compete Agreements

D. Performance Appraisals (5.10%, 4.60%)
1. Performance Measurement- The Criterion
2. Criterion Problems
3. Documenting Employee Performance
4. Category Rating Appraisal Methods
5. Comparative Appraisal Methods
6. Narrative Appraisal Methods
7. Special Appraisal Methods: MBO, BARS, BOS
8. Types of Appraisals
9. Rating Errors
10. Appraisal Interview
11. Linking Appraisals to Employment Decisions
12. Legal Constraints on Performance Appraisal
13. Documentation

E. Workplace Behavior Problems (1.90%, 1.55%)
1. Discipline
2. Absenteeism and Tardiness
3. Sexual Harassment
4. Drug and Alcohol Use
5. Off-duty Conduct

F. Employee Attitudes, Opinions and Satisfaction (2.01%, 2.11%)
1. Measurement
2. Results Analysis
3. Interpretation
4. Feedback
5. Intervention
6. Confidentiality and Anonymity of Surveys

III. STAFFING (19%, 15%)

A. Equal Employment Opportunity/Affirmative Action (3.56%, 2.99%)
1. Legal Endorsement of EEO: Supreme Court Decisions
2. Equal Employment Opportunity Programs
3. Affirmative Action Plans
4. Special Programs to Eliminate Discrimination
5. Fairness Issues: Reverse Discrimination, Quota Hiring vs. Merit Hiring

B. Recruitment (2.84%, 2.22%)
1. Determining Recruitment Needs and Objectives
2. Identifying Selection Criteria
3. Internal Sourcing
4. External Sourcing
5. Evaluating Recruiting Effectiveness

C. Selection (5.94%, 4.39%)
1. Application Process
2. Interviewing
3. Pre-employment Testing
4. Background Investigation
5. Medical Examination
6. Hiring Applicants with Disabilities
7. Illegal Use of Drugs and Alcohol
8. Validation and Evaluation of Selection Process Components

D. Career Planning and Development (2.06%, 1.84%)
1. Accommodating Organizational and Individual Needs
2. Mobility Within the Organization
3. Managing Transitions

E. Organizational Exit (4.60%, 3.56%)
1. General Issues
2. Layoffs/Reductions-in-Force
3. Constructive Discharge
4. Retaliatory
5. Retirement
6. Employer Defenses Against Litigation

IV. HUMAN RESOURCE DEVELOPMENT (11%, 12%)

A. HR Training and the Organization (3.06%, 3.72%)
1. The Learning Organization, Linking Training to Organizational Goals, Objectives, and Strategies
2. Human Resources Development as an Organizational Component
3. Funding the Training Function
4. Cost/Benefit Analysis of Training

B. Training Needs Analysis (1.52%, 1.52%)
1. Training Needs Analysis Process
2. Methods for Assessing Training Needs

C. Training and Development Programs (4.42%, 4.50%)
1. Trainer Selection
2. Design Considerations and Learning Principles
3. Types of Training Programs
4. Instructional Methods and Processes
5. Training Facilities Planning
6. Training Materials

D. Evaluation of Training Effectiveness (2.00%, 2.26%)
1. Sources for Evaluation
2. Research Methods for Evaluation
3. Criteria for Evaluating Training

V. COMPENSATION AND BENEFITS (19%, 15%)

A. Tax & Accounting Treatment of Compensation & Benefit Programs (.57%, .53%)
  1. FASB Regulation
  2. IRS Regulations

B. Economic Factors Affecting Compensation (2.09%, 1.77%)
  1. Inflation
  2. Interest Rates
  3. Industry Competition
  4. Foreign Competition
  5. Economic Growth
  6. Labor Market Trends/Demographics

C. Compensation Philosophy, Strategy, and Policy (1.81%, 1.55%)
  1. Fitting Strategy & Policy to the External Environment and to an Organization's Culture, Structure, & Objectives
  2. Training in and Communication of Compensation Programs
  3. Making Compensation Programs Achieve Organizational Objectives
  4. Establishing Administrative Controls

D. Compensation Programs: Types, Characteristics, and Advantages/Disadvantages (1.71%, 1.20%)
  1. Base Pay
  2. Differential Pay
  3. Incentive Pay
  4. Pay Programs for Selected Employees

E. Job Evaluation Methods (2.20%, 1.60%)
  1. Compensable Factors
  2. Ranking Method
  3. Classification/Grading Method
  4. Factor Comparison Method
  5. Point Method
  6. Guide Chart-Profile Method (Hay Method)

F. Job Pricing, Pay Structures, and Pay Rate Administration (2.14%, 1.49%)
  1. Job Pricing and Pay Structures
  2. Individual Pay Rate Determination
  3. Utilizing Performance Appraisal in Pay Administration
  4. Reflecting Market Influences in Pay Structures
  5. Wage Surveys

G. Employee Benefit Programs: Types, Objectives, Characteristics, and Advantages/Disadvantages (3.42%, 2.17%)
  1. Legally Required Programs/Payments
  2. Income Replacement
  3. Insurance and Income Protection
  4. Deferred Pay
  5. Pay for Time Not Worked
  6. Unpaid Leave
  7. Flexible Benefit Plans
  8. Recognition and Achievement Awards

H. Managing Employee Benefit Programs (3.75%, 3.43%)
  1. Employee Benefits Philosophy, Planning, and Strategy
  2. Employee Need/Preference Assessment: Surveys
  3. Administrative Systems
  4. Funding/Investment Responsibilities
  5. Coordination with Plan Trustees, Insurers, Health Service Providers and Third-Party Administrators
  6. Utilization Review
  7. Cost-Benefit Analysis and Cost Management
  8. Communicating Benefit Programs/Individual Annual Benefits Reports
  9. Monitoring Compensation/Benefits Legal Compliance Programs

I. Evaluating Total Compensation Strategy & Program Effectiveness (1.32%, 1.26%)
  1. Budgeting
  2. Cost Management
  3. Assessment of Methods and Processes

VI. EMPLOYEE AND LABOR RELATIONS (11%, 14%)

A. Union Representation of Employees (1.52%, 1.98%)
  1. Scope of the Labor Management Relations (Taft-Hartley) Act (1947)
  2. Achieving Representative Status
  3. Petitioning for an NLRB Election
  4. Election Campaign
  5. Union Security

B. Employer Unfair Labor Practices (1.68%, 1.91%)
  1. Procedures for Processing Charges of Unfair Labor Practices
  2. Interference, Restraint, and Coercion
  3. Domination and Unlawful Support of Labor Organization
  4. Employee Discrimination to Discourage Union Membership
  5. Retaliation
  6. Remedies

C. Union Unfair Labor Practices, Strikes, and Boycotts (1.96%, 2.60%)
  1. Responsibility for Acts of Union Agents
  2. Union Restraint or Coercion
  3. Duty of Fair Representation
  4. Inducing Unlawful Discrimination by Employer
  5. Excessive or Discriminatory Membership Fees
  6. Strikes and Secondary Boycotts
  7. Strike Preparation

D. Collective Bargaining (2.94%, 4.06%)
  1. Bargaining Issues and Concepts
  2. Negotiation Strategies
  3. Good Faith Requirements
  4. Notice Requirements
  5. Unilateral Changes in Terms of Employment
  6. Duty to Successor Employers or Unions: Buyouts, Mergers, or Bankruptcy
  7. Enforcement Provisions
  8. Injunctions
  9. Mediation and Conciliation
  10. National Emergency Strikes

E. Managing Organization-Union Relations (.88%, 1.16%)
   1. Building and Maintaining Union-Organization Relationships: Cooperative Programs
   2. Grievance Processes and Procedures
   3. Dispute Resolution
F. Maintaining Nonunion Status (.79%, .91%)
   1. Reasons
   2. Strategies
G. Public Sector Labor Relations (1.12%, 1.38%)
   1. Right to Organize
   2. Federal Labor Relations Council
   3. Limitations on Strikes
   4. Mediation and Conciliation

VII. HEALTH, SAFETY, AND SECURITY (6%, 6%)
   A. Health (2.41%, 2.22%)
      1. Employee Assistance Programs
      2. Employee Wellness Programs
      3. Reproductive Health Policies
      4. Chemical Dependency
      5. Communicable Diseases in the Workplace
      6. Employer Liabilities
      7. Stress Management
      8. Smoking Policies
      9. Recordkeeping and Reporting

   B. Safety (2.05%, 2.04%)
      1. Areas of Concern
      2. Organization of Safety Program
      3. Safety Promotion
      4. Accident Investigation
      5. Safety Inspections
      6. Human Factors Engineering (Ergonomics)
      7. Special Safety Considerations
      8. Sources of Assistance

   C. Security (1.54%, 1.74%)
      1. Organization of Security
      2. Control Systems
      3. Protection of Proprietary Information
      4. Crisis Management and Contingency Planning
      5. Theft and Fraud
      6. Investigations and Preventive Corrections

Selected Competencies in the IPMA HR Competency Model

KNOWS MISSION

Understands the purpose of the organization including its statutory mandate, its customers, its products and/or services, and its measures of mission effectiveness. Is able to articulate the relationship between human resources activities and successful mission accomplishment. Keeps current with factors which may have a future impact on mission.

UNDERSTANDS BUSINESS PROCESS AND HOW TO
CHANGE TO IMPROVE EFFICIENCY AND EFFECTIVENESS

Approaches assigned HR program responsibilities with a broad perspective of the way business is done within an organization. Able to recognize and implement change to enhance efficiency and effectiveness.

UNDERSTANDS CLIENTS AND ORGANIZATIONAL CULTURE

Researches unique characteristics of client organizations to ensure that assistance and consultations are appropriate to the situations. Maintains awareness of differing cultures and provides service that is tailored to the requirements of the culture.

UNDERSTANDS PUBLIC SERVICE ENVIRONMENT

Keeps current on political and legislative activities which may affect the organization and/or the HR community. Seeks to understand the intent as well as the letter of laws, orders, and regulations which result from the political process so that implementation is consistent with the intended outcomes of legal and policy changes.

UNDERSTANDS TEAM BEHAVIOR

Applies knowledge of team behavior to help achieve organizational goals and objectives. Maintains currency with new approaches to human motivation and teamwork that may apply to the organization.

COMMUNICATES WELL

Expresses ideas and exchanges information clearly and persuasively. Speaks in terms of business results and goals rather than HR technical terms. Communicates effectively with all levels of the organization.

POSSESSES THE ABILITY TO BE INNOVATIVE
AND CREATES A RISK TAKING ENVIRONMENT

Thinks outside the box. Creates and presents new approaches which are outside the context of current policies when warranted by mission needs. Understands and applies techniques which are designed to encourage creativity and innovations. Creates an environment where risk taking is valued.

ASSESSES AND BALANCES COMPETING VALUES

Manages competing priorities and work assignments by continuously evaluating the needs of the organization's mission against pending work. Maintains contact with senior management to ensure a clear understanding of mission priorities. Explains priorities to key customers to ensure that they understand the rationale for decisions regarding work priorities.

APPLIES ORGANIZATIONAL DEVELOPMENT PRINCIPLES

Maintains knowledge of social science and human behavior strategies which can be used to improve organizational performance. Establishes strategies to promote greater learning within the organization. Provides advice that supports creating opportunities for employees to grow.

KNOWS BUSINESS SYSTEM THINKING

Applies whole systems thinking to HR work processes by ensuring consideration of all external and internal environmental factors in providing advice and solutions to customers.

APPLIES INFORMATION TECHNOLOGY
TO HUMAN RESOURCE MANAGEMENT

Maintains awareness of current and emerging technologies which have potential to improve the efficiency and/or effectiveness of HRM within the organization. Develops proposals to implement new HR-based technology within the organization when justified.

POSSESSES GOOD ANALYTICAL SKILLS INCLUDING
THE ABILITY TO THINK STRATEGICALLY AND CREATIVELY

Analyzes a multiplicity of data and information from several sources and arrives at logical conclusions. Recognizes the gaps in available data and suggests other ways to obtain the needed information.

DESIGNS AND IMPLEMENTS CHANGE PROCESS
Ability to recognize the potential benefits of change, and create an infrastructure which supports change. Is flexible and open to new ideas and encourages others to value change.

USES CONSULTATION AND NEGOTIATION
SKILLS INCLUDING DISPUTE RESOLUTION
Takes the initiative in solving or helping to resolve problems. Knows a variety of problem-solving techniques and uses them or recommends them to involved parties.

POSSESSES THE ABILITY TO BUILD TRUST RELATIONSHIPS
Has integrity and demonstrates professional behavior to gain the trust and confidence of customer. Follows up on commitments made on a timely, accurate, and complete basis. Can keep confidences and does not abuse the privilege of accessibility to confidential information.

POSSESSES MARKETING AND REPRESENTATIONAL SKILLS
Persuades internal and external customers of the needs and beneficial outcomes of particular programs or actions. Develops the pros and cons of an issue and persuades interested parties of the best course of action. Ensures that customers are aware of the importance of the HR role.

USES CONSENSUS AND COALITION BUILDING SKILLS
Enhances collaboration among individuals and groups by using consensus building skills. Objectives summarizes opposing points of view. Incorporates all points of view and assists in arriving at a consensual position or agreement. Reconciles disagreements with officials through reasoning and presentation of the facts. Uses differences of opinion to build alternative solutions to problems or concerns. Understands when and how to elevate issues to higher level line officials when actions being taken are inconsistent with legal or higher level policy requirements. Has courage to take a stand when an issue is considered important to the well-being of the organization's mission or reputation.

KNOWS HUMAN RESOURCE LAWS AND POLICIES
Keeps current and understands statutory and regulatory requirements affecting HR programs. Sees and uses intent of requirements as an HR tool to assist in managing resources.

LINKS HUMAN RESOURCES TO THE
ORGANIZATION'S MISSION AND SERVICE OUTCOME
Understands mission needs and context in terms of people needs. Understands the HR role(s) within the organization and adapts behaviors and approaches that are consistent with the role(s).

DEMONSTRATES CUSTOMER SERVICE ORIENTATION
Keeps abreast of organizational climate and mission changes and is keenly sensitive to customer needs and concerns. Responds to client needs, questions, and concerns in an accurately timely manner.

UNDERSTANDS, VALUES AND PROMOTES DIVERSITY

Understands the potential contributions that a diverse workforce can make to the success of the organization. Is aware of the potential impact of HR processes and assures that diversity needs are considered.

PRACTICES AND PROMOTES INTEGRITY
AND ETHICAL BEHAVIOR

Behaves in ways that demonstrate trust and gain confidence. Treats customers fairly and courteously and effectively responds to their needs regardless of organizational location or grade level. Promotes and maintains a high level of integrity.

Source: International Personnel Management Association, 1617 Duke Street, Alexandria, VA 22314 (2001). Copyright © IPMA. Reprinted by permission.

APPENDIX D

ORGANIZATIONS AND GOVERNMENT AGENCIES IN HR MANAGEMENT

ASSOCIATIONS

WorldatWork (formerly American Compensation Association)
14040 North Northsight Boulevard
Scottsdale, AZ 10020
http://www.acaonline.org

American Management Association
1601 Broadway
New York, NY 10019-7420
http://www.amanet.org

American Payroll Association
30 East 33rd Street, 5th Floor
New York, NY 10016-5386
http://www.americanpayroll.org

American Society for Industrial Security
1624 Prince Street
Arlington, VA 22314
http://www.asisonline.org

American Society for Public Administration
1120 G Street, NW, Suite 700
Washington, DC 20005
http://www.aspanet.org

American Society for Training and Development
1640 King Street
P.O. Box 1443
Alexandria, VA 22313-2043
http://www.astd.org

American Society of Safety Engineers
1800 East Oakton
Des Plaines, IL 60018
http://www.asse.org

Employee Benefit Research Institute
2121 K Street, NW, Suite 600
Washington, DC 20037-1896
http://www.ebri.org

ESOP Association
1726 M Street NW, Suite 501
Washington, DC 20036
http://www.the-esop-emplowner.org

Human Resource Certification Institute
1800 Duke Street
Alexandria, VA 22314
http://www.shrm.org/hrci

Human Resource Planning Society
317 Madison Avenue, Suite 1509
New York, NY 10017
http://www.hrps.org

International Association for HR Information Management
401 North Michigan Avenue
Chicago, IL 60611
http://www.ihrim.org

International Foundation of Employee Benefit Plans
18700 Bluemound Road
Brookfield, WI 53008-0069
http://www.ifebp.org

International Personnel Management Association
1617 Duke Street
Alexandria, VA 22314
http://www.ipma-hr.org

National Association of Temporary and Staffing Services
119 South Saint Asaph Street
Alexandria, VA 22314-3119
http://www.natss.org

Society for Human Resource Management
1800 Duke Street
Alexandria, VA 22314
http://www.shrm.org

Wellness Councils of America
Community Health Plaza, Suite 311
7101 Newport Avenue
Omaha, NE 68152
http://www.welcoa.org

NONPROFIT AND GOVERNMENTAL TECHNICAL ASSISTANCE PROVIDERS

Cooperative Personnel Services
191 Lathrop Way, Suite A
Sacramento, CA 95815
http://www.cps.ca.gov

The Center for Local Government Studies
Historic Boise Depot
2603 West Eastover Terrace
Boise, ID 83706
http://www.clgsonline.com

Local Government Institute
4009 Bridgeport Way West, Suite E
Tacoma, WA 98466-4326
http://www.lgi.org

National Center for Small Communities
444 North Capitol Street, NE, Suite 208
Washington, DC 20001-1202
http://www.natat.org/ncsc

U.S. DEPARTMENT OF LABOR AGENCIES

U.S. Department of Labor
200 Constitution Avenue, NW
Washington, DC 20210
http://www.dol.gov

Bureau of Labor Statistics
http://www.bls.gov

Wage and Hour Division
Employment Standards Administration
http://www.dol.gov/esa/public/whd-org.htm

Occupational Safety and Health Administration (OSHA)
http://www.osha.gov

Office of Federal Contract Compliance Programs (OFCCP)
http://www.dol.gov/dol/esa/public/ofcp_org.htm

OTHER GOVERNMENT AGENCIES

Equal Employment Opportunity Commission (EEOC)
1801 L Street
Washington, DC 20507
http://www.eeoc.gov

Federal Meditation and Conciliation Service
2100 K Street NW
Washington, DC 20427
http://www.fmcs.gov

Office of Personnel Management
1900 E. Street NW
Washington, DC 20415-0001
http://www.opm.gov

PUBLICATIONS IN HR MANAGEMENT

There are a number of publications available that allow HR professionals and other managers in local government to add to their foundation of knowledge in the field. These publications provide information on research findings, applications in organizational settings, and emerging developments.

PUBLICATIONS THAT SPECIALIZE IN HR MANAGEMENT

Books that cover the HR function

Robert L. Mathis and John H. Jackson, *Human Resource Management*, 9th ed. (Cincinnati: South-Western, 2000).

Jay M. Shafritz, Norma M. Riccuci, David H. Rosenbloom, and Albert C. Hyde, *Personnel Management in Government*, 5th ed. (New York: Marcel Dekker, 2001, forthcoming).

Books and other references that cover specialized HR topics

Marci Z. Balge and Gary R, Kreiger, eds., *Occupational Health & Safety*, 3d ed. (Washington, DC: National Safety Council, 2000).

Ivan E. Bodensteiner and Rosalie Berger Levinson, *State and Local Government Civil Rights Liability* (Eagan, Minn.: West, 2000), vols. 1, 2, and 3 as updated.

Julius E. Eitington, *The Winning Trainer*, 3d ed. (Houston: Gulf, 1996).

Dick Grote, *The Complete Guide to Performance Appraisal* (New York: American Management Association, 1996).

Robert D. Gatewood and Hubert S. Feild, *Human Resource Selection*, 5th ed. (Chicago: Dryden, 2001).

Richard C. Kearney with David G. Carnevale, *Labor Relations in the Public Sector*, 3d ed. (New York: Marcel Dekker, 2001).

George T. Milkovich and Jerry M. Newman, *Compensation*, 6th ed. (Boston: Irwin/McGraw-Hill, 1999).

Stephen P. Robbins, *Organizational Behavior*, 8th ed. (Upper Saddle River, N.J.: Prentice-Hall, 1998).

Periodicals with professional orientation
Compensation and Benefits Review
Employee Relations Law Journal
HRFocus (formerly Personnel)
HR Magazine (formerly Personnel Administrator)
HR News (formerly Resource)
IPMA News
Labor Law Journal
Occupational Health and Safety
Personnel Journal
Public Personnel Management
Professional Safety
Review of Public Personnel Administration
Training and Development Journal
Workspan (formerly ACA News)
WorldatWork Journal (formerly ACA Journal)

Periodicals with academic orientation
Personnel Psychology
Journal of Applied Psychology
Journal of Occupational and Organizational Psychology
Journal of Vocational Behavior
Human Resource Planning

BUSINESS AND MANAGEMENT PUBLICATIONS THAT OFTEN INCLUDE HR ARTICLES

Periodicals with professional and managerial orientation
Academy of Management Executive
American City & County
Business Week
Forbes
Fortune
Harvard Business Review
Public Management
Public Administration Review
SAM Advanced Management Journal
Supervisory Management
The Wall Street Journal

Periodicals with academic orientation
Academy of Management Journal
Academy of Management Review
Journal of Organizational Behavior
Group and Organizational Management
Human Relations

APPENDIX F

ANNUAL REPORT FORM EEO-4

EQUAL EMPLOYMENT OPPORTUNITY COMMISSION
STATE AND LOCAL GOVERNMENT INFORMATION (EEO-4)
EXCLUDE SCHOOL SYSTEMS AND EDUCATIONAL INSTITUTIONS
(Read attached instructions prior to completing this form)

APPROVED BY
OMB
3046-0008
EXPIRES 6/30/2000

DO NOT ALTER INFORMATION PRINTED IN THIS BOX

SAMPLE

MAIL COMPLETED FORM TO:

A. TYPE OF GOVERNMENT (Check one box only)

☐ 1. State   ☐ 2. County   ☐ 3. City   ☐ 4. Township   ☐ 5. Special District

☐ 6. Other (Specify) _____

B. IDENTIFICATION

1. NAME OF POLITICAL JURISDICTION (If same as label, skip to Item C)

	EEOC USE ONLY
	A

2. Address—Number and Street | CITY/TOWN | COUNTY | STATE/ZIP | B

C. FUNCTION

(Check one box to indicate the function(s) for which this form is being submitted. Data should be reported for all departments and agencies in your government covered by the function(s) indicated. If you cannot supply the data for every agency within the function(s), please attach a list showing name and address of agencies whose data are not included.)

1. FINANCIAL ADMINISTRATION. Tax assessing, tax billing and collection, budgeting, purchasing, central accounting and similar financial administration carried on by a treasurer's, auditor's or comptroller's office and

GENERAL CONTROL. Duties usually performed by boards of supervisors or commissioners, central administrative offices and agencies, central personnel or planning agencies, all judicial offices and employees (judges, magistrates, bailiffs, etc.)

2. STREETS AND HIGHWAYS. Maintenance, repair, construction and administration of streets, alleys, sidewalks, roads, highways and bridges.

3. PUBLIC WELFARE. Maintenance of homes and other institutions for the needy; administration of public assistance. (Hospitals and sanatoriums should be reported as item 7.)

4. POLICE PROTECTION. Duties of a police department sheriff's, constable's, coroner's office, etc., including technical and clerical employees engaged in police activities.

5. FIRE PROTECTION. Duties of the uniformed fire force and clerical employees. (Report any forest fire protection activities as item 6.)

6. NATURAL RESOURCES. Agriculture, forestry, forest fire protection, irrigation drainage, flood control, etc., and

PARKS AND RECREATION. Provision, maintenance and operation of parks, playgrounds, swimming pools, auditoriums, museums, marinas, zoos, etc.

7. HOSPITALS AND SANATORIUMS. Operation and maintenance of institutions for inpatient medical care.

8. HEALTH. Provision of public health services, out-patient clinics, visiting nurses, food and sanitary inspections, mental health, alcohol rehabilitation service, etc.

9. HOUSING. Code enforcement, low rent public housing, fair housing ordinance enforcement, housing for elderly, housing rehabilitation, rent control.

10. COMMUNITY DEVELOPMENT. Planning, zoning, land development, open space, beautification, preservation.

11. CORRECTIONS. Jails, reformatories, detention homes, half-way houses, prisons, parole and probation activities

12. UTILITIES AND TRANSPORTATION. Includes water supply, electric power, transit, gas, airports, water transportation and terminals

13. SANITATION AND SEWAGE. Street cleaning, garbage and refuse collection and disposal. Provision, maintenance and operation of sanitary and storm sewer systems and sewage disposal plants.

14. EMPLOYMENT SECURITY STATE GOVERNMENTS ONLY

15. OTHER (Specify on Page Four)

APPENDIX F

453

D. EMPLOYMENT DATA AS OF JUNE 30 (Cont.)
(Do not include elected/appointed officials. Blanks will be counted as zero)

1. FULL-TIME EMPLOYEES (Temporary employees not included)

JOB CATEGORIES	ANNUAL SALARY (In thousands 000)	TOTAL (COLUMNS B-K) A	MALE					FEMALE				
			NON-HISPANIC ORIGIN		HISPANIC	ASIAN OR PACIFIC ISLANDER	AMERICAN INDIAN OR ALASKAN NATIVE	NON-HISPANIC ORIGIN		HISPANIC	ASIAN OR PACIFIC ISLANDER	AMERICAN INDIAN OR ALASKAN NATIVE
			WHITE B	BLACK C	D	E	F	WHITE G	BLACK H	I	J	K
SKILLED CRAFT	49. $0.1-15.9											
	50. 16.0-19.9											
	51. 20.0-24.9											
	52. 25.0-32.9											
	53. 33.0-42.9											
	54. 43.0-54.9											
	55. 55.0-69.9											
	56. 70.0 PLUS											
SERVICE/ MAINTENANCE	57. $0.1-15.9											
	58. 16.0-19.9											
	59. 20.0-24.9											
	60. 25.0-32.9											
	61. 33.0-42.9											
	62. 43.0-54.9											
	63. 55.0-69.9											
	64. 70.0 PLUS											
65. TOTAL FULL TIME (LINES 1-64)												

2. OTHER THAN FULL-TIME EMPLOYEES (Include temporary employees)

66. OFFICIALS/ADMIN.												
67. PROFESSIONALS												
68. TECHNICIANS												
69. PROTECTIVE SERV												
70. PARA-PROFESSIONAL												
71. ADMIN. SUPPORT												
72. SKILLED CRAFT												
73. SERV./MAINT.												
74. TOTAL OTHER THAN FULL TIME (LINES 66-73)												

3. NEW HIRES DURING FISCAL YEAR - Permanent full time only JULY 1 - JUNE 30

75. OFFICIALS/ADMIN.												
76. PROFESSIONALS												
77. TECHNICIANS												
78. PROTECTIVE SERV.												
79. PARA-PROFESSIONAL												
80. ADMIN. SUPPORT												
81. SKILLED CRAFT												
82. SERV./MAINT.												
83. TOTAL NEW HIRES (LINES 75-82)												

EEOC FORM 164, FEB 97 (Previous Editions are Obsolete)   EEOC COPY   PAGE 3

D. EMPLOYMENT DATA AS OF JUNE 30
(Do not include elected/appointed officials. Blanks will be counted as zero)

1. FULL-TIME EMPLOYEES (Temporary employees not included)

JOB CATEGORIES	ANNUAL SALARY (In thousands 000)	TOTAL (COLUMNS B-K)	MALE NON-HISPANIC ORIGIN WHITE	BLACK	HISPANIC	ASIAN OR PACIFIC ISLANDER	AMERICAN INDIAN OR ALASKAN NATIVE	FEMALE NON-HISPANIC ORIGIN WHITE	BLACK	HISPANIC	ASIAN OR PACIFIC ISLANDER	AMERICAN INDIAN OR ALASKAN NATIVE
		A	B	C	D	E	F	G	H	I	J	K
OFFICIALS/ ADMINISTRATORS	1. $ 0.1-15.9											
	2. 16.0-19.9											
	3. 20.0-24.9											
	4. 25.0-32.9											
	5. 33.0-42.9											
	6. 43.0-54.9											
	7. 55.0-69.9											
	8. 70.0 PLUS											
PROFESSIONALS	9. $0.1-15.9											
	10. 16.0-19.9											
	11. 20.0-24.9											
	12. 25.0-32.9											
	13. 33.0-42.9											
	14. 43.0-54.9											
	15. 55.9-69.9											
	16. 70.0 PLUS											
TECHNICIANS	17. $0.1-15.9											
	18. 16.0-19.9											
	19. 20.0-24.9											
	20. 25.0-32.9											
	21. 33.0-42.9											
	22. 43.0-54.9											
	23. 55.0-69.9											
	24. 70.0 PLUS											
PROTECTIVE SERVICE	25. $0.1-15.9											
	26. 16.0-19.9											
	27. 20.0-24.9											
	28. 25.0-32.9											
	29. 33.0-42.9											
	30. 43.0-54.9											
	31. 55.0-69.9											
	32. 70.0 PLUS											
PARA- PROFESSIONALS	33. $0.1-15.9											
	34. 16.0-19.9											
	35. 20.0-24.9											
	36. 25.0-32.9											
	37. 33.0-42.9											
	38. 43.0-54.9											
	39. 55.0-69.9											
	40. 70.0 PLUS											
ADMINISTRATIVE SUPPORT	41. $0.1-15.9											
	42. 16.0-19.9											
	43. 20.0-24.9											
	44. 25.0-32.9											
	45. 33.0-42.9											
	46. 43.0-54.9											
	47. 55.0-69.9											
	48. 70.0 PLUS											

EEOC FORM 164, FEB 95 (Previous Editions are Obsolete)   **EEOC COPY**

REMARKS (List National Crime Information Center (NCIC) numbers assigned to any Criminal Justice Agencies whose data are included in this report.)

SAMPLE

LISTING AGENCIES INCLUDED ON THIS FORM

CERTIFICATION. I certify that the information given in this report is correct and true to the best of my knowledge and was reported in accordance with accompanying instructions. (Willfully false statements on this report are punishable by law, U.S. Code, Title 18, Section 1001.)

NAME OF PERSON TO CONTACT REGARDING THIS FORM	TITLE
ADDRESS (Number and Street, City, State, Zip Code)	TELEPHONE NUMBER AREA CODE

DATE	TYPED NAME/TITLE OF AUTHORIZED OFFICIAL	SIGNATURE

EEOC FORM 164, FEB 95 (Previous Editions are Obsolete)   EEOC COPY   PAGE 4

JOB DESCRIPTION FOR HR DIRECTOR
IN SMALL MUNICIPALITY

IDENTIFICATION

Job Title: Human Resource Director   **FLSA Status:** Exempt

Department: Human Resources   **Code:** 13005A

Location: Municipal Building   **Reports to:** City Manager

JOB SUMMARY

Plans and implements HR function and coordinates HR activities for city: Develops HR policies to implement strategic objectives, develops and submits budget, and prepares plans and programs. Organizes, staffs, and supervises HR department. Directs HR research, records management, reporting, and service activities. Coordinates job analysis, recruiting, selection, training and development, performance appraisal, compensation, and employee relations activities and programs. Coordinates HR component of health, safety, and security programs. Performs related services as required.

RESPONSIBILITIES AND TASKS

A. Planning (10%)—Participates with executive leadership and elected officials in strategic planning process. Develops and obtains approval for HR policies to implement strategic objectives. Develops and submits budget for HR activities. Determines competencies required to meet objectives, estimates HR requirements, and develops plans to meet anticipated HR needs. Develops and updates city affirmative action plan. Develops related HR plans and programs as required.

B. HR Administration (10%)—Determines organization of HR department. Assigns responsibilities to professional and clerical staff. Selects, trains, and supervises staff. Maintains current information on HR practices and legal requirements through research of published material and Internet sites. May authorize subscriptions to professional journals and reporting services. Implements human resource information system. Directs the maintenance of records and preparation of reports including reporting of employee data to payroll section. Develops requests for proposals, recommends awards, and administers contracts with consultants as required. In cooperation with city attorney, responds to HR legal issues.

C. Staffing (20%)—Coordinates on-site analysis of jobs and preparation of job descriptions. Approves job announcements and directs recruiting activities. Approves selection procedures such as application blanks, ability and work-sample tests, supplemental application forms, structured oral interviews, and background investigations. May coordinate validation studies. Directs screening of applicants and referral to supervisors. Reviews recommendations for compliance with EEO laws and regulations and city affirmative action plan. Coordinates postoffer procedures such as drug testing and physical examinations.

D. Training and Development (10%)—In cooperation with city departments, implements orientation programs for new employees. Analyzes performance ratings, surveys, supervisory recommendations, and other sources of data to assess training needs. Establishes training objectives and arranges for training using internal and external sources. May personally conduct training. Ensures that employee training records are maintained. Uses participant surveys, on-site behavioral measures, and results to assess effectiveness of training.

E. Performance Appraisal (10%)—Approves performance appraisal instruments. May coordinate validation studies. Ensures that raters receive necessary training. Schedules and monitors performance appraisal process in departments. Assists supervisors in observing performance, counseling employees, and correcting performance problems and rating performance. Administers ratings appeal process. Reviews ratings for compliance with EEO laws and regulations. Compiles and analyzes appraisal data needed to support other HR activities.

F. Compensation (20%)—Obtains approval for pay structures. Coordinates job evaluation and grade placements. Reviews requests for reclassification. Coordinates compensation surveys. Coordinates periodic updates and revisions to pay structures. Develops procedures and guidelines for periodic pay adjustments. Reviews recommendations for pay actions for compliance with guidelines. Ensures that pay is administered in accordance with wage/hour and EEO laws and regulations. Administers employee benefits programs. Conducts periodic audits of compensation program to ensure compliance with policy objectives.

G. Employee Relations (10%)—Coordinates periodic assessments of employee morale and satisfaction. Recommends and obtains approval for actions needed to address problem areas. Maintains and updates policy manual and employee handbook. Coordinates publication of employee newsletter. Administers employee awards and recognition program. Administers employee assistance program. Administers progressive disciplinary procedures and approves recommended disciplinary actions. Administers grievance and disciplinary appeal procedures.

H. Health, Safety, and Security (5%)—Cooperates with risk manager in implementing programs and procedures to manage and reduce the incidence of work-related injuries and diseases. Ensures that supervisors and employees receive safety training. Implements HR component of workplace security program.

I. Related Services (5%)—Serves on committees and task forces as required. Establishes and maintains liaison with organizations and agencies in HR management. Represents the city in the community and promotes the city's mission and values in community activities.

JOB SPECIFICATIONS

Knowledges, Skills, and Abilities
Knowledge of concepts, theories, and techniques of HR management. Knowledge of organization and administration of HR function. Knowledge of employment law including federal and state statutes regulating EEO, wages and hours, and safety and health. Knowledge of administrative agency guidelines and enforcement procedures. Knowledge of constitutional provisions applying to city employees. Knowledge of city ordinances, policies, and rules relating to HR. Verbal communications skills to lead subordinates, counsel employees, conduct training, deliver presentations, and speak to external groups. Reading skills to comprehend professional literature, laws and regulations, legal documents, and related theoretical and/or technical material. Writing skills to develop business correspondence, policies, procedures, proposals, brochures, and news articles. Math skills to prepare budgets and perform statistical analyses. Computer skills to use word processing, spreadsheet, database, and specialized human resource information systems programs. Ability to identify HR dimensions of organizational problems, evaluate alternatives, and develop solutions. Ability to relate to people with diverse ethnic, racial, and socioeconomic characteristics to initiate action,

clarify understanding, build consensus, or resolve differences. Ability to build partnerships with line managers. Ability to develop and implement HR strategies that
achieve city's mission and objectives.

Credentials and Experience
Degree in human management or closely related field from accredited college or university. Minimum of seven years professional experience in HR field, including management of a major HR activity (graduate study may be substituted for up to two years
experience). Professional certification by the Human Resource Certification Institute
or Public Human Resource Certification Council.

Special Requirements
Willingness to work during nonduty hours, holidays, and weekends when necessary to
achieve goals. Willingness to travel overnight to attend and participate in meetings
and conferences. Willingness to maintain appropriate national and local professional
affiliations. Commitment to city's mission, values, and strategic goals. Strong personal
and professional ethics.

APPROVALS

	City Manager	November 9, 2000
Name	Title	Date

Source: Southeastern municipality of 40,000. Yolanda E. Jackson, JPR Recruiting, 337 East Magnolia Avenue,
Auburn, AL 36830. Reproduced by permission.

GLOSSARY

A

ability A present competence to perform an observable behavior or a behavior that results in an observable product.

ability test A test, usually of the paper-and-pencil type, used to assess mental, mechanical, physical, or clerical ability.

absenteeism An employee's failure to report to work at scheduled times.

administrative law Regulations issued by government agencies established to enforce the law.

adult learning principles Principles, referred to as andragogy, pioneered by Malcolm Knolls. They appeal to the need to know the reason for learning something, the desire for control over learning, and application to real-life situations.

affirmative action A process in which employers identify underutilization of protected groups, determine availability in the relevant labor market, and set hiring goals.

agency shop A union security provision requiring an employee to pay a service fee to the union if he or she does not become a member.

alternate form method A reliability estimate using two different random samples of questions drawn from a larger pool.

alternative dispute resolution (ADR) A nonjudicial method of settling a charge of discrimination through mediation by an impartial third party.

attitude survey A survey that measures employees' perceptions of pay, promotional opportunities, task clarity and significance, skills utilization, organizational commitment, and relationships with supervisors and coworkers.

authority The right to command action from others.

autonomous work groups A design strategy that allows a group of employees to control their work.

autonomy The extent to which employees are free to schedule their own activities, decide work procedures, and select necessary equipment.

B

bargaining unit The specific group of employees determined to be eligible for union representation.

base pay Cash compensation in the form of wages paid based on hours actually worked or salary computed on some other basis.

behavior modeling A form of role-playing in which a trainee observes some other individual and imitates his or her behavior.

behavior modification Influencing behavior through positive or negative reinforcement (rewards or punishments).

behaviorally-based criteria Criteria that measure the degree to which an employee carried out expected behaviors, used for performance appraisal.

benchmark jobs A sample of representative jobs found in other organizations, to be used in a compensation survey.

benefits Rewards to employees for membership in the organization, such as health insurance and retirement plans.

bloodborne pathogens Viruses that have their highest viral load in the blood of infected people.

broadbanding Consolidation of several traditional grades into a single band with one maximum and one minimum rate of pay.

building-related illness (BRI) Symptoms that can be clinically diagnosed and linked to a source in a building.

bureaus of municipal research Privately sponsored organizations that promoted the theories of scientific management in the government sector.

burnout A precipitous drop in job performance caused by high stress levels or accumulated stress.

C

career A profession or occupation that an employee trains for and pursues as a normal life activity.

career growth An employee's progressive acceptance of new roles and responsibilities within the same organization.

case law The collective set of court decisions in a judicial system.

certification Recognition of a union as the exclusive bargaining agent for employees in a unit, usually after a representation election.

checklist appraisal A performance appraisal format that requires the rater to check items most representative of the employee's characteristics and work contributions.

checkoff A union security provision allowing employees to request payroll deduction of union dues.

class A group of jobs that are similar in duties, responsibilities, requirements, and pay.

class series A vertical grouping of two or more classes on the basis of type of work and level of difficulty.

class specification A description of a group of jobs that are similar in duties and responsibilities, have the same entrance requirements, and receive the same rate of pay.

classification method A system that divides jobs into broad groups such as executive and clerical and then into smaller classes within the groups.

classroom type lecture Presentation of factual information to a group of people.

closed shop A union security provision requiring an employee to become a member of the representing union before hire (an illegal provision).

collective bargaining An approach to labor relations in which the employer has a compulsory duty to bargain with the recognized employee union under established procedures.

common law A body of law other than federal statutory and constitutional law, case law, and administrative law.

common rater errors Systematic errors in judgment that occur when an individual observes and rates the performance of an employee. The most frequently described errors include recency, first impression, halo, central tendency, rater patterns, similar-to-me effect, contrast effects, and stereotyping.

comparable worth A doctrine that maintains that jobs held primarily by women should be paid the same as jobs held by men having the same internal value; advocates suggest that the **equal pay for equal work** perpetuates pay inequities based on the labor market.

compa-ratio A ratio (average rate paid/range midpoint) that indicates whether actual pay is what the pay policy intends.

comparative appraisal methods Measurement of individuals against each other, resulting in a list of individuals ranked in order of performance.

compensable factors Factors used in the **point method**, such as skill, effort, responsibility, and working conditions.

compensation survey A survey of compensation paid by employers in the relevant labor market, used to develop a competitive pay structure.

compensatory approach A method of selection in which high levels in some qualifications may offset or compensate for the lack of other qualifications.

compensatory time Time off, awarded at time-and-one-half, in lieu of overtime pay.

competency Knowledge, skill, and ability that affect a major part of a job.

competency model A validated decision tool, correlated to job activities, that describes key knowledge, skills, and abilities for performing a specific job.

competency-based appraisal Performance appraisal based on observable behaviors that indicate the employee's level of performance in applying certain competencies.

competency-based pay A pay structure based on a wide range of employee attributes and skills.

compressed work schedules A job design strategy that allows the employee flexibility in the number of days worked during a workweek.

computer-assisted training A quick and efficient training method provided through the use of computer programs.

concurrent validity Method of establishing validity by administering a test to current employees and correlating test scores with performance measures.

constitutional law Law developed from the U.S. Constitution.

construct validation A showing that a test identifies a psychological trait that underlies successful performance on the job and measures the presence and degree of the trait.

content validation A showing that a selection procedure samples all the significant parts of a job and only those parts.

core competency A central and important capacity of an organization.

correlation A statistical technique for showing the relationship between variables.

criterion-related validation A showing of statistical correlation between scores on a test and measures of job performance.

critical incidents Reports made by knowledgeable observers of action taken by individuals who were especially effective or ineffective in accomplishing their jobs.

cross-training Training employees in different tasks within the organization; creates more flexibility in staffing.

cumulative trauma disorders (CTDs) Physical problems caused by repetitive use of the same muscles to perform tasks.

D

decertification Removal of a union as bargaining agent after losing a decertification election.

defined benefit plan Retirement plan in which the employer agrees to provide a specific level of retirement income.

defined contribution plan Retirement plan in which the employer contributes a fixed amount and the benefit depends on how the funds are invested.

Delphi technique A planning method that uses responses from a panel of experts to develop a consensus.

demand The amount of resources needed by an organization.

departmental orientation Orientation that covers topics unique to the new employee's department and job.

development program Preparation of individuals to take on future responsibilities.

disability A physical or mental impairment that substantially limits a person in the performance of major life activities; preferable to the term handicapped.

discipline Action taken against an individual for misconduct that he or she has the ability to correct.

disparate impact Using selection standards or decision rules that appear to be neutral, but have an adverse effect on members of protected groups; also known as unintentional discrimination.

disparate treatment Using selection standards or decision rules that explicitly treat protected group members differently than other applicants or employees; also known as intentional discrimination.

distance learning methods Any training an employee receives where the trainer and the employee are separated by location and/or time.

diversity Differences among people in regard to race, ethnicity, age, gender, culture, and other factors; also the principle that organizations respect and appreciate such differences.

drug testing Screening of applicants for drug use.

due process In an organizational setting, the procedure that allows an employee facing disciplinary action to explain and defend his or her conduct before a disinterested person or group; also known as **procedural due process**.

E

80 percent rule Rule stating that a **prima facie** case of disparate treatment discrimination is established when the selection rate for protected groups is less than 80 percent of the selection rate for the highest group; also known as the 4/5ths rule.

employee assistance program (EAP) A program designed to assist in the identification and resolution of productivity problems associated with employees impaired by health, marital, family, financial, alcohol, drug, legal, emotional, and other concerns that adversely affect job performance.

employee factors Characteristics of employees, including ability, motivation, and attitude toward work.

equal employment opportunity (EEO) The concept, grounded in law, that states that employees and applicants should not be discriminated against in employment actions based on race, color, religion, national origin, sex, or disability; also known as fair employment.

equal pay for equal work A standard that defines equal jobs as those with equal skill, effort, responsibility, and are performed under similar working conditions and requires that these jobs must receive equal pay. Unlike **comparable worth**, this is a legal standard.

ergonomics A body of knowledge about human abilities, limitations, and other characteristics that are relevant to the work system.

essay appraisal A format that rates the employee's job performance in a narrative discussion.

evaluation Measurement of an outcome against stated objectives.

executive responsibility A human resource function in which the chief executive maintains a high degree of control in order to carry out the mandates of the electorate.

exempt employees Certain employees exempt from the minimum wage and overtime provisions of the Fair Labor Standards Act.

expert power Authority based on the possession of valued knowledge.

F

fact-finding A dispute resolution procedure involving a hearing and nonbinding recommendation by a neutral third party.

flextime A design strategy that allows an individual some flexibility in the hours of work.

G

gainsharing Giving employees part of the amount saved when labor costs are less than expected.

gap analysis Identification of the gap between where employees' skills are and where they should be.

grade A group of jobs considered substantially equal for pay purposes.

graphic rating scale A format used to rate performance on a continuum of scale points.

group discussion A technique that involves groups of trainees in the generation and discussion of material to be learned.

H

hazing A form of initiation that uses harassment.

health The prevention of illness and maintenance of overall well-being.

health maintenance organization (HMO) Alternative to traditional medical insurance that provides a range of medical services to employees for a fixed cost.

honesty tests Tests used to identify and eliminate potentially dishonest people from consideration.

horizontal job loading Alternate term for **job enlargement**.

HR Abbreviation for human resources.

HRM Abbreviation for human resource management.

human resource information system (HRIS) Technological system used to collect, store, and retrieve employee data.

human resource management Design and implementation of systems in an organization to ensure the efficient and effective use of human talent to accomplish organizational goals.

human resource planning (HRP) A process that attempts to maintain an appropriate staff of qualified employees at all times.

human resource/staff ratio The number of full-time equivalent employees assigned to HR for each 100 employees on the payroll.

human resources The managerial, professional, and operating employees of an organization.

I

incidence rate The number of injuries and illnesses per 100 full-time employees during a given period.

industrial psychology Earlier forms included the study of how to match workers' qualifications with jobs.

industrial welfare movement Attempts by employers during the late 1800s to improve conditions for employees, both in the workplace and in their lives away from the job.

infectious diseases Diseases caused by viruses or bacteria, such as hepatitis B, HIV, and tuberculosis.

interactive video Training that allows trainers and trainees at different sites to see and hear each other in real time. Also called videoconferencing.

interest arbitration A judicial type of dispute resolution in which an arbitrator hears evidence and makes an award, either binding or nonbinding.

internal consistency method Reliability estimate using a statistical calculation of internal consistency of question formats in selection tests.

J

job A basic set of responsibilities and tasks in an organization; may be carried out by more than one position.

job analysis The process of collecting and organizing job information relating to work content and worker requirements.

job descriptions Documents that provide comprehensive information on the various jobs within an organization.

job design The organization of duties and responsibilities into a unit of work to achieve a particular objective.

job enlargement A job design strategy that focuses on increasing the number and variety of an employee's tasks.

job enrichment A job design strategy that focuses on the needs of the individual employee by allowing greater responsibility for the work.

job evaluation Assessment of the relative worth of jobs in an organization.

job instruction training (JIT) Learning by observation of an experienced employee and work with the actual equipment and materials used on the job.

job posting Publicizing a notice of job openings in the organization.

job rotation A job design strategy that shifts employees from one job to another in the organization.

job satisfaction A person's attitude concerning aspects of the work environment such as the level of pay, relationships with coworkers and supervisors, and working conditions.

job sharing A design strategy that allows more than one employee to share one position.

job specialization A system of job design where an employee does only one limited part of the organization's total work.

job specifications Outline of what an applicant must be able to do before being hired.

K

knowledge A body of information applied directly to the performance of a function.

L

labor market analysis The process of monitoring external staffing sources, considering the unemployment rate, characteristics of the labor force, and local training programs.

laissez-faire A capitalistic philosophy holding that business owners were entitled to complete control over employees.

legislation and regulation Federal, state, and local laws and regulations that affect the performance of a job.

M

maintenance-of-membership A union security provision requiring an employee to remain a member of the union after joining.

managed care Plan under which employees receive comprehensive health care from designated providers that have negotiated a flat rate contract with the employer.

management by objectives (MBO) A performance appraisal system that sets organizational goals and measures actual accomplishments against them.

management rights Issues reserved to management that are related to the organization's mission, not subject to bargaining.

management philosophy The mission and vision of an organization and how it treats employees.

managerial forecasting The process of estimating what resources will be needed by an organization.

mandatory bargaining issues Terms and conditions of employment such as wages and hours that must be bargained for.

Markov analysis A method of estimating how many employees will move into, out of, and between jobs in a given time period.

mediation A dispute resolution procedure using a neutral third party to facilitate communication and persuade the parties to reach agreement.

medical savings account (MSA) Employer-funded account from which the employee may pay out-of-pocket medical expenses.

meet and confer An approach to labor relations in which the employer consents to a discussion with representatives of employees regarding terms and conditions of employment; less favorable to the union than **collective bargaining**.

mentor A person more senior in position or experience who coaches a junior person or protege.

mentoring In training, a method that utilizes a **mentor**.

merit principles Principles requiring fair treatment and high standards in public employment; part of Civil Service Reform Act.

merit system Appointments to government jobs based on character and fitness, with removals made only for cause.

midpoint A target rate of pay within a grade for a fully-trained employee, performing at a satisfactory level, typically at or near the rate paid for the same skills in the relevant labor market.

minimum wage A minimum hourly wage that must be paid to any employee covered by the Fair Labor Standards Act.

motivation Predisposition to behave in a purposeful manner to satisfy specific, unmet needs.

multiple-gate A variety of the noncompensatory approach to selection in which a candidate faces selection procedures all at once.

multiple-hurdle A variety of the noncompensatory approach to selection in which a candidate faces selection procedures one after the other.

multiple-linear regression A statistical procedure used in the compensatory selection approach that uses the total of weighted scores to predict job performance.

N

negligent hiring A situation in which an employer does not investigate the background of a potential employee and exposes coworkers or others to the risk of harm.

neutral competence Governmental human resource function free of political patronage, exemplified by an independent civil service board.

noncompensatory approach A method of selection in which there are minimum qualifications that cannot be compensated for by high qualifications in other areas.

O

occupational group Classes grouped together according to the general functional nature or character of duties.

off-the-job training methods Any training an employee receives on the job site but not on the actual job, or at a location other than the job site.

on-the-job training methods Any training the employee receives on the job while under direct supervision.

operant conditioning Alternate term for **behavior modification**.

organizational behavior (OB) Study of how people act in organizations and how behavior and attitudes affect organizational performance.

organizational capacity The ability of a local government to pursue and maintain a competitive advantage for the products and services it offers.

organizational climate Collective perception of employees regarding their job content and environment.

organizational commitment An attitude of employees who identify with the organization's values, beliefs, and traditions.

organizational orientation Orientation that covers matters relevant to all employees.

orientation A program designed to welcome new employees and introduce them to their jobs.

outcome-based criteria Measurable results used as a basis for performance appraisal.

overtime pay Payment at the rate of one and one-half times the employee's regular rate for hours in excess of 40 in a workweek, required by the Fair Labor Standards Act.

P

paper-and-pencil tests Written tests for employee assessment that are inexpensive and easy to administer.

participative decision making (PDM) In labor-management relations, an approach in which employee views and suggestions are given serious consideration by management; a cooperative, rather than adversarial process.

pay policy line The level at which an organization decides to set pay scales, either matching, leading, or lagging the market rate.

pay range The range between the maximum and minimum pay rates within a **grade**.

performance appraisal A formal, written assessment of employee work contributions and the communication that takes place with employees before, during, and after the assessment.

performance feedback Information that employees receive about how well they are doing their jobs; may be systematic or informal.

performance standards Statements of what is considered acceptable and attainable on a particular job.

permissive issues Issues that are neither **mandatory** nor **prohibited** under collective bargaining.

personal protective equipment (PPE) Equipment that will promote workplace safety, such as safety shoes, gloves, and goggles.

personality tests Tests used to identify employee characteristics or traits that may be associated with job performance.

planning Process of determining organizational objectives and selecting a future course of action.

point method A job evaluation method that assigns points to jobs based on scaled and weighted compensable factors such as skill, effort, responsibility, and working conditions.

policy General statement that guides decision making.

polygraph tests A method of assessing honesty by using the polygraph machine.

position A collection of duties and responsibilities carried out by one person.

predictive validity Method of establishing validity by administering a test or "predictor" to applicants, hiring these applicants without regard to test scores, measuring performance at a later time, and correlating test scores with performance measures.

preferred provider organization (PPO) Plan under which various health care providers contract with the employer to provide services at competitive rates.

prima facie Proof legally sufficient to establish a case.

procedural due process Alternate term for **due process**.

procedure Guide to action used to achieve a given purpose; prescribes exactly what actions to take in a specific situation.

prohibited issues Issues not subject to bargaining, usually covered by civil service regulations.

Q

quality circles (QCs) Small groups of employees who meet regularly to identify work problems and recommend solutions.

quality of worklife (QWL) Management activities that promote such values as fairness, meaningful work, employee empowerment, and balance between family and worklife.

R

recruiting The process of generating a sufficiently large group of qualified applicants in order to select the best-qualified individuals for available jobs.

reengineering Management approach that uses process as a major organizing principle, redesigning jobs and rethinking how employees carry out their duties.

referent power Authority based on admiration of the individual.

reform movement Political movement during the mid- to late-1800s designed to end the spoils system of appointing people to government jobs.

regression A statistical method of estimating the value of a variable when given the values of other variables.

reinventing government Public sector counterpart of reengineering.

reliability The stability, consistency, and dependability of the results of a selection measure.

resources Advantages available to management, including economic, financial, physical, human, and information.

responsibility A group of related tasks that make up a major work activity of a job; also known as accountability, domain, and work behavior. Most jobs contain from three to eight responsibilities.

"right-to-work" laws State laws forbidding unions and

employers to agree on **union or agency shops;** permitted under the Taft-Hartley Act.

role-playing A training method in which trainees assume different identities and practice a typical work situation.

rule Requirement that an individual must follow; narrow in scope and application and leaves little to discretion.

S

safety The avoidance of injury-causing accidents.

safety regulations Regulations that influence worker safety on the job.

scientific management Theory of management that stressed planning, job design, and efficiency.

security Efforts to reduce the risk of violence, specifically to employees in the workplace.

selection The process whereby job-related information is collected from applicants and offers of employment are given to those applicants who are most likely to be successful.

sexual harassment Unwelcome sexual advances or requests for sexual favors that are intended as an exchange for a job benefit or that create a hostile work environment.

sick building syndrome (SBS) Health and comfort problems that appear to be associated with working in a building; the specific cause cannot be identified.

simulation methods Training methods designed to duplicate the work situation and environment as much as possible.

skill A present, observable competence to perform a learned psychomotor act.

skill obsolescence The situation in which a skill is no longer needed, often because of changes in technology.

skill variety The extent to which a job demands the performance of a wide range of activities.

skill-based pay Pay structures based on the number of skills that employees have mastered rather than the tasks they are assigned to perform.

skills inventory A collection of information on the qualifications of all employees in an organization.

Social Security Federal program providing retirement, disability, death, survivor, and health insurance benefits, funded by employer and employee contributions.

spoils patronage Appointments to government jobs based on political influence.

staffing table A chart showing estimated future vacancies in different types of jobs.

standing plan Policies, procedures, and rules used repeatedly to guide HR activities.

statutory law Federal laws and executive orders.

strategic planning Process of determining strategic

objectives and actions needed to achieve the organization's mission.

stress A condition in which an individual is confronted with opportunities, constraints, and demands and the outcome is both important and uncertain.

strike A work stoppage used by employees to pressure employers to meet union demands; illegal for many public employees.

subject matter expert (SME) Experienced job incumbents and supervisors who provide advice on work content, worker requirements, and performance standards to job analysts and test developers.

substantive due process A form of **due process** that places an additional requirement on an employer to show a compelling government interest in a disciplinary action against an employee for exercising his or her constitutionally protected rights.

succession chart A list showing the readiness of different candidates for promotion to key positions in an organization.

supply The amount of resources available to an organization.

synergy The creation of a whole that is greater than the sum of its parts.

T

task A single identifiable job activity.

task identity The extent to which a job allows employees to perform an entire piece of work and to clearly identify the outcome of their effort.

task significance The extent to which the job impacts the lives and work of others.

technology The means by which an organization transforms resources into outputs.

telecommuting A job design strategy that allows employees to work primarily out of their homes.

test/retest A reliability estimate using the correlation between scores on the same test given to the same people twice.

Theory Z Style of management that involves participative management, employee empowerment, and focuses on customer satisfaction; component of **total quality management**.

total quality management (TQM) Approach to management that uses statistical methods, benchmarking against industry standards, participative management, employee empowerment, and a focus on customer satisfaction.

training A process by which people acquire knowledge and skills needed for performance in their current assignments.

training needs assessment (TNA) The process of outlining the training project, analyzing jobs, and identifying KSAO deficiencies.

trait-based criteria Personal characteristics or attributes of individuals used as a basis for performance appraisal.

trend analysis The use of past patterns to predict needs in the future.

turnover The permanent separation of employees from the organization, because of resignation, retirement, layoff, or discharge.

U

unemployment compensation A partial wage replacement program for employees laid off through no fault of their own who are willing to accept a similar job.

union security provisions Certain arrangements intended to strengthen the position of unions. See **closed shop, union shop, agency shop, maintenance-of-membership**, and **checkoff**.

union shop A union security provision requiring an employee to become a union member after hire.

unions Associations of employees formed to represent members in collective bargaining with employers over wages and conditions of employment.

utility analysis Determination of how much a valid selection procedure improves the quality of applicants selected versus a procedure that has not been validated.

V

validity The degree to which a test actually measures the quality it is designed to measure.

variable pay Cash compensation linked to factors such as performance, seniority, and skills.

vertical job loading Alternate term for **job enrichment**.

videoconferencing training Two-way video transmission of training sessions held at multiple locations.

W

web-based training Training provided through a website that allows employees to take individual training at a convenient time and location.

welfare secretaries Members of business firms who helped workers with education, housing, medical care, and other personal matters.

whole job ranking An ordering of jobs from highest to lowest based on an overall definition of content and/or value.

work behavior Term used in the "Uniform Guidelines" for job **responsibility**.

work/life initiatives Programs designed to promote personal health and deal with related family concerns such as elder care and financial planning.

workers' compensation Insurance that provides a percentage of lost wages and medical and rehabilitation expenses resulting from on-the-job accidents and illnesses.

work-sample test A test in which applicants perform duties that closely approximate those of the actual work situation.

URL INDEX

CHAPTER 1
http://www.ipma-hr.org/training/certification.html
http://www.hrconsultant. com/hrm/glossary.html
http://www.aspanet.org
http://www.ipma-hr.org/
http://www.shrm.org

CHAPTER 2
http://www.nlc.org/
http://www.natat.org
http://www.theroundtable.org/
http://www.cce.cornell.edu/programs/restructuring

CHAPTER 3
http://www.eeoc.gov/
http://www.eeoc.gov/stats/charges.html
http://fairmeasures.com/sh.html
http://www.usdoj.gov/crt/ada/adahom1.htm
http://www.law.cornell.edu/

CHAPTER 4
http://www.mapnp.org/library/guiding/motivate/motivate.htm
http://www.calib.com/nccanch/pubs/usermanuals/supercps/satisfy.htm
http://www.andromeda.rutgers.edu/~ncpp

CHAPTER 5
http://www.pti.nw.dc.us/
http://www.acinet.org/acinet/
http://www.bls.gov/
http://www.census.gov/
http://www.ci.westminster.co.us/
http://www.ihrim.org/

CHAPTER 6
http://www.usmayors.org/USCM/best_practices/bp_volume_2/redmond.htm
http://www.ci.redmond.wa.us/
http://stats.bls.gov/soc/soc_home.htm
http://www.lni.wa.gov/wisha/ergo/officerg/offergr2.htm
http://www.nwlink.com/~donclark/leader/jobsurvey.html
http://www.accel-team.com/work_design/
http://stats.bls.gov/soc/soc_home.htm

CHAPTER 7
http://www.pstc.com/
http://www.job-analysis.net/
http://www.oalj.dol.gov/libdot.htm
http://www.doleta.gov/programs/onet/

CHAPTER 8
http://www.aimd.org/
http://www.apa.org/ppo/aa.html
http://www.ipma-hr.org/private/research/diversity/divlinks.html
http://www.shrm.org/hrmagazine/articles/0800cov.htm

CHAPTER 9
http://www.cheyennecity.org/
http://www.monsterboard.com
http://www.corporate-screening.com/employment_screening.htm
http://www.ci.broomfield.co.us/jobs/index.shtml
http://www.job-interview.net/
http://www.governmentexecutive.com/dailyfed/0699/062299k1.htm
http://exams.spb.ca.gov/

CHAPTER 10
http://www.ci.concord.ca.us/hr/org-train-dev.htm
http://www.orientxpress.com/
http://www.astd.org/
http://www.shrm.org/whitepapers/documents/61313.asp
http://www.trainingsupersite.com
http://www.keirsey.com/cgi-bin/newkts.cgi

CHAPTER 11
http://www.performanceappraisal.com/
http://www.performance-appraisal.com/
http://work911.com/performance/index.htm
http://doleta.wdsc.org/jobs/prfguide.html

CHAPTER 12
http://www.gov/fedclass/html/draft.htm
http://www.acinet.org/acinet/

http://stats.bls.gov/blshome.htm
http://erieri.com/codes/
http://hr-guide.com

CHAPTER 13
http://www.dol.gov/dol/esa/public/whd_org.htm
http://www.opm.gov/
http://www.dol.gov/dol/esa/public/regs/compliance/ofccp/compdata.htm
http://www.flsa.com/
http://www.epf.org/pay_equity.htm
http://www.eeoc.gov/laws/adea.html

CHAPTER 14
http://nadm.org/
http://www.jobstresshelp.com/
http://www.eap-association.com/
http://www.joe.org/joe/1987winter/a5.html
http://www.shrm.org/

CHAPTER 15
http://www.nea.org/
http://www.afscme.org/
http://www.nrtw.org/
http://www.nlrb.gov/index.html
http://www.doi.gov/hrm
http://www.aflcio/org/
http://www.fop.org/
http://www.teamster.org/
http://www.ana.org/

CHAPTER 16
http://www.osha.gov/
http://www.clgsonline.com
http://www.shrm.org
http://gopher.law.cornell.edu/topics/workers_compensation.html
http://infoventures.com/osh/
http://eapage.com/

CHAPTER 17
http://www.mapnp.org/library/plan_dec/str_plan/str_plan.htm
http://www.eoa.org

APPENDICES
http://www.shrm.org/hrci/
http://www.acaonline.org
http://www.amanet.org
http://www.americanpayroll.org
http://www.asisonline.org
http://www.aspanet.org
http://www.astd.org
http://www.asse.org
http://www.ebri.org
http://www.the-esop-emplowner.org
http://www.hrps.org
http://www.ihrim.org

http://www.ifebp.org
http://www.ipma-hr.org
http://www.natss.org
http://www.welcoa.org
http://www.cps.ca.gov
http://www.lgi.org
http://www.natat.org/ncsc
http://www.dol.gov
http://www.bls.gov
http://www.dol.gov/esa/public/whd-org.html
http://www.osha.gov
http://www.dol.gov/dol/esa/public/ofcp_org.htm
http://www.eeoc.gov
http://www.fmcs.gov
http://www.opm.gov
http://207.106.209.11/publications/pdf/440000.pdf
http://www.shrm.org/hrci/

NAME INDEX

SUBJECT INDEX